CERVANTES
A BIOGRAPHY

William Byron

CERVANTES
A BIOGRAPHY

CASSELL
London

CASSELL LTD.
35 Red Lion Square, London WC1R 4SG
and at Sydney, Auckland, Toronto, Johannesburg,
an affiliate of
Macmillan Publishing Co., Inc.,
New York

First published in Great Britain 1979

ISBN 0 304 30466 2

Printed and bound at William Clowes & Sons Limited
Beccles and London

To Liz

Contents

Part III: APPRENTICESHIP

Part IV: FREEDOM'S CAPTIVE

Part V: THE JOURNEYMAN

Illustrations

Prelude

The countryside around Alcalá de Henares, some twenty miles from Madrid, is homely and plain as an old farm kitchen. Eroded hills sit in it like crabbed peasant elders eyeing their land with sour detachment. But the soil is fertile. Rolling swells of wheat have grown there since Roman times. The wine taken from its vineyards is acrid and bumptious, but the trout from the Jarama River are famous, and plump sheep graze under the poplars on the banks of the Henares.

It seems not dramatic enough, this land, to house the bones that lie in it—Albas' and Olivares' and the older lime of Trajan's legionaries—but the sky is endlessly high and broad, a sky for mystics to strain at. The weather is harsh, the famous nine months of winter and three months of hell which make most of New Castile a trial to visitors. This is the northeastern section of that amorphous region known as La Mancha, and there is not much that is soft about it, but it breeds men who are tough and enduring. To them, the earth is the enemy, to be tamed and dominated like a mule which, they say, will serve you faithfully for ten years for the pleasure of kicking your brains out at the end of it.

The city of Alcalá de Henares is like its landscape, unremarkable except for its arcaded, now rather too grand main street. And, like the countryside, it is an ossuary of history: the Roman Complutum, probably built on the ruins of an earlier Greek colony, it was the cradle of Spanish law, the birthplace of Catherine of Aragon, of the poet-archpriest of Hita, of the Emperor Ferdinand of Austria. Scattered through it are the mummified remains of its great university. The single building of the original foundation which remains intact, the college of San Ildefonso with its marvelous plateresque façade and its austere patios, is too silent and lifeless to give us any idea of what it once had been. The long, straight back streets, lined with tidily decrepit palaces and convents, tell us more, for here some of the flesh is left on the skeleton of a sixteenth-century boom town.

On October 9, 1547, the town was at full boil. The inns were crowded. Later in the day, the taverns would begin filling up, the students and their whores would gather at the Venta de Viveros, outside the city walls, where "if the innkeeper is Christian, the wine is Moorish,"[1] and the gambling would get under way at Vilhán's place near the Santiago Gate, not far from the house at No. 2 Calle de la Imagen, in the converso quarter of Alcalá, where the child Miguel de Cervantes was born.[2] The Morisco and "Jewish" moneylenders were already stirring behind their modest doors in the main thoroughfare, the Calle Mayor. By the evening the streets would be rowdy with the brawling of young men, for the students were to elect a new chancellor and more than a score of new faculty members a week hence, and the city was awash in professorial cash. The only empty place in town that week was the granite gibbet outside the Vado Gate, although that would doubtless resume business as usual once the school year formally began on October 18, the day the registration notices went up on the two main doors of San Ildefonso.

Outside the already venerable church of Santa María la Mayor, the morning was crisp and bright, but the little group standing at the hemispherical baptismal font in the dark Oidór chapel probably could feel the cold rising through their legs from the stone floor. Led by the stentorian bronze bells of San Ildefonso, the bells in the city's forest of towers, like great bronze muezzins, were already sounding the call to mass. They were close enough so that even Rodrigo de Cervantes, the father of the infant being baptized that morning, could hear them despite his gathering deafness. While the parish priest, Bartolomé Serrano, and the child's godfather, Juan Pardo, passed the tiny creature between them like a small, wet bird, Rodrigo may have speculated with professional interest on the commotion in the streets. He was a barber-surgeon by trade—that is, he was one of the slightly clownish figures of the age, standing in relation to a physician as, say, a plumber does to an engineer; the drinking and fighting were sure to produce a few broken bones and sword wounds and an ailing kidney or two for him to treat. If only the victims were not too poor to pay, for the Lord knew he needed the fees. The infant being christened Miguel at the font meant another mouth to feed; "a little brother more, a little slice less," the saying went, and the slices were none too plentiful as it was.

Still, Rodrigo would have found reason enough to love the infant. His wife, Doña Leonor de Cortinas, had presented him with a boy this time, apparently a healthy one, to replace his first-born, Andrés, who had squinted at the world with sickly eyes and then had quickly died. Andrea, who was nearly three, and Luisa, born in 1546, were fine little girls, but a son, now, a son was essential, especially to a poor man with no money to pay out in dowries.

Although a baptismal record exists for Miguel de Cervantes Saavedra, we do not know on what day he was born.[3] That he was christened Miguel has occasioned speculation that he was born on September 29,* St. Michael's day, but there is no other evidence of this, and in that age of awesome infant mortality, when a child had less than one chance in three of surviving his birth and then only a 60-40 chance of reaching his first birthday, his parents may not have risked endangering the child's soul by delaying his baptism for as long as ten days. He may have been named for a great-uncle, a draper named Miguel Díaz de Cervantes.

Until relatively recently, much confusion surrounded even the question of where the child was born, but this was largely because of Spaniards' gift for fantasy and their distaste for the demeaning restraints of evidence. Cervantes' baptismal registration was found and published as long ago as 1753; in an affidavit drawn up in Algiers in 1580 and published for the first time in 1905, Cervantes referred to himself as a "prominent hidalgo of Alcalá de Henares."[4] True, he would later swear before a notary in Seville that he was a "resident of Madrid and a native of Córdoba," but that was for tactical reasons in a culture in which legal documents were weapons in the individual's guerrilla war against bureaucracy.

Over the centuries, ten cities and towns other than Alcalá[5] have claimed to be *the* place, none so seriously as Alcázar de San Juan, where an entry in parish records for November 9, 1558, recorded the baptism of one Miguel, son of Blas de Cervantes Sabeydra and Catalina López. Written in the margin alongside it was the exclamation, "This was the author of the story of Don Quixote." The inscription is now recognized to be an eighteenth-century forgery, no doubt by some forgotten patriot who obviously suspected he was on to a good thing. Were it correct, Cervantes would have been less than ten years old when he wrote his first published poems and, even more improbably, not quite thirteen when he fought as a squad leader at Lepanto. This did not discourage one writer from objecting, in defense of Alcázar de San Juan, "Was not the humble shepherd David under fourteen when he vanquished the blasphemous and impious Goliath?"[6]

This was a pardonable foolishness, perhaps, because there was the

* In the Julian calendar. The Gregorian correction (March 1582) to the old calendar added ten days to dates up to the year 1700. Spain accepted the correction immediately, but not all of Europe did so; Britain, for example, did not endorse the new system until 1751. Pre-1582 dates mentioned in this book follow the Julian system; dates after March 1582 are given according to the Gregorian calendar.

stuff of legend in Miguel de Cervantes' life. The child at the font in Alcalá de Henares on that October day in 1547 would suffer from all the disadvantages we consider desirable in heroes: he would be poor, largely self-educated, physically mutilated, a slave, a jailbird, a social outcast, throughout most of his life an obscure failure. From this hardship-enriched soil, late in his life, books would grow to bring him fame—an unpalatable kind of fame, to be sure, but satisfying all the same.

For those who miss the sterner virtues of moral heroism in this relatively simple folk legend, a more austere sequel is available in the Cervantes we shall see in the last decade of his life. Ill, still poor, still thwarted in his dearest hopes, he will embark on a great intellectual and spiritual adventure, a voyage of exploration across the line dividing art from life in search of vindication in this world and redemption in the next.

On the way, with sweetness and wit and unfailing honesty, he will piece the shards and splinters of his absurd life into an epic of splendid humanity.

Part I
THE FAMILY

So Vast a Dream

For those who enjoy the game of historical portents, 1547 was crowded with weighty *faits-divers*. God removed Francis I from the European chessboard that year, opening France to half a century of religious turmoil for Spain to exploit. That year, too, He swept away that pushy heretic Henry VIII as summarily as, the year before, He had silenced Martin Luther in mid-sermon, thus demonstrating His enthusiasm for the Spanish cause. In April of 1547, as though to confirm Spain's understanding with the deity, Emperor Charles V, clad in his gold-embossed armor, his bearded Habsburg jaw thrust forward like a lance in its rest, led the Catholic forces to victory over the massed Protestant armies at Mühlberg, in central Germany; in his explanation that "I came, I saw and God conquered" there is no hint that little was won there for the Catholic cause.

Almost a continent away, Ivan the Terrible of Muscovy, unnoticed by most Spaniards, assumed the title of Tsar in 1547. In European politics, no wind left the tree unshaken. Ivan's pressure on the Baltic region and on Turkey forced Habsburg attention to refocus on Flanders, where Cervantes' brother Rodrigo would die in battle, and on the Mediterranean, where Russian policy so alarmed the Turkish sultan that the battle of Lepanto was delayed until Miguel was of an age to fight in it.

There were other, less titanic, transitions that year. A physician's son, Mateo Alemán, was born in Seville into a life which would produce a monumental novel called *Guzmán de Alfarache* which angrily questioned God's bounteousness. Alonso López-Pinciano, whose Spanish-language commentary on Aristotelian poetics profoundly influenced Cervantes' writing, was born in Valladolid. Hernán Cortés, "who added a New Spain to the Spanish crown,"[1] died within sight of the walls of Seville,

Spain's gateway to the New World; the age of the conquistadors died
with him, although more than a generation would pass before the fact became public knowledge.

Among the minor events of 1547, some are of special interest to us.
The first Spanish translation appeared of Jacopo Sannazaro's *Arcadia*,
the Italian pastoral novel on which Cervantes' first major work was
largely patterned. That was also the year when Jacques Aymot, the
French classical scholar, presented his version of a Byzantine romance,
the *Aethiopica*, by a writer named Heliodorus; the work was to be the
model for Cervantes' last novel as, with only slightly less unfortunate results, the Greek romances would be for some of Shakespeare's late plays.

A cultural event of some scope occurred only weeks before the birth of
Spain's most famous writer: on September 1, 1547, Spanish Inquisitional
courts were provided with their first printed *Index of Prohibited Books*,
reproducing the list issued the year before at the Catholic University of
Louvain, in Flanders, and adding a memorial of works specially dis-
tasteful to the Spanish authorities.[2] It would be followed by a more complete *Index* in 1551 which would include, among other works, much of
the writing of Erasmus of Rotterdam as well as all Bibles in vernacular
tongues, on the grounds that wide reading of Scripture was an inex-
haustible source of heresy. The Golden Century of Spanish art had hardly
gotten under way, but the Platinum Age of intellectual freedom was all
but over.

In Spain more than anywhere else in Europe, free, speculative thought
was a victim of the central movement of ideas in the sixteenth and seventeenth centuries, the pressure of modern scientific skepticism on established systems of thought; this produced what has been called the tension between the stabilizing classical forces of the past and the dynamic
romantic forces expressed in the term "baroque."[3] The rigid universe
erected by "St. Aristotle" and endorsed by the Council of Trent was beginning to crumble before a newly inquisitive "St. Socrates."

The tension touched every basic aspect of life. It was felt in the warnings of the "arbiters"—they had not yet arrogated the title of economists
to themselves—that wealth lay in productivity, not in hoarding money. It
would surface in the agonized and frequently dangerous debates of the
late sixteenth and early seventeenth centuries over the extent to which
Aristotelian poetics must govern literary form—in other words, where in
fiction the "lie" of history ends and the "truth" of poetry begins. That
boundary might also be expressed as the line between seeing and knowing
which is the essential issue of religious faith.

Part One of Cervantes' *Don Quixote*, which attempted to fix that line,
appeared in 1605, the same year as Bacon's *The Advancement of Learning* and Kepler's ambiguous *Astronomia Nova*. This was also the year in

which one of the last of Spain's great mystics, Luis de la Puente, published his *Meditations on the Mysteries of Our Holy Faith,* a guide to the
spiritual exercises needed to achieve "a perfect union of love."⁴ Before
Part Two of the *Quixote* was published, in 1615, the first information
was deposited against Galileo by the Holy Roman and Universal Inquisition. And in 1616, the year of Cervantes' death, the first formal prohibition was issued against public demonstration of the Copernican cosmology.

It was, in short, a confusing time for a thinking man, and it must go
far toward explaining the reputation for indecisiveness with which
scholars would burden Cervantes. For if, until the last two decades of his
life, he seemed not to know what face to turn to the world, this must be
at least partly explained by the multiplicity of faces his world turned to
him. Ambition would lead him in his youth to play a variety of more or
less convincing roles: he would be the tragic poet-warrior, the conquis-
tador without conquests, a Pizarro without a Peru. In this he was to obey
the imperatives of the archaic values his generation inherited, the already
etiolated standards of a medieval world of immutable revealed truth. In
his ripeness, Cervantes would be found, virtually alone, exploring in un-
fashionable prose a strange region in which truth and illusion touch and
recoil, absorb and reject each other. Between these two outposts lay a
journey through a daily Spanish world where, economically, politically,
spiritually, and intellectually, the real and the illusory were becoming increasingly indistinct.

Change, however, is a surreptitious process. Seen through the eyes of,
say, a Valladolid banker, things had never looked better for Spain than
they did in 1547. The country was rich, powerful, feared, its people enterprising and vigorous. It was the pedestal supporting the Habsburg
Empire, the largest the world had ever known. Spain was the coffer of
the Catholic Christian faith, the catapult from which dominion sprang,
the very seat of honor. Its armies were triumphant, its wool was the finest
in Europe, its universities flourished. The whole edifice was rinsed by a
torrent of silver shot with rivulets of gold pouring across the Atlantic
from the Americas. Spain was exalted by its values: purity and unity of
faith, a missionary impulsion carried forward in a spirit of knightliness. It
had a sense of leadership and achievement, of moral probity, of a time
when all things, like the discovery of new worlds, were possible.

This, our banker would have assured us, was how it had been ever
since the Reconquest. Granada, the last of the Moslem principalities on
Iberian soil, had fallen in 1492 to Spanish armies, 781 years after the first
Moslem invaders from North Africa landed near Gibraltar. The victory,
followed by Columbus' almost simultaneous conquest of the unknown
ocean on his voyages of discovery, released in the Spanish a tide of mili-

tant energy. Long centuries of frontier spirit had already made them feel larger than life, possessed by a consciousness of their own mythic grandeur which pushed them on to new efforts, more astonishing conquests.

Spain's social paragon was the aristocratic warrior-knight of the Reconquest, the proud resistance figure, direct heir of the fierce Iberians who had defied Roman domination for two hundred years. He was Lancelot and Amadis of Gaul, St. George and St. James the Moorslayer, the model of honor: noble, brave, generous, of untainted Spanish Christian lineage. This, at any rate, was the image, occasionally accurate, with which every man in Spain identified. The romances of chivalry had a special meaning to the Spanish, for what had they done, those Rolands and Percivals, that Spain's knights had not done and, for that matter, were still doing? Men like Cortés and Francisco Pizarro were not merely fleeing from poverty at home, they were carrying on the Reconquest in new theaters. So were the Spanish armies which had added great chunks of Italy to the national heritage; by the logic of the righteous, moral rectitude authorized political expansion.

At the head of this nation of cavaliers was Charles, the First of Spain, Fifth of the Holy Roman Empire, lord of the four kingdoms of Spain,[5] most of Germany and Italy, modern Benelux, large tracks of what is now northern and eastern France, Sardinia, Sicily, bits of North Africa and nearly half the Western Hemisphere.

With his coming, Spain's—particularly Castile's—sense of national purpose was submerged in a movement of imperial destiny. In spite of their objections to Flemish-born Charles's extravagance and foreign ways, Spaniards approved the prospects opening before them. "God," Charles was assured by his grand chancellor Mercurino Gattinara, "has set you on the path towards a world monarchy."[6] Once Charles decided that he was really more Spanish, from his mother's side, than he was Teutonic, from his father's, the people of Spain swallowed their misgivings and settled down to cherish him, dazzled by the splendor of

> that Spain which, for a brief day,
> two worlds could not contain,
> for the globe was a small place
> to hold so vast a dream
> of valor and nobility.[7]

Meanwhile, our banker might have informed us, affairs at home were in capital shape. In the important cities of the peninsula, a skilled workman could earn up to 110 ducats a year in a period when a comfortable house and garden could be rented for 20. This was not, of course, to be compared with the incomes of the country's greatest magnates—up to 170,000 a year for the D'Avalos family, for example—but it was more money than a laborer had ever earned before. Farmers supplying the main urburn centers with produce confidently mortgaged their lands to buy more land, more seed and stock. The arrangement seemed to suit everybody: the farmer whose marginal earnings made capital accumulation almost impossible; the state, which relied for its tax revenues chiefly on the peasantry; city dwellers, who thought to find in it a risk-proof haven for their new capital which would allow them to live on the proceeds from other people's labor, as befitted gentlemen.

The rich were growing so much richer that they began to worry lest their wealth keep them out of paradise; the difficulty was frequently resolved by the expenditure of a ducat or so to hire squadrons of candle-bearing poor (children, if possible) to escort their coffins to their tombs as intercessors with the Great Inspector.

Building was booming; the luxury tradesmen—the silversmiths, jewelers, workers in tooled leather, sculptors, fancy tailors, painters and altar makers, apothecaries and importers of fine Holland cloth—could hardly keep up with the demand, for consumption was most highly valued when it was most conspicuous. People with money hung their walls with Córdoban leather in the summer and expensive tapestries in winter, decked their tables with silver and their wives with silks and jewels. Much was given to the Church and its appendages; fortunes were lavished on gold and silver ornaments for the *cofradías,* or lay brotherhoods. Scholars spent great sums to influence voters in elections to lucrative university chairs. Some cities devoted considerable money to helping the poor, caring for the sick, raising foundlings, marrying off orphans and burying the dead.

Spanish thought was wide-ranging and extraordinarily unrestrained in the early sixteenth century; it had made as much of an impact on European letters as the Spanish military presence had on its politics. A working knowledge of Spanish was as indispensable to foreigners then as a grasp of English is today. Europe affected Spanish fashions, imitated Spanish manners, grumbled about Spanish influence and condemned its literature as rude and barbaric, a sure sign of cultural penetration. The Spanish theater, possibly the most vigorous in Europe then, was being rough-hewn by such men as Bartolomé de Torres Naharro and Lope de Rueda. The stream of Italian Renaissance culture first channeled into Spain by such men as the poet Garcilaso de la Vega converged with Humanist thought from the North, exemplified by Luis Vives,[8] to create a recognizably national intellectual style. There is no doubt that the fifteenth and sixteenth centuries were the most prodigious incubators of artistic talent in Spanish history; all the great literary figures of the Golden Century, all its remembered architects and musicians, all but one (Murillo) of its major painters were born before 1601.

> Immense century! Century of giants!
> Opened by Columbus and closed by Cervantes![9]

A brilliant picture, and a true one. But truths are like proverbs: for every penny saved which is a penny earned, there is one you can't take with you. It would be just as accurate to depict a hemophiliac Spain which, in 1547, was slowly dying of internal hemorrhages. The country's economy was the most fragile in Europe. Its people were conservative, incurious, wary of new ideas. The Castilian pedestal, already cracked and wobbly, trembled under the weight of an empire it was not strong enough to support. Its agriculture was showing signs of ruination and its armies were largely fed by the landless and the dispossessed. Knightliness was degenerating into vulgar patricianism, the sense of mission into sclerotic orthodoxy, unity of faith into racialism. Despite its power, Spain was increasingly becoming the victim rather than the perpetrator of events.

And the torrents of silver, for the most part, rushed through the country into foreign hands without fertilizing the economy they washed—so rapidly, in fact, that the Spanish state would declare itself bankrupt four times in the course of the sixteenth century.

Throughout the period, a steadily increasing tax burden, made heavier by inflation which quadrupled prices within a century, fell mainly on the tenant farmers least able to support it. Not only were the hidalgo class and the clergy immune from direct taxation, but so was much of the small (under 4 per cent of the population) but relatively moneyed middle class—civil servants, teachers, students, etc. Statistics compiled in Burgos in 1591, for example, showed that only 17 per cent of the city's population was taxable.[10]

Despite centuries of hymns by Iberian writers in adoration of the country's natural wealth, Spain has always been a poor country, mountainous, not overly endowed with mineral wealth or energy sources, traversed by unruly rivers which seem to spurn any middle state between drought and flood. Roman irrigation had nevertheless turned the peninsula into an imperial granary, and elaborate development of that system had enabled Moslem farmers to nurse the reluctant earth into luxuriant flower. The water wheel, wrote the twelfth-century Hispano-Arab poet Ibn Waddah, molded silver ingots from the water of the pond, and made them grow in the garden as coins.[11]

But irrigation, like bathing and an abhorrence of pork, was a Moorish habit and, while not altogether abandoned, was much neglected by Christian farmers. Moreover, the departure into exile of tens of thousands of Moors, fleeing the Reconquering Christians, had stripped the fields of much skilled labor.

Many of the farmers who managed to bear the heavy burden of mortgages, crop failures, lack of water and overtaxation were driven into beggary by the Mesta, the sheep-breeders' association which produced the Merino wool that was Spain's leading export. Its flocks, numbering in the millions of head, were allowed free passage over any land, regardless of what was growing on it. Fencing land against them was a crime, and in case of litigation, the Mesta itself was the magistrate. Fields lying in the broad paths between plain and mountain taken by the sheep in their twice-yearly transhumance were often trampled into muddy wastes.

By the end of the century, agricultural production would drop so radically that the granary would become a net importer of wheat; debtors' prisons would be so full of peasants that the Cortes (parliament) of Castile would ask for a prohibition of further arrests for debt among the peasantry, and the roads were as alive with beggars as a soldier's breeches were with vermin.

That the process was well under way by the time Cervantes was born can be judged from a letter written in 1545 by Prince Philip to Charles V. "The common people," he warned, "on whom the burden of paying taxes falls, are reduced to such extreme calamity and poverty that many of them go naked, lacking what to cover themselves with, and the damage is so universal that this poverty extends not only to Your Majesty's (common) subjects, but is even greater among the gentry, to whom (the peasantry) cannot pay their rents . . . and the prisons are full, and all of them are going to be lost." The letter compares Spain's situation with that of France, observing that "the fertility of those kingdoms is so great that they can suffer (crop failure) and survive," but such is the sterility of Spain that "a bad year leaves the people so poor that they cannot raise their heads for many years afterward."[12]

Urban prosperity was taking a slower path down the same hill. Expulsion of the Jews in 1492 and the emigration of tens, perhaps hundreds, of thousands of Moslems who rejected conversion to Christianity deprived the country of many of its business and financial leaders, its finest artisans, its best scientists, much of its dynamic capital. Few Spaniards could be found to take their places in activities considered menial. Local industry was strangled by heavy taxation, suffocated by minute regulation. The crown favored a policy of encouraging imports, chiefly from its colonies, and restricting exports on the theory that they drained the nation's wealth.

Spain, of course, has no patent on internal contradictions. But, like everything Spanish, its dualism seems more grandiose, more theatrical, more tragic than other countries'; its contrasts, like its light, appear sharper and its vitality, for good and evil, more vibrant. Spain's rise and fall was vertiginous—less than a century elapsed from the end of the Reconquest to the defeat of the Spanish Armada—so that the very compactness of its imperial career contributed to Spain's cultural shock.

After nearly a millennium during which, with rare and limited exceptions, the country had lived closed in on itself, cut off from Europe by the absorbing enormity of its own problems, the end of the Reconquest brought a dizzying rush to make up for lost time, to catch up, culturally and politically, with the rest of the world. The intellectual mood of the early sixteenth century was critical; everything was re-examined, analyzed, compared. The spread of printing vulgarized ideas, took criticism out of the cloister and made it available to anyone who could read. In other countries, the growth of institutions had been slow, evolutionary; Spain was hustled from medievalism to modernity in a generation. Every source of stability was shaken, every certainty pierced. The relatively simple principles of the Reconquest were giving way to the doubts and complexities of Renovation, Renaissance and Reform. Confusion was deepened, moreover, by the fact that the country's weaknesses, like its strengths, grew in large measure from the Reconquest.

The Christian campaign to drive the Moslems back into the sea had been a halting process, partly because of the immense military and economic problems it presented and in the internal rivalries in the leadership of both sides, but partly, too, because, in nearly eight centuries of promiscuity, Christian, Moor and the Moslems' Jewish allies had become blood brothers to a degree none of them cared to admit. Reconquest Spain was a profoundly disunited land of differing laws, customs, languages, dress and religions, administered mainly by local lords who were sovereign in their own territories.

In some areas, the conquered peoples were left alone to practice their own religions; in others, authorities forced conversions. Thousands more adopted Christianity for reasons of convenience, and still other thousands were sincerely converted by the passionate militancy of Reconquest Christianity.

Wherever they went, the Moors maintained a high ethnic profile, clinging openly to Moorish habits and manners, marrying among themselves, speaking Arabic; many Moriscos—Moslems converted to Christianity—remained secretly faithful to Islam. Their social status was equivocal: in some regions, notably the rich farming country around Valencia, they were reduced to what amounted to serfdom; in others, they grew rich as innkeepers, artisans, shopkeepers, manufacturers. But they neither sought nor attained political or social influence in a society they detested.

This had also been true of those Jews who spurned apostasy; with most of the normal avenues of advancement closed to them—they were barred, for example, from the army, the civil service, most of the craft guilds—they had maintained their traditional roles as businessmen and financiers. But Jewish converts to Christianity, called *conversos* when the disparagement intended was mild, *marranos* (swine) when it was more heartfelt, rapidly achieved positions of influence in the government, in business, industry, the professions, the arts, the Catholic Church. Not only were numerous abbacies occupied by conversos, but so were the bishoprics of Segovia and Burgos, the archbishoprics of Granada and Seville and even, some scholars believe, the primatial archbishopric of Toledo. New Christians collected the crown's taxes and administered its finances; they were the powerful royal secretaries, the jurists who drew up the nation's laws; they taught in the universities, their physicians martyred the sick with potions composed by converso apothecaries. And, often, they were the spiritual police who pursued their own defectors: Tomás de Torquemada, the grim, ascetic Dominican monk who was Isabel's first Inquisitor General, may have been of New Christian lineage; his successor, Diego de Deza, certainly was. The Jewish intellectual-mystical tradition found what it at first thought to be a safe home in theology; it expressed itself in a range of Christian thought which covered Vives' Erasmian moralizations and the Counter-Reformational orthodoxy of Melchor Cano; Fray Luis de León's biblical exegesis and the pseudo-Lutheran liberalizations of Agustín de Cazalla; the bustling mysticism of St. Teresa of Ávila and the revivalist ecstasies of the Illuminists (*alumbrados*).

It was a medieval truism that religious tolerance begot civil disorder; the axiom was self-enforcing, because the efforts of a missionary Church to impose conformity on minority sects which were frequently messianic and separatist usually did promote violence. Especially to the Spanish Church, its reflexes formed by eight centuries of aggressive evangelism, spiritual safety lay in a monolithic unity of faith. In this it was generally —though not uniformly—supported by the crown, already faced with more disorder than it could cope with.

A decade before the fall of Granada, the Catholic Kings had created a new arm of the state, the Council of the Supreme and General Inquisition, to replace the Papal Inquisition which had existed in Spain since 1238. After the Reconquest was completed, the crown set about the work of unification. Too weak to impose more than a token discipline on its arrogant nobility, too poor for a concerted move against hypocritical conversos whose income-producing capabilities it valued, too conscientious to punish unjustly those converts whose Christianity was genuine, the throne could and did try to allay popular resentment by giving first the Jews, then the Moslems, a choice of exile or conversion.

So far, we have a standard medieval situation; there was not a country in the Old World which had not taken turns in expelling its Jews and persecuting its dissidents, rightly so in the current thinking, for disagreement with the crown's religion implied criticism of the sovereign, which made dissidence treason as well as heresy. But at this point the picture is changed by a specifically Spanish exaggeration, the national code of honor, a deadly serious parody within a parody which, like religion, for which it was often mistaken, left no corner of Spanish life untouched.

One historian defines honor as "a metaphysical entity deposited, so to speak, in the valor of the man and in the fidelity of the woman," combining the fundamental aspects of emotional life: sex, reputation, face-saving, patriotism and the insecurity of temporal and eternal welfare.[13] The aristocracy lived by it in every country in Europe, but only Spain made it the spool around which all other ethical values were wrapped.

It involved, first of all, adoption by the commonalty of the Reconquest warrior-knight's tradition of chivalry. This imposed on Spanish daily life a set of artificial values designed for a military caste in a wartime situation, and it made any pragmatic examination of the country's real problems appear vulgar and dishonorable. The code's emphasis on violence caricatured the knight's courage in battle; knightly pride was burlesqued in its exaggerated sensitivity to offense, just as the courtly love of the Middle Ages was unwittingly ridiculed in the popular feeling on woman's virtue.

> Honor is a pure crystal
> which even a breath can tarnish.[14]

Lope de Vega summarized the popular opinion in *Los comendadores de Córdoba:*

> Honor is that which consists in others' esteem.
> No man is honored for his inner qualities,
> but from others does he receive honor.
> For a man to be virtuous and to possess merit
> is not to be honored, though it prepares the way
> for those who treat with him to grant him honor.

It underlay that mysterious egalitarianism which raises the "essential man" in every Spaniard to equality with the greatest in the land. "I am your tenant, not your slave," the beauteous Dorothea tells the lordly Don Fernando in *Don Quixote*. "And I, a peasant and farm girl, esteem myself as highly as you, a lord and a gentleman, do yourself."[15]

Honor had its farcical side. A sixteenth-century writer reported the indignation of a Spanish recruit in Italy who was not getting the treatment he thought he deserved. "Don't you know who I am, you men?" he demanded. "This is no way to treat men of honor."

"Who are you, by your life?" he was asked.

"I am," came the haughty reply, "the polisher-in-chief of the Count of Benavente's vermeil."[16]

As often as not, the farce ended in bloodshed. The "laws" of honor were thought to be universal and immutable, prescribing a subtle code of responses to violations. Take the case of a woman courted by a king: her honor and that of all the males in her family were stained even if she refused his attentions. But, since a subject could not be offended by a monarch, whose person was sacred, there was only one way to remove the blemish, and that was to remove the innocent lady from this life.

Violence was honor's constant companion, stylized belligerency raised to the dignity of social ideal. Calderón's protagonist in *The Doctor of His Honor* forces a surgeon to bleed to death his unjustly suspected wife: "Love adores you, but honor abhors you." Cervantes, whose irony is merciless in its treatment of conventional honor, tells of the soldier in *The Labors of Persiles and Sigismunda* who sank Arnaldo's ship in a plot to rape Sigismunda; when his plot failed, he killed himself and his mate, not out of remorse for his evil ways but because his failure dishonored him. El Cid Campeador declined into Don Juan Tenorio.

What dishonored a man? Work, for one thing, not only "low or mechanical labor," which meant any manual activity from wielding a scythe to stitching a slipper, but, in general, living from the proceeds of one's own efforts. Trade and commerce, any capital investment except in land, livestock or valuables, were dishonorable. So was intellectual work as a livelihood, although it was tolerable in teachers and ecclesiastics. The Aristotelian dictate that all paid employments absorb and degrade the mind was far better heeded in that Christian society than St. Paul's admonition, "If anyone will not work, let him not eat."

When Cervantes chose a knight and a peasant as the protagonists of his novel in praise of folly, he went directly to the heart of the Spanish social myth. The situation can also be expressed statistically: the aristocracy, comprising less than 2 per cent of the population, owned better than 95 per cent of the land; the peasantry made up nearly 95 per cent of the population. Distribution of rights and privileges was in direct proportion to land ownership.

"The fields go untended," a Spanish critic would complain early in the seventeenth century, "as do the mechanical arts, business and commerce, to which our nation scorns to apply itself, because its haughty and vainglorious spirit, even among the common people, is dissatisfied with the state in which nature placed it, and aspires to nobility, despising all those occupations which it holds to contradict that state."[17]

A sixteenth-century German traveler marveled that Spaniards "all appear to be kinsmen of the king, or at least Spanish grandees, when they are really only porters or poor goatherds."[18] The Frenchman Bartolomé Joly, who, it is true, found little to admire in Spain, observed with Gallic superiority the artisans at the court of Philip III who worked "disdainfully, as though to get it over with; some, especially the silversmiths, can be seen seated contemptuously at their work with their capes on and, two or three hours after the midday meal, go strolling with their swords at their sides,[19] and as soon as they scrape together two or three hundred reales, there they are, gentry! There is no reason for them to do any more work until, having spent it all, they are obliged to return to their benches. . . ."[20]

At the same time, the aristocracy—the chivalric tradition's titular occupant—relieved of the pressure of an infidel on its doorstep, sloughed off its political responsibilities with its coat of mail, encouraged in this by a monarchy anxious to centralize power in itself. In compensation, the nobles presented their bill for blood and treasure expended in the war of liberation—with eight centuries of accrued interest—and undertook a competition to determine which was the most noble, the richest, the most splendid. They spent themselves in court intrigues, in gallantries, in maintaining the armies of servants made stylish by the emperor's Burgundian courtiers. They bought fine horses and rich equipments for war when the occasion arose and, in peacetime, remained largely decorative. "The majority of great noblemen are more suited for ceremonial missions than for negotiations," one foreign diplomatic observer would note. "It is on the occasion of some baptism, marriage, death or birth, or the ratification of a treaty, that they really shine. They can pay compliments as to the manner born, but they will neither take the trouble nor have the inclination to transact business."[21] They nonetheless thought of themselves as the country's natural administrators, looking with languid disdain on the growing number of low-born professionals peopling the royal bureaucracy.

Honor's prime conditions were *hidalguía* (gentility) and *limpieza de sangre* (purity of blood—without Moorish or Jewish admixture). They were related, but by no means synonymous.

Legally, hidalguía was the simpler of the two states to attain. Although its most satisfactory proof was a properly executed patent of nobility, duly sealed and beribboned and emblazoned with the family crest, it could be proved by attestations that the candidate's family was and had been generally reputed to be gentry. It was no empty honor. Even if it was a recent purchase from a needy monarch it conveyed, along with honor, exemption from direct taxation, immunity from imprisonment for debt and from the disgrace of the gibbet should the occasion arise. The law could be delicate with a hidalgo's honor. Execution of a noble was by beheading, as it was elsewhere in Europe, but, in Spain, the gentry were decapitated from the front; only traitors were beheaded from behind.

Honor was tainted by poverty. The literature of the period is saturated with derision of poor but proud hidalgos. There is the gentleman in the anonymously written novel *Lazarillo de Tormes* who survived on the crusts of bread scrounged by his urchin squire but who affirmed that a hidalgo "owes nothing to anyone but God and his King, nor is it seemly that a gentleman neglect his self-esteem, even for a moment."[22] Paredes, Quevedo's gentleman in *La vida del buscón*, "shaves the beard of his cloak" (trims its frayed edges) he sees shadowed by the sunlight. Don Quixote makes fun of the hidalgo who goes into the street picking his teeth rather than admit he has nothing in his house to eat, but the knight himself is obeying the imperatives of honor when he refuses to pay his bills at an inn because, he insists, what knight-errant "has ever paid poll tax, sales tax, queen's patten money, statutory tax, toll or ferry? What tailor ever collected his wage from him for a suit of clothes? What warden ever received him in his castle and made him pay for his keep?"[23]

In all Spain, no spendthrift was more prodigal than the state. It was buying itself more expensive luxuries: preservation of an empire against the corrosion of nationalism and mercantilism, integrity of the faith against foreign sectarianism. Its taste in royal adornments was on the showy side—a Holy Roman crown, later an Escorial. That Spain was living beyond its means was a concept incompatible with honor—dynastic, aristocratic, national, Catholic—and honor was worth more than life itself. This helps to explain why, with his tax revenues already in pawn for years ahead, Charles V could permit himself to confiscate all treasure from the Indies in the spring of 1547, instead of the usual royal fifth, to finance his victory at Mühlberg. It is why, when he finally resigned the throne to his son in 1556, it was buried under a national debt of some 40 million ducats, and it is why Philip II would feel himself entitled to more than double that debt in the ensuing four decades. If the crown was reduced to juggling its finances like a shady housing promoter with the law at his heels—why, this was material to the national destiny.

There was, however, one luxury with which Spain felt it could dispense: intellectual adventuring.

While the Church had been unenthusiastic about what it saw as an alien intellectual excitement in Spain, for a time it tolerated and occasionally sponsored speculative thought in the hope of controlling it. Even this tentative fling at liberalization was cut short by Luther's rebellion against Rome. A campaign by Spanish theologians to discredit Erasmism quickly overrode isolated protests, convincing Spaniards that Erasmian doctrine and Lutheran heresy were merely the white and the yolk of the same rotten egg.

Spain's masses, needful of the stability which orthodoxy gave, were overwhelmingly in favor of the Church offensive. Then, as now, the word *novedades* (literally, novelties) had pejorative connotations. In 1551, Bishop Antonio de Guevara of Palencia, a writer of some standing, recommended that authorities in Granada not "attempt or introduce new things, because novelties always bring trouble to those who effect them and engender disturbances among the people."[24] This was in line with a continuing tradition: even Seneca had warned that "wishing to know more than is necessary is a kind of intemperance."[25]

As a result of the campaign, the country's leading Humanists either fled abroad, were jailed as heretics or were forced to renounce the ideas on which they had based their whole system of thought. The case of Pedro de Lerma, the first chancellor of the University of Alcalá de Henares, was typical.

While still a young man, Lerma had left Alcalá, ultimately becoming dean of the Faculty of Theology at the Sorbonne, in Paris, and a close friend of Erasmus'. Then he returned to Alcalá—one of the strongest redoubts of Humanist thought in Spain and a converso center—to spend his last years among his own people. In 1537 he retired, but despite his seventy years, he was shortly afterward imprisoned by the Inquisition for heresy; after a long trial on a charge of preaching Erasmian doctrines, he was forced to make public abjuration, in all the principal towns of Spain where he had preached, of the eleven Erasmian propositions the Inquisition considered heretical and scandalous. In addition, he was required to declare that the said doctrines were diabolically inspired to sow evil in the Church.[26] The old man preferred to trek back across the Pyrenees to die in exile rather than live in a country which, he charged, was unfit for the learned to inhabit.

Vives had already taken refuge in Flanders, where he alleged that "we live in difficult times, in which we can neither speak nor remain silent without danger."[27] In 1533 Rodrigo Manrique, son of Inquisitor General Alfonso de Manrique, whose support of Erasmus had earned him banishment from the Imperial court, wrote Vives from Paris: "You are right. Our country is a land of pride and envy; you may add: of barbarism. For now it is clear that down there one cannot possess any culture without being suspected of heresy, error and Judaism. Thus silence has been imposed on the learned. As for those who take refuge in erudition, they have been filled, as you say, with great terror. . . . At Alcalá they are trying to uproot the study of Greek completely."[28]

The Spanish door swung irresistibly shut against foreign contamination. In 1558 it was decreed that the punishment for importing unauthorized foreign books in Spanish translation would be death. In 1559 Spaniards were forbidden to study abroad in any but approved schools in Italy and Portugal. In 1576 the University of Salamanca would discontinue the study of anatomy as unchristian and unclassical, but the action was motivated by the same fear of unbridled thought that would cause it to suspend the study of mathematics early in the seventeenth century. The Inquisition, meanwhile, continued to investigate persons who sold horses outside the kingdom (on the grounds that they not only deprived Spain of the stallions of which it was so proud, but risked contact with heretics in the process). Acrobats whose prowess exceeded what was believed natural and animal trainers whose beasts seemed so preternaturally clever as to suggest that the devil had a hand in their training were subjected to clerical scrutiny. As long as Spain was protected by the "impenetrable wall" of the Inquisition, affirmed Diego Cardinal de Espinosa, the Spanish would continue to be "the beloved of God and the chosen people of its Church and would triumph over our enemies."[29]

Two other factors help account for the acerbity of Spanish anti-intellectualism: honor's requirement of blood purity and the strong Jewish current in the humanities.

It was the Reconquest, again, that provided the momentum for the insistence on limpieza de sangre, the desire to wash away all taint of the former enemy, to leave the Spanish soul clean and whole; Spain sought a warrior's clear and blameless conscience. Conversion to Christianity by Moors and Jews, rather than healing old wounds, reopened them; once a heathen, the feeling went, always a heathen, regardless of the antiquity of a family's conversion.

Inevitably, intolerance in principle was compounded by all the sullen resentments of racial and religious prejudice. Old Christians envied converso wealth and influence; they were indignant at the conversos' easy access to—even intermarriage with—the greatest houses in the land. They believed the Moriscos were spying for the predatory Turks, and some of them were, especially for the Turkish-ruled Barbary pirates of North Africa who ravaged the Spanish Mediterranean coasts. Old Christians charged, again rightly, that exiled Jews were conspiring against Spain with its enemies. Later, with the rise of Protestantism, New Christians were accused of importing the Lutheran heresy into Spain, and, in fact, a combination of Erasmian simplicity and Protestant directness did color the thinking of some conversos. On the other hand, Christians of Jewish ancestry were suspected of secret Judaizing in cynical contempt of their new religion. Some certainly were contemptuous of a religion they felt they had been forced to adopt; others, like the forebears of St. Teresa, slipped in and out of Judaism as though it were a protective suit of armor, according to the temper of the times. In Lope de Rueda's mid-sixteenth-century play *Medora,* the comic lackey Gargullo muses that, when he grows rich, "I shall have my family murdered . . . so that my lineage may not be known."[30]

None of these New Christian transgressions were widespread enough to justify the fear of subversion which moved the country, but they provided the handle for all the traditional baggage of prejudice. The conversos, said the envious Old Christians, "possess the fat of the land and live in greater prosperity than the natives, though neither tilling and sowing, nor building and fighting, nor engaging in any honest labor."[31] Moriscos were witches and sexual libertines, Jews kidnapped Christian children and sacrificed them on Christian altars, they brought plague to Spain, etc., etc. Marranos, protested a chronicler at the court of the Catholic Kings, ate "stews of onions and garlic and meat cooked in oil . . . a thing which gives a foul odor to the breath" and a rancid smell to the house.[32] He would have been appalled to know that these malodorous practices in time would become the Spanish national cuisine.

That the complaints were chiefly aimed at the conversos was made clear in the religious riots which occurred in Spain's major cities in the late fourteenth century and at intervals throughout the fifteenth; in almost every case, Moslems and Jews who had remained faithful to their religions were little molested; many conversos saved their lives by taking refuge in the comparative safety of the Jewish quarters.

Understandably, mannerisms, habits, values associated with Moorishness or Jewishness were automatically suspect. A man might be called on to explain himself for bathing on Saturday. Faith itself could be dangerous: St. Ignatius of Loyola was for a time accused of Judaizing because of the strictness of his religious practices. Trade and labor were more than merely antiaristocratic, they were characteristic of Moors and Jews. Certain occupations were "impure": blacksmiths, tailors, cobblers, innkeepers, muleteers, for example, were "Moorish"; physicians, apothecaries, drapers, scholars were "Jewish." The story is told of Joselito the tailor in the province of Jaén who was married for his money by an impoverished gentlewoman and promptly gave up tailoring as dishonorable, thus reducing the family to poverty.[33] Only the peasantry by and large escaped suspicion of "taint," a distinction which both flattered their egalitarian feelings and soothed their envy of lordly opulence; a "pure" peasant could—privately—feel himself superior to a noble of "shameful" lineage.

While limpieza conferred few of the material privileges of hidalguía, it was not without its practical advantages. Statutes requiring blood purity as a precondition to civil rights had begun to appear in the fifteenth century. The most famous was that issued by the magistrates of Toledo declaring conversos, "descendants of the perverse lineage of the Jews," to be "infamous, ineligible, inept and unworthy" to hold any public or private office in the city or to exercise their civil rights. Despite hesitation by the crown and the Vatican—canon law contained no such prohibition—Toledo's example was followed over the succeeding two centuries by a growing number of cities, monastic orders, lay brotherhoods and craft guilds.

Application of the edicts was often lax at first, but in the 1540s and 1550s attitudes began to harden under the pressure of Counter-Reformationist zeal and economic tensions which thrust New Christian successes into higher relief. To comply with the edicts, an aspirant to a restricted position had to submit a certificate of limpieza de sangre proving the spotlessness of his ancestry for three generations back in the sixteenth century, four in the seventeenth. The loophole they opened was wide enough for most conversos of means to slip through: like hidalguía, blood purity could be established, officially at least, by repute.

Fear of Lutheranism focused attention on the role converts from Judaism played in the country's cultural life. "Jews" had not only deeply infiltrated the Church, they were disproportionately influential in Spanish scholarship, philosophy and letters. Vives was of New Christian stock, for example, as were the twins Juan and Francisco de Vergara, whom many considered the nation's most widely cultivated men. Mateo Alemán was "Jewish" and so was Fernando de Rojas, who wrote the dialogue most widely known as *La Celestina,* ranked just behind *Don Quixote* as the period's most brilliant prose masterpiece. We will explore in a later chapter the belief of some modern scholars that Cervantes himself was of converso lineage. If so, he was in distinguished company; other "Jews" in the arts included architect Diego de Siloë, who designed the Granada cathedral; Andrés Laguna, the botanist and naturalist who became physician to Pope Julius III; Torres Naharro, Fray Luis de León, poet-composer Juan del Encina, mathematician Pedro Nunes, perhaps even St. John of the Cross—the list could go on for pages. Humanism was heretical and "Jewish"; "Jews" were intellectuals and artists; intellectualism, therefore, was heretical.

The syllogism made literacy itself unwholesome, an attitude Cervantes would satirize savagely and repeatedly. In his interlude *Choosing a Councilman in Dagonza,* the college graduate Pesuña asks candidate Humillos if he can read. He answers:

"Certainly not, nor will you ever come across a kinsman of mine so weak-minded as to try to learn those chimeras which send men to the stake and women to the whorehouse. I don't know how to read, but I know other things lots better than reading."

"What are they?"

"I know all four prayers by heart, and I recite them four or five times every week."

"You think that's all you need to be a councilman?"

"With that, and with my being an Old Christian, I'd dare to be a Roman senator."

The question inevitably arises: how could a Golden Century in art have blossomed in such stifling air? It has been suggested that the danger was to academic, not artistic freedom, that speculative and experimental science were choked off, but creation and contemplation were unhampered.[84] One wonders how many artists would agree that the creative process is so sealed off from the intellectual life around it that the mind may roam freely in some areas but not in others.

Many—most—of Cervantes' contemporaries probably saw nothing wrong with the situation. The theater was dominated by such men, writers of undoubted dramatic and poetic genius who subscribed to orthodox attitudes acceptable to a sensation-hungry but intellectually passive public. They saw their responsibility as celebrating, not criticizing, the national virtues. Besides, serious artists were supposed to concern themselves with aesthetic issues of form, style, coloring, suitability, with the very nature of the artistic function. Politics was unworthy of art.

Social criticism, in the circumstances, was muted, but by no means silenced. Such writers as Alemán, Quevedo, above all Cervantes, contrived a literature that could survive in a dungeon, slipping controversial ideas between the lines of their books where skillful readers knew to look for them. It is nevertheless true that to social problems, even they returned moral and ethical, not institutional, responses.

It is difficult today to understand how narrow the field was for social criticism in the sixteenth and seventeenth centuries. There were few options. The apparatus by which collective problems are analyzed or even identified hardly existed. Economics was a rudimentary art, as gimcrack as Leonardo's flying machine. No viable alternative was recognized to traditional political structures; true revolution, we remember, was an eighteenth-century invention. No wonder, then, that men still wandering on the misty frontiers of the Middle Ages should think of social ills as the products not of a system, but of sinful humanity's faltering will to choose good instead of evil.

Of them all, Cervantes is the one who speaks most cogently to us today. As we read his stories, we perceive that there was something tangential about the way his people thought and behaved, a sly unorthodoxy in their approach to the truths Spain was sensitive about, like the nature of honor, the wisdom of the mighty and the gallantry of what his country thought of as its historic mission. Disconformity is evident in Cervantes' scorn of superstition, his rejection of Tridentine populism, his softening of the Counter-Reformation's neo-Aristotelian severity with an older Platonic tolerance. When Quixote, in his very first adventure, "rescues" the boy Andrés from a whipping by a rich peasant, when he frees a chain gang of galley slaves, he is clearly administering crude social justice. References to magisterial venality, the dishonor of poverty, the unfairness of emphasis on lineage swarm in his books like flies in August. The idle cruelties of the duke and duchess and their retinue in the *Quixote* reflect the lopsided viciousness of Spain's social structure. The Church takes its lumps: clergymen seem to find themselves facing lances and verbal barbs with uncommon frequency, they are compared to women, indicted as wastrels. *The Dogs' Colloquy* can be read as a satire on Church corruption; the novella called *The Jealous Extremaduran* can pass for a warning to a Spain at pains to perfect its spiritual isolation. The *Quixote* has been seen as, among many other things, an allegory on the futility of Spanish imperial dreams.

Cervantes is thought of as the most Spanish of Spain's novelists. This is partly because more of his Spain is actually encountered in his stories—its people, inns, roads, its illusions and confusions—than in the work of any of his contemporaries. More important, Don Quixote and Sancho Panza have been accepted as what has been called "the national sigh of Spain,"[35] the epitome of Spanishness and consequently, to his fellow countrymen, the essence of what is best in mankind. Having elected itself a nation of anarchist poets, Spain rightly recognizes Quixote as the great anarchic poet of literature and offers him as the nation's ambassador to the rest of humanity. "Never," the knight warns Sancho, "be guided by arbitrary law, which generally has great influence with the ignorant who would appear clever. . . ."[36]

Because it has saddled him with the unwelcome role of national spokesman at a critical period in his country's history, this very Spanishness has contributed to Cervantes' reputation for ambiguity. Later ages eager to ascribe praise or blame for the conduct of Philippine Spain have searched his work for indications of how he stood on political and social issues. They have come up with a full range of portraits: Cervantes the proto-Marxist social revolutionary, Cervantes the reactionary, the anticlerical crypto-Protestant, the apologist for the Counter-Reformation, a champion of ethnic minorities, a jingoist anti-Semite, a clown, an intellectual alive to the spiritual anguish of his time.

Yet, after all, Cervantes was an artist, not a political commentator. Social criticism in his books became an element of style, the texture into which a moral message was woven. He understood that life constantly protests against itself and that, by capturing life whole in his work, he would give injustice its organic place in a total Cervantine world, as natural and outrageous a phenomenon as death or malice.

That, at his best, he succeeded in doing precisely this was his conquest, his Peru. In a Spain grown old, tired, petulant and poor this old, poor, tired man would retain his moral buoyancy, and the intellectual vitality to pursue a triumphant dream.

] 2 [

Holes in the Family Coat

If Rodrigo de Cervantes thought at all, as he clutched his tiny son Miguel in the echoing Oidór chapel, about his first trip to the ancient stone font in Santa María,[1] reflection would have had a bitter taste. He had been carried then in the arms of *his* father, Juan de Cervantes. That had been in 1509 or early 1510, when Juan, then a young lawyer, arrived in Alcalá de Henares from Córdoba to serve as deputy *corregidor*.*

His father had been everything Rodrigo was not. Juan was university-trained, well to do, an important person in the town, a man with a future. To judge from his subsequent career, he was also rapacious, self-important and vain, but these qualities may not have been so evident then.

Something in the family genetic code seems to have gone haywire when Rodrigo was born. He inherited neither the Cervantes ambition nor the waspish shrewdness of his mother's line. He loved to sing and play his vihuela, after the manner of barbers of the day, and to act the gentleman, which was not easy on his income. He probably stayed out of his wife's way as best he could, for Doña Leonor seems to have wielded the strong hand in the family. She is seen as fiercely possessive, highhanded, resilient, energetic, decisive—things might have gone better had she been the man in the family. If she was resentful of the way her marriage had turned out, she left no record of it, although the persistent absence of any other Cortinas from Cervantes family events suggests what her people thought about it.

There had been a time when she might have thought she was making a good match, for Rodrigo had been rich when she met him, a spoiled dandy who raced through the muddy back streets of Alcalá on fine horses and, on feast days, fought in the mock tourneys where the gentlemen used

* A royal magistrate appointed to oversee a city's affairs.

cane spears instead of lances. Not bad, for the grandson of a Córdoban cloth merchant.

A Córdoban cloth merchant? A converso's trade in a converts' town. Were Cervantes' ancestors "Jews," then? The question seems to make some Cervantes scholars skittish, as though the notion were vaguely unsavory. Many who accept other obscure but important "facts" about Cervantes' life with, as we shall see, fewer proofs or none at all back away from this one. Besides, what difference does it make to us today if Miguel de Cervantes, who lived four centuries ago, was a gentleman, or had Semitic blood in his veins? The kind of man he was, how his life affects ours—these are what matter. Yet it does make a difference to us because it did to his contemporaries and surely would have to him. In a society scrambling for handholds in the past, judging men by ungenerous standards, the judged often perplexedly concur in their own guilt.

Barely enough evidence has been found to allow for a working hypothesis that Miguel de Cervantes was descended from New Christians, that this was publicly known and that it colored his attitudes toward life and his society. But the available evidence does not authorize the security with which some modern scholars have seized on it to explain a number of mysteries: why were Cervantes women so frequently loved and so seldom married? Why was Miguel de Cervantes pinned so firmly to the margin of society and why was his company so little cultivated even by those, like the anti-converso Quevedo, who openly admired his work? How explain Cervantes' intense, austere religiosity? Above all, what were the secret springs of his style, that gentle, elastic irony, so delicately different from his contemporaries' burlesques that it might, today, be identified as Jewish humor?

In fact, we cannot pinpoint a single incident in Cervantes' life as having happened the way it did because of his supposedly Jewish ancestry. Such proofs of it as exist are circumstantial and inconclusive, but they do exist and, while they can be countered, they cannot be dismissed. We can do no more than ponder them, and wonder.

Oceans of ink and ingenuity have flowed in trying to trace the family's ancestry, with minimal success. Attempts to prove its aristocracy have been stubbornly unproductive.[2] The Cervantes line may have originated in Galicia, may have migrated to Andalusia via Talavera de la Reina, near Toledo. The very scarcity of authentic records prods doubt about the solidity of the family's hidalgo and Old Christian identity; aristocracy, when it truly existed, was usually traceable; blood purity, in families with pasts to hide, usually was not.

The Cervantes family's gentility has always been accepted as it was asserted by Miguel and his father. It ought nevertheless to be noted that their hidalguía was entirely a matter of repute. To win his release from debtors' prison, Cervantes' father was obliged to collect testimonials in Alcalá de Henares, Madrid and Guadalajara, where the family's roots were shallow, to show that he was a gentleman. None was sought in places—Córdoba, for example—where those roots might have gone deeper. None of the witnesses admitted to knowing the family for more than twenty-six years—that is, nothing was said of Miguel's ancestors beyond his grandfather Juan—and none had actually seen a patent of nobility, with its "ad perpetuam rei memoriam and (its) leaden seals,"[3] made out in the name of Cervantes. All declared that Juan and his son Rodrigo "had been held" to be gentlemen—because, as one witness specified, "of their clothes and way of living."[4]

Allusions in Cervantes' works to the cult of lineage and honor are often, so to speak, pointedly ambiguous. "There are only two lineages in the world, as my grandma said, the haves and the have-nots";[5] "Every man is the son of his own works";[6] "Know you, Sancho, that no one is more of a man than another if he does no more than another";[7] "Where is the family in the world, however good its lineage, but you may pick some holes in its coat?"[8]

Many of the passages in his work refer clearly to religion. "I am an Old Christian," says Sancho, "and as far as I am concerned, that is good enough to make an earl."[9] "It is quite true that I am a bit malicious," the squire declares, "and I show some of the marks of a rogue, but all this is covered and hidden under my great cloak of simplicity . . . and if only for the fact that I believe firmly and truly in God and in all the tenets and beliefs of the Holy Roman Catholic Church, and for being a mortal enemy of the Jews, the historians should have mercy on me."[10] As governor, Sancho is called on to judge if a swineherd's hands be *"limpia o no"* —clean or not;[11] such wordplay cannot be considered capricious in a writer as deliberate as Cervantes or in a society as alert to such nuances as Cervantes' Spain.[12]

Allusions to the Pauline doctrine of virtue as a qualification for divine grace toward unbelievers are obsessively frequent in Cervantes' writings. "I may say that Dulcinea is the daughter of her works, that virtues improve the blood and that the virtuous and humble are more to be esteemed and prized than exalted wickedness . . ."[13] ". . . True nobility lies in virtue," Dorotea informs Don Fernando.[14]

St. Paul, as Christianity's puritan intellectual, was popular in a Europe made hungry for purification by the sixteenth century's religious and philosophical conflicts. He was also the spiritual master of converts anxious to find the unadorned Word their forefathers revered amid the unfamiliar and not always welcome trappings of Catholicism. The "born again" impact of Paul's conversion worked powerfully on Jews seeking to justify their apostasy. Which of these currents was Cervantes riding when he sent the protagonists of his novel *The Labors of Persiles and Sigis-munda,* his archsymbols of spiritual regeneration, not to the Church of St. Peter in Rome, but to St. Paul's? Cervantes' dedication is made explicit when Quixote praises St. Paul: "In his time he was the worst enemy Our Lord's Church had, and the best champion it will ever have; a knight-errant in life and in death a staunch saint, a tireless toiler in the Lord's vineyard and teacher of the Gentiles."[15]

To some, the abundance of crypto-identities (crypto-Moslems and Christians, aristocratic changelings, saintly hoodlums and sanctimonious scoundrels) should be read as a continuing defense of genealogical ambiguity, especially his own. There is a danger here of being too subtle; Cervantes' philosophy of literature was, after all, based on the idea that all worldly truth is ambiguous.

Literal reading of Cervantes' work has produced charges against him of bigotry, racism, anti-Semitism. His sermons against the Moriscos, for example, do sound as though he wholeheartedly endorsed Spain's blunderbuss expulsion of its Moriscos, an estimated 150,000 to 300,000 of them, early in the seventeenth century. In *Don Quixote,* in the *Persiles,* in *The Dogs' Colloquy,* strident support is given for the popular notion, so prevalent as to become national policy, of the ineradicable corruption of the Moslem soul. We may have to admit that Cervantes never unlearned the hatred of Moslems he acquired as a captive in Algiers and a veteran of the Turkish wars. Yet even in this, his most violent prejudice, his respect for truth asserted itself.

Cervantes' Moriscos are often damned a little too loudly by Morisco characters drawn with careful sympathy. Their diatribes are often double-edged. The heat with which the Christianized "jadraque" in the *Persiles* proclaims his wish that "my eyes, before they close, (may) see this land free of these thorns and evils which oppress it"[16] obscures the irony of his invitation to the frivolous and incompetent King Philip III: "Come, then, O fortunate youth and prudent king, and execute the gallant decree of exile, and do not be stayed by the fear that it must leave this land deserted and depopulated. . . ." The passage was almost certainly written after the decree was carried out; Cervantes would have known that it had in fact left some of Spain's richest farming regions "deserted and depopulated."

The Morisco Christian Ricote in *Don Quixote* fulminates with equal energy against his kind. But then he lauds Germany, where he has found refuge, as a place "where one can live with more freedom, for its inhabitants do not peer too closely at fine points: every man does as he pleases, because in most places there, people live with free consciences."[17] This can be taken as a hint of the kind of New Christian flirtation with Lutheranism that led men to the flames; it can also be read as an appeal for liberty of conscience by a Catholic confident of his faith's force of attraction.

Forgetting a basic fact—that no other writer's work in Inquisitorial Spain is so saturated in ironic ambiguity as Cervantes', so elaborately encoded in the intellectual cryptography of the time—has led some Jews to accuse him of anti-Semitism. "O effeminate folk, infamous and of little worth," a Christian calls them in Cervantes' play *The Dungeons of Algiers*. But their persecution nevertheless "moves me to compassion," the Christian goes on. Cervantes' Jews obey the imperatives of Inquisitorial orthodoxy; they are taunted and bullied and made fools of. But they are never deprived of their humanity, never caricatured as the bestial, unrelievedly evil monstrosities we see in so much Spanish and Flemish painting of the fifteenth and sixteenth centuries. The cruelty of their predicament is never lost from sight.

The plight of the Jews Cervantes saw in Algiers, perhaps the only avowed Jews he ever saw, was pitiable. Although the wealth they had brought with them into exile from Spain had largely contributed to North African prosperity, and although (perhaps partly because) they covertly controlled the Turkish provinces' trade, they were hated by the Moslems with whom they had sought refuge. Moslem religious tolerance toward them was barely that—tolerance. Jews were obliged to dress in distinct black; anyone, even a slave, could beat them publicly with impunity. Cervantes obliges his audience by making the Jews in his plays derisory; they cringe and fawn on their tormentors. But Cervantes' pity for them (and, by extension, for their kinsmen in Europe) is concealed by the flimsiest of veils.

What in fact does happen to the Jews in *The Dungeons of Algiers?* A captive Christian sacristan steals their food, filches their possessions, disrupts their Sabbath, even kidnaps one of their children. He may be a wag, our sacristan, but he is undisguisedly insolent and malicious. Yet what is he doing that his Church has not done to the Jews in Spain? He has stolen their treasure, deprived them of their sustenance, trampled their sacred institutions. The kidnapping is a pointed burlesque of the Christian folk tales of ritual abductions of Christian children by the Jews.

This kind of autopsy can be pushed too far, of course; efforts to read *Don Quixote* as a cabalistic treatise on the Old Testament are ingenious but not at all persuasive. It can be argued that a man with Cervantes' grand vision could have adopted decent, commonsensical attitudes without being pushed into them by the prod of an equivocal past. But when all this has been noted, there remains what the sixteenth century might have thought of as a distinctly garlicky tone to Cervantine double-think: his ascetic, critical earnestness, his irony, his defensiveness, the simple loftiness of his Christianity, his puritanism and his almost self-justifying insistence on the fecklessness of any but spiritual purity, the extraordinary depth of his tolerance.

How much historical evidence is there to support the theory of his supposed New Christian descent? None a lawyer could be satisfied with. Efforts to extract clues from Cervantes' life often sound more like wish fulfillment than research. His permanent grasp on society's outer fringes is blamed on general knowledge of his "Jewishness" and not, as it might easily be, on his poverty and temperament. He was a tax collector and that was traditionally a converso occupation; it was also a job offered when he needed one, an escape from an unfortunate marriage, a flight from premature burial in a dull Manchegan village. Cervantes would comment wryly that the trade had its attraction for a poor man: at least it involved handling money.[18] A remark by Lope de Vega, whose Old Christianity has never been questioned, that Cervantes was a "pig on the hoof"[19]—the choice of epithets made the meaning of the insult clear—is cited. But this could have been no more than a gratuitous calumny (in contemporary terms) by a man never known for his taste in human relations. "As well," Cervantes observed, "try to put doors to an open field as tie up the tongues of slander."[20] Proponents of the converso theory note that all of Miguel's immediate family, including his mother and sisters, could read and write, a rare enough situation in any family in the period and more so in families of his social and economic group—except in converso families with a tradition of literacy.

The verifiable past of the Cervantes family begins in Córdoba with Miguel's great-grandfather, Ruy or Rodrigo Díaz de Cervantes, a draper who is thought to have been born in the 1430s. He married a Catalina de Cabrera about whom nothing at all is known. The family was probably prosperous. There was money enough, in any event, to send Miguel's grandfather Juan, who must have been born in the late 1470s, to read law at Salamanca. Up to this point, the converso theory, vaguely activated by Ruy Díaz's trade in a town where more than half the population was New Christian, remains sluggish. It comes alive with a start, however, late in 1503 or early in 1504, when Juan, then two or three years out of university and working as a petty magistrate handling fiscal questions for the Inquisition tribunal in Córdoba, married Miguel's grandmother, Leonor Fernández de Torreblanca, the eldest daughter of a Córdoban physician and possibly Juan's cousin.

The first reference to a Torreblanca of interest here crops up in 1473. Córdoba, once the brilliant capital of the Western Caliphate but now shrunk to a middle-sized provincial town, had long been divided between its Old Christians and its conversos. On March 14, 1473, the second Sunday of Lent, a religious procession carrying a statue of the Virgin Mary wound through flower-strewn streets beneath balconies hung with tapestries. As it passed the house of a rich converso, a girl emptied a pitcher of water from a window over the head of the Virgin, presumably inadvertently. A cry of desecration arose from the marchers when one Alonso Rodríguez insisted that the liquid was urine and not water. The converso squire of a local magistrate tried to reason with the crowd; in the ensuing scuffle, he was stabbed to death. His name was Pedro de Torreblanca and the incident blew up into a three-day anti-converso riot in which hundreds of New Christians were killed and their homes and shops burned by the mob.

The next meaningful date in the story is 1486, when Christopher Columbus arrived in Córdoba for a stay of several months while awaiting the arrival there of King Ferdinand and Queen Isabel. He brought with him introductions to two brothers of Genoese origin, Leonardo and Lucian Esbarroya, both apothecaries. Their little shop was the meeting place for Columbus and the circle of friends which quickly formed around him, a circle which included the Torreblancas, the Martínez family to which they were tied by marriage and, probably, Ruy Díaz de Cervantes and his clan. There were others, too, like the Spinola family of Genoese merchant bankers; Luis de Santángel, *escribano de ración*—a sort of finance minister—to Ferdinand; Diego Enríquez de Arana, already a follower of the navigator, and his cousin Beatriz, a dark-haired beauty of twenty who would give the explorer a son two years later. It is easy to imagine Columbus, his ruddy face glowing with emphasis, his pale blue eyes, the eyes of a beleaguered fanatic, glaring with the intensity of his conviction as he preached to the little group that men could defy the open sea and survive.

When we focus on the individual members of that group in the Esbarroyas' shop, the "smell" of New Christianity becomes powerful, if not overwhelming. First, there was Juan Díaz de Torreblanca, a physician, the son of a physician named Rodrigo Díaz de Torreblanca and, to compound the confusion, father of another Juan, also a doctor. Wealthy, successful, well connected in Córdoba, reputedly an excellent scientist, he was passionately interested in physics and astrology, which in those days included the study of astronomy, navigation and the allied disciplines. He was also irascible, greedy, unscrupulous and violent; he is said to have threatened to murder his wife, Isabel Fernández, because she refused to allow him to use her dowry to put over a shady business deal. Juan Díaz was a sharp enough businessman to amass a fortune in real estate and other non-medical income.

Then there was Juan Sánchez, "Maese (Master) Juan," Juan Díaz's stepfather, also a physician, also respected for his scientific learning, something of a visionary. He was so singed by the orator's fire that, despite his advanced age, he threw away home, career, ease and security to follow Columbus, pausing only to marry his children off properly and make adequate provision for his wife. He was one of the thirty-nine men left at La Navidad by Columbus in 1493, under the command of Diego Enríquez de Arana, who perished in an Indian massacre.

Juan Díaz's wife Isabel was the daughter of Diego Martínez, a wealthy merchant. Her brother Luis was another leading Córdoban doctor—there is still a street in Córdoba named "Maese Luis" in his honor. Her sister Inés was married to Leonardo Esbarroya. Another brother, Diego, was a saddler; Rodrigo de Torreblanca, Juan Díaz's son, ran a workshop that turned out tooled Córdoban leather.

Medicine was notoriously a converso profession, and here, in Cervantes' grandmother's family, we find five prominent doctors. The Esbarroyas, as apothecaries, practiced another pre-eminently New Christian office, as did the family leatherworkers. Many if not most of the successful merchants in Córdoba—a description which fits both Diego Martínez and Ruy Díaz de Cervantes—were of converso ancestry. Even the group's interest in science was, in Spain, a mark of New Christianity.

It is not entering the argument about Columbus' alleged Jewish ancestry to recall how much help he received from known conversos like the Dominican Diego de Deza and Santángel, whose family had once been implicated in a plot to murder a Córdoban inquisitor. New Christians tended to band together, to intermarry, to form a tight defensive palisade; friendship with Santángel would have established, in their contemporaries' eyes, an immediate presumption against the Torreblancas and, accordingly, against their friends the Cervanteses.

None of this constitutes proof. Not *all* physicians, apothecaries, saddlers, merchants were New Christians; intellectualism was typical of the converso caste, but certainly not exclusive to it.

Nothing illuminating is known of Miguel's mother's family. Her parents were apparently small landowners in Arganda, near Madrid, who moved to Barajas, where the Madrid airport now stands, before she was born. Her grandfather, Diego Sánchez de Cortinas, was once governor of a fortress in the province of Toledo; he was best known locally as the man vain enough to pay the then unheard-of price of 1,125 reales for tomb space in the Arganda church of San Juan Bautista.

If all this—Cervantes' ancestors' "Jewish" activities and associations, his indulgence of unorthodoxy and his tolerance for the outcasts of Spanish society, his Pauline intellectualism—establishes at least a suspicion of New Christian descent, it cannot be twisted to cast doubt on the sincerity of Cervantes' Catholic devotion. It may, however, help to explain the special substance of his faith.

His was not the catechistically rigid Christianity of the Counter-Reformation. Rather it was an essential Christianity, an obligation to be honorable before God. Through the ambiguity of Cervantes' attitudes runs a consistent idea: no sin, no error cannot be redeemed by recognition of the Truth—the ideal, the Good, whose sum he thought of as the Roman Catholic deity. He saw Christianity as a metaphor for the absolute good, the perfect harmony of love, to which all other conditions aspire, and he insisted that non-Christians may share in "Christian" attributes. Thus people are worthy or unworthy of love and pity as they approach or recede from virtue.

Man's will is free; the assertion is central to Cervantes philosophy: "no witchery in the world can move or force the will, as some simple-minded people believe, for our will is free . . .";[21] "I am almost forced to follow (my) path and I must keep to it in spite of anyone, and you will weary yourselves in vain trying to convince me to resist what Heaven wills, Fortune ordains and Reason requires and, above all, what my will desires. . . ."[22] But its freedom was the freedom to find its way to God, a search for which the Catholic faith, whatever the imperfections of its Church, was the official guide.

There is nothing unorthodox in this, nothing the Church could not endorse. It blended smoothly with the attempt of Renaissance Christianity to redefine humanity's relationship with God as an active partnership in the enterprise of salvation. True, Cervantes' God was too grand, too broadly understanding to fit in the iron maiden of orthodoxy the Inquisition had fashioned for Him. But such differences as might exist up to this point between Cervantes' God and the Church's were negotiable.

There is, however, another strain running through Cervantine theology which muddies the clear stream of freedom and reasonableness: a mystical sense of blood, the ancestral blood which will claim its own over the pages, across the generations. The blood of little Luis in *The Call of Blood* speaking to the blood of his unknown grandparents; the aristocratic blood enforcing its delicacy on Preciosa in *The Little Gypsy Girl* and on Christina in *The Illustrious Serving Wench*. It is not difficult to see this intimate language of the blood dictating Cervantes' stern but sorrowful sympathy for the Jews.

He was convinced the Moslems and the Jews, especially the Jews, the olive tree on which, Paul said, Christianity was the graft, were wrong in rejecting Christ; he was impatient at what he saw as their persistence in error. But there is something of the sound of a family quarrel in his attitude toward the Jews. He was ready to join St. Paul in welcoming them unreservedly to the ranks of the wholly "virtuous" once they had found the path. If his own forebears had declared belatedly for Christ, it was surely a satisfaction to him. For if Cervantes' writing represented—at least in one of its multiple aspects—a pilgrimage toward human-Christian truth, he then could proudly say that *his* people had started long ago on the journey to the New Jerusalem.

] 3 [

The Unmaking of a Gentleman

Shortly after his fiftieth birthday, Miguel de Cervantes would be bundled into prison by a venal judge in Andalusia. Eight years later, another dishonorable magistrate would pack him and his family off to prison in Valladolid. On both occasions, he might have wondered if he was being made in some mysterious way to do penance for the sins of his ancestors. Especially for those of his grandfather, Juan de Cervantes.

Juan began and ended his career as a law licentiate as a specialist in fiscal law for the Inquisition. In the intervening four decades he functioned as a minor magistrate—roughly on the level of a small-town alderman—in nearly a dozen cities from Córdoba to Cuenca. At various times during that period he was accused of nearly every form of malfeasance, from peculation to illegal arrest and torture. The charges may not always have been true; corruption of the system of local justice within which he worked exposed the bench to the crudest kind of political blackmail. But Juan's way of mixing his unadmirable private life with his public duties indicates a conviction that justice was not so much a beast of society's burden as a goat to be milked for his personal benefit.

Nowhere was this more evident than in Guadalajara, near Madrid, where in four gloriously cynical years, from 1527 to 1531, he seems to have laid the foundation for his personal fortune by (1) acting as procurer for his employer, the Duke of Infantado, and (2) conniving in an illicit but profitable love affair between his daughter María and the duke's bastard son Martín de Mendoza, a priest known because of his antecedents as "the Gypsy." The experience cost Juan a week's imprisonment in Valladolid, but when he emerged with an endorsement by the local magistrates as "a very honorable and upstanding person," he was ready and equipped—with 600,000 maravedis[1] and a haul of jewels and other treasure elicited from Don Martín—to lead the good life he clearly felt he owed himself.

Only months later, Juan, his wife Leonor, their daughter María and their sons Juan, Rodrigo and Andrés were to be found acting as pillars of society in Alcalá de Henares, living like lords, keeping servants and slaves, always "very highly regarded and finely arrayed and with many silks and other rich accoutrements and with good horses, pages and grooms. . . ."[2] María bought the house known as La Calzonera, in the Calle de la Imagen, near the place where the synagogue had once stood; facing the house, on the corner of the Calle Mayor, was another home owned by Juan. The scale on which they lived could not have been bought for 600,000 maravedis. There may very well have been some basis for the charges of corruption laid against Juan in Guadalajara.

For Juan's son Rodrigo this was probably the only happy period in his life. If he had ever dreamed of going to university and becoming a physician like his Torreblanca kinsmen, he had probably abandoned it by then. He was twenty-three years old, and his partial deafness would have been an impediment in a school system relying chiefly on lectures. Besides, his father had never shown much interest in the children's education. He had seen to it that they could read and write and do sums and had a smattering of Latin and then had let them run as wild as they could on a magistrate's income. Why bother with schooling now, in any case? They were rich. Rodrigo and his brothers were regular participants in the tourneys and equestrian games so popular among hidalgos, they knew the best people—such local celebrities, for example, as Don Alvaro do Sande, a regimental commander on leave from his unit in Italy. As for Juan de Cervantes, he spent the three years from 1532 to 1535 investing his money in real estate[3] and doubtless congratulating himself on being able to show the Alcalainos how magnificent their former deputy corregidor had grown.

By 1535, however, the well of his contentment began to go brackish. He and his wife quarreled; approaching age, inflated vanity and the man's unwavering adherence to his own desires may have made life with Doña Leonor unattractive. In 1536–37 he lived alone in Ocaña, serving as a magistrate. In 1538 he was back in Alcalá with his family, but he apparently had not refreshed the family finances, for in that year we find María pawning "a rosary with over one hundred Oriental pearls" and a "satin sleeve with sixty-one gold loops, each set with three pearls,"[4] surely relics of the Gypsy's devotion.

The wily licentiate engineered one final coup on behalf of his family. When his wealthy friend Hernando de Córdoba died, Hernando's daughter María was left in ward to Juan de Cervantes. In 1538, over her family's opposition, the lawyer married the girl to his oldest son Juan, then thirty-four and unprepared for any office other than that of husband to an heiress.

Shortly after the newlyweds moved into La Calzonera, old Juan withdrew to Córdoba; only his youngest son, Andrés, went with him. Taking a former mistress named María Díaz as his "housekeeper," Juan at once set about savoring his second youth. This seems to have been the period when Rodrigo met Leonor de Cortinas.

Was the girl aware of how frail the family's security was? She may have suspected it, but she was surely unaware of how critical their situation became after Juan's departure. And what had she to look forward to in Barajas? A grubby life as a landowner's wife, working as hard as her servants? With Rodrigo she could envision herself as a lady of fashion in a fashionable city, as Alcalá must have seemed to the small-town girl she was. Rodrigo was dashing and sweet-natured and gay, not at all like the grave Castilian peasants she knew at home. It may be, too, that her cavalier believed her family fortune to be greater than it was. Whether for love or money, they were married, it is believed, early in 1543.

It was probably around 1547, the year of Miguel's birth, that the precarious Cervantes economy collapsed. Rodrigo's brother Juan died and his wife removed herself and her fortune from the family's grasp. Rodrigo, as titular head of the household, could now survey a Calzonera stuffed to the eaves with dependents: his sister María and her illegitimate daughter, named Martina de Mendoza to make her parentage clear; Leonor de Torreblanca and her black slave Luis, whom she stubbornly refused to give up; Leonor de Cortinas, of course, and his children, Andrea, Luisa and now Miguel. Someone had to provide a living for them all.

Someone? Who but Rodrigo? But how? Tilting with cane spears, countless hours of idle tavern conversation had qualified him to spend money, not to earn it. There was no point in asking his father for help. Juan is not thought to have attended Rodrigo's wedding, nor did he witness the baptism of any of Rodrigo's children. This would explain the mute war of names Rodrigo waged against his father. Tradition required that his first-born be named Juan; he was christened Andrés instead, when the child died, the next to arrive was named Andrea. If Miguel was in fact named for Juan's brother Miguel Díaz de Cervantes—whom Rodrigo may never even have known—the implied reproach of an errant parent was evident.

Rodrigo must have known a spell of panic, a time when he was tempted to run away as his father had done. Instead, he recalled his medical ambitions. If not a physician, then he at least could be a surgeon. University training was not demanded of those lowly practitioners, and the examinations for a license were relatively simple. So he called on his friends at the university for coaching and he bought the three books he needed for the trade: Antonio Nebrija's Latin grammar, Vigo's *Practice of Surgery* and Lobrera de Avila's *The Four Diseases*. If the chronology we are following is correct, it was in 1547 or early 1548 that gentleman Rodrigo de Cervantes embarked, no doubt clumsily, on a career of splinting broken limbs, administering purges and poultices, bleeding for fever, treating for stone.

He must soon have perceived that trying to earn a living as a neophyte surgeon in Alcalá was like standing on one foot for a week: more tiring than productive. Surgeons were the manual laborers of medicine. Consider their method of setting a dislocated shoulder. The patient was hoisted up on, say, an open door, with the armpit of the offending shoulder saddling the door. A stout cross-pole was attached to his feet and a rope was fastened just below the dislocation. At the practitioner's command, an assistant pulled the rope taut while the surgeon pressed with all his strength on the cross-pole. If the patient was lucky, the pressure snapped the bone back into place. A physician, by contrast, did little more than take a sufferer's pulse and inspect his urine, wherein all medical secrets, like fortunes in a crystal ball, were thought to be revealed to those competent to read them.

Occasionally, the surgeon found a well-to-do patient who might give him three or four reales; the same patient would pay a physician a dozen. Wealthy students had no need of him at all; they would bring their personal physicians and surgeons with them.[5] More often than not, it was the poor who needed Rodrigo's services; from them, if he got anything but promises, he might collect a few maravedis, enough to buy a wheel of bread for his family, or a worn but still wearable pair of breeches.

Competition among medical men was ferocious in Acalá. The university was a center for medical studies and the town was full of white-gloved doctors riding their white mules, flashing their huge thumb rings and draping their flowing satin yokes arrogantly over their shoulders. It was just as full of surgeons, chiefly medical students who had failed to win their degrees. Benefiting from the old-school network, most of these worked regularly in the service of established doctors; newcomers like Rodrigo took the miserable leavings of a picked-over practice, or skirted the law by treating those who needed clandestinity: thieves, abortion victims, prostitutes, students wounded in illegal duels. They were derided by the public and despised by physicians. "What is a surgeon's work when it is done in a neat and Christian manner?" a physician is asked in the dialogue in *Journey from Turkey*. "The same as an executioner's," comes the reply.[6]

By the autumn of 1550, the family was convinced that life in Alcalá promised too little. Rodrigo had been relieved of responsibility for Martina de Mendoza, who that year married Diego Díaz de Talavera, the influential financial officer for the Archbishop of Toledo (and almost certainly of New Christian origin). But in June, Doña Leonor gave birth to another son, christened Rodrigo.[7] At about the same time, an incident involving a local nobleman left the surgeon publicly branded as an incompetent.

Commentators eager to find deep roots for *Don Quixote* have viewed Rodrigo's flight from Alcalá as—precisely—quixotic, the action of a dreamer following a hopelessly impractical lure of success to the next day, the next town, to the city across the plain. Yet the decision can be looked at as being so hardheaded that it may not have been Rodrigo's at all. A thoroughly practical María de Cervantes, an equally down-to-earth Leonor de Cortinas may very well have decided that it made sense for Rodrigo to start over elsewhere, in a place where he was not known as a bungler. Then too, elsewhere was a place where they had not lost honor, where they were not avoided by the people who once had been pleased to consort with them, where Rodrigo would not feel, as he must have felt, like slinking furtively through the streets with his kit of leeches and lancets and splints and basins.

On January 10, 1551, Juan de Cervantes, then a magistrate in charge of confiscated property for the Inquisition in Córdoba, authorized his daughter to sell the family property in Alcalá. María, still the family banker, was making provision for the move. The destination chosen: the royal court city of Valladolid, 40 leagues (about 160 miles) northwest of Alcalá de Henares.

It may not have occurred to the migrants that they were simply following the crowd. Less pious than Toledo, less exclusively mercantile than Burgos, Valladolid was the most aristocratic city in Castile, the place where the purest Spanish is said to be spoken, where even the prostitutes —"those lovely ladies, scented, whitened and arrayed like princesses of France"[8]—were so arrogant that they would besiege the noble houses to solicit custom. It was the most populous of the northern cities, with some thirty thousand inhabitants, not counting slaves, working wives, non-working widows, ecclesiastics or apprentices.[9]

The royal councils and tribunals had long been fixed there; even the normally peripatetic court seemed to have settled down more or less permanently in Valladolid. The city, consequently, drew the whole pushy swarm of royal hangers-on, led by the nobility. It's university made it an intellectual center and its Italian merchant-bankers had turned it into a financial capital. In no city in the region did fewer people actually labor for a living; lawyers and jurists alone outnumbered the laboring population by four to one.

Unlike most cities, where the poor were considered a pestilence and the rule was work or leave, Valladolid had a reputation for kindness to them. It was a place where the rich bought masses for their slaves' souls and the poor were cared for from the public purse, except in time of epidemics, when those who could walk were given a bundle of provisions and hustled out onto the highways. Naturally, the dispossessed hastened to Valladolid from all over Castile with the desperate optimism of the sick rushing to a new faith healer. With them, in March or early April of 1551, came Rodrigo dé Cervantes, his women, children, bedding, linens, sausages, cheeses, chests and bundles piled into one of the long, covered two-wheeled carts known as "galleys" which he had hired for the jolting, eight-day trip from Alcalá.

The moment he entered Valladolid, Rodrigo may have thought his money troubles were over. The very air would have seemed to glow with a soft, golden sheen. The smell of wealth rose even higher than the reek of refuse in the church squares. His first walk around the town would have bolstered the impression as he pushed through throngs of merchants, lawyers, litigants, diplomats, actors, monks, students, beggars, soldiers, servants, slaves, civil servants, petitioners, jobseekers, hurrying apprentices, peasants come to sell their wares and court ladies with their faces elegantly plastered over with coats of almond or pineapple paste. Even the artisans' wives chinked and twittered with gold rings, gold bracelets, gold collars, gold toothpicks, chains of jet, of crystal, of ebony, coral, pearls, agate. Many of the men, and not always the richest, wore diamonds on their fingers; some displayed chains worth six thousand ducats, more than Miguel de Cervantes would earn in a lifetime. Clothes were embroidered in gold, stiff lace collars were tipped with it.

Pigs rooted happily in the trash at the entrance to the aristocratic Corredera de San Pablo—Valladolid was known as a place where one ate well—but the street was commonly reputed to represent some 150 million maravedis a year in income. Nowhere was the medieval confusion of splendor and squalor more visible than in Valladolid. The city, sneered one sixteenth-century commentator from tidy Holland, had an abundance of *"picaros, putas, pleytos, polvos, piedras, puercos, perros, piojos, pulgas"*—rogues, whores, lawsuits, dust, stones, swine, dogs, lice and fleas.[10] But the laborers who gathered before dawn in the Plaza Santa María to seek day work could count on earning as much as seventy maravedis a day if they were hired, for wages were still rising faster than prices in 1551. If there were a place in all Castile where a man could find his feet, it was Valladolid.

Unless the man were Rodrigo de Cervantes.

It was not simply that Valladolid's university turned out even more doctors than Alcalá's; Rodrigo had brought his ineptitudes with him. A scattering of Cervantine documents for the remainder of 1551 tells its story of irony, optimism and impotence. On November 5, Rodrigo signed an obligation to one Gregorio Romano for 44,472 maravedis, payable on the following St. John's Day, June 24; the debt took the form of an obviously fictitious sale of silver candlesticks and other valuables. The guarantors of the loan were a Pedro García, hosier, and María de Cervantes, who may have been García's mistress. María, it seemed, worked faster than Rodrigo did. It was María, again, who leased a two-story house owned by Diego de Gormaz outside the city walls for all of 1552. It must have been a sizable place because the rent was sixteen thousand maravedis in a district where a decent house and garden could be rented for half that. María and her mother took over the upstairs apartment, leaving the ground floor to Rodrigo and his family.

It is hard to see what Rodrigo could have done to head off disaster. He might have found a haven outside the city; many smaller towns ran a crude social-security system, hiring a physician on a yearly retainer to treat their citizens, and those towns which could not afford a doctor often supported a resident surgeon. But he did not. There were other means of survival—hiring on as a building laborer, for example—that a forty-three-year-old hidalgo would not have considered. Predictably, the arrival of St. John's Day found the clan without even the twenty ducats they needed to pay the rent.

To fend off the landlord, María and her mother sold off a few of their remaining possessions. Gormaz, for the moment, was left holding María's black velvet skirt. But on July 2, 1552, Romano sued. The possessions of Rodrigo and his sister were ordered attached. The unfortunate surgeon was imprisoned for debt. He would not have been lodged in the same cell his father had once occupied, but it took him a good deal longer to get out of jail.

Valladolid provided free legal aid to its poor. Perhaps it was his lawyer, Francisco de Pedrosa, who reminded Rodrigo that a hidalgo could not be imprisoned for debt. A patent of hidalguía would have procured instant release, but there was no patent to show. Rodrigo requested thirty days' freedom to prove his claim and find the cash to pay his debt. Romano objected, doubtless reasoning that a commoner would be easier to dun than a gentleman. Rodrigo's request was denied.

At home, meanwhile, Miguel and his sisters were receiving their first real lesson in poverty. Two days after their father's arrest, a deputy magistrate and a notary showed up at their house with a group of witnesses to distrain the family's goods. The list makes sorry reading: worn blankets, worn clothing, mattresses, Rodrigo's three-book library, his sword and vihuela, a jewel case, a Christ child in a wooden box, a single table and three chairs (two of them broken), a cloth bearing a mysterious coat of arms of a castle and crosses which were not the Cervantes arms, a velvet hat with a silk band . . .

Doña Leonor de Torreblanca reacted swiftly. That very day she affirmed before witnesses that the furnishings on the upper floor were hers, not her daughter's, and thus not subject to embargo. We learn two minor facts from her declaration: Doña Leonor, despite her family's prominence, could not write, and María de Cervantes, although she was past forty, had aged well enough to pass for a minor under the age of twenty-eight. Gallantry in unlikely circumstances is a Spanish specialty.

When the officials returned the following day to collect the furnishings on the top floor, they found the pickings lean but the premises crowded, for the whole tribe had moved upstairs. At least there was a bed for Doña Leonor de Cortinas to lie on when she gave birth to the baby she was carrying, an event which is believed to have occurred on July 22. The child was a girl and she was christened Magdalena.

On July 11, Rodrigo was released for six days to complete collection of evidence of his hidalguía. It should have been enough to satisfy the court and a judge did order Rodrigo discharged on August 13, but a new suit, this time by Pedro García, sent him back to his cell. He was out again on November 7, in again on December 17, out just after Christmas. On January 5, 1553, he left for Alcalá de Henares to collect further testimony, but on January 26 he returned to prison. At no point in any of the legal proceedings was Rodrigo's trade mentioned. It is easy to understand why he would have kept silent about an office which might have brought his gentility into question; why the plaintiffs failed to bring it up is less fathomable—unless Rodrigo had never even begun to practice in Valladolid.

His children were almost certainly brought to see him in the prison where Miguel was also to be lodged half a century later. The visits may help to explain the girls' subsequent preoccupation with material security; Luisa would find it in a nunnery; Andrea, as strong-willed as her mother and as contemptuous of conventional morality as her Aunt María, would seek it in a series of more or less profitable love affairs.

Papa was finally discharged early in February. To forestall further attempts at seizures, the family deposited most of its possessions with sympathetic neighbors, all of whom swore they had received the items before June 1552, which made them immune from distrainment. Landlord Gormaz was pacified with a few more of María's clothes. The scattered belongings were secretly sold off. Two years after their arrival in El Dorado, Rodrigo and his family returned, destitute, to Alcalá de Henares to live with Martina de Mendoza and her husband.

What happened next can be guessed from the cold notarial language of a document drawn up in Córdoba on October 30, 1553:

Know by all these present that I, Rodrigo de Cervantes, son of the licentiate Cervantes, native of Alcalá de Henares, being at present in Córdoba, know and concede that I owe and must pay to Alonso Rodríguez, merchant, native of this city of Córdoba . . . the value of twelve *varas (about eleven yards)* of Rouen *(cloth)*, eighteen and two-thirds varas of Holland *(cloth)*, with which said merchandise I concede and hold myself to be satisfied. . . .[11]

With no future for him in Alcalá, Rodrigo must have taken the only step still open to him: he had written to his father, probably also to his brother Andrés, with whom he was still on good terms and whose marriage to an heiress had made him a person of consequence in the Córdoba region. And Juan de Cervantes had consented, probably after a good deal of coaxing, to sponsor his fool of a son. Rodrigo may have waited until the fall harvest was in, when he could realize the income from his sole remaining real asset, a plot of wheatland near Alcalá. Then, sometime in late September or early October, the family had made the trip, by the regular Alcalá-Madrid-Córdoba cart service. They did not need a special conveyance this time; there were so few possessions to take with them.

] 4 [

The Fathers

Until the family reached Córdoba, Miguel de Cervantes is hardly visible even to the imagination. He might simply have been another of the multitude of bundles the family trundled from one economically deserted island to another. But Córdoba would have been different. There we can think of Miguel finding his feet, feeling that he had come at last to a place that claimed him.

True, he would have had to go through an interview with the formidable grandfather he probably had never seen, and it may not have been a joyous meeting. A pale child, probably thin, certainly nervous, his tongue in knots—it is easy to imagine the old man eyeing this unprepossessing young specimen as just what might have been expected to issue from Rodrigo, as though he, Juan, held nothing but a watching brief in the case.

With that over, however, there was nothing to prevent Miguel from abandoning himself to his childhood for the first time. Córdoba was different from any city he had ever seen, more workaday, prosperous but provincial, and it probably soothed him. The proverbial "granddaughter of Seneca, daughter of the Caliphs," the city still displayed its family heirlooms, built in appropriately golden stone: the Roman bridge, for example, and the great mosque, now holding the new cathedral in its abdomen like a battle casualty clutching a shrapnel wound.

To a six-year-old boy with a lively imagination, it may have seemed that even nature was trying to emphasize that this was an exciting place. In December 1553 and again in January 1554 the Guadalquivir River overflowed its banks for his amusement, washing peremptorily into his new playground in the Plaza del Potro, the center of old Córdoba and its commercial heart, ringed with inns and crawling with *pícaros*.*

* An untranslatable word which covers the whole range of social parasites, from beggars and hustlers to thieves and cutthroats.

The square was a constant carnival, a turmoil of traders to be importuned, visitors to be stared at, muleteers to trick. Miguel almost certainly saw his first puppet show there in 1554, when one of the most celebrated masters in Andalusia, Sebastián Hay, set his stage up in the square to show "figures from the Old Testament and part of the New."[1] The show stuck in Cervantes' mind. Half a century later we will find his protagonist in *The Glass Scholar* objecting sourly that puppeteers were "vagabonds who treated divine things indecently, because, by the figures they exhibited in their shows, they changed devotion to laughter, and . . . they sometimes stuffed . . . the figures of the Old and New Testaments into a sack which they sat on when they ate and drank in grog-shops or taverns." Hay must have been a precious rogue; all of the puppeteers Cervantes describes are rascals for whom he had obvious sympathy. Maese Pedro, whose puppets are beheaded by Don Quixote in a fit of helpfulness, is a bandit in disguise. In the interlude *The Wonder Show,* the fast-talking Chanfalla eviscerates notions of blood purity by convincing a village audience that none but legitimately begotten Old Christians can see the marvels in his empty puppet theater.

Probably for the first time, too, the boy made friends, some of them for life. One was Tomás Gutiérrez de Castro, the son of a master hosier, who would go through phases as a tradesman, soldier, actor and theatrical producer before buying an inn in Seville where, more than thirty years later, a rootless Cervantes would find shelter. To join them around the Potro fountain, with its figure of a rearing colt, were Miguel's distant cousins Gonzalo Gómez de Luque, Alonso de Cervantes Sotomayor and Gonzalo de Cervantes Saavedra; the latter two would be Miguel's companions in the battle of Lepanto. There was Juan Rufo Gutiérrez, a dyer's son, who would also fight at Lepanto and who was to become almost as famous as a gambler, adventurer, lover and politician as he would for his epic poem *La Austriada.* The stones of Córdoba were saturated with poetry: Pedro Sanz de Soria and Jerónimo de Lómas Cantoral, both to be mentioned approvingly as poets in Cervantes' novel *La Galatea,* were children in Córdoba then. So was Juan de Aguayo Castillo, whose book *The Perfect Alderman* is believed echoed in Don Quixote's advice to Sancho Panza on the government of Sancho's island.

A vague impression of strain may have shadowed these heady discoveries. Rodrigo doubtless adjusted quickly to his role as the family's burden. His father may have arranged for him to practice as a surgeon in the Inquisition prison. More work may have been available at the Charity Hospital in the Plaza del Potro. It has been suggested that Rodrigo was given a minor administrative post to spare his father, who was now an attorney for the city of Córdoba, the indignity of having a surgeon for a son. Whatever he was doing, Rodrigo was earning a living, not a lavish one, but enough to allow him the luxury of repaying draper Rodríguez. At least, there is no record of a lawsuit.

Miguel's mother would not have been so easily appeased. Córdoba itself probably sent Doña Leonor's guard up, and not simply because it was Cervantes territory. There is still an African secrecy about the city. It sits in its landscape of oranges and olives like a Damascene garden walled by the high Sierra Morena to the north. Córdobans are formal, a little dry, a shade muted as Andalusians go, the "Castilians" of the south. But they nevertheless display the soft, volatile Andalusian gaiety which was a permanent lure—and thus an affront—to Castilian sobriety. St. Teresa described the Andalusian climate as one in which "it seems as if the devils are better able to lead us into temptation";[2] she declared in a letter that she had consoled John of the Cross "for his pain at finding himself in Andalusia (for he cannot stand those people). . . ."[3]

Any hopes Leonor de Cortinas might have had for a grand family reunion were probably soon squelched. She may have tried, as an investment in the future, to placate her father-in-law Juan. Perhaps it was her idea that the son born to her, probably in 1554 or 1555, should be named Juan; nothing is known of the boy except that he was alive in 1585 (he is mentioned in Rodrigo's will) and dead before 1593. If so, the gesture was wasted. For Leonor and old Juan it must have been loathe at first sight. They had a good deal in common—their firmness, their shrewdness, their shared recognition that Rodrigo was . . . Rodrigo. But this impertinent female with her Castilian small-town self-importance—no, Juan would have thought, decidedly not. And however hard she tried, Leonor could not have hidden her resentment at Rodrigo's dispossession, nor her disgust at this foolish grandfather's infatuation with his triumphant housekeeper-mistress, María Díaz.

In such an atmosphere, Doña Leonor surely reared herself as a wall between her family and those Andalusian devils. She would have risen to her responsibility devotedly and diligently, as a peasant fights to hold what is his. She would have been all mother and three-fourths father to her children. Did she resent the burden?

In a one-act play by Cervantes called *The Divorce Court Judge*, Minjaca, a surgeon's wife, protests that "I was fooled when I married him because he told me he was a genuine, pulse-taking physician and he turned out to be a surgeon, a man who fixes splints and cures minor ailments, which makes him worth half a doctor in value . . ." Are we listening to a wifely reproach recalled from the author's childhood? Not textually, perhaps; it is unlikely that Rodrigo's medical ambitions survived his *caballero* period. But it may express Doña Leonor's line of attack: "If only you had become a doctor . . ." How much admonition was there to her children not to wind up "like your father," how many reminders that "there are better things in this world . . ."? Rodrigo would gradually dwindle until, with Miguel in Algerian captivity, we find him actually pretending to be dead so that his "widow" could raise ransom money more efficiently.

In any event, there was apparently no grand family reconciliation in Córdoba; Juan continued to live with María Díaz, while Rodrigo moved his nomads into a large house owned by his mother's family in the parish of San Nicolás de Ajerquía. It was not a caballero district. San Nicolás was the leatherworkers' parish; it was here, near the Plaza del Potro, that the gilded, painted, worked leather was made for the rich to hang on their walls. The tanneries surrounding the shops made it the filthiest, most fetid sector of the city.

For Miguel, these surroundings may have been ventilated by the purity of Latin grammar and the airiness of classical mythology. He reached school age in 1554 or 1555 and, while no documentary evidence has so far been found to place him in school anywhere as a boy, he almost certainly received some early education and Córdoba is the likeliest place for that to have happened.

Objections, based largely on the documentary void, that he may not have set foot in a classroom until he was nearly twenty years old are difficult to accept. True, he could have learned to read at home, as his sisters did. A boy who avidly read "even scraps of paper in the street"[4] could conceivably have taught himself rudimentary Latin. We are reminded that the mature Cervantes was a dilettante, an opsimath, self-educated and embarrassed by the fact. He made occasional mistakes in his classical allusions. His Latin was shaky. His knowledge of Latin literature, though wide, was chiefly drawn from Spanish translations. His background in philosophy was at best unsystematic and eclectic. In short, little can be seen in his work of the formal dialectical structure that gave erudite writing of the day its surface authority. The prologue to Part One of the *Quixote* even pokes uneasy fun at academic pretensions.

Yet he would turn up in Madrid in 1567 as an advanced student in a Madrid academy, which presupposes some previous training in the humanities. From that period, too, would date the first of his poems to come down to us and they show a familiarity with classical mythology and a technical sophistication one is reluctant to attribute to private reading alone. Cervantes' dilettantism can more easily be explained by incomplete schooling than by none at all.

Facilities were notoriously scant in Córdoba then. In October 1553 a Cervantes kinsman, Fray Alonso de Vieras, then choirmaster of the city's cathedral, opened a school to teach church boys reading, writing and music and Miguel may have gone there briefly. But when the Jesuits opened their new academy in Córdoba on October 18, 1555, Miguel, just turned eight, may very well have been there in the preparatory course, with his slate and his buttered bread and dried figs in a basket, sitting cross-legged on the floor to submit to Cicero and Virgil. A frequently quoted passage in *The Dogs' Colloquy* may reveal how he felt about it:

> I was pleased to see the love, the solicitude and industry with which those blessed fathers and masters taught those boys, training the tender young twigs of their youth to prevent them from growing crooked or departing from the path of virtue, which they learned along with their letters. I observed how gently they scolded them, how mercifully they punished them, how they inspired them with examples, gave them prizes as incentives and how prudently they indulged them; and, finally, how they pictured for them the ugliness and horror of vice and depicted the beauty of virtue. . . .

As rector of the school, Ignatius de Loyola had personally chosen a timid but enthusiastic young educator, Father Pedro Pablo de Acevedo. The new Jesuit teaching system put great stress on public performance— recitations and dramatic productions—to bring morality alive. Acevedo was a specialist at this. In the prologue to his play *Metanoea* he tells of his early love for the theater, reporting that before entering orders he had written profane plays which he later regretted as "soul-chilling."[5] Now he devoted his talents to taking Renaissance plays out of the university patios and appropriating religious dramas, the *autos sacramentales,* from the churches and combining them into edifying spectacles for young Catholic minds.

Twenty-five of Acevedo's works have survived, earnest, erudite exercises, occasionally beautiful, in which morality was obviously more important than theatricality. They won praise from his audiences although, because the plays were in Latin, few listeners other than the clergy could understand a word of them. Acevedo would hide for days after a play of his was given, to avoid congratulations. He was apparently very popular with the boys.

If these were among the models for Cervantes' early plays (we are told in *Don Quixote* that "from my boyhood I have loved the stage and, as a youth, I would gaze longingly at a players' company,"[6] it is not surprising that he failed to ignite the theatrical world of Madrid. They were obsolescent even in Cervantes' youth, with their Olympian sentiments and their allegorical figures, personifications of such traits as pride and avarice. At a time when Lope de Rueda was creating a muscular new style of theater based on credible dialogue and human conflict, the Jesuit form was more archaic than ever.

How far through the four-year academic program Miguel went is impossible to know. Perhaps no more than a year or so. Cervantes' mature thinking does not carry the stamp of full Jesuit indoctrination which four crucial years in a child's formation might have impressed indelibly on it. The Jesuit emphasis on virtue is there, doubtless bolstered by Doña Leonor's northern homilies. But it lacks the Jesuits' militant rigidity. Cervantes' Catholicism was gentler, accommodating on all but the fundamental core of belief. The spirit of Ignatius' avowal to the Inquisition that he was ready to declare black was white if the Church would have it so was a long step away from Don Quixote's position that, in effect, black is white if *he* so chose. The spirit of sweet forgiveness which invests his books owed little to the somber *psychomachia* of the Jesuits.

In 1557, the Cervantes family vanishes from sight in Córdoba. Old Juan de Cervantes had died on March 11, 1556. His wife, Leonor de Torreblanca, pursued him to the grave slightly over a year later, her Christian conscience encumbered by her lack of generosity in having sold rather than freed her slave Luis, then twenty-two years old and "tawny in color."[7] That year, 1557, was one of famine and drought followed by "the usual calamity of plague, which almost always follows that of hunger."[8] Food was so scarce that, said the proverb, "if a lark wants to cross Castile, it has to carry its grain with it."[9] The Cervanteses may have fled to the protection of Juan's brother Andrés de Cervantes in Cabra, a country town some forty miles from Córdoba, where food was more plentiful and the air reputedly cleaner.

Cabra was an overgrown village, not substantially smaller then than it is now. Ten-year-old Miguel de Cervantes needed schools and books; there were no schools in Cabra, probably not many books. Visions have been projected of Miguel as a kind of Iberian Huckleberry Finn, exploring the mysterious Cabra cavern with his cousin Juan, Andrés' son. The cave may even have been the model for the cave of Montesinos, where Quixote dreams his surrealistic dream of a down-at-heels world of chivalry. If so, it was small profit from seven years of wasted boyhood that no amount of poetizing about pastoral simplicity and the slowly revolving kaleidoscope of the seasons can repay. Did the experience at least cultivate a love of nature in him? Cervantes would later describe nature as God's handmaiden, but the nature he had in mind was stylized, idealized; except as an abstraction, nature in his books is usually a malignant presence, God's angry handmaiden. It is to be noted that Cervantes would never again choose to linger snugly in a country town when he could think of an excuse for flight to the big city.

An effort has been made to convert the Duke of Sessa, lord of Cabra, into Rodrigo's benefactor and Miguel's intellectual patron. The notion is extravagant. Sessa had once employed Juan de Cervantes, but the licentiate had not found the job to his liking and he hadn't stayed long. The same Sessa would, years later, give a letter recommending soldier Miguel de Cervantes to King Philip II.

From 1558 to 1560 Sessa was in Italy, serving as governor of Milan. He was a professional courtier who spent little of his time in Cabra. Conceivably, on one of his visits there, the intercession of Andrés de Cervantes might have moved him to open his library to the boy who already showed his love for the poetry the duke prized highly. It is not a likelihood to bet on.

Just when this venture into limbo ended is not known for certain. Presumably, the initiative for change came from brother Andrés, whose purse and social standing must have been equally frayed by the surgeon's hungry brood. Seville was big enough for Rodrigo to vanish into, far enough to force him to make his own way. Andrés would help. The record in Seville begins, as it would end, with what by now seems a wearisome inevitability: a lawsuit. On October 30, 1564, we find Rodrigo, as agent for a group of houses in the elite San Salvador district, winning an action against one Juan Mateo de Ureña for three months' back rent. Since Rodrigo and his family lived in the lower-class San Miguel quarter, it is to be assumed the houses in question were owned by Andrés, who appeared as a character witness for his brother. This suggests that Rodrigo needed vouching for, either because he was a newcomer and still little known, or because he had been there for some time and was all too well known. The first hypothesis is slightly more likely and considerably more charitable.

] 5 [

Great Babylonia

To Miguel's sister Andrea, the move to Seville may have seemed a kind
of deliverance. She was a good-looking girl, perhaps even beautiful if her
lively amatory career is any guide; vivacious; probably physically precocious. And willful. To such a girl, Córdoba would have been merely a
patio facing inward on the Spanish edifice and Cabra, if she had lived
there, no more than an unfurnished room. Life, she would have thought,
must hold something better than what she was presumably headed for:
marriage with some saddler or tailor, a haphazard clatch of children
released aimlessly into a world of pointless privation. The Church? That
was all right for her whey-faced sister Luisa with her pinched little features and her depressed patience. But Andrea, one can be sure, enjoyed
her body too sweetly to consign it to the embraces of a straw pallet and a
homespun robe. Mystic marriages were not her style; she would have had
something more robust in mind.

Whether any program so ambitious as marriage with Nicolás de
Ovando formed in her mind is a risky guess. Her life demonstrates a
strong streak of Cortinas shrewdness, a peasant's atavistic hunger for independence. But there was a healthy swatch of Cervantes impulsiveness
there, too. She may have thought, as she murmured in Ovando's arms,
that poor girls sometimes married wealthy aristocrats, but rarely, rarely;
she probably thought more often of Tía María's affair with Martín de
Mendoza.

Just how and when Andrea met Ovando is not known. A crossing of
glances in a candlelit church nave? A trace of a smile at a stall in the
fashionable Calle de las Sierpes? By 1565, at any rate, the two were established lovers. "Mother, oh my mother," runs the popular Sevillian ballad in Cervantes' novella *The Jealous Extremaduran,*

you watch over me,
but if I don't watch myself,
your guard will be useless.
They say it is written,
and so true it is,
that it is privation
that whets the appetite;
love that is confined
grows to infinity,
and so it is better
that you not shut me in. . . .

What little we think we know about Nicolás de Ovando describes an "ordinary" Andalusian aristocrat, charming, spendthrift, well connected. He seems to have been of mediocre intelligence, made up for by a lavish share of arrogance.

In 1564, his uncle, Juan de Ovando, vicar-general of Seville, was sent to Alcalá de Henares to inject a dose of Tridentine rigor into the lax doctrinal bones of the university. The vicar took with him his nineteen-year-old secretary, Mateo Vázquez de Leca, who here makes the first of several appearances in Cervantes' life.

A queer bird, Mateo, with a queer background. He was allegedly the son of a pseudo-aristocratic Corsican adventurer named Ambrogino de Leca and a Corsican Christian slave in Algiers named Isabel de Luchiano; rivals at court would later sneer at Mateo as a "Moorish dog." Don Santo Ambrogino, who probably had no more right to the *Don* than he did to the *de Leca* in his name, was befriended by Diego Vázquez de Alderete, then canon of the Seville cathedral, and by Juan de Ovando. Somehow, Mateo wound up as Mateo Vázquez de Leca, and Juan's protégé. The vicar seems to have doted on him with more than patronal intensity, to have conceived one of those affections that impecunious young men sometimes know so well how to cultivate in solitary older men; letters from the fifty-one-year-old vicar remain to us, addressed, a little sadly, to *"El magnífico señor mi hermano Mateo Vázquez. . . ."*[1]

It was Juan de Ovando, apparently, who installed the young *magnífico* as a student in the university at Alcalá in 1564. To the boy's place as his secretary he called his nephew, Nicolás. The picture emerges of a powerful aristocrat's son, spoiled, living comfortably on a sinecure while awaiting the expected inheritance from his papa. Andrea helped him wait.

We are a long way from a liberated woman here. Such liaisons were common in this period of strict moral principles and routine moral insouciance, when one child in eighteen was conceived out of wedlock. This was especially true in Seville, the capital of Spanish sin, despite horrendous laws against immorality.

The story is told of the public punishment meted out to a woman taken in adultery with a mulatto. They had spent two years in prison before being turned over to her tavernkeeper husband on January 10, 1565, that he might do justice as he saw fit. The pair was led to a public platform in the Plaza de San Francisco, alongside the court building. The huge square was jammed with spectators as the unfortunate pair sank to their knees. The innkeeper arrived, followed by a cortege of Franciscan and Jesuit fathers. He mounted the platform. So did the monks, begging him to forgive the sinners, but he insisted that only blood could wash out the stain on his honor. Drawing a knife from his boot, he stabbed them both repeatedly until, sated with vengeance, he turned to descend from the platform. "The mulatto is still moving," called a voice from the crowd. The innkeeper grabbed a spectator's sword and hacked at the prostrate bodies. Then, facing the crowd, he waved his hat triumphantly; "Off with the horns," he shouted, tossing the hat into the crowd.[2]

There may be some connection between him and the Pole in Cervantes' *Persiles* who plans to stab his adulterous wife to death despite the prayers of the hero (Periandro) for mercy. Cervantes himself was almost certainly away from Seville at the time, but members of his family may have been in the Plaza de San Francisco that day and described the scene to him. Periandro's plea shows us how far Cervantes was in spirit from the prevailing attitudes toward honor. "What do you think will happen when the authorities hand your enemies over to you, bound and broken, on a public stage, in view of an infinite throng, while you twirl your knife above the platform, threatening to slash their throats, as though their blood might, as you put it, cleanse your honor?" he reasoned. "What can happen to you, except that your injury is made more public? For vengeance punishes, but does not expunge blame; and the sins committed in such cases, since reparation does not proceed from the free will (of the guilty), remain intact. . . . I would have you consider that you are going to commit a mortal sin in taking their lives which may not be done for all the gain that the world's honor may offer."[3]

In a suit to force Nicolás to pay for his pleasure, Andrea later described herself as "betrothed and promised" to him. Betrothed, surely not. Promised? Most likely; the device is ageless. It is hard to believe that the family expected anything better.

The daughter born to Andrea in 1565 or early 1566—who would style herself either Constanza de Ovando or Constanza de Figueroa in reference to an august Ovando family connection—probably was not conceived under the Cervantine roof, if only because, then as now, separate bedrooms were an unknown luxury for the children of the poor. But that

Andrea could fulfill the assignation bespeaks undeniable parental indulgence.

Poor Leonor! She must have swayed like a carrack in a storm, alternating frothy reproaches to daughter and husband with shrewd calculation of what profit the affair might be expected to produce. As usual, Papa Rodrigo seems to have had little to say in the business. He would appear later in Andrea's petition for legal guardianship of her daughter, but he was already little more than a true-to-life legal fiction to his womenfolk.

What effect these tensions had on seventeen-year-old Miguel can only be guessed at. Enough of a concordance can, however, be traced between the known facts of his later life and the patterns of thought about sex and its social implications in his work to raise the question of whether Cervantes was not as much a sexual as a social misfit. If he was, Andrea's casual seduction and betrayal by an aristocratic young idler may have dramatically confirmed his feelings of alienation on both counts.

Nothing we know about his boyhood provides an answer. He said he stuttered: "my stammering and almost silent tongue," he calls it in the *Epistle to Mateo Vázquez;* "I have no choice," we are told in his prologue to the *Exemplary Stories,* "but to use my tongue, which, although it stutters, will not do so in speaking truths." We cannot assume he meant this literally rather than literarily; even if the defect was physical, we may not point knowingly at it from our psychoanalytical armchairs as a sign of sexual disturbance; neurological or medical explanations may serve as well.

What is recorded of Cervantes' real-life sexual relationships is provocative but unsatisfying. They were, so to speak, conducted at arm's length. The single premarital adventure on record was conducted with a tavernkeeper's wife, his social inferior; she might be said to have played the Andrea to his Ovando. The very existence of the illegitimate daughter the affair produced, his only acknowledged child, may have been concealed from his sisters for over a decade and from his wife for nearly twenty years. His marriage was for all practical purposes abandoned after less than three years of desultory cohabitation; except for sporadic visits, he was not to be reunited with his wife or any other woman, as far as is known, for some sixteen years.

This torpid sexual career becomes more suggestive when it is viewed in a family context. Of the six children Doña Leonor de Cortinas raised to adulthood, Miguel was the only one known to have married. Every one of the women of her progeniture—Andrea and her daughter Constanza, Magdalena, Miguel's daughter Isabel—would turn out to be what pre-liberation morality would unhesitatingly have described as a whore. Iron-ribbed Doña Leonor, in more or less voluntary combination with a mercurial Rodrigo, whelped children of a curious alloy, emotionally dense but sexually fragile.

Searching Cervantes' works for clues to his sexual attitudes takes us into the fitfully lit recesses of Cervantine ambiguity. He evidently liked women and sympathized with them. A French writer[4] has pointed to the amazingly varied gallery of women in Cervantes' stories. They can be primly sensuous, like the Little Gypsy Girl with the white spot under her left breast and the web between the last two toes of her right foot, or as incandescently chaste as the nun-like Sigismunda in the *Persiles*. There are prostitutes like La Repulida in *The Widowed Ruffian*. Women of good family like Leocadia in *The Call of Blood* and Cornelia Bentibolli in *The Lady Cornelia* proudly present their bastards to us. There is the Christian witch Cañizares and her Morisca colleague Zenotia, the sin-rotted Rosamunda and the exemplary Constanza, the Illustrious Serving Wench who is the fruit of an aristocratic rape. Fabulous Dulcinea, on the one occasion on which she materializes as the peasant girl Aldonza Lorenzo, winnowing grain and smelling of sweat, radiates so much good-humored, lusty, animal seduction that one understands old Quixote's infatuation with her. Only in the anomalously ill-natured play called *La Entretenida* (*The Dalliance*), with its overtones of sibling incest, are the women shown as dull or vicious; it is a peculiarly disagreeable piece of work, as though Cervantes had written it compulsively but with distaste.

The women he created are often more "real," more alive than the men they confront. They are always intensely feminine; in all of them, even the most sketchily drawn, even the most pious, runs an undercurrent of sensuousness. It is Cervantes' men who so often are prudish, jealous, sexually either brutish or immature, his women who are tolerant, worldly-wise, compassionate of the erring. And an astonishing number of them not only make hash of conventional morality, but live happily ever after on the dish. Cervantine stories are littered with harquebus weddings like that of Leocadia to the man who raped her. Through seventy-nine of the eighty chapters in the *Persiles,* the lovers' passion is preserved unspent by the frigid trinity of chastity, continence and guilt, but even in this sanitary atmosphere a father is prevailed upon to overlook his objections to his pregnant daughter's wedding because "we must not disturb our celebration with such childishness."[5]

Sexual delinquency, inevitably, is seen as a matter of honor.

> A woman must be good
> and, more important, seem so.[6]

But honor is a class attribute. Among women of noble breeding, honor is subject to accommodation: "More harm comes from an ounce of public

dishonor," Leocadia's father affirms, "than an *arroba*⁷ of secret infamy. . . . True dishonor lies in sin, true honor in virtue; it is with word,
wish and deed that one offends God and, since you have not offended
Him in word, thought or action, hold yourself to be honorable. . . ." No
such facility is available to the sturdy, healthy women of the lower classes
who are prematurely bedded. In the eyes of their (usually aristocratic)
seducers, the poor and the obscure had no honor but that to which they
might accede by marriage to their social betters. To their credit, they
manage, by their courage, resourcefulness—and innocence—to defend
their rights.

Contrapuntal to this romantic line of bedding and bastardy is a more
than literary, more than contemporary preoccupation with sexual guilt,
expiation and penance. In "The Tale of Foolish Curiosity," as told in
Don Quixote, Anselmo trots out his wife's virtue as a stable owner shows
off his best horse; by impiously trying to "force her to work miracles" to
prove her chastity, by seeking forbidden knowledge for worldly satisfaction, he destroys himself, his friend and his wife. A dread of sin pervades *The Great Sultana,* a deceptively simple tale of a beautiful Spanish
girl held captive in Constantinople. There, like some female Joseph, she is
hidden for seven years from the sultan's lust by a crypto-Christian
eunuch. Despite her conviction that martyrdom, not marriage, should be
her choice, she finally becomes the sultan's number-one wife—and
improbably sets about evangelizing him. The hero of Cervantes' play *The
Happy Rogue* is a rake struck as suddenly as St. Paul was by divine
grace; he becomes a saintly monk who, to absolve a sinner of her
(presumably sexual) sins, takes them on himself. He is a Job-like figure
at the end, leprous and disfigured by the woman's guilt, but cleansed of
his own. In *The Jealous Extremaduran,* the child bride Leonora, who
was good but did not seem so, ends her life in a convent.

The note of Christian redemption is central to the *Persiles,* the story of
a pilgrimage to Rome by the lovers Persiles and Sigismunda in expiation
for their betrayal of Persiles' brother, to whom the heroine was betrothed.
The book is full of subplots and incidents in which lust is identified with
the powers of darkness: Zenotia, thwarted in her unholy love for the
Christian Antonio, causes the murder of the satyr Clodio, who has grown
sweaty thinking about Sigismunda; Rutilio stabs to death a lubricious
witch who turns into a werewolf in mid-embrace, etc., etc. Retribution is
ineluctable: Zenotia is put to death for her wickedness; Rutilio elects to
live as a hermit on a desert island; Rosamunda—*rosa inmunda*—the ad-
vocation of trial marriage and apostle of sex as pleasure, dies in haggard
rage after being rejected by the impregnable Antonio.

Cervantes' symbolism is frequently sexual: sometimes it is a prostitute who does the Lord's work (*The Happy Rogue*); in *The Great Sultana,* the Christian eunuch triumphs over a renegade Christian. A black slave, representing the darker, more primitive—and poetic—side of man's nature, is the divine vehicle in *The Jealous Extremaduran.* Perhaps equally meaningful is the fact that Cervantes' Ideal Women—Galatea, the shepherdess Marcela in *Don Quixote,* Dulcinea herself—are intellectualized, sexless creatures, Platonically perfect and literally untouchable.

Clichés of a century struggling to reconcile its raging sexual appetite with its exacerbated sense of sin? Only partly. Images leap from Cervantes' pages which hint at a searingly personal sense of sexual guilt, even of revulsion. What, for example, are we to think of the Glass Scholar, who believes he has been turned to glass by the charm of a prostitute? Or of a Quixote who, because he has rebuffed the advances of a hussy, is badly mauled by cats in the darkness of his chamber and forced to cower in his bed? There is nothing haphazard about the incident's sexual implications; the Middle Ages had already developed an elaborate popular symbolism relating cats with Eve the temptress, with witches and forbidden knowledge. In a coarse age, Cervantes the artist was oddly prissy about sex itself, a trait which makes the occasional scatological or coital jokes in his stories unexpectedly shocking. He was even bothered about sexual explicitness in other people's work: *La Celestina,* he thought, would be a divine book if it were less overtly carnal.[8]

If we read the signs right, Miguel's immediate reaction to this first of Andrea's forays into sin was no doubt a compound of shame, embarrassment, bafflement, even disgust. Perhaps other, inadmissible things— jealousy, a kind of dispossession. Probably, too, a feeling of complicity. Andrea the hussy and prissy Miguel were, after all, very much brother and sister, sharing a common hunger for life, not improbably a common conviction that they were meant for better things than those life seemed to have reserved for them. But the incident may already have given him a confused perception of love as

nothing more than desire, and as such it is the chief source and origin from which all our passions flow, as any stream from its source, and it is because of this that, whenever the desire for something ignites in our hearts, we are moved to pursue it and seek it and, seeking and pursuing it, we are led to a thousand unruly ends. It is this desire that incites the brother to seek the abominable caress of his beloved sister, the stepmother her stepson and, worse still, the very father his own daughter. It is this desire that transports our thoughts toward painful perils. Nor is it deflected by the barrier of our reason, for although we recognize our evil with perfect clarity, we do not for that reason withdraw from it.[9]

That source Cervantes was apparently to deviate into a transmuted sensuality of art and a safely dispersed love of humanity. Sex would become a central symbol of that worldliness he would increasingly come to see as the root of evil, the degeneration of humanity's divine essence. Perhaps, like his Happy Rogue, he took some of his sister's guilt on himself. Or was there some stone on which an entire family's affective edge was blunted?

We may not choose to go as far as the German psychoanalyst who identified Don Quixote's horse Rocinante as Cervantes' mother figure because of the wretched animal's failure to "support" or "nourish" its rider.[10] We are nevertheless curious about another puzzle: was it affection that prompted Doña Leonor's son to use the name Leonor or some variant of it again and again in his stories, although not a single character named Rodrigo was created in all the million and a half words Cervantes wrote? Or was it the length of that matriarchal shadow?

Seville in the sixteenth century was an exhilarating, unsettling place for any boy fresh from the country. It was the big town, as big as Paris, bigger than London, in a class with Venice and Constantinople. Sevillians were proud of themselves, contemptuous of everyone else. Hercules built their city, the legend said, and Caesar girdled it with strong walls. It called itself the "Athens of Spain" for the number of its schools and tried, with infuriating lack of success, to wrest from Toledo the distinction of being the "new Rome" because of the number of its churches. *"Quien no vió Sevilla no vió maravilla,"* the people said—who has not seen Seville has never seen a wonder. Eight rivers, they clamored, flowed into the city, of water, wine, oil, milk, honey, sugar, gold and silver. Round and fat it sat, its five miles of walls studded with 160 towers, the symbol of the exuberance and vitality of the Spanish empire, the place where, sometimes, even the beggars went on horseback.

It had all of a potentate's vices, too; it was licentious, unruly, frivolous, violent, mercurial, vain, ostentatious, with that insularity peculiar to all great cities. *Quien no vió New York* (or Paris or London or Tokyo) *no vió maravilla.* . . . Its monopoly on commercial traffic with the New World made it incomparably rich, garishly cosmopolitan. It was, sang a contemporary romance, the

> great Babylon of Spain, map of all nations
> where the Fleming finds his Ghent
> and the Englishman his London.[11]

Money made Seville, and Seville made money.

> Never doubt that money is the be-all and end-all;
> it is the prince, the noble, the gentleman,
> it is blue blood and Gothic ancestry. . . .

said Lope de Vega in *La prueba de los amigos*. In Seville, even the nobility plunged feverishly into trade. Indeed, many had been tradesmen before they bought, won or married a title. A caballero in Seville with no drop of merchant's blood in his veins was, it was said, a second wonder. For that matter, even Spanish blood was sparse in the veins of not a few of them.

The city's star turn was the wheeling of the silver fleets in their transatlantic orbit. Every spring and every fall, scores of ships massed in the Guadalquivir to load supplies for the colonists of the New World; every fall, scores more would arrive, pressed deep in the water by their loads of precious metals, hides, pearls, ambergris, timber, medicinal plants, spices, sugar. Around them, like bee-eaters around a hive, flitted vessels from all Europe; iron for tools and weapons came from Biscay, woolens from Holland, fine cambrics from France, brocades from Italy, dried herrings and hemp from the Baltic, to be exchanged for oil and soap and pearls, capers and marmalade, wine and cochineal. Streets swarmed with Portuguese, Bretons, Flemings, Ragusans, Moriscos, blacks. The world came to Seville; the rhythm of the city's life was as finely tuned to the fleets' movements as a monk's to his devotional schedule. The timing of Rodrigo's suit for back rent, in late October, suggests that the fleet's arrival had put the defendant back in the money. It is impossible not to imagine the Cervantes boys, fresh from the country, gawking openmouthed at the perpetual carnival around them.

Sailing day was a semi-annual world's fair. As many as a hundred ships —most of them of under one hundred tons' displacement, with an occasional thousand-ton monster hulking over them like the fat boy in a street gang—would be moored in the port in a labyrinth of sails and masts and cables. Wares still lay heaped on the wharves built out over the beaches ("all this sand," commented Lope de Vega, "is money"[12]). In the hot, bright, Andalusian morning, the sun glinted on the Torre de Oro and glowed warmly on the scaffolding atop the Giralda, the already ancient Moorish minaret which was then being coiffed with a new Renaissance cupola. Gallants strolled along the beaches dressed for the occasion in doublets of silver cloth and shirts of damask embellished with diamonds and pearls, black velvet hose lit with gold embroidery, velvet caps decorated with gold and plumes; gold chains thumped on their breasts and hands rested on gold sword hilts. Seville's internationalism was reflected in men's fashions: high-collared Italian capes, long Turkish surcoats, hose slashed like the Germans', baggy breeches in the Moorish style. These were mostly the India men, displaying their new wealth, flirting with the ladies who shot inviting glances over the complaisant heads of duennas and pages.

The women of Seville were an imposing breed, grave in manner, mincing in step, mysterious in their narrow-brimmed hats and shawls that covered their faces but left one bright, inquiring eye unveiled. While there was a liberal sprinkling of crones like Aguello in Cervantes' story *The Illustrious Serving Wench,* who wore false teeth and a wig and covered her face with so much white lead that it looked like a plaster mask, Sevillian women were famous for their daintiness. Contemporary commentators remarked in wonder on their cleanliness: Agustín de Rojas in his *El viaje entretenida* declared he knew a woman in Seville "who goes to the baths every Saturday even if the sky collapses with water"; Alonso Morgado said "they often go to the baths, since there were two such houses in Seville"[13] (open to women only during the daytime and to men only at night).

Around these heraldic lions and leopards turned the lesser fauna of Seville, poor gentry in search of patrons, out-of-work servants in search of masters, vulpine French traders who wore their plumes on the right side of their bonnets, like soldiers, in smug defiance of the Sevillians, whose feathers sprouted on the heart side. And, everywhere, the toughs, smoothing their moustaches and glaring out of their cowls at the crowds, looking for a purse to cut, a silk kerchief to filch, perhaps a commission to dispatch a gallant's rival in love, business or honor. From where they stood, they could also see the six prison galleys in the harbor and, like Cervantes' Rinconete and Cortadillo, the sight probably made them "sigh and dread the day when they might make a mistake that would cause them to spend the rest of their lives in them."

From the day the fleet sailed for the Americas until the moment in late summer or early autumn when the eastbound ships arrived in the mouth of the Guadalquivir, Seville held its breath. Disaster to the fleet could spread financial panic as far away as Riga. But a safe return touched off an explosion of joy, luxury and riches in the city. Suddenly, Seville was full of money. The stalls of the Alcaicería, the old Moorish souk, were gorged with gold and silver objects, pearls, crystal, jewels, silks. In the fine houses lining the nine hundred paces from the Alcaicería to the Jerez gate, the celebration went on night and day. The flea market outside the Arsenal gate bulged with contraband bargains. Most spectacular of all were the bullion convoys, files of hundreds of bullock carts creaking under loads of metal and precious stones.[14]

But this was only the climax of the show; the Sevillian Follies was a permanent spectacle for wide-eyed adolescents. The city, Zúñiga tells us, was "at the peak of its greatest opulence"[15] and it was rapidly changing its personality. The old, still predominantly Moorish town with its secretive, twisting, often vaulted streets lined with blank-walled, inward-turning houses was retreating before a wave of fine, new Western-style buildings with tall, grilled windows. At the end of the Calle de las Sierpes, the royal prison was being enlarged to accommodate its rapidly expanding clientele. Luckily, the artistic mind is no more clairvoyant than any other; Miguel still had no suspicion that it was one day to be another of the many dungeons he would inhabit. He would still have been able to gaze with bewildered delectation at the *hampa,* the brotherhood of the underworld, as it went earnestly about winning admission to the new jail.

Certainly he watched the underlife of Seville with the fascinated attentiveness of a naturalist in an aquarium; his plays and stories are among historians' prime sources of information on the subject, especially the amiable *Rinconete and Cortadillo,* about a pair of teen-aged delinquents whose natural talent for skulduggery earns them membership in the clearinghouse of crime led by Monipodio, a funnier, less frightening original for Fagin in Dickens' *Oliver Twist.* So sunny, so youthfully sympathetic is Cervantes toward the two young rascals with their "breeches of coarse stuff and their hose of flesh," their shoes so "torn and soleless that they served more as shackles than as shoes," that one suspects they were dredged up from his memories of this first, wondering experience of Seville. He may have seen them across the river, at the slaughterhouse near the church of San Salvador, lounging alongside their baskets and their linen bags waiting for commissions as delivery boys. Or perhaps it was on the steps surrounding the cathedral, that fortress of Christianity built to make the world marvel at its size, that he watched silently while two cheerful young derelicts picked the sacristan's pocket.

Oh, there was a great deal for a young man to watch: pastry cooks making frog pies, or the horse fairs in the Plaza de Santa Catalina. And there were the special occasions when he could peek at the women working through the night to dress statues of the Virgin for Holy Week; he could watch the ruinously elaborate Corpus Christi festivals, when players' companies acting from carts moved from square to square to declaim both eucharistic dramas, the autos sacramentales, and scabrous farces: when the scandalous *zarabanda* was danced in the holy processions—and even, it was said, by the nuns in their convents. In October there was the wine fair, two weeks of autumnal madness of which we hear a muffled echo in the portrait of the whore in *The Dogs' Colloquy* whose specialty was fleecing the northerners off the ships coming to Seville for wine.

It must not, of course, be thought that Satan reigned unopposed in Seville. The years Cervantes spent there in his youth held edifying moments in which we must dutifully suppose he shared. The Council of Trent had ended in 1563 "with universal benefit to Christiantity" and its decrees, ratified by Pope Pius IV early the following year, were read from the cathedral pulpit at high mass that August.[16] That young Cervantes was one of the crowd standing in the giant nave to hear them is easy to imagine; it takes rather more piety to suppose that the resounding contentions of the Counter-Reformation had much of an impact on him then.

The Inquisition's autos-da-fé were another matter. Seville was a center of Spanish Lutheranism in the sixteenth century—a notion which should not create images of city-wide ferment: the Lutheran and crypto-Lutheran "reformism" which so terrified populace and authorities alike touched only a tiny minority. But some of the century's most spectacular autos were held in Seville, among them the controversial ritual in 1564 in which six Flemish Protestants were executed, and another in 1565. It is unimaginable that Cervantes, who surely had never seen one before, should not have been drawn at least to one of them, by sheer curiosity if nothing else.

Cervantes did not love the Inquisition. His parody of an auto-da-fé in *Don Quixote,* when the priest and the barber Nicolás, representing religious and secular law, try and "relax" books for burning,[17] is only the most obvious of a series of ironies at the Inquisition's expense that are scattered throughout his works.

He deplored the Inquisition practice of perpetuating a sinner's infamy through succeeding generations. In the *Persiles,* the dead Clodio's wickedness is hidden by the pious Auristela because "she did not wish the sins of the dead to come to light, an impulse as prudent as it is Christian."[18] Don Quixote laughs at a Sancho dressed in the painted robe, the *sanbenito,* of the Inquisition's convicts; he stands silently by when his squire plunks his penitential miter on his ass's head.[19] Cervantes would later refer to Inquisitors as "mastiffs"; it was the pejorative word the hampa used for the police.

The intensity of his mature judgment, clearly, was rooted in the kind of emotional disgust most acutely felt in youth. That he witnessed, and was repelled by, an auto-da-fé seems more than likely; sheer opportunity places the scene in Seville.

It was a frightful spectacle, not at all unique in its cruelty in an age of public bestiality, but staged with crushing dignity and unsurpassed dramatic skill. From the moment the procession began moving across the great wooden bridge over the Guadalquivir to the sound of trumpets blaring the Call to Justice, until a climax came before the huge wooden cross in the Plaza de San Francisco, a Sevillian auto was a perfect lesson in neo-Aristotelian theatrics. The holiday crowds came away from it consumed and renewed with a righteous horror. Miguel undoubtedly preferred a more smiling form of stagecraft. He found it in the plays of Lope de Rueda.

Rueda is sometimes called the father of Spanish drama as well as, and more rashly, Cervantes' literary father. Both titles must be shared with others. To today's ear, the verse written by this Seville-born goldbeater turned strolling player would sound about as compulsive as the dialogue from a 1904 minstrel show; but in his day it was considered as light and shimmering as the gold leaf Rueda once worked. More important, Rueda's work reflects the popular theater's struggle to free itself of the Aristotelian tradition which made the personages of fiction instruments of the gods. In his plays we see them emerging, still indistinctly, as characters in action, possessed of free will and capable of decisions arising from their specific natures, a process Cervantes would carry over the threshold of modern literature in *Don Quixote*.

In the prologue to his volume of *Eight Plays and Eight Interludes*, Cervantes recalls that Rueda's plays "were dialogues, like eclogues, between two or three shepherds and some shepherdess or other; these were embellished and padded out with two or three interludes involving a comic—a Negro or a rogue or a yokel or a Biscayan[20]—and all these four figures and many more were portrayed by the said Lope with the highest imaginable excellence and fitness."

Performances in those times were given on improvised platforms in the patios of inns, in the palaces of the rich, in taverns, on carts or wagons drawn up in a public square. Within less than a decade, these would evolve into the "corrals," patios or courtyards arranged as primitive theaters. But in 1564, when Rueda returned to Seville from the new capital in Madrid, such luxury was still in the future. "In the days of this celebrated Spaniard," we learn from Cervantes, "all of a playwright's baggage was contained in a sack and added up more or less to four sheepskins backed with gilded leather, four beards and wigs and four shepherd's crooks. . . . The theatrical decor was an old blanket drawn apart by two cords . . . and behind this were the musicians, singing some old romance without guitar accompaniment."[21]

Over the years, Cervantes obviously read and reread the collection of Rueda's plays published for the first time in 1567 by the printer-poet Juan de Timoneda, a venture which earned Timoneda verse accolades from Cervantes. He knew them well enough to dip into them with respectful liberality and fish out thirty-five verses from a now lost Rueda play to incorporate in his own drama *The Dungeons of Algiers*.

Did Miguel ever see the great Lope perform? The actor had a twelve-day run in Seville in 1564, the year before his death in Córdoba. It would be fine to think that Miguel found the half real he needed to stand and watch one of those performances. For Lope is thought to have become a cult figure to Miguel, perhaps chiefly because the playwright represented the glamorous vagabondage Cervantes would later find was neither so glamorous nor so carefree as a seventeen-year-old boy might have supposed.

Rueda's career was an object lesson in the sixteenth-century truism that literature and money were hardly on speaking terms. After a decade of national celebrity, he was still to be found pawning his costumes to escape debtors' prison. Only once, for a brief period, had he been able to sample a beggar's version of the good life, a three-year-long joyride on his wife's dowry.[22]

Biographers have pictured Miguel loitering at street corners where the stocky, muscular figure was likely to pass, hoping for a nod, a casual greeting of "Go with God," even—oh, impossible!—a chance to express the admiration the boy was too timid to volunteer. We are free, too, to imagine him hanging back in the cool shadows in the church of San Miguel on July 18, watching the baptism of Rueda's second wife, a Morisca, and their child, then following the splendidly dressed party of players and aristocratic hangers-on into the sticky-hot sunlight outside.

At least two of the men he may have seen there that day were to play important parts in Miguel's life. One, a silk weaver named Pedro Montiel who helped Rueda stage his farces, was to become Cervantes' close friend, possibly his agent in dealing with Madrid's theater managers. Montiel could have been instrumental twenty years later in bringing Cervantes together with his tavernkeeper mistress. Cervantes would leave an affectionate portrtrait of him as Chanfalla in the interlude *The Wonder Show*. The other was Alonso Getino de Guzmán, a musician and dancer who, as a royal bailiff, was to become the Cervantes family's adviser in their efforts to raise money for Miguel's ransom from Algerian captivity.

But what, in fact, was Miguel doing skulking in churches and hanging around on street corners? Why wasn't he in school? Although some Cervantists think he was, the evidence is brittle and fragmentary. His uncle Andrés is known to have left his son Juan with the family in Seville around the start of the 1564 school year. It is unlikely, the reasoning goes, that Juan would attend school while Miguel did not. Nothing has been found, however, to establish that either boy attended classes then.

Father Acevedo, who had headed the Jesuit school we suppose Miguel attended in Córdoba, was now headmaster of the order's academy in Seville. What more natural than that the youngster should have picked up where he left off . . . seven years before? Astrana Marín noted that the cast for a school play on Corpus Christi Day in 1564 includes a "Miguel"—no family name is given—and, arguing that the name was uncommon in the city then, he suggests the reference must have been to Cervantes.

If Rodrigo were as anxious as he is supposed to have been to see to Miguel's education, would he have felt free, as he is thought to have done, to pull his son out of classes in the middle of the school year to accompany him on a months-long trip to Alcalá de Henares? Why was Miguel not sent to a university, to Alcalá, say, where he could have lived with his family? Money was not an insurmountable problem; the universities often helped the decently born poor, even finding jobs for them in the entourage of some more prosperous student. And why, if Miguel were a graduate of the sophisticated Jesuit system, do we find him four years later in a Madrid school which was no more advanced than the institutions he is supposed already to have attended?

We are left, for answers, with the statistical absurdity of trying to guess the number of Miguels in Seville versus the numbers of Juans, Antonios and Franciscos. It is less of a strain on the imagination to suppose that the family did not care enough to push the project, that Miguel was simply allowed to drift as his father had. "I was at the gates of grammar, which are those through which one enters into the other sciences,"[23] he would say half a century later; the remark has the flavor of warmed-over regret, the hindsight of a man who had yet to prove he was an artist in terms his better-schooled contemporaries would accept.

Well, if he did not attend school, what did he do in those years in Seville? No trade is spoken of familiarly in his works except war and the kind of practical jurisprudence his own experience would have taught him. He apparently did know something about medicine, however; there were doctors among his later acquaintances in Seville. Could he not have acquired them while helping his deaf father on his surgical rounds? This might also help to explain his intimate knowledge of Seville's underworld and its demimonde.

On October 30, 1564, Rodrigo granted a power of attorney to Doña Leonor and to his nephew Juan, but not to Miguel, to collect any moneys anyone was fool enough to owe him. Andrés de Cervantes witnessed the act. On this document is based the belief that Miguel had been chosen to accompany his father to Alcalá de Henares to see his sister Luisa take the veil in the Reformed Carmelite convent newly founded there. Why Miguel should have gone is not clear. Supposedly it was to help his deaf father negotiate the trip and arrange for Luisa's dowry as a new bride of

Christ. But Andrés traveled as far as Córdoba with his brother. And there were plenty of people, including his sister María and her family, who could have acted for Rodrigo.

Whatever the reason, father and son are pictured setting out early in November along the usual route, through Córdoba and across the Mancha, where, at that season, the air was acrid with the odor of Manchegan wine fermenting in the huge earthenware vats made by the potters in El Toboso. Via Toledo the route led to Madrid; from there to Alcalá was a day's ride.

The roads of Spain held a special symbolism for the sixteenth century. To writers like Vicente Espinel and Mateo Alemán, and especially to Cervantes, they were Spain in concentrated form, where Juan Everyman could be glimpsed, like a figure in a painting, poised in the act of existence. The roads and the wayside inns, called *ventas,* which marked the stages of each day's travel—for no one would brave the terrors of the night out of doors if he could help it—would give Cervantes more than just the setting and the raw material for most of his stories, more even than the panoramic vision or that sense of the unexpected workings of fate he so brilliantly exploited. They were his way on the literary pilgrimage he followed through his books. They helped unify his work as they did his country and his people.

The unifying influence of Spanish roads is no mere bookish metaphor. Traditionally an urban people, the Spanish sheltered by night in their towns, emerging by day to raid the surrounding earth of its riches. The highways were bridges between the towns, ribbons of relatively safe commotion stretching across vast, silent, largely deserted landscapes ruled by bands of highwaymen which were often as big, and as predatory, as army squadrons.

It was on the roads that most Spaniards met one another and encountered those strange creatures, travelers from abroad. Before the end of the century, when carriages came into fashion and the diligence began to convey passengers at too brisk a pace to allow for chatting, people journeyed by cart, on mules and horses, in litters, on foot, according to their station, progressing slowly; a courier might cover 40 leagues (some 140 miles) a day, but a cart, even on the cart roads which took maximum advantage of the terrain, seldom did more than a fifth of that. People talked and argued and perorated as they rode. News raced by word of mouth along the roads; it rode in the interminable caravans of pack animals almost invisible under incredible loads of salt, wood, pottery, grain, passengers, melons, works of art, wool, hams, everything that moved in trade by land.

Broadway, Piccadilly, the Champs-Elysées and the Gran Via compressed together into dirt channels often not wide enough for two carts to pass abreast, running for hundreds of miles across a semi-wilderness where bears and boars roamed free and wolves prowled even in the suburbs of great cities. It is no wonder that contemporary minds were excited by them. Sometimes it seemed that the entire nation was on the move on any given day—merchants trying not to seem too invitingly wealthy, an army sergeant shepherding a frowsy group of recruits to an embarkation port, priests, tax collectors, dandies, dispossessed peasants on their way to the towns to seek work or simply moving because they had no idea of where to stop, convicts on their way to the galleys in Seville under the guard of green-uniformed officers of the Holy Brotherhood, itinerant magistrates and, always, the muleteers, strong, sly, stupid men, the despots of the highways. "It is comical," recorded a German traveler, "to see a Spaniard riding his stallion, usually daggerless, bootless and spurless, with his servants trailing at his horse's heels and, before him, a world of trunks, boxes, chests and hats which completely blot out any sight of the road."[24] Joly remarked on horsemen's *cornes à pisser,* instruments which functioned as gutters to cast a rider's urine far enough off to prevent its dripping into his boot. Riders also, he tells us, wore protective straw covers over their hats, and masks and goggles to shield their faces from the summer's dust and from the mud that covered a traveler like icing on a cake in the rainy season.

It was in the long nights at the inns, around a common table, before a common fire, that Spain on the move convened. Perhaps it was there that the Spanish developed the florid art of making a little conversation go a long way, embellishing an idea with intricate arabesques of phrasing the way a flamenco singer adorns a simple couplet. Sometimes a cartload of players or a puppeteer would collect enough coins from the company to warrant an impromptu performance. Stories would be told or read before the fire. Each of the nearly two dozen major ventas along the main cart road from Madrid to Seville was a world of its own which, like the world outside it, was often a hard, unaccommodating place.

Foreigners were generally unenthusiastic about Spanish ventas. "On the roads one sometimes comes across a miserable-looking hovel, furnished with a sturdy enough table, but with nothing on it to set one's hand to," one of them grumbled. "If a person sits down, though it might only be to rest a little from the fatigue of the journey, the hosteler must be paid even for that, although one had ordered nothing to eat or drink. . . ."[25]

Wise travelers brought their bedding with them; the egalitarianism of venta vermin was as notorious as the judicious impartiality with which innkeepers fleeced their guests. Bedclothing was rarely changed more than twice a month, regardless of the occupancy rate, unless the guests

were important and able to pay. Only a veteran of the roads could understand the fine gradations of hostly attentions; in *The Illustrious Serving
Wench*, Carriazo and Avendaño are given a room which was "neither for
caballeros nor for servants, but for folk who fit between the two extremes." Lesser persons slept in beds in dormitory rooms, or, like Don
Quixote, on the ground in patios, stables, even kitchens.

Few inns offered any food; the traveler was expected to bring his own.
Personnel of the inn would cook it for him, exacting a tithe for the landlord's own table or for a favored guest. Joly the unquenchable griper
complained about the cooking. The meat, he said, was "a great cinder,
half roasted, half dragged through the ashes." He was probably lucky at
that. When food was available, it was usually highly doubtful; Don Quixote is offered a bit of blackened codfish at one venta; at another he is
promised a feast in the form of a cow's foot. Bacon was rancid, salads
mostly wilted radish leaves bathed in stale oil and carnivorous vinegar,
meat pies were slops baked in dough, the tripe came from unknown animals and the slices of cheese usually resembled fine lace. Wine was customarily stored in skins rather than barrels, which brought frequent protests from foreign visitors that the stuff tasted more like cod's blood than
grape juice.

None of this would have troubled the Cervanteses much; they had
been trained in poverty. But the cost must have hurt: four reales a night
for table service and towels, another real per bed and candle, still
another real to have the bed made and a lunch prepared for the next
day. There was no set tariff on the after-dark services of the inn's maids,
which, to judge by the description of Maritornes in *Don Quixote*, were as
unpleasant as they were illegal. Broad-faced, she was, and flat-nosed, with
a head like a wedge from which peered one blind eye and another not
much sharper. Her breath smelled of "yesterday's stale salad" and her
hair was like a horse's mane; "her delightful body made up for her other
faults," although "being a touch round-shouldered made her look at the
floor more than she might have wished."[26]

Neither Cervantes, presumably, had call for such services on the trip to
Alcalá. Rodrigo's mood is hard to guess. He was returning to a place
where every street mocked his present decadence. Still, he was revisiting
his youth, too, and he seems to have had a faculty for shutting unpleasantness out of his mind.

The Luisa he found when he got there was not likely to cheer him. She
had been left—when?—in the care of her godfather, the devout lawyer
Christóbal Bermúdez, who had chosen her friends for their piety and
who had steadily, perhaps realistically, directed her toward the Church.
Everyone called her "Santita," little saint. She was now a quiet, muffled
girl of eighteen, more than usually glum because of the recent death of

her dearest friend, Bermúdez's son Alvaro. Yes, the Church was the place for her.

Rodrigo's relief was probably tempered by vexation at the expense her betrothal involved. What with her dowry and entry fee (to cover the cost of candles and celebrational feasts), the figure could very well have exceeded two hundred ducats, three years' income for a working man. We may suppose that most of the money was begged or borrowed. For it was a matter of great formal rejoicing that Luisa was to enter upon a life as harsh as a galley slave's.

The convent had been founded only two years before by St. Teresa's friend María de Jesús, whose desire to reform the Carmelite order had seized her in 1562, the same year in which the ambition was born to Teresa of Ávila. An illiterate widow who had already been expelled from a Carmelite community in her native Granada and threatened with public whipping for her "delusions,"[27] she had walked barefoot to Rome to seek permission from Pope Pius IV to found a Carmelite house according to the fundamental rule, without mitigation. Teresa, a frequent visitor at the Alcalá house, called her "a little corner of God."[28]

The fundamental rule was unmitigated purgatory for the "little nuns" of the Discalced Carmelite Convent of the Holy Image. They went barefoot the year round (sandals were not authorized by Teresa until 1576), slept on sacks filled with grapevine cuttings, wore skin-lacerating habits of coarse cloth which, in the event of demonstrable need, could be changed once a year. The habits were never doffed and prayers were constant to the Lord to kill the *mala gente*—the evil folk—which cohabited in them. The nuns' lives were filled with begging for alms, prayer, ceaseless hard labor and perpetual silence within the thick stone walls of the fifteenth-century palace in which the community was installed. They rose at 5 A.M. in summer and six in winter, ate no meat except in cases of severe illness, were forbidden personal property of any kind. The death rate was high.

It was they who made famous the candied almonds of Alcalá which families returning from a baptism were expected to distribute to the hordes of children who followed them through the streets crying, "Godfather, godfather, untie your little purse."[29] Anyone ringing the ancient convent bell today can still buy a bag of the sweets from an unseen successor to Luisa who will pass it through the conventual turnstile.

Not until February 11, 1565, did Luisa enter the convent—it was located only a few doors away from the house in which she was born—as the novice Luisa de Belén. The nuns, probably fewer than a dozen then, had been busy since the previous day making the arrangements. On the morning of the eleventh, they gathered behind the locutory grille, their faces yellowish-white in the candlelit gloom. Their spiritual adviser slowly read the venerable Carmelite rule as it had been framed in Palestine three centuries earlier. Then Luisa took the vows of humility, chastity, poverty and obedience. With that, the family watched her disappear into the choir while the nuns sang a hymn of grace.

Neither Miguel nor Rodrigo is likely ever to have seen her again. She was confirmed as a novice six days later and probably professed in 1567 or 1568. In her more than half-century of conventual existence, she was subprioress of the Alcalá convent twice and prioress twice, in 1602–5 and again in 1620. The only utterance by her which comes down to us is probably apocryphal but not at all untypical; when informed of her brothers' captivity by Barbary pirates, she is reported to have said: "They will redeem their guilt and their sins, professing their Christian faith, and if they are sacrificed, they will accede to Holy Glory in a single bound."[30] Despite the harshness of Camelite rule, this frail, tough, lackluster little woman, the black-haired ugly duckling in a brood of blonds, was her family's last survivor; she died in 1620 or 1621, aged seventy-four or seventy-five.

Rodrigo and Miguel lingered for some weeks more in the home Rodrigo's sister María shared with her daughter Martina de Mendoza and Martina's husband, Diego de Talavera. By March they were back in Córdoba, where they may have arrived in time to see the imposing funeral held for Lope de Rueda, who "because he was an excellent and famous man . . . was buried in the cathedral in Córdoba, between the two choirs. . . ."[31] We know they were still there on April 10; there is a record of a purchase on that date, on credit of course, of an extravagant length of fine black cloth—thirty-eight varas, over a hundred yards—payable by the end of May. No record exists of payment.

Out of the frying pan and into the fire: on his return to Seville, Rodrigo found that one Francisco de Chaves had moved to embargo his possessions for debt. Andrea had been shrewd enough to block seizure of his goods by filing a counterclaim alleging her ownership of part of them, a move which kept the suit going until her father's return. She declared her age to be seventeen, a fiction the notary amiably supports with the formula, "and so she seemed by her aspect"; she was, in fact, twenty and may already have begun to swell with Doña Constanza.

Rodrigo applied the now automatic solution to his problems: flight. The destination this time was Madrid, because the court was there, because his mother-in-law had lately died and left some small inheritance to Doña Leonor, because Nicolás de Ovando was in Madrid. And, too, because he was running out of places to hide in Andalusia. By early 1566, the family was installed in the new capital of all the Spains.

6

Turning Point

Miguel would have had to shout to make himself heard. The din of voices and cart wheels and the squeals of animals swirling on the clouds of yellow dust at the Puerta de Moros, the Moors' Gate, made it a chaos from early morning until the gate was shut again at dusk. From it led a jumble of streets inherited from Madrid's Moorish past, a labyrinth mockingly summarized in the name of one alley called *Sal si puedes*—Get Out If You Can.

But Miguel had been in the capital before, if only briefly. We can imagine him nudging his brother Rodrigo with, perhaps, a faintly patronizing air, and pointing toward the Alcázar, the old Moorish fortress high on a hill overlooking the gate. This was now the royal palace; to Spaniards it was the center of the world. From the road, the boys in the cart could see the double-eagle royal standard flying over the battlements to announce that King Philip II was, as usual, in residence.

For all three of them—the two boys in the dust below and the black-clad prince in the glowering castle on the hill—that year, 1566, was a turning point. Some scholars believe Miguel's life as a wanderer began with a minor scandal in the palace grounds; Rodrigo's death was to be an absurdly casual result of the decisions the king was then formulating, decisions which would enfeeble the empire Philip was resolved to strengthen. And, improbable as the conjunction would have seemed to any of them that day, Miguel the barber's son and King Philip would converge in history as the archsymbols of their time and place.

Philip II was enraged. His courtiers could hear it in the ominously soft voice; they could see it in the chilling little smile they said was only a step away from the knife; the blue eyes, red-rimmed from nights of sacrificial toil in the interests of Spanish hegemony, bulged farther out of the pale face that, with its neat blond beard, rose like a cloud-hung moon above the black clothes the king habitually wore.

He had lost patience with his smugly prosperous Flemish burghers. For five years they had bombarded him with complaints—about his soldiers, his bishops, his narrow trading policies. Their real grievance was economic colonization by Spain, but Philip, Duke of Brabant and Count of Flanders, had made his own diagnosis: creeping Protestantism. Now, in 1566, Flemish aristocrats had leagued to present a bill of indictment against him which amounted to a manifesto of rebellion. Worse, his agents had warned him that the Calvinists were stirring the Dutch with sermons sustaining a people's right to depose a tyrannical ruler. Even the policy of moderation he thought he was following there was being spurned as "murderation."[1]

He had already sent the Spanish Inquisition to tighten his control over the disgruntled provinces. That had only aggravated the complaints. In August of 1566, Flemish anger burst like a plague swelling. Hundreds of churches were sacked, the holy images desecrated. In the cathedral at Antwerp, the venerable statue of the Black Madonna was ravaged by a mob. Calvinists in Amsterdam, Utrecht, Leyden, Delft, all Catholic towns, had seized control of municipal governments. Philip had already asserted his preference to lose his crown rather than "rule over a nation of heretics odious to God."[2] He took a long step in that direction with the appointment of the Duke of Alba to squelch Flemish impertinence once and for all.

Philip did not trust Alba; he did not trust anyone who was too strong or too bright or too popular. But Alba was a man he understood, a simple man of blood and iron who could be counted on to share the king's outrage. Indeed, two years later, when the imprudence of Spanish policy was already becoming evident to keener minds in Spain, the violent duke would assure his master that "it is much better to preserve, through war for God and for the king, an impoverished and even ruined kingdom than to maintain it intact without (war) for the devil and his satellites the heretics."[3] Which proves, at the very least, that Philip was a more concise stylist than Alba.

Mediocre intelligence was less than ever permissible in a monarch in that period of ballooning national rivalries. Cautious, slow-thinking Philip was never to perceive that the policies he inherited from his father Charles V—absolutism in faith and authority, crown imperialism, a metal economy—were beyond his power to enforce. Northern preferences for expanded trade and productivity were deemed unworthy of Castilian pride and Philip's dynastic heritage. His subjects generally agreed with him; they were as entrapped in their national image as he was. And the door of the trap was beginning to swing shut. The ravishment of the Black Madonna of Antwerp was the first overt act in a struggle which would go on for an incredible eighty-two years. It would bleed Spain white; by the early 1620s, the Dutch war alone would be consuming a third of the Spanish crown's total annual budget. It would lead to rebellion within the peninsula itself. When the Netherlands' independence was finally conceded in 1648, Spain would be a nation riddled with self-doubt, militarily exhausted, a country with a memory where its soul had been.

To the Cervantes family, newly arrived from the magnificence of Seville, Madrid would have been an unprepossessing place, a mean city of mean streets lined with jerry-built houses, most of them only one story high to evade having court officials billeted in their second stories. Bare patches were already showing on the wooded hills around the city where the rock had been shorn of its coat of pine, oak, chestnut, walnut, elm and poplar to provide emergency housing for the whores and hangers-on pouring into the capital. In five years, the population had grown from twelve thousand to sixty thousand.

When Philip had begun to transfer his administration there to establish the nation's first fixed capital in 1561, Madrid was a sheltered town, famous for its even climate. Now the wind brought the newly exposed dust of the mountains whistling down into the town to seep in at doors and unglazed windows, stripping the varnish from oaken tables. Winters had become noticeably colder; the poor, standing ankle-deep in noxious muck, shivered as they waited for the free soup that was passed every day at noon through a tiny barred window of the little church of San Luis.

For Rodrigo de Cervantes, a bitter winter was giving on a hopeful spring. His lawsuit in the winter of 1566–67 to collect a heritage left to his wife by her mother in Arganda leaves a legal cairn by which we can follow the family to Madrid. For once, the law seems to have sided with the Cervanteses: the next two years would find them living in comfort so unaccustomed that Rodrigo would *lend* the impressive sum of eight hundred ducats to a smooth-talking deadbeat named Pedro Sánchez de Córdoba. Years later, when the money was desperately needed, Rodrigo would still be trying in vain to collect on the debt; barber-surgeon Cervantes had been too hidalgo to insist on co-signers.

No thanks for the family's prosperity went to the honorable Nicolás de Ovando. His expectations of a rich inheritance were to be shattered by the revelation at his father's death that his family was bankrupt if not broke. Despite his moderately rapid climb, mostly on the shoulders of

Mateo Vázquez, to a post as a royal chamberlain, Nicolás was launched on a life of genteel poverty which made the breach-of-promise suit Andrea filed merely an academic exercise.[4]

In *Don Quixote*, Cervantes would arrange matters more to his taste: Don Fernando would, after all, marry the Dorotea he had "promised" and debauched. Andrea, meanwhile, seems to have found consolation nearer at hand.

The Cervantes household had become a headquarters for a group of Italians, probably exchange agents for Italian merchant-bankers. Such men as Pirro Boqui, Francesco Musaqui and Antonio Lomelin or Lomellino would act as witnesses for Rodrigo in his dealings with the law. Just what they were doing there is not clear. Rodrigo may, like most surgeons of the day, have opened a barbershop which became a meeting place for the underoccupied who made up much of the city's population. A more probable explanation is that, as the legal tussling over Leonor's heritage dragged on, the Cervantes family took in boarders to supplement Rodrigo's earnings, and the habit stuck.

Among the group was Gian Francesco Locadelo. He seems quickly to have acquired a privileged position in the house, so much so that, on June 9, 1568, he appeared with Andrea before a Madrid notary to execute what may have been a genuine act of gratitude on his part or, as realism obliges us to suppose, merely a legal fiction. "Whereas I am much obliged and indebted," he averred, "to Señora Doña Andrea de Cervantes . . . for having, when I was in this land far from my native country, favored me and nursed me through certain sicknesses I suffered, and because she and her father did other things for me and for my benefit which I am obliged to remunerate and reward," Locadelo made her a gift worthy of a prosperous banker.[5]

The list is long of lengths of cloth, of jeweled clothes, cloth of silver and gold, silken cloaks and crystals, as well as what amounted to complete furnishings for a decent home, from bed sheets of Rouen cloth to walnut tables and a set of pewter plates. There was even a viol, not to mention a host of such smaller objects as fifty crystal buttons—and three hundred gold escudos.

Locadelo's gift speaks to us of a lonely man, aging, perhaps, who had once established himself, or planned to, as a man of substance; the inventory suggests not only that he had means, but also the refined taste of an Italian of good family. That secretary, those marquetry chests for coifs, the mattresses and chests and cushions of green velvet. Something had gone wrong. Had he been married to a woman now dead? In any case, he had come to the end of things in Spain; he was—we can be almost certain of it—going home. Locadelo must have been fond of Andrea, and suspicious of her parents. His deed of gift, witnessed by that same Pedro

Sánchez de Córdoba who was to fleece Rodrigo, contained a provision that it was offered as a dowry "so that no other person, neither her parents nor brothers nor any one of them might oppose any obstacle whatsoever to the said Doña Andrea's wishes. . . ." The gift was hers alone, to be withdrawn should it tempt her family to cause her any "difficulty or vexation."⁶ Obviously, there was tension between Andrea and her parents; she was shortly to be found away from the family in what, to judge from the forty-ducat-a-year rent she paid for it, must have been an extremely comfortable house, but earning her living, at least officially, as a seamstress.

Whether Miguel's sympathy covered Andrea's new affair is not recorded; the specific reference to "her brothers" in Locadelo's non-intervention clause sets one to musing. But Miguel by that time had other fish to fry. He was too deeply involved in his own *madrileño* life to brood over his sister's amusements. He was in the center of things, the place that moved the world. Madrid then was like an egg, with the court as the yolk; anything that shook the center made the white vibrate. And in 1567–68, the egg was practically scrambled.

For one thing, there was trouble brewing among the Moriscos in the old kingdom of Granada. With the expiration of the forty-year agreement concluded with them by Charles V, Philip and his choleric chancellor, Espinosa, had imposed a humilating new code nullifying what few rights to ethnic identity the Moriscos had retained. It was made a crime for them to read, write or speak Arabic, to patronize their baths, to use Moorish surnames or wear Moorish clothes. The new regulations reflected in part the fear felt by Old Christian Spaniards for an "enemy" population.

There were other plague spots. The king almost precipitated a rebellion in Catalonia by reacting violently to a wholly imaginary Calvinist uprising there. As in Granada, as in Flanders, Philip II identified compromise in Catalonia with weakness, concession with apostasy.

That myopia was increasing his problems in Flanders as well. On September 19, 1567, word arrived in Madrid that Alba had captured the dissident leaders Counts Egmont and Horn. On the same day, Philip ordered the arrest of Baron de Montigny, who was on a peace mission from Flanders and who, until the moment of his arrest, was convinced that a peaceful solution to the Flemish problem was possible. Egmont and Horn were publicly executed; Montigny was judicially murdered.⁷

The keystone of the Black Legend surrounding Philip II, however, was the imprisonment and death of his mad son, the infante Don Carlos. Ever since the trepanning the prince had undergone after a head-first fall down a flight of stairs—the treatment was supplemented by depositing the remains of a beatified monk in his bed—bizarre stories had been circulating about the prince's strange conduct. He had girls whipped for pleasure, it was said; he tortured animals. He tried to throw his treasurer, Juan de Lobón, through a window. He drew a dagger against Espinosa and publicly called great ladies whores. His gluttony was said to encompass even the swallowing of diamonds and pearls.

All Madrid seemed to peer over Philip's shoulder as, with increasing anxiety, he watched the degeneration of this hunched, misshapen boy who is said to have hated him. Theories that the prince was a crypto-Protestant may be discounted, along with those alleging a romance with his stepmother, Elisabeth de Valois, only four years older than he and originally destined to be the bride of Carlos, not his father. But when he tried to enlist the king's bastard brother, Don Juan of Austria, and Montigny in a plot to establish an independent kingdom in the Netherlands with himself on the throne, his madness became treason.

On January 15, 1568, Philip asked that prayers be said in all the city's churches and monasteries for divine guidance in a grave enterprise. All mail into and out of the court was held, and no one was allowed to leave or enter the city except on official business. Madrid held its breath.

For three days, the king consulted with jurists and theologians. Then, at eleven o'clock on the night of January 18, a small group of courtiers led by an armed and helmeted Philip burst into the infante's room in the Alcázar. The boy was terrified understandably. "What would Your Majesty want with me?" one contemporary account reports him as asking. "Now you will see," came the answer. The windows and doors of the room were boarded up. The boy who was then Philip's only male heir became a prisoner.[8]

On July 24, 1568, Don Carlos died, almost certainly of natural causes. He had been on a hunger strike; he had been sleeping through the humid, malarial Madrid summer in a bed packed with ice brought down on muleback from the peaks of the Sierra de Guadarrama. His health had always been delicate.

But the charge has never quite been dismissed that his father had him put to death. The dreaded word poison immediately flashed around the Continent, as it always did when a prominent person died mysteriously. Philip's explanatory letters were vague, but his motives were probably those he outlined to his sister María: "I wished in this to make sacrifice to God of my own flesh and blood, preferring His service and the universal benefit and welfare to other human considerations."[9] That his kingdom, his subjects, the imperial destiny he had inherited from his father the emperor and his great-grandparents the Catholic Kings should pass into such hands as his son's may have been a possibility more painful to the monarch than that of the boy's death was to the father.

Young Cervantes may have been better informed of these developments than some of his fellow madrileños. There is reason to believe that he had struck up friendships with a number of poets including Gabriel López Maldonado and Luis Gálvez de Montalvo. One special new friend was Pedro Laínez, an older man, chamberlain to Don Carlos, whom Cervantes would later acknowledge, to the doubtful glory of both, as his master in the art of poetry.

In 1567 Miguel even established himself as a poet of sorts. His sonnet was not published, exactly; it was hung, with dozens more, on a flimsy triumphal arch, to tremble in the sharp October wind. Madrid was in dubious festival that autumn. On October 10, the queen gave birth to her second daughter. The child's sex dismayed Philip in view of his preoccupation over Don Carlos. Nevertheless, a festival was ordered. To design and direct it the king named the Cervanteses' friend Alonso Getino de Guzmán and his partner, Diego de Ostia. Erection of triumphal arches at strategic places in the city was standard in such celebrations; to have a congratulatory verse hung on them was not only a poet's patriotic duty but, in a city with only one printer,[10] it was a rare opportunity to get one's poems read.

Getino's invitation to Miguel to contribute one of these efforts has been taken as acknowledgment that the boy was already recognized as a poet in full standing. Not likely. Not, at any rate, if the sonnet in question is a sample of his work at the time. It is pompous, forced, lackluster. Admittedly, the occasion was not all that inspiring. And the verse does show a rudimentary familiarity with the rules of poetic composition. Miguel clearly had been reading and listening to public recitals of poetry as well as writing it; there are echoes of the nationalistic bombast of such Establishment poets as Hernando de Acuna and the finer, cleaner, but no less imperial poems of Diego Hurtado de Mendoza.

What is, perhaps, most depressing about this sonnet is not so much its amateurishness—how could it be otherwise?—as the fact that more than a generation later, a middle-aged Cervantes would be turning out sonnets very little better, just as forced, just as tedious. October 1567 marks the official beginning of a frustration—artistic, professional and, finally, personal—that would pursue him to his grave. To the sixteenth century, literary greatness was for poets—not novelists, not entertainers. And a verse poet Cervantes would never be, despite an occasional spasm of happy inspiration. That much is obvious from the opening lines of

> Most Serene Queen, in whom is found
> all that God can give to a human being . . .

He did have other reasons to be pleased with himself that year. He had also arrived at the "gates of grammar," or so we suppose. In any event, it was in Madrid in 1567–68 that he received the only formal schooling to which he is definitely known to have been exposed.

There is, nevertheless, something equivocal about his position in the Estudio de la Villa, an academy financed by the city on what is now the Calle de la Villa. He was twenty, absurdly old for normal public enrollment. Was he a private student? Did he receive lessons in return for work done around the place? Why, when other boys his age, those who were not well along in university studies, had long since begun to earn their own living, was he in school at all? Had a wave of prosperity suggested to his parents that Miguel might, after all, be apt for a career in letters or in the Church? We cannot even be sure of what Miguel himself thought about it. That he would go through later life feeling cruelly inferior to the less talented but more elaborately schooled men around him is not necessarily a clue to his feelings at twenty. Probably he was pleased to have the education then. Madrid, the center of Spanish civilization, crammed to its bulging walls with men of vast culture, thinkers, theologians, men of law and poets—Madrid would have taught him suddenly to need the background these men had. He would have seen for himself how impossible a curiosity he was in the period, an ignorant poet, one of the very animals he would deride—with more bravado than conviction—nearly half a century later as buffoons

> who have little to do
> with skill, wisdom and knowledge.[11]

The institution in question had existed for many years; it had been endowed by Ferdinand and Isabel. But it had lately fallen on hard times and in the autumn of 1566 it had been closed for lack of a rector. Committees were sent throughout the region to seek a new headmaster. At Alcalá de Henares, in Talavera de la Reina, everywhere, the answer was no until at last, in March 1567, one Francisco del Bayo was hired. The city endowed the school with a miserable subsidy of 25,000 maravedis a year and set the fee for paying pupils—the poor were to be admitted free —at 2 reales a month. Cervantes may have entered the school then, perhaps in the advanced poetics class, translating the classics, doing Latin composition and commenting on themes in prose and verse.

Bayo lasted in the job only until that October, when the school was shut down again. On March 9, 1568, a new rector was finally appointed: Juan López de Hoyos, parish priest at the Madrid church of San Andrés; his pay was slightly better than Bayo's—30,000 maravedis a year plus a *cahiz* (about eighteen bushels) of wheat.

Cervantists have found in López de Hoyos the thinker who was to shape Miguel's thought for life, supposedly along Erasmian lines. "Master, affectionate admirer, protector, editor, friend," Astrana Marín called him, ignoring his own calculation that, what with vacations and delays in the school opening, Cervantes may have had less than eight months of course time.[12]

López de Hoyos was a gentle, cultivated man with a lofty if pedestrian mind, well thought of in Madrid and, despite his mildly Erasmian leanings, a protégé of the terrible Cardinal Espinosa. In the fifteen years he directed the Estudio de la Villa he is not known to have produced a single notable alumnus other than Cervantes. He was kindly, tactful, generous of praise, lived alone with his mother and was apparently the kind of good man the great find easy to patronize.

There is no doubt that López de Hoyos had been and continued to be an Erasmian. That Cervantes' writings, especially *Don Quixote,* show signs of Erasmian seasoning is hard to deny. But to complete the syllogism by making the good priest of Madrid his Erasmian godfather smacks of art historians' conceit. Even if the master had possessed the flamboyant, electric, aggressive mind to light philosophic fires in a boy's brain—and no evidence comes to us that this was true—he simply hadn't the time. True, he may have put across his admiration for Erasmus, may have planted a name and an aspiration in the boy's memory. But such Erasmism as may be found in *Don Quixote* was almost certainly acquired by Cervantes later, on his own, as most of what he knew was acquired.

"Master, affectionate admirer. . . ." That surely. Although López de Hoyos was too polished a critic not to have recognized Miguel's poetry for the daub it was, he seems to have seen enough in the young man to encourage his love of verse. This became obvious in October 1568 when Queen Elisabeth, under the respectful guidance of the court physicians, finally died after months of illness. López de Hoyos, as the city's intellectual-in-residence, was ordered by municipal authorities to compose the funeral allegories, the inscriptions to be hung around her tomb in the newly built church of the Descalzas Reales, as well as a "history and true account of the illness, pious passing and sumptuous obsequies of the Most Serene Queen of Spain, Doña Isabel de Valoys our Lady."[13] Something similar had been done at the school on the death of Don Carlos; "in our Studium," the rector recorded, "the students composed many very good funeral orations, elegies, verses, sonnets." None are distinguishable as Miguel's.

The book honoring the queen took six months to prepare. And this time the star performer, if there was one, was Miguel. He is mentioned specifically four times: for an "epitaph in sonnet form with a *copla Castellana* done by Miguel de Cervantes, my beloved disciple"; four *redondillas* by Miguel de Cervantes, "our dear and beloved disciple"; an elegy in folio 157 bears the notation that it was composed "in the name of all of us . . . by the aforesaid (Cervantes) . . . the which, in most elegant style, contains things worthy of being remembered"; and finally, in the Table of Notable Items, we are directed to the "elegy by Miguel de Cervantes in Castilian meter to the Cardinal (Espinosa, to whom the book was dedicated) on the death of the queen; in it, very curious things are treated in delicate conceits."[14]

This praise has been explained as a generous attempt to win judicial leniency for a "disciple" who, by the time the book was printed in September 1569, is believed to have been a fugitive from justice. No such rationalization is needed. At twenty-one, Miguel was surely the oldest boy in the school, very probably the brightest. Perhaps, too, the most troubled. It seems only natural that good, stuffy, kindly López de Hoyos should have found him the easiest to talk to, should have seen something in the stammering, disoriented young man that challenged his mind and seized at his heart. It is affection that glows through the dust of centuries in the book in the Spanish National Library. López de Hoyos had, in a sense, become Cervantes' first patron. Did he envision guiding the young man into orders? Did he perhaps see Miguel as his successor, or was he grooming his student for introduction to the mighty Espinosa, whose dependents already included Mateo Vázquez and Nicolás de Ovando as well as López de Hoyos himself? Through the priest's interest, and the apparent prosperity of the Cervantes family, we glimpse the now silted-over foundations of a comfortable, productive career for a young man of letters. If it be unfeeling of us to thank heaven that it never came about, that he escaped a slough of security which would have left us an unread library of earnest, pedantic works but never a *Don Quixote,* never the greatest of the *Exemplary Stories*—why, then, so be it! We are, the rest of us, merchant bankers of the mind: genius owes us its fruition, whatever the cost.

Exactly what happened to Cervantes in 1569 is one of the most tantalizing mysteries of his mysterious life. Such facts as we have are merely provoking. On September 15, 1569, a royal order was issued that a bailiff be sent, armed with the official staff to justice, to pursue and arrest Miguel de Cervantes, last reported seen in Seville, for having wounded Antonio de Sigura in a clash of arms. The said Cervantes, when apprehended, was to be brought back to Madrid, where his right hand was to be chopped off by the public hangman; if he survived this exemplary punishment, he was to be exiled from "my kingdoms" for ten years and subjected to "other penalties contained in the said sentence."[15]

We hear next, documentally, from Miguel de Cervantes just before Christmas of the same year; he is in Rome awaiting a certification of blood purity he has asked his father to obtain for him as a precondition of employment.

Do the two documents refer to the same Miguel de Cervantes?

Probably they do. The purity certification was certainly destined for the author of *Don Quixote*. No other document pertaining to the criminal case is thought to have survived the later sale of court records as scrap paper, and Cervantes was a common name in Spain. But it was not so common in Madrid in 1569. Doubt rasps at the skin of probability, is chased and returns to bare its teeth again, yet no other solution seems adequate to the problem: why was a young man on the lip of life suddenly wrenched from stability and tossed spinning into uncertainty? Some rebellious movement of the blood, an abrupt terror of looming dullness, a wish to see the world uncurtained by the matriarchal shadow of Doña Leonor de Cortinas? An unexpected offer of a career abroad which, when tasted, would quickly be found unpalatable? Or a dramatic, unlooked-for crisis?

When the warrant was discovered, toward the middle of the nineteenth century, it was greeted with shocked disbelief, as though the brawling readily permitted to Lope de Vega, Quevedo, Calderón de la Barca were too embarrassing to the Spanish image of Cervantes as a man of almost unearthly benevolence. Gradually, however, the Spanish psychosexual obsession found in the fight a new source of pride in the national idol, for now he could be melded with that other paragon of Spanish compulsiveness, Don Juan Tenorio. St. Miguel de Cervantes became a rake, a lady's man. The duel—for a duel it had become—had to be over a woman.

Some Cervantists, the most reserved, have suggested that Miguel reacted to a slighting reference to his sister Andrea's love affairs, as though the sexual forays of an obscure surgeon's daughter were so prominent in Madrid gossip that they would arise in an unlikely conversation with a man Miguel could hardly have known. One biographer posits a love affair with a lady of quality who was as inaccessible as the heroine of any chivalric romance and was the model for Quixote's Dulcinea. Another sees Miguel as somehow involved in the hopeless courtship of one of the queen's ladies-in-waiting by his friend the aristocratic poet Luis Gálvez de Montalvo. The affair, with Magdalena de Girón, did take place, with its concomitant bribing of pages to carry notes, its skulking in corridors pining for a tender glance, its serenades and amorous graffiti.

This romantic atmosphere fostered an elaboration of the scenario: because the sentence was considered too harsh a response to the kind of street brawl that might have flared at almost any hour in the muck-swamped alleys of Madrid, the row must have occurred in the royal palace grounds. This would have been an affront to the king's majesty for which not even nobles or court officials went unpunished; court chronicler Luis Cabrera de Córdoba, it was noted, was exiled in 1601 for merely putting his hand to his sword in the king's presence. This is gratuitous swashbuckling; since the fourteenth century, the law had prescribed loss of a man's sword hand for spilling blood unless the offended party pardoned his assailant, for money or for charity.

A fight could nevertheless have started in the arcaded palace courtyard. This was a favorite *mentidero*—a place to gather and gossip and, as the word indicates, to lie—for madrileños of every class. Under the tile-roofed galleries bordering the patios swarmed idlers, petitioners, tipsters with doubtful information to whisper, peddlers of questionable influence. In the corners, ministers' aides and magistrates dealt with suppliants and litigants, taking their bribes, selling documents required by the state or the Inquisition, arranging for the purchase of offices or titles or privileges. There, too, the poets were drawn in the early part of the day to spout their verses and chip away at each other's reputations. Cervantes might have encountered Sigura there. But why cross swords with him?

The man has been identified as an illiterate member of a Madrid family of master masons who later made a modest living as superintendent of construction for the royal palaces in Aranjuez, Madrid and El Pardo. An ordinary fellow with a sullen peasant's mind; a codicil in his will revising his bequests suggests a countryman counting his ducats and scowling at the heirs waiting to receive them. He does not sound like the man to proffer insults in connection with a minor palace intrigue to a young man who, at best, was scarcely more than privy to it. A quarrel would have arisen from a personal grievance. Did a Cervantes too impressed with his new friendships tease Sigura for his illiteracy? Did Sigura riposte with a sneering comment on the pretentiousness of schoolboys playing at being great gentlemen? Or was there a crude gibe at the young man's virility, pointed enough to release the mechanism of sexual disorientation in Cervantes' heart? Something to bring a clumsy gush of arrogance welling up, under the pressure of new friends, a new life, the need for achievement, from some deep-lying stratum of pride, defiance. Perhaps a burst of unreasoning self-assertiveness from a young man anxious to replace an ineffectual father.

Cervantes was never to refer directly to the incident in his writing; it was nothing to be proud of. The theme of dueling does recur in his stories, however, and such patterns sometimes point to personal experience. In his play *The Gallant Spanishwoman,* a character named Saavedra wounds a man in a duel and is forced to flee to Italy. The *Persiles* is full of duels, one of which has rung a bell to scholars seeking evidence of Cervantes' brawl (one hesitates to qualify so squalid a set-to as a duel) with Sigura. It concerns the barbarous Spaniard Antonio de Villaseñor, who wounds a man in a foolish quarrel over protocol. "I retired to my parents' house," the character explains, "and told them of the event and, aware of the danger I was in, they provided me with money and a good horse, advising me to hide because I had earned many powerful and influential enemies. This I did, and in two days I crossed the line to

Aragon, where I rested a bit from my unprecedented haste."[16] There is evidence, however, that the incident may have been based on an actual duel involving a real-life Villaseñor in La Mancha, and not on Cervantes' personal experience.

Why would Miguel have run away at all? Spanish good sense had made pardon for a price in a blood offense an almost routine solution. Sigura, for the moment, appears to have refused pardon. Perhaps the price had not been right. Or was the offense so grave as to have atrophied the Siguran sense of charity?

If we subscribe, however reluctantly, to the theory that the arrest warrant concerned *the* Miguel de Cervantes, then the choice of Italy as a place of refuge was natural. To a man on the run, it was enough like home to be attractive. Naples and the Two Sicilies, Milan were Spanish territory; Genoa, though nominally independent, was a client state, but even there the grasp of Spanish justice was feeble. In the sovereign states, in Rome, Venice, Tuscany, a man was safe. True, Catalonia was a safe place too; a Castilian writ still had no force in Aragon then. But to a young man dazzled by the brilliance of Renaissance learning, eager to steep himself in the warm spring of southern humanist letters, sober, workaday Catalonia was not the place to stop.

Italy, then, probably via the standard exit, Barcelona,[17] where it is "the natural and peculiar characteristic of the Catalonian nobility to be friendly and to favor strangers who have some need of them . . . the flower of the world's fine cities . . . hostel and haven for strangers. . . ."[18] It is easy to see Cervantes feeling almost gay as he stood on the beach there and, for the first time, watched the sea clamor at the walls rising from the water's edge. The harbor would have been clogged with galleys skittering like monstrous centipedes over the water. In *Don Quixote* we glimpse the port at daybreak.

> Don Quixote and Sancho gazed in all directions; they saw the sea, which until then they had never seen; it seemed to them very spacious and broad, much more so than the lagoons of Ruidera which they had seen in La Mancha; they saw the galleys lying in to the beach; their awnings were down, uncovering a host of streamers and pennants which fluttered in the wind, kissing and sweeping the water. From on board there sounded clarions, trumpets and pipes which filled the surrounding air with sweet and martial accents.[19]

It was probably in one of these floating torture chambers that Miguel joined a voracious community of vermin on the six-day voyage along the coasts of France and the Milanese to Genoa. He may not have expected to be away long.

Part II
KNIGHT-ERRANT

7

The Cardinal's Chamberlain

. . . The things which, as though in prophecy, I often heard said of Your Most Illustrious Grace to Cardinal Acquaviva when I was his chamberlain in Rome. . . .

This passing reference in Cervantes' dedication of his novel *La Galatea* is all Cervantes ever said directly about his employment in Rome, and this fact alone should make us wary; he could be as taciturn about the experiences he regretted as he was talkative about those that interested him. His short career in a Vatican household was probably of the regrettable kind.

He may have been lodging with one of the Spanish families concentrated in the Via dei Banchi[1] when his purity certification reached Rome, probably early in February 1570. With it may have come word of publication of the Studium book containing his poems, although he is not likely to have received a copy of the book; at the going price of mail (a two-page letter from, say, Madrid to Toledo, a distance of less than fifty miles, could set a workingman back more than a week's wages), the cost would have been prohibitive for the likes of Rodrigo de Cervantes. Correspondence was effectively reserved for officials, merchants and the idle rich.

Armed now with a formal guarantee that none in his family were or had been "Moors, Jews, conversos nor reconciled by the Holy Office of the Inquisition" but were "Old Christians, clean of any stain,"[2] Cervantes was free to look for work.[3] He found it with Giulio Acquaviva y Aragon, thanks, according to one source,[4] to Acquaviva's friend and fellow cleric Gaspar de Cervantes y Gaete, identified as Miguel's kinsman. Why Don Gaspar did not take his supposed protégé into his own household is not clear.

Acquaviva was the second son of the Duke of Atri and Teramo and the nephew of a general of the Jesuit order. Miguel's senior by only a year, he was reputed "a very virtuous and cultivated lad" of whom "much could be expected."[5] Pope Pius V had sent him to Madrid in 1568 to extend pontifical condolences on the death of Don Carlos. The embassy went off badly, through no fault of his. He seems to have spent much of his time acquiring Spanish handicrafts like any other tourist; the exit visa issued to him on December 2, 1568, grants him export rights for such items as five dozen pairs of perfumed gloves and a dozen pairs of silk hose. His failure seems not to have damaged his career. When Miguel went to work for him in the late winter of 1570, Acquaviva was preparing for the May 17 ceremony at which both he and Don Gaspar were to become cardinals.

A sight of soul-expanding speculation surrounds Cervantes' appointment as Acquaviva's *camarero*, or chamberlain: the cultivated young churchman is popularly seen as conceiving a spontaneous sympathy for the exiled young poet; literary conversations are heard at monsignore's table. Cervantes' duties are thought of as combining those of secretary, major-domo, confidant, arranging his lord's correspondence, receiving his guests. The notion that he may have been no more than a domestic servant makes Spanish cheeks quiver with indignation.

Definitions of a chamberlain's function varied widely then, partly because a noble house mustered chamberlains and chamberlains' chamberlains in a descending order from the high chamberlain, the lord's principal fiscal officer and often his chief lieutenant. Even at the lowest level, a camarero was by no means the humblest of the two to three hundred hirelings in a great household. He was a good step on the staff ladder above the pages; he may have had servants of his own. But it is nonsense to imagine a twenty-two-year-old nobody suddenly wandering in off the street, with or without the recommendation of a relative he did not know, to head the household of a dignitary who had never before set eyes on him.

A number of contemporary accounts exist to tell us what Cervantes' work may have been like. One of the most concise was written in Naples in 1519 by Roberto de Nola in the introduction to his cookbook, the first to appear in Spanish. It was the camarero's duty, he informs us, to "keep his lord's chamber neat and tidy, and when his lord wishes to rest or lie down, always to be at his side, without failing even once in this, unless he is sent (on an errand) by his lord . . . always to be present at his lord's lying down and rising up, with his clothes ready, and to put the clothes he wears to air on sunless days . . . (to) keep his bed well made and the linens very clean, and whenever the sheets and pillowslips are changed to perfume them and the shirts to be worn and the handkerchiefs, sprinkling them with musk. . . ." He is to store the master's silks and linens in chests in orderly fashion, everything to be noted in a ledger.

We are a long way here from airy literary conversations at the signorial table. But there is communication of a sort, for Nola warns that a chamberlain must be "honest and secret and reverent to his lord," admonishing that "though (the master) may jest with him and allow him broad license," he "be not remiss in respecting (him) all the more," and "to humble himself and to be discreet and not garrulous, and if his lord do some disorderly thing he should know how to hide it and never speak ill of him in public or in private. . . ."[6] Literally, a gentleman's gentleman.

An ambiguous position at best. One not made easier by the reflection that the master he served, whose cloak he patiently held and whose bed sheets he patiently counted, was hardly older than the servant. Nor should we seek much satisfaction in monsignore's "jests" or the "broad license" he may have extended to his chamberlain; they were not likely to be invitations to serious discussion of poetry or anything else. Yes, monsignore; no, monsignore; oh indeed, monsignore. . . . His Youthful Eminence may hardly have been aware of Miguel's presence.

Is this what Cervantes had come to Italy for? He had come to consort with men like Torquato Tasso, then twenty-five and already famous for his chivalric epic *Rinaldo,* or the incendiary Dominican poet Giordano Bruno; he had come to sit in the academies, the literary clubs of the day, and nestle in the heart of poetry. He surely wanted to build a life he may vaguely have imagined as a drifting through golden halls of learning, a dream of Grecian dialogues.

Well, the golden halls were there; so were the marble libraries and the paintings. He could see them, perhaps, as he trotted in his master's velvet-sheathed shadow at the Vatican, or wandered the city alone in those few hours when Acquaviva had no need of him. There were plenty of people in Rome he might have liked to meet. El Greco was there then, for example, staying as an honored guest with Cardinal Farnese, but even had the painter not been too prosperous, too fanatical, too odd, too Byzantine to have had anything in common with Cervantes, he would not have considered consorting with a mere servant. No, Cervantes' dreams were escaping him. What were real were the bowing and genuflecting; the laundry lists were real, and so were the scatological practical jokes of the lower servants. For despite Nola's recommendations of reverence, this was a trade for rogues and thieves. It took a Guzmán de Alfarache to thrive in it, someone who could lie to his master's face and steal behind his back. His lordship might dine on fowl simmered in almond milk and ginger, on livers stewed in sweet wine and cinnamon and meat pies cooked with cheese and spiced with saffron "because it gladdens the heart,"[7] but Guzmán, who in Alemán's novel also serves a Roman cardinal, complains of eating "cold in winter and hot in summer, little, bad and late."[8]

Discovering that the Romans did not like him because he was a Spaniard could only have intensified Cervantes' dissatisfaction. Although Rome pops up more than seventy times in his writing, the impression clings that he did not like the "queen of cities and Lady of the world."[9] Most of the references are demotic or conventionally pious. There is an occasional touch of irony, as in the lament of the robbery victim in *The Two Maidens* who regrets the loss of "the trunkful of agnus (dei) he had brought from Rome more than anything else he had." Even in the *Persiles,* where it symbolizes man's highest aspiration, his worldly ideal and his otherworldly yearning, Cervantes' attitude toward the city is distant, strained, cold.

To the Romans—indeed, to most Italians—the Spanish were arrogant, pompous, quarrelsome and crude. In the *Persiles,* Cervantes has the runaway servant Bartolomé El Manchego plead to be hanged in Spain rather than in Rome, "because here, those to be hanged are not treated with the proper formality . . . hardly anyone watches and so there is hardly anyone to say a 'Hail Mary,' especially if it is a Spaniard who is being hanged."[10]

Although their own literary energy was waning, Italians deprecated Spanish literature as primitive and mannered. They were the cultural Old World and the Spanish the vulgarians from the West. Spanish protocol was deemed so hilarious that for centuries afterward, doing things Spanish style was a popular locution for pretentiousness.

Not even Spaniards' faith was safe from Italian sneers. Accustomed to think of themselves as the treasurers of Roman Catholic piety, they were shocked to find themselves viewed by their subject peoples as crypto-heretics mongrelized by centuries of promiscuity with Jews and Moors. "Marrano" was the common Italian insult for all Spaniards. The very existence of the Spanish Inquisition was taken as proof of Spanish religious instability. Just as Erasmus could declare that "there are hardly any Christians in Spain,"[11] so the Italians could affirm with Pope Julius II, no friend of Spain, to be sure, that Spaniards were "sprouts of Jews and Marranos . . . a people as abject as they are base . . . heretics, schismatics, accursed of God."[12] In short, any virtue which could be withheld from a dominant power by its subordinate states was denied the Spanish. Italy felt itself exploited, drained, but it was at least confident of colonizing the conqueror's culture—an Italian Greece to Spain's Rome.

The Spanish, naturally, responded in kind. *Guzmán de Alfarache* applies the common Spanish epithet of "white Moors" to the Genoese, who, it was said, carried their consciences in their wallets. A letter from

Gálvez de Montalvo in Rome to the Duke of Francavila in 1587 sets the tone: "Life in Rome, sir, is uncommonly hard, and not all the great kindness done to me by the cardinal (Ascanio Colonna) suffices to make it tolerable. It is so depraved, so innately wicked that one doubtless must be an evil man to be content here: lies, flattery, bad faith, deceit . . . the prisons, full of Spaniards; the Italians seem like muleteers, spending their lives singing insults at us. The streets (are) full of whores, both married and available for marriage; there are twelve thousand on the (official) list. . . . Sodomy is taken less, far less, gravely than eating an egg on Friday! A fine thing, here, where you bump into a vicar of Christ at every step. . . ."[13]

Cervantes' literary observations on Italy mainly range from the merely testimonial to the enthusiastic, but an occasional dry recollection shows that he had felt the sting of the Italian wasp. In the *Persiles* he remarks on Lucca as a city where "more than anywhere else, the Spanish are well treated and regarded because there they do not command, they request, and since they never spend more than a day there, they have no opportunity to display their character, which is considered arrogant."[14]

If his position was as humble as Nola's description suggests, Cervantes could not very convincingly have replied to Italian disdain with Spanish haughtiness. Yet it should not be assumed that he once resolved that, no, this would not do. Or that the military fire at which he later warmed himself was ignited spontaneously.

This is the point in his career at which the heroic myth which began forming around the theory of his duel in Madrid enters its epic phase. Cervantes' noble mind, it is urged, was outraged at the humiliation of household service; his quixotic nature enticed him in search of adventure, in pursuit of an ideal. The quintessential mythic requirement, poverty, drove him to seek his future in war because he was unsuited to subepical enterprise. This effort to compress him into the mold cast for every Spanish folk idol gives him a slightly silly stance, a sort of Siegfried stuffed into the tight pants and flowing cravat of Puccini's Rodolfo. The Cervantes of the right-thinking is uncomfortably close to caricature.

The soul which, we are told, was mortified by his domestic duties was the same substance—admittedly a little crisped at the edges by then—which, later on, would accept the even seamier career of commissary and tax collector and stick to it for a decade. There is an aggrieved air about quite a number of the remarks in his books which suggests he was as capable as the next man of feeling sorry for himself: Cervantes the unsuccessful office seeker broods that some people "bribe, importune, solicit, rise early, beg, pester and still fail to achieve what they aspire to, and then someone else appears and without knowing how or why, finds himself with the post many others wanted."[15] There is Cervantes the writer only too well aware of how dilatory he has been: ". . . half of the divine gifts and thoughts of a poor poet are scattered by his anxiety to earn his daily bread."[16]

It was only toward the end of his life that, like his Quixote, "stumbling here, falling there, hurled down here and picking myself up once again," Cervantes nevertheless succeeded in "carrying out a great part of my design."[17]

The cardinal objection to the fairy-tale Cervantes is that it diminishes rather than augments him as a man. If we find reason for vicarious pride in Cervantes' life, surely it is because, whittled by friction with defeat and surrender, he should still have had the will to shake himself, to look for and find the strength of character he needed to work in a way he had never worked before. This mining of spiritual reserves where no reserves should be is the essence of heroism. It is no achievement for a chronic hero to be heroic.

The heroic myth is not disparaged, in any case, if we say that, in Rome, Cervantes was a young man on the make. In common with so many others in that vast Spanish class of genteel poor to which he belonged, he was hungry to get somewhere, to be somebody. If we consider the possibility of his Jewish ancestry, the very word "ambition" sets up a resonance as inchoately compulsive as the roar of a rioting mob heard through a closed window. He would never disguise his eagerness for fame or hide his disappointment when it eluded him. "The desire to win fame," Don Quixote assures Sancho,

"is a mighty impulse. What do you suppose made Horatius cast himself down from the bridge, clad in full armor, into the depths of the Tiber? What was it that burned Mutius' arm and hand? What impelled Curtius to throw himself into the deep and flaming chasm which appeared in the middle of Rome? What made Caesar cross the Rubicon in defiance of all the omens that appeared against it? . . . All these and other great and varied deeds were and will be the handiwork of Fame, for which mortals yearn as the prize they win by their high achievements: a share of immortality."[18]

Cervantes recognized that service in a great household was an open corridor to prominence. In *Don Quixote,* a page boy bound for the wars is asked if he receives an allowance.

"If I had served a grandee of Spain or some other important personage," the lad replied, "I should most certainly have one, for that is what comes of serving good masters: from the servants' hall you may rise to be an ensign or a captain or accede to some other privilege. But

my wretched luck has always attached me to some upstart or hanger-
on whose pay and rations were so lean and miserable that starching a
single ruff would consume the half of them."[19]

The progress from servants' hall to sinecure was tedious going, however; the toadying, petty deviousness it imposed on its pilgrims required a
special kind of soul—one, as Fitzmaurice-Kelly pointed out, like Pietro
Aretino's, tough and commanding; in his play *La cortegiana*, published
in Venice in 1535, Aretino noted authoritatively that a courtier must be
"invidious, whorish, heretical, adulterous, backbiting, ungrateful, ignorant," he must know when to strike and when to be watchful and patient.
Cervantes' grandfather Juan had been up to the test. But then, Juan de
Cervantes had perhaps been a little like an immigrant's son: closer to the
family's origins, readier to fight the battle on the terms offered.

This was not Miguel's way. "I am no good for palaces," protests
Tomás Rodaja in *The Glass Scholar*, "for I have a sense of shame and I
do not know how to flatter." The objection recurs regularly in Cervantes'
work. "Happy is he to whom Heaven has given a crust of bread," Quixote declares, "without the obligation of offering thanks for it to any but
Heaven itself."[20] Cervantes lacked the single-minded, sterilizing stamina
to cut his way through the political undergrowth of the Vatican jungle.

He was twenty-three years old and probably eager for excitement, for
some clear, grand line of action, not the muffled, smarmy environment of
a prelate's entourage. It is even likely that a sense of high personal destiny
was growing on him. The feeling is not unusual at twenty-three. And,
however modestly it may face the world, genius is usually aware of itself;
" '. . . for there is no poet,' said Don Quixote, 'who is not arrogant, and
who does not think of himself as the best in the world.'

" 'There is no rule without exceptions' answered Don Lorenzo, 'and
there may be some who are and yet do not think so.'

" 'Few,' said Don Quixote. . . ."[21]

Cervantes probably did not look to a future in literature. Not in a
world where no writer could live by his art, not even the tireless Lope de
Vega, whose prodigious production kept his popularity at its peak almost
throughout his lifetime. Literature was a gentlemanly accomplishment
then, an added grace, but not a serious occupation nor even quite a respectable one for a man of consequence to live by. Besides, the Cervantes
of 1570 cannot be thought of as a poet. He was a young man with a literary affectation which, had fate given him his way, might never have become anything more than that. *Don Quixote* escaped premature disaster
probably more often than any other Western masterpiece.

Iglesia o mar o casa real was the popular prescription for the ambitious
poor—the Church, the sea or a royal court. It may have been his experi-

ence in Rome which steered Cervantes away from the Church. The sea? Too capricious a mistress for any but merchants and pirates to risk romancing. And even if we discount the probability of the duel and his status as a fugitive, there were no strings at court to fit his hand.

For the moment, he was probably low on funds and short of ideas. One imagines him, like Berganza the talking dog, "carried away by my natural goodness," deciding to "do my duty to my master, for I was drawing my wages from him and eating his food. After all, this is the duty . . . of all who serve."[22] Something else would come up.

History was already working on the problem.

] 8 [

The King's Crumbs

A militant Eastern superpower on permanent ideological crusade, having already swallowed up part of Eastern Europe and established its supremacy in the Middle East, presses relentlessly against the West, exploiting every rivalry, probing at every weakness. Most of Europe shelters, reluctantly, behind the military shield of a Western superpower convinced that civilization is threatened by Eastern barbarism. France, more fearful of suffocation by its ideological brother than of aggression from across the Continent, remains aloof from the Western alliance, choosing instead to cultivate its friendship with the Eastern colossus in the hope of maintaining a power balance.

So the half-century-long struggle between Christian Europe and the Ottoman Turks. For most of that time, Europe had been on the defensive. The combined Spanish-Venetian-papal offensive launched in the late summer of 1570—in which Cervantes is believed by some historians to have begun his career as a soldier—was only the latest in a series of Christian attempts to contain Turkish expansion. It may qualify as the most clownish of those efforts; certainly it was one of the most tragic.

From the day in 1521 when Sultan Suleiman the Magnificent captured Belgrade until his death in 1566, the size of Turkey's empire doubled; it covered an area reaching from southern Russia to the Gulf of Aden, from Bagdad to the Atlantic beaches of Morocco. Its capital at Constantinople was more populous than Spain's ten biggest cities combined. From the Balkans, Suleiman had laid siege to Vienna and flicked a tentative fist at northern Germany. Only a thin strip of the Dalmatian coast and a fragile thread of Aegean islands were left in Venetian hands as a corridor for East-West trade. Some of the more inflamed Christian heads thought they could see the Porte's objectives clearly: first Italy, then the archrival,

Spain; after that, the rest of Europe would drop like flying fish on a deck. The death of Christianity.

Neither side felt strong enough to strike decisive blows at the enemy, but the Turks jabbed at the Christian heartland through the Barbary pirates in their North African protectorates, savaging Western shipping and clawing at the coasts of Italy and Spain from bases in Algiers, Tripoli, Tetuán, Salé, Bizerta, Tunis. The West had periodically replied with what were really little more than raids in force: a Holy League fleet of Spanish, Venetian and papal ships had sailed grandly off in 1538, but internal rivalries and the exaggerated concern of Spain's Genoese admiral, Andrea Doria, for the ships he was renting to the emperor led to a defeat at Preveza, in Albania. Charles V himself led an army to Algiers in 1541; he lost more than half his force in a week and barely escaped with his life. In 1560, Philip II essayed a ponderous and costly strike at Tripoli; the force, under Doria's nephew, Gian Andrea, was destroyed in a day at the Tunisian island of Djerba. The record of defeat was not unrelieved. Spain did manage to hang on to the North African outposts Philip's great-grandfather, Ferdinand the Catholic, had begun collecting, although they remained no more than exposed blisters on the African hide; a Spanish relief mission did succeed in beating back a Turkish attempt to invade Malta in 1565.

When Suleiman's death delivered the Ottoman throne to his son Selim II, most of Europe sighed with relief. Selim was effeminate, vain, a drunkard who doted on Cypriot wine, a man manifestly incapable, it was thought, of maintaining his father's momentum. True, it was in that year, 1566, that the Turks took the rich island of Chios, exacted tribute from the Venetian colony of Ragusa, pillaged the Adriatic coast of Italy as far north as Trieste, panicking Venetians into believing that, as the saying went, they would wake the next morning to hear the cock crow in Turkish. In 1567 they took Naxos, leaving Venice nothing in the Aegean but Cyprus and Crete. Still, Philip II, knowing that Selim was having as much trouble with uprisings in Persia as Spain was in the Low Countries, listened only distractedly to the pleas of the new pope, Pius V, for a revived Holy League to crusade against the Porte and liberate Jerusalem from the infidels.

An anachronism, Pius V, a reminder of how close the times still were to the spirit of St. Bernard and St. Louis. As Grand Inquisitor, the terrible "Fra Michele dell' Inquisizione" had even appalled his protector, Pope Pius IV, by his severity. His elevation to the papacy in 1566 has been seen as the enthronement of the Inquisition. Naïve, brusque, stubborn, a political innocent, he shocked a papal court accustomed to the delicacy of Italian diplomacy. Having set the tone of his administration at once by spurning the rich inaugural vestments in favor of his worn, rough-spun Dominican robe, he proceeded immediately to drive the money-changers out of the Roman temple. Nepotism and favoritism were banned; Rome's prostitutes were expelled or herded into ghettos; convents became models of rigorous conformity and the court itself a paragon of sobriety. In 1569 he expelled the Jews from the Papal States, although they were allowed, for regrettable commercial reasons, to maintain a humiliating presence in Rome and Ancona.

Fra Michele Ghislieri, this ascetic who lived almost exclusively on boiled herbs and who, contemporaries noted, looked more dead than alive, saw Christianity's problem very simply: there were two enemies, heresy and the Turk. Both were to be extirpated. Having analyzed the situation and prescribed the remedy, he set about applying the treatment. His campaign against what he saw as heretical literature drove hundreds of printers out of Italy to refuge in Germany and Switzerland. He egged Philip II on in the Netherlands and so worked on the already gorged conscience of Catherine de Medici that he is considered by many to have contributed to the 1572 St. Bartholomew's Day massacre of Protestants in France. He excommunicated Elizabeth I of England in 1570 and dabbled enthusiastically in Catholic plots all over Europe. He was altogether a "strange union of singleness of purpose, magnanimity, austerity and profound religious feeling with sour bigotry, relentless hatred and bloody persecution."[1]

Pius' plan for a crusade against the Turks was scaled to his invincible naïveté. Nothing would do but a revived Holy League with massive power, for—he was realistic enough to see this—only a united Europe could face the Asian giant. Although reluctant to admit any merely political obstacle to the achievement of this grand design, certain obstructions did arise: France, for the moment, was not only tolerating its Huguenots, but was actually allied with the Porte; Austria was at truce with the Turks; Ivan the Terrible of Muscovy was too deeply involved in butchering his metropolitan Philip of Moscow and destroying his city of Great Novgorod to respond to the pope's call. There was nowhere for Pius to turn but to Spain.

Philip II sympathized, but, infuriatingly, Philip also temporized. By 1570, however, with France once more contorted with religious spasms, the Low Countries seemingly pacified and England absorbed in domestic political upheaval, the king of Spain was at least ready to listen, if not necessarily to agree. Spanish passions and fears had been aroused by the still raging Morisco rising in the Alpujarras; within months, they would be heightened by the fall of Tunis to Euldj Ali, perhaps the wiliest of the Ottoman sea wolves.

Then, in May, the Turks fell on Cyprus. Selim on his own might have been too indolent to fight a war, but his advisers were not. They convinced him that his glory required conquests, that, once slowed, the pendulum of power would swing against him.

Venice leaped into a frantic diplomatic offensive, agitating in Europe for immediate rescue of the island while putting out peace feelers to Turkey through France. The Republic had good reason to want peace with Constantinople. It lacked the men and materiel for a major war; it had no wish to lose what was left of the Eastern trade in silks and spices on which its declining wealth was based; the very grain it needed to feed its citizens came from Russia and the Balkans.

Unhappily for the Signory, its historical role as everyone's middleman had earned everyone's distrust. No one had forgotten that it was Venice's separate peace with the Turks that had scuttled the first Holy League. For their part, the Venetians, mindful of what they believed had been Doria's treachery at Preveza, strongly suspected Spain of wishing to use Venetian ships and spill Venetian blood to consolidate Spain's hold on the western Mediterranean.

Philip nevertheless recognized that Spain's first line of defense on the East ran through the Venetian possessions in the Aegean. Unwillingly, he assigned Gian Andrea Doria and the fifty-one galleys of the Sicilian squadron to join an expedition to relieve Cyprus. It was a clumsy choice. As a Genoese and the heir of Andrea Doria, Philip's captain was detested by the Venetians; Doria was openly contemptuous of the Venetians. Although the crafty, autocratic Genoese lord was reputed to be the best naval commander in Italy, he was to be subordinate to the papal commander, Marcantonio Colonna, his junior, whose sympathy for Venice was flagrant and who, Philip had been warned by Cardinal Granvelle, knew "no more about the sea than I do."[2]

When the allied admirals met in Suda Bay, in Crete, on September 1, they disagreed at once on the fleet's objectives. Venice's Girolamo Zanne wanted to make straight for Cyprus. Doria, who like most naval strategists of the day was disinclined to fight unless his force clearly outnumbered the enemy's, insisted that a direct clash with the Turkish fleet was too risky. Colonna's mediation finally produced a plan for a diversionary action, and the entire battle group sailed off to raid Rhodes.

It never got there. On September 11, the commanders learned that the Cypriot town of Nicosia had fallen two days earlier; as many as twenty thousand of its inhabitants, it was said, had been put to the sword. The Sultan's army now held everything on the island except Famagusta, and that was now under siege. No one in the Christian fleet knew that the Turkish ring around the bastion was still loose enough to be vulnerable to a bold attack, a stroke which would almost certainly have avoided the hecatomb at Lepanto a year later.

Doria may never have intended to do any fighting on that expedition; he may even have received specific orders to that effect from his royal master, who was not so rich that he could write off half his active navy in an action from which Spain would derive no profit. The news from Cyprus gave the Genoese the excuse he sought. Insisting that it was too late in the year to begin an offensive, he peremptorily turned his ships around and sailed for Sicily. He was right about the weather, at any rate. The violent squalls which annually swept the Mediterranean clear of all but the most urgent shipping from October until late March began early that year. By the time his allies got under way, the storms were upon them; only remnants of the Italian squadrons reached home safely.

On his return to Venice, Zanne was whisked into prison. Lack of daring was the charge, along with weakness of character and avarice, presumably for concern with that part of the Venetian squadron which he had equipped out of his own pocket. His death in chains a few months later spared the Republic the embarrassment of hearing his defense.

Was Cervantes really a witness to this grotesque exercise? Just when did he enlist, and why?

An infantryman, wrote Bernardino de Mendoza in 1592, "enlisted willingly, moved by a youthful desire to seek adventure, by the vision of improved fortune and condition, perhaps even (by a need) to flee from the workings of justice. . . . From the moment he enlisted, he esteemed himself a nobleman, despising all artisanal trades. . . . Not in vain did a general or colonel, when fortune buffeted him in battle, often enlist to recover or purify his honor in the ranks of that infantry, serving with a pike; not for nothing were the first ranks always crowded with captains and other officers discharged or deprived of command, with gentleman prodigals, ruined noblemen. . . . The ranks of such an infantry were true schools and safe havens for honor."[3]

Although Mendoza was talking about the early part of the sixteenth century, the spirit he described still prevailed. Another commentator, writing in 1639, agreed that "two things impel a man to leave his country to be a soldier: the first, an inclination to arms and the winning of honor in exercising them; the second, because he is poor and cannot support himself in the style he considers proper."[4]

Such explanations were sneered at by Spain's less bellicose neighbors. "The Italians say it is a small thing that the Spaniards risk their lives," a contemporary source remarked, "since their lives are so wretched that, in losing them, they lose little, for they are barefoot, naked and ill-treated, while (the Italians) are well clothed, rich and (have) beautiful women and so they fear to die."[5]

Cervantes acknowledged the centrifugal force of poverty; the page boy in *Don Quixote* sang the refrain of the poor recruit:

> My poverty leads me to war, but, you know,
> If I had any money I never would go.

But it would be a mistake to see this as Cervantes' only motive for becoming a soldier. His romantic yen to be a full participant in life, rather than simply a spectator, is better summed up in Periandro's exhortation in the *Persiles* to the poor fishermen he rallies to his army:

> "If they have doubts, those who dig in the earth, earning barely enough reward to sustain themselves for a day while gaining no glory at all, why not exchange their spades for lances and, fearless of the sun's heat or of any of the heavens' inclemencies, strive to earn, along with their keep, a glory that will aggrandize them above all other men?"[6]

The poet-warrior was a stock figure of Renaissance romanticism, most glamorously represented in England's Sir Philip Sidney and in his Spanish alter ego, Garcilaso de la Vega. Jorge Manríque, Lope de Vega, Fernando de Herrera, Juan Rufo—the list is nearly a Spanish literary pantheon—all chose to spend part of their lives preferring, as the maxim prescribed, "the king's crumbs to a nobleman's feast."

The game of guessing when Cervantes enlisted has delighted scholars for centuries. In the dedication of *La Galatea,* he wrote that he had "for several years followed the victorious banners of that military sun," Marcantonio Colonna. Affidavits advanced by the family in 1576 and 1578, and by Cervantes himself in 1580 and 1590, suggest that he might have enlisted as early as 1568. One witness to the 1578 document was Mateo de Santiestéban, a companion of Cervantes' at the battle of Lepanto, who declared that "the said Miguel de Cervantes was serving a year earlier (than the battle) in the said company, because this witness himself saw him . . . being a soldier in the same company."[7]

Cervantes' verse epistle to Mateo Vázquez, written in 1577, affirmed that

> For ten years have I suited my pace to the commands of service to our great sovereign Philip . . .

which would have put his enlistment back to 1567. Although the span of choices was confusing, nineteenth-century biographers confident of Cervantes' almost journalistic accuracy[8] set about making what they hoped were definitive guesses on his actions. Reviews of the history of each Spanish brigade, almost every company, produced assurances that Cervantes had enlisted in 1567, in 1568, in 1569, in the Spanish army, the papal forces—a whole, now abandoned, garden of theories.

Not until early in the twentieth century was the irritating discovery made that Cervantes could not have been in Italy in 1568 because he was still López de Hoyos' "beloved disciple" in Madrid at the time. Nor could he have enlisted in 1569, because his request for blood-purity certification, required for entry into a noble household but not for military service, was not issued until December of that year.

The conclusion had to be faced: Cervantes and his family, apparently working on the assumption that in Philip II's sixty-thousand-man bureaucracy the right and left hands were uncompromisingly estranged, had cooked the record in order to reinforce his claims to royal assistance. Miguel's record is deliberately confused with that of his brother Rodrigo to make his military career more impressive; it was claimed, for example, that he served in the 1583 assault on the Azores in which Rodrigo was cited for heroism, when hundreds of witnesses could have certified his presence in Madrid at the time. We will find him lying about other facts as well, with an innocence that seems incredible now. But then, as any Mediterranean-area taxpayer will quickly affirm, lying to the government is not really lying at all; it is merely an act of self-defense, a maneuver in the play of suspicions by which the Latin citizen and his rulers keep each other in balance.

A newer theory plumped for June or July of 1570. The reasoning: a golden opportunity presented itself in the form of Don Alvaro de Sande, the "old friend" of Cervantes Sr., who was then the colonel in command of the tercio of Naples. Sande, it was felt, would have offered too precious a chance for preferment for Cervantes to have passed up.

Well, what preference was he shown? The pikemen, traditionally the front-line assault troops, were still the army's elite. A steel blade was considered a gentleman's weapon, the idealist's arm, by contrast with the still relatively new, inaccurate and faintly dishonorable firearm, which killed from a distance instead of bravely in personal combat. Cervantes subscribed to the notion, damning the invention of artillery, with which the harquebus and musket were then classed: "Blessed were the times which lacked the dreadful fury of those diabolical engines, the artillery," says Don Quixote, "whose inventor I firmly believe is now receiving the reward for his devilish invention in hell; an invention which allows a base and cowardly hand to take the life of a knight. . . . Although no danger frightens me, still it causes me misgivings to think that powder and lead may deprive me of the chance to win fame and renown by the strength of my arm and the edge of my sword. . . ."[9]

But was Cervantes assigned to the elite body of pikemen? He was not. He carried a gun, like any other anonymous recruit with nothing to recommend him but youth and energy and enthusiasm. True, the harquebus was more respected in Philip's day than it had been in his father's, but it was still the assassin's weapon, still assigned to the commonest of soldiers. There is no indication that Cervantes was given extra pay or rank; no evidence is available that Don Alvaro followed the young soldier's career with paternal benevolence, this "old friend" who, a generation earlier, had known Rodrigo Sr. for part of a summer and who is not known to have seen him afterward. Indeed, the colonel himself is not heard from again in connection with his supposed protégé; he had, in fact, quickly vanished from the scene.

There are other objections. The famine in Naples in 1570 was one of the most intense of the century: speculators in rotten grain were driving prices far out of reach of the poor, who were making their bread of beans or chestnuts, even of tree bark. Cervantes, in Rome, would have known this. It is difficult to believe he would have chosen that particular time to go to Naples. One may have eaten badly in the cardinal's household, but no one starved.

None of the accounts of Cervantes' life have omitted to cite his recollections of Naples, the headquarters city of the Spanish army in Italy "whose streets," he tells us in the *Voyage to Parnassus*, "I trod for better than a year." Since it seems free of the inflationary tendencies noted in the affidavits, there is no reason not to take this statement, vague as it is, for the literal truth. Simple arithmetic demonstrates that placing him in Naples in the summer of 1570 would have given him a total sojourn of almost *three* years there. It is harsh to be asked to put basic arithmetic before insight; it smacks of calculation. It is uncongenial. But there it is; if we assume that his enlistment did not take place until the summer of 1571, we can account for about a year and a half of Cervantes' time as having been spent in Naples. It is impossible that he should have reached there later than that summer, for in early September he was among the troops massed in Sicily for the Holy League's first official campaign.

What would have been his *immediate* incentive in 1570? As the hot, dry summer burned its way into a frighteningly hot autumn, few people, probably, other than the pope really believed the Holy League would ever come into being. In Venice, Doria's "treachery" had strengthened the peace party's hand. While secret negotiations began in Constantinople— not so secret that Philip failed to learn of them—the Republic's negotiators stalled in Rome. Its chief delegate, Michele Suriano, attended meetings or not, as the mood took him; Venetian demands on her prospective allies grew preposterous. There was wrangling over the leadership of the combined force; Don Juan of Austria was chosen as the commander, but he would be bound to act on the counsel of three generals, one from each power. Colonna was designated as his second-in-command. Venice insisted that the League's mandate be enlarged to include recovery of the provinces the Republic had already lost in the eastern Mediterranean. Spain refused. Philip demanded that the League move against the Barbary states as well as Turkey proper. Venice refused. So the months wore on: the dickering in both Constantinople and Rome collapsed, was revived, collapsed again; in Cyprus, the defenders of Famagusta scanned the sea for signs of the promised relief. By late April 1571, the general opinion was that, true to its mercantile morality, Venice was about to sink the Holy League project. Only the pope refused to admit that the negotiations had failed.

Cervantes, from his vantage point in a Vatican household, must have been thoroughly aware of the conference's tidal variations, must have shared in the general pessimism. And with no war in the offing for Spanish forces, the attractions of military life would have appeared decidedly bottom-drawer. Cervantes' later anthems to the glory of soldiering probably reflect the apotheosis conferred on him by the experience of war, not the early vocation he is so often accorded. But without prospects for fast advancement, he might very well have pondered the drawbacks of army life as well as its virtues. The hardship of a Spanish soldier's life was common knowledge. In his *Carlo famoso*, Luis Zapata wrote:

> I think there is no more piteous condition
> than the miserable profession of soldiering:
> always in battle, never paid, and as his reward,
> great infamy, if he escapes his sentence of death.

Don Quixote spoke from his creator's experience when he described a soldier's life:

". . . he is the poorest of the poor. For he is limited to his wretched pay, which comes either late or never, or to what he can loot with his own hands, at considerable danger to his life and conscience. Sometimes he is so naked that a slashed doublet serves him at once as uniform and shirt, and in midwinter, if he is in open country, his usual protection against the inclemencies of heaven is nothing more than the breath from his mouth which, since it comes from an empty place, I know for a fact comes out cold, against all the laws of nature. Watch him waiting for nightfall, when he may find respite from all these discomforts in the bed that awaits him, which, unless through his own fault, will never sin by being too narrow. For he can measure out as many feet of the earth as he likes, and toss and turn in its as he pleases without rumpling the sheets. Finally, after all of this, the day and the hour arrive for him to receive his professional degree; that day the battle comes, and that is when they will cover his head with a doctor's cap of lint to heal some bullet wound that may have pierced his temples or left him maimed in arm or leg. And if this does not happen and a merciful Heaven keeps and preserves him alive and unhurt, he may very well remain as poor as he was before; and then he will have to go through more skirmishes, through battle after battle and emerge victorious from all of them before he has some chance of bettering his lot; but such miracles are seldom seen. But tell me, gentlemen, if you have ever thought about it: how many more have perished by war than have profited by it?"[10]

On May 6, 1571, however, news arrived that alchemized the conference in Rome from leaden defeatism to brightest optimism: a report from Famagusta that one hundred more galleys had left Constantinople en route for Cyprus. Selim had just been playing for time. The peace talks in Turkey popped like a harpooned blowfish. Suddenly, the recalcitrant Venetians in Rome became effusively conciliatory. In two weeks, eleven months of problems were solved or, when solution defied even the pope's fervid mediation, merely ignored. On May 19 a treaty covering the first three years' operation of the "perpetual alliance" was concluded.

The treaty was proclaimed, along with a universal jubilee, in a ceremony in St. Peter's Basilica on May 25, 1571, in the presence of His Holiness and the college of cardinals. The three signatories swore to maintain the treaty forever. In case this resolution flagged, the pope was to arbitrate any interallied dispute threatening to compromise the League's military effectiveness—a recourse which was to prove entirely ineffective in resolving disputes at sea, where the tactical decisions were made, but which did extend a papery awning over the principal allies' mutual distrust.

After all the months of doubt, the agreement touched off an explosion of popular enthusiasm. For weeks, while preparations for the coming campaign crawled ahead, churches were filled with people praying for victory, and the streets of scores of cities were brilliant with jubilee processions. So magnificent were the celebrations in Venice that they filled the news flyers all over Europe. Every city in Italy prepared to send its contingent to the League force; in Spain, recruiting was stepped up to fill the gaps left in Philip's line regiments by disease, desertions and the casualties of the Alpujarra war.

What is more logical to suppose than that it was this vital current of joy which jolted a hesitant Cervantes into enlisting in Don Juan's new army?

There is a kind of subplot to the mystery of Cervantes' military debut, another question to which no documentary answer exists. Cervantes' younger brother Rodrigo also fought at Lepanto, almost certainly in the same galley—at least the family later swore he did. If so, he served in Miguel's unit. Not much is known about young Rodrigo; he suddenly materializes at Lepanto, a private soldier like his elder brother. When and where did he enter the army? When did he arrive in Italy and where were the brothers reunited?

In 1570, Rodrigo was just twenty years old, the minimum enlistment age for the Spanish army then. It is true that no documentary proof of age was required; candidates merely had to have "the aspect" of a twenty-year-old as judged by the not overly discriminating eye of a recruiting sergeant anxious to fill his quota. But it is unlikely that Rodrigo would have joined the army in Spain in 1570 without seeing action in the Alpujarras, and even more improbably, if he had, that the family would not have mentioned it afterward. No such experience is recorded. If he enlisted in 1570, then, it would have had to be in Italy, with Miguel. But although pay records have been found for the military careers of both brothers dating from 1572 on, none have turned up for 1570.

The brothers fought at Lepanto in a company commanded by one Diego de Urbina in a tercio led by Miguel de Moncada. The unit had suffered heavy casualties in the Alpujarras. It was not, however, until late 1570 or early 1571 that a serious effort was made to flesh out its depleted ranks. Customarily, captains returned to their home towns to look for new men. Urbina was a "neighbor" of the Cervantes family from Guadalajara, an easy morning's mule ride from Alcalá de Henares and less than a day from Madrid. He might even have known the Cervanteses; at the very least, they would have had acquaintances in common. If Rodrigo had thought about enlisting, whether on his own or at Miguel's urging, he would probably have elected to join a local company, led by a man known to him and containing other local recruits, rather than be an anonymous newcomer to a totally strange command.

Urbina's detachment did not reach Italy until July 26, 1571, with the new commander in chief, Don Juan of Austria. The new men were not even equipped until they reached Naples a week later. It is a good bet that Rodrigo was one of those recruits, a Rodrigo awed by the hardened, battle-tested veterans who made up the unit's core, still dazzled by his view of Don Juan's splendid suite.

It is difficult not to believe that Miguel knew he was coming, that the two young men planned to serve together, that they were reunited either in Genoa, where the tercio paused briefly before proceeding south for reoutfitting, or in Naples itself, and that wherever they met was where Miguel de Cervantes enlisted in the Spanish army.

Events, meanwhile, seemed to be picking up speed. On June 16, 1571, while the defenders of Famagusta beat back wave after wave of assaults against the city's crumbling walls, Don Juan entered Barcelona to the roar of cannon pounding out salutes from the forts along the seafront and the warships at anchor in the bay. Surrounded by municipal officials and Catalan nobles, he rode through streets shaded with garlands. Like a modern bullfighter making a triumphal tour of the ring, he rode under cascades of flowers poured down by Catalan girls from balconies bedecked with blossoms and gay with tapestries and shawls.

Once Don Juan got down to work, he perceived that the speed with which preparations were advancing was largely a fiction. For more than a month, while the suspicious Venetians fumed and appealed to the pope against what they saw as Spanish perfidy, the generalissimo marked time in Barcelona, trying to cut his way through the inertia of cynical workmen, royal bureaucrats and military confusion. Don Juan's chaperon, Luis de Requesens, remarked in a letter to his brother, Juan de Zúñiga, Philip's ambassador to the Holy See, that "the Original Sin of our Court of never accomplishing or doing anything in time or season has increased immeasurably since you were here, and is increasing daily."[11] A Spanish proverb puts it more succinctly: "In Spain, everything starts late and never ends."

Nor was Don Juan's mental comfort enhanced by a coldly instructive letter from the king ordering him to decline the style of "Highness" which the prince's entourage was so eager to accord him. Philip's instructions to his brother in Barcelona reflect the monarch's lack of enthusiasm for Spain's new commitment: the commander in chief was to seek battle as quickly as possible, Philip said, but he was not to expose the fleet unless he was virtually certain to win.

Philip rarely appears less likable than when he pressed a restraining thumb on the Imperial bastard's glamorous blond head. It was one of Philip's tragedies that he never seemed to be doing the right thing even when he was. When he wisely discouraged Don Juan's dreams of an empire which the king knew neither Juan nor Castile could sustain, he was accused of envying his brother's dash, of being jealous of his brother's success with women, of harboring the dreariest kind of bureaucratic power lust. No conscientious monarch can compete in popular affection with a daredevil hero who, if he lost any sleep, did so in some beauty's bed. Philip was a "have," Don Juan, at least in hierarchical terms, a "have-not"; Philip was cautious where Juan was bold, clerkish rather than athletic. That he was also statesmanlike where Juan was reckless is passed over impatiently in the general evaluation.

On July 20, Juan sailed for Italy, reaching Genoa six days later. His reception there could not have sweetened his temper. All the signs of respect were scrupulously observed: the greeting at the port by the Genoese

Senate, the homage of ambassadors from Savoy, Parma, Florence, Mantua, even Venice; the princely quarters set aside for him in the Palazzo Doria; the sumptuous official reception that evening. But French intrigues had almost convinced the Genoese that it was in Italy, not in the eastern sea, that Don Juan saw the new kingdom he was so intent on manufacturing for himself. Genoese leaders inquired coldly how long he planned to stay; they urged him to limit the number of attendants he took into the city.

Early in August, he left for Naples. With him were Prince Alexander Farnese of Parma, his old school friend, perhaps the most astute general of the period, and Francesco della Rovere, the son of the Duke of Urbino, who had volunteered for the coming campaign. Behind their crusaders' crosses, the condottieri were finally on the move.

] 9 [

An Army of Parrots

When Cervantes reached Naples, presumably in the summer of 1571, the city was like a fat woman on the verge of apoplexy. An influx of country people attracted by its luxuriant aristocracy had already made it the biggest city in Italy after Rome, and it was rapidly spreading inland. Whole new urban quarters were sprouting on what until recently had been small farms. Now the place was packed with thousands of new soldiers as well. While the taverns along the Via Margherita breathed out gusts of noise-laden heat, grave-looking gentlemen rode up to the great Spanish mansions in the Calle de Toledo, today's Via Roma, which ran through the old town to the port like the cleavage of a large bosom straining at a small bodice.

Had he been given time, he must have enjoyed this "richest and most sinful of Spanish cities"[1] (surely not as Spanish as Toledo, as has been averred, but as Spanish as it was Italian). Probably he had little time at this juncture to do any more than try and learn the rudiments of soldiering in the few weeks left before the big push. The fleet would have to sail in early September at the latest to avoid being caught by the winter storms.

The army Cervantes joined was organized around polyvalent companies of roughly 250 men each. From ten to eighteen of these companies formed a tercio, something akin to a modern brigade in its flexibility, but closer in size to a regiment, led by a *maestro de campo* already, in Cervantes' day, coming to be called colonel.

And what an army it was! A burlesque of an army, by today's reckoning, but with a deadly sting, an army of Cyranos. Cutthroats from the slums of Seville, disinherited second sons of noblemen, landless farm boys fleeing slow starvation at home, students who had run out of money or who found scholarship too cool a potion for the hot longings of youth, poets out to see what life was like; there were Italian musketeers and Swiss pikemen, Burgundian harquebusiers, German lancers, Irish soldiers of fortune.

Like most armies of the time, it fattened on graft: officers took bribes, paymasters pocketed a slice of the soldiers' pay, captains collected tombstone wages. The men were no better than their officers. Soldiers frequently deserted, out of resentment of discipline, out of fear or boredom, for a woman, sometimes simply to collect another enlistment bonus by signing up elsewhere before melting back into the landscape. In Naples, men called to guard duty in peacetime not uncommonly had to rent weapons from an armorer to replace those they had sold or gambled away.

Women were a commander's curse. One military manual of the period recommended that women follow the army at a ratio of eight women to one hundred men. In what was then called the Spanish Barracks Quarter of Naples, stretching from the church of Santa Ana del Palacio to the Magnacavéllo, thousands of Spanish soldiers were billeted in private houses so crowded with women they were more brothels than barracks. For all we know, that may have been where Cervantes was quartered. Or he may have been in another island of troops facing the Castelnuovo, only a musket shot from the Street of the Deserters, a no man's land which even the king's discipline preferred to ignore.

"A good soldier must realize," cautioned Marcos de Isaba, "that the day he enters his name on the king's register and draws his pay and begins to enjoy that high honor of being a soldier, on that day he must understand that he . . . may do nothing evil or harmful. . . . The good soldier needs much patience, if his salary or pay is held up. . . . The soldier must be courteous and well bred. . . ."[2]

In fact, when his pay failed to arrive, as happened more often than not, the good soldier, responsible for keeping himself fed and clothed in the plumes, sashes, capes which satisfied his vanity and hid the patches in his uniform, generally raised hell, terrorizing the countryside, begging, pillaging, wrecking. When money at last did arrive, most of the men immediately drank it up and gambled it away, then returned to their thieving and begging. Their penchant for armed robbery became proverbial. Even the Spanish hand-kissing habit was sarcastically seen as a way of "stealing rings like the Gypsies."[3] Pleas for tighter discipline were constant; if they were better supervised, it was urged, "they would not insult people nor rob them so brazenly, nor would they break in doors or windows at night, destroying shops and stalls . . . to such a point that, when night falls, no one dares to leave his house (and) the law is powerless. . . ."[4] Patrols spent most of their time in brothels and taverns—as customers, not custodians.

Yet the magical result of this permanent riot was honor. Isaba, raising the running sixteenth-century argument about the superiority of arms versus letters, naturally opts for arms because—his clinching argument— "no noble or gentleman who has ever entered the world will confess that his ancestry or lineage descends from merchants or doctors or notaries or landlords or other low callings, but (claims it) from an ancient trunk or branch which began to be a lineage in the army" risking its life cheerfully for king and God, while those of lower office "sweetly and calmly, at the fire in winter and drinking cooling drinks in the shade in summer busied themselves . . . swindling their fellows."[5]

Neither his few months in the remoteness of a Madrid academy nor his service in a cardinal's palace would, one presumes, have prepared Cervantes fully for such raucous companionship. He was never, in fact, to have many illusions about the glamour of soldiering. The soldiers in his stories are almost without exception quarrelsome, boastful, beggarly. But he could treat them with a gentle irony of which none of his contemporaries was capable. At one point, for example, he describes a company in which there "was no quartermaster to restrain us; the captain was a lad, but a fine gentleman and devout Christian; the ensign was only a few months gone from the court and a servants' dining room; the sergeant was cunning, wise and a great harrier of companies from the place where they are recruited to the embarkation point. The company was full of gossipy rogues who committed a number of impertinences in the places we went through, which redounded in curses on him (the king) who did not deserve them."[6]

Cervantes was a harquebusier, not quite the lowest of the low in pay scales; he did earn more than the men in the fife and drum corps. He had a gorgeous new uniform: ruff, leather doublet with cape sleeves over a red shirt with slashed leg-of-mutton sleeves, bands of yellow and red stripes on his slashed knee breeches, red hose and buckle shoes, narrow-brimmed steel helmet and a long sword at his side which he may not have known how to use. *Papagayos*—parrots—the Spanish troopers were called, and no wonder.* But he was a harquebusier. It was all very well for Antonio Gallo to recommend against giving the weapon "to persons of small strength and little brio"; no doubt the firepower it provided was a major factor in the conquering sweep of Spanish arms against the massed cavalry and archers of more tradition-minded opponents. The

---

* This vestimentary fanfare, it seems, had a more aggressive function than mere display; in 1586, Martín de Eguílez affirmed: "It is very clear that ten thousand armed soldiers in colorful clothes will excite more fear than twenty thousand in black," which, he sniffed, was for "town men or apothecaries."

fact remained that the thing was a nuisance, inaccurate, dangerous to handle; it could send a one-and-one-half-ounce roundball 180 yards, but the chances of hitting anything at over 100 were discouraging. Its chief value was to sweep enemy ranks at point-blank range, disorganizing their formation before the pikes and swordsmen moved in to the kill.

Everything about it was clumsy. It weighed only about twelve pounds, but it was nearly five feet long. It took an eternity to load and fire; although the wheel lock was already well developed, the Spanish were still using the serpentine for quick-match firing. A picture comes to mind of Cervantes, his chestnut hair plastered to his broad forehead, the sweat rolling down under his already soiled finery in the muggy August heat as he swings the gun down quickly to the right, yanks back the serpentine, holding it with two fingers of his left hand while his right fumbles at his belt, over the bullet extractor and the wad hook and the flint and steel for lighting the serpentine, to his wooden powder flasks, pouring the powder into the muzzle, then the wad, then ramming in the ball, uncovering the priming pan, pouring in the powder, squeezing the trigger gently, smoldering serpentine snapping down to ignite the priming powder and set off the main charge, the heavy kick of the gun bruising his townsman's shoulder. On board ship, if he could steady himself against the roll long enough even to load the beast, and if the damp and the spray did not put the match out, he'd be lucky to hit the hull in front of him. For the moment, the important thing was to learn to use it. Preferably without allowing the iron barrel to blow up in his hand.

It is probably safe to assume that Cervantes was at the port of Naples to see Don Juan go ashore at the great naval base on the morning of August 8, 1571; by all accounts, virtually all of Spanish Naples turned out to welcome the handsome, blond, blue-eyed hero of the Alpujarras in his scarlet brocade suit and cheer him along his way to the Castelnuovo. On August 14, after a Te Deum and mass in the Franciscan convent of Santa Clara, the young generalissimo—he was almost exactly the age of recruit Miguel de Cervantes—knelt before the high altar to receive the gold-and-jewel-encrusted baton of Holy League command, along with the standard and—perhaps of greatest significance to Don Juan himself—a papal message delivered in Latin, Spanish and Venetian dialect: "Take, happy prince,[7] the insignia of the true Word made man; take the living symbol of the Holy Faith, whose defender you are in this enterprise. May it give glorious victory over the impious foe, and may his arrogance be humbled by your hand."[8]

Moved as much, no doubt, by the generosity of His Holiness' language as by the solemnity of the moment, Don Juan immediately hurried to the port, followed by cheering thousands of Neapolitans and Spaniards. There, standing at attention as the fleet's artillery and all its riflemen crashed out a salute, he watched Count Gentile Saxatelo hoist the heavy silk banner to the masthead of the *Real*, Don Juan's flagship. The count was rewarded for his labors with a gold chain worth four hundred escudos—a sum that would have paid Cervantes' three-escudo distinguished-service bonus for over eleven years. It was an imposing standard, a twenty-four-by-thirteen-foot expanse of gold-fringed blue damask bearing a huge image of the crucified Christ above the papal, Venetian and Spanish escutcheons linked by an embroidered gold chain from which Don Juan's personal arms depended.[9]

Don Juan was given a new reason to speed his departure a few days later: the Count of Priego returned from his mission to Rome with a papal promise: ". . . fight well, assure God's victory, and I promise you the first state you win from the Turk."[10] Never mind that His Holiness had no states but his own to give; he knew what nourishment the hero's spirit required.

On the afternoon of August 25, the *caudillo*'s flotilla arrived to a frenzied welcome in the sheltered harbor of Messina. As the *Real* wheeled about and rested its oars beside the waiting Venetian and papal galleys, the standards of St. Mark and St. Peter dipped in salute, and volley on volley thundered out from coastal batteries. Sir William Stirling-Maxwell, in his biography of Don Juan, described the scene enthusiastically:

> In the harbour, in front of the landing-place, there had been reared a huge square edifice, of three orders, with broad steps descending to the level of the waters, each of its sides displaying three arches, a host of heraldic devices, and a great wealth of Latin prose and verse. On leaving his barge, Don John passed up the steps and beneath the arches, where there stood waiting his arrival a noble charger covered with trappings of massive silver, the gift of the city. Mounting, amidst the cheers of the multitude and the roar of cannon, and attended by his staff and the chief Sicilian nobility, he rode along the Via Maestra to the Cathedral of La Nunziatella, one of those noble piles in which the Norman has displayed the religious architecture of the north, side by side with columned temples of Grecian art. From the harbour to the cathedral, and from the cathedral to the palace, the balconies glowed and gleamed with the usual display of beauty and festal tapestry; and the streets were spanned with arches, rich in arms and trophies, sculptured virtues and graces, inscriptions, couplets, all combining to one general result—assurance that the banner of Messina, a red cross on a field of gold, would follow wherever the Austrian eagle might lead, and that Venus and Neptune, and the other heathen deities, concurred with the Blessed Virgin and Saint Rosalia in favouring the League and detesting the Morisco and Turk. At night the general enthusiasm again

burst forth in an illumination of the city, and the countless shipping in the vast basin of the harbour. No fugitive from Famagusta had yet arrived to cast a gloom over the exultation of the Christian host.[11]

Don Juan immediately got down to business. After sending out two reconnaissance galleys under Gil de Andrada and the Venetian Chico Pisani, to spy out the Turkish strength and probable movement, he began to inspect the Allied fleet. What he found horrified him: Colonna's papal squadron was in line order, but the Signory had supplied little more than a paper fleet. "Your Grace could not believe how ill-equipped they are in fighting men and sailors," he wrote to his military mentor, García de Toledo, on August 30. "They have arms and artillery, but since they cannot fight without men, I was distressed to realize that conditions forced me to do something quickly, counting the galleys by number and not by quality. . . . I should add a word about an even worse fact with which the Venetians have presented us, which is that there is no discipline whatever; rather, each galley goes off where it pleases."[12]

No such high concerns troubled Cervantes. The great campaign had brought scores of friends and relatives to Messina, among them his cousins Alonso de Cervantes Sotomayor and Alonso's brother Gonzalo de Cervantes Saavedra, a mediocre poet on whom Miguel would lavish a kinsman's praise; the brothers had been forced to flee from Córdoba because Gonzalo had wounded a man in a duel. Juan Rufo was in Messina, and Gabriel López Maldonado; Laínez, too, and the Valencian poet Cristóbal de Virués, and Anton Rey de Artieda, another Valencian, who, like Cervantes, would be wounded three times at Lepanto. They were all, except for Laínez, about the same age, all poets, all now wearing the parrot's gaudy plumage. Whether they all made contact in that chaotic staging area is unknown. But it is stimulating to imagine them chattering excitedly together, speculating on the coming action.

It may have been one of them who informed Cervantes that his sisters were at it again. On August 27, 1571, a young nobleman named Alonso Pacheco Portocarrero acknowledged before a notary that he owed Doña Andrea de Cervantes five hundred ducats for "a large gold necklace with its pearls and gems, rubies and emeralds and diamonds, and a long gold chain with a gold agnus dei and a crystal rosary" which she had allegedly lent him.[13] A month later, Andrea sued for the value of "certain maravedis and jewels"; the suit named not Alonso but his younger brother Pedro Portocarrero, whose scandalous conduct had earned him the nickname La Muerte—Death—and would bring him a sentence to the prison galleys despite his aristocratic lineage. Apparently a case of neo-Ovandism—except that the injured party in the case, or one of them, was the youngest Cervantes daughter, Magdalena, then seventeen. Was

Andrea's suit designed merely to shield her sister's good name? Or had the Pacheco brothers shared the sisters?

Alonso, as the family heir, would twist his way through a decade of promises—to pay when he came into his estate, to pay when the next batch of cork was sold, to pay tomorrow, two years later, five years later —wiggling out of breach-of-promise suits by both Andrea and a Magdalena who by then would, for the effect, be styling herself "Doña Magdalena Pimentel de Sotomayor." Andrea would eventually get 250 ducats, her outraged sister nothing, Alonso a new wife and a comfortable fortune. Young Pedro would survive the holocaust of the Invincible Armada to become, despite his criminal record, a Knight of Santiago and a gentleman of the royal household.

A proud lot, the Portocarreros, among the most arrogant of the great Andalusian families. It was an earlier Portocarrero who, as mayor of Seville, appealed to Charles V against the city council's denial of his mayoral title because he had refused to check his sword at the city hall door. Now, in the late summer of 1571, Don Pedro Portocarrero, the father of playboys Alonso and Pedro and the man whose death could bring fortune to his sons and, so it then seemed, to Cervantes' sisters, was in Messina with Miguel, preparing to fight the Turks.

In Sicily, affairs were progressing at what, given the circumstances, might be considered fair speed. Papal delegates scurried into Messina bearing gifts and encouragement for Don Juan, rosaries for the men and plenary indulgences for everybody involved. To impress the seriousness of the mission on the men, the commander in chief banned women from the fleet,† and ordered the death penalty for blasphemy. A dangerous split between the commanders led by Doria and Requesens, who were for satisfying honor by a series of raids but avoiding the main Turkish force, and those supporting Don Juan and the Venetians, who insisted on an all-out fight, was resolved when the respected Alvaro de Bazán, Marquis of Santa Cruz, voted with the caudillo. Orders were given to sail September 10 to seek and destroy the Turkish fleet.

The fleet did not sail on September 10. On September 10 it huddled in Messina harbor, sheltering against one of the sudden, vicious squalls for which the Mediterranean is famous. For four days, as many men as lived in the cities of Madrid and Valladolid combined lay packed in the cramped, stinking ships, nerves crawling and stomachs rebelling against the rocking of the light hulls. Not until September 16 was the huge force able to maneuver into position and weigh anchor.

The Latin love of color and splendor was orgiastically requited that

† Some women did manage to sneak aboard, of course. One of them, Maria "la Bailaora," went disguised as a soldier. She carried the masquerade to the extreme of fighting so well in battle that she was later placed on the king's payroll—as a trooper in Cervantes' tercio.

day. From the shifting, bustling forest of masts, hundreds of pennons, en-
signs, banners snapped in the still smart wind, dominated by the yellow
and white papal standard over Colonna's galley, the Lion of Venice, the
Cross of Malta, the red and gold flag of Spain, the heraldic bearings of
Sicily, Naples, Milan, Genoa, Savoy, squadron commanders' personal em-
blems and divisional pennons. Over them all the blue and gold banner of
the Holy League soared above the crimson and gold *Real,* throwing violent bursts of shadow over Don Juan standing on the forecastle roof in his
gold embossed armor. Banks of yellow and green and scarlet uniforms
lined the decks. A rippling carpet of giant oars whipped the surface of
the bay to a creamy iridescence as the vessels darted into line: galleys, the
fleet's assault vessels, 170 tons of purely utilitarian craft, floating perches
for the parrots on the decks; six mighty galleasses, looming high in the
water in what seemed then like the awesome invincibility of their
172-foot length and their combined total of some three hundred guns;
and a cloud of auxiliary craft, patrol and escort ships, fighting galiots.

The noise must have been hallucinatory. Chains thundered, hulls
creaked, sails boomed, skippers' mallets rhythmically thudded to give the
stroke to the rowers. Orders were shouted in a dozen languages while an
immense crowd cheered feverishly, as though the blood of all Christendom had rushed to its head there in the port of Messina. Harbor batteries pounded out a military benediction as the mass of timber and iron
and leather and rope and silk resolved itself into a line ten miles long.
From the ships rose a hum of prayer, for they swarmed with monks,
Franciscans sent by Philip II, Capuchins delegated by the pope and
Jesuits sent by no one in particular, although one of them did deliver a
crucifix, the blackened Christ of Lepanto now hanging in Barcelona's cathedral, to Don Juan from Pius V. And as the fleet stood slowly out to
sea, it passed an anchored papal brigantine from whose deck a nuncio
tirelessly made the sign of the cross.

First out were the eight galleys of the vanguard under Juan de Cardona, flying streamers emblazoned with the arms of Philip II. The main
fleet came out in the order of its "horns" or wings, led by Doria's right
horn of fifty-four galleys flying green flags. Next came the center or "battle," sixty-four galleys headed by the towering *Real* with the papal and
Venetian flagships at its flanks, all displaying blue standards. The Venetian left horn of sixty-three galleys under Agustín Barbarigo's command
followed, showing yellow pennons; near the head of the Venetian line
sailed Doria's galley *Marquesa,* with Miguel de Cervantes and, presumably, Rodrigo aboard. About a mile behind the main force followed Santa
Cruz's rear guard of thirty galleys, showing white flags. Last out was a
squad of twenty-six sailing ships—supply vessels—along with the galleasses, moving two by two. Altogether, the force probably included 308

ships of all types mounting a total of roughly 1,800 cannon, some 28,000 soldiers of whom 20,000 were in the pay of the King of Spain but only 8,100 of whom were Spanish. Trumpet bands, doctors, apothecaries, sailors, rowers, commissaries, paymasters, gunners, cooks, butchers, armorers, carpenters, sailmakers, priests—all the miscellaneous craftsmen of a fighting fleet—brought the total manpower up to approximately 80,000 men.[14] Like Cervantes, most of this (for the period) awesome host was about to discover the horror of life aboard a war galley.

] 10 [

The Sea Eagles

"Want to learn to pray?" asked a proverb of the day. "Then go to sea."[1]

Crowded, filthy, alive with vermin, so dangerously hard to handle that a storm would send it scurrying for the nearest shelter, the galley had nevertheless been the eagle of the sea[2] since well before the Trojan War; indeed, its long, sleek, menacing profile had changed little from that of the ships in which Octavian and Marc Antony battled for control of the ancient world fifteen centuries before Lepanto. Like the horse on land, it dictated the era's sense of space. Most men feel distance in terms of the time needed to traverse it. To a traveler spending six weeks on the road getting from Venice to Madrid, to a seaman who might, in bad weather, take eight months to cover the 2,700 miles from Turkey to Gibraltar, Europe and the Mediterranean were as vast as the whole world is to us. The spirit of adventure needed a shorter operating range then.

In its basic form a galley was a shallow-draught, single-decked, oared wooden vessel with two masts, lateen sails and high castles or super-structures fore and aft, capable of speeds under oars alone, in brief spurts, of up to six and one half knots. It might in fact be easier to think of the Lepanto galleys as sea wasps rather than eagles: 120 to 170 feet long from stern to the tip of their bronze-sheathed rams, 12 to 20 feet wide; 50 of them would fit on the flight deck of a modern supercarrier. On each of the 30- to 40-foot oars hauled three to six men, rammed closely together on benches bolted to the hull. A narrow shelf, called the *crujía,* ran the length of the ship between and slightly above the rower's benches. Five cannon were mounted in the bow to give point-blank fire.[3]

"Life in a galley—God grant it to whoever wants it," said another proverb. With a wartime complement of up to 400 men aboard, a galley gave each man a statistical space about twice that of a coffin in which to sit, stand, eat, sleep and relieve himself. Even to noses accustomed to constant reminders of life's pungency, the stench was abominable. In his *Arte de navegar*, Antonio de Guevara advised passengers aboard commercial galleys to carry a supply of perfumes (sweet gum, amber, aloes) to avoid fainting and nausea from the contaminated air.[4] Cervantes called them "maritime dwellings where one is most often abused by the bedbugs, robbed by the criminals, angered by the sailors, ravaged by rats and wearied by insects"; the crews, he observed, "are diligent in profiting by good fortune, lazy in a gale; in a storm they command freely and obey little; their god is their sea chest . . . and their pastime is watching the passengers being seasick."[5] The bedbugs, at any rate, could be useful: with cards and dice forbidden on board, the men gambled on bedbug races. Eugenio de Salazar, a member of Philip II's Privy Council, expressed the general feeling when he observed that a galley contains "naught that is good or seems good, but . . . it is like women—a necessary evil."[6]

Cervantes could be wry about most aspects of galley life, but the treatment of the oarsmen outraged him. His compassion was boundless for these men—mostly convicts, with a sprinkling of Moorish slaves and volunteers—whose punishment was, as a rule, immeasurably more violent than their crimes. (Murderers and thieves there were, but also bigamists, procurers, counterfeiters, makers and sellers of dice, blasphemers.) Decades later they were to become key symbols not only of Quixote's anarchic preference for justice over law, of Cervantes' lament for humanity's rejection of its own divinity, but of man's right to exercise his individual will. To row in a galley was a negation of human dignity, the climax of a long process of breaking a man's spirit preparatory to breaking his strength, which Cervantes found intolerable.

The rowing was bad enough; the men's hands were turned to shell by wear and salt water, thighs and buttocks were worn raw by the bullock hides covering the benches, backs and shoulders charred by sun and salt spray. Worse was the constant dread of punishment in which they lived. To impose the drummer's cadence, to encourage laggards to pull their weight, boatswains marched up and down the crujía wielding fists or a whip of bull sinews or whatever came to hand. A rebellious slave was strung up by the wrists, beaten with whips and staves, then cut down and his wounds rubbed with salt and vinegar before he was sent back to his oar. There was no limit to the punishment but the officer's sense of economy, for if a slave died under the whip, his executioner owed his market price to the king's treasury.

In compensation for his ordeal, the galley slave was—when the rules were obeyed—given a seaman's pay of two crowns a month and a seaman's rations, twenty-six ounces of rotting biscuit a day, three ounces of beans, half an ounce of oil. Four times a year, at Christmas, Mardi Gras,

Easter and Pentecost, he was regaled with a smoked herring, a half pound of meat or dried codfish beaten with vinegar, and a pint of wine, rewards which also fell to those going into battle or assigned to specially exhausting labor.* Sick men were sometimes fed broth, almonds, raisins and preserves by medical prescription only.

Decent officers tried to treat their galley slaves as fairly as any lion tamer would treat his dangerous cats. Most often, however, the men were cheated of their food, forced to pay all-too-real fines for fictitious offenses dreamed up to withhold pay the officers had already spent. When their time was up, they were frequently cheated of their freedom: they were billed for court costs, for transportation, barber services, the very bullocks' hides they sat on; small loans would be made to them which they could pay off only by work at the oars. Freedom, for many, came only with death. They died easily, of the cold and the heat, of starvation, injuries, battle wounds, exhaustion, of gangrene caused by frostbite, of lack of medical care. In storms and battle, they went down with their ships.

Rebellion was always incipient. One Mateo Lujan Sayavedra stabbed his captain to death in retaliation for a blow. As his victim expired on the deck, the murderer called out: "Hey—lower the yardarm, for I know they must hang me, and I care not a stick, for I have avenged my heart."[7]

Cervantes would recognize Quixote's liberation of a galley gang en route to port as an Aristotelian sin of ignorance (we would be more likely today to think of it in Marxist terms, as an objective error) and he would duly see to it that the knight was punished. But he was in no doubt that Quixote had done the right thing. Later in the book, Sancho watches a boatswain at work and his Spanish pride wonders "how a lone man striding (along the gangway) and whistling dared to whip so many people."[8]

In "The Captain's Tale," a semi-independent story grafted into *Don Quixote*, we read of an incident that occurred during the Holy League's 1572 campaign, in which Cervantes took part:

> In this campaign the galley named the *Prize* was taken; its captain was a son of that famous corsair Barbarossa. Its captor was the flagship of the Neapolitan squadron, called the *Sea Wolf*, commanded by that thunderbolt of war, that father of his soldiers, that fortunate and never-vanquished captain Don Alvaro de Bazán, Marquis of Santa

---

* Cervantes would have had more generous rations. Soldiers were normally given twenty-six ounces of hardtack a day, plus twelve ounces of more or less fresh meat three times a week, six ounces of cheese and as much fish, two pints of wine, two ounces of oil and four of vinegar, as well as chick-peas, rice and garlic. When supplies ran short, everyone but the officers ate an iniquitous *mazamorra* of hardtack crumbs and garlic stewed in oil and thinned with water. Salt was rationed, other spices undreamed of.

Cruz. . . . So cruel was Barbarossa's son, and so harshly did he treat his captives that, when the oarsmen saw the galley *Sea Wolf* coming down on them and closing in, they all downed their oars at once and, grabbing hold of their captain as he stood at his post shouting at them to row faster, they passed him down the benches from poop to prow, biting him as he went, so that his soul had already gone to hell by the time he had gone but a little way past the mainmast. . . .[9]

Such scenes of violence were still largely imaginary for Cervantes as the *Marquesa* ran before a brisk easterly wind toward Corfu. It may be that his first taste of war came in the reminiscences of the veterans aboard. Perhaps, as he listened, he felt the grudging, guilt-infected admiration intellectuals often feel for the professionally violent. But he may also, as he watches the rowers then, have reflected that heroism in battle may be no more than an approved phase of bestiality.

The fleet reached Corfu eleven days later. For once, the Corfiotes, usually not fond of their hard-fisted Venetian rulers, were pleased to see them. As the League troops filed ashore their startled eyes took in a scene of wreckage and desolation. The masts of sunken boats poked up through the greasy surface of the bay; razed churches and homes, empty corrals, the rubble of battle were everywhere. Turkish troops had attacked the island ten days earlier, virtually destroying the port. Only the bravery of the four thousand Italian troops on the island had prevented its capture.

There were other ill omens for Don Juan. The Venetian galleys were beginning to show their scars. In the older ones, rotting timbers betrayed the Venetian habit of keeping their galleys in dry dock when not actually in use; splitting seams showed how hurriedly the new ones had been built. A hastily convened council of war aboard the *Real* produced the customary divisions of opinion, and once again, the more timorous captains were shamed into agreeing to seek a showdown with the marauding Turks. Don Juan and his advisers would have been surprised to learn that Turkish military opinion was just as divided as the Europeans'; captains like Euldj Ali were as fearful of Christian strength as the Europeans were of the Turks'. Nor did the Christians know that Selim had already issued orders to his fleet admiral, Ali Pasha, to intercept and destroy the Holy League's forces.

Unconcerned by, if not oblivious to, the narrow writhings of history around him, Cervantes joined the rush of men toward the river that emptied into the harbor. Perhaps, as imaginative biographers have suggested, he was enchanted by the shades of white-armed Nausicaa and her father King Alcinous, who were so hospitable to Jason and Medea on their quest for the Golden Fleece, and who restored the shipwrecked Ulysses, for Corfu was identified in local legend then with the Homeric isle of Scheria. Himself embarked on a crusade against the Turk, he may even have recalled that Richard the Lion-Heart spent some months there on his return from the Holy Land four centuries earlier. He also needed a bath.

The monstrous late-summer Mediterranean mosquitoes may have seemed benign by contrast with the voracious wildlife he was busily exterminating on his body and clothing. It was probably not until later that evening, on his return to the ship, that he began to feel feverish. By the time the fleet moved downcoast to Gumenitza, where it anchored on September 30, he was aching, shivering, burning with malaria on a plank beneath the forecastle. He would get no peace from the boisterous men around him, too accustomed to suffering to concern themselves much with a sick recruit. Rodrigo, one supposes, was there to nurse him, to bring him the food he was too miserable to eat, to hold the common water dipper to his cracked lips. He must have dozed repeatedly, sometimes rousing up to kick feebly at a rat nibbling at his boots, wrapping himself more tightly in his flea-infested blanket against the unassailable chill in his blood.

Don Juan, meanwhile, was agitated by another ague: battle fever. He had just learned that the Turkish fleet was sheltering under the guns of the fort at Lepanto. Immediately he made an inspection of the fleet; cannon and harquebus volleys fired in his honor caused so many casualties that firing a weapon during inspections was made a capital offense.

Less immediately mortal, but potentially far more lethal, was the resurfacing of the enmity among the allies. The example was given by the Venetian commander, Sebastiano Veniero. Almost legendary in Italy, Veniero was dynamic, cultivated, brave as a mongoose and extravagantly honest. In some ways this seventy-five-year-old curmudgeon resembled Philip II: although he was modest with his intimates and as tender as could be expected of a man who claimed descent from Aurelian, he could be pigheaded, even cruel where the Republic's interests were involved. Don Juan's fleet inspection appeared to him to be one of those times.

The caudillo had clumsily delegated Doria to visit the Venetian ships. Veniero refused to allow the hated Genoese to board his galley; he was personally offended, he later reported to the doge in Venice, at Doria's "coming aboard to see whether a vessel commanded by one of Your Serenity's generals was in good order."[10] The irascible Venetian went so far as to threaten the generalissimo's deputy with death if he so much as set foot on the Venetian flagship's deck. The incident had hardly been smoothed over—Don Juan, realizing his mistake, was easily mollified— when a second and far worse explosion threatened to splinter the fragile Holy League.

To bring the depleted complements of troops aboard the Venetian galleys up to something like fighting strength, Veniero and his second-in-command, Agustín Barbarigo, had reluctantly agreed to take four thousand of King Philip's soldiers, mostly Italians, into his ships. A dispute arose between one of these troopers and a Venetian sailor which quickly turned into a free-for-all that left an unrecorded number of dead and wounded. When a Milanese officer offered to mediate in the row, the outraged Veniero warned him off. "By the blood of Christ," he roared, "take no such action, unless you wish me to sink your galley and all on board. I will bring these dogs to heel without your assistance."[11]

While the incident was being reported to Don Juan, a squad of Venetian musketeers overcame the rebellious soldiers. Four of them were summarily hanged. As far as Veniero was concerned, that was that. But the commander in chief was enraged by the implied affront to his authority. "By God," he swore, "I will no longer tolerate the arrogance of this old fool. . . ."[12] After a few moments of wild talk about arresting the Venetian, even opening fire on the Venetian galleys, Colonna, backed by Barbarigo and Santa Cruz, managed to calm things down. Don Juan settled for refusing to have anything to do with the haughty old Venetian, and there the matter ended, temporarily. But the ill feeling it generated lingered on.

On October 4, the fleet sailed in battle order from Cephalonia, only to be driven by poor weather into a small port on the island's northern tip. More bad news caught up with them there. A Venetian brigantine which had slipped through the tight Turkish blockade brought news of the fall of Famagusta on August 2. Cyprus, to whose rescue they were heading, was lost.

For two months, a garrison of some five thousand Greeks and Italians, convinced that relief was on the way, had replied so lustily to Turkish general Mustapha Pasha's forces that in two weeks, according to contemporary accounts, they killed thirty thousand attackers. The figure may be inflated, but it indicates a sufficiently ample slaughter to explain Mustapha's subsequent fury in dealing with his captives. By July 31, with hope of relief gone and starvation raising a threat of plague, Famagusta's governor, Nestor Baglioni, and its military commander, Marcantonio Bragadino, had sued for surrender.

The terms of capitulation were generous—suspiciously so. Hostages were to be exchanged; safe passage to Crete with full military honors and retention of their weapons was promised for all soldiers and gentlemen in the city.

On August 6, Bragadino and a number of his officers visited Mustapha's tent to say good-by. The Turkish commander casually asked them what security they offered for the safe return of his ships. Bragadino replied that none was given and none needed: Mustapha had the word of a Venetian gentleman. The Turkish commander pointed to Antonio Quirini, the son of a Nicosian captain, and demanded that he be left as hostage. Bragadino refused. In a sudden—probably feigned—rage, Mustapha accused the defenders of massacring Turkish prisoners. The Venetian officers were ordered executed at once. The entire garrison, already embarked for passage to safety, was sent into slavery in Constantinople. Special treatment was decided on for Bragadino himself. It began with the slicing off of his nose and ears. He was whipped daily, given hard and humiliating labor, forced to kiss the earth under the Turkish general's feet. His teeth were broken. On August 17, in the city's central square, the dying man was flayed alive. His voice, reciting the *Miserere mei, Deus,* gradually weakened. He was dead by the time his executioners' knives reached the groin. His skin was stuffed with straw, hung from the mast of Mustapha's flagship and passed in triumph along the Cypriot coast.

The effect of the news was to prove disastrous for Ottoman hopes; it so enraged the Christians that all differences among them were suspended until the atrocity could be avenged.

Old and ancient resonances echo from the council of war called aboard the *Real* in response to the news, like the muted clanking of a knight waiting in a deep forest. Despite differences in strategic estimates, a plan was hammered out: on the morning of October 7, the fleet was to deploy some fifteen miles out from the mouth of the Gulf of Patras, the western end of the Gulf of Corinth. If, within two hours of that time, the enemy failed to appear, a general salvo of cannon and small arms was to be fired and all flags unfurled. If the Turks still refused to come and fight, the operation was to be considered ended, since it was thought to be suicidal to try to pursue the enemy within range of the guns installed on both sides of the channel at Lepanto.† But Christian honor would be satisfied.

Don Juan issued final orders to the fleet: artillerymen and harquebusiers were ordered to hold their fire until the very instant when the galleys rammed their opponents, on the theory that greater fear was instilled in the enemy if the noise of shattering oars and cracking hulls coincided with the roar of weapons. His final order—which some say was issued on the advice of Doria, while others credit García de Toledo—was to saw off all the galleys' beaks to allow the prow guns to fire on a level rather than at elevation, so delivering a deadlier, more accurate point-blank fire. It would also mean impaling the Turkish ships at closer quarters, giving boarders a few priceless seconds' head start in launching their attack while the enemy was still reforming his ranks.

† The Italian name for the Greek port of Naupaktos and the adjacent straits separating the Greek mainland from the Peloponnesus.

For naval warfare in the sixteenth century was, in its essentials, land warfare on water, minus the mass formations of a land battle, but made more terrible by the conditions under which it was fought. Francisco Manuel de Melo observed that "naval combat is usually the stubbornest, the bloodiest, the most horrible of all."[13]

Cervantes has Don Quixote describe the dangers of a head-on engagement in the open sea:

". . . All the space the soldier has is that allowed by two feet of planking on the beak. With all that, seeing himself faced with as many ministers of death as there are artillery pieces aimed at him from the other side, no more than a lance's length from his body, and seeing that at his first misstep he will go down to visit the deep bosom of Neptune, he yet, with intrepid heart, borne by the honor driving him on, will offer himself as a target for all the harquebuses and will try to cross that narrow passage to the enemy ship. And what is more amazing is that no sooner has one man fallen to a place from which he can never rise until the world's end, than another takes his place. And if he, too, falls into the sea lurking in wait for him like an enemy, another and still another will follow as fast as they can die; this is the highest bravery and daring to be found in all the hazards of wars."[14]

When the weather finally cleared on the morning of October 6, the fleet crept gingerly around the southern tip of Ithaca, Ulysses' homeland, toward the Curzolarian Islands, Homer's Echinean Isles, off the Albanian coast north of Preveza, the base for the battle of Actium. At the same time, the Turkish fleet was edging its cautious way through the gulf. Both forces were probing warily, each a blinded Cyclops feeling furiously for its Ulysses.

Two hours before dawn on October 7, the day of St. Mark, patron of Venice, the Christian galleys moved slowly out toward the Gulf of Patras. Silently they slid through the pre-dawn mist, exploring every inlet, every promontory that could provide a place of ambush. At 7 A.M., as the fleet rounded Point Scropha, lookouts spotted the tips of masts thrusting toward them, looking like a procession of flaming torches in the first gleams of sunlight. They were coming fast, driven by a fresh wind off the gulf. Ali Pasha had been hurrying to try to jump the Christian fleet before it could prepare for action.

The fleets were still about fifteen miles apart—some two hours' sailing time at best. A square green flag broke out on the mainmast of the *Real* and a gun boomed the signal to assume battle stations. On the galleys' decks, preparations were hectic. Guns were loaded; decks were powdered with fresh sand; barrels of water were strategically disposed to fight fires.

Leather bulwarks were strung up around the galleys' flanks to provide protection from enemy arrows—a protection which the Turks, to their discomfort, disdained. Soldiers oiled the blades of pikes and swords. Stones and javelins were hauled to the tops of masts to hurl down on boarders. Barrels of powder covered with damp sacking were set out, along with vats of watered wine and oil. Carpenters readied planks and nails for emergency repairs, replacements for sails and rigging were broken out.

Aboard the *Real,* benches were taken up to provide more space for the troops, who now numbered four hundred. The oarsmen were replaced by fresh men from the transports. At Don Juan's order, the chains were struck from the legs of all non-Moslem galley slaves, and the men were armed and promised their freedom if the day should bring victory to the Christian cause. Small boats trailing the galleys were cut loose to clear the sea for action.

A final council of war was hastily summoned aboard the *Real,* where 360 knights, all of noble familes, formed the caudillo's personal guard. The grave, proud, taciturn Doria, whose conduct in the battle was to be severely criticized, urged the commander to avoid a fight. But even as he spoke, he may have glanced resignedly at the painting of Nemesis, the goddess who punishes human ambition, on the wall of the sumptuously decorated cabin, and mentally shrugged. It is hard to believe that he seriously meant to stand up against the eager young man whose eyes glittered with excitement in the gilded gloom as he announced impatiently: "The time for talking is past, gentlemen; this is a time for fighting."[15]

11

Lepanto

On his plank belowdeck in the *Marquesa,* a still feverish Miguel de Cervantes would have been aware of a bustle around him, would have heard the cries of "To arms! To arms!" and the boatswain's commands, *"Avante Boo-ooga"*—all ahead, ro-ow. He would have felt the hull shudder under the sudden, fierce beat of the oars as the galleys began to scramble from their line-ahead sailing formation to line-abreast battle stations.

This was to be a day lighted by thousands of flashes of individual courage. But the first of them on that calm, sunny October morning may have been Cervantes' appearance in the entrance to the hatch. Disheveled, weaving on cottony legs, eyes blinking painfully in the expanding sunlight after a week in the penumbral hold, his helmet jammed on his head, he bawled for his gun and his orders. All his senses were certainly heightened by his fever, by the danger and the excitement.

Some of the men tried to dissuade him—Santiestéban, Gabriel de Castañeda, perhaps Rodrigo. He was in no condition to fight, they urged. Look at him! He could hardly stand! A sick man was a nuisance in a fight; worse, he was unreliable and therefore dangerous. But Miguel could see the Turkish flags advancing, hear the music of Turkish pipes floating across the water, a muted tumult as the fleets deployed. "It was amazing," said one witness, "to see that expanse of sea covered with galleys with their proud castles and flags of every color and all that noise."[1] Go below? Abandon his post and his comrades? All Cervantes' pride, his sense of duty, his hopes, ambitions, the lurking lust for glory surely milled in his mind with a sheer herd instinct and the nameless, febrile exaltation of a long-awaited danger finally faced.

"What?" he reportedly shouted. "What will they say of me! They'll say

I did not do my duty! But I would rather die fighting for God and my king than nurse my health." Still his fellows, now joined by the *Marquesa*'s captain, Francisco Sancto Pietro, begged him to retire. It was no use. "What will they say of me?" indeed. Might they say with Capacho in *The Wonder Show* that "conversos and bastards are never brave?" Miguel grew testy: "Gentlemen," he exclaimed, "on every occasion up to today on which His Majesty has been offered a fight into which I have been ordered, I have served well, as a good soldier; I shall do no less now, even though I am sick and feverish. Better that I fight in the service of God and His Majesty and die for them than to skulk below deck. . . . Captain, put me in the most dangerous post there is—I will stick to it and die fighting!"

Even admitting the young Cervantes' taste for resounding rhetoric, it all sounds a bit stagy. This may be because we do not have it from Cervantes himself or, in fact, from any other disinterested witness. The sole source is the testimony given more than six years later, in March 1578, by Santiestéban and Castañeda, as witnesses to an *información* or affidavit executed by the Cervantes family.

In the document, Ensign Santiestéban declared that "he knew to be the truth that when the Turkish fleet was sighted in the said naval battle, the said Miguel de Cerbantes (sic) was sick and had a fever, and his said captain and this witness and many other friends of his told him 'that since he was sick and had a fever, that he should remain quiet below in the galley's hold' and that the said Miguel de Cerbantes replied 'what would they say of him, and that he was not doing his duty and that he would rather die fighting for God and for his king than hide under cover and nurse his health'; and so this witness saw him fight like a valiant soldier with the said Turks in the said battle at the pinnace, as his captain ordered, and he was given command of other soldiers. . . . He was a soldier in Captain Diego de Urbina's company in the galley *Marquesa* in the land-side horn."[2]

Castañeda's testimony supported Santiestéban's, with the added details that Cervantes had twelve men under him and that he was wounded in the chest by a harquebus bullet and that his hand was damaged. The testimony is reproduced in two other Cervantes documents compiled in 1580 and 1590.

Something like what he is supposed to have said was doubtless stammered out by a feverish and excited Cervantes, but we will probably never know exactly what he really did say. There is, in any case, no reason to question the general circumstances, that he was ill, that he nevertheless insisted on serving. He hints at his condition in the *Epistle to Mateo Vázquez:*

> With fear and effort together
> I was present at the event,
> armed more with hope than with steel.

His commander refused to put Miguel at the prow, where the bitterest action might be expected, but he did put him in the waist of the ship, at the pinnace, at a point where the second of three temporary defensive traverses crossed the deck.[3] Whether the young man was actually in charge of the twelve-man squad or whether his command was simply an invention of witnesses anxious to inflate his record is impossible to know. Perhaps the ship's cripples were congregated there. Certainly the position was exposed. Torres y Aguilera called the skiff "the highest and most exposed part of the whole galley and the most dangerous"[4]—open to enemy ships preferring to bypass the deadly prow to attack at the weaker points amidships, or to a flanking attack in support of another galley already engaged at the bow. Accounts of such actions at Lepanto are plentiful. The most crushing single blow to the Turkish forces that day, the capture of their flagship *Sultana,* would be delivered by a rush of reserve troops across the ship's waist. The harquebus fire was particularly telling at Lepanto, said a contemporary chronicler, "at the cookstove and the pinnace where they never stopped firing," leaving the Turkish galleys "full of dead bodies."[5]

The enemy fleet was in full view now, scudding under all sail like sinister whippets before the strong wind. Selim had mustered nearly three hundred ships, a force variously estimated at from 80,000 to 120,000 men. On the mainmast of Ali Pasha's *Sultana* Selim's flag was clearly visible, a green expanse embroidered with the Sultan's monogram and verses from the Koran in yellow. Alongside it surged the flags of Algiers, Tripoli, Anatolia, Negroponte, Egypt, Constantinople, all of the Ottoman provinces.

Straining at their oars, the Christian galley gangs brought their ships around into line facing the enemy. The left horn under Barbarigo reached toward the Curzolarian shoals and the Etolian coast, while Doria, whose squadron had the farthest to go, moved his ships, now numbering sixty-four south to sea to take the right horn. In the center, Colonna brought his galley alongside the *Real*'s right flank while Veniero wheeled around to its left[6] and Requesens' vessel closed up behind, making the *Real* a floating bastion complete with outworks, a malevolent ruby set in gold in the middle of a four-mile-long necklace of ships.

Don Juan, accompanied by his master of the horse, Luis de Córdoba, and his secretary, Juan de Soto, boarded a frigate for a final tour of inspection. As he raced from ship to ship, he warned the troops not to panic at the sound, reportedly blood-chilling, of the Turks' battle yells; he distributed religious medals, scapulars and rosaries as freely as he did exhortations, reminding the men of the plenary indulgence promised to all combatants. To the Spanish the twenty-four-year-old caudillo said: "My sons, we came here to die, to triumph, if heaven so ordains. Do not give the enemy occasion to ask, with impious arrogance, where is God? But fight in His holy name for, dead or victorious, you will enjoy immortality. Show them we are gentlemen and Christians." To the Venetians: "Today is the day to avenge affronts: the remedy for your ills is in your hands, wield your swords with brio and fury."[7]

Cheers and shouting greeted his words. The men revered him—he was believed capable of anything, even of swimming in full armor—and they snatched at his cap, his gloves. His presence was so heartening that soldiers of all nations embraced each other, swearing to fight to the death. As the frigate reached Veniero's poop, the white-bearded old man, his eyes filled with tears, exchanged a friendly greeting with the dashing young generalissimo.

At about the same time, Ali Pasha, who was only slightly Don Juan's senior and who had a reputation for humane treatment of his captives, was promising his Christian slaves freedom if the Turks won. "Friends," he said in Spanish, "I expect you to do your duty by me, in return for what I have done for you. If I win the battle, I promise you your liberty; if the day is yours, God has given it to you. But my trust is in the destiny of Islam."[8]

Over three hours had now passed since the enemy was first sighted. Don Juan knelt to receive absolution and plenary indulgence in the name of Pope Pius V. All through the fleet, men dropped to their knees as though stricken with terror. Except for the babble of the platoons of monks, the Christian fleet was silent, making the noise of the Turkish approach seem even more frenzied. The Moslem soldiers—one commentator said they were riding high on hashish—fired wildly in the air, gesticulating and dancing to a blaring of horns and a crashing of cymbals.

Barbarigo, nervously eying the forbidding channel between the sand bars and the Etolian coast on his left, pressed steadily ahead of the lumbering galleasses, driven by his fear of encirclement. He was unfamiliar with these shores, but the enemy knew them as they knew their own decks. A warning from the *Toscana* slowed him down. Slowly, ponderously, the two giant fortresses were towed forward into position about three quarters of a mile in front of the wing, like champions before a line of medieval cavalry. The Turks had never faced them before, and the sight is said to have confused them.

From where he waited—the *Marquesa* was some five hundred yards up the line toward the center—Cervantes could see the fifty-six galleys of Mehemet Sirocco's (Shoräq's) squadron forcing the pace so hard they seemed to be gliding on a sea of snow. He may have shivered as the fresh morning breeze chilled the sweat running under his doublet and dripping icily through the red woolen hose, but it is not likely he noticed it. "The two armies were terrified as they moved toward the clash," we are told by a Girolamo Diedo impressed by "the gleaming helmets, the shining breastplates of our men, the steel bucklers like mirrors and the other weapons sparkling in the sun's rays, as well as the naked swords. . . . The enemy was no less menacing and caused as much fright in our side as it aroused marvel and wonder by the gold of all those resplendent lanterns and banners, remarkable for the variety of their thousand handsome colors. Although the two corps were still far apart, Ali, the captain of the sea . . . ordered an artillery salvo fired so that His Highness might reply. . . . By addressing himself to the captain generalissimo of the Christians and to no one else, he was asking for a reply in kind, so that . . . learning where the chief galley of the baptized was placed, he could go and encounter it, as he later did."[9]

As the men rose from prayer, the wind abruptly changed and began blowing from the west. The Christian oarsmen were able to rest on their oars the Christian sails bellied in the breeze. Cries of "Victory" went up from the galleys, for the change was seen as a sign from heaven, proof that God was, after all, a Christian.[10] Like a knight winding his horn in answer to a challenge, Don Juan fired a shot from the *Real*.

Then a single puff of smoke popped out from the huge, bronze eighty-pounder in the bow of Ambrosio Bragadino's galleass, the one nearest the shore, testing the range. Still too short. The whole fleet knew that for Ambrosio and his brother Antonio, who captained the other galleass on the left, this was a personal fight: they were kinsmen of the unfortunate commander at Famagusta. Now a sound like a flood rushing through a narrow street coiled back to the line: the galleasses on the left and center had opened fire. As the Turkish ranks split to bypass them, their broadside cannon roared in fury, while torrents of fire lashed out from the harquebusiers—three hundred of them to each fortress—stationed behind the big ships' high, protecting sides.

Two Turkish galleys went down at once. Again the shout of "Victory!" went up from the League army and, for a moment, it seemed as though they might already have been right.[11] The drums beating the stroke aboard the Turkish galleys faltered, went silent. But their hesitation was only momentary. The Turkish captains had little trouble rekindling the courage of Ottoman troops convinced of their invincibility. The neat order of the Turkish formation was splintered, but that was unimportant now. The galleasses, they mistakenly judged, were already behind them, out of the fight for all practical purposes. The big ships had delivered their message to future naval strategists that high firepower had made

oared warships obsolete and that, henceforth, sails and broadsides
would replace oars and frontal attack.

But this day was still to be fought. "Mehemet Sirocco . . . and Caur
Ali, outdistancing the rest of the Turkish detachment in their furious
ardor, hugged the Etolian shore; at the head of their right wing, they
rushed one behind the other between the sandbanks and the river mouth
. . . they were attempting to turn our galleys by slipping behind them.
With four or five of their ships, they tried to attack us from the rear,
while their other vessels were ordered to pass outside the banks to take us
from the front. But the excellent Barbarigo was unfailingly vigilant; he
spun his galley around, along with those others nearest him. . . . Nevertheless, five galleys succeeded in enveloping us, and from them came a
cloud of arrows."[12]

At this point in a sixteenth-century sea fight, all semblance of tactics
was lost. Galley closed with galley in a cacophony of splintering wood
and coughing cannon, the rush of arrows and incendiary pine cones and
the popping of harquebuses; ships waded into battle as flamboyantly as
drunks into a tavern brawl. The range was so short that harquebusiers
were spattered with their victims' blood. Spanish fire was specially effective because the Sultan's galleys, without pavisades or traverses, left the
unarmored Turkish soldiers as exposed as flames before a firehose.

All along the line, the galleys wheeled and rammed. The *Marquesa*
was in the thick of the fighting.* The League's left wing was to suffer the
highest casualties of any Christian squadron that day; on its fate would
depend the outcome of the battle. With Doria and Euldj Ali fencing far
to the south, the threat of a breakthrough at this crucial early stage was
concentrated on the left. While no record has been found to tell us
whether the *Marquesa* was actually boarded at any point, the casualty total—forty killed and probably three times that many wounded—suggests
that the Turks did manage to put men aboard.

The carnage at Lepanto is almost unimaginable. In a strip of sea less
than five miles across and a few hundred yards deep, more than sixty
thousand fighting men hacked and flailed with swords, pikes, daggers,
maces, javelins. They blasted away at point-blank range with bows and
poisoned arrows or crude firearms emitting pellets that disintegrated with
a kind of shotgun effect. Contemporary commentators again and again
evoke with awe the noise and ferocity of such combat. Fernando de
Herrera tells us the fight was waged "with such a great clamor that it
seemed that not only were the galleys breaking up in pieces, but the very

* The redistribution of the Spanish and papal forces to beef up the undermanned
Venetian galleys—and to head off desertions by independent Italian captains—
meant not only putting Philip's troops into Venetian ships, but dotting the Venetian line with Spanish galleys. It was this reshuffling which put Cervantes in the
Republic's wing.

sea bawled, unable to bear that terrifying din, churning its foam-laden waves which, only a little time before, were so tranquil. And the men, beside themselves, could not hear each other and the sky scorched their eyes with the smoky darkness of those flames."[13]

Diedo, too, was stunned, though not to inarticulateness, by the racket: "The sound of trumpets, of clappers, of drums became terrible, but still more so the noise of the harquebuses clacking, and the thunder of artillery. So piercing were the cries, so intense the clamor rising from the multitude that everything crackled horribly, one was bewildered with terror. Thick waves of arrows, sheets of artificial fire fly or float in the air. Their dense smoke spreads like a nearly continuous web which blots out everything. All we could see, entirely encircling us, were ships in various and bizarre postures, as the caprices of combat arranged them. The sea over a stretch of nearly eight miles was entirely covered, not so much with masts, yards, oars, the debris of broken things, as with an infinite number of cadavers: they transformed the sea into blood. This chaos of innumerable and fantastic monstrosities somehow tears men out of themselves, metamorphoses them and makes them live in an alien world. . . . The men are mad, they shout, howl, laugh, weep."[14]

Every man at Lepanto saw the Demon that day, touched something that moaned and writhed at the core of life. No wonder Cervantes would remember the "naval," as the battle came simply to be called. In this cataclysm, as savagely disproportionate to man's sense of measure as an upheaval of nature, he would have known a kind of mindless elation of terror he would never feel again. This was something to abandon oneself to, to lose oneself in; no intensity of private emotion, no scope of particular imagination could meet this total immersion in violence on equal terms. One blended with it as a mystic in a storm blends with the universe, and became, for an hour, a giant. Cervantes told about it in stately tercets in the *Epistle to Mateo Vázquez:*

> I marked the shattered host melt like a flood,
> And a thousand spots upon old Neptune's breast
> Dyed red with heathen and with Christian blood;
> Death, like a fury, running with foul zest
> Hither and thither, sending crowds in ire
> To lingering torture, or to speedy rest;
> The cries confused, the horrid din and dire,
> The mortal writhings of the desperate
> Who breathed their last 'mid water and 'mid fire,
> The deep-drawn sighs, the groanings loud and great
> That sped from wounded breasts, in many a throe
> Cursing their bitter and detested fate.[15]

1. An alleged portrait of Cervantes, attributed to his friend Juan de Jáuregui but almost certainly a twentieth-century forgery based on a verbal self-portrait in the prologue to the *Exemplary Stories*. No reliable likeness is known to exist. (Photo MAS)

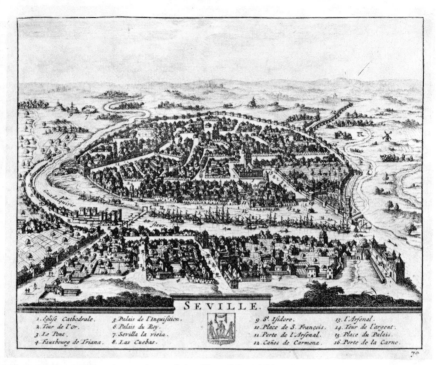

SEVILLE.

1. Eglise Cathedrale.   5. Palais de l'Inquisition.   9. S.t Isidore.   13. l'Arsenal.
2. Tour de l'Or.   6. Palais du Roy.   10. Place de S. François.   14. Tour de l'argent.
3. Le Pont.   7. Sevilla la vieia.   11. Porte de l'Arsenal.   15. Place du Palais.
4. Fauxbourg de Triana. 8. Las Cuevas.   12. Caños de Carmona.   16. Porte de la Carne.

2. A sixteenth-century view of Seville. (The Hispanic Society of America, New York)

PHILIP II. KING of SPAIN, NAPLES, SICILIE &c.

3.
King Philip II of Spain as an old man. (The Hispanic Society of America, New York)

4.

Elisabeth de Valois, the third of Philip's four queens. It was her death in 1568 that prompted the first of Cervantes' known writings. (The Hispanic Society of America, New York)

5.

Madrid in the late sixteenth century, after it became Spain's first fixed capital. (The Hispanic Society of America, New York)

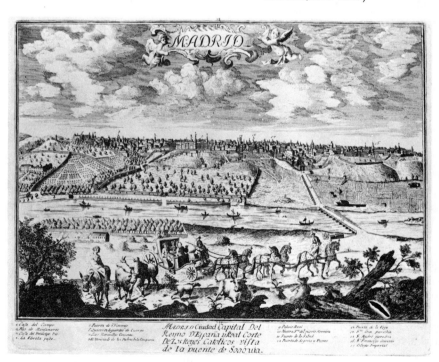

6. Three sixteenth-century Spanish infantrymen. The harquebusier in the middle wears the "parrot" uniform and the gear in which Cervantes fought at Lepanto. (The Hispanic Society of America, New York)

7.
Don Juan of Austria, bastard half brother to Philip II and the last, and least, of the medieval paladins. He commanded the Christian fleet at Lepanto. (The Hispanic Society of America, New York)

Tintoretto pinx

Sebastian Veniero.
R.¹ Museo de Pinturas nᵒ 919.

8.

Sebastian Veniero, commander of the Venetian forces at Lepanto. Cervantes served in a Genoese galley in the Venetian wing. (The Hispanic Society of America, New York)

9.   A contemporary painting of the battle of Lepanto, the "noblest occasion that centuries past have seen and those to come can hope to see," according to Cervantes. He was wounded three times in the fighting. (The Hispanic Society of America, New York)

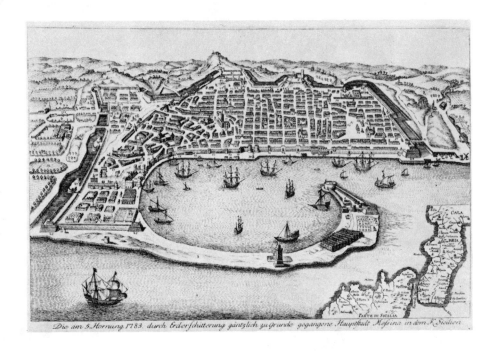

Die am 5. Hornung 1783. durch Erderschütterung gäntzlich zu grunde gegangene Hauptstadt Messina in dem K. Sicilien.

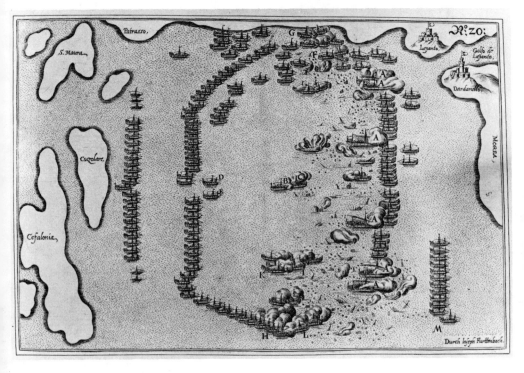

Durch Iosppn Furttmbach.

10. *Top:* A view of Messina, home port for the Holy League fleet. (Copyright British Museum)

11. *Bottom:* A contemporary engraving showing the battle orders of the Christian (left) and Turkish fleets at Lepanto. The *Marquesa,* in which Cervantes fought, was in the Christian right "horn," nearest the Morean coast. (The Hispanic Society of America, New York)

12. Algiers at the end of the sixteenth century. (New York Public Library Picture Collection)

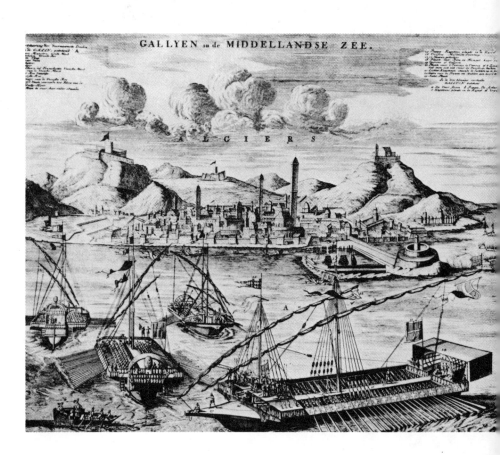

Pedimento de CERVANTES para la información de su cautiverio y rescate en Argel. Madrid, 18 de Diciembre de 1580.

13. The introduction to the 1580 affidavit describing Cervantes' record during his captivity in Algiers. It may or may not be in his hand, but the signature is certainly authentic. (Archivo General de Indias, Seville)

At the extreme left of the Christian line, the hazards of war were sorting themselves out with fiendish energy. After an hour of defensive fighting, Barbarigo was finally able to counterattack. Sirocco's Alexandrian flagship was captured. The bey himself, wounded in three places, fled the ship and struggled toward shore only to be captured by pursuing Christian troops. ". . . Barbarigo ordered the boarding of the galley of Caur Ali, whose merit as a warrior is well known," reported Diedo. "He took the famous captain prisoner. Seeing this, the *reis* (Moslem captains) nearby elected to save themselves, only too happy to be so close to their own country. They rushed toward the Villa di Marino rocks. But not all could reach them. In their headlong flight they rammed each other, became tangled, ensnared. This pileup soon formed a kind of bridge, a blessing for the fugitives who, scrambling over it, reached the reefs. . . . A good many of these desperate men were exterminated by ours before they could set foot on land. Others, in their frenzy to save themselves, shoved each other aside, hurled themselves over their comrades, fell in the sea and drowned. In the midst of this fight to the death, Barbarigo was wounded by an arrow in the left eye. That happened while he was directing operations; realizing that he was not being heard because his helmet was covering his face, he threw up the visor so that his voice might carry better. It was at that very instant that the enemy let fly his arrows with the greatest ardor. He was warned of the danger. 'It is a lesser peril to run that risk than to be misunderstood at such a moment.' Soon he was hit."[16]

Although he refused to allow himself to be carried below, Barbarigo was out of action for good. He would linger in speechless agony for more than twenty-four hours before he died. His rival, Sirocco, survived him by only a day before he was decapitated—at his own request, Spanish historians say, to end his suffering.

In many of the Turkish galleys, the remnants of the soldiery were annihilated by their Christian slaves, who hacked away their chains with abandoned weapons and fell ferociously on their former masters; twelve to fifteen thousand of them regained their freedom that day. At least five thousand others perished with their ships.

As the Turkish right weakened, Ottoman troops farthest from the shore, seeing their fleeing comrades streaming over the rocks and knowing that, to them, this avenue of escape was closed, fought with desperate fury. Martín de Eguilez told of Turks transpierced by pike blades and already dead, sliding down the eighteen-foot-long shafts to strike with their swords, like fighting bulls with their aortas cut giving a last, blind charge before dropping.

Cervantes was wounded three times at Lepanto—how, and in what sequence, we can only guess from scattered references in his writings. The

Epistle to Mateo Vázquez suggests that he took two harquebus wounds in the chest, despite the heavy leather jerkin he wore, before a ball shattered his hand:

> within my breast a cruel blow had made
> a deep and gaping wound, and my left hand
> was bruised and shattered past all human aid . . .

Presumably he dropped his gun under the shock of the impact. He may have fallen, but he must have been up again at once, before the numbness could wear off, for he tells us he continued to fight with his sword, indicating that he was involved in hand-to-hand combat:

> . . . I, unlucky, stood
> with one hand buckled firmly to my blade,
> the other dripping downward streams of blood . . .

He also tells us he fainted:

> And yet, it conveyed such sovereign satisfaction
> to my soul to witness the debasement
> of that barbarous, heathen folk by the Christian
> that I failed to pay attention to my wounds' lament,
> although, in truth, so fiercely did my pain assail
> me that, more than once, my very consciousness did fail.

There is even a possibility that he accidentally shot himself. In an early version of *The Jealous Extremaduran,* Loaysa, frantic because his mistress has decided to enter a convent, "is said to have enlisted in a famous campaign Spain was conducting against the infidels, where it is believed certain that he was killed by a harquebus that burst in his hands, and so was punished for his prodigal life."[17] In the final version, Loaysa merely goes off to the Indies. Was Cervantes masking a fact that would have cast a slightly ridiculous shadow over his glory? Or simply declining to connect indignity with any Spanish soldier, however sinful?

The Turkish right-horn galleys now massed for a final, frantic effort to reverse the tide of battle. "They hurled themselves savagely against our left," Diedo recounted. "The enemy was furious to see that our artillery was creating disorder in his galleys. He tried to take us on the flank. We closed. The galleass of Signore Ambrogio Bragadino . . . was at that moment facing the coast. Leaving its neighbor, which could still attack the right end of the enemy's *battaglia,* it moved inshore and succeeded in piling the Turkish galleys one upon the other with its artillery. Some of them would founder on the shoals, others on the banks. Some of our vessels in this zone had not yet made contact with the adversary. Keeping formation as best they could, they faced left and turned their prows toward the shore. This highly skillful maneuver allowed them to charge vigorously down on the enemy, who found himself surrounded, hemmed in as in a harbor. A horrible massacre ensued."[18]

Although legend focused on the battle that by now was building up around Don Juan and Ali Pasha in the center of the line, the outcome of the battle of Lepanto had already been decided.

By 11 A.M., Ali had made his first serious mistake: he had tried to delay the battle in the center until his wings could turn the Christian line. Now his galleys were perfect targets for the enormous firepower massed in the Christian center. The first shot from Francesco Duodo's galleass brought down the *Sultana*'s lantern. An evil omen. The League's galleys glided slowly forward, sparing the oarsmen as much as possible. The high prows of the Turkish galleys forced the Moslem gunners to send their projectiles whistling harmlessly over their enemies' heads, while the massed Christian cannonry, firing over their sawed-off spurs, committed a terrible slaughter among the Turks. Enraged, Ali whipped up his oarsmen, shooting two galley-lengths ahead of his line in an apparent frenzy to engage Don Juan in single combat. The *Sultana* rammed the *Real* so violently, we are told, that the two vessels were embedded in each other. Grappling irons snaked out from both sides.

Descriptions of the fighting become blurred here. The two sides were about evenly matched, with some five hundred fighting men in each flagship. Ali had six galleys lying under his quarters to feed fresh men into the grinder; Don Juan had only two, but Ali had dispensed with his reserve, while the galleys in Santa Cruz's reserve squadron were free to attack where they were needed. Aboard the *Real* was the entire Spanish general staff, including the two most experienced commanders in the force, Miguel de Moncada, Cervantes' colonel, and Lope de Figueroa, whom William of Nassau once called the most dangerous soldier in the Spanish army and who was now seeking revenge for the three years he had spent as a slave rowing in a Turkish galley.

The fighting was furious. Ali himself wielded a sword in one hand and a dagger in the other. Boarders surged back and forth across the decks, with each side reaching the other's mainmast three times before being hurled back. Aboard the Venetian flagship, Veniero, carrying his seventy-five years gallantly, wore a helmet and cuirass, but his feet were slippered for a better grip on the deck. Abandoning his steeply slanting poop, he stood amidships firing a crossbow—there was an attendant by him to rewind it—and doing great damage with his iron bolts. A mass of ships coagulated around the *Real*—twenty-five or thirty of them in a space 150 yards by 250. Galleys had to force their way through the mass of oars, broken timbers and bodies to reach the fighting. Colonna's papal flagship was dueling with Turkish army commander Pertev Pasha's galley. Santa Cruz, "small in quantity, in valor superhuman,"[19] was everywhere at once, sinking one Turkish galley by pouring cannon shot into its poop, grappling with another and putting its men to the sword.

"Horrendous was the confusion," Luis Cabrera de Córdoba wrote, "the fear, the hope, the fury, the pride, tenacity, rage, the pitiful deaths of friends, the rousing, the wounding, killing, capturing, burning, the flight into the sea of heads, legs, arms, bodies; wretched men, some breathing their last, some gravely wounded, were being finished off by Christian bullets. Others, swimming in the water and grasping hold of the galleys to save their lives even at the cost of their freedom, clutching oars, rudders, ropes and pleading for mercy in pitiful voices, were dashed away by the furious victors, who cut off their hands without remorse. . . ."[20]

The slaughter went on for over an hour with no decisive advantage to either side. At one point, Ali and Don Juan are said to have set out toward each other, the low-born muezzin who had sung his way to command via the sultana's heart, and the dancer's bastard searching for a throne. Both were under thirty, each fighting for glory, for his future and against the humility of his past. But the confusion was too great even for the power of legend; their advance was blocked by the mass of men between them. The sky was dark with smoke from the piñatas, the earthenware pots filled with fireballs and thrown by hand; naked oarsmen screamed with pain when pots of quicklime were dumped on them; the oil-smeared decks were ignited by pots of flaming liquid; nails were scattered to halt barefoot sailors and armed oarsmen already skidding on the soft soap hurled by the enemy.

The sensation of horror was to remain deeply impressed in men's memories of Lepanto. "So bloody and horrendous" was the battle, said Torres y Aguilera, "that it seemed as though the sea and the fire were all one. . . . There was nothing but *aljubas* (coats), turbans, quivers, arrows, bows, shields, boots, helmets and some masts and antennae and an infinity of other debris of war, and especially, many human bodies. . . ."[21] Casualty levels were awesome: seventy-five of the hundred men in the *Real*'s prow fell within ten minutes.

Tales of individual heroism that day are as countless as they are incredible. Aboard the *Doncella*, Federigo Venusta of Lodi, captain of Philip II's artillery, seized a grenade. It exploded in his hand. Thrusting his artilleryman's knife, used for cutting wick, at an oarsman, he ordered him to sever the hand, but the man fainted. Venusta sliced it off himself, rushed into the hold, seized a hen and, pushing the bloody stump into the bird's body, ordered it tied to his wrist. Implored to go below, he retorted that this was no day for a man to stop fighting, especially since his right was still in condition to avenge the left. Then he plunged back into the melee.[22]

Martín Muñoz, aboard the *San Juan* of Sicily, was, like Cervantes, ill with fever. He, too, wrenched himself to his feet and rushed aboard a Turkish vessel, reaching the mainmast with nine arrows in him and one leg shot away. Dying, he sank down on a barrel and, watching the life flow hotly out of him, called out: "Gentlemen, let every one of you do as much." Then he rolled over.[23]

Paolo Ghislieri, a kinsman of Pius V's, was the first man to jump into the galley of Kara Baivel. The two men had often met when Ghislieri, then the slave of a Moslem corsair captain, dragged his leg chains glumly through the streets of Algiers. Kara, as a man of arms, was sympathetic, Ghislieri remembered. Now, spying the corsair in the thick of the fighting, he called: "If you want to save your life, jump into the sea." Kara's only reply was to brandish his sword. Ghislieri slowly lowered the harquebus he was carrying and shot him in the chest. Then he cut off the dying man's head to end his agony.[24]

A Spanish Capuchin friar, an old soldier, tied a crucifix to a halberd and, crying that Christ would fight for his faith, led a boarding party into a Turkish galley, emerging victorious and unharmed. A Roman priest of the same order, finding that his flock was getting the worst of the fray, seized a boathook and killed seven Turks, driving the rest from the deck.

Few of these stories can be proved, of course, but they are at least symbolic of what Torres y Aguilera called the "incredible spirit" of the combatants at Lepanto. No action since the Reconquest had produced so rich a body of heroic legend. Not until Verdun would its aura of futile, frightful gallantry be surpassed.

The turning point unquestionably came with the death of Ali Pasha. There are virtually as many versions of it as there were witnesses. To Aurelio Scetti, rowing as a convict in the Venetian galley *San Giovanni Battista,* the scene was exemplary: "Don Juan, sword in hand, hewed and slew the enemies of the faith of Christ one after the other. With no less ardor, Marcantonio Colonna did the same, as did the Grand Commander of Spain (Requesens) and Don Juan de Cardona. They fought more furiously still when they learned of the death of the Venetian general Barbarigo. Ali Pasha's flagship defended itself strongly. The Christians proved stronger: in no time at all, they put three hundred janissaries to the sword. Ali Pasha fell into a towering rage at seeing himself destroyed and vanquished by the Christian enemies. He killed himself by stabbing himself in the throat. He preferred to die rather than to be a prisoner of the Christians. However, his two sons and other persons in his suite were taken prisoner."[25]

Another version has Ali, wounded, offering his jeweled sword or, variously, a gold collar, a casket of jewels, a pile of gold, to a Spanish soldier who, disdaining present rewards in the hope, presumably, of richer spoils to come, struck off his head. Swimming with it to the *Real*, he presented it to the generalissimo. "What am I to do with it?" Don Juan is said to have replied coldly, dismayed at the indignity to a worthy foe. "Throw it into the sea."[26]

Most historians agree that Ali was struck, probably in the head, by a harquebus ball, that a soldier from Málaga saw him fall, severed the head and held it aloft for all to see. It was then stuck up on a pike by order of Don Juan, where it remained for about an hour before tumbling into the sea. Posterity, of course, was not to be put off with any such dismissal.

No recital was so satisfying as the Fordian drama presented by the Englishman Richard Knolles, writing in the reign of James II. "The bassa, deadly wounded in the head with a shot, and all imbrued with blood, was taken, and as a joyful spectacle, brought to Don John, who, seeing him ready to breathe his last, commanded him to be despoiled of his armour and his head struck off. Which presently set upon the point of a spear, he for a space held up aloft with his own hand as a trophy of his victory, as also with the sight thereof to strike a terror in the minds of the other Turks, who in the other galleys fast by fought yet right valiantly; neither was he therein deceived."[27]

Leaderless, effectively cut off from flight, the Turks locked into the center fought on furiously for nearly an hour after the commander-pasha's death. But by 2 P.M. the last resistance collapsed. So, with it, did military discipline. Victorious soldiers rushed forward to pillage the enemy vessels, leaving their own unmanned.

Although, far out to the south, where Euldj Ali was making a fool of prudent Doria, the fighting continued for two more hours, there was nothing the wily renegade could do to reverse the tide of battle. Christian reinforcements from the center overwhelmed his line; by the time Don Juan himself, limping on a wounded heel (this was indeed a Homeric day), rushed to Doria's rescue, the Christians were back in control of the situation. Finally, with thirteen galleys, Euldj Ali slipped under Santa Cruz's prow toward Preveza, running virtually through the entire, plunder-crazy Christian fleet to escape.[28] Don Juan, Santa Cruz and a few other commanders tried to chase him, but their oarsmen were exhausted, the sky was turning a sickly gray and they broke off the chase. Some thirty-five other Ottoman vessels fled to the shelter of the forts at Lepanto. These, with the Algerine's thirteen, were the only Turkish survivors. The time was approximately 4 P.M. The orgy of extermination was complete.

> The sounds triumphant ringing loud and clear
> bore through the smitten air, in jubilant flood,
> the Christians' victory from ear to ear![29]

Nearly thirty years later, Cervantes would distill from the ferment of blood and pride, faith and plunder, the most poignant passage ever written about Lepanto, in "The Captive's Tale" in *Don Quixote:*

". . . I was present at that glorious battle, being already a captain of infantry . . . that day, so fortunate for Christianity because it showed the world and all its nations how mistaken was their belief that the Turks were invincible on the sea. On that day, I say, when the Ottoman pride and arrogance were broken, among the many fortunate men there—because the Christians who died there were luckier than those who remained alive and victorious—I alone was unlucky; for, contrary to the naval crown I might have expected in Roman times, I found myself on the night following that famous day with my feet in chains and my hands handcuffed. And this was how it happened: after Euldj Ali, the bey of Algiers and a bold and fortunate corsair, had charged and captured the Maltese flagship, leaving only three knights alive in it and those badly wounded, Gian Andrea's *capitana,* with me and my company aboard, went to its relief; and, doing what I was supposed to do in such a situation, I jumped into the enemy galley which, veering away from its attacker, prevented my soldiers from following me and left me alone among my enemies. Resistance was impossible against so many; at last, covered with wounds, I surrendered. And since, as you will all have heard, gentlemen, Euldj Ali escaped with all his squadron, I remained in his power, a captive; only I was sad among so many happy men, only I a prisoner among so many who were freed. . . ."[30]

Looting, meanwhile, was pressed with renewed frenzy. ". . . The soldiers, sailors and convicts pillaged joyously until nightfall," one source observed. "There was great booty because of the abundance of gold and silver and rich ornaments which were in the Turkish galleys, especially in those of the pashas."[31] Then, under a sky blackening with ominously more than October darkness, the fleet bumbled north toward the small port of Petala, above Point Scropha, each galley towing either a galleass or a Turkish prize. Behind them, burning hulks lighted the whole gulf like funeral pyres, illuminating the wreckage on the convulsed surface of the sea.

Once in harbor, the chief officers crowded aboard the *Real* to congratulate each other, embracing, kissing, capering on the bloodstained decks. Informed of the victory, Barbarigo, deprived of speech, raised his hands to heaven in sign of thanks to God. Don Juan sent for Ali's two captured sons, thirteen-year-old Mohammed, and Sain, seventeen, to console them on their father's death. All noted that the great standard of the Holy League, alone of all the fleet's flags, was untouched by shot or arrow. Only Veniero hesitated to join in the celebration until he was summoned by the generalissimo. Don Juan met the proud old man, who was hobbled by an arrow wound in the leg, at the *Real*'s gilded boarding ladder. He hugged him, calling him "most excellent father" and declaring that "I rejoice with you, Excellency, over this great victory."[32] A witness to the scene, Alvise Soranzo, reported: "His Highness told him he had fully noticed what the Venetian galleys had done, and that certainly His Highness and all the Spanish lords had been astonished." Veniero, mute with emotion, said virtually nothing. Both men wept.

Just how much of a hecatomb the battle had been grew clearer in the days that followed. True, the enemy fleet had been virtually wiped out: 130 ships captured, 62 sunk in battle, 50 more destroyed as unseaworthy by the Christians. Estimates of Turkish dead and wounded range up to 35,000, the number of captured at 7,200 and perhaps really twice that many. Christian boasting helped obscure the already murky facts; it has been calculated that the number of captures claimed would have given the Turks 800 ships. The Christians, too, had "drunken of things Lethean, and fed on the fullness of death":[33] of the roughly 28,000 men who fought in this last crusade, 7,500 were killed in battle, 15,000 were wounded and nearly 4,000 of these died in the following weeks of the poison on Turkish arrows, of loss of blood, of gangrene, not a few of the doctors' care.[34]

How much Cervantes was aware of all this can only be imagined. One hopes, for his sake, that he was at least conscious on the day after the battle to see a gravely affectionate Don Juan threading his way among the wounded, stopping with a word or a smile for every man, calling them his sons, helping them with his own hand, listening to their stories. "He is a lucky soldier who fights knowing his prince is watching him."[35] Cervantes' pay records show that Miguel was made a *soldado aventajado*, literally a privileged soldier, a citation which carried a three-escudo-a-month pay raise to give weight to the honor. Of Rodrigo's part in the battle we hear nothing, but military pay records for 1572 show that he got a *four-escudo* raise, presumably for valor at Lepanto. Honors among the *Marquesa*'s men, in fact, were so frequent as to indicate how distinguished the galley's service had been. Whether Rodrigo, too, was wounded is not known. The family's later obfuscation of the record is more than usually confusing on the point. In a petition in 1578, Doña Leonor swore that one of her sons "had his hand cut off and the other had one crippled."[36] Other testimony said it was Rodrigo who had lost the use of his hand, but in the prologue to the *Exemplary Stories* Cervantes states that he "lost his left hand to a harquebus shot in the naval battle of Lepanto, a wound which, although it may seem ugly, he considers handsome for having been received in the most memorable and noblest occasion that centuries past have seen and those to come can hope to see. . . ." Testimony by Beltrân del Salto in 1578 stating that Miguel was left with a crippled left hand "which he could not control" was probably accurate.[37] And since Rodrigo went on to a heroic, if not particularly rewarding, military career, it can be assumed that he suffered no disabling wound at Lepanto.

In the allied fleet, the comradeship of battle lasted barely three days. Bickering over the spoils had left everyone feeling cheated, including the noble but greedy volunteers. Although both Don Juan and the Venetian Senate were eager to follow up the sea victory with a land conquest which would give some military meaning to the battle, at least by assuring the League a strong advance base for future campaigns, the Spanish commander was forced to bow to the facts of his position: a reconnaissance in force led by Doria showed that Turkish forts in the area were still formidable; the winter storms were beginning; there were so many sick and wounded that the fleet was little more than a floating hospital, and supplies were short. Only the provisions taken from the Turkish ships saved the Christians from starvation. League supply ships left in Corfu to prevent them from slowing down the battle fleet were still unheard from. They would be found still idling in Corfu on the fleet's return there, because of a misunderstanding of Don Juan's orders.

Worst of all, mistrust and jealousy once more fragmented the League. Charges of treason were already being heard against Doria. Veniero and Don Juan squabbled angrily over a petty point of protocol. The caudillo's permanently blistered sensibilities were rasped because the impulsive old Venetian, whose vaingloriousness was as hardy as his physique, had sent word of the victory to the doge and the people of Venice without waiting for the commander in chief to make the first announcement to the world. In retaliation, Don Juan highhandedly ordered all Veniero's mail seized and brought to him for censorship. It often takes a considerable effort of will not to look at history with the helplessness of children watching an endless divorce-court wrangle.

12

"For the Greater Glory of the Right"

From a Cervantes in constant pain, suffocated by the stink of infection around him, appalled by the screams of agony and, through his own flickering consciousness, watching men die, seeing their bodies dropped naked into the sea—from this young man busy with his suffering, we have no right to expect any clear recollections of that three-week voyage back to Messina. He was lucky enough—he had survived the battle. And he was surviving the doctors as well.

While Veniero and the Venetian fleet, on insanely logical orders from the Senate, remained in the Adriatic—they would spend six months trying with inadequate and undisciplined forces to achieve a land victory, finally to return home in something like disgrace—the Spanish and papal forces set their course for Italy, Don Juan proceeding directly to Messina on royal orders, while Colonna ducked briefly up to Rome to receive his hero's welcome before rejoining the fleet in Sicily.

For the moment, all the Christian world shared deliriously in Cervantes' conviction of a world made safe for Christianity. In Venice, the Piazza San Marco was draped in captured Turkish banners. ". . . Everything was joyous," we are told, "everyone trying in his own way to demonstrate his delight, even the merchants who, like bellringers, did not cease all that week to strike their anvils with hammers, and the spice dealers to strike their mortars with their pestles, so that the noise was so great that one could not hear anyone speak, nor even go out into the town. Every (high) place, steeples and houses, was amply decked with lights and fireworks and many cannon were fired. And to complete the celebration, distribution was made to the poor in every quarter of the sum of four thousand ducats aside from wine and flour."[1] Walls in the ducal palace were covered with painted scenes of the battle. Everywhere, statues were carved, coins and medals struck, songs composed.

Legend tells us that Rome was better prepared for the news than its allies: on the afternoon of the day of Lepanto, while sitting at work with his treasurer, Pius V suddenly rose, opened a window and gazed out as though his ear had caught some distant sound. Then he dismissed his subordinate with the admonition: "God be with you; this is no time for business, but for giving thanks to God, for at this moment our fleet is victorious." As the man retired from the room, his master prostrated himself before a crucifix. It was a time for miracles; the treasurer noted the day and hour of the occurrence, which were afterward found to coincide with tolerable precision with the moment when Ali Pasha fell and the shout of triumph rang through the *Real*.[2] In the days which elapsed before the arrival of the Count of Priego, Don Juan's messenger to the pope, His Holiness frequently expressed his surprise at the delay of the news in reaching him. When it did arrive, he is said to have praised Don Juan in the words of the Evangelist: *"Fuit homo missus a Deo, cui nomen erat Joannes"* (There was a man sent from God, whose name was John).[3] A day of celebration was declared which is still observed in the church of Santa Maria Maggiore on the anniversary of the battle.

For Colonna, Rome was Rome still, and he was received with a slightly shriveled version of the honors of an ancient conqueror. New Latin inscriptions on the Arch of Constantine compared him to the first Christian emperor. He and his family had, in fact, prepared a full triumph, but the pope, concerned for his allies' sensibilities, persuaded him to trim it down to an ovation. "Along the Appian Way," notes Stirling-Maxwell, "beneath the venerable arches of the Emperors, and through streets hung with trophies and tapestries, Colonna was therefore obliged to content himself with passing to the Capitol and the Vatican, not in an antique car and clad in armor, but riding on a white genet, and wearing the Order of the Fleece, the robe of furred velvet, the crimson breeches and the white boots of daily life."[4] Even the stone gladiator in the Capitol square had his role in the rejoicing: in his right hand he held a naked sword, and in his left, a facsimile of Selim the Ottoman's head with a great wound in the brow.

Only in Spain was the rejoicing muted. Lope de Figueroa did not reach the court at Madrid until November 22, three weeks after Philip had received the news from the Venetian ambassador, Leonardo Loredano. That gentleman had hurried to the palace to find the king seated behind the curtain of his gallery in the chapel, hearing the service for the eve of All Saints'. Like his father when informed of the victory of Pavia, Philip received the news without expression and heard the service out to the end, but he did then order the *Te Deum* to be sung and presented Loredano with a fine jewel in reward for his news. The word flew from mouth to mouth, and in the evening there was a voluntary, unpremeditated and certainly unauthorized illumination by bonfires in the principal streets. The Cervanteses were by no means the only family in Madrid whose sons had fought the Turks; surely it requires little license to imagine Andrea, or Magdalena, their father, perhaps all three at separate times, rushing out to announce the news, or to picture a family group before the hearth, chattering excitedly of the great event and wondering anxiously how Miguel and young Rodrigo had come out of it. With minor differences in the number of candles lit and the commodiousness of the benches occupied, one supposes the essentials of that scene repeated as in a play of mirrors in a thousand rooms in the city.

But Philip, although pleased with this feat of Spanish arms, was too concerned with the loss of Spanish wealth and the lack of corresponding gain to Spanish ambitions to lose himself in celebration, even if he were capable of such exuberance. Only in Seville, because Don Juan's *Real* had been partly built there, were the festivities conducted on any scale; the silken hangings for the celebration there cost over seven thousand ducats, and the money spent for candles alone would have covered almost all the back pay Cervantes had not yet received. In Toledo, dean and chapter have faithfully since that day obeyed the king's instruction to institute in the cathedral a service of thanksgiving to be performed every October 7 forever. Philip also bestowed various crosses of knighthood, commanderies, rents and money rewards upon the more distinguished officers of his fleet and troops who had been engaged at Lepanto. To Don Juan his gratitude was displayed in a moderately fraternal letter. His Majesty even persuaded the aged Titian, who had declined or evaded the invitation of the doge and the Venetian Senate to commemorate the victory in the ducal palace, to execute a picture on the subject for him—or, at least, there is a picture by Titian in the Prado at Madrid which tradition has connected with Lepanto. Some years afterward, Lucas Cambiaso, a now largely forgotten Genoese painter, was employed by Philip to execute six huge canvases on the theme for the Escorial, where they can still be seen in all their martial mediocrity in the Hall of Battles. Pictures were painted on many Spanish walls to record the triumph, from Santa Cruz's country palace in La Mancha to a gaggle of Dominican convents interested in immortalizing the role of the Dominican Pius V in the victory of Christ.

Even in England, the Christian victory made so deep an impression that, a generation later, Shakespeare established a tumultuous background for *Othello* by excited rumors of Turkish fleet movements on Cyprus, the beginning of the campaign that ended at Lepanto. James VI of Scotland wrote a doggerel narrative of the battle of over 1,100 lines when, according to the preface, he was only twelve or thirteen years old and stirred a furious row over tribute to a "foreign Papist bastard."[5]

Lepanto has frequently appealed to minor English poets as a source of inspiration, usually with notably unvictorious results. There was, for example, Abraham Holland's "Naumachia, or a poeticall description of the cruel and bloudy sea-fight or battaile of Lepanto," published in London in 1632, which ran to such effects as

> That horrid noise the battell made was such,
> Hearing heard nothing, 'cause it heard so much.[6]

Quixote himself would have rejoiced in the

> Stiff flags straining in the night-blasts cold
> In the gloom black-purple, in the glint old-gold;
> Torchlight crimson on the copper kettledrums,
> Then the tuckets, then the trumpets then the cannons . . .

in G. K. Chesterton's nineteenth-century ballad "Lepanto."

News of the disaster was more than two weeks in reaching the Sultan. When he did hear about it, he stayed out of sight for six days and was with difficulty restrained from massacring all his Spanish and Venetian slaves. Confusion over the extent of Turkish losses, rumors of Christian invasion forces on the move sent thousands of families fleeing in panic from Constantinople. Scattered rebellions broke out in the Balkans in the year following the battle, encouraged by the scantiness of the garrisons in the Turkish forts. A French observer remarked that the appearance of fifty Christian galleys before the Turkish capital would have emptied the city—which is, in fact, what Don Juan had hoped to do.

The welcome given the Spanish galleys on their return to Messina may not have been decorous, but it was certainly noisy. The generalissimo, with part of the Spanish squadron, arrived there late in the afternoon of November 1, All Saints' Day. By the next day, the rest of the Spanish detachment and the papal galleys had huddled inside the long, protecting arm of the mole in Messina harbor. The wounded could probably hear the shouting and cheering from the crowds massed on the quays, along the shore and on the heights overlooking the port. It is to be supposed that the commander's order for a victory review was less enthusiastically received by the filthy, pain-weary men in their reeking ships. The fleet nevertheless put out to sea again, returning in two columns in precise order, with standards and banners flying, towing the captive Turkish ships stern first with their antennae reversed and their colors trailing in the water. A brave sight, if one didn't look too closely or smell too keenly. Cervantes may have felt as much as heard the salvo of greeting from the fleet's guns that made the very sea under him slip and rear with the impact, followed by the roar of response from the shore batteries and the armed merchantmen in the harbor.

As far as can be made out, it was only then that the wounded were taken off and carted to the hospital, a musket-shot from the port. What expressions did Cervantes see in the faces of the crowd as the carriers filed through? Sympathy? Pity? Smiles of tribute, or a sudden turning away from the reality of that day? Since this man with almost total recall never alluded to the scene at all in his work, we must assume that he was too feverish, too sick and exhausted to absorb any impression beyond a swirling blur and a great din; relief at being ashore again may have obliterated every other feeling, perhaps even anesthetizing the sudden dread of the hospital. For, as was well known—the notion survives to this day in much of the Spanish countryside—a hospital is where one goes to die.

In any case, there were more cheerful events to occupy the crowd. The caudillo and Colonna, fresh from his extravaganza in Rome, landed upon a specially erected and sumptuously decorated platform to be received by the city's clergy and magistrates. Beneath an embroidered canopy, amid the roar of cannon, rattle of musketry, clash of military music and shouting of the multitude, he proceeded to the ancient cathedral to hear the *Te Deum*. Don Juan then was lodged in the palace, where the municipality waited on him the next day with a splendid gift, including a white charger and a sum of thirty thousand crowns which, with his usual cavalier grace, he ordered divided between the hospital and the soldiers who had been wounded or distinguished in battle.[7] Messina, almost as rich as Naples in taverns, brothels and churches, was in a festival fever; the city rang with a golden clangor as the returning troops rioted in triumph— although most of their money, it must be admitted, was looted from the Turks, for their own back pay had, as usual, not yet appeared. According to Venetian Bartolomeo Sereno, who had been aboard Honorato Caetani's *Grifona* at Lepanto, some of the men who had behaved badly in the fight bought trophies and, clothed in Turkish jackets, strutted cockily about like so many Latin Falstaffs. And, he adds in an obvious thrust at Doria, "I know a great captain, whom I saw, who to counterbalance the testimony which his own conscience gave, went about purchasing praise from writers and asked for false accounts, hoping to conceal his vileness by such glory."[8]

The only hint of the revelry to penetrate the thick walls of the hospital would have come from the carrying in of some celebrant cut up in a tavern brawl or left for dead in one of the obscure streets near the port. Inside those walls, life was grim and life was earnest. Astrana Marín observed in his biography that Cervantes served all the apprenticeships of misery—hospital, slavery and prison—and that they were all stages of the same horror. At least Cervantes had a bed to himself. In many hospitals, patients were crowded four and five to a large bed regardless of their ailments.

Although the more enlightened institutions isolated some infectious diseases, notably plague and typhus, others imposed a more democratic sharing of vermin: pregnant women lay with victims of gunshot wounds and venereal disease and cholera, often in feather beds with feather comforters which functioned as incubators of bacteria. If a patient upset his inevitable cup of herb tea, he and his bedmates lay in the wet until it dried of itself, for linens were only occasionally changed. Chamber pots between the beds helped spread infection, filling the cracks in the floors. Such operations as were performed were carried out in the wards, the patient having been psychologically prepared for his ordeal by the sight of the instruments—the saws and mallets and knives which enterprising surgeons later in the century took pains to keep sharp—laid out beside him ready for use. Not surprisingly, more hospital patients died of their cures than died of their ills. And those whom medicine spared had other dangers to fear. Men died of hunger for lack of a friend to help them. For a man without money, a hospital was little more than a mortuary. But if he did have some, he was considered fair game for the hospital wolves, orderlies ignorant of medicine but adroit in rascality, and the professional thieves who feigned illness—it was easy then, when the doctors knew hardly any more about disease than the patients—so that, from their hospital beds, they could reconnoiter and rob the living, the dying and the dead. In *The Life and Deeds of Estebanillo González*, the anonymous seventeenth-century author of this most cynical of all memoirs describes his brief service, after some three months of disastrous apprenticeship to a Roman barber-surgeon, as a licensed surgeon in the Santiago de los Españoles Hospital in Naples.

His first duty was to bleed a patient at the chief surgeon's orders. "Reaching the sick man's bed," he recounts,

I bared his right arm and, rubbing it gently, I strangled it with a shoelace I had acquired from a wench in an inn along the road. I got out the lancet and, since I had read, while leafing through the books (on surgery) of my late master, that the vein must be well pierced if a bleeding is to succeed, (and since) I was master more by science than by experience, I cut it so thoroughly that the wound looked more like a crooked stroke from a Moor's lance than an upright barber's lancet slash. In the end, I came out of this so well that the sufferer lost only that arm, but his left remained sound because it had not been touched by the point of my blade, from which God deliver all faithful Christians.[9]

A few days later, a malarial soldier who threatened to expose Estebanillo's lack of zeal was quickly dispatched to the next world by a dose of icy water.

Finally, Estebanillo struck gold:

> One night when I was on duty, I happened to pay several brief visits to a student because I saw that he was very tired and extremely nauseous, and since my eyes were lynx-like and my hands like dragnets, when I raised his head and bent him over double to see whether, by so doing, I could relieve a cough that was suffocating him, I spied a purse he had (placed) under his pillow, with twelve *doblas* forming the column and fifty *reales de a ocho* as the capital. I realized that he was on the alert and so I deferred the stroke to a better time, and so that he might not grow suspicious of me, as soon as I had done with my errand I cleared out of there like a company of harquebusiers and, when he was overcome by a mortal faintness, the patients nearest his bed raised a shout, bidding me rush to help this scholar to die comfortably and to bring him a confessor.
>
> I, seeing that his hour to account to God had come and mine to account for his purse, sent a comrade of mine to fetch the chaplain, while I, playing the hypocrite to the hilt, more for the money than for the half-dead student, threw myself headlong over the pillow and intoned:
>
> *"Jesus, Maria, in manus tuas, Domine, commendo spiritum meum,"* while my hand stole under the pillow. And for my hand to seize the little mine of such precious metals and to slip it into my own pouch was all one gesture, as I repeated:
>
> "Jesus, Jesus, God go with thee."
>
> The onlookers thought the "God go with thee" was said for the patient, but it was nothing of the sort, for I said it to the purse, on account of the danger it ran from the bed to its tomb in my breeches . . . later I had two masses said for him . . . since I had been left his legitimate heir.[10]

A burlesque, of course, but less invented than merely elliptical. Cervantes faced fewer dangers because he was in what had become a military hospital. And, we suppose, his brother Rodrigo was able to wangle leave to care for him, at least until he was out of danger. The hospital's reputation, however, had led Don Juan to assign his surgeon general, Don Gregorio López Madera, to supervise the care of the wounded. He was a distinguished figure, surgeon general also to Philip II as he had been to the Emperor Charles V, and one of the first in Spain to accept the new theory that bullet wounds were not poisonous after all, and that a ball in a non-vital organ could safely be removed. He had also accepted the theories most conspicuously championed by the renowned French barber-surgeon Ambroise Paré dispensing with direct cauterization of a bullet wound with a hot iron or boiling oil in favor of soothing applications of a balm of egg yolks, oil of roses and turpentine.

Navarro y Ledesma conjures a moving image of López Madera in his flat, black doctor's bonnet (unadorned, however, by the physician's feather, as his thumb was unhampered by the physician's huge ring) and his black gown, filing through the ward in which Cervantes lay, followed by aides carrying his surgical kit and his bag of unguents. The biographer pictures him reassuring the wounded poet, peering down at him through his spectacles as he cleans and dresses his wounds while Cervantes bites his lip in pain.[11]

Another image recurs in books by Spanish writers dazzled by the juxtaposition of two of Spain's most glamorous figures, the Prince of Wits and the bastard Prince of Austria, Don Juan. The commander visited the hospital some ten days after his return to Messina to cheer his men. It is standard to assume some mystic communion between the stricken, blond young poet and his dashing, blond young chieftain, as though Juan were a pleasingly urbane John the Baptist paying premonitory homage to the Master of Spanish Letters. But all aside from the question of Don Juan's transcendental powers, the place was, as we have seen, alive with heroes. Quite possibly the general's morale-boosting tour of the wounded included a stop at Miguel's bedside—the man's wounds *were* grave, after all—as it did at a score of others. Miguel must already have been a lonely figure, dutiful and earnest, but withdrawn and timid, his—hereditary?—shield of indulgent irony still untempered by time and indignity. It is easier to think that he was liked by the few who bothered to know him for the sweetness of his manner, his cheerful optimism, his decency and uprightness, than to imagine him, as so many biographers do, as some tavern spellbinder who could charm the gold out of a Neapolitan whore's teeth. And this may indeed have persuaded, say, an officer who knew him to whisper into the caudillo's ear that "here's a decent fellow, sir, and a brave fighter" whose wounds merited a word of encouragement. Mystical empathy was never in Miguel's line; to invent it merely beclouds the subtler, truer, more appealing youthfulness of spirit that nourished him throughout a notably unrewarding life.

For the moment, he had troubles for which a kindly murmur, from any source unless it were the king himself, could provide only a poor ointment. As the autumn evenings lengthened into winter darkness, Miguel must surely have been so sickened with fear and chagrin as with the persistent pain and the fever. By Christmas he would presumably have known he wasn't going to die. That much was off his mind. His hand still bled; it would be bleeding yet two years later when

> . . . the blood still flowing from the chiefest wound, though two more there were, I wished to go, to be present to see the Moor defeated . . .[12]

in Don Juan's brief conquest of Tunis. Worse still, the damned hand refused to respond to his will. At least it was his left hand. But it is not hard to read his thoughts as he lay there and stared at that misery of a hand lying useless on the blanket, good only to give him pain. Staring into the great fire at one side of the ward, staring at the altar under the gilt retable at the foot of the room, staring at the smudged light filtering through the dirt of the high windows, the terrible conviction would gradually have pushed its way into his mind that his hopes were as dead as those fingers. What kind of a future was there for a one-handed soldier? An administrative job? With no glory, precious little advancement and no fortune but what he could steal? Better go back to holding Acquaviva's towels. Had he fled from Madrid to save his right hand only to lose his left? Much later on he would find rationalizations for the exchange: in the *Voyage to Parnasus* he would proclaim that the movement of his left hand had been sacrificed "to the greater glory of the right."

That he would dandle the day in his memory, showing it off with an almost pathetic satisfaction as a day when honor prevailed, is an irony worthy of him. Recurrent assertions, as in *Don Quixote,* in *The Faithful Sentinel,* in the *Persiles,* that a soldier's life is nobler than a scholar's have been generally taken at face value. Fitzmaurice-Kelly saw in Cervantes' simple, innocent pride in his record of Lepanto an assurance of immortality which not even "the lapse of forty haggard years (could) wither in its infinite variety."[13]

Cervantes did have a way of seeing himself in categories; he was the Soldier coetaneously with the Poet, the Playmaker, the Novelist, the Captive. And grand at all of them, an opinion in which he frequently invites us to concur. Of all these acquired identities, the most vivid was surely that of the Soldier, for, after all, he had only to look down to be reminded of it.

Yet he had learned lessons in those forty haggard years which jar against this activist image. He had, for one thing, perceived the emptiness of Spain's heroic myth with its arrogant impatience of failure; through Quixote he tells us that neither power nor success is important—only purity of heart and the will's survival. War he was to pronounce as an "impious" thing, for it

. . . destroys the native and the foreigner.
It consumes, burns, hurls down
kingdoms and populous empires
and exiles most beauteous peace,
and its proud ministers, more covetous
of golden metal than of any other thing,
disturb our contentment and repose,
and in bloody, perilous war . . .
hold her in prison's bound
to see if we will promise, for her ransom,
our miserable, hard-won wealth.[14]

The mature Cervantes can be seen in his work as a man mistrustful of violence in all its forms. In Philippine Spain, Lope de Vega's Spain, where there was seldom any question that the sword was at least as mighty as the pen, surprisingly few of Cervantes' characters live by violence. Most of these are criminals, burlesques, cardboard heroes. Overt violence is clownish, a slapstick indictment of the underlying violence of life itself and of death as the ultimate absurdity, never triumphant, seldom satisfying. When a Cervantes character dies—rarely by violence—his death is so stylized, so ritual, almost choreographic, that a reader's reaction is more aesthetic than visceral. Only twice, when Don Quixote dies and when Carrizales expires in *The Jealous Extremaduran,* is death a real presence in Cervantes' work.

Why, then, did this pacific, life-celebrating, violence-hating man, this theoretician, keep coming back to his soldiering days? Almost certainly he suffered from common author's *angoisse,* the intellectual's resentment of his role as a spectator, the feeling of being cheated of "real" life that so often generates activist fantasies. Then again, as he and his country aged, Cervantes' growing sensitivity to the decaying Spanish world around him may have become associated in his mind with his own "forty haggard years." What more natural than to identify his youth with what seemed to have been a golden age of established values and simple virtues? Is it any wonder that his mind should have periodically retreated over the decades of despair to the crude, comforting purity of physical heroism and youthful daring? Is it surprising that he should have recalled the rapt wholeness of that hopeful, eager time—a time when patriotism was more genuine than it ever would be again—with an almost incredulous pride? How remote, how unreal those flamboyant days must have seemed to him, and how necessary their assertion. He did so with restraint: his debt to Lepanto was discharged in fewer than a dozen pages among all the thousands he wrote. He had learned, by that time, the harsher, weightier heroism of endurance.

How important was the battle of Lepanto to Western history? It did not destroy Turkish power. By the following summer, a new fleet of some 250 ships was on the water, built largely of green timber and manned by green crews who so trembled at tales of Lepanto that they had to be driven aboard with sticks, but nonetheless a presence to be reckoned with. Venice would soon be little more than a Turkish tributary. The Ottoman Empire was intact and undiminished.

Nevertheless, in halting the momentum of Turkish expansionism, Lepanto probably began the century-long process of Ottoman disintegration. Equally significant was the destruction of the myth of Turkish invincibility. Now it was the world's turn to fear Spanish "invincibility" until that myth, too, drowned in the waters around Britian with the "Invincible Armada." Certainly Catherine de Medici was frightened in France; by detaching her from Coligny's anti-Spanish policy, Lepanto probably contributed to the St. Bartholomew's Day Massacre. Indeed, the recession of the Moslem-Christian rivalry turned the spotlight on the antagonism between Catholics and Protestants. The center of European history moved from the Mediterranean into the Atlantic.

In disengaging from its Western operations, the Porte was also obliged to alter its policy toward its Western provinces. Turkish discipline in the Barbary states necessarily slackened, not only because it was harder to enforce, but because the empire's energies were distracted by new troubles on its eastern frontiers. The Barbary corsairs roamed almost at will, functioning as Ottoman privateers, waging a hit-and-run guerrilla fight against the Christian powers to supply the deficiency of a full Turkish fleet. Neither a weakened Venice nor a distracted Spain whose attention was being increasingly diverted toward the Low Countries was capable of effectively policing the Mediterranean against the North African raiders —a fact which, even as the spring of 1572 approached, was working to change Cervantes' life.

By late February, Miguel was probably able to move shakily about the ward on his own, freeing Rodrigo to rejoin Diego de Urbina's company in winter quarters in Calabria. So the news that entered his bleak, damp little world would most likely have been fragmentary. Just as well: it was all bad.

Distrust among the allies was reaching a crisis, effectively annulling any hope of a united crusade. Both Venice and Spain were trying to pull the League in different directions, Venice toward the Levant, Spain toward North Africa, leaving an already failing pope the only advocate of holy war. Pius was still influential enough to persuade the allies to muster a fleet in Messina harbor in early spring. But the effort exhausted him.

On May 1, 1572, he died (with the aid, it is said, of a dose of curdled ass's milk which brought on a fatal fever) in his sixty-eighth year.

Philip immediately ordered Don Juan to suspend action, on the partly spurious grounds of an imminent rupture with France. It is true that French feints in Italy, combined with French threats to intervene on the side of the rebels in the uprising which had broken out in Flanders in April of that year, required a Spanish riposte. But Philip was well aware that a France divided by internal religious struggles and enfeebled by a succession of military defeats was in no position to make serious trouble for the strongest nation on earth. Unenthusiastic about draining Spanish resources to fight Venice's battles, he was maneuvering instead for a blow at Algiers, hoping to realize the old dynastic dream of making the Western Mediterranean a Spanish lake.

Venetian howls of treason would have been justified had not Venice itself been contemplating treason; at the brink of ruin from high taxes and loss of trade, it was even then dickering, through the good offices of the French ambassador to Constantinople, for a separate peace. For the time being, the Sultan's terms were too stiff. Philip, convinced it would serve no good end but under pressure from every quarter, at last agreed to a League expedition against the Morea. He insisted, however, that Don Juan, with part of the Spanish fleet, remain in Palermo to parry any French mischief in Italy.

In April, Cervantes was finally released from the hospital. We know only that he spent the next two to three months in Messina, posted to Lope de Figueroa's tercio while Rodrigo remained in Miguel de Moncada's unit. The general assumption, based on no evidence, is that despite his useless hand he returned to the ranks as an active, gun-toting infantryman. It is not impossible to fire a harquebus with one hand, probably no more difficult than climbing a ship's ladder on skis. But it is more reasonable to suppose that he was given some sort of non-combatant duties.

He was, in any case, well enough to play a bit part in the next act of the Holy League comedy. On July 7, 1572, while a petulant Don Juan waited in Palermo for a French move that never came, fifty-eight papal and Spanish vessels sailed to a rendezvous at Corfu with the Venetian fleet to begin the League's "spring" campaign. At Spanish insistence, Veniero had been replaced as the Republic's commander by Jacopo Foscarini, a pompous veteran of senatorial infighting whose principal claim to command was the ability to deploy a shade more tact in his dealings with the Spanish than his predecessor could summon. Both the Cervantes brothers were in the Spanish squadron under Gil de Andrada's command, as we know from Miguel's 1590 memorandum to Philip II: ". . . and the following year he (Miguel) was at Navarino and later in (the expedition) to Tunis and La Goleta . . . and (so was) a brother of his, who also served His Majesty in the same campaigns."

For weeks, a combined force of 13 papal, 22 Spanish and 105 Venetian galleys, 6 Venetian galleasses, 24 supply ships, 21,000 troops and 30,000 crewmen fiddled in Corfu while Don Juan burned. Then, just as the fleet prepared to leave for Gumenitza, a letter arrived from the caudillo; a victory over the French in Flanders had persuaded King Philip to release him for duty; he was free and impatient to assume the glorious command of this glorious expedition for the conquest of further glory. Leaving Doria in Sicily with a police patrol, he scampered almost immediately to Corfu. He would be there, his letter advised, within two weeks with 55 more galleys, 2 Tuscan galleasses, 40 transports and 15,000 men. The fleet was to wait in Corfu until he arrived.

On August 14, he sailed into a virtually empty harbor at Corfu. The fleet? Gone chasing the Turks. Almost apoplectic with rage, the commander in chief vowed to punish Colonna, swore to have Andrada's head for insubordination. He dispatched Santa Cruz to find his errant squadrons and bring them back to Corfu.

Colonna had received his commander's letter on July 29, just as his ships were getting under way. He conferred briefly with Andrada and Foscarini. The fleet's orders had been to bring the Turkish armada to action, but not to besiege any fortress if it left the unprotected ships exposed to a surprise attack. Foscarini pressed lightly but effectively on the hesitant Colonna and Andrada an ambiguous authorization in Don Juan's letter for advance units to proceed without him if any Venetian island was threatened. Were not all Venetian islands threatened? The fleet hurried out of port to begin a solemnly farcical game of hide-and-seek which would leave everyone but the slippery Euldj Ali steaming with frustration.

On August 4 they reached the island of Kythera, where they were told the Turkish fleet was at Malvasia, thirty-five miles away on the east coast of the Elso peninsula. Foscarini, alleging the weakness and lack of confidence of the Turks, urged immediate pursuit. In fact, the Turkish force outnumbered the Christian in ships and men, although its speed and firepower were decidedly inferior.

With more imagination than science, Colonna insisted that the guns of the sailing ships be used in support of the line of galleys. There ensued an orgy of maneuvering which proved to everyone's satisfaction but his that sailing ships and oared galleys could not work together. While the Christians advanced to the Dragoniere Islands, Euldj Ali, leading a fleet of some 210 vessels whose weaknesses he knew too well to want to commit them to battle, ran down to Cape Malea, on the southeastern tip of the Morea. On August 7, the Christians sighted the Turkish fleet hugging the shore as it slipped around the cape. As quickly as they could, the League's captains formed up in battle order similar to the Lepanto formation, except that the sailing ships were interposed between the galleasses and the galleys, where they could create maximum chaos in the Christian operation. Euldj Ali crossed over to Kythera, his long line almost filling the channel; his objective was to gain the regular noon breeze from the west and run down on the League line when the sailing ships were helpless. But the breeze betrayed him; under a brisk east wind, the Christian line began to close in on him. The Turkish commander retreated, ordering his ships to row backward to disguise his flight. The fleets were still miles apart when, in the late afternoon, the wind failed entirely, leaving the sailing ships becalmed. Euldj Ali drew up his line, willing to fight the galleys alone, counting on his numerical superiority to make up for his second-rate equipment. But Colonna, his honor at stake, refused to leave the sailing ships behind; opinion in the fleet, he asserted, would not allow it. Forty-eight galleys were diverted to tow them. As the Christians majestically advanced, the Turks backed water. This elephantine saraband continued until dusk when, with all lights out and under cover of a salvo for a smoke screen, the Turkish galleys disappeared. Sending a message back to Don Juan, the Christians returned to port to take on fresh water.

The posse set out again on August 9, sailing westward in pursuit of the enemy. Finding nothing, its leaders that night decided to return to Corfu to protect Don Juan's smaller force. But, on the following morning, the Sultan's navy was spied approaching Cape Matapan. Challenge shots were exchanged at once. This time the fleets bombarded each other, a display in which the Turkish gunners brilliantly proved their incompetence, but the day's performance closely adhered to the scenario of the fleets' previous encounter. Once more, the Turks literally vanished in a puff of smoke and fled to Quaglia.

The confrontation did persuade Colonna that his precious sailing ships were useless in a fight. With or without a breeze, they could be outmaneuvered by the more agile galleys because their guns did not have the power to hold the enemy at a respectful distance. He now decided that the only hope of accomplishing anything on the expedition lay in rejoining Don Juan. Within thirty-six hours, the fleet reached Zante. Colonna, at least, was keenly aware of having made a fool of himself.

When the joint fleet assembled in Corfu on September 1, there was much saluting and elaborate ceremonial, somewhat spoiled in effect by the young generalissimo's temper tantrum. Because Andrada stood up to him, and there was no question of severity with the already defiant Venetians, Don Juan made Colonna his scapegoat. He heaped abuse on that mild-mannered man's bald head. The papal commander was too dispirited even to remind his superior that, since he and Foscarini constituted a majority of the high command, they had a right to carry out any decision they chose to make.

When the supreme commander had worked off his spleen, a surly council of war was held aboard the *Real* on September 6. With the fighting season so far advanced, Don Juan agreed to give up any hope of the land campaign which had been the expedition's primary objective. Instead, they would seek another final battle with the Turkish fleet. On the following day, most of the sailing ships were dispatched with the horses, land artillery and siege machinery to shelter under the guns of the fort on Zante. The rest of the fleet at last got going on the eleventh. After two months at sea, Miguel de Cervantes must have felt as foul as he doubtless smelled. But he and his fellow crusaders were still a long, weary, feckless way from home.

At Cephalonia, the Christians learned that the Turkish fleet, still short-handed and weakened by sickness, was split between Modon and Na-varino (Pylos), seven miles apart on the southeastern tip of the Pelopon-nesus. Taking on eight days' worth of water and several boatloads of throwing stones, the League force moved to trap the Turks while they were still divided, in the hopes of polishing off the two segments sepa-rately. Some thirty miles from Modon it pulled up, staying out of sight so as not to startle the enemy into rejoining forces prematurely. The Chris-tian captains calculated that a night's rowing would bring them to Modon at dawn on September 16, bottling up the seventy Turkish galleys there. The plan would have succeeded had not the *Real*'s pilots gotten lost and brought the armada eight miles too far to the west. When the ex-asperated Christians finally sighted Modon, they could do no more than watch impotently as the Turkish detachment from Navarino filed into the harbor.[15]

The backing and filling, hardly even enlivened by a fruitless attempt to capture Navarino, went on for three more weeks. On October 6, with supplies low and rain sheeting down like a curtain falling after the sum-mer's exit, the Christians sailed for Italy.

This was not quite the end. Euldj Ali came out of Modon to try to capture two Christian supply ships waiting to be towed out. There was a brief skirmish in which Santa Cruz's *Loba* captured Mamut Bey's galley, as recounted in *Don Quixote*. It was the sole prize in a three-month cam-paign by 76,000 men.

] 13 [

The Sand Castles

For most of Lope de Figueroa's 2,668 men, Naples in the winter of 1572–73 was a sour place. The weather was cold and wet, giving the Mediterranean a sullen, rumpled look. The summer's fiasco had left everyone feeling flat. When the men's back pay arrived at all, it came in driblets. An official order on February 11, 1573, authorized payment of ten escudos to Miguel de Çerbantes,* soldier in the company of Don Manuel Ponce de Leon "on account of what is owed him." Ten more were disbursed on February 14 and on March 6 he received another "twenty escudos he claimed are owed him"; twenty more reached him a few weeks later. Everyone scrabbled to keep himself in gambling money. Most of the soldiers lived on handouts, loans, thefts until the next installment came, often as much as a year late and never in full. "All or most things in war involve asperity, harshness and inconvenience," Cervantes later recalled.[1] He probably welcomed the rest, however; the past eighteen months had been more than moderately charged with asperity, etc., and his wounds were still troubling him. But, like most of his comrades, he was probably eager for action to erase the record of Modon and Navarino.

Don Juan was determined to get an early start that year. The rendezvous was set for April 15 in Corfu. Philip and the Venetians had agreed on a force of three hundred galleys for the coming campaign; every shipyard in Spain was busy turning out the 150 ships needed for the Spanish contingent. Venice, meanwhile, made a lively show of recruiting large numbers of infantrymen to fill its unfillable quota.

The serenissima's brisk preparations made the blow all the more shocking when it came. On March 7, for the second time in a generation,

* Miguel spelled his name with the *b*, but without the cedilla under the *C*.

Venice secretly signed a separate peace with Constantinople. The news
was formally announced in Venice April 4, when the papal nuncio and
the Spanish ambassador were summoned to the doge's palace to hear the
Republic's reasons. The ambassador, predictably, bewailed the day Spain
had agreed to support the perfidious Venetians; the pope, when he heard
the news, threatened to excommunicate the entire Republic. When, three
days later, a ducal emissary arrived in Naples to inform Don Juan of the
terms of the "black peace," he was refused audience. Instead, the
generalissimo hurried to the port and ordered the Holy League colors removed from the mast of the *Real* and the flag of Spain raised in its place.
Bitterly he remarked to Juan de Zúñiga that bad habits are lost late or
never.

This sense of outraged virtue has been carefully preserved by Spanish
historians, although to King Philip's credit must be laid his mildness
when news of the treaty reached Madrid on April 17. He recognized that
Venice had good reasons for seeking peace. It had been keenly disappointed at what it felt was its allies' lack of support. The trade it lived on
was crippled; despite the high taxes which the pinched Venetian merchants increasingly resented, its treasury was empty. Most telling of all,
perhaps, was a pervasive feeling that there was no way to win this war,
even at the cost of national ruin. The Mediterranean was too big, the Ottoman Empire too rich and too remote. The practical Venetians had decided to cut their losses. The thirty-year treaty, virtually a declaration of
surrender to the Porte, gave Venice back its trade, at usurious cost, including the payment of reparations of 300,000 gold sequins. Turkey was
confirmed in its possession of Cyprus. Venice was not to man more than
sixty galleys a year. Even Philip's poise must have been shaken, however,
by one Turkish concession: the Sultan promised to defend Venice against
any attack by her former allies.

In the long run, Philip was probably more pleased than offended.
Discharged of his obligation to the Holy League, relieved for the moment
of the need for further slaughter of the Dutch, he was able to turn to
more congenial pursuits. That spring, the translation of royal remains to
the half-completed monastery of San Lorenzo del Escorial began in a
series of solemn funerals. The body of Elisabeth de Valois, Cervantes'
"most serene Queen," went first, followed by that of the unfortunate Don
Carlos and, finally, by the remains of Emperor Charles V in a huge ma-
hogany casket.

Housing his relatives in a suitably imperial mausoleum was, however, a
private pleasure. Urged on by Don Juan, who was running out of potential kingdoms to conquer, Philip elected to try to subjugate North Africa
and neutralize the Barbary corsairs.

Piracy was not an exclusively Spanish preoccupation. No Christian coastline in the Mediterranean was safe from North African raiders; no lone Christian merchant ship was immune from fear of that dreaded moment when

> . . . some distant sail a speck supplies
> with all the thirsting eye of Enterprize . . .[2]

Only France, allied with the Porte, was relatively free from harassment. But because only Spain could stand up to the Sultan's guerrilla navy in the West, life on the coasts of Spain and its Mediterranean possessions was specially precarious. Whole stretches of coast were deserted by people who fled inland to escape the raids.

The North Africans were by no means the only pirates in the area; the Mediterranean was as lawless a thoroughfare as any back street in Barcelona or Marseilles. Christian raiders stuffed the markets of the region with loot; Uskoks, the water bandits of the Adriatic, operated from impregnable bases near Fiume. The French, the Florentines, the Dutch, the English, the papacy all engaged in Mediterranean piracy at one or another period. The galleys of the Knights of Malta, with Spanish backing, functioned almost exclusively as a pirate fleet in peacetime; the Order of St. Stephen, a company of international adventurers, theoretically limited its raids to Moslem shipping, but it was not above torturing a Christian captain into saying his ship was Turkish in order to justify pillage. Ships fitted out as "privateers" by the wife of the Viceroy of Naples had to tow a captive home on one raid because "its wealth could not be contained in their vessels"; privateers were welcomed back to Naples "like conquerors, with bonfires and celebrations, just as if they had returned after winning a decisive victory over a mighty and terrible foe."[3] By 1580, so many slaves had been taken by Christian corsairs, chiefly from Spain and Spanish Italy, that the price of slaves collapsed on local markets. Christians even lent their Barbary competitors a hand when the price was right; Tunisian pirates, in agreement with the Grand Duke of Tuscany, set up a warehouse in Livorno where Christian slaves were deposited to await ransoming in reasonably humane conditions. Long before then, the Venetians ran a brisk trade in Christian slaves with the Turks. But then, Cervantes would later note, "no one who lends himself to such activities, of whatever faith or nation, has anything but a cruel and insolent nature."[4]

Nevertheless, Christian privateers (the term describes any pirate operating for *our* side) were to the Barbary pirates (the noun for any privateer operating for *their* side) what a Sicilian shoplifter is to a New York vice lord. Organized in pre-Roman times as a defense force against marauding Europeans, by the sixteenth century the North African pirate fleets were compact military establishments which provided the bulk of the Barbary states' official revenues. The damage they did was enormous; in one season alone, they made off with more than fifty ships in the Strait of Gibraltar and off the Atlantic coasts of Iberia. By the 1570s, roughly 250,000 Christian slaves were held in Algeria alone. It has been calculated that, from its founding in 1198 to 1789, the Trinitarian Order of monks alone ransomed over 900,000 Europeans from Barbary captivity, including St. Louis of France.

Yet the corsairs were always vulnerable to Spanish attack at any time Spain might choose to press one. Imperial problems—lack of funds and manpower for concentrated action in one area—had so far restricted Spanish efforts to little more than raids in force. Now Philip, with a powerful fleet at his disposal, may have dreamed of a full-fledged war, one that could achieve a triple objective: to wipe out the Barbary plague, turn the western Mediterranean into a Spanish pond and effectively close the southern gap in Spain's ring around France. It would also, he reasoned, cement the loyalty to him of Spain's Moriscos by cutting them off from Turkish encouragement.

The first question was where to strike. Santa Cruz favored an immediate offensive against Algeria, the strongest and richest of the Sultan's western provinces. Philip turned the idea down. Perhaps he had in mind the ordeal his father had undergone there a generation earlier. More probably, he rejected the idea because he rejected the source.

Don Juan urged the capture of Tunis. He had been thinking a great deal about Tunis lately, and about the papal promise, reaffirmed by Gregory XIII, to anoint him king of the first land he conquered. In 1572 he had sent Don Jaime de Losada there, ostensibly to arrange for an exchange of prisoners, but in fact to spy out the situation. And, however much Philip might have preferred to disregard his brother's suggestions, there was a lot going for the idea.

Spanish troops occupied La Goleta, the fort perched fiercely, like a great gray falcon on a hunter's arm, on a spit of land facing the narrow inlet opening into the Lake of Tunis. The wealth of the place rivaled that of Algiers, but its defenses did not. Its former king, Muley Hamida, "the cruelest and most valiant Moor to be found in the world" according to Cervantes,[5] had been chased from his throne by Euldj Ali in 1570 and was currently in La Goleta plotting his revenge.

Discussion of the proposal dragged on into the summer. Naples, meanwhile, was busy but confused. A bewildered Fray Miguel de Servía (Don Juan's confessor) complained that "no one knows where the campaign will be, but great preparations go on. Many mills and ovens have been installed in Naples. . . ."[6]

For the moment, this contentious game of blindman's buff left little time or energy for the cultural entertainments we must suppose attracted Cervantes and his friends in Italy. The talk in the taverns and the barracks was chiefly of the coming campaign, or about the generalissimo's magnificence; when he loaded a crowd of friends and a pride of Neapolitan beauties into twelve galleys and sailed out of Naples harbor to celebrate his saint's day in a friend's gardens in Pozzuoli, the whole city stopped to goggle with pleasure. And all but a few dour souls slapped their ragged thighs in approval when the Paladin of Christendom, despite his complaints of destitution, returned a gift sent by the Sultan's sister as ransom for the two sons of Ali Pasha captured at Lepanto. She had forwarded enough ermines and sables, rubies, turquoises, damascene swords, porcelains and other such cosies to keep every trooper in Naples in luxury for a month. One of the boys had died of a fever, Don Juan regretfully informed her; he was sending the other home, with her gifts, "because the greatness of my ancestors has accustomed me not to receive gifts from those in need of favors, but to give them and to show largesse."[7]

Philip finally agreed to attack Tunis, but under conditions which offered no satisfaction to his brother. The king, after all, had no intention of conquering Tunis, which he realized would mean simply one more endless drain on the Spanish treasury. What he had in mind was a raid to restore Muley Hamida to the throne, thus giving Spain an ally in Tunis. His specific orders to Don Juan were to capture the city, dismantle its defenses, restore the fugitive king and get out. To make his meaning unmistakable, Philip fired Don Juan's secretary, Juan de Soto, whom he suspected of fostering the Bastard's royal ambitions; in his place he would show more resistance to the paladin's charm.

Since none of the rank and file knew of these restrictions but all knew of the caudillo's ambitions, twenty thousand Cervanteses were elated when news of the campaign leaked down to their level. All of them hoped that if they distinguished themselves in the fight and Don Juan did become king of Tunis, their futures would be made.

On August 1, 1573, the commander moved his forces to Messina, picking up Santa Cruz's galleys and trying unsuccessfully to pry loose from Granvelle, the viceroy of Naples, at least part of the 150,000 escudos advanced by Philip for the expedition. On the fifteenth the fleet continued on to Palermo. Doria, with forty-eight galleys, was left there on sentry duty. The rest of the fleet finally sailed September 24, over two hundred vessels and nearly twenty thousand soldiers.

It got as far as Trapani before a storm scattered it. Once more, a project proposed in the spring was being carried out in the stormy autumn. Trapani had been expecting the generalissimo. A new quay had been built for him, hung with the red and gold Spanish colors flapping wetly in the wind. A triumphal arch was emblazoned with the royal arms, the city's escutcheon and Don Juan's personal bearings. He was given another horse, a fine gray stallion this time with black and gold trappings, along with an offering of fruits and vegetables.

Not until October 7, the second anniversary of the battle of Lepanto, was the force able to begin the last lap of the crossing to La Goleta, anchoring under its walls on the evening of the eighth.

The sight of a fleet three times as big as anything even Algiers could muster threw the population of Tunis into a panic. As the tercios disembarked near the ruins of Carthage, the three thousand janissaries garrisoning the town, along with the bey and most of the adult population, fled to the mountains, stopping only long enough to loot the town before the Christian dogs could get to it. The news delighted Don Juan; it probably disappointed the soldiers. When the vanguard entered Tunis that evening, filing through the olive orchards where Charles V had won so futile a victory half a century earlier, they found the place deserted, Don Juan wrote to King Philip, except by men and women too old to fly and, in the fort, a couple of Moors with a governor who said he was keeping the place for the king, Muley Hamida. The men had strict orders: no unnecessary killing, no slave-taking, but pillaging at will. Furious at finding no dark-eyed Tunisian women huddled in the houses, even more injured at finding that the Turks had skimmed the cream of the treasure, the troops tore at the walls of golden mud with their pikes, probed the wells with their ships' grappling irons in search of hidden wealth. They ravaged the royal palace, tore apart the ancient mosque with its jasper and porphyry pillars. Someone came across a tame lion cub and presented it to Don Juan; it became his companion and symbol duirng the shockingly little life that remained to him. A few days later, Bizerta surrendered even before Don Juan could move against it.

Backed by his council, the caudillo decided to install Muley Mohammed, Hamida's more malleable brother, as governor as a sign of displeasure at Hamida's shows of independence. The deposed king, weeping in rage and disbelief, was bundled aboard a galley to exile in Spain.

Don Juan, by now half-crazed by thwarted ambition, then proved how right the king had been to distrust him. "In Spain," says the proverb, "the law is observed but not obeyed." Faced with the alternative of razing the fortifications, as he had been ordered to do, or preserving the city as a Spanish and Christian enclave, as the pope had urged, Don Juan chose to lay what he saw as the foundations for his future kingdom. That there was not a hope of milking the Spanish treasury, much less the papal coffers, for the money he would need to conquer and maintain the country against the enemies surrounding it apparently never entered his head. He not only refused to dismantle the fortifications, but ordered the Milanese military architect Gabriele Serbelloni to design and build a huge new fortress on the edge of the salt lake fronting the city. To garrison it, he gave Serbelloni four thousand Spanish and four thousand Italian troops as well as two thousand sappers and one hundred cavalrymen. Governorship of La Goleta was entrusted to Don Pedro Portocarrero, the ineffectual but patriotic father of the Cervantes sisters' seducers in Madrid.

Fortunately for Cervantes' peace of mind, he had received no word from home for many months, perhaps for years. It would have been no comfort to him to learn of his sisters' picaresque adventures, still less to know that his family was penniless again unless some fee could be wrung from the Portocarreros.

Andrea had set herself and her daughter up in separate lodgings and was earning what money she could as a seamstress. Two documents tell us how humbly the family was faring. The first is dated September 1, 1573, and sets forth the terms by which Andrea agreed to take an apprentice, Isabel de Alvear, for two years, promising "to give her food and drink, to clothe and shoe her respectably . . . to house her and give her a bed to sleep in and to wash her clothes and care for her sicknesses" while teaching her to sew.[8] At the end of the contractual period, during which little Isabel would learn more about scrubbing clothes than she would about making them, Andrea guaranteed that the girl would have made herself twenty ducats' worth of finery and would go home to the widow Alvear with six thousand maravedis in cash. Andrea was apparently counting on her lawsuit to supply the money.

The second document, infinitely sadder than the first, is dated September 16, 1573. While Miguel and Rodrigo marked time in Palermo dreaming of repairing the family fortunes once Don Juan should establish his royal household in Tunis, their parents swore before notary Baltasar de Jos to pay a Madrid cloth merchant, Hernando de Bárcenas, twelve ducats in Castilian silver on account of a larger debt. The total amount is unspecified, but it was already overdue. Doña Leonor even pledged to cede the money from her (by that time) largely or wholly non-existent dowry. Rodrigo and his dependents, then, did not even own the clothes on their backs; and given the brief interval, a mere two months, he was allowed for payment, Rodrigo's credit was obviously disappearing faster than the silver from a nobleman's pantry. "This thing called need," Don Quixote would comment, "is to be found everywhere, extends to every region and reaches everyone. . . ."[9] Old Rodrigo—sixty-five was old then —was sinking deeper into his deafness, into a self-sealing isolation into which not even his vihuela could any longer intrude. He may not have been unhappy; one suspects he was past that, past struggling, no longer capable of outrage or despair. This soft, floppy cabbage of a man seems at the end to have finally allowed himself to subside, as he had probably always wanted to do, into a vague semiexistence maintained with, no doubt, affectionate impatience by the sedulous Doña Leonor and his equally resolute daughter Andrea. Only Magdalenita, pliable, ineffectual Magdalena, may have been close to him. It is in Rodrigo's . . . evaporation . . . that we see most clearly why old Juan had so little use for his second son. The buzzard had begot a finch.

In any case, the irony of the Cervantes family situation in that autumn of 1573 was appropriately Cervantine. Miguel may have been convinced that Don Juan had found a promised land for both of them. The last two tercets of his *Epistle to Mateo Vázquez,* written at a time when death seemed his only alternative to slavery, tell us he would have stayed with the Tunis garrison if he could have. Perhaps he went so far as to volunteer; if so, the plea was turned down:

> God knows if I had earnest wish or not
> to share my brave and gallant comrades' fate
> and live or die with them, whate'er their lot!
> But destiny, in her relentless hate,
> willed not that I, in this renowned affair,
> should end my being and my sufferings great.[10]

Still, Don Pedro's continued good health and prosperity were as cheerfully desired by Miguel as they were deplored by his family in Madrid. And when Don Pedro died little more than a year later, the event brought no loss to Miguel and no gain to his sisters.

On October 24, 1573, Don Juan sent half the fleet ahead to Palermo with Santa Cruz; the generalissimo sailed with the rest of his ships before dawn of the following day. He was at sea only a few hours before storms drove him into the coast and pinned him there for a week. It was there that he learned of the death of his half sister, Juana of Austria, who, it was said, was more like him than anyone else on earth. When the *Real* reached Palermo on November 12, to the now customary fanfare, its crimson-and-gold splendor was draped in black and the paladin was dressed in mourning.

An Island Idyll

The men in Lope de Figueroa's tercio groaned when they learned they were to winter in Sardinia. The place had an evil reputation, as the Italians in Palermo gleefully confirmed. It was a place of exile, lonely, rotten with malaria, infected with a poverty so incurable that banditry was, after animal husbandry, the island's principal industry. Its climate was harsh; its dwarf men and dwarf beasts lived in rude, mud-brick houses with hearth-holes in the roofs instead of proper chimneys. And boring, my lads, oh how boring! There was not, people declared, a single thing to do on that obscenity of an island but train your fleas to race and wait for spring.

Yet Sardinia had a mythic quality that may have worked on Cervantes' imagination. It was still Arcadian then, a mysterious, unworldly garden of shepherds and ancient customs, even more tightly clannish than Sicily, primitive to a point of paganism. In Sardinia, the Holy Mother was still closer in nature to Artemis than she was to the Christians' Virgin Mary, and the thousands of brooding stone *nuraghe*—the protohistoric fortified dwellings lying hard by the stone pre-Roman tombs—made even the Huntress seem a latecomer. The Middle Ages sat like a porous shell over the older, darker life of the island; the Renaissance, already senescent on the mainland, had never succeeded in crossing the narrow Tyrrhenian Sea to Cagliari. Sardinians were kindly enough, grave, as quick as Spaniards to take offense. But they kept their distance from the tercios, as though waiting for them, too, to pass away. Besides, they spoke an odd, Latinish language that not even the Neapolitans could understand.

It would be surprising if Cervantes enjoyed being there. Islands in his stories are usually bleak, stony places, cold and desolate and full of unknown terrors. And the Italians had been right; there was absolutely nothing to do there, nowhere to go. Occasionally, on feast days, there was dancing in the villages, and bareback riders raced their stunted horses through the streets. But, mostly, time was a narrow, gray strip of light between the sagging sky and the mud underfoot.

Cervantes probably did make two brief escapes to Naples; there are pay records allotting him thirty escudos on February 15, 1574, and as much again on March 10. There must have been time in Naples for reunion with old friends. We know that Laínez was there because Cervantes tells us so in the curious pastoral code in his novel *La Galatea*. It was the habit of poets in this period of classical rediscovery to adopt pseudonyms from Greek and Latin poetry. A listing discovered some years ago in the Spanish National Library cites some of them: Lope de Vega, for example, called himself Belardo, Cervantes' friend Francisco de Figueroa was Tirsi (taken from Virgil's *Eclogues*), Laínez took his Damon from the same source. Cervantes himself was Lauso. The choice is interesting; in Virgil's *Aeneid*, Mezentius, the father of Lausus, is slain in battle by Aeneas. Lausus, though badly outmatched, rushes to exact vengeance. Despite Aeneas' reluctance—"Why rush upon death, and overdare thy strength?" he reasons; "love fools thee into rashness"—Lausus persists until he is killed.[1]

In Cervantes' *La Galatea*, which, like all pastoral novels of the period, was a *roman à clef*, Damon (Laínez) is revealed as being one of the three persons who knew Lauso's mistress, which, if the theory of Cervantes' Neapolitan love affair is admitted, puts Laínez in Naples in 1574–75, probably along with Tirsi (Figueroa), Cervantes' neighbor from Alcalá de Henares. Rey de Artieda, the boy wonder—at fourteen he had already earned praise as a poet from the great Gaspar Gil Polo—may have come on leave from La Goleta. They doubtless filled him in on such literary gossip as the row over Torquato Tasso's *Aminta,* one of the greatest of the Italian pastoral dramas, recently published and then being eagerly vivisected in the academies, reviving the argument over the relative merits of Tasso and Ariosto.

One may question how seriously Cervantes was taken by his friends. Both Laínez and Figueroa were considerably older men, and both had already acquired reputations as poets; Tirsi, who had attended universities in Italy, was respected even there for the melancholy Petrarchist verses he wrote in both Spanish and Italian. Rey de Artieda, although younger than Miguel, was not only a precocious poet and scholar, but a captain in the army to boot. It may be that the still unknown youngsters—Cervantes, Cristóbal de Virués and others—were the group's mascots, received with parental indulgence. For they had the important things in common: they had all been through the horror of war, they were all

(like most literary Spaniards) convinced of the superiority of Italian letters. And they shared an almost mystical reverence for poetry,

> . . . glory of the heavens and of the earth,
> the very stuff of the muses' delectation;
> it opens all secrets, and it encloses all. . . .
> Be thou more eager in its presence. . . .[2]

These Neapolitan interludes were brief, however. There was a steady
shuttle of Lope de Figueroa's troopers moving between Sardinia and the
mainland on similar errands and Cervantes would have had to return to
base promptly to let another man take his turn. After the easy distractions
of cosmopolitan Naples, the sodden tedium of Sardinia must have been
excruciating. Perhaps it was there, in the endless barracks card games and
dice marathons, that Cervantes cultivated the taste for gambling that
stayed with him for the rest of his life. He later declared that it was soldiering that taught him to be "liberal"[3]—the word in Spanish has a sense
of easy-come-easy-go carelessness about money. But he almost certainly
returned from Naples with another antidote for boredom in which few of
his comrades are likely to have joined him: poetry.

No manuscript remains to us to prove this. But the probability is strong
that *La Galatea* began to take shape in the pastoral simplicity of Sardinia. This was a period when Cervantes' mind was greedily engorging
what chunks of Italian Renaissance culture it could scrounge; references
to Italy, to Italian poets, to classical literature, are threaded through his
writing like the fat in a salami. With his brain stuffed with barely
digested classical titbits, his self-esteem encouraged by older, recognized
artists, and his hand wanting any labor more arduous than clutching a
deck of cards, it would be surprising had he not ceded to his poetic yearnings. Thinking about, perhaps reading, the *Aminta* may very well have
moved him to speculate, as he watched the squat, taciturn Sard herdsmen
drive their flocks through the village streets in the wintry dusk, whether
he might do, if not as well, at any rate as much. One imagines a work—
perhaps a play, perhaps a book—beginning to take shape in his thoughts,
a rough kind of shape, perhaps hardly more than an idea and an aspiration, beating in the stately rhythms of pastoral verse. Picture him sitting
apart from the others, staring with wide, vacant eyes at the shadows cast
by the light from the oil lamps on rough, whitewashed walls, his paralyzed hand clamped heavily across a sheet of paper, his shoulders shrug-
ging distractedly at the sarcasms from the cardplayers across the room as
he pieces together the elegant puzzle of an Arcadian poem.

There is a hint in all this that he was in no cheerful frame of mind that winter. After three major campaigns he was still a nobody, a one-handed nobody at that. And cloistered as he was on a miasmic mudhole of an island, he was out of sight and out of the minds of the august personages who might have pushed him ahead. As his expectations withered, all the prickles of his squalid history must have stung his ambition raw: his loneliness, the sense of injustice and ineffectiveness which were his father's sole bequests to him, his rasping consciousness of poverty and, worse, of anonymity. Perhaps he stuttered more than usual that winter. He probably had few friends; both he and the other men would have sensed that, for all his gambling and his joking, he was somehow different from the rest. But it may have been just that sense that provided a counterpoise to his heavy depression.

"Do not mock my desires," says the protagonist of Cervantes' play *Pedro de Urdemales,* "for, from afar, a hope shows itself to me in which I see such a light as invests me and carries me toward the good I desire."

Spring comes early to the Mediterranean. In March, flowering apple and pear and plum trees begin to frost the greening lowlands with white blossoms. There, the fighting season began in April. The troops were beginning to stir like shrews poking inquiring noses out of their burrows after a winter's hibernation.

On the mainland, plans were ripening, or so it seemed. Despite the months-long fiesta arranged by the Neapolitan aristocracy for its golden prince, Don Juan had spent an anxious winter engineering his return to Spain in the spring to consult with his brother on the future of what he thought of hopefully as his Tunisian kingdom. The silence from Madrid had so far been disheartening. Money was arriving so sluggishly that the generalissimo had been obliged to give over part of his forty-thousand-ducat-a-year allowance, and even to pawn some of his plate and jewels, to provide a little ready cash for the men. A fresh outbreak of rebellion in the Netherlands had turned Philip's attention away from the south; he was close to bankruptcy again, in no position, even had he been in the mood, to build new empires when he had all he could do to hold together the existing one.

Some of the omens were read as good. On March 21, Pope Gregory, a man as good as his word when it came to disposing of other people's territory, assured Don Juan of Rome's support for his sovereignty over Tunisia and awarded him the Order of the Golden Rose "as a perennial testimony of flowering and gentle virtue. . . ."[4] In April, royal permission was received for Don Juan's return to Madrid. He set off at once.

He got as far as Gaeta. There orders reached him from Philip to proceed to Genoa to put down what were presented as serious civil disturbances. The row was between Doria's Spanish-backed faction and a group of French-supported nobles for control of the Republic of Genoa.

Don Juan was beside himself with rage. He was no diplomat, heaven knew. And he resented the role of policeman. Besides, there were interesting proposals afloat in case Tunis escaped him. The pope's son, Jacopo Buoncompagni, had met him in Gaeta with a papal suggestion that Don Juan aid in a plot to depose Elizabeth of England and set Mary Stuart on the throne. Don Juan would lead a Spanish invasion force to England, conquer the kingdom and, like the knights in the tales of chivalry, receive the hand of the new queen in marriage. When the plan was presented to Philip by the papal nuncio in Madrid, the king was tempted. But his good sense soon persuaded him that, with France fomenting trouble at every weak point in his empire and the Castilian treasury as empty as a papal promise, this was no time for war with England. The proposal served chiefly to make his Genoese mission even more odious to Don Juan, who was reported to be suffering from frequent stomach-aches.

At La Spezia, a letter arrived from Philip renewing his order to dismantle the Tunis fortifications before "we lose our reputation and the people" in the place, which he perceived was indefensible against a concerted Turkish attack.[5] Philip went on to retail reports that the new fort ordered built by Don Juan was inadequate and short of water. The caudillo replied angrily that Serbelloni was a genius at his trade and should know what he was doing; moreover, he declared, he did not expect the Sultan to try for Tunis that year. Philip was right. The walls of the new fort were still only a dozen feet high and without defensive works. The king's insight was hardly surprising; he had kept so tight a rein on money and supplies to Tunis, items which Don Juan airily considered his brother's problems, that Serbelloni would have had to be a magician as well as a genius to have carried out his orders. Philip was taking a typically Philippine approach to the Tunis question. Contemporary chronicles report that he was more surprised than vexed by his brother's disobedience. He did not summarily order the forts demolished. The garrison was not pulled out. He merely pressed an Imperial finger on the flow of funds to Serbelloni and let events follow their course. If the Turks failed to counterattack, then Spain might be free to consolidate its advantage there. If Turkish strength was as refreshed as the king believed it was, why throw good money after bad?

It has been widely alleged that Philip's treatment of Don Juan was motivated by petty jealousy of his more glamorous brother's heroism in battle, his popularity, his success with women, his good looks and dashing manners. Yet, despite the best efforts of Don Juan's enemies at court, led by the king's first secretary, Antonio Pérez, Philip's treatment of his brother was usually gentle and as considerate of his feelings as the national interest would allow. Nothing obliged him to softness; Philip was deeply convinced of his absolute right to execute private and secret judgment, and so, by and large, was Don Juan. It is more reasonable to suppose that the family loyalty for which the king was known extended to his charming, improvident brother. Philip's firm but mild handling of Don Juan even suggests something more than affection—respect, perhaps, even a faintly wistful admiration for this appealing man-child.

From La Spezia, Don Juan sent forty galleys under Marcelo Doria to pick up the troops in Sardinia and bring them north. When he arrived in Genoa he found, to his disgust, that there was nothing for him to do there. The winter had been hard in Lombardy, famine acute. It is difficult now to realize how close even rich cities were then to the edge of disaster. Months before, Gian Andrea Doria had written to Don Juan: "Your Highness probably knows that, since no wheat is harvested in the territory of Genoa, and very little of what, other than wheat, is necessary to feed men, there is in consequence much poverty, not only in the mountains but in the city itself. To such a point that the poor are hard pressed to stay alive, especially in winter, when you add to the lack of bread their need to clothe themselves and the impossibility of finding work. . . ."[6]

The coming of spring had relieved the distress; there was work again, the port was abustle after the winter doldrums and Genoa was too busy for politics.

The caudillo, however, was to use his authority to settle trouble arriving in an unexpected quarter. As Fray Miguel de Servía tells it: "This day (June 2) word arrived that the Genoese galleys which had gone to Sardinia to bring up the squadrons of Don Lope's tercio wintering there had been in a row with the soldiers, who tried to embark in so (tumultuous) a way that the galley captains, to protect their seamen . . . set up an armed guard with naked blades, and the soldiers on land moved to protect themselves as well, and they ganged up in such a way that the struggle grew fierce. The galleys turned their prows inshore and fired off many rounds of shots. The Spanish captains quickly retired their soldiers . . . leaving many dead on both sides. . . . When the news of the riot became known in Genoa, the people, none of whom saw in the Spaniard more than a person who killed or wounded, were furious. . . ."[7]

Don Juan sent a delegate to restore order. Two men were hanged and several punished less severely, including the captains and owners of some of the galleys. The Geonese declared themselves satisfied.

Despite a certain tension in the air, then, the months of June and July 1574 were pure pleasure for Cervantes. The record he leaves of his delight in Lombardy is bright and relaxed. Witness his loving inventory of the wines Tomás Rodaja sampled in *The Glass Scholar:* "They arrived

in the handsome and splendid city of Genoa and, disembarking in its
sheltered artificial port and after visiting a church, the captain and all his
comrades repaired to an inn . . . there they discovered the suavity of
Trebiano, the forthrightness of Montefrascón, the power of Asperino, the
headiness of the two Greeks, Candía and Soma, the grandeur of the
Cinco Viñas, the sweetness and gentleness of the lady Guarnacha, the rusticity of Chéntola; among all these gentry, the lowly Romanesco dared
not even appear.[8] And, having reviewed so many and so different wines,
the host offered (the Spanish) a Madrigal, a Coca, an Alaejos and (a
wine from) the more Imperial than Royal City,[9] the antechamber of the
God of Laughter. And all these were honest, not merely names painted
on a map, but real and true; he offered Alanis, Cazalla, Guadalcanal and
Membrilla, nor did he forget Ribadavia and Descargamaria. . . .

"Tomás also admired the Genoese women's blond hair and the kindly
and gallant manners of the men, the admirable beauty of the city; its
houses seem to have been set in the hills like diamonds in gold." The
weather, we may conclude, was fine, for in *La Galatea* we are told that
the city was "full of decorated gardens, white houses and glittering spires
which, wounded by the sun's rays, reverberated with such fiery beams
that they could barely be looked at."[10] The taverns in the Via della
Maddalena were full; little knots of plumed and pantalooned troopers
stood in what is now the Piazza Fossatello to murmur elaborate Spanish
compliments to the serving girls going by. A Riviera holiday.

An incident occurred in Genoa that spring. It was not an important
event: the sea picked up a small vessel and flipped it over on the beach
with its mast in the sand and its keel in the air. Rescuers rushed to the
spot, cut a hole in the hull and released the imprisoned captain and four
crewmen. End of incident. Cervantes may only have heard about it, but it
is more probably that he was one of a crowd that witnessed the scene.
And, like virtually everything he ever saw, it stuck in his mind. It pops up
as a mere paragraph, a gleaning, in *The Glass Scholar,* written a quarter
of a century later. But in his *Persiles,* which was not completed until
1616, we find it blown up into a major sequence climaxing the first chapter of Book Two, in which a storm at sea flips a ship carrying Auristela-
Sigismunda over on the shore of an island where she will be reunited with
her lover.

There is a clue here not only to the way his mind worked, his keen eye
and astonishingly adhesive memory, but to how relatively little formal
schooling he received (and how much private reading he did) in an era
when only arms or the university could atone for the original sin of poverty among the humbly born. There is a defensive pride in the literary
gold he was able to mine from his experience: ". . . the lessons received
from books often create a profounder experience of things than is per-

ceived by the very persons who have seen them," he comments in the *Persiles*, "because he who looks at things attentively over and over gives substance to what he has read, while those who look heedlessly retain nothing, and this is why observation is superior to reading."[11] A few chapters farther along in the novel, the hermit Soldino cries proudly—disingenuously, too—that he can foretell the future although he is "without books, with only the experience I have acquired in the time of my solitude. . . ."[12]

For Don Juan, however, it was an anxious interlude. Increasingly urgent warnings were coming in from Serbelloni that the Turks were massing forces; a Turkish fleet had been sighted off Modon. Don Juan appealed to Philip, to Granvelle in Naples, to the viceroy in Palermo to rush reinforcements to Tunis. But he already owed the viceroy of Sicily well over a million scudi, and the able but envious cardinal viceroy of Naples saw no reason to contribute to Don Juan's private ambitions.

The caudillo did what he could on his own, sending a detachment under Don Juan de Cardona and Don Bernardo de Velasco with twenty Neapolitan ships loaded with supplies and four companies of Italian infantry to reinforce Serbelloni. When he saw the state of the Tunis defenses, Cardona removed the three-hundred-man garrison from Bizerta, along with their artillery, to La Goleta, from whence he and Velasco embarked the Goleta contingent in their ships and returned to Sicily, leaving old Portocarrero with some five hundred soldiers, a few skiffs and a couple of hundred oarsmen.

On July 1, Granvelle warned Serbelloni that the Sultan's armada was making for Tunis. The warning came too late, however. On July 13, Euldj Ali led a fleet of three hundred sail, carrying forty thousand soldiers, into the roads of Carthage.

Word of the attack reached Genoa around the end of July. Without waiting for authorization, with no money and practically no supplies, Don Juan put what troops he could muster aboard his galleys—García de Mendoza's Spanish infantry, Lope de Figueroa's tercio and a miscellany of Lombard companies—and embarked at La Spezia August 7. Stops in Naples to pick up more men and at Palermo to wait for sixty-five more galleys to join him chewed up more weeks. It was well into September before the fleet at last filed past the western hump of Sicily toward Africa.

Beyond the Gulf of Castellammare, the fleet ran into a storm that drove it back to Palermo for a week. When it abated, Andrada was sent ahead with four galleys on a scouting mission. The remaining 101 vessels nosed out toward the open sea . . . and almost immediately were slapped onto the island of Trapani, within sight of the Sicilian coast, by another gale even more violent than the first. Andrada was hurled all the way back to Sardinia and was not heard from again for nearly three weeks.

It is no wonder Cervantes was chary of islands; he had caught malaria on Corfu, glloping boredom on Sardinia, and now he was stranded on a point of rock, raging as furiously as the storm. His star was hitched tightly to Don Juan's; if Tunis were lost, he would have to begin all over again maneuvering for advancement. He was, of course, unaware that his ill wind was blowing someone good in Madrid.

Don Pedro Portocarrero had made a will. The commander at La Goleta had been openly terrified for months, ever since he had first received word that Euldj Ali had left Constantinople. On June 20, he had summoned his witnesses and drawn up a document leaving all of his considerable fortune to his oldest son Alonso. Of Pedro "la Muerte" there was no mention. The will reached Madrid around the time Don Juan got word of the attack on Tunis. Now, while their brother fretted on a Sicilian outcropping, Andrea and Magdalena placidly hoped for the worst in Tunis. They had stiff competition; the moneylenders had also heard the news and they were clustering around Don Alonso like fleas on a chicken.

By September 29, the weather looked as though it might be calming, and the fleet was preparing to try again. As the men trooped wearily aboard their ships, a sail was sighted making for Trapani. It was a leaky, storm-battered French hulk. Aboard it were Don Juan Zanoguera and fifty men, all who were left of the more than eight thousand in the Tunis garrison, to inform Don Juan that he was too late, that he had been too late long before he left Palermo. Tunis had been one of the worst disasters of the century for Spanish arms.

Portocarrero had sent a frantic plea for help to Don Juan; perhaps he already suspected that he was to be made the goat of this business. The process was not long in getting under way; on August 3, Don Juan wrote to Granvelle, "I have always taken Don Pedro Portocarrero for a poor soldier and so I have written to His Majesty more than once, but I never thought this defect would reach so deep as to allow the governor of so important a fortress to permit the enemy to approach so quickly and easily while he does nothing but shelter behind the walls; from one who begins with so little spirit I do not know what we should expect. . . ."[13]

On August 23, La Goleta was stormed and taken, with the slaughter of hundreds of Spanish soldiers. Three weeks later, Tunis fell. Zanoguera, who had been waging a last-ditch fight near La Goleta with three hundred men, was offered his freedom if he would lay down his arms. When the time came for the Turkish commander to keep his promise, he refused to release more than fifty men, chiefly to spread the word of the Turkish victory. When Zanoguera protested, the Turk showed him the severed head of Pagan Doria, commander of the Italian troops in Tunis, and inquired which offer he preferred. Those who were not killed in action or put to the sword afterward were shipped back to slavery in Constantinople. Among these were Serbelloni, whom Zanoguera had seen beaten as he was led, bound, before the Turkish commander's horse toward the port. Another was Don Pedro Portocarrero, who obliged everyone by dying on the journey to Turkey.

Just about everyone in authority at the time has been spattered with blame for the loss of Tunis: Granvelle and his Sicilian counterpart for refusing to send help in time, Philip for his refusal to fix a policy, Portocarrero of course. Don Juan must be considered the guiltiest of them all. In disobeying the king's orders, in preferring to amuse himself in Naples rather than keep his troops in readiness, above all in focusing so ardently on his dreams of what might be that he neglected utterly to defend what had already been won. *"Don Juan con la raqueta y Granvela con la bragueta perdieron la Goleta,"* went the popular doggerel of the day— Don Juan with his racket and Granvelle with his codpiece lost La Goleta.

The Turks did blow up La Goleta, but they completed the fortifications of Tunis itself; then they sailed proudly back to Constantinople, having once more frightened the West with a display of Ottoman power on its doorstep. It was the last time a Turkish force seriously threatened the peace of the West. Within months, Selim fell while drunk on his beloved Cypriot wine and cracked his skull on the marble floor of his baths. The ensuing dynastic struggle and the uprisings it caused in Turkey's eastern provinces began the process of decline; subsequent years of inactivity so decayed the Ottoman fleet that, by the end of the sixteenth century, it virtually ceased to exist. Only the North African pirate fleets maintained the old tradition.

Don Juan led his forces, now diminished by some hundreds drowned in the storm, out of Trapani on the evening of Zanoguera's arrival. On September 30, or October 1, Cervantes' company went ashore in Palermo. Was it there that he learned, surely bemused, that Acquaviva had died in Rome July 21, in his bed, at the age of twenty-eight?

"For it is certain," says Cardenio in *Don Quixote*, "that when the stars in their courses bring disaster, no power on earth can stop them, no human ingenuity avert them."[14]

] 15 [
"Such Points of Despite"

" 'Life and a lover,' " murmurs Orlando, and "going to her writing table she dipped her pen in the ink. . . ."[1] "Life and a lover," might Cervantes have cried, dipping his pen in the ink in Naples in 1574.

Did he, in the Naples of the soft nights, love a tempestuous, dissolute Neapolitan beauty? Did he immerse himself in literature, listen ferociously to the young Italian poets in the Pozzuoli and Portici taverns? Did he gorge himself and his love on "la macatela," "li polastri," "li macaroni," "manigoldo"[2] and other such tender trifles of Italian gastronomy? Did he write a novel that died on a trash heap in Algiers and was reincarnated in *La Galatea?* Did he have a son by the woman we know, or suspect we know, as Silena? And did his unhappiness at the end of what surely would have been his first affair help to drive him out of Italy, out of the army and into slavery?

Well, why not? He was passably good-looking, a dreamer, still boyish, with a reservoir of gaiety chuggering up in streams of laughter from under the layer of disappointment in his mind. Strong-willed women would have found him appealing, would have responded to that youthful capacity for adoration, the untapped passion, the elegant wit that saved him from being too fatuously earnest. Yet here he was, at twenty-seven, a Ulysses without a Penelope, a Dante who had never seen his Beatrice. He had time, even a little money: the Duke of Sessa, in command of the army with Don Juan in Madrid, issued an order on November 15 allotting him twenty-five escudos against what was owed him, the best that could be done for the moment with the military cashbox again as dry as a miser's eye.

No one knows who Silena was, nor how Cervantes met her, if she existed at all. Not many of his contemporaries knew, either: ". . . although he believed no one understood his song because the disguised name of Silena meant nothing to them," he hints in *La Galatea*, "more than three of those who were there did know her. . . ." That she did exist is induced from the trail of clues Cervantes left through his work, chiefly in *La Galatea* and the *Voyage to Parnassus*. Like the cryptic clues in a treasure hunt, comments and poems, all oblique, closely guarded, seem to tell us that she was probably a Neapolitan; ". . . since Lauso named Silena in his song," we are told offhandedly, "and no shepherdess by that name was known, and since Lauso had traveled through many parts of Spain and even all of Asia and Europe, the shepherdess who had conquered his will was probably a foreigner."

Cervantes says she was a beauty, "more beautiful than beauty itself," and clever, "wiser than wisdom itself." She was, at least for a while,

> sun to my eyes and star to my sea. . . .
> In thee, Silena, I hope, in thee I trust,
> Silena, glory of my thoughts,
> north toward which my desire tends. . . .
> What good does your presence not assure?
> What evils not exile? . . .

He seems to have been dazzled, flattered that so demanding a creature should have accepted him. If so, he paid heavily for the privilege in pain and humiliation, but the pride he once felt never entirely died. "And you may be certain, friend Lauso," Tirsi says in Book Five of *La Galatea*, "there is not in the world a breast so inflamed with love that disdain and pardoned arrogance may not cool it and even move it to retract its ill-centered thoughts; and I am brought the more to believe this truth by knowing who Silena is, though you have never told me, and by knowing her fickleness, her wild impulses and the easiness, not to call it by another name, of her desires, qualities for which, were they not tempered and disguised by the peerless beauty with which heaven has endowed her, she would be universally abhorred."

Lauso is an elusive figure in *La Galatea*. He materializes and dematerializes without ever bearing very heavily on the surface action. Yet he emerges as the most authentic person among a gallery of more or less symbolic pastoral types. The poetry in which Lauso sings his anguished love is some of the best Cervantes ever produced, fresh, intense as the pain of a new wound rather than the dull, stiff ache of a half-forgotten scar. It sounds very much as though it had been written in Naples or, at the latest, in Algiers, where thoughts of Italy stuck like arrows in his memory. By what miracle did the wounds remain open, not only through the five years of his enslavement, but through the healing three years of intense activity that followed it? There may be a fugitive clue in the *Voyage to Parnassus*, in which he boasts that

> . . . my *Filena* gay
> hath caroled through the woods, whose leafy land
> gave back many a merry lay.

No *Filena* by him survives. It was obviously a pastoral, quite possibly begun or even completed in Naples in 1575. It may have been lost in the Algerian debacle and re-created from memory later on. But most of the memories which surface in his works were, by an enzyme of Cervantine mockery, made clearly retrospective; the verses relating to Silena in *La Galatea* come to us unscreened, intact, as cries of a present anguish, not a past and already processed deception:

> Love, which has raised me to such dizzy heights,
> do not tumble me with heavy hand
> into the dark, forgetful depths!
> Be a lord to me, and not a tyrant.

Laínez was in Naples until mid-June 1575. In the half-dozen months they were together, Cervantes presumably turned out pages of poetry for the master's criticism, over flagons of wine in a tavern, perhaps around a table before the hearth in Silena's kitchen, dipping their fingers or their spoons (forks were just coming into fashion then, but they had not yet made much of a dent on military manners) into the common bowl of, say, fritters of roasted goats' livers pounded with bread and vinegar and mint and eggs. Silena may very well have had a voice in the discussion; sexual equality, at least in matters of the intellect, was widely espoused then by the Italian poets.

> Now I have new being, now I am alive,
> now I can win the name in every land
> of illustrious, unarguable, admitted fame. . . .

Even then, the self-doubt in sexual matters he probably always felt crept in:

> I hope that your [Silena's] unrivaled understanding
> inspires you to reckon how much faith
> supplies my worth where merit fails. . . .

Compare the transparent passion of that verse from *La Galatea* with the weary nostalgia of the passage from *Voyage to Parnassus* on which some Cervantists base the theory that he had a son by Silena. The lines were written more than a generation later, shortly after Cervantes missed

his last chance for an easy old age when he was refused a place in the retinue of poets accompanying his patron, the Count of Lemos, to the
count's new post as viceroy of Naples. In Chapter Eight of the poem, he
recounts a dream of Naples in which there came

> a friend of mine, named Promontorio,
> youthful in years, but a fine soldier.
> My wonder grew at seeing him there,
> truly and palpably alive in Naples,
> a ghostly accessory of my past. . . .

(The line, *"espanto a los pasados accesorio,"* could also be read "a ghost
of my past couplings." Such baldness was unlike Cervantes; the associa-
tive suggestion has nevertheless to be retained.)

> My friend gave me a tender hug
> and, holding me in his arms, said
> that he could hardly believe I was there;
> he called me father, and I called him son;
> in this lay the point of truth which,
> here, can be called a fixed point.
> Said Promontorio to me, "I warrant,
> "Father, that some great event brings you
> "so far, though you are gray and already half dead."
> "My son, in my fresh and early morning
> "I dwelt in this land," I told him,
> "and I was more gay and lusty then.
> "But that Will, which rules us all,
> "I mean the Will of heaven, has brought me
> "to a place that gladdens more than it afflicts me."

In the poem, Cervantes is interrupted by a splendid pageant which
gives him occasion to pay tribute to some of the leading figures of the
day. Promontorio vanishes; Cervantes, denied what he asserts to be his
rightful place among the great, leaves, "full of indignation."

Was Promontorio his son? The name was common enough in southern
Italy then, too common to allow for historical confirmation. Cervantes
seems to insist on the truth of what he says. But his concern for verisimilitude in art frequently led him to declare the truth of things which were
sometimes verifiably true and, as often, patently untrue, as in the fictitious
Cidi Hamete Berengeli's "true" history of Don Quixote.

There is, moreover, no indication that Cervantes had any contact with
Naples after 1575, astonishing negligence if Promontorio was his only son.

The explanation has been offered that Cervantes preferred to hide the boy's existence from Catalina de Palacios, the woman he married in 1584, just as, for years, he concealed from her the existence in Madrid of his only known child, his illegitimate daughter Isabel. Isabel was finally pressed on Doña Catalina, but Cervantes' reluctance to play the father might explain why no such effort was made on his son's behalf. It is true that a perceptible percentage of the world's population is composed of bastards left behind and forgotten by foreign soldiers after they return home. And the bitterness of his separation from Silena could have made him unwilling to contact her again, for any reason. But why is there no mention of Promontorio in *La Galatea,* where Silena is so vivid, if invisible, a personage?

Promontorio's entire known existence is contained in the few tercets in a poem about a dream written by Cervantes when he was old and sick and already feeling the appraising fingers of death upon him. Perhaps the unanswered and unanswerable questions are stilled if, for a faceless, forgotten bastard of the Neapolitan slums, we substitute an imaginary son whom Cervantes might have wished to father but never did. He remains an immense symbol of Cervantes' "fresh and early morning." What the poet is probably telling us is that, for him, his soldier youth was the "promontory" of his life, when all things were possible, when Apollo, the god of poetry, had not yet refused him a seat among the elect.

Whether or not he succeeded in fertilizing Silena, he certainly fertilized his mind. The mass of material to be read was huge—Aretino, the Tassos, Ariosto, Machiavelli, Boccaccio, Petrarch, Sannazzaro, Pulci, Boiardo, Bembo—and although much of it was not read until years later, in Spain, he must have made a beginning on it in Naples. Italian literature provided him with an education and, in keeping with the habits of the time, a storehouse from which to borrow plots, situations, even characters. Such petty thievery was not only commonplace but recommended in the interests of artistic continuity—provided the jewels were then artfully recut.

Just what books Cervantes did read in Italy is uncertifiable. Some he read, or heard, in manuscript form; these were regularly passed from hand to hand, sometimes for decades, before they found a publisher. Nor is it safe to affirm that because he spent the better part of five years in Italy and was, after all, a bright young fellow, his mastery of Italian was firm enough to support understanding of complicated works except in translation; he is known, for example, to have read a Spanish version of Leone Ebreo's *Dialoghi d'amore,* the Neoplatonist work which weighed so heavily in *La Galatea.* That he was up to reading some books in Italian, however, is clear from later allusions; in the book-burning sequence in *Don Quixote,* for example, he gently criticizes the Spanish translation of

Orlando furioso, and he later observed that "translating from one language to another, when one is not dealing with the queens of language, Greek and Latin, is like looking at the back of a Flemish tapestry. . . . But I do not wish to imply that the exercise of translation is not laudable; a man could do worse things which bring him less benefit."[3]

That he ever read Plato or Aristotle directly is doubtful; their respective interpreters, Leone for Plato and, in Spain, Alonso López-Pinciano for Aristotle, were read later on and so, probably, were Spanish translations of most of the classical works—by Virgil, Livy, Pliny, Apuleius, Homer, Horace, Lucan—whose ideas resonate in his writing.

Critics lately have liked to think that the publication in 1596 of López-Pinciano's *Philosophia antigua poética,* the first Spanish-language commentary on Aristotle's *Poetics,* supplied the formal shock that generated *Don Quixote.* It's a neat formula, devised to explain why Cervantes returned to letters at that period after his years in the literary wilderness. There is no doubt that he read the book; passages from it can be found almost whole in *Don Quixote,* and it is essential to a formal understanding of the *Persiles.* But, as an explanation, it may be more elegant than substantial. There were other stimuli for the production of Cervantes' masterpiece, and among the factors the theory elides is the neo-Aristotelian indoctrination to which he was probably exposed in Italy.

The debate over Aristotelian rules, made more urgent by the Council of Trent's endorsement of Aristotelian ethics, was ferocious in the 1570s —precisely because Aristotle's century-old grip on Italian literary form was beginning to loosen. In 1570, Benedetto Varchi asserted that Dante might be considered superior to Homer. The literary Old Guard, for whom the Latin and Greek writers were as venerable as vernacularists like Dante were trifling, immediately sprang to their defense against the moderns' suggestion that times were changing and the classical rules could no longer be absolute. Although still more than a decade away from a head, the debate was already generating prerevolutionary heat.

That Cervantes was privy to the controversy is likely. Much of his early writing, notably his play *The Siege of Numantia,* shows some familiarity with the neo-Aristotelian paraphernalia of literary construction. Objections have been raised that there is no sign of the debates in *La Galatea,* that the writer is not, as he would later be in *Don Quixote* and the *Persiles,* preoccupied with the problem of truth in fiction. Yet one of the new original aspects of Cervantes' pastoral novel is indeed his effort to stiffen the soft Platonic framework of the traditional pastoral with an injection of neo-Aristotelian verisimilitude. Perhaps the answer is that he was introduced to Aristotelian formal problems in Italy, that he understood them incompletely, perhaps even unwillingly, and that he experimented with them tentatively in his early works. Subsequent reading, as we shall see, would then have clarified and solidified his understanding of them, exciting him to more daring experimentation in his later work. It may nonetheless be true that his early loyalties were to softer forms. Thus, in *The Liberal Lover,* he would recite the credo of the Renaissance, ". . . its parts with the whole and the whole with its parts made one marvelous and concerted harmony . . . I adored it and served it with as much solicitude as though there were no other deity on earth or in heaven to serve or adore." Yet even while he sang verse after verse of his hymn to the Golden Age, he was moving toward the troubled, ambiguous Second Part of *Don Quixote* and the *Persiles,* following the path proposed in Italy in the late sixteenth and early seventeenth centuries, with the same courage and the same regrets.

It was probably Cervantes' contact with the circle of Spanish and Italian poets in Naples that brought him to the attention of the Duke of Sessa (assuming the unlikelihood of their having formed an attachment in Cabra in Cervantes' adolescence). Sessa was an appealing figure. Count of Cabra, Viscount of Iznájar, a hero of the Alpujarras, former governor of Milan, now viceroy of Sicily on temporary assignment to Don Juan, Sessa was all the things a Spanish nobleman was expected to be and seldom was: a brave fighter, polished courtier, shrewd tactician, skillful administrator. He was known as "the Magnanimous." But there was something a little off in him, a weariness, almost a flabbiness of spirit that he was sensitive enough to recognize in himself. Generous to a point of prodigality, a lover of masques and tourneys, he had so dissipated his immense fortune that Philip II was obliged to put him on a carefully supervised pension of two thousand escudos a month. He wrote excellent poetry, an entirely seemly accomplishment in a gentleman, and surrounded himself with artists wherever he went; "illustrious example in arms, science, wit, style and art," the poet Jorge de Montemayor called him.[4] But he was a prophet of disillusionment before it became epidemic in Spain. To his peers, he lacked the extra grain of folly, of fierce blindness to probabilities, that had pushed men like Cortés and Pizarro and his own grandfather to achieve their logically impossible feats of bravado. What was left after this cooling of the blood was a cultivated, responsible, intellectually fastidious man:

> I lost myself to learn the Courtier's art
> and I succeeded in learning it,
> since I have come out bereft of illusions. . . .[5]

He was old now and, with a grand Córdoban stoicism, almost impatient of living:

> No more, now, life; it is a wearying thing,
> keeping the soul on guard to preserve you. . . .[6]

Whether Cervantes was a regular visitor to the salons and the library of Sessa's house in Naples is not known, but it is likely. It was Sessa who had appointed Juan de Cervantes as chief magistrate of Baena in 1541, who had named Miguel's uncle Andrés mayor of Cabra and had kept him in the city government, where he was still officiating in 1575. He had known Cervantes' parents and he would have been totally indifferent to any question of their ancestry. The distinction of Miguel's speech and manner, the delicacy of his mind, would have been all that was needed to recommend the young man. Sessa might even have made some small financial contribution to his hungry friend's maintenance.

Life was rich, life was full: a beautiful mistress, friends, books and talk of books, work, enough money to keep him out of the line of soldiers begging in the streets, perhaps even enough to indulge in small extravagances, such as visiting the kitchens of the English ambassador's house to buy delicacies from the cook.

There was, of course, one stone in his shoe: he was no further ahead in his career than he had been three years before. Although this fact undoubtedly nagged at his mind, he may have been having too good a time to let it dominate him. And then, suddenly, it began to matter very much indeed. Because, early that summer, things began to go haywire.

In mid-June, Don Juan came back from Spain, where he had been kindly received by the king despite his having left Italy without royal permission. He now held the title of Philip's lieutenant general for Italy, which placed him, at least nominally, over all the Spanish governors and viceroys there. This had been dispensed as a sop after the king had refused him the title of *infante*, which, in the absence of an heir apparent—Philip III was not born until 1578—would have put him in line for the throne, a prospect from which the king recoiled. A starvation diet was imposed on Don Juan's dynastic appetites, and rumors were already afloat that he would soon be sent to Flanders to fight the king's war there.

It was all well and good for kings and princes to swim in this tide of grand events, but pebbles like Cervantes were merely stranded on the beach and left to dry in the sun. Don Juan's future was uncertain; Sessa, no longer needed in Naples, returned to his palace in Palermo. Laínez had left, too, and heaven knows how many others. Worst of all, it was probably in the high summer of 1575 that Cervantes' idyll with Silena was broken.

Silena, apparently, was a woman who changed her loves as she did her linens, with the seasons. Even a more experienced lover than Cervantes would have had trouble keeping her in hand, and on the evidence of two brief and unsatisfactory affairs later on and a marriage which was never more than a loose conjunction of sympathies, in sexual matters he seems to have been more Shetland pony than Arab stallion. Perhaps he had Silena in mind when he observed in *La Galatea* that "gold and gifts are among the sharpest of love's arrows, the ones with which the greatest number of hearts are made subject";[7] the reflection recurred when, at the end of his life, he commented in the *Persiles* that "a penniless lover, unless full-handed fortune favors him, can almost never bring his desires to happy end."[8] He may have been expecting too much of fortune. The son of a father who must always have seemed to be apologizing for his own existence, Miguel may well have been one of those men who explained his doubts to women who were impatient of explanations and contemptuous of doubt. It would, of course, be presumptuous to affirm that he was an incompetent bedmate. But it is fair to observe that nowhere in the life or work of this superlatively civilized man is there any hint of the predatory, self-aggrandizing savagery so often characteristic of the great semenizers of history. Nothing is so destructive of sexual abandonment as Cervantes' implacable self-consciousness, unless it be a piercing sense of one's own ridiculousness or, worst of all, a haunting suspicion of one's own inadequacy. A man can stammer in love as he does in conversation.

The breakup seems to have happened gradually, like a shelf pulling slowly out of a wall:

> Fortunate he who is beloved by thee,
> Silena, with constant purity, without
> tasting the bitterness of jealousy. . . .

There were quarrels, reconciliations:

> I wandered everywhere, aimlessly; I could not see
> the sky; I went among sharp thorns, among thistles I walked,
> but then, at the very instant when my soul was touched
> by your clusters of bright rays, I saw before me,
> revealed in the sudden light, the beckoning,
> illuminated pathway to my heart's delight. . . .

Silena's "fickle nature" soon closed that pathway for good:

> Heavenly Silena, and my own—
> it is how I often spoke to her,
> because such beauty made it appear
> as though she were come from heaven;
> but now, cleansed of my fear, I see

I can more clearly recognize
Silena not as come from Paradise
but as a false siren of the sea.

To thine eyes, to thy pen [sic],
to thy truths and games, succumbs
an innumerable sum
of vain and blinded men.
The last to come with thee is always first,
and, in the end, he who loves thee best
is by thee as cruelly oppressed
as the accurst first by thee is cherished. . . .

I speak not as one aggrieved,
for that would be still to love;
I speak as a man deceived
and, blameless, made mock of. . . .

That thou sing in praise of liberty
is just, and thou art right to do it,
but see, thou dost preserve it
with nothing but cruelty. . . .

No more, Silena, for I am laid
on such points of despite,
the smallest of them has the power
to leave me lifeless or mad. . . .

We are treated, still in *La Galatea*, to a final flourish of youthful bravura.
Lauso is depicted as rushing up to Damon and hugging him gleefully. To
his friend's astonished inquiry as to the reason for such satisfaction, he
replies:

"Far better (than success in love) is the good I bring, my true friend
Damon, for the cause which to others often means despair and death has
to me brought hope and life, namely, the reproachful disdain and coldly
civil mockery I saw in my shepherdess (Silena), which have restored me
to my former self. No longer, shepherd, no longer do I feel the heavy
yoke of love on my weary neck; now has the burdensome machinery of
thought that had crushed me been dismantled; now I shall renew my interrupted converse with my friends, now the green grass and fragrant
flowers of these peaceful fields will exist for me. . . . Now I feel me free
and master of my will. . . .

With bended knee pressed firmly to the rocky soil,
my hands upraised in humble supplication
and my heart replete with an honorable zeal,

I worship thee, holy disdain; in thee are counted
all the causes of this sweet celebration. . . .
The love I gave, though it was honest, was not so feeble
that, for but a single spurning, it could have been dashed
　　to earth;
no, a hundred thousand rebuffs it first required. . . ."

All this is admirable humbug. Cervantes never forgot his Silena. Jealousy sings its discordant theme from end to end of Cervantes' work, far more stridently than could be justified by the prevalence of the jealous lover in the literature of that time. Later on, in the period of the *Exemplary Stories* and the *Interludes,* his anger would be gentled by age and tolerance and a measure of popular success; Cervantes' sympathy for jealousy's victims spares them the merciless scorn the age traditionally reserved for cuckolds.

With his friends gone, his affair ended, the summer dwindling and his future blank, Cervantes brought himself to act on a resolution he may have been nursing for some time: to return to Madrid to solicit royal favor. Besides, he may have known that affairs at home were in their usual mess. The Portocarrero business had come alive again with Don Pedro's death. On May 7, 1575, Alonso Pacheco formally confirmed "my obligation to give and pay to you, Señora Magdalena Pimentel de Sotomayor, now present in this capital . . . the sum of 500 ducats, worth 187,500 maravedis, which I owe you because I was indebted to you for it through a donation I made and granted in your favor, for which I bestowed and sent the sum for the reasons and obligations I had, and I pledged myself to pay you the said sum when I inherited the goods and estate to which I would succeed on the end and death of Don Pedro Portocarrero, my lord and father; and thus it has occurred that my said father is dead and gone from this present life, and I thus have succeeded to his goods and possessions, as his legitimate son, and now that the delay accorded in my obligation to pay the said 500 ducats has expired and you are desirous of receiving them from me . . . and to facilitate matters for me that I may arrange my affairs you have seen fit to delay payment. . . ."[9]

This was the opening rush in a legal scrimmage which, in late September, found the Cervantes sisters not only unpaid, but out the costs of a muddle-headed court complaint against Alonso as well.

In 1576 Alonso's wife died. A year later he remarried; Magdalena and Andrea became Things of the Past. Magdalena would try once more, in 1578, to collect her five hundred ducats; by that time, the money was desperately needed for Miguel's ransom. Alonso remained unmoved. As far as is known, he never paid either sister a single maravedi.

It is unlikely that the case increased Cervantes' anxiety to return home;

he had problems of his own to solve. He requested and was granted a leave of absence for himself and his brother. Whether he had an audience with Don Juan is not known, but when, in late August or early September, he was received by Sessa in the viceregal palace in Palermo, he was given letters of recommendation to the king from both the duke and the caudillo.

Suppositions that he was going home to seek a captaincy are hard to take seriously. He must have known that his military career was finished, that his superiors were relieved to see him go. The wording of a petition by Doña Leonor to raise money for Miguel's ransom is significant: "because he was maimed (*estropeado*), my lord Don Juan gave him license to come to Spain. . . ."[10] Still, the young man must have been pleased. The letters, he could reasonably expect, were his passports to royal favor.

They were, in fact, his patents of poverty.

] 16 [

Capture

The weather had been fine when the galley *Sol* sailed from Naples, in convoy with the *Higuera,* the *Mendoza* and a fourth vessel, sometime in the third week in September. But, with Barcelona only two days away, storms in the Gulf of Lions had thrown the *Sol* all the way back to Corsica, separating it from the other ships. Most of those aboard were soldiers on leave, like the Cervantes brothers; still, these were no waters for a Spanish ship to be in alone; the *Sol* was now beating up the French coast, trying to catch up with the others.

During the night of September 26, 1575, off the mouth of the Rhone River and within sight of Les Saintes Maries de la Mer, a lookout spotted three ships bearing toward the *Sol.* Probably there was a moment of suspense when everyone aboard hoped the sails were friendly, that the squadron's commander, Don Sancho de Leiva, had come looking for them. But as the vessels drew closer, their sleek, light shapes revealed them as corsair galleys.

Cervantists have tried to piece together what happened then from the descriptions of sea fights with pirate galleys in Cervantes' stories, *La Galatea, The Liberal Lover,* the *Persiles, Don Quixote, The Spanish Englishwoman.* They would have the skipper ordering full sail in an attempt to outrun the attackers (*The Spanish Englishwoman*), a sixteen-hour battle (*La Galatea*). But the accounts are no more than evocative; none fit the circumstances of Cervantes' capture tightly enough to support a factual narrative. It is thought that the pirates lay alongside the *Sol* until dawn before attacking. That they first put out a small boat to demand surrender (*La Galatea*) is unlikely, since they were facing a single galley and not, as in the novel, a heavily armed sailing ship.

Outnumbered by more than three to one, the men in the *Sol* fought because there was no help for it. A heavy Spanish galley, crowded, probably overloaded, could not hope to win a race with well-greased, stripped-down North African vessels which probably were reinforced—having six men on an oar instead of the usual three or four. According to later testimony, the battle lasted for some hours. Sea fights usually did; every foot of deck space meant a man's life and liberty and was defended with a ferocity in keeping with the stakes. A number of defenders were killed and many others were wounded, but Cervantes probably was not; if he had been, he would have told us about it, at length.

> For in the galley *Sol,* whose luster fell
> by my ill fortune, I was doomed to see
> my comrades' ruin and mine own as well.
> At first our valour shone in high degree,
> until by sad experience we awoke
> to see how mad was all our bravery![1]

There had really never been a doubt of how the fight would end. The pirate *reis*—captains—came aboard, led by Arnaute Mamí, an Albanian renegade who was captain of the Algerian fleet, and his lieutenant and rival Dalí Mamí, a Greek renegade nicknamed *El Cojo*—the Gimp. Both men had a reputation for gratuitous cruelty—Cervantes insists on this in every one of his piracy stories—which they shared with most of the renegades fighting for the Turks. They were, after all, soldiers of fortune; of the thirty-five ships listed in the Algerian fleet in 1588, twenty-four were captained by renegades or their sons. Violent, anarchic, greedy, accountable to no one except in matters of religion, they showed little mercy to Christians lest their own apostasy be put in question.

"But fickle fortune, of whose character no constancy can be expected, envious of our success, sought to disturb it with the greatest mischance imaginable. . . ."[2] Complaints of his bad luck flourish in Cervantes' stories and the crop is particularly luxuriant in his accounts of Moslem captivity. More often than not, as he would wryly admit in the *Voyage to Parnassus,* his misfortunes were of his own making. But his grumbling against "the deep and ancient sea, which has played so many tricks on me,"[3] must be fully allowed. The sea had already cost him a hand, had literally sprayed cold water on his dreams of advancement. This time it was to cost him "one of the most precious gifts the gods gave to man,"[4] his freedom.

In *The Spanish Englishwoman,* Recaredo recounts that "when they boarded (our galiots), they stripped us to the skin. They took whatever there was in the boats and set them adrift. . . ." Some such scene may have been enacted in the *Sol*. It was probably on the blood-spattered Spanish deck, in any case, that the spoils were roughly divided. Rodrigo went with the one seventh of the booty reserved for Ramadan Pasha, the dey* of Algiers. Miguel fell to Dalí Mamí.

Those letters! Miguel apparently lacked the opportunity or the presence of mind to get rid of them. Now it was too late. Navarro y Ledesma pictured Dalí examining the signatures of Don Juan and the Duke of Sessa, running appraising eyes over Miguel from head to foot: a one-handed man, not much good as a worker, but important, the papers proved that, worth a fine ransom. One can even imagine the Greek finding the letters, saying nothing, allowing the maimed trooper to be fobbed off on him, perhaps protesting for the form, grinning inwardly at the reflection that the Captain of the Sea had outfoxed himself this time.

Transfer of the captives to the corsair ships was under way when the rest of Leiva's squadron appeared over the horizon in search of the *Sol*. The captors hustled back to their ships and cut the Spanish galley loose, leaving some prisoners still aboard. Then they fled.

Miguel and Rodrigo were not among those left behind.

"Blows aplenty and cuffs they gave me to make me tell them if I had any money," recalled the author of *Voyage to Turkey* of his capture by pirates. ". . . In such a turmoil had they thrown me, and so terrified was I at what fortune had suddenly done to me, that I did not know whether to cry or laugh or wonder, or (realize) where I was; my companions said they wept copiously, that they were amazed because I did not seem to feel it any more than if I had been free, and this is true—that of the sorry turn in my fortune I felt nothing . . . because I could not believe, could not convince myself that it had happened."[5]

So may Cervantes have felt, at least at first. Conviction would have come when, because he was thought to be a valuable property, irons were clapped on his wrists and ankles, perhaps his neck as well. His first glimpse across the water of Algiers, rising up its hill like a milky morning mist, released the full tide of bitterness in his heart:

> When I arrived in chains and saw the place,
> so noted in the world, whose teeming breast
> hath nursed the fierce swarms of a pirate race,
> my bitter lamentation found no rest,
> and ere I knew, the tears coursed at their ease
> down my haggard cheeks, and unrepressed.

* The title given to governors of Algeria before 1830.

My straining eyes were fixed upon the seas,
the strand, and hill . . .
. . . my tears seemed charged with fire
and shame, at thought of that disastrous day.[6]

As soon as the ships dropped anchor in Algiers harbor, oars, sails and tiller were locked in a heavily guarded warehouse to prevent any Christian attempt to flee while the loot was being unloaded. A festival mood spread through the city, as it always did when a squadron returned from a successful mission, and the beach was quickly filled with curious onlookers. One can imagine the prisoners, many of them wounded, most of them chained, huddled on the beach while the spoils were distributed, staring in bleak confusion at the crowd of black-clad Jews, Algerian shopkeepers, prostitutes in long tunics, of janissaries dandling the short, vicious clubs with which they would casually brain anyone who annoyed or displeased them. Equally confusing would have been the chaos of languages around them, Turkish, Arabic, Spanish, Italian, Maltese, Croatian, Kabyle, Russian, the bastard lingua franca of the Mediterranean ports and, shrilling over them all through the heavy air, the garbled *la ilaha illa'allah*—"*lah lah lu la leh*"—of the Algerian women's victory cry.

Little sympathy the prisoners would have read in those appraising faces. Some of the men, the poorest, would soon appear in the vast, arcaded slave market, where they would be paraded naked before a throng of country people shopping for laborers, made to walk, jump, be beaten with sticks to see if rheumatism slowed their reactions, spit on and rubbed to uncover hidden scars and have their palms read to reveal their longevity.

Perhaps the true horror of their situation came home to the prisoners at the sight of the slaves in the crowd, some with faces puckered by the loss of nose, ears or lips, their eyes turned inward on their own rage.

At last the prisoners were led out into the town. As they clumped clumsily up the Street of the Souk, the city's main thoroughfare, toward the dungeons on the hill, children ran alongside them, pelting them with filth, chanting children's mindless insults:

Thieving Christian,
not ransom, not escape;
Don Juan not come here;
here die,
dog, here die![7]

Those consigned to the dey were deposited in the largest of the city's four public prisons, the royal bagnio, a warren of small, vaulted rooms on three stories around a patio with a cistern in the center, where the inmates, as many as two thousand at a time, shared space on the stone floors with scorpions, snakes, lizards and the inevitable bugs. At one end of the courtyard, a table, bare of images, served as an altar on high holy days, when Christians from all over the city gathered to hear mass said before an image of the Virgin painted on a card or a cross torn from a rosary, to trade gossip and hawk their dreams of liberation. Except for the lack of bedding and the captives' relative freedom to come and go during the day, it might have been any royal prison in Spain.

Miguel was in the contingent confined in Dalí Mamí's private slave quarters. For the time being, all were left in chains under heavy guard to stew in their own grief, the first step in the softening-up process leading to ransom negotiations. Later they would find that the irons were more symbolic than confining, except for disciplinary cases and those whose ransom value warranted extra precautions.

That night, while they lay in their cells, Algiers celebrated, the reis in their homes, the men, like as not, in the taverns the Christians ran in the prisons, the only places in the city where drinking was openly permitted. "It was all eating and drinking and triumphing," scowled Bishop Diego de Haedo.[8] On such occasions, the reis would dress their pages—"their bearded wives," Haedo called them—in women's clothes, "satin and velvet, chains of gold and silver, damascened poignards at their belts and, in a word, (they) would adorn them more coquettishly than if they had been beautiful women . . . and send them out to sashay through the city in troupes for (the reis') amusement and pride."[9]

Fray Diego's outraged male arrogance is of more than folkloric interest. That homosexuality was at home in Moslem society, even officially encouraged in the warrior caste (government food and housing, for example, were denied to janissaries who married, and their sons were barred from the militia and all public office), baffled and horrified Europeans to whom female prostitution was both normal and useful, if not positively virtuous. For life in North Africa offered a mirror image—distorted, to be sure—of European cultures in which perceptive Europeans might have seen themselves but seldom did.

In appearance Algiers was not so different from the Mediterranean towns they knew. It was as Roman as Palermo, as Moorish as Córdoba, bearing as many reminders of Vandalism as Toledo or Burgos. Here, too, narrow brooks of streets, narrower even than the alleys of Granada, rambled erratically between banks of low, spotlessly white houses with flat roofs rising from the sea in terraced ranks. As in Spain, the play of color was regal. The battlemented ramparts were built of soft, golden stone like the walls of Jerez de los Caballeros, but in Algiers they curved like a drawn bow, with the long mole an arrow aimed at Mallorca; in the farms and the huge country-house gardens around the city, citrus trees, palms, cypresses, cedars, vines, mulberries made deep green splotches like enamel inlays on the red hills, as they do around Jaén. Algiers had been a rich city for half a millennium, a place of abundant honey and butter and fowl, chick-peas and lentils and wheat tiling the land in gold and green, reaching out toward the city itself, where green and yellow tiles glistened on fountains, in cool patios, on the roofs of mosques. Espaliers in the hills echoed the double arcade of the dey's palace with its rows of slender marble and porphyry columns that recalled the tooled elegance of Santo Domingo de Silos.

It was a bigger city than it looked to be; in the roughly one square mile within the walls—the Al-Djzaïr where the sheep of the Beni-Mezranna had grazed for centuries—one hundred thousand or more people lived, prayed in its hundred mosques, splashed in its sixty baths, including the two marbled splendors (oh shades of Vespasian!) where even Christians could go if they had a silver coin for the attendants who doused them with hot water out of bronze jugs.

Yét in European eyes it was all wrong. Here it was the Christians who worked the land the Moslems hated to till. Here there were no inns, no hospitals. Because the Turks wore metal insets in the soles of their slippers and animals were never shod, Spaniards said that here it was the men who wore iron and the horses that went barefoot. As in Europe, madmen were held to be holy, as though too badly burned in the divine fire, but their madness could take extravagant forms; if one of them saw a handsome woman on the street, we are told, he might hurl himself upon her and take her there and then, "whereupon all kiss his hands and head as though he had done a holy work."[10] Rarely were the flagellants in Spain's Easter processions recalled by the sight of Moslem holy men burning their scalps with hot irons, slashing their breasts and arms with knives, burning rags on their arms. Nor, perhaps understandably, were priestly raids on European virginity evoked by the sight of Algerian marabouts sodomizing boys in the souk or in the streets, to the general approval. There were *haji* who put out their own eyes after seeing Mecca and others, less extreme, who shaved their heads save for a single long lock of hair to serve as a handle by which the angels might pull them up to heaven—an odd sight to Europeans to whom a tonsure was acceptable. Europeans devoted to the medical practice of waving a saintly thighbone over a sickbed were shocked by those housewives who, bathed and perfumed to bewitch the spirits, danced themselves into a trance at the bedside of the sick to seduce occult healers to the victim's aid. And even a Cervantes who abhorred the cruelty of a Spanish auto-da-fé probably rated it lower on the scale of atrocity than the public impalement in Algiers of a relapsed convert to Mohammedanism.

The term of Miguel's initial confinement was brief, probably no more than a week or two. Then the softening-up routine began. New prisoners were issued uniforms: short blue cassock with rounded neck and half-sleeves, coarse linen breeches, black-and-white-striped djelaba, blue cap, white stockings and straw-soled slippers; the vermin were international. Then, like most of the ransomable prisoners when they were not working, they were allowed to roam the city freely, wearing irons on legs and wrists, to find out for themselves what lay in store for the unransomed.

Modern apologists have likened the lot of Christian slaves in North Africa to that of prisoners of war, evoking echoes of the Geneva Convention and for-the-duration internment. We are advised of the inappropriateness of applying such epithets as "hopeless" and "degrading" to their condition. Christian slaves, by such accounts, were viewed as victims of temporary misfortune involving no contempt of human dignity; whether they were better off as slaves than as free men in their own countries, we are told, depended on "circumstances."[11]

The circumstances described by contemporary witnesses, however, do not support this benign vision. "The slave is not a man, but a monster . . . to enslave a man is a most signal evil, and the most vituperous affront which can be given a man," wrote a captive Portuguese priest, Dr. Antonio Sosa.[12] In substantiation, he provided an endless list of executions, disfigurements, atrocities. "Malice and cruelty there (in Algiers) are given absolute empire," wrote another witness early in the seventeenth century, "and, through the blindness of hate or boredom, execution is decreed for those undeserving of it. . . . (Turks and corsairs) are more passionate partisans of cruelty than of justice. . . . I must confess that, in describing misery, my pen falls from my hand and that, having seen it, I cannot but weep to recall it."[13]

Most of the men had to work, of course; slaves were expected to earn what keep they were given. Captives assigned to the "warehouse" were owned by the city administration and were assigned to public works. Privately owned slaves functioned as gardeners, farmers, quarrymen, house servants, masons. They collected refuse, sold water and fruit through the streets and, like the children of Israel in Joseph's Egypt, they made bricks. Christians greased the hulls of corsair ships and calked their seams. All but one of the city's surgeons were Europeans and so were the public executioners, for it was shameful for a Moslem to spill Moslem blood; besides, death by a Christian hand was thought to give the victim merit in the eyes of Allah.

There seems to be nothing atrocious in all this, until one looks more closely, at men harnessed like oxen to carts loaded with stone or to plows on the hilly upland farms; to men—and women—working under a constant rain of blows and threats until they dropped of exhaustion, beaten if they stopped to rest or to shift the weight of their chains. Hungry, dressed in rags, working in every weather, they filled the city's streets "so sick, so thin, so wasted, so worn and so disfigured that they were barely able to stand,"[14] begging for their food on Fridays because their Moslem masters refused to provide for them on the Sabbath. Sick men were driven to work with cattle prods and whips. If one was suspected of malingering, as they almost always were, his captors would build a bonfire and threaten to throw him into it; when, hobbled, he attempted to flee in panic, they would laugh and jeer: "See how well my barbarian is, and how easily he can cure himself, so that now he can run swiftly. . . .[15] Unless he were valuable, a slave would be worked until disease or exhaustion felled him, when he would very likely be dumped outside the walls for the dogs to finish in proper Old Testament fashion.

The horror quotient was even higher at sea. Galley slaves returning to port were said to have a "blank and wild look, as though they did not know themselves," and were "so wholly diminished that nothing is left of them but skin and bones, so that, though they are alive, one could, just by looking at them, draw an anatomy of all their bones, nerves, veins, arteries and cartilage."[16] The reis were accustomed to dealing out summary punishments to relieve their nervous tension. Arnaute Mamí was the most feared—"who, in his house and on his ships, has more Christians missing their ears and noses?"[17]—only because he was the most powerful. On every galley, oarsmen were whipped until the blood ran, lost eyes, arms, even heads for trivial causes. They perished of hunger, or died bloated with sea water. Hired Moorish rowers (who received hardly milder treatment) might take out their fury on the Christians, rising from their benches to "rip off their ears and noses with their teeth."[18]

For a Christian, death and the threat of violence were constant at sea or in port, not merely as punishment for major offenses, but as exaggerated responses to everyday irritations. The burning and lapidation in 1577 of Fray Miguel de Aranda in random reprisal for the execution of a corsair in Valencia inspired one of the most passionate speeches in Cervantes' play *Life in Algiers*, for "I saw the servant of God . . . amid the unjust mob, his manner mild and humble, die happily for God. . . ."[19] Algerians made irate by the loss of a fellow countryman would beg alms in the streets with which to buy a slave for retaliatory execution. Slaves were mutilated for snapping a branch from a tree, strangled on the mere suspicion of stealing a pot, impaled by inches for daring to raise their hands to a Turk. With Algiers always vulnerable to a concerted attack, false rumors would periodically sweep the city of invasion or of revolt by the slaves. In Act III of *The Dungeons of Algiers*, Cervantes recounts the janissaries' "cruelty and stupidity" when, panicked by a cloud formation they took to be a Christian fleet with "your dead Prophet on the prow of a ship," they ran wild in the streets, killing any Christians they found, until at last "the sun disbanded the armada." It is a mark of Cervantes' measure that the criticism is uttered not by a captive, but by a disgusted Moorish prison guard—the same jailer who cynically exacts an entry fee from Christians converging on the prison to hear mass.

So prevalent was the climate of violence that even the European traders went in fear for their skins. Haedo tells of a Venetian shipowner in Algiers harbor who was condemned to the stake for defending his cargo against a marauding janissary and who, to the bishop's scorn, was converted to Islam "to save his miserable life."[20]

Against such a background, statements that slaves were often treated as members of the family resound sardonically. No doubt this was occasionally true, especially on the back-country farms. No doubt captives of high retail value were more mildly treated; those in the dey's bagnio were seldom put to work at all. Certainly the Orient had no monopoly on gratuitous cruelty. On October 17, 1584, the commander of Venetian convict galleys captured a Turkish vessel carrying Ramadan Pasha's son and mother to Tripoli; all the crew—50 Moors, 75 Turks, 174 Christian renegades and 45 women in the official retinue—were hacked to pieces. When the Spaniard Juan de Cañamares was punished for attempting to assassinate King Ferdinand, "first they cut off the hand that was raised against the king, then, with red-hot iron pincers, they tore out a nipple, then an eye, then they cut off the other hand, then they tore out the other eye. . . ." So exceptional was the case that even the chronicler was moved to remark that the victim's death was "very cruel."[21]

It is equally true that there were few objective witnesses to conditions in North Africa. What testimony we have comes either from the Catholics or their clerical champions. When Cervantes proclaims that

> . . . the poor man who finds himself
> in this rabble's hands is sure
> to come to harm, and he must look to God
> for his freedom, or, though living,
> yet count himself as dead . . .[22]

he was not being absolutely impartial.

But even biased testimony must finally be believed when the weight of specific citation becomes overwhelming. No one of good faith challenges the accounts that came out of Buchenwald, nor those still emerging from the Soviet slave-labor camps, simply because the reports come from former inmates. In these, as in North Africa, the horror of a captive's life was in direct proportion to his captors' disdain of him, to the institutionalization, the scale of brutality and to the jailers' lack of positive moral accountability to any outside authority. No amount of insistence on the Moslems' kindness to each other, their fairness in dealing with coreligionaries, the good order of their cities, their unquestioning obedience to authority, their abhorrence of blasphemy or the number of public baths they maintained can alter the grim fact of whole cities, whole regions turned into what, today, we would call slave-labor camps.

It is against this background that the elaborate bargaining over ransoms began almost at once. For while Cervantes and his comrades were learning the facts of life in Algiers, their masters were going to some pains to estimate the captives' cash value, questioning, spying, examining clothing and possessions.

Prices were always inflated at first. And, at first, the prisoners were carefully surrounded with smiles, gestures of friendship, avowals of confidence. Just a business arrangement among friends. They were well, even ceremoniously fed on couscous and fruited pilaff. Questions of money were airily evaded.

Then, some days later, the tone would change. The prisoner would be informed that, by God, his true identity has been discovered, that he is a grandee of Spain, cousin to the king, master of Alcántara—anything. Sosa recounted that "of their own authority . . . they made me, a poor priest, a bishop, and then private secretary to the pope. . . . Next they made me a cardinal, then governor of the Castelnuovo in Naples, and now I am confessor and (spiritual) director to the queen of Spain, and for their purpose they suborned Turks and Moors who affirmed this."[23] At one point he was confronted with a crowd of Turks who alleged that they were newly returned from Naples, where they had been slaves in his vast palace.

Captives who declined such promotion were simply considered to be bargaining properly. The standard counterploy was imprisonment in chains. One chronicler observed that some captives were loaded with as much as one hundred pounds of iron and forced to drag it through the streets. If the victim affected an attitude of haughty pride, the treatment was made even harsher: he would be thrown into a solitary cell, his neck, arms and legs almost immobilized under the weight of his chains. For food he was given moldy bread and fetid water. He was sometimes gagged, frequently beaten. After some months of this, he would resemble "the living dead, eyes sunken, his flesh stuck to his bones, covered with hair and gray of skin."[24]

Rodrigo's negotiations with Ramadan had gotten off to a brisk start. The dey was not an unusually greedy man. Indeed, this former Sardinian goatherd was reported to be just, upright, gentle and benign in judgment and prudence. The relativity of that gentleness may be perceived in the fact that it was Ramadan who personally dragged one Andrés de Iaca through the streets tied to the tail of his horse, who had Antonio de la Mantia killed on the hook and—albeit reluctantly—consented to the burning of Fray Miguel de Aranda. Still, as tyrants go, he was a reasonable sort. He only wanted a fair return on the heavy investment he had made in buying his governorship, and this meant keeping the turnover of merchandise brisk. As the brother of a man carrying letters from Don Juan and the viceroy of Sicily, Rodrigo might have been assessed at far more than the three hundred escudos Ramadan set as a bargaining price.

El Cojo, a stupider man who lacked the dey's keen eye for quality, put his faith in the precious letters and, insisting that Miguel was a "gentleman of quality," priced him at five hundred gold escudos. It may even have been a bargain at that; seven thousand was not an unusual ransom for a nobleman, and the tariff could climb to fifty thousand for a grandee.

Naturally, Miguel protested that he was just a poor soldier. Just as naturally, he was disbelieved and put in irons to bring him to his senses. Testimony taken in Algiers in 1850 for the *Información de Argel*, the affidavit on which is based most of what is known of his captivity, recounts that "Daliman" had him "shut up and weighted with shackles and chains." Hernando de Vega, another of "Alimami's" slaves, said Cervantes was "fettered and loaded with irons and guarded, vexed and troubled, all so that he might ransom himself. . . ."

There was a way out: conversion to Islam. An act unthinkable, but often done. For religion was the heart of the Algerian matter. Barbary was a battleground where a sullen war for souls was fought, a sequel to Lepanto and Tunis waged in the streets and in the prisons. The number of renegades in Cervantes' captivity tales obliquely suggests how many defections there were from Christianity—some six thousand in Algiers alone in 1568, perhaps eight thousand by the early seventeenth century. True, many came from the Balkans, where poverty, Turkish dominance, resentment of Venetian colonial policy and its Roman Catholicism made any alternative acceptable. From the hardship areas of the Western Mediterranean, from Corsica, Sardinia, Reggio Calabria, Mallorca, rural Spain, the poor came to profit from the Moslems' eager invitation to convert and prosper. More sophisticated in international dealings than their new coreligionaries, often better educated, more skillful sailors and subtler negotiators, they became Islam's colonial governors, its sea captains, its agents. Ramadan Pasha was a renegade; so was his successor Hassan Pasha, protégé of the renegade Euldj Ali. The great Barbarossa, who had brought the Western provinces into the Ottoman Empire, was the son of a Lesbian potter.

Among the enslaved, the pressure to convert was hard to resist. Moslem proselytizing was incessant. Children, the weak-willed, the self-indulgent and resentful were alternatively seduced and brutalized. While it may not have brought instant release (slaves often remained slaves), conversion did confer important privileges: better treatment, for Moslems did not, as a rule, mistreat other Moslems; exoneration from galley service and from wearing chains; freedom to consort with Moslem women, forbidden to Christians under pain of torture or death for both man and concubine. Conversion entailed a general absolution for past sins, which in practice meant annulment of money debts to Christians, and sometimes sudden wealth through congratulatory gifts from the faithful.

To the Christians in North Africa, every conversion to Islam was a battle lost. It was not merely that defection represented a physical danger because renegades' efforts to prove the sincerity of their conversion often made them cruel masters and treacherous friends. A defection slipped a knot that secured all Christians to their universe. Their faith was their identity, the last redoubt of their resistance, and they felt toward converts the same sorrowful contempt soldiers feel toward a man who deserts his post under fire.

Into this caldron Cervantes cast his leaden stock of guilt and pride and outrage, to be syncretized into a pervasive religious impulse. His quest for expiation, the private and Catholic need for purification by sacrifice, fused with his courage and despair to produce his gestures of renunciation, his heroics, his evangelistic sense of responsibility toward all the world. The apparent hopelessness of his captivity—five hundred escudos! Why not five million?—blended with his doctrine of free will as a lever to salvation. Don Quixote contemplates the galley slaves he is about to liberate and declares that "it seems harsh to me to make slaves of men whom God and Nature created free. . . ."[25]

This is guessing, of course. But without such an explanation we cannot fathom what has been called his "complete moral sovereignty" in Algiers;[26] we are left with a Cervantes whose courage was mere robot masculinity embalmed in reflex pietism, a figure huge but hollow, like the lath-and-plaster giants in Spanish festival processions: we know there is a man inside the grimacing, bouncing, shuffling effigy, but we cannot see him.

There is a documentary frame for a missionary portrait. To judge from the *Información de Argel*, the free-handed, roistering soldier from Naples became something of an evangelist in captivity. Not only was he active in "honest, upright things" and noted for the "clean and honorable thoughts" characteristic of an "honorable and virtuous Christian,"[27] but, testified Diego Castellano, he "succored poor Christians, helping them to pay their wages and survive." (Slaves were routinely hired out for day wages which they were obliged to turn over to their owners.) Juan de Valcázar, a friend since the Tunis campaign, said Cervantes talked a number of renegades who had taken up piracy into reconverting and jumping ship in Christian territory, comforting them and encouraging them. "If it had not been for the industry and good spirit of Miguel de Cervantes," he declared, "the boys would still be in Algiers and would be Moors and persisting in their evil ways. . . ." Valcázar confirmed that Cervantes gave alms to poor captives, "giving them the wherewithal to buy food and paying their wages to prevent their being maltreated by beatings and other mistreatment." Witness Luis de Pedrosa had "never seen anyone who so consistently did good to other captives," conduct which brought him "great fame, praise, honor and glory among the Christians."

He took his proselytizing seriously. There is unmistakable satisfaction in the success of a clearly autobiographical character named Saavedra, in Act IV of *Life in Algiers,* in dissuading his friend Pedro from apostatizing. Pedro protests that he would "neither reject Christ nor believe in Mohammed" and asserts that only "with voice and costume I'll be a Moor to gain the goal I seek," explaining that his plan is to become a pirate merely to jump ship on Christian land "and not unburdened with treasure." Saavedra is ahead of him on the declining path of choice. "Greedy snares are these, and vain," he warns, ". . . for you shall always be waiting for the how and when: 'Not this year; the next will be surer. . . .' " The argument ends with Pedro bestowing blessings "for your teachings of wholesome firmness."

He couldn't win them all. That Saavedra comes off very much second best in an exchange with a turncoat captive named Leonardo is oddly reassuring, for it suggests that Cervantes' sense of the ridiculous saved him from being self-righteously windy. Here he stands off and deflates himself with wry candor. The scene in Act II presents Saavedra lamenting his bad luck with typical Cervantine relish:

> . . . Ay, hard, iniquitous, inexorable star!
> How you have dragged me by the hair
> to the fearful anguish that besets me!

"Laments at times like these are useless," retorts another prisoner, Leonardo, "for if weeping could soften heaven, my tears would already have moved it." He believes in showing "a happy face to sad misfortune," but Saavedra will have none of this. Acquiesce in his disgrace? Better death than "depart by a single point from a righteous way of living." Leonardo replies:

> If I were to imitate your ways
> I would have no choice but to hurl
> myself at once into hunger's arms.

> I know full well captivity holds
> no contentment, but I would not enforce
> my belief in my own distress by dwelling on it.
> I hold my master for a friend; you can see
> how he treats me; I am free to roam.
> Let him who takes pleasure in it
> protest that "I am a captive."

And when Saavedra persists in his censure, Leonardo snaps, "Friend Saavedra,

> if you will drive yourself
> to preach, this is not the soil
> in which you'll reap the fruit you desire. . . ."

Cervantes' humor is in this, but so are his sorrow and the sincerity of his faith. Later, the long nights alone in strange towns, the long, reflective days spent urging a hired mule over the Andalusian hills would shape this faith into something more flexible, more harmonious, still exhortatory, but gentler, an ointment for the guilt of frailty and the aching likelihood of failure.

But that was later. In Algiers his faith was sharper, a weapon to wield in defense of the Lord's honor. Slavery, like war, like art, like existence itself, was a challenge, personal and immediate.

By Christmas, he seems to have persuaded Dalí Mamí to bring him out of confinement; the Greek may even have begun to suspect that, as the Spanish say, he had taken a cat for a hare. Miguel's shattered hand saved him from the galleys, and El Cojo's lingering illusions probably spared the captive from having to do heavy work. Cervantes may have been added to the renegade's household staff, but it is most probable that he was given no work of any kind. He began to circulate, and immediately encountered familiar faces: Gabriel de Castañeda, his companion at Lepanto who was captured in the fall of La Goleta, taken to Constantinople and then to Algiers; Beltrán del Salto; Alférez Ríos; Juan Navarrete, who had already lost his ears in one unsuccessful escape attempt; Andrés Muñoz, who was taken in the *Sol* with Cervantes and who would be among the few in Algiers with whom Miguel would maintain contact in later years. And, of course, Rodrigo.

The plotting to escape began at once.

] 17 [

"Be Thou a Shepherd"

Twenty-five thousand captives; twenty-five thousand dreams of escape, freedom, vengeance. For a Christian caught trying to escape, punishments were often exemplary; ears were lost, noses vanished, floggings were commonplace, the fatal hook* and the slow fire not unusual. The penalty was generally scaled to the fugitive's usefulness or his ransom value, but rarely did he escape unpunished.

Attempts were nevertheless frequent, successful ones less so. Even men who could look forward to being ransomed tried it, out of rage or daring. Despite the captives' relative freedom inside the city, flight was not easy. The more audacious, and expensive, route was by sea. Cervantes and his friends ruled this out; it was considered suicidal in midwinter, when the sea itself was against them and traffic was light enough to make the Algerians' elaborate security system impermeable. Besides, it could take weeks, perhaps months, to arrange for a ship, and they were in a hurry.

Escape by land was even more difficult. The nearest haven was Spanish Oran, some 220 miles to the west. But the coast was infested with Algerian patrols up to the Oranese border and the inland track ran through a region of bramble-covered hills and shale desert, a dead land peopled by nomad tribes who hunted fugitives for bounty. Wolves, hyenas, an occasional lion prowled the underbrush. Armed patrols, though less regular than along the seafront, were frequent everywhere in the area.

This, however, was the route chosen. Cervantes apparently organized the break; in any case, he is known to have selected the Moor who was bribed to guide the party of eight fugitives to Oran. Sometime in January or February 1576, at nightfall, when a group of slaves would pass un-

---

* A method of execution which consisted of dropping a naked, bound man from a height onto a large iron hook and letting him dangle from wherever it caught him until he expired.

noticed among the crowds of Christians returning home from work, they filtered through the truck farms on the city's southwestern edge. Each man carried a supply of biscuit, a package of edible herbs and a paste of flour, eggs and honey. Ahead of them lay ten to fourteen days of walking across rugged terrain, scuttling like lizards into the brush at the sound of a voice or a hoofbeat or the distant flash of the sun on a white burnoose.

How far they got is unclear, but they had been gone for several days, according to the *Información,* before the guide deserted them. An echo of their anguish, if not of their predicament, is heard in the lament of the lost fugitive in *Life in Algiers:*

> This long way,
> so much heath and mountain
> and the continuous roaring
> of man-eating beasts
> has put me in such a state
> that I think to end it with my death.
> My bread is soggy
> and my clothes torn by brambles;
> my shoes rent,
> my resolution consumed
> so that I cannot advance one foot
> a toe's length before the other.
> Now hunger afflicts me
> and insufferable thirst torments me,
> already my strength is waning,
> already I can see that this misfortune
> will end in my surrender
> to whoever may want to recapture me.
> My judgment is gone;
> I no longer know which is the sure way
> to Oran; no path, no road
> is pointed by my sorry plight—
> more: so weary am I that I could not move
> a step though I should find it.

After discussing the problem, they decided against trying to continue on their own; an unknown land held more terrors for them than the known perils behind them. They trekked back, each to his prison, to face punishment from their individual owners. Miguel, who took full responsibility for leading the attempt, may have been beaten. Diego Castellano says he was treated "much worse than before, with clubs and chains";

elsewhere we learn that "from then on he was held in more chains and more closely guarded and confined."

It was in Algiers, Cervantes tells us, that he "learned to have patience in adversity."[1]

In March 1576, Castañeda was ransomed along with a Valencian notary named Antonio Marco. When the soldier returned to Madrid, he carried letters to the Cervantes family containing the first news they had of the brothers' captivity.

So much is farce in the grim drama of Cervantes' redemption that one inclines to see it as a shadow play in the two-level form of sixteenth-century theater. On a balcony, the ragged captives move furtively from man to man, whispering gravely, clapping one on the shoulder, arguing with another, edging warily away from a third, freezing into tense attitudes of enmity as turbaned figures enter and exit. On the planks below them, a conspiratorial Doña Leonor and a frantically posturing Rodrigo dash blindly against a ring of gray-faced men in rusty black suits—the royal bureaucrats. They are seen as decent men, not heartless, but made so papery by the dusty universe they inhabit that even their charity seems mean-spirited, miserable.

As soon as his sons' letters arrived, Rodrigo hurriedly worked up a petition for aid and presented it to the Council of Castile. He must have been rebuffed, because the action is followed some weeks later by another plea, this one to the Royal Council. But his was only one such appeal among too many. Again the answer was no. He turned to still another body, the Council of the Cruzada, which administered a subsidy granted the Spanish crown by the papacy. Here he was told that his petition was incomplete. On November 9, 1576, nearly six months after the letters' arrival and a year after his sons' capture, Rodrigo took testimony before a Madrid notary from Castañeda and Marco confirming the Cervantes brothers' captivity. The result, apparently, was still another refusal.

The family's desperation was heightened that summer by the announcement that the Order of Mercy was planning a ransom mission to Algiers for the following spring.[2] That it was to be a major effort was emphasized by the appointment of no fewer than three Mercenarian prefects to make the voyage, Fray Jorge del Olivar of Valencia, Fray Jorge de Ongay of Pamplona and Fray Jerónimo Antich of Mallorca. Olivar was expected shortly in the capital to seek funds there for the mission.

Doña Leonor rose determinedly to the occasion, and Rodrigo fell to it as nobly. Whose idea it was for Rodrigo to "die" so that Leonor, swathed in widow's black, could work more effectively on the sympathy of the Cruzada's functionaries is not known. Navarro y Ledesma favored old friend Alonso Getino de Guzmán, the ex-dancer turned royal bailiff; he had the right sense of fantasy, and his job gave him an insight into official thinking. But in its easy negation of Rodrigo's identity there is more than a whiff of Cortinas shrewdness. The important thing was that the scheme worked, more or less. Doña Leonor, perhaps exaggerating ever so slightly the heaviness of her weeds as she exaggerated her sons' wounds ("one of them had his hand cut off and the other lacked an arm"), petitioned for aid in liberating her sons, the sole supports of a widowed mother. . . .[3]

On November 28, the Cruzada approved a grant of sixty escudos of four hundred maravedis, thirty escudos for each son. The conditions attached to the grant—it was absurdly small, but it was something, well meant, undoubtedly all that could be given—were nastily governmental: a guarantor must be provided (Getino volunteered); unless a signed receipt was submitted within one year by the captives themselves testifying to their liberation, the money was to be refunded to the council.

The family's cash reserve was tiny. And every other source of revenue seemed closed. Andrea and Magdalena could hope for nothing from the Pachecos for at least two more years. Rodrigo tried to collect on his eight-hundred-ducat loan to Pedro Sánchez de Córdoba; he was simply ignored. Only one possibility, the most desperate, was left to them, and sometime in the late autumn, they sold all but their most essential household goods. The only record of this is contained in a petition Doña Leonor submitted to the Cruzada in 1579: "If Your Sanctity does not grant me this charity, the result will be that my said son will not be ransomed, for I have no resources, having sold such goods as I possess to ransom Rodrigo de Cervantes, my son. . . ."[4] We do not know how much the sale produced, probably not a great deal, but it was added to the sixty escudos Doña Leonor finally collected on December 16 and immediately turned over to Fray Jorge.

Andrea, too, went to law for money, but probably not on her brothers' behalf. In October 1576 she petitioned for legal guardianship of her daughter "Constanza de Figueroa" in order to "pursue her lawsuits . . . and collect her goods and treasure."[5] Why is the child's father not named in the petition? What "goods and treasure" was she after? Were the Ovandos blocking a grant, perhaps a bequest, to Nicolás' daughter? Andrea was granted the guardianship, but there is no evidence that Constanza ever came into her mysterious estate.

One other item of note occurred in Madrid that winter to swell the volume of news in the letters the Cervanteses sent to their sons with the Mercenarian fathers: the appointment of Mateo Vázquez de Leca as a secretary to King Philip II.

In Algiers, meanwhile, the arrival of spring meant an easier time for Miguel. With El Cojo off raiding, he was again free to roam the city. Most of what he saw there could only have inflamed his anger. The con-

stant rattle of chains, the casual insults, the occasional blow or rude shove
may have been less soul-shriveling than the sight of new captives stumbling off returned corsair galleys, in their eyes the same frightened impotence he would so well have remembered as his own only a few months—
only months?—before. We may catch a glimpse of Cervantes himself
among the captives on the beach in *The Dungeons of Algiers* who, "gaz-
ing toward their country with eyes of desire," sang to the music of the
waves lapping at the sand *"cuan cara eres de haber, O dulce España!"*—
how dear to be with you, oh sweet Spain![6]

It was not all straining and sorrow, of course. Cervantes was a curious
man and the wealth of detail he brought into his stories concerning
Moslem clothes, customs and manners indicates how enrapt he must frequently have been in studying them. Fitzmaurice-Kelly imagines that,
"while his captors watched two tattoed Moors, oiled from head to foot,
wrestle amid a clash of cymbals and drums, Cervantes may have stolen to
the marketplace to hear the Ráwi, the Arab trouvère, tell the 'Tale of
King Omar bin al Núuman and his sons,' in which Kanmakan and
Sabbáh seem the Oriental analogues of Don Quixote and Sancho."[7] He
observed the children fondling their talismans—a bit of lion's skin, a tur-
tle bone, a chameleon's head, silver tablets inscribed with passages from
the Koran. There were the wedding parties, to be climaxed by that triumphant moment when the door of the bridal chamber opened just wide
enough to allow the bridegroom to hurl the bride's bloodstained drawers
to her waiting kinswomen for exultant exhibition. He saw newly married
women going masked in sign of mourning for their virginity. Almost
surely he encountered a party of students helping a woman through a
difficult childbirth by chanting orations through the streets while clutching an extended bedsheet on which trembled a single egg and entreating
the women of the town to douse the egg with jars of water in the belief
that the child would be born when the water broke the egg.

From the houses he passed might come the sound of music made cool
and soothing by its rubbing against porphyry columns and mosaic fountains. Perhaps he watched the women dance with ponderous grace in
their patios, for so negligible were Christians considered that none but the
most dignified of Moslem matrons objected to being seen by them. Algerian women were reputed beautiful and, if they were prosperous, their
lives were a long and languid celebration. As girls, they were fattened for
marriage "like turkeys, occasionally dying under the spoon";[8] once wed,
they maintained their seductiveness by munching endless quantities of
sweets, which, with an aversion to any exercise more strenuous than an
undulant excursion to some holy man's tomb outside the walls, preserved
them in that ideal state still revered in the more remote Andalusian villages: *gorda, blanca y tierna*—fat, white and tender.

That Cervantes ever succumbed to these attractions to the point of including an Algerian mistress among his distractions is highly unlikely. Aside from his private hesitancy toward sex, perhaps only recently reinforced by a disastrous Neapolitan affair, he points out in Act II of *The Dungeons of Algiers* that

> Labor and sorrow
> kill lascivious appetites,
> and the great fear of punishment
> for our guilt restrains us all. . . .

Familiarity with Algerian daily life seems to have tempered but not dissolved Cervantes' hatred of all things "Turkish." Like Sancho Panza, reproached as a poor Christian for nursing a grudge, he could retort that that was all well and good, but his shoulders remembered their injuries.[9] Cervantes' very last work, the *Persiles,* opens with the "barbarian" Corsicurbo shouting down into "the narrow mouth of a deep dungeon, more tomb than prison of the many living dead entombed there. . . ."

If read uncritically, his captivity plays could be viewed as anti-Moslem propaganda, and some of his changes in reworking *Life in Algiers* into the *Dungeons* have been seen as confirmation of this function. Consider the scene in Act III of the first version in which Francisquito, a boy precociously amenable to martyrdom, moves to embrace his brother Juanico. The younger child rebuffs him with infantile importance in imitation of his new benefactors:

> Brother? Since when?
> Be off with the dog;
> let him not touch me!
> FRANCISCO: Why do you *convert*[10] my joy
> into tears, my brother?
> JUAN: You are very stupid.
> Is aught more pleasant than to be a Moor?
> Look at this fine robe
> that my friend gave me—
> and I have another, of brocade,
> stranger still and more resplendent.
> I eat savory couscous,
> sugary sherbet I drink. . . .[11]
> And you shall labor in vain
> to move me with your tears,
> but if you want to be a Moor
> I swear you can achieve it.
> Take my sage advice

and you will see your lot bettered.
Farewell, for it is a great sin
to converse so much with Christians.

But Spanish theater audiences did not welcome the notion that their innocents were vulnerable to heathen bribery. In the *Dungeons*—which was never staged—Juanico is straitened into joining his inflexible brother as a symbol of Christian constancy:

FRANCISCO:	Why, brother, be thou a shepherd, strong and brave, for behind you will joyfully follow a little sinner made innocent by the grace of our Lord. . . . this strange obstinacy with which tyranny musters all its fury shall draw from my lips no more than . . .
JUAN:	What?
FRANCISCO:	An Ave Maria.
CARAHOJA(Turk):	Let us go in, for gifts shall yet do more to change their minds than the whip and the rod.
CADI:	A hundred thousand signs tell me my campaign is failing . . . I shall be accursed of Mohammed himself if I do not rule these rogues.
FRANCISCO:	Are you not afraid of him?
JUAN:	I am not afraid of him.[12]

Propaganda? Perhaps. Yet in the same act Cervantes presents a Moorish crowd as being moved to tears by the martyrdom of a relapsed renegade who, a Moslem witness declares, died "so happy that I believe he did not die." In Act III, Cervantes' assertion of Turkish cruelty is softened by his surprise at their tolerance. We see the prisoners preparing an Easter play to accompany the mass and wondering that

these faithless dogs allow us,
as you see, to keep our religion.
They give us freedom to say
our mass, though secretly.

Algiers, Cervantes remarks, is "a miniature Noah's ark of every kind of trade and talent, of disguised virtues," sometimes all too well disguised. The character named Ossorio recounts that

> once, the consecrated priest
> was taken from his altar
> and dragged through the streets
> of the town, and so cruelly
> did they use him that, on the way,
> he left his freedom and his life.

In Act II of *Life in Algiers* Cervantes fulminates against

> these people, in whom goodness has no home,
> (who) never gave a word they kept,
> being false, lawless, faithless and treacherous.

And he seems to be following the same track nearly two decades later when, in introducing Cide Hamete Benengeli as the "author" of *Don Quixote*, he apologizes for any "inaccuracies" in the story because the narrator was an Arab, "it being characteristic of those of that nation to be liars." If anything good is missing from the story, we are warned, "I am certain it was because of its dog of an author. . . ."[13]

It takes us a while to realize that Cervantes is being playful. For the "dog of an author" is, after all, Cervantes, and he persistently thereafter guarantees Cide Hamete as being "very accurate at all times," a "meticulous investigator," etc.[14] He gives the game away at one point: "Cide Hamete, chronicler of this great history, begins this chapter with these words: 'I swear as a Catholic Christian . . . ,' to which his translator comments that in swearing as a Catholic Christian when he is a Moor, as he doubtless was, Cide Hamete wished only to say that, since a Catholic Christian when he swears, swears or should swear truthfully. . . ."[15]

Miguel's circle of friends (Rodrigo, as usual, is a phantom presence) must have been wide in Algiers. He found them even among the renegades, for we know he enlisted one of them as an intermediary in a wildly ambitious escape plan and that he may have owed his life to the intercession of another when the attempt failed. Much is made in the *Información de Argel* of the fact that "the said miguel de serbantes [sic] . . . always and continuously associated, communicated and conversed with the leading Christians, such as priests, lawyers, nobles and others in His Majesty's service, with much familiarity, all of whom were delighted to have him as a friend and to converse with him; and particularly . . . that the very reverend Redemptionist fathers . . . associated, communicated and conversed with him, having him at their table and holding him in close friendship."

It is not surprising that hidalgo Cervantes frequented the gentry among the captives; one hardly sees him drinking himself sodden on home brew in the prison taverns, still less joining the masked Christians who danced for coin at Moorish gatherings or shot oranges off each other's heads with arrows. Yet he seems to have endeared himself even to the humblest among his fellow slaves. Hernando de Vega tells us it was "public and notorious to this witness as to the other Christians in Algiers that, because the said Miguel de Cervantes was a leading and illustrious person in addition to being wise and of good inclinations and habits, all were pleased and delighted to associate and communicate with him . . . noblemen, captains, ecclesiastics and soldiers, and such is he that he is not only cherished, loved and esteemed by all those I have mentioned, but all the other persons in the community cherish, love and prize him because he is the type of person they admire, amiable and noble and gentle with everyone. . . ."

Cervantes' pride in his acceptance, even his lionization, by the leading citizens of this slave commonwealth would be pitiable if it were less noble. The gentry seemed to have recognized in him that impulse to sacrifice himself for the general good which motivates the finest public servants. And they were ready to exploit it. They were willing to be included in the escape plans organized and carried forward by humble soldier Cervantes; they were equally content to let him take the blame on himself when the plans went haywire. Years later, when his petitions for royal favor were being consistently rejected, we find no evidence that any of these influential personages came forth to point out how mistaken King Philip was in depriving himself of so faithful a servant.

By the summer of 1577 there were over 70 captives among the 25,000 slaves in Algeria who could be counted as intellectuals—by which, in the context, is often simply meant the instructed. The proportion was considered high by Haedo. Many were priests and/or jurists, but even among these there were or would be poets and authors of learned works, such men as that "clear current"[16] Dr. Domingo Becerra, who in 1585 would publish his *Galateo, or Treatise on Customs,* and Bartholomeo Ruffino de Chiambery, the soldier, doctor of both canon and civil law, whose treatise on the fall of La Goleta and Tunis, written in captivity while he was shuttled from Tunis to Constantinople to Algiers, finally perished in a fire in the Turin Library in 1904.

These were Cervantes' true intimates, for of such consolations as were available to him, poetry, as the most absorbing, must have been the most therapeutic. That he wrote poems in Algiers is documented; a few of them survive in identifiable "Algerian period" form and many others are certainly, though not verifiably, embedded in *La Galatea* and in the captivity stories. Some of his earliest stories—*The Liberal Lover,* for example —may have been outlined or even drafted in Algiers, though they were not published until over a generation later. If he wrote any plays for the prisoners' festivals they have been lost, or were blended into works composed after his liberation. Sosa testified that he "often worked at composing verses in praise of Our Lord and His Blessed Mother and of the Holy Sacrament and other holy and pious subjects, some of which he made a special point of showing to me, sending them to me that I might see them."

It was Ruffino's manuscript which elicited the first poems we know Cervantes wrote in Algiers, probably late in 1576. Ruffino showed him or read him the work and, with the spontaneous generosity Cervantes usually displayed on such occasions, he composed two sonnets in praise of the work and its author:

> With ever green laurel shall you be
> crowned, unless I miss my guess,
> if once our fortune and cruel fate
> removes you from such sad and low estate.

Not good; not even adequate. But there is triumph in the first stumbling steps a child takes unsupported, admiration for a shoot which defies the cold winds of early spring to burst, incredibly, through the crusted earth.

The Mercenarian mission arrived in Algiers April 20, 1577, with "a great abundance of money and other types of merchandise."[17] On April 27 the first ransom agreements were reached. At best, the news the monks brought Miguel and Rodrigo from home must have been depressing. Word from Olivar of their mother's "widowhood" may have startled them at first, but the letters he carried would have reassured them about their father. What was clear from the meagerness of the sum the family had been able to raise was that the moderately prosperous family the brothers had left behind them in Madrid had reverted to its normal state of indigence.

Negotiations with Ramadan Pasha had brought Rodrigo's price down to a still exorbitant three hundred ducats. The dey was at the end of his three-year term of office and eager to convert his remaining "properties" into cash before the arrival of his successor, Hassan Veneciano. But Dalí Mamí, then in Constantinople bribing his way into the captaincy of the Algerian fleet, had left strict orders: the tariff of Miguel was still five hundred gold escudos. None of El Cojo's deputies dared to settle for less.

Although, as the eldest son, Miguel had first claim on any money available, he renounced his rights to Rodrigo. Doubtless he calculated that the Mercenarians' funds might be stretched to cover Rodrigo's three hundred ducats, but they were surely not elastic enough to reach his five hundred escudos, much less to free both of them.

However logical, the decision must have struck both of them as tantamount to a death sentence on Miguel. Now hope and escape were synonymous, and they knew what the odds were against survival, let alone success in such ventures. Miguel nevertheless immediately set about his plans, "for the hope of gaining my freedom never deserted me, and when . . . the outcome failed to coincide with my intent, I never gave up, but proceeded to invent and pretend to some new hope to sustain me, no matter how frail and weak it might be."[18]

He accordingly "gave orders that a brother of his named rrodrigo de servantes [sic], who was ransomed from this Algiers in the month of August of the same year with the same money provided for the ransom of the said miguel de serbantes, that he arrange for and dispatch from Valencia and Mallorca and Ibiza an armed frigate to carry . . . Christians to Spain; and to better effectuate this, he availed himself of the favor of Don Antonio de Toledo[19] and of Don Francisco de Valencia, knights of St. John, who were then captives in this Algiers, who gave (Rodrigo) letters to the viceroys of Valencia and Mallorca and Ibiza, charging and begging them to favor the transaction."

The classic plot: recruiting a fast ship of eight to ten oars manned by skilled mariners of the Mediterranean islands who knew the Barbary coasts. Disguised as Turks, the rescuers would beach the craft on the sand some two miles from the city; those who spoke the local language best would go ashore at dusk to seek the waiting captives while the vessel stood out to sea under cover of darkness. It was a dangerous business, fatal to anyone who had once been a slave and who was caught in what the Turks not unnaturally viewed as an act of sabotage. Prices were as high as the risk, certainly too high for the Cervantes brothers to attempt on their own. Thus the need for Miguel to associate as many distinguished persons as possible with the venture and hope that all this marooned gentility could pass a large enough hat among the authorities in the Balearics to pay the operation's costs.

The timing seemed perfect. With Ramadan Pasha wholly engrossed in his liquidation sale and Dalí Mamí and Arnaute Mamí both absent, no one was paying too much attention to those prisoners who had been disqualified in the ransom sweepstakes.

Miguel, "awaiting the said frigate, ordered fourteen of the highest-ranking prisoners . . . to hide in a cave which he had found and arranged for outside the city, where some of the said Christians were hidden for six months, and others less, and there he supplied and obtained provision for them and had other persons provide the necessary for them, with the said Miguel de Cervantes having the daily care of sending supplies to all of them, for which he ran in great peril of his life and of being put on the hook and burned alive. . . ."

Admirable, heroic, devoted. And puzzling. The cave was in the grounds of an estate owned by an Alcaide Hassan some three miles east of the city, near the sea. How did Cervantes manage to get supples to the men in it every day for months? Where did the money for provisions come from? Certainly not from Cervantes himself; Valcázar said he often heard Cervantes complain that he had to borrow money for his own sustenance because Dalí Mamí "gave him nothing to eat, nor clothes to wear," and this is repeated in testimony later taken in Madrid. The disappearance of so many valuable captives must have been noticed; did the authorities assume they had all escaped? This is hard to believe; in any case, no search seems to have been made for them.

Too many witnesses agree on the basic facts of the episode to doubt its accuracy. According to some testimony, Cervantes borrowed over one thousand reales from Christian traders and other visitors to Algiers; the men in the cave may have been able to pay some of the expenses. But the ingenuity and organization needed to carry out such an operation still leave us openmouthed in wonder. True, El Cojo's absence made it easier for Cervantes to scheme, to beg, probably to steal, risking his life, ignoring the bagpipe and drums of the *mensuar*† sounding the curfew from the palace grounds two and a half hours after dark, (from then until the same signal was sounded two and a half hours before dawn, any Christian found on the streets was liable to severe punishment) to carry food to the fugitives. Some of that borrowed money must have gone in bribes to jailers and watchmen. The experience that teaches a man to move with a stoat's cunning is quickly acquired in a prison camp. Cervantes would have seen his devotion and his peril as the cost of his own freedom, and considered it cheap at the price.

The men in the cave might never have agreed to the plan had they thought they would have to spend more than a few weeks in hiding. It is inconceivable that anyone went into hiding before early May, when Rodrigo's release seemed assured. Had everything gone according to plan, the frigate would have arrived to take them off sometime in July. While the "six months" cited in testimony is merely one more example of the documentary inflation to which the Cervantes family was prone, some of the fugitives were to spend nearly five months in their self-allotted dungeon.

† The common hangman.

They cannot be blamed for their innocence. No one seems to have anticipated what was about to happen, not the busy Mercenarian fathers, not the captives they had ransomed, perhaps not Ramadan Pasha himself.

What happened was Hassan Veneciano.

A cataclysm on legs, cruel as a hurricane is cruel—naturally, coldly, arrogantly.

On Sts. Peter and Paul Day, June 29, 1577, Ramadan led an official procession to the port to receive his successor. He may have been a little nervous; Hassan, a former Venetian scribe, was Euldj Ali's protégé; the security of such powerful protection allowed him to make his greed and ruthlessness almost legendary throughout the Ottoman Empire.

Father Dan gives us a picture of a transfer of power in 1634 which, although the Algerian power structure had changed somewhat by then, may help us visualize the scene in the port in 1577. All the officers of the government, some fifteen hundred in 1634, were massed in the port. As the new pasha went ashore, cannon from all the ships in the harbor joined the guns of the forts in a salvo of salute. A procession of janissaries and militiamen marched in escort to the sound of music "more capable of inspiring fear than giving pleasure." The newcomer, clad in a flowing white tunic in sign of peace—one wonders if Hassan troubled himself with such gestures—rode a horse with a jeweled silver saddle and stirrups, holding a silken bridle woven with turquoises.[20]

Cervantes picks up the description here. Although *The Liberal Lover* is set in Nicosia after the Turkish conquest of Cyprus, and the time element is deliberately fudged, his description of a new pasha's accession may have been based on recollections of Hassan's arrival in Algiers. In the story, Ricardo and his crypto-Christian friend Mahamut reach the beach in time to see the outgoing dey greet his successor:

> Ali Pasha (for so he who was leaving the government was named) was accompanied by all the janissaries normally stationed in Nicosia . . . they marched in two wings or files, some carrying muskets and the others naked scimitars. Arriving at the tent of the new pasha, Hassan, they formed ranks around him and Ali Pasha, bowing, did reverence to Hassan, and (Hassan) greeted him with a slighter bow.

The contrast between their counterparts in Algiers as they exchanged greetings must have been shocking. The relatively mild-mannered Ramadan was around fifty years old; his crest of black hair and his full black beard were already edged with gray, and years of indolent authority and luxury had covered his robust frame with a layer of unmilitary fat. The man before him was in his early thirties, "tall, lean, with large, burning eyes, an aquiline nose, small mouth, sparsely bearded, with chestnut hair and a sallow, yellowish complexion, all indications of his evil nature."[21] He was said to have curbed his tendency to corpulence by schooling himself to eat only once every four or five days. This enforced asceticsim may have helped generate the nervous energy with which he "every day hanged this man, impaled another, cut another's ears, and this for so little cause, or none at all, that the Turks knew he did so for pleasure, and because he was naturally inclined to murder the whole human species."[22]

Let us return to the scene as Ricardo and Mahamut saw it:

> Then Ali entered Hassan's pavilion and the Turks put (Hassan) on a powerful, richly adorned horse and, leading him around the circle of tents and then on a broader circuit of terrain, shouted and cheered and said in their language, "Viva, viva Suleiman the Sultan, and Hassan, Pasha in his name!" They repeated this many times, with increased vigor, and then led him back to the tent where Ali Pasha had been waiting. Then Ali, the Cadi‡ and Hassan enclosed themselves in the tent alone for the space of an hour.
>
> Mahamut told Ricardo that they had retired to discuss what needed doing in the city in connection with the projects Ali had begun. Shortly thereafter, the Cadi came to the tent opening and, in Turkish, Arabic and Greek, loudly proclaimed that all those wishing to enter to ask justice, or who had any other complaint against Ali Pasha, might enter freely, that there was Hassan Pasha, sent by the Great Lord as viceroy . . . and who would see to all right and justice. With this warning, the janissaries stepped away from the entrance and made way for all who wished to enter.

Ramadan—certainly the model for Ali Pasha—must have been a shaken man by then. Hassan Veneciano's concern for right and justice in Algiers was entirely personal. He at once set the tone for his administration by illegally pre-empting jurisdiction over all captives up for ransom who were held by the corsair captains and by Ramadan. All previous ransom agreements were nullified and made subject to renegotiation with him alone.

The news fell on Cervantes and his friends like a cudgel blow. If Rodrigo's ransom agreement failed to survive renegotiation, the escape plot collapsed. And what of the men in the cave, meanwhile? They could not simply saunter back to their prisons as though they had been out sight-seeing. At the very least, Hassan's order could mean that the Mercenarians' work would drag on indefinitely. Yet as long as there was any

‡ A Turkish civil magistrate.

hope of escape, Miguel had to keep funneling supplies and encouragement to his new dependents.

For those who had a choice, the new situation was too risky to gamble on. Antonio de Toledo and Francisco de Valencia, whose influence was so vital to the success of Cervantes' plot, secretly negotiated their ransoms with their owners, who feared that Hassan would confiscate these rich prizes. The two men fled to Tétuan.

When he learned of this, the new dey was enraged: seven thousand ducats for Toledo, a nephew of the Duke of Alba! Hassan would have demanded fifty thousand. The scene is imagined in *Life in Algiers,* when the dey roars that

> I cannot speak for grief and anger. . . .
> For so vile a price, vile rabble, did you trade
> so illustrious and rich a knight? So greedy
> were you for money, so great seemed the fee
> that you even threw in a companion
> who alone could have paid the price?[23]

He demanded the execution of two captives on the pretext that they had insulted Moslem slaveowners. Fray Jorge del Olivar had them spirited out of the country and, when Hassan threatened wholesale executions in reprisal, the friar offered himself as a hostage instead. Hassan was only too pleased to accept the bargain: as a Mercenarian prefect, Olivar was worth far more than the two men he had saved. The gesture is duly commemorated by Cervantes:

> . . . after disbursing the full twenty thousand ducats
> he had brought, (he) remained in pawn
> for seven thousand more. O rare charity!
> O holy heart![24]

Tension was raised still higher by the news that the mad king of Portugal, eighteen-year-old Sebastian I, had sailed from Lisbon at the head of seventeen thousand men (plus, despite the king's religious fanaticism, some nine thousand camp followers) to wage holy war against the emperor of Morocco. A single thought bred hope among the Christians and terror among the Moslems in Algiers: that a victorious Christian army might then turn against the strongest of the Barbary provinces. To forestall the slave insurrection that was a constant Algerian nightmare, surveillance was stiffened; guards were reinforced in all prisons. No Christian felt safe in the streets and with reason; panicky mobs killed several who had allowed the sudden surge of hope in their hearts to show in their faces.

The security measures, along with the return of Dalí Mamí to Algiers with Hassan, sharply curtailed Cervantes' freedom of movement. It may have been at this point that he recruited an assistant known by the nickname of "El Dorador." Not yet twenty years old, the youth was one of the rootless, oddly unsubstantial characters who flitted so sadly through the slave towns, unstable, wretched, without pasts or futures, virtually without identities. He was apparently born in Melilla, already a Spanish enclave in Morocco; a baptismal certificate for him is dated September 29, 1557, perhaps ten years to the day after the birth of Cervantes, and he had been christened Miguel. His father had been the town's Spanish chief magistrate, Bartolomé Dorador, and his mother a black slave named Juana. Miguel is believed to have been the second of three children Dorador fathered on his slave; the relationship apparently was approved by Spanish society in Melilla, for the baptismal records list some of the town's leading citizens as witnesses.

Bartolomé Dorador died in 1559, when documentation on his slave family ends; Juana and her three children presumably vanished into the family estate and the group eventually disintegrated. Miguel, born a Christian, seems to have converted to Islam, then returned to Christianity.

It is easy to understand the appeal to Cervantes of this boy who, with no legitimate name of his own, had adopted his father's as his nickname. Here was a chance to rescue a drowning soul, perhaps to set him on some constructive path. They could help each other: if El Dorador would convey the provisions Cervantes furnished to the cave in Alcaide Hassan's garden, a place would be made for him on the frigate for Spain. Any doubts in his mind about the youth's reliability were probably overruled by Cervantes' need and his compassion.

By early August, the pace of ransom negotiations had picked up. They had been spurred by reports from Morocco: in a single four-hour battle, eight thousand Portuguese had been slain, Sebastian among them; fifteen thousand Christians were captured. Portugal's treasury was emptied and its throne deserted. The news made even Hassan feel relatively benign, and impatient to go off raiding on his own.

On August 24, 1577, Rodrigo was one of 106 captives who sailed from Algiers. Wearing the Mercenarian scapular in grateful advertisement of his redeemer's order, he entered Valencia September 1; twenty-four hours later, with the signing of his act of redemption, he was a free man.

He wasted no time in delivering his letters to the viceroys of Valencia, Mallorca and Ibiza, waiting, probably in Mallorca, while arrangements were made with a Mallorcan named Viana to attempt the rescue. From there he headed for Madrid, for Miguel had entrusted one more document to him for delivery, the letter which, to modern eyes, may be the strangest of all his writings. This was the *Epistle in Tercets from Miguel de Cervantes, Captive, to M. Vázquez, My Lord,* a poem in eighty tercets and one quatrain.

Most of the first ninety lines are devoted to buttering up the junior royal secretary with what seems to be curiously un-Cervantine flattery, phrased with a suavity worthy of a practiced courtier. They recall the men's former friendship, when Vázquez was

> inexpert and new
> at things which, now, he weighs and treats of
> so well that I am envious. . . .

Mateo, the poem asserts, did not win his position by haunting the favorite's door

> breakfastless, after a hungry night,
> but through virtue alone. . . .

It apologizes that

> the muted tones of my rustic flute,
> my lord, have not reached your ears,
> though it is time it had a better sound . . .

but in a lengthy review of Cervantes' career to date, it pleads that this

> . . . was not for lack of effort
> but for the excess of it (which) led me
> on a strange and deviated path. . . .

The poem's climax is an impassioned appeal to Philip II on behalf of "twenty thousand doomed Christians" to invade Algeria:

> may the insolence with which this miserable outpost
> continually seeks to do you outrage
> awaken a great fury in your royal breast. . . .
> In number they are many, but slight in power,
> exposed, ill-armed, with no strong wall
> nor rock for their defense. . . .

The mere knowledge of your coming
will terrify this enemy folk, which
already foresees itself as broken and lost.

The *Epistle* is neither so odd nor so impertinent a document as one
might think. As every subject's father, a monarch was accustomed to receiving every kind of private petition, though only those considered valuable because of the source or the information they contained were allowed to filter through the secretarial screen. And the habit of setting
matter-of-fact material in verse was widespread then. At the age of
twenty-five, Francisco López de Villalobos, a physician to Emperor
Charles V, wrote *A Summary of Medicine with a Treatise on the Pes-
tiferous Bubos* (that is, on syphilis) entirely in verse. Besides, the form
would have flattered Vázquez, who wrote pedestrian verse himself and
who was already beginning to set himself up as a minor patron of the arts
with a personal court of second-rate poets.

But did Cervantes write the *Epistle?* The document, not in Cervantes'
handwriting, was discovered in 1863 in the Madrid archives of the Count
of Altamira, whose wife's family had been connected with Vázquez. It
was never authenticated and the manuscript vanished again soon after its
publication when, along with a quantity of Mateo's correspondence and
state papers, it was disposed of as scrap.

We know that the last section, the appeal to Philip, is genuine because,
with minor changes, it is spoken by Saavedra in Act I of *Life in Algiers.*
Occasional lines from the poem turn up in *La Galatea.* Cervantes was
parsimonious of his verse lines; he was also Mozartian in his willingness
to borrow themes from himself and rework them, to watch them change
their colors in the altered light of new literary atmospheres. Sonnets,
songs, ballads appear in his stories which had obviously spent years wandering in search of a fixed abode.

At least one modern Cervantist dismisses the poem as "apparently a
modern forgery."[25] No reason is given for the judgment except the peculiar manner of its discovery and disappearance and the doubtful theory
that Cervantes would have had no time in Algiers to write a long work
(although it was precisely then, in the enforced idleness imposed by his
captor's return to Algiers, that he might have had the time to do so).

If the poem is a fake, it is an astonishingly good one, stylistically and
psychologically. The forger, if there was one, was a master mimic, able to
capture Cervantes' tone, his rhetoric, even his awkwardness. More: he
seized the very note one might expect to hear resonate in the poem—Cervantes' feeling of helpless anger, the bafflement that drives a man to seek
relief in foolish ways for an unrelievable ill. It is a poem in which Cer-

vantes—for we may conclude it *was* Cervantes'—figuratively stamps his foot and tears his hair.

There is no record that Vázquez acknowledged receipt of the poem, no proof even that he saw it. In any case, he was busy at his own plotting: murky dealings involving Don Juan of Austria, then governor of Flanders, and the Bastard's secretary Juan de Escovedo, had perhaps shown Mateo a way to unseat the man he hated most at court, the king's archsecretary, Antonio Pérez. The feud would crop up repeatedly to bedevil Cervantes.

A long-standing enmity between the two royal clerks had been coming increasingly into the open. They were too much alike for the subtle Pérez to misunderstand the threat his underling posed. Like Vázquez, Pérez was illegitimate, the son of a priest who had also been a secretary to Philip. His rapid rise to the position of Spain's wealthiest and most powerful civil servant had been fostered by the king's Portuguese crony, Ruy Gómez da Silva, Duke of Eboli. By way of thanks, Pérez had taken the duchess, Ana de la Cerda, as his mistress.

Some historians have suspected the duchess of seeking to run Spain through Pérez. She may have been foolish enough to think she could. She was apparently a beauty, "a jewel encrusted in all the enamels of nature and fortune,"[26] Pérez once wrote in a lyrical moment, despite her brood of children (ten births, six survivors) and the black patch she wore over a crossed eye. Haughty, arbitrary, domineering, foul-mouthed and violent she may have been, but the sensual mouth and the seductiveness gleaming in her one good eye from the portraits remaining of her seem to have conveyed a world of sexual intelligence. Philip himself is said to have read the message eagerly, only to be offended in his Hispanic masculinity by Ana's assertion that she preferred Pérez's ass to the king's whole person. It may indeed have been this imprudence that cooled Pérez's passion for her; it was certainly an added stimulus to Philip's unrelenting persecution of the pair. His Most Catholic Majesty never forgot, never pardoned a sexual rebuff. It probably helps to explain why he was willing to listen to Vázquez's murmured hints that Pérez and his Ana were guilty of extortion, fraud and, worst of all, treason.

It should surprise no one, then, that an importunate poem from a remote North African prison may simply have been tossed unread into the oblivion of an antechamber drawer. The author himself could have expected no better.

In Algiers, luck seemed to be with Cervantes and his co-conspirators in the cave. Dalí Mamí, at the head of a nine-ship squadron, had gone raiding at the end of August and surveillance of his captives was relaxed. When word of Viana's departure from Mallorca reached Miguel on September 19, he at once left El Cojo's house to join the men in the grotto, stopping only to urge Sosa one last time to join him. Sosa again refused, fearful that his physical debility might endanger the others. He had spent months in a cell in the house of a renegade Jew, the Alcaide Mahamet, chained to a stone sunk in the cell floor, half-naked and nearly starved; the damp and darkness had given him a wracking cough. The two friends said good-by for what they may both have believed was the last time. Moments later, Miguel slipped through the Bab-Azun Gate toward the grotto.

He found some of the men nearly as weak as Sosa after their months in the cell-like cave. Cervantes' news, his very presence, would have cheered them. The ordeal was nearly over. But, as the rendezvous hour approached, the tension in the cave must have become nearly unbearable.

The frigate was due on the night of September 28. The waiting men saw no sign of it that night, nor on the twenty-ninth. Moreover, that day, September 29, El Dorador failed to show up with food. It was only later that the fifteen waiting men learned that "the said frigate arrived as ordered by the said Miguel de Cervantes, and at the time indicated, and having arrived a second night at the same spot, the sailors' courage failed them and, because no one was willing to go ashore to notify the hidden men, the escape failed."[27]

This was the official version of what happened, but it was probably not the true story. Other testimony in the same document indicates that at least some of Viana's men did live up to their bargain, that they did go ashore and were captured. Alonso Aragonés declared that "the frigate came in twice and was lost on the second try, and this witness spoke to the very Christians who came in her, and they told how they had come for the said Miguel de Cervantes and his companions." According to Cristóbal de Villalón, when the vessel came inshore its men "spied a fishing boat, which they considered highly compromising, and they withdrew to safety. . . ." Sosa affirmed that "I personally talked later with seamen who told me they had come in that frigate and were captured and they described at length how they came twice and why they were afraid and how narrowly the thing came to naught."

Finally, there is Haedo's version: "The misfortune was that at the very place and moment the frigate . . . ran its prow ashore, some Moors happened to be passing there and, despite the darkness, they spied the boat and the Christians from it, and the Moors then began to shout and call for help, yelling, 'Christians! Christians! Boat! Boat!' When those from the vessel saw and heard this, they were forced to put to sea to escape. . . ."[28]

In the cave, the anxious men knew nothing of what was happening. But one conspirator was still in circulation and his already uncertain sta-

bility apparently cracked under the strain. By weaving the pieces of testimony into the tissue of probabilites, we perceive a jittery El Dorador
watching from the beach on the night of September 28 as the frigate
came inshore, spotted the fishing boat and beat a hasty retreat out to sea.
Convinced the attempt had failed, El Dorador's first thought was to
save his own skin. This "bad Christian" may have wrestled with his conscience throughout the night before going to the dey and declaring his
eagerness to return to Islam. To prove his good faith, he gave his companions away, identifying Cervantes as the "author of the plot and the
one who devised it," but, it would seem, naming no one else in the group;
Miguel may have been circumspect enough to have withheld that information, and El Dorador always delivered the supplies he brought to Juan
Navarro, Alcaide Hassan's gardener.

The dey immediately had the garden surrounded. It is reasonable to
suppose that the frigate did return on the following night, that a shore
party fell into the hands of the waiting soldiers and that, seeing or hearing what had happened, the men aboard the craft fled in panic.

On the following morning, a squad of "armed Turks and Moors,
mounted and on foot," surged into the garden and "forcing their way into (the cave)," arrested the conspirators. "Miguel de Cervantes, seeing
they were discovered, told all his companions to throw the blame on him,
promising them that he would implicate no one but himself because he
wished to save all the others; and so, while the Moors were binding
them, the said Miguel de Cervantes declared loudly so that the Turks
and Moors heard him, 'None of the Christians here are guilty in this
business, because I alone was the author of it and I persuaded them to
flee,' thus placing himself in manifest danger of death, because King
Hassan was so cruel that, because a Christian attempted to escape, or
because someone helped or promoted the flight, he would order a man
hanged or at least that his ears and nose be cut off. . . ."

At about the same moment, said Sosa, "thinking that I, too, was waiting for that frigate so as to leave in it," El Dorador went to Sosa's cell
"and began with false and misleading words to excuse himself so that he
might not be blamed for that treachery; and I know that, as he had
promised others that he would become a Moor, so he afterward became
and lived three years as a Moor, until he died on the same date on which
he had disclosed this affair to King Hassan, which was St. Jerome's Day,
the last of September. . . ."

We may catch a glimpse of the wretched youth in the character of
Pedro in *Life in Algiers*, when he confesses to having earned three gold
escudos by informing the dey of the high lineage of the play's hero and
heroine. When Saavedra chides him for his treachery, Pedro asks if he,
who can barely survive, must "respect and honor those who are well able

to pay their ransom? There is no such prayer in my litany!"[29] He goes on to boast of having swindled another slave of four more escudos by pretending he had a boat in which "surely the fool thought he could gain his freedom." Saavedra, now furious, warns him he is sailing in dangerous waters, but Pedro retorts that "other feet must climb the bitter hill of my travail. . . ."[30]

Other feet—Cervantes'—were climbing it now. ". . . The said Turks, having sent a horseman to the King to report all that had occurred, and that the said Miguel de Cervantes had declared himself to be the author of that concealment and flight, the King ordered that he alone be brought to him, and so they brought him, bound and on foot, with many blows and insults along the way from the Turks and Moors."

"And they spit upon him and took the reed, and smote him on the head," says the Gospel of St. Matthew. The analogy of Cervantes with Christ seems contrived until we remember that so Miguel must have seen himself, a martyr climbing to Golgotha. It was on that darkening hill that the Cervantes legend in Algiers began.

Hassan, we are told, "uttered many threats of death and torture in order to learn the truth of that affair, and he (Cervantes) steadfastly persevered in telling the said King that he alone was the author of the said business, and that if His Highness had to punish anyone, that it be him only. And despite all the (King's) questions and threats, he refused to implicate or name anyone else. By so doing, he surely delivered many other Christians from death, and others from heavy punishment to whom the said King ascribed blame. And this was especially the reason why the very reverend father Fray Jorge de Olivar . . . was spared the harm the King wished him, convinced he was behind the business. . . ."

Amazingly, Cervantes walked out of the interview not only alive but unhurt. One can only suppose that he was spared martyrdom by Hassan's sense of property. With the other men from the cave, all appropriated by the dey, he was confined in the royal prison.

Three days later, they were led out to Alcaide Hassan's garden. There was indeed to be a victim, but not the valuable Cervantes nor his commercially viable companions. Juan Navarro, the gardener, was a poor peasant with no hope of finding his ransom, and so expendable. While his co-conspirators watched helplessly, the man was strung up to a tree by one foot—Hassan himself hauled on the rope—and dashed down, hauled up, dashed again for hours until he expired, strangled in his own blood.

The episode, complete with plot, cave and frigate, is re-created in *The Dungeons of Algiers*. With the difference that, in the play, the conspiracy succeeds.

The Author of It All

For two years the world had stopped turning for young Rodrigo; in Algiers he had certainly been so intent on surviving his captivity that his return to Madrid late in 1577 must have given him a feeling of unreality. Life was so normal, Madrid so unconcerned with what he had suffered, what Miguel was still suffering. Most fantastically normal was his family: the same old poverty, the same futile love affairs.

Magdalena was about to break or had just broken off relations with a nobleman named Fernando de Lodeña after a two-year romance, on promise of what was becoming the standard breach-of-promise fee: three hundred ducats. Years later, on her deathbed, Magdalena would recall having gone to Lodeña's house after his marriage to one Ana María de Urbina to reclaim the money she had "lent" him in his bachelor days (the proprieties were being observed even before those who knew perfectly well she had never in her life owned three hundred ducats to lend anyone). He acknowledged the debt, she declared, but "threatened her repeatedly, saying she would never collect a céntimo unless she gave him a signed statement that he owed her nothing, and, when they were alone, promising that as long as she lived, he would provide her with food, and that if she outlived him, he would leave her enough to live on."[1] Unwillingly, she gave him the paper. Like the Pachecos, Lodeña apparently never delivered anything but promises in return, for in her testament she would assert that he still owed her three hundred ducats, which hypothetical sum she would bequeath to her brother Miguel and her niece Constanza.

By early 1578, her genius for choosing companions who offered no real danger of marriage may already have led her to the bed of a Basque gentleman, Juan Pérez de Alcega, lord of the obscure village of Vicuña and a

court official of correspondingly unimposing stature whose major accomplishment seems to have been to acquire a reputation for philandery.
We are nearly three years away from Magdalena's breach-of-promise suit
against *him* (three hundred ducats again, requested on October 26,
1580); the by now slightly tacky pleasures of courtship were still before
her.

Andrea seems to have been more discreet. Rodrigo found her set up
with Constanza in her own establishment, away from her parents, working as a seamstress. The house she rented must have been large and lavish; the 140 ducats a year she paid for it was nearly five times what her
parents were paying for the tiny house into which they were crowded
with Magdalena and, presumably, their invisible youngest son, Juan. It
was too large and lavish, perhaps, to house a seamstress and her daughter.
Some biographers have charitably concluded that her lawsuit against
Nicolás de Ovando must have been moderately successful. But is it really
charitable to suppose that, with her brother in mortal danger and her
parents in poverty, she would have diverted so much of her own money to
the indulgence of a luxurious whim? A deeper morality prompts the conclusion that she shared the house with a new benefactor and that the 140
ducats merely passed through her hands to maintain appearances. His
anonymity, along with Andrea's comfort, suggests that he was already
married, well-to-do, with an established position and, within the plastic
limits of adulterous honor, honorable.

None of this seems to have tempted Rodrigo to make his life in
Madrid. Besides, he had only one trade, soldiering. As soon as this business of Miguel's liberation was disposed of . . .

News of the mission's failure may have reached the Cervantes family as
early as November, through Viana, or as late as February from Miguel
himself. It was all to be done over again. Rodrigo Sr., the family Lazarus,
was officially revived for the effort. On March 17, 1578, he began the
process of petitioning the court for funds on the basis of Miguel's "ten
years of service"—no more than a routine inflation of the record. To establish his brother's merit, young Rodrigo rounded up four witnesses,
Mateo de Santiestéban, Antonio Godinez de Monsalve (who had known
Miguel since Tunis and was ransomed with Rodrigo), Gabriel de Castañeda and Beltrán del Salto y Castilla, both of them Miguel's companions
in the unsuccessful attempt to walk to Oran.

We have already noted the substance of their testimony, chiefly concerning Miguel's heroism at Lepanto and its recognition by Don Juan.
The rest of what they had to offer was functionally vague. Santiestéban
affirmed having known Miguel eight years, but he could not remember
which of his hands had been injured. Godinez had "heard it said by
creditable persons, soldiers and captains,"[2] that Cervantes had served ten

years to date. Salto, too, volunteered that bit of gossip, gleaned from soldiers whose names he, no more than Godinez, could recall. Finally, we have an assertion by Castañeda that he had read Miguel's letter from Don Juan in Algiers, without explaining how he could have seen a document which had been confiscated by Dalí Mamí even before it arrived in Algiers.

One wonders whether anyone but Cervantes' biographers has ever taken this legalistic marzipan seriously. The Royal Council, at any rate, did not. The petition was rejected; the councilors had seen too many others like it. Yet money was needed now, at once, for there was a chance the thing could be done quickly. The family had been informed by the Mercenarians that a Valencian trader Hernando de Torres, was thought to be leaving shortly for North Africa; the fathers said he sometimes undertook ransom negotiations.

It is at this point in the proceedings that a gesture is recorded which, ever since, has made Cervantophile hearts pound with Latin pride. The family, in Miguel's words, contributed "its entire fortune, and the dowries of my maiden sisters, leaving them impoverished in order to ransom their brothers."[3] Splendid! The image of these two maidens sacrificing their hopes for marriage along with their bridal portions is so fine a concept, so generous an impulse, that it is almost cruel to recall that neither sister was a damsel any longer, that both were beyond any realistic hope of marriage, that neither, probably, had a dowry to dispose of. The girls gave what they could, 1,077 reales, slightly under 100 ducats; most or all of it, probably, was Andrea's, possibly from the same mysterious treasury that provided her 140-ducat rental. Andrea further signed a promissory note for 200 ducats more. Then, on June 9, the family agreed in writing to pay anything over the subscribed sum that might be needed to complete the ransom payment. All this was generous enough; surely it represented every maravedi they could beg or borrow. We do not now need, to be touched, the theatrical hokum aimed at piercing bureaucratic hearts.

The money was deposited with the Mercenarians, who acted as intermediaries in such cases and who still held the royal order for thirty escudos to be applied to Miguel's ransom. But the mission never came off. Torres may not have gone to Algiers at all, or he may have refused to risk his own money in the affair, given the Cervantes family's obvious inability to pay.

The next step was a petition from Doña Leonor to the War Council in July for a license to export eight thousand ducats in merchandise to Algiers. Because the request mentioned the letters Miguel received from Don Juan and the Duke of Sessa, the council, impressed by the big names, asked to see them. Leonor had to explain that the letter from Don Juan was gone forever, but she did produce certification from Sessa that the letters had been written. The duke confirmed that Cervantes "lost a hand fighting like a good soldier," that he had "fought well" against the corsairs who captured him and, therefore, that "because he was taken while on His Majesty's service and because he had lost a hand in the said service, he deserves His Majesty's fullest favor and help. . . ."[4]

Grudgingly, His Majesty agreed, perhaps more as a favor to Sessa than to Cervantes. On November 30, the council granted Doña Leonor license to export a mere two thousand ducats in merchandise within eight months. In the margin of the petition, the words *"está bien"* express the royal approval. The handwriting is Mateo Vázquez's.

Astrana Marín notes angrily that Mateo did not even try to prevent the shaving down of the authorization Doña Leonor had asked. There is, of course, no way of knowing this, but it is a reasonable assumption. Once more, and not for the last time, the national scandal surrounding Antonio Pérez had run athwart Miguel's private ambition.

On the night of March 31, 1578, Juan de Escovedo was returning to his house facing the Eboli palace when he was set upon by six bravos. One of them ran Escovedo through the chest with a sword. He died where he lay. The killers were paid in jewels by Pérez, who used signed, blank orders from the king to obtain military posts for them in safely distant Italy.

Vázquez, only recently ordained a priest, was absorbed in the secular business of bringing Pérez down. He was out in the open now, whispering into Philip's ear the charges of murder and treason all Madrid retailed against the archsecretary and his noble mistress, choosing his words carefully, no doubt, to skirt the allegation that the murderers had Philip's at least tacit approval.

Philip, for the time being, played his usual double game. He showed Pérez a bill of particulars Vázquez had prepared against him, assuring Pérez that "as long as I live there is nothing to fear,"[5] but doing nothing to stop Vázquez from egging Escovedo's family on to press charges against the pair. Escovedo's murder may even have been part of an elaborate Philippine scheme to rid himself of Pérez, punish the scornful Eboli and curb, perhaps discredit, Don Juan. Even to his contemporaries, Philip's motives were unclear; the Escovedo family is known to have doubted the king's complicity in the plot, for, they said, "if this was the king's doing, he had only to hush it up, for he had the power to do so."[6] Perhaps this only testifies to the king's deviousness. By covering Pérez he covered himself, gradually allowing himself to be reluctantly "convinced" by the "facts" Vázquez and others were so diligently accumulating. Meanwhile, the protests of innocence from Pérez and Eboli, their threats against Vázquez, helped him to preserve his pose of Solomonic impartiality.

In the circumstances, it seems excessive to castigate the "virtuous" Mateo for his seeming indifference to the fate of his acquaintance Cervantes. The secretary was learning from his masters the art of carrying on business as usual in times of great strain, but too much detachment should not be expected of him.

The export license awareded Doña Leonor was, theoretically, worth at least fifty ducats to the Cervantes family if they could sell it to a merchant. But, with no one to stand as guarantor for the sum, no trader could be found to touch it. There was no help for it: Rodrigo *père* would have to pay another visit to the great beyond. Sometime early in 1579, her widow's weeds still fresh from their previous airing, Doña Leonor returned to the council to plead for exemption from the guaranty provision. In a decree dated March 5, acknowledging that "because she is a widow and poor she can find no guarantor,"[7] the councilors ordered the provision waived.

Trouble now had to be dealt with in another corner of the bureaucracy. In the fuss that followed young Rodrigo's return, Leonor had neglected some of the legal formalities expected of her. On Febrary 28, 1579, noting that no evidence of either son's ransom had been presented, the Cruzada ordered restitution of the entire sum it had granted the Cervanteses, threatening an embargo against the property of guarantor Getino de Guzmán.

To return the money before Miguel was ransomed was unthinkable. But an official seal on the lock of Getino's door would be intolerable. On March 17, Leonor appealed against the seizure and asked an extension of the grant. The council backed and filled, but it finally responded to a second petition submitted a week later. Niggling to the last, it agreed to suspend action in the case . . . for four months.

The incident was alarming. Perhaps the safest place for the thirty escudos was at home. But the Mercenarians were dragging their feet about returning it, fearing that it might come into the hands of the rival Trinitarians; competition between the two redemptionist orders had already led to countless lawsuits. Accordingly, on March 28 the "widow" Cervantes returned to the Cruzada and obtained an order restoring the money to her possession.

"One of the definitions of man," Cervantes remarks in the *Persiles*, "is that he is risible because only man, and no other animal, laughs, and I say that he can also be called a piteous animal, an animal that weeps. . . ."[8]

The dey's bagnio was an excellent place in which to reflect on one's past errors and future possibilities. In Cervantes' case, there was a considerable imbalance between the two. It was all very well to tell oneself that "it is impossible for good or evil to last indefinitely"[9] and that "when the limit of your trials does not lead to your death, which is the end of them all, change must ensue, not from bad to worse, but from bad to good and from good to better."[10] The fact was that, as far as he could be expected to see, bad had perversely led to worse and change was taking its own sweet time in ensuing. Any early optimism regarding his chances of escape would, one might suppose, have been seriously blunted by then; he had only to glance at any one of fourteen other faces in that prison to remind himself of how tragically he had failed. He had offered himself for martyrdom and had been rejected, only to watch another man die horribly in his place.

Cervantes was ready to try again.

And since Fate, whose business it is to provide obstacles for cavaliers to overcome, had made it difficult for him to go to Spain, then Spain must come to him. The *Epistle to Mateo Vázquez* had been the first summons. Now a second invitation was to be issued, to a nearer neighbor this time.

The *Información de Argel* tells us that Hassan had "ordered (Cervantes) confined in his bagnio loaded with chains and irons, still with intent to punish him; at the end of five months, the said Miguel de Cervantes, with the same zeal in the service of God and His Majesty and in the benefaction of (other) Christians, imprisoned as he was, sent a Moor secretly to Oran with letters to Señor Marqués Don Martín de Córdoba, general (governor) of Oran and of its forces, and to other prominent persons, his friends and acquaintances in Oran, to the end that they might send a spy or spies and (other) persons of trust with the said Moor to Algiers to bear him away with three other distinguished noblemen who the King was holding in his bagnio."

Nothing less! And how, "imprisoned as he was," did he find and treat with his messenger? The phrase suggests that Cervantes recognized how incredible the account sounds, but no hint of explanation is given. Was the man a prison guard? His later steadfastness argues that he was not. A Moslem intent on conversion to Christianity? The odds against this are astronomical. How was he to be rewarded, and by whom? At least one biographer has seen a woman's hand in the business, presumably that of "Zoraida," the mistress Spaniards are so eager to assign Cervantes.[11] If the Moor were a servant of a powerful woman (for not just any woman will do), it might, the theory goes, explain the man's silence on the stake. The hypothesis is like Cervantes' plan: improvised, wistful and full of holes; it explains nothing,[12] and it plunges us back into the myth of Cervantes the heavy-lidded Latin lover. A modern critic has pointed out that there are two types of verse in the captivity plays: strong, natural, almost epic when dealing with Cervantes' own experience; labored and self-conscious when dealing with love affairs.[13]

In Don Martín de Córdoba, it is true, Cervantes had chosen a correspondent who might have sympathized with his appeal. Córdoba had himself been a captive twenty years earlier and had tried to organize an uprising of the Christians in Algiers; the plan was betrayed, and many captives died. Don Martín had been ransomed not long afterward for 23,000 escudos.

In the event, he never had the chance to respond to Cervantes' call. "The said Moor, bearing the said letters to Oran, was stopped by other Moors at the entrance to Oran who, suspecting the worst because of the letters they found, took him and brought him to this Algiers, to Hassan Pasha, who, seeing the letters and the name and signature of the said Miguel de Cervantes, ordered the Moor impaled; he died with great constancy, without revealing anything. And for the said Miguel de Cervantes, two thousand strokes of the rod were ordered."

Two thousand strokes! Three times as many as a strong man could survive. But not one of them was ever laid on. Why not? It was certainly not because Hassan had gone soft; only weeks before, on December 12, 1578, the dey himself had beaten a Mallorcan named Pedro Soler to death in his palace for trying to escape to Oran; on December 24, 1579, Juan Vizcaíno would die for the same reason. A man named Lorenzo was whipped so severely on May 29, 1580, that he succumbed to his injuries two days later.

Alonso Aragonés testified that he was in Algiers when the Moor was impaled "and thus knows that Hassan Pasha . . . was highly indignant against the said Miguel de Cervantes for seeking to carry off his caballeros, and so he decreed two thousand strokes of the rod for him . . . and if he did not deliver them, it was because of kindly mediators. . . ." Diego Castellano declared that "many entreated for him."

We do not know who interceded for Cervantes on this occasion. Among them may have been Morato Maltrapillo, a Murcian renegade, successful corsair captain and close friend of Hassan's. Morato is known to have pleaded for the prisoner on Cervantes' subsequent attempt to escape, and perhaps he did so on this one as well. Or Hassan may have bowed to pressure from Dalí Mamí, who was reclaiming his property undamaged. Cervantes was in fact returned to the Greek soon afterward.

Cervantes himself marveled at his luck. "The only man who made out well with him (Hassan)," the Captive recalls in *Don Quixote*, "was a Spanish soldier named Something de Saavedra; though he did things to win his freedom which will remain in those people's memories for many years, yet (Hassan) never beat him, nor ordered him beaten, nor said a harsh word to him, although for the slightest of the things he did any of us would have been impaled, as he himself feared to be more than once."[14]

There is an excuse for thinking that Cervantes may have begun almost literally to enchant the dey. Even the Christians appeared to view Cervantes as a kind of sacred fool and to treat him with the curious indulgence, a compound of fear, awe and reverence, which the Middle Ages accorded to the possessed. Hassan, as superstitious as any Turk, may have eyed this foolhardy, stubborn man uneasily; in the sixteenth century, still invested with wonders fey and threatening, one did not tamper lightly with a wight. Especially in the spring of 1579, when famine was filling the streets of Algiers with the dead and dying, Hassan was sensitive to omens. In May, during the processions organized to pray for rain, his holy men urged the dey to forbid the saying of Christian mass and he readily consented. For good measure, three sacred images taken from captured Christian ships and believed by the marabouts to be responsible for the drought were dragged, bound by the feet, to the palace gate, where they were chopped up and burned.

The dey could have considered Cervantes a fourth such image and eliminated him, too. But this might also have been to tempt fate. Besides, Hassan was a soldier. A grudging respect for the fool's courage was probably an ingredient in his gingerly treatment of Cervantes. "Do not weary yourself," he advises the furious Cadi in Act III of *The Dungeons of Algiers,*

> for he is Spanish, and not all your gifts,
> your rages, your punishments, your promises
> can make him turn from his intention.
> How little you know the stubborn swine,
> obstinate, fierce, proud, arrogant,
> opinionated, indomitable and bold. . . .

Whatever may have been in Hassan's mind, it gave Cervantes considerably more liberty in which to plot again, to write again (sonnets to the Virgin, probably pastorals; what else could so succinctly express his longing for freedom, for the harmonious and tender simplicity now so utterly denied him?), generally to draw "a comfortless consolation from feigning wan and distant hopes to sustain the life I now abhorred."[15] And, when no balm was strong enough to soothe his anger, to wander alone to the beach to contemplate "the sky, the sea, the sand and this silence, interrupted only by my sighs. . . ."[16]

Probably even the sacred fool thought it prudent to lie low for a while. Besides, there was an interesting new arrival in Algiers. On April 25, Antonio Veneziano was captured while en route to Spain from Palermo. Now virtually forgotten by all but a few literary historians, Veneziano was famous in his day as humanist, poet and balladeer. To some Italian critics, he was the father of Sicilian poetry. At the time of his capture he was already beginning to build the legend as a popular satirist which would ultimately lead him to a Palermo prison and, there, to his death in a fire in 1593.

While word of his wizardry may not yet have leaked into the Algerian literary world, Veneziano quickly established himself as a poet by undertaking a 289-stanza lyric poem expressing his anguished love for "Celia." Cervantes was drawn to him at once; there were not so many practicing poets in Algiers that the arrival of one more was not an event.

They probably saw a lot of each other during the dry, torrid summer of 1579. The city was almost empty; the corsair captains were frequently at sea, and the city dwellers' habitual summer migration to the cooler hills around the town had been encouraged that year by fear of plague. It was an atmosphere conducive to melancholy discourse and the quiet exploration of technical poetic problems. They read each other's poems, perhaps compared their griefs over Celia and Silena. Veneziano was only four years older than Cervantes and both had hopes of preferment at the Spanish court—after their liberation.

That Veneziano had any lasting literary influence on Cervantes is doubtful. The Sicilian shared his friend's support for the vernacular literature in which Cervantes' genius would find its medium. But the younger man would have been of two minds about Veneziano's anti-Aristotelianism and his wish to see art move closer to life, away from the classical conventions in which imaginative literature was encased. This was a natural enough attitude in the Sicilian, whose talent for popular verse, for ballads and songs, was not really up to the writing of poetry on a heroic scale. Cervantes may have sensed this, and Cervantes aspired to a place among the giants. Prose fiction, he would have argued, should indeed be "historical"—true to life, should be looser and freer to look around itself at everyday people and things. But poetry was serious literature, for which only the grand machinery of Aristotelian formalism was appropriate.

This was indeed the fashionable view and, as we have seen, Cervantes had an emotional need to be in the mainstream of poetical theory, to show that he could match canons with the best of them despite his lack of schooling. Perhaps, though, he had an even deeper objection to Veneziano's principles: somewhere in his mind the conviction may already have prowled that he did not, would never fathom what metered poetry was really all about, what subtle concatenation of sounds, structures, symbols and images distinguished metrical discourse from prose. Veneziano might say what he liked about the stultifying rigidity of Aristotelian rules; that very rigidity was the crutch on which Cervantes' poetry leaned.

Well, well . . . this was all stimulating, no doubt, not to say disturbing. But as the long summer of 1579 seeped slowly toward the autumn, Cervantes grew restless. The shackles on their wrists were of real iron, these were real dungeons and liberation was a real, not a theoretical, problem. Cervantes may already have been turning a new escape plan over in his mind, one bolder and more grandiose than any he had yet devised. It was in September that he found the instrument to bring it to life, in the person of "a renegade of Spanish nationality, who said that his father was from Osuna and that he was a native of Granada, and that when he was a Christian his name was the Licentiate Girón, who brought himself to become a Moor in this land of Algiers and that as a Moor his name was Abderrahmen; seeing that the said renegade showed repentance for what he had done in becoming a Moor, and a desire to return to Spain, the said Miguel de Cervantes repeatedly encouraged and exhorted him to return to the faith of Our Lord Jesus Christ, and to this end he arranged for Onofre Exarque, a Valencian merchant then in Algiers, to donate money, which he gave, more than one thousand three hundred *doblas*,[17] for the purchase of an armed frigate, persuading him that nothing he could do would be more honorable nor more agreeable to God and His Majesty. . . ."

Once stung, twice wary, however. Cervantes was taking no chances on placing himself at the mercy of a second Dorador. A discreet investigation was made. Among those interviewed was a stocky, red-bearded man named Luis de Pedrosa,[18] who came from the Andalusian town of Osuna and who declared himself to have been "one of the principal accomplices in this affair, in two ways: first, because the renegade was from the same region and town as this witness, and, second, because Cervantes told him secretly to be ready at the hour (he) indicated. . . ."

Pedrosa testified that "before setting out to . . . put the plan into operation, the said Miguel de Cervantes, like a discreet, wise and steadfast person, in order to satisy and inform himself and to satisfy his friends and the person who was to donate the money for the frigate . . . came to this witness one day and, calling him out in great secrecy and taking him aside, asked him what kind of a person the renegade was . . . and whether he had the will to want to return to Christian land. He asked this witness to talk to (Girón) and find all this out, since we were both from the same region, and . . . this witness replied that he (Girón) was gifted and well-intended, that by seeking him out secretly and discreetly . . . they could discuss the business together and (Cervantes) could see then what was in his heart . . . and from then on the business went forward honorably."

"Yet confidence lives," exclaims Constanza in *The Dungeons of Algiers,* "that while life lasts, it is known foolishness to despair of good fortune."[19] Confidence must have radiated from Cervantes if he was able to talk a hardheaded trader into parting with a small fortune, at extravagant personal risk, on the strength of vague promises of future advantage. That he succeeded tells us much of his persuasiveness and of the credit he had amassed among the Christians in Algiers.

Things went forward briskly. Under the pretense of equipping himself for piracy, "the said renegade bought the said frigate, of twelve benches, and made it ready, following the advice and orders of . . . Cervantes in everything." Meanwhile, "wishing to serve God and His Majesty and do mercy to Christians, as is his nature, (Cervantes) secretly gave word of the venture to many gentlemen, jurists, priests and (other) Christians . . . to be prepared and alert for a certain day, with the intention of embarking them all and taking them to a Christian land; there were sixty Christians (involved), the flower of those in Algiers. . . ."

Sixty? As well have hired a band and marched out singing. The man's defiance clearly had kept pace with his swelling rage. This time, it seems, he was determined not only to be free, but to deal the Turks a blow that would be felt all the way to the Bosporus. "I am so eager to be free that . . . I will lend myself to anything that promises me that joy," asserts a captive in Act I of the *Dungeons* who has already lost his ears in an escape attempt. And, he warns, "unless you cut off my feet, there will be no stopping me from running away."

Excitement crackled in the sparkling autumn air that October. Fernando de Vega testified that "he and the others (in the plot) spent many happy days, looking forward to their liberation"; Fray Feliciano Enríquez even "contributed some money for provisions because this witness believed that his freedom was within his grasp. . . ." There was a great coming and going as Cervantes "solicited, arranged for and procured everything, as the author of it all"; Sosa, making himself important, affirmed that "nothing was agreed on in this affair that (Cervantes) and the said merchants did not inform me of and ask my opinion and advice about," but he magnanimously insisted that "much is owed to the bravery of Miguel de Cervantes."

Thinking big, of course, implies big risks. In the *Dungeons,* Vivanco voices the all-too-common fear in Algiers: that a plot will fail "if many know of it, for nothing comes smoothly to fruition here when many are privy to it."[20]

Cervantes could not have known that, in Madrid, a new effort was taking shape to obtain his release, one more promising than any to date. On July 31, when his plot still had no more substance, probably, than a few quiet words spoken absently to Veneziano or Sosa, the procurator-general of the Trinitarian Order in Spain, Fray Juan Gil, issued a receipt to

Doña Leonor de Cortinas, "widow, once wife of Rodrigo de Cervantes, defunct, may he be in heaven," for the sum of 250 ducats. On the same day, a second receipt was delivered to Andrea de Cervantes for an additional 50 ducats. The friars contributed some 45 ducats more—a total of 3,800 reales or 280 escudos—but withheld the usual understanding that they would advance as much more as was needed toward Cervantes' ransom. The receipt to Doña Leonor details that the money deposited was all in coins, *"reales de a ocho y de a cuatro, doblones de a cuatro e ducados e escudos"*[21]—the very miscellany attests to how painfully it was collected, how austerely hoarded. The mission was announced for the spring of 1580, but word of it had not yet reached Algiers.

On August 19, still in mourning clothes, Doña Leonor returned to the War Council and won another six-month extension of her export license.[22] Less than two weeks later, on August 31, an order came from the Escorial to the Cruzada's bursar to grant Fray Juan Gil 190,000 maravedis toward the ransoms of Spaniards taken in the crown's service; a half million more came from the Councils of the Indies and of the Military Orders. Every maravedi helped. It began to look as though Cervantes' luck had finally turned.

In Algiers, with "everything ready and at the point of departure, which with the help of God would come about thanks to the good order . . . Cervantes had established, and with all the Christians happy and gay, seeing how prosperously the business had gone up to then, and that only two days remained before the said departure was to take place," the witness, Aragonés, learned from Cervantes that "one of the king's renegades, who called himself Caiban, had learned of the affair and had reported it to the king, and later it became public knowledge that one Juan Blanco de Paz, a captive of the king himself . . . whom this witness had heard describe himself as a monk of (the order of) St. Dominic . . . had betrayed the plan and that for this he had been given a gold escudo and a jar of lard. . . ." His action "put . . . Cervantes in peril of losing his life, for it was he who was chiefly accused by Juan Blanco de Paz as the author of it all. . . ."

Rodrigo de Chaves, another of the men cheated of his freedom, recounted that, although he was "a close friend of Dr. Juan Blanco de Paz . . . from whom he had no secrets," he nevertheless berated the monk later "for being so evil as to deprive so many Christians, distinguished and honorable persons, of their liberty."

No discernible spark of amiability lights the memory of Juan Blanco de Paz; like a scorpion petrified in plastic, it lies embedded in four centuries of malediction. This alone might explain the faint prick of pity one feels for him. He seems to have been one of those unlucky men so lacking in character, advantage, charm, even intellect, as to allow any of us to despise him comfortably.

The country around Montemolín, in southern Extremadura, where he was born in 1538, is fit for goats, cork oak, the hardiest of fighting bulls and not much else. Montemolín was then a tightly inbred village of four hundred souls where close intermarriage was the rule: Juan was the son of Juana Gómez and Juan Blanco and, on his father's side, the grandson of another Juana Gómez and Juan Blanco. According to Astrana Marín, Blanco was a common name among Moriscos in Extremadura.[23] Moreover, the name of Paz, which Juan Blanco took when he joined the Dominican order, was often taken in his district by relapsed but reconciled Judaizers. It is to be noted that Rodrigo de Chaves reported having heard in the dey's bagnio that "the said Juan Blanco de Paz was a *Mudéjar*." If all of these indications—a virtually incestuous, Judeo-Morisco ancestry in a region of intense poverty—apply to his case, Juan Blanco was born with a taste of ashes and gall in his mouth.

Where, or even whether, he took his degree in theology and was ordained a priest is not known; in any event, he entered the Dominican monastery of San Esteban, in Salamanca, was expelled from there for now undeterminable reasons and returned for a while to his native village. In 1575 he reappeared with a request to be named titulary commissioner of the Inquisition court at Llerena; the request was granted, after a routine investigation, on January 31, 1576. Soon after that he went to Rome, perhaps, it has been suggested, to seek revenge against the Salamancan Dominicans, as, years later, he would calumniate the Trinitarians who redeemed him.[24] It was on his return to Spain from Italy that he was captured, in August 1577.

In Algiers, he immediately set about making himself unpopular. Aragonés, who had no reason to spare the man, called him a "backbiting, slanderous, arrogant man of evil inclinations"; to Domingo Lopino he was "a man of evil conscience apart from God's way" and a man of "bad reputation and little credit." He at once represented himself as an official of the Holy Office, a claim to which he had a nominal but not a functional right, and did his best to terrorize his fellow prisoners. He cuffed a priest who remonstrated with him, and kicked another. In the more than two years since his capture, this priest had "been a mischievous man, everyone's enemy," had "never said mass . . . nor was he seen to recite prayers at the canonical hours, nor take confession, nor visit or console sick Christians, as other Christian priests were wont to do. . . ." Lopino's accusation suggests that "Mudéjar" Blanco was suspected of relapsing from the faith. Under the pressure of religious fervor in Algiers, such suspicions would certainly have been voiced. This may have been behind his scuffles with his fellow priests in the dey's bagnio; at the least, it whispers of the atmosphere of contempt in which he moved.

One understands what drove this stunted man, with his burden of hatred, envy, resentment, stupidity, to his companions' betrayal. As far as is known, he was not included in the plot. His jealousy of Cervantes seems to have been obsessive. Cervantes was respected and liked, his energy and leadership were applauded, his company solicited in the democracy of captivity by persons of rank. To Blanco de Paz, shunned, ignored when he was not actively despised, Cervantes apparently had become a symbol of the recognition he, Blanco, was denied. The mentality is all too sadly familiar. It is the mentality of the professional gunman, the pathological killer. Its objective is power, its tools are fear and cruelty. Blanco's threats to invoke the power of the Holy Office against those who rejected him had been largely unsuccessful. Now he held a weapon of unhoped-for effectiveness: his knowledge of the conspiracy. This was power, not over one or two men, not over the hated Cervantes alone, but over sixty men, most of them precisely those persons of rank to whom he was so maddeningly invisible. One can imagine him, his blue eyes bulging with self-importance, the breath hissing excitedly through the gap left by two missing front teeth, as he hurried to detonate his monstrous petard.

When his betrayal became known, everyone's first impulse was to panic. Girón fled to Morocco. Even Cervantes was swept up in the movement. For the first time, he went into hiding, in a place provided by Diego Castellano, "until he could see what the king did. . . ."

Hassan waited as long as he could to spring his trap, hoping to snare as many of the conspirators as possible. When it became evident that the secret was out, he issued an edict of death for anyone caught sheltering Cervantes, "and all the Christians and Turks who knew of the affair . . . took it for granted that if he fell into the king's hands he would not escape with his life, or at the least without losing his nose and ears. . . ."

Even in hiding, Cervantes maintained his control over the situation, converting his hiding place into a sort of secret command post from which messages of reassurance streamed out to his co-conspirators, exhorting them to keep up their courage. Exarque was terrified that "the king . . . would use torture and that . . . Cervantes, as the guiltiest of all, would reveal who was in the plot, and the said Onofre Exarque would lose his fortune, his freedom and perhaps his life." He "urged and beseeched and argued that . . . Cervantes go to Spain in some ships which were about to sail and that he (Exarque) would pay his ransom."

Cervantes refused. He promised the merchant that he could be "sure no torment, not even death itself, would be enough to make him condemn anyone but himself; and he told the same thing to all those who knew of the affair, encouraging them not to be afraid, because he would take the whole burden of that business on himself, though he was certain to die for it. . . ."

To Pedrosa he not only repeated this promise, but bid him pass the word that if any of the others were caught "they should always throw the blame on . . . Cervantes." He urged Cristóbal de Villalón "not to hide or be in any wise afraid," that even under torture he would "behave as men of valor, spirit and constancy ought to do; and because of this, this witness composed himself and did not run away, and took good heart."

His refusal to save himself was not mere grandstanding. As he explained it, "seeing . . . the cruel edict issued against anyone hiding him and so that no harm might come to a Christian who concealed him, and also fearing that if he did not appear, the king would look for someone else to torture or from whom he could learn the whole truth of the case, he then of his own free will gave himself up to the king. . . ."

Cervantes took what precautions he could. Prudently, he did not give himself up directly to the king, but to Morato Maltrapillo, the corsair who had befriended him. Morato is seen several times in the captivity stories. He is surely the pirate to whom Biedma entrusted himself in *Don Quixote,*

who swore he was a great friend of mine and who had exchanged vows with me which bound him to keep any secret I might entrust to him. Some renegades who intend to return to Christian lands often take with them testimonials from prominent captives in which they swear, however they can, that the renegade in question is a good man, has always been a benefactor to Christians and is eager to escape at the first possible opportunity. Some collect these testimonials with good intentions; others deliberately keep them for emergencies: if they are unlucky enough to be lost or captured while raiding in Christian lands, they haul out these certificates and claim the papers show why they came, which was to remain on Christian soil. . . . Then, when they see their chance, they return to Barbary to carry on as they had before. . . . One of these renegades was this friend of mine, who had testimonials from all our comrades in which we praised him lavishly, and if the Moors had found those papers on him, they would have burned him alive.[25]

Maltrapillo may have had such a collection of testimonials, though his record suggests that he would have used them as insurance only. In the event, he did show himself to be a good friend by pleading for Cervantes' life.

Hassan displayed a savage delight at seeing the now familiar Spanish face and the crippled hand, "believing that now he could . . . destroy Onofre Exarque and Baltasar de Torres."[26] To frighten Cervantes, "he ordered that a rope be put around his neck and his hands tied behind him, as though they were going to hang him," but the prisoner "never sought to name or condemn anyone, telling the king, with great steadfastness, only that he was responsible along with four other caballeros who had already left (Algiers) as free men, and that it was they who were to go with him, and if they had planned to take anyone else, no one knew it or was to know it until the day of sailing. . . . The said king was very angry with him, seeing how his answers differed from what he had been told by . . . Dr. Juan Blanco. . . ."

Nor did cajolery serve where threats had failed. Cervantes, "defying the cruel threats uttered and the promises promised, refused to implicate anyone, steering the business so adroitly, so twisting the questions he answered that the said king was confused and balked. . . . And this witness (Aragonés) holds it as certain that had . . . Cervantes told what he knew, many gentlemen involved in the affair, who are known as poor by their masters and owners, would have been discovered and would have fallen into the hands of Hassan . . . and would never have been ransomed save at excessive prices. . . ."

Obviously bemused despite his anger, Hassan had this "obstinate . . . arrogant . . . indomitable" Spaniard confined in the royal bagnio, where he "held him closely and under heavy guard, in chains and irons, for five months. . . ." No one else was ever arrested or punished in the plot. Cervantes' conduct was known "to all the Christians captive in Algiers," for which he was "praised and held in more esteem and honor than ever."

Cervantes himself may have been as startled by his temerity as he was by his survival. There was always a quality of fantasy about his activist side, as though, despite the evidence, he never quite believed it. "For me alone," says Cide Hamete Ben Cervantes in the last paragraph of *Don Quixote,* "was Don Quixote born and I for him; action was his role, writing mine. . . ."

That even as he lay chained in the dey's prison he was thinking of the next attempt is hinted in a letter he wrote from there to Veneziano on November 6, 1579, along with two glum poems in tribute to "Celia": "I swear to your worship as a Christian that it was *the many fancies wearying me* which prevented me from completing these verses as well as I would have wished, but I am sending them to your worship as a mark of the great willingness I have to serve you; since you have inspired me to such an untimely revelation of my poor wits' faults, I trust the keenness of your worship's (wits) will accept this apology as I intend it, and so will encourage me not to forget, *at a more tranquil time,*[27] to celebrate as I can the heaven which holds your worship so discontented in this land.

May God pluck us from it,[28] and may your worship reach that land where Celia lives."

Veneziano, obviously moved, replied in a sonnet in Italian to Signor Michele de Cervantes thanking him for the consolation he offered, assuring him that he had indeed "fulfilled that of which we spoke together" and urging that

> If suddenly a danger should arise,
> let us close ranks that we may vanquish it,
> my doctor, friend and grand practitioner.[29]

Had Cervantes been executed, or even grievously punished, Blanco de Paz might well have been murdered by his fellow prisoners. As it was, feeling against him was ferocious. Pedrosa said that all of those betrayed, leaders as well as "other common folk, sturdy men whom (Cervantes) had brought in as rowers . . . moaned and cursed their fate, uttering great groans . . . against the said Juan Blanco de Paz, so that some said: 'O damned captivity, even when you want to take revenge on people and pay off those who deserve it, you cannot.' And others: 'If only Juan Blanco de Paz were not a priest so that I could get my hands on him and give him his deserts. . . .'" Sosa said he was "much hated and reviled by everyone" and that "some Christians told me they were ready to stab him . . . and I especially heard that he was most hated by the said merchants who gave the money. . . ." Blanco de Paz's owner even locked the man up briefly for his own protection after he quarreled with fellow priests who had called him a fool. Cervantes, naturally, "from that time on remained on terms of great enmity" with him.

Cervantes was out of prison by Easter, though still in chains. And he had a new owner: Hassan Pasha had bought him for the five hundred gold escudos El Cojo demanded. If being sold as a slave is a "misfortune to which no other can be compared,"[30] being sold to the dey was disaster. The posted price on him immediately went up to a thousand escudos, which in effect meant, if Hassan was serious about it, that Cervantes could never look forward to ransom. One wonders if Hassan *was* serious about it; a different motive was reported by Haedo: "Hassan Pasha, King of Algiers, said that as long as he held the lamed Spaniard, his Christians, his ships and even the whole city were secure."[31] But Cervantes and his friends firmly believed that the dey intended to "take him to Constantinople, where . . . he could never regain his freedom."

"I am so unlucky," groans Ricardo in *The Liberal Lover,* "that not only had I no chance as a free man, but as a captive I neither have it nor hope for it."

] 19 [

Freedom

In Algiers' Christian community, a ghetto within a ghetto, emotions were always volatile, but events in the winter and spring of 1579–80 were making them yaw like rafts in a storm.

Two years of drought had brought famine of disastrous proportions; Haedo reports that between mid-January and mid-February of 1580 it killed 5,656 Algerian poor. While townspeople spread out over the crevassed countryside in search of food, hungry janissaries pillaged private homes in the city.

The crisis had brought out Hassan's qualities of leadership. He had his own way of rationing basic foodstuffs; he cornered the market on them, on flour, butter, oil, honey, wheat and vegetables, and sold them through the souk at black-market prices. Only onions and cabbages escaped his administration—the janissaries, whose staples they were, had warned him away from them. Prices had been rising in any case since the dey debased the Algerian currency, using the silver thus conserved to play the lucrative silver market in Constantinople. His technique for fostering foreign trade was equally distinctive: he insisted on first call on all goods brought by Christian traders, at his own price—often a consignment of rotting hides—or, like as not, no price at all. Charges against shipowners visiting the city were sometimes trumped up if Hassan coveted their ships; the vessels would be confiscated and captain and crew sent off to row in the corsair galleys. Nor did his subjects' fiscal well-being escape the dey's attention. He established a new estate tax which, in effect, made him almost everyone's principal heir. Despite successive crop failures which had left the country's agriculture in ruins, he increased taxes on land and livestock and sent troops to collect them when the indigent tribes refused to pay.

When a committee of leading citizens called for redress of their grievances, he responded with characteristic swagger: he would see to it, he
promised, that every corpse had a burlap winding sheet.

The malcontents sent a delegation to the Porte to complain to the Sultan, but Hassan, with the help of his protector, Euldj Ali, outmaneuvered
them. Hassan's term of office was to expire in the autumn of 1580. By the
time his successor, a relatively mild-mannered Hungarian renegade
named Djafer, arrived in Algiers in late August with twenty thousand of
Hassan's escudos in his chest for "traveling expenses," the new dey-desig-
nate would be in too mellow a mood to ask for more than a token accounting.

Two other occurrences had agitated the manic-depression in Algiers.
First came word of the redemptionist missions to the city; the Trinitarians were to be joined by a party of Portuguese Jesuits and the ransom
effort, it was rumored, would be a major one.

On May 29, the Spanish fathers arrived, led by their procurator-
general, Fray Juan Gil, and Fray Antón de la Bella. With them, in addition to some thirty thousand ducats in cash, they brought a quantity of
merchandise—forty dozen Toledan caps, bolts of fine, pomegranate-dyed
stuffs, cases of sugar plum—to be used as gifts to the slaveowners and to
be sold in the souk. On May 31 they paid their formal visit to Hassan, sitting on rich Persian carpets and, as was the custom, touching their hearts
and clasping hands in greeting. It was also the custom to exchange gifts
(a later dey is recorded as having sent a French mission one steer, six
sheep, two dozen chickens, four dozen loaves of bread still warm from the
oven and a dozen wax candles), but it is to be feared that Hassan considered the gift of his presence ample for the occasion. The fathers paid the
equally customary entry fee, 10 per cent of all the money they had
brought, less 2,415 gold escudos of which Fray Juan prudently omitted
mention in order not to inflate Hassan's greed. In return, they received
the dey's safe-conduct for the mission.

The friars' problem was complicated by the season. This was the heart
of the raiding period, and most of the corsair captains, with whom much
of the negotiation would have to be held, were at sea; with them, at their
galleys' oars, were fully seven thousand Christians.

In the first days of June, reports of a second event reached the city
which were to turn the ransom efforts into a life-and-death lottery: a
Spanish fleet was assembling in the peninsula's southern ports, chiefly in
Cádiz, while Spanish troops were massing near Badajoz. The fear that
trembled under the surface of Algerian life, of a concentrated Spanish assault, immediately flared into panic. The dey rushed to fortify the city's
defenses and appealed to Constantinople for reinforcements; once more,
Algerians vented their terror on their defenseless captives with beatings

and an occasional butchery. A few days later, word came that King
Philip's show of force was aimed at Portugal, not at the Moslems. With
the Portuguese throne vacant, Philip was grasping the chance to imple-
ment a long-dormant Spanish ambition to unite the peninsula under the
Castilian crown. But the scare seriously disrupted ransom procedures in
Algiers. Mindful of their patriotic duty, the corsair captains at sea had
scattered; many would remain away from their home ports throughout
the summer and into the following winter. This in turn meant that
money destined for the purchase of some of their captives would have to
be diverted to ransoming others in Algiers. But which? Moreover, there
was always an open fund which the friars were empowered to use at their
discretion in cases of special hardship. And what captive in Algiers did
not consider his a special case? A lottery.

While negotiations got under way for the men on the scene for whom
commissions were held, Fray Juan probed to discover which of the captives deserved extra consideration by the mission. He would soon have
heard about Cervantes, and what he heard would have predisposed him,
when they met, to the affection he later showed for this intrepid young
rebel. He also met Juan Blanco de Paz.

Blanco was a busy man at that moment. For, "seeing that he was
abhorred by everyone, shamed and abused and blinded by fury, (he)
threatened the said Miguel de Cervantes, saying that he would collect information against him to deprive him of all credit and of any pretension
he had to His Majesty's favor for what he had done and tried to do in
this Algiers. . . . To carry out his evil intention, thinking thus to deprive
. . . Cervantes of his good repute, the said Juan Blanco de Paz began
collecting statements as a commissioner for Holy Office, as (he) claimed
to be, and especially against those for whom he had a particular hatred
and enmity, and against . . . Cervantes, inquiring into his life and
habits. . . ." And "so that . . . Cervantes would not make public in
Spain the betrayal perpetrated by Juan Blanco de Paz, he tried . . . to
frighten him."

Blind with fury he must have been, else not even his insensitivity would
have allowed him, for example, to burst uninvited into Sosa's quarters,
knowing him to be a friend of Cervantes, and demand to be recognized
as an Inquisitorial officer. When Sosa insisted on seeing his commission,
Blanco admitted he did not have it with him. Sosa angrily ordered him
off with a warning against abusing the name of the Holy Office to "collect
information and administer oaths, because great scandal could result"
from it.

The Dominican also approached Fray Feliciano Enríquez, asking if he
knew of anyone "who had any vices" he could swear to. The Carmelite
replied that whether he knew of such or not, he was not about to say so,

and that if he ever returned to Spain he would take it up with the Inquisition there. The incident is revealing of the general attitude toward Blanco because Enríquez admitted under questioning that he had, for reasons unexplained, "for a while been a strong enemy of . . . Cervantes; and because of this, this witness heard a certain person (presumably Blanco) say some vicious and ugly things against the said . . . Cervantes, and it was then that this witness sought with perseverance everywhere in Algiers to inquire and learn if there were any ugly or dishonest thing against . . . Cervantes to stain his character, and I found that what the certain person had said was a great lie. . . . May this witness be burned alive if everything spoken against . . . Cervantes were not all a great lie, for . . . all we captives are devoted to the said . . . Cervantes and are rather inclined to envy his noble, Christian, upright and virtuous ways. . . ."

With even his former friends now against him, Blanco turned to bribery. The *Información* not only charges him with attempting to suborn witnesses, but produces testimony to an actual attempt. Amazingly, at least one of the men he tried to corrupt, Captain Domingo Lopinio, had been a conspirator in the escape attempt Blanco betrayed. As Lopino told the story, Blanco came to see him one day. Lopino was "in a *calabozo* in his master's house with two heavy chains about him, one around his chest and the other, the heaviest in Algiers, on his left leg, with his master not allowing him to leave the house." Blanco de Paz, "knowing that this witness thought ill of him for the business of revealing about the frigate . . . was there to visit and console him, encouraging him greatly, inquiring wh ether he needed anything." He then informed the captain of "certain testimony he had taken against certain persons," especially showing him a statement against Cervantes. When Lopino asked why he was doing this, he was told that it was "because he (Cervantes) wished him ill and was his enemy, since he went about speaking so ill of him." Lopino then objected that if Cervantes was his only enemy, he ought not to be collecting testimony against others as well. "This," explained Blanco, "was done as a trick, involving many, to give color (to the affair) so that if they talk in Spain of the evil he (Blanco) had done in destroying so many people, their testimony would be discounted because they were his mortal enemies."

Blanco returned another day, urging that Lopino "speak up if he needed any service, or money, that he was not to be abashed, that he was ready only to serve him." Eventually, he got to the point: "Señor Captain, I need Your Worship's favor to complete the condemnations in two indictments." One of them was against Cervantes. Lopino said "it weighed heavily on him that Juan Blanco had got into the business of calumniating such a person, being, as he (Cervantes) is, a generous, virtuous and very brave gentleman, whose function in Algiers was to favor and help all Christians who recommended themselves to him." He warned Blanco that "everything he was doing would be of little value, that he should not get mixed up in this, that it weighed on his soul and conscience and that he would have to account for it all to God." The retort was prompt: "Señor Captain, I have already bared my breast to Your Worship as an important person and a friend; I swear to you that, when anyone wounds me and does me ill, as they say they must, I must hurt and damage him as much as I can, though I act against my own father; because here in Algiers I will find witnesses at every step at little cost."

Although the bigger fish were eluding him, the Dominican's invocation of the Inquisition seems nevertheless to have frightened some simpler souls into his net, for, we are told, "with it all, the said Juan Blanco . . . collected many statements against many people, especially those who were his enemies, and against Cervantes. . . ."

Blanco immediately managed to alienate the redemptionist friars—just those persons who might have been able to help him. To both the Spanish Trinitarians and, even more ineptly at that juncture, the Portuguese Jesuits, who were nervy about claims of Spanish authority, Blanco represented himself as an officer of the Inquisition with a (wholly fictitious) mandate from King Philip. "Having been challenged . . . by Fray Juan Gil, whom he summoned to give him the obedience due to a general commissioner (of the Holy Office), and the redemptionist friars here present, to show them the said powers if he had them, he said he neither had them nor would show them. . . ." The friars sent him packing, as the priests captive in Algiers already had done. In this ransom lottery, he was the first loser.[1]

The winners began to emerge on June 12, when Hassan contracted to release thirteen of his captives for one hundred escudos each. Hassan was being sticky about his more valuable properties, however, refusing to accept less than five hundred gold escudos for any of them and insisting on one thousand each for Cervantes and aristocrat Jerónimo de Palafox. Gil had nothing like that kind of money to spend. Dickering over Cervantes was stalled despite the "many prayers and importunings" to which the friar was "moved by his compassion for the prospect of the many perils that beset him and the many trials he had already undergone."[2] But the Cervantes family had pledged only a little over a quarter of the sum asked, and the conditions of Gil's mission forbade his contributing seven hundred escudos from the general fund to any single captive's ransom.

Besides, this ascetic man who "set an example of great Christianity and great wisdom" had other battles to fight, sometimes literally. In one of Sosa's dialogues with Antonio González[3] we learn of two incidents in which Gil almost lost his life. One involved a twenty-five-year-old Murcian woman named Dorotea whom the friar had just ransomed from her Turkish owner. A few days after the woman's release, the Turk informed Gil that the deal was off; he had been drunk when the contract was signed, he argued, and anyway the woman was a convert to Islam and could not be ransomed. The case finally went to court.

As Sosa told the story, "the magistrate, whom the Turks call the Cadi, ordered the Fathers to bring Dorotea before him. Hardly had she arrived . . . when the Turk began an outrageous bawling, saying: 'Give me my Christian. I want my Christian.'" And when he saw that the case was going against him, he played his trump:

"'This woman is a Moor and a Mohammedan, not a Christian.'"

"When poor Dorotea, who was trembling with fear, heard so false and infamous an accusation," huffs Sosa, "she began with Christian intrepidity to proclaim, 'I am a Christian, I have always been a Christian and Christian I wish to be all my life.'"

"Her owner could not tolerate so frank and valiant a reply . . . and, rushing on her like a fierce and angry lion, and beating her, he said, 'Dog, you will return to my power and you will see how you will pay for this.'"

The Cadi managed to restore order. He then commanded the Turk to prove the woman was a Moslem. The man tore angrily out into the street and, within minutes, was back with two Moors "as furious as he" who swore she was a Moslem. Dorotea, shedding "such copious tears that it was a great pity to see her," repeated her protest: "'The witnesses are false, because I am a Christian.'" At this the Turk "seized her and gave her a terrible blow and would have given her many more had not Fray Juan Gil . . . grabbed him, saying, 'Mind what you do before this Tribunal . . . since this woman is not your slave, but free and a Chrisitan.'"

This was too much for the Turk. "'I am a janissary,'" he shouted, "'and the papist struck me . . . and so, in conformity with our customs and uses, he must be hanged, or at least have his right hand cut off.'"

Sosa's account sputters with indignation at this point: "And so that you might see what a vile rabble all these people are, there were even Moors there who confirmed this lie and insisted to the Cadi that the Turk was right, pressing him to punish the papist and return the Christian to her former master. The Cadi, stunned by so much shouting and commotion, ordered: 'Let justice be done now, then, and cut off his right hand.'

"Already the Moors, of whom a goodly number were there, and some Turks laid hands on Father Gil . . . when another prominent Moor, a scholar and co-administrator with the Cadi in the administration of justice, stopped them, saying:

"'Do not cut off the papist's arm, but if he struck the Turk, let him be given stern blows in return, and whip him out of here, and so let the one repay the other.'

"It was half laughable and half pitiable to see how eagerly (they) . . . rushed at Fray Juan and, each as he could, delivered so many blows to his face and body and felled him so heavily that we brought him out of there half dead. . . ." The unhappy Dorotea was "condemned to return to her master and was forced to become a Moor."

Not many days later, the battered friar was set upon in the souk by another Turk whose slave had run away. This time, a royal officer present arrested the assailant and brought him before a magistrate, who ordered that the Turk be spread out on the ground forthwith and given six hundred blows of the rod. Whereupon, reported Sosa, Gil threw himself upon the Turk's prostrate form and, shrouding him in his mantle, he cried, " 'Lay the blows upon me, Señor Cadi, and not upon him.' And so insistently did he repeat this prayer that the Turk at last was pardoned, and everyone was amazed and astounded by such a thing. . . ."

Cervantes, his neck in a noose, defying Hassan to save his friends; Juan Gil shielding the body of a prostrate enemy; Juan Blanco de Paz clutching his gold piece and his pot of lard: this is a medieval passion play come to life, a tale of chivalry of biblical grandeur. But the suffering was real.

On August 3, Fray Antón de la Bella led 108 ransomed captives, men and women, aboard two ships bound for Valencia.

Cervantes was not among them.

Preparations for Hassan's departure were already far advanced; packed chests and hide sacks littered the palace corridors. If Cervantes was in the port to watch the liberated prisoners leave, he had only to glance around to see the four ships in Hassan's convoy being readied for sea. To be taken to Constantinople—Cervantes seems to have seen that as a death sentence. The notion strums ominously through the *Información:* ". . . intending to take him to Constantinople, where . . . he could never gain his freedom . . ."; ". . . surely he would have been taken to Constantinople and would never have gained his freedom," etc. The idea was firmly rooted in his mind; years later, Recaredo would affirm in *The Spanish Englishwoman* that "had they given me to the Sultan it would have meant never being free for the rest of my life." This was not necessarily true, but the point is that Cervantes thought it was. What wild projects boiled up into his mind it is useless to try to guess, but his history should assure us that whatever he contemplated was bold and probably fatal.

Jolly conversations he must have had with Fray Juan. For the friar, in his turn, had grown fond of Cervantes that summer, showing him "great favor, discussing his affairs and having him at his table and bestowing

great friendship upon him." Conversations bristling with oppressve silences, like cell-block dialogues between a condemned man and his prison
chaplain. Cervantes was game; he even acted as witness to ransom contracts for other captives. One was a young aristocrat named Diego de
Benavides, of a wealthy Baeza family. Tall, his thin, sparsely bearded
face still scarred by the wound he had received before his capture at
Tunis in 1574, Benavides had been brought by Djafer Pasha from
Constantinople and ransomed five days later—for 250 escudos, a
fourth of what Hassan was asking for Cervantes.

On September 19, in the morning, Hassan moved his slaves and the
last of his effects to the waiting galleys; the tide would be early that day,
around 3 P.M., and a dozen vessels were ready to sail on it. Shortly before
10 A.M., the file of captives was herded down through the city to the port.
Cervantes was fastened to a bench, reported Alonso Aragonés, "with two
chains and several shackles." Palafox was in the same galley, a few
benches away. Then Hassan went aboard. Fray Juan was with him; he
still held commissions for nine of the men in the galleys, and he was making a last attempt to beat Hassan's prices down closer to his budget. But
the dey was obdurate; these were all important men, he repeated
placidly, all gentlemen.

A miracle which is phenomenologically explicable may nevertheless
have all the functional value of a miracle. For Hassan suddenly changed
his mind on one price and only one—Cervantes'. Did it occur to him, as
his eyes ran calculatingly over the ranks of huddled men, that a rebellious, one-handed slave might bring more trouble than profit? Did he understand that this man would try again and again to be free, and that,
sooner or later, Hassan would have to get rid of him or kill him? Whatever the reason, Hassan told Gil that he would let Cervantes go for half
price, five hundred escudos, on condition that the money be paid in
Spanish gold escudos.

Fray Juan may have seen the hand of God at work, may even have
been nudging it as much as he dared. There was still a snag: he had only
280 gold escudos left of the 2,415 he had so tactfully concealed from Hassan; the rest of his capital was in Algerian silver doblas. The Moslem
would not consider accepting these; who knew better than he how worthless Algerian currency had lately become? And there was still the question of how much cash Gil could properly advance toward Cervantes'
ransom above the 3,800 reales subscribed for him in Madrid. The friar's
solution was mildly illegal: he would grant Cervantes roughly one thousand reales from the general fund; the rest would be lent to him from
funds reserved for other captives, notably Palafox—no question of paying
one thousand escudos for him—whom for one reason or another he could
not then ransom.

Time was a factor now. The tide was beginning to swell; the sun had already tilted obliquely down toward the sea. At a run, Gil fled through the port and into the city, making the rounds of the Moorish money-changers who, despite the "Papaz's" obvious need, gouged him only moderately deeply, taking commissions of ten silver aspers on the escudo instead of the customary four. When he had amassed his pile of gold, he sped back to the galleys. Moments later, the air rang with the sound of hammer on iron. Fray Juan, meanwhile, was paying out the first of the seventeen traditional "fees" needed to legalize the liberation, to the galley master, the customs officers, the guards, scribes, magistrates, sergeants at arms and Djafer Pasha; the total amounted to nearly 20 per cent of the ransom price.

Navarro y Ledesma imagined Cervantes and Palafox exchanging glances, the tall, swarthy young aristocrats' eyes burning—reproachfully?—into those of the stocky, fair hidalgo.[4] Perhaps. Cervantes' glance may have been a shade glassy. When the last fetter fell, he raced to the galley's side and leaped ashore.

Moments later, the great triangular sails were broken out and the twelve galleys began to move slowly out of the harbor.[5]

Later that day, Cervantes signed a promissory note to the Trinitarian Order for two thousand reales Gil had lent him.[6] He found lodging with Benavides, who seems to have clung to him with filial tenacity. Indeed, the Baezan later testified that, after regaining his freedom, he "asked other Christians what . . . prominent persons there were in Algiers with whom one could communicate, and they answered that there was first of all one, just, noble and virtuous, of very good standing and friend of other gentlemen, who was Miguel de Cervantes; and thus this witness sought and looked for him . . . being a stranger in the land, (and) found in him father and mother. . . ."

There was still a major item of unfinished business to be dealt with: if he was going to appeal to the king for favor, it would be useful to go armed with documentary evidence of his conduct in Algiers which was firm enough to counteract the malice of Blanco de Paz.[7] Accordingly, on October 10 he presented a petition to Gil as the legitimate representative in Algiers of the Spanish crown and the papacy asking that the friar receive testimony on Cervantes' "captivity, life and habits . . . to be presented if need be to His Majesty's council." Later he would deride those "who, free of Turkish enslavement, wearing over their shoulders the chains struck from their legs, recount their ill fortune with piteous voices and humble supplications in Christian lands,"[8] but in 1580 it seemed a good idea to do so, and in writing.

Interrogation of the dozen witnesses he rounded up went on for twelve days before apostolic notary Pedro de Rivera. On October 24, he sailed with five other newly liberated captives (including witnesses Chaves and Benavides) for Spain.[9] Gil, who remained in Algiers until March 1581, accompanied them to the port, gave them the traditional blessing and issued the order for the ship to weigh anchor.

"There is no contentment on earth, to my way of thinking, to equal the recovery of one's lost liberty."[10] At least there was that for Cervantes, along with a sheaf of poems and a file of memories on which to draw for his stories. There was a sprinkling of friendships,[11] a solid sense of intimacy with the Holy Family and a more satisfying knowledge of his own stature as a man. He had learned how men behave when they are stripped to their naked humanity and how sustaining an ideal can be against the probabilities of rational reality. It was little enough to show for sixty-one months of hell, and it was all the compensation his world would ever grant him. Yet of the thousands upon thousands of men and women who survived that ordeal in the thousand-year history of Barbary captivity, only one, Cervantes, found and followed the thread of immortality which ran through it.

Part III

APPRENTICESHIP

] 20 [

Diplomatic Interlude

"Before them they saw the longed-for and beloved homeland; joy rebounded in their hearts, their spirits swelled with their new happiness, one of the greatest to be had in this life: to arrive safe and sound in one's homeland after long captivity."[1]

Even today, the hills behind Denia, south of Valencia, seem to touch a knee in welcome to the broad carpet of beach before the town. So it may have seemed to Cervantes after eleven years of exile. *"Cuan cara eres de haber, O dulce España."*

After a day's rest, the six liberated captives proceeded on to Valencia, arriving there on or about October 30, 1580. They went first to the Trinitarian monastery, where, while preparations went forward for their formal release forty-eight hours later, they were cleaned and soothing ointment was applied to the galls their irons had left on arms and legs.

Valencia was in fiesta to welcome them. This was Morisco country and a favorite target for Barbary raiders; the Valencians shared the captives' feeling that every liberation was a victory over the enemy. So, as the ceremonial procession flowed into the city under the massive arch of the Torres de Serrano on the morning of November 1, people rushed out of their houses to cheer them. Monks from all the city's religious orders except the rival Mercenarians walked with the little knot of haggard men who, like Recaredo in *The Spanish Englishwoman,* wore the Trinitarian scapular—a blue cross on a red-trimmed ground of white linen—over their blue captives' uniforms. Minstrels accompanied the line, their pipes and drums making a chirping echo to the "plat" of firecrackers and the complacent pounding of the Micalet, the great bell in the cathedral tower.

In the vast, taper-lit nave, its Gothic fabric still free of the anticli-

mactic eighteenth-century mask it wears today, a *Te Deum* was sung.
Then the procession filed along the aisles to hear mass in the apse, stopping on the way to kneel before the jeweled cup of purple agate
venerated in Valencia as the Holy Grail. After listening, on their knees, to
a sermon recounting their captivity, the six men were escorted back to the
monastery while Trinitarian friars solicited alms for them from the
Valencian gentry. In the afternoon, each man was given clean clothing, a
share of the money collected and his official *patente* of liberation. The
long ordeal was over. They were free to go home.

Or, at least, some of them were. For men in debt to their redeemers, it
was customary to furnish some pledge of repayment before leaving Valencia. In addition to the two thousand reales he owed the friars, Cervantes
had borrowed over a thousand more from Christian—chiefly Valencian—
merchants in Algiers; according to testimony taken in Madrid, the money
had gone to buy food because "the Moor who held him captive gave him
neither food nor clothing."[2] It would have done him no good then to
know that this was more money than he would ever have in his life at
any one time. Certainly there was no hope of such help from his family.
In a letter to his parents, dispatched with fellow prisoner Juan de
Estéfano, he asked them to prepare a petition for a subsidy from the
Royal Council. He may also have wanted assurances that his old quarrel
with Antonio de Sigura had been settled and that Castilian justice no
longer had designs on his one good hand. Until an answer arrived, the
former prisoner was virtually a prisoner in Valencia.

This was a benign captivity, however. To the end of his life, Cervantes
was warmed by memories of Valencia, of "the grandeur of its site, the excellence of its lodgings, the charm of its surroundings" where pilgrims
found "not merely an inn in which to take shelter, but all the houses of
the town invited them with pleasant hospitality"; he praised "the beauty
of its women and its extreme cleanliness," was soothed by its "charming
language,[3] rivaled only by Portuguese in sweetness and agreeableness."[4]
This was clearly a time to luxuriate in the pure delight of freedom, of
safety, a return to life. Perhaps a time for building castles in the air, although this is open to question. Despite a general desire to "Quixotize"
Cervantes, there were few occasions in his life when he was any more
than optimistic. He does seem to have hoped in Valencia that the miracle
of his liberation would be a continuing benediction, that his record was
good enough to force justice to pay his claim. It would have seemed only
realistic to a man with no money and no marketable skills to try to parlay
his few visible assets—his record and his handful of influential friends—
into a career.

The time probably seemed right to do that. Spain's annexation of Portugal was now an actual if not a legal fact. The takeover had gone off
relatively smoothly. Before his death on January 31, 1580, at the very

hour of a lunar eclipse, the last reigning king of the Avis dynasty, the aged, epileptic Cardinal Enríque, Sebastian's uncle, had endorsed Philip's candidacy to succeed him; the Regency Council had voted in the Spaniard's favor. Most of the Portuguese nobility, along with the mercantile middle class, had good financial reasons to welcome absorption into the Spanish empire and, on the whole, the higher clergy was Philip's either by sympathy or by purchase. The people and the lower clergy had persisted in seeing all things Spanish as abominations and had backed the claim to the throne of one Don Antonio, prior of Crato; in his support, the Bishop of Guarda had mustered an army of thirty thousand peasants and the prior had been proclaimed king by a cobbler in a field near Santarém. An almost bloodless campaign by a Spanish force under the Duke of Alba disposed of serious opposition to the Spanish pretension within two months. Don Antonio escaped to Calais, taking the Portuguese crown jewels with him. Portugal, its vast overseas possessions and its primacy along the Asian trading routes were in Spanish hands. Only the Azores held out for Don Antonio.

Cervantes may have reasoned that a golden age of Castilian carpetbagging was beginning in Lisbon. His old patrons, Don Juan and Sessa, were both dead, but he might still hope for the help of two men at court. One was Don Antonio de Toledo, his co-conspirator in Algiers, who had since become King Philip's master of the horse. The other, of course, was Mateo Vázquez. Cervantes did not yet know that the very Portuguese affair on which he was counting for advancement had already beclouded Mateo's star at court.

The secretary's scheming had not worked out as he hoped it would. Philip had indeed finally allowed himself to be persuaded that Antonio Pérez was not only a personal threat, but also a potential obstacle to the crown's Portuguese ambitions. In March 1579 Pérez had been placed under house arrest. But Mateo had not succeeded to the archsecretariat. Rightly or wrongly, the king suspected him of having violated a royal confidence during the maneuvering over the Portuguese coup. Despite the secretary's protestations of innocence, Philip would not be reassured. Juan de Idiáquez was appointed to Pérez's place. Vázquez was not dismissed, but he would never succeed in emerging from the probationary shadow to which the king's mistrust had consigned him.

It was not until December 1 that Cervantes' father, now definitively relieved of the need to play dead, could start up the machinery for the subsidy petition. He presumably sent word to Valencia at once for his son to show his creditors as an earnest of the family's good intentions. By December 9 Cervantes was on his way to Madrid.

The plans he hatched in Valencia must have taken on a look of acute urgency when Cervantes returned home about December 15. Perhaps it had not registered fully on his mind until then how much of a burden the brothers' captivity had been on the family, or how deeply his absence had been felt. His father, aged as much by uselessness, no doubt, as he was by time, no longer pretended to earn a living; such funds as the family had presumably came from Andrea and, possibly, brother Juan.

If his parents had hoped that Miguel would settle in with them, find a trade, function as a responsible elder son, they were disappointed. It was not merely that, as was surely the case, he recognized that his best hope of helping them lay in a profitable association with some powerful sponsor. Like many veterans home from the wars, he must have felt stifled by the prospect of a small and dutiful existence. The atmosphere at home, thin and rancid as a tenement mattress, would have impelled him in the same direction taken, each in his own way, by his brothers and sisters: escape.

Rodrigo had reenlisted as soon as he could; he was now with Alba's troops in Portugal. Andrea was still living away from the family, whether with a companion is not known. Magdalena, still pompously styling herself Doña Magdalena Pimentel de Sotomayor, had left home spiritually if not physically, being then deep in "amorous converse," as the phrase went, with Juan Pérez de Alcega.

All of this must have seemed pointless and squalid, and the sooner Miguel did something about it the better. On December 18, he personally submitted his petition. The next day he returned a favor by testifying for his witness, Chaves, in a similar cause. No record of the council's responses has come down to us, but the answer was probably no in both cases. Its good will had already been picked clean by flock of Lepanto heroes and hordes of liberated captives. Madrid's streets were full of the bogus captives satirized so wryly in Book Three of the *Persiles*. The old soldiers' adage was fully operative:

> Our God and soldiers we alike adore,
> But only when in danger, not before;
> After deliverance, both alike requited,
> Our God forgotten and our soldiers slighted.[5]

Cervantes may not have been too surprised. But the rebuff probably confirmed him in the conviction that, if there were a future for him in the royal service, it would have to be fashioned through such acquaintances as he had at court. These were with the royal personage, who was then smiling his way through southern Portugal at a stately pace made even more deliberate by unusually heavy rains which turned the roads into agents of passive Portuguese resistance. Philip had convoked a Cortes in Thomar at the beginning of April at which he was to be formally declared king, and it may have been there that Cervantes

caught up with him, armed with all his oaths and petitions and affidavits.

No one, except perhaps Vázquez, ever saw them. When Cervantes arrived at court, he found that the miracle of Algiers was accomplished; his
luck was turning back into its old, silted channel. Don Antonio de Toledo
was dead, probably of influenza. Vázquez was not eager to press the
claims of an obscure supplicant. Worst of all, from Cervantes' point of
view, while the carpetbagging he had been led to believe was thriving in
Portugal was as lucrative as advertised, its rewards were being reserved
almost exclusively for the Portuguese. In his effort to ingratiate himself
with his new subjects, Philip had adopted a "liberal" policy. Portugal was
to be virtually autonomous. Not only did the king swear in Thomar to
observe all the laws and customs of the realm, but he also promised to ap-
point only Portuguese to posts in their own country and its colonies, and
Portuguese were to be given places in the royal household. At the court,
disgruntled Spaniards sulkily eyed the crowd of satisfied Portuguese petitioners. Survivors of Sebastian's Army of Morocco were given precedence
over the veterans of Spain's own wars. Was there money to be spent?
Philip had so arranged his finances with his creditors that, despite a recent bankruptcy, he felt free to pawn Castile for a further 600,000 ducats
with which to buy Portuguese affection. Only one Spanish institution followed Philip into Portugal in force: the Inquisition, anxious to deal with
the marranos, many of them Spanish refugees or their descendants, who
were among Philip's bitterest opponents.

We do not know what kind of a post Cervantes was after, although we
may presume he sought a civilian sinecure in which, as a gentleman, he
could explore the gentlemanly estate of poetry. What he got was a polite
dismissal, with a minor courier's assignment as consolation.

On May 21, 1581, a royal order was issued to pay fifty escudos to
Miguel de Cervantes on account of one hundred allotted for expenses
for a royal mission to Oran, the remainder to be paid on his return. On
May 23, he collected his money from Royal Navy paymaster Lope Giner
in Cádiz and left at once for North Africa.

Some effort had been made to invest the mission with an importance it
probably did not have. Philip, we are told, was concerned over two problems affecting the security of his southern flank: instability among Portuguese colonial officials hostile to his coronation, and Turkish fleet movements in the western Mediterranean. As an expert in North African
affairs—oh yes!—Cervantes was to confer in Oran with Don Martín de
Córdoba, the governor to whom he had appealed for help in escaping
from Algiers. Don Martín, presumably because of the vague wording in
the *Información de Argel*, is sometimes presented to us as a personal
friend of Cervantes', although theories are noticeably scarce on how such

a friendship might have come about. From Oran, the fact-finding mission was to move to Mostaganem to confer with officials there before returning to Portugal to report to the throne.

Certainly the mission was dangerous. It is not hard to imagine how queasy Cervantes probably felt about crossing the Mediterranean in the corsair season, this time carrying letters from the king himself. Nor can we know how much personal initiative was allowed Cervantes; his report to the court has never turned up, although it may have survived under the mountains of still unclassified documents in Spanish archives.

But we do know that Philip's supposed worries about the region were no more than peripheral. Except in the Azores, the Portuguese empire rallied to him without demur. And he could afford now to forget about the Turks; a recent agreement had demilitarized the western Mediterranean, and Philip knew that Turkish weakness made the truce self-enforcing.[6] If there was to be trouble with anyone, it would be with the English and the Dutch, who were probing with increasing insistence into Spanish-Portuguese trading areas. Philip's area of concern had turned to the north and west; his battleground was the Atlantic, not the Mediterranean. Cervantes was sent into the pacified south, not the turbulent north.

It was probably July before he returned to Portugal to report. He found the city in fiesta; an epidemic of plague had receded, the treasure fleet had come back early and safe from the Indies and the king was being painstakingly winning, even going so far as to abandon his usual black costume to don a white brocade suit and wearing his beard trimmed round in the new fashion.

Cervantes probably enjoyed himself, at least for a while; there is a fatuous tribute to Lisbon in the *Persiles*—to its courtesy, its women, language, importance—all the standard paraphernalia of praise to testify that, in his old age, the disagreements of those months had been absorbed into the crevasses of his thinking, leaving pleasant memories like chunks of fool's gold on the surface. His early biographers, alert to his slightest hints, staunchly read a mysterious Portuguese mistress into his tribute (in Chapter Four of the *Voyage to Parnassus*) to "Milan for pomp, Lusitania for love." Some, free of the documentary impedimenta discovered later, gave the maternity of Cervantes' daughter to this gentlewoman, a dishonor we now know she did not deserve. The theory of his romance in Lisbon is gratuitous, but it is amiable enough, harmless, as impossible to contradict as to confirm; those whom it comforts are free to fondle it.

Cervantes' Oran mission may have been presented to him as a step to higher functions, and he may have believed this. By early fall, however, it was obvious that the puddle of preferment had dried up for him in Lisbon. The net profit to him of nearly a year of expectation and effort consisted of a few escudos, a dusting of memories of Oran in his stories—the name Chiquiznaque, an Oranese river, for a character in *Rinconete and Cortadillo;* a snatch of dialogue in *Life in Algiers* detailing the geography between Algiers and Oran; and the story of *The Spanish Gallant,* supposedly based on Don Martín de Córdoba's epic defense of Oran and Mers-el-Kebir. These and, presumably, a renewed conviction that "I am not for palaces, for I have a sense of shame and I do not know how to flatter."

This should not be taken to mean, as it often has, that his disgust with bureaucratic scavenging thrust him at once into an Arcadian mood. A great deal of romantic cant has been offered to explain why Cervantes finally ventured into literary professionalism in the early 1580s. It comes down to the notion that, disgusted with the worldliness of the court and the fickleness of royal favor, he turned inward toward a fairer world, to the flower-strewn, sunlit fields of his artistic sensibility. It is tiresome to be presented with a portrait of Cervantes as an apprentice Quixote, brooding himself into Arcadian trances like some secular John of the Cross when the going got rough. As though he had ever seen a bureaucratic career as anything more than a foundation for his literary ambition.

His disappointment in Lisbon is more likely to have convinced him that, for the time being, there was no easy channel to poetic eminence; he would have to take the plunge unbelted by any life-preserving sinecure. He would owe his failure ever to find security to pride and bad luck and the times, to his lack of university credentials and contacts; it is this equation which has been viewed as quixotry, Arcadianism, all the patronizing explications available to those who think of art, like indigestion, as something spontaneous and abnormal which an artist, by his self-indulgence, brings upon himself.

In the late autumn of 1581, Cervantes not only continued his job-hunting, but there is reason to think that he had not even wholly abandoned his courtship of Vázquez. In Book Four of *La Galatea* there appears a poem which is in effect a second *Epistle to Mateo Vázquez,* "composed and sent to the celebrated Larsileo, who in the court's business has had a long and practiced career." Larsileo was Vázquez's poetic pseudonym, and the poem may have been written in Lisbon in 1581 or in Madrid soon after Cervantes' return there.

In the hendecasyllables of rhetorical gravity, Cervantes bewails the "false, the deceitful world promissory of joyous satisfactions" embodied in the "wary life of the courtesan" which tempts "human hope, frail and piteous, in fleeting pleasures occupied wherein it seeks, but does not find, a measure of repose." He invites Larsileo to hear "the sad groans of a disdained, afflicted breast against which fire, air, sea, earth wage continuous war, conspiring all in his misfortune." He has turned, he says, to the "robust, pastoral, simple and wholesome life" of the shepherd (that is, to the writing of *La Galatea*) to forget "in all its aspects the false abjection" of the courtier's. Lauso-Cervantes derides "the favorite's grave mien, which feigns to show that he commands where he is not obeyed"; he jeers at the "suave voice of the false adulator." The shepherd, he asserts more pointedly, need not suffer "the cunning secretary's persistent disdain," watch "the brazen men of ambition with addled wits trail after favor, nor after the favorite, though they have never dyed sword or lance in Turkish or in Moorish blood." "Who would not despise such a life?" Lauso asks—and implies that he might be willing to tolerate it all the same. For the poem nevertheless ends with a supplicatory reminder that "my trust is in you and in your good wishes."

At the same time, we find Cervantes exploring still another avenue of preferment. If the Spanish well was dry, at least for the moment, there might still be America. "Refuge and support of the desperate of Spain," he called the Indies in *The Jealous Extremaduran*, and the description was beginning to fit him uncomfortably closely.

His first petition for employment in the colonies must have been made in October or November of 1581, to judge from a letter, one of the two by Cervantes known to exist, discovered in the Archivos de Simancas in 1954. It is dated February 17, 1582, from Madrid, and is addressed to "The Illustrious señor Antonio de Eraso, my lord, of the Council of the Indies, in Lisbon."[7]

"Illustrious señor:"[8] Cervantes wrote in his small, neat script, "Secretary Balmaseda[9] has shown me what, as your favor required, I had hoped (from him), but neither his solicitude nor my diligence can compete with my misfortune; the outcome of my dealing was that His Majesty has not provided for the office I sought and so I have no choice but to await the dispatch boat to see if it brings anything about a vacancy. All those that were available here have already been filled, according to what I was told by señor Balmaseda, who I know truly wished to find something for which I could apply. I beg your grace to express in his (letters) the gratitude this good will merits, if only that he might know I am not ungrateful. In the meanwhile, I am amusing myself by breeding my *Galatea*, which is the book I told your grace I was composing. When it has grown enough, it will go to kiss your grace's hands and receive the correction and amendment which I did not know how to give it. May Our Lord keep the illustrious person of your grace as He can, and prosper you. . . . I kiss your grace's hands. Your faithful servant, Miguel de Cervantes."[10]

"My *Galatea*" . . . this is a pied piper of a line, leading a procession of implications. The bustle of the year which had elapsed since his liberation had left Cervantes so little time for writing that he must, as we suspected, have made at least a start on his first big book before he left Algiers. In a sense, then, *La Galatea* may be looked at as a companion document to the *Información de Argel,* detailing the adventures of his soul as the affidavit recorded his struggles against physical captivity. The chains on his wrists, we see, had no hold on his mind; he had, after all, escaped again and again in his imagination. How awesome, the ungovernable power of Cervantes' creative energy! As a Turkish wrestler might fling away a presumptuous dwarf, it brushed off imprisonment, fear, even hunger; it was unhurt by the strains of conspiracy, nourished by failure, undistracted by his strivings and disappointments in Madrid and Portugal. Here, surely, lies the secret of his "love affair" in Lisbon, with the most elusive of mistresses: a novelist's first heroine.

Other echoes vibrate from the letter. Although Eraso was not the humanist and man of letters his father had been, he seems to have been won over by Cervantes' enthusiasm. The heavy demands made on the Council of the Indies by the annexation of Portugal made the secretary one of the busiest men in Lisbon, yet he had taken the time to chat about the young man's novel. Eraso seems honestly to have wanted to help his supplicant, suggesting a specific post for Cervantes to solicit and giving him a letter of recommendation to Balmaseda in the administrative headquarters in Madrid. Either as an economy measure or because of his usual dilatoriness, Philip had neither ordered the office formally posted nor provided funding for it.

Despite his declared ineptitude for "palaces," Cervantes had learned something of the courtier's art in Portugal; his promise to send his novel to Eraso for "correction and amendment" would have been enormously flattering to the secretary. Yet behind the flattery, behind the obvious disappointment the letter evokes, there glows a shy but genuine appreciation, as though there had been a moment of real contact between the two men. Eraso may even have been genuinely sorry things had not worked out as Cervantes had hoped; perhaps he followed the fledgling writer's career. When the royal "privilege" or license for publication was granted for *La Galatea* on February 2, 1584, it was signed by Antonio de Eraso.

What if Cervantes had gone to America? Would he have vanished into colonial obscurity, as Mateo Alemán did? Would he have turned up in Spain years later, impoverished and importunate, as did Juan de Maestranza Rivera, ex-prosecutor for the royal tribunal in Guatemala, ex-mayor of Trinidad City, praised by Cervantes in *La Galatea* as a poet of "erudition, grace and artifice"?[11] Or would he, like his own Jealous Extremaduran, have returned rich, old and anxious to revive a lost dream? It is often postulated that the Indies might have cheated the world of *Don Quixote,* of *The Siege of Numantia,* of the *Exemplary Stories.* But why suppose that New Spain would have been more fatal to Cervantes' creative impulse than even Algiers had been? No, a *Don Quixote* we might still have had. A different knight, perhaps, trotting over a more exotic landscape than the placid flatness of the Mancha, in pursuit—who knows?—of an even more spacious vision of innocence defiled. But something of that life would have remained to us. Oblivion was not among Cervantes' options.

] 21 [

The Hyperboreans

In September 1583 Miguel de Cervantes pawned five rolls of red and yellow taffeta for thirty ducats. The cloth, given him by his sister, Magdalena, is recognizable as part of the "dowry" Andrea had received from Locadelo fifteen years earlier. The situation is equally recognizable: nearly two years after his return from Lisbon, Cervantes was still jobless, living on his sisters' handouts.

When he reached Madrid with the remains of his hundred-ducat fee for his errand to Oran he found his family financially afloat, but treading bitter water. On August 12, 1581, Juan Pérez de Alcega had agreed to pay Magdalena one hundred ducats down and two hundred more within a year; she in turn consented to drop her marriage claim against him.

Magdalena may have been legally satisfied, but she was not consoled. She seems to have taken all her love affairs seriously; she was apparently one of those people who need someone to adore, and Alcega had brought out all her capacity for love and puppy-like self-surrender. When the affair collapsed she was around twenty-nine years old. This had been her last battle against spinsterhood, and she had lost it. Now, hurt and disoriented, she declared her life all but physiologically ended. She put off all ornament, took to wearing the black clothes of mourning which she soon changed for the homespun of a lay Franciscan sister. Henceforth, she was consecrated to piety and good works. Magdalena Pimentel de Sotomayor, née Cervantes de Saavedra, virtually ceased to exist; Sister Magdalena de Jesús had not yet quite materialized, but that still misty form already headed a religious procession most of her family was eventually to join.

The whole business was probably pushed well to the back of Cervantes' mind. His homecoming was away from home. The welcome given him by

Madrid's perfervid literary society must have warmed him like early spring sunshine flooding into an unheated room. A sonnet in his honor by Gálvez de Montalvo exults that Spain, "nearly widowed" by Cervantes' brushes with death, now rejoiced in the recovery of the "lost muses" inhabiting his "wholesome soul"; not even the poem's inflated artifice can disguise the real pleasure generated by this reunion of old friends.

Indeed, many in that small but ebullient universe were old friends and companions in arms: Rufo, who was readying his *Austriada* for the printer; López Maldonado, at work on his *Cancionero*. Gálvez de Montalvo's *El pastor de Filida* was about to appear and we can imagine him reading the manuscript excitedly to Cervantes: the plot of this pastoral romance is a thinly veiled account of his courtship of Magdalena de Girón; who better than Cervantes could bring instantaneous understanding to every obscure reference, each deliberate ambiguity?

Cervantes may have renewed his relationship with López de Hoyos, still master of the local academy, and had his first look at the Latin encomium the municipal laureate had composed ten years earlier in honor of the victory at Lepanto. That there was the cordial reweaving of old ties so sentimentally postulated by some biographers is at least open to question. Thirteen years of separation is a severe test of a brief friendship, if in fact something more than a formal attachment had ever existed. López de Hoyos was old, probably ill. When he died in the summer of 1583 he left a considerable estate, but nothing was left in his will to his "beloved disciple," not a book of the nearly five hundred he owned, not a keepsake.

The reunion with Francisco de Figueroa makes for more pleasant contemplation. Cervantes surely heard some of Figueroa's elegantly crafted verse; three of his sonnets turn up in *La Galatea*, a gesture to be looked upon as tribute, not plagiarism, since they were well known among the Madrid poets. Figueroa was still a remote figure, even more mysteriously legendary than he had been in Italy. He was married now and lived in deep retirement in Alcalá de Henares, working slowly and painstakingly on the poetry he would burn (as unworthy of a disciple of Virgil's) before he died, but there were sporadic visits to the capital. On these occasions, his courtly wit and limitless erudition would turn the literary scene into a brilliantly lit festival. The visits were always brief; when they ended, it was as though Madrid had been left in the half-light cast by the few candles still guttering when a ball is over.

Above all, for Cervantes, there was Laínez. At nearly fifty, he was a father figure to that brood of young poets, an Establishment man who functioned as a royal censor; it was Laínez who bestowed official approval on *La Austriada*, *El pastor de Filida* and a book of pastoral eclogues by

Pedro de Padilla which would earn Padilla a reputation as one of the best of the new crop of poets.* Laínez's rakehell tendencies (he is said once to have broken a leg fleeing through a lady's bedroom window) had been curbed if not extinguished by his new wife, a girl of Mozarabic ancestry named Juana Gaitán who was less than half his age. Now, under the approving eyes of the moneylenders to whom he had been in thrall despite the generous pension granted him by Philip II, Laínez had settled down to manage his own estate and the property Juana owned in Esquivias, a village near Toledo. He was even getting back to work on the two volumes of poetry he had been piecing together for years.

Was it chiefly in Laínez's library that Cervantes caught up on some of the reading he had missed in Algiers—the Spanish version of Camoëns' *Os Lusiadas*, Torquato Tasso's *Jerusalem Liberated*, the first Spanish translation of Aesop's *Fables* and dozens more? It was chiefly the younger man's "old and true friend"[1] who read the work Cervantes was turning out, criticizing, teaching, pressing him to polish. Laínez's rhetoric rings loud in Cervantes' poetry, informs the stately Italianate hendecasyllables of *The Siege of Numantia*. He probably saw to it that Cervantes made the literary rounds, meeting the current collection of bright young men.

Padilla was one of these. Then in his early forties, he had been a child prodigy, a scholarship graduate of the University of Granada at fourteen, already known as a poet when he entered the university at Alcalá de Henares the following year. A gentle, sweet-natured, quiet man, Padilla, with a strong religious calling soon to be satisfied (to his friends' astonishment) by his ordination as a Carmelite monk.

Luis de Vargas Manrique was the most boyish of the new boy wonders; he was eighteen years old in 1582 and already the author of several plays. Wealthy, with a distinguished name and easy entry into aristocratic circles, he was the very pattern of the gentleman glory-hunter. When, in 1588, he embarked with his eight servants in the Invincible Armada (along with his friend Lope de Vega), it would be as an adventurer. He wrote as he did everything else: for pleasure. A Cervantes who, at nearly

---

* The approval was by no means unanimous, as witness the verse critique by Cervantes' friend, the satirical poet Baltasar del Alcázar:

> *Padilla, see here! How awful:*
> *The book you've written—*
> *some call it lightweight*
> *and others say it weighs a quintal.*
> *As your friend, I*
> *am of a contrary opinion . . .*
> *for there is nothing at all in it*
> *that weighs as much as a feather . . .*
> *(and) nothing at all in it*
> *that is not heavier than lead.*

(From *The Collected Poems*, Madrid, 1910.)

twice his age, had already known more than a normal share of heartbreak and disappointment, whose purse probably could not support the buying of a round of drinks with anything like the regularity pride required, might have had good cause to detest a young man who had always had everything going for him. It is to the credit of both that they grew to be close friends.

Cervantes may nevertheless have felt more at home with Lucás Gracián Dantisco, who belonged to one of the great families of Spanish humanists. One of Lucás' brothers was Fray Jerónimo Gracián, famous as a writer, more famous now as the confessor and confidant of St. Teresa. Lucás himself was a popular author and, as librarian of the Escorial, a man of some influence. He probably read parts of *La Galatea* long before he gave it official approval on February 1, 1584.

There were dozens, scores more, most of them obscure, praised with indiscriminate benignity in *La Galatea*. Most lived from hand to mouth, hoping for the miraculous day when their talent—they had no doubts about their talent—would attract a faithful patron. They vanished one by one; the sheaves of scribbled-over paper were sold for scrap, or put to homelier uses.

Cervantes was beginning to make a name for himself as a working poet. Laudatory sonnets, those conventional tributes with which most books were prefaced then and which Cervantes would satirize in *Don Quixote*, were being requested from him by other writers—by Padilla for his *Romancero* and, later, for his *Spiritual Garden*, by Gálvez de Montalvo for the *Filida*, for Rufo's *Austriada* and López Maldonado's *Cancionero*.

La Galatea was completed by the late spring or summer of 1583. The success of Gálvez de Montalvo's pastorals, which appeared in 1582, and the Padilla eclogues which appeared later has been credited with reviving the moribund pastoral fad in Spain, giving Cervantes high hopes for the reception of his novel. In fact, the form did not dictate to the times; it was the times which recalled the form to life.

Hazlitt saw pastorals as reading "a pragmatical, self-sufficient lecture over the dead body of nature."[2] Schlegel, on the other hand, summarized the Romantics' delight in them when he referred to *La Galatea* as "a garland of the flowers of innocence."[3] Fitzmaurice-Kelly has left us a wickedly accurate picture of them as "a land of spells and of enchantment where, by the melodious murmur of sapphire waves, in magic caverns or amid banks of fern and asphodel, under rustling palm or lisping elms, the beauteous-voiced shepherds sang their lays disconsolate or fleeted the time carelessly as they did in the golden world. Here the songs of Apollo silenced the harsh words of Mercury, and from dawn until night life was spent in grove and glen that echoed perpetually to the charmed sound of lute and canzonet. It is the land of perpetual mid-summer. . . . With these blameless Hyperboreans, life floats on as in a sylvan dream . . . (in) a world of pleasurable sadness and aromatic de-sondency. . . ."4

No one reacts to pastoral romances any more because hardly anyone reads them. This is not because their preoccupations do not concern us; today's communal experiments and the more urbane enthusiasm for ecol-ogy are surprisingly close in spirit to the pastorals' natural ideal. It has also been noted that "any book in which an ideal society of intersexual equality is described centuries before it became a social fact cannot be dismissed as infantile."5

But there is a formidable array of barriers between the pastorals and modern readers. The novels' form, poetry linked by narrative prose pas-sages like the recitatives and arias in a cantata, no longer appeals to us. To separate those elements of Renaissance idealism in them which still attract us from the archaic apparatus of technical and ideological values they promote takes a considerable labor of literary archaeology. Most of them are about real people living real events to which most of the keys have been lost, so that they seem to us today to be as unreal as Meissen porcelain shepherds.

Nevertheless, they should be viewed as serious attempts to state a seri-ous problem: how to reconcile in art the ugliness of reality with Renais-sance ideals of beauty and harmony. They sought an art both true and moral. Pastorals have been called the literature of a waning civilization and, especially in the post-Tridentine Mediterranean world, the problem they faced seemed urgent.

In Spain in the 1580s there was a current of uneasiness running. The country was still proud of itself, still the strongest in the West. But the old confidence was shaken, the old dynamism slowed. The marauding of English privateers, notably Sir Francis Drake, whom the Spanish called El Draque and whom they feared as a demon, had left merchants fearful about the safety of their investments in colonial trade. War in the Low Countries dragged on with no sign of ending, straining Spanish resources and disrupting the vital commerce in wool with the Flemish manufac-turies. Catholic orthodoxy, so recently reconditioned in the Council of Trent, was manifestly failing to rout the Protestant heresy. At home, the already crowded slums of the big cities, especially Madrid, were swelling like new bruises as increasing numbers of ruined farm families fled the land. In Castile, particularly, the situation was becoming critical. Prices were rising faster than wages. Cottage industry was declining in favor of city workshops. A progressively lopsided tax structure, symbolized by the notorious *alcabala*,† was being tacked together in an effort, chronically unsuccessful, to pay the costs of Philip's Imperial policy. The rising curve of defaults on mortgages and annuities illustrates the crumbling of the harsh, rigid structure of rural society. Because the Castilian economy was primarily agrarian, the crisis on the land was beginning to show itself in a business recession in the towns whose prosperity depended on the well-being of their hinterlands.

In Spanish intellectual life, too, the sap was running sluggish, frozen by an increasingly protectionist Church. The big questions concerning God and man's relation to Him and to the cosmos had been given stern official answers which choked off further inquiry. New questions, lesser ones, were being asked; economics was beginning to replace theology as a safe field for speculation, partly because few people took the economists very seriously.

It would be simplistic to affirm that the arts bore witness to this muddling of intellectual inquiry. We can only note as a provocative coincidence the fact that in the 1580s all but one of the arts showed a marked lack of vigor in Spain. The explosion of creative experimentation in music which had produced such original talents as those of Miguel de Fuenllana and Francisco Guerrero was jelling into formalized repetition of approved patterns.[6] Few buildings of interest distinguish the architecture of the period; work was within a year of completion at the Escorial, but that sinusitic exhalation of the Counter-Reformation had been designed nearly a quarter century earlier. Only a few sturdy plants—Juan Martínez Montañés, Juan de Juní—remained in the once flourishing garden of Spanish sculpture. In painting, the patchy undergrowth of minor figures of the period is obscured by the tremendous shadow of El Greco—an Italian-trained Cretan whose vision was perhaps less specifically Spanish than it was Mediterranean.

Literature, however, was pulling hard against the undertow. True, it was becoming popularized, secularized as never before. There was a demand for escapist literature; after a generation out of fashion, the romances of chivalry were coming back into vogue. This was the movement which was also bringing pastorals to the fore again after twenty years in limbo; between 1559(?), when Jorge de Montemayor's *Diana* appeared, until Gabriel del Corral closed the cycle in 1629 with *La Cintia de Aranjuez*, more than forty pastoral romances were published. They were

† A sales tax, originally of 10 per cent but raised to 14 per cent in the second half of the sixteenth century, on every transaction in retail trade. A single hide, for example, would be taxed when the farmer sold it, taxed again when the tanner sold it to the saddler, still again when it went to the consumer and again if it was later flogged at second hand.

hugely successful (the *Diana* went through some twenty-six editions before 1600), largely because they gave a narcotic refuge in a mythically pure, natural world to people who increasingly saw life in the edemic cities as evil and corrupt and grotesquely complex; they expressed the longing of the time for an ideal, ordered society. The quest was not peculiar to Spain. This was the period when, in Italy, Torquato Tasso was struggling in his *Jerusalem Liberated* to marry classical ideals with the religious anxieties of the time; in England, the efforts of Sir Philip Sidney and Edmund Spenser to adapt their Puritanism to medieval ideals of chivalry as seen through a filter of Neoplatonic mysticism were darkly reflected in *The Faerie Queene*. But in England the problem was to invest an expanding, aggressive society with an ethic; the problem in the Mediterranean was to rationalize a declining world.

Was it hazard or a nice sense of the public mood which in 1582 led to the publication of a volume of poems by a minor writer of converso ancestry named Gregorio Silvestre, who, before he died in 1569, had been the first of the Castilian-language *desengañado*—disillusioned—poets? His theme, that disillusionment is the necessary response to whatever the world may offer, softly echoed the work of the one genuinely original verse genius of the time, Luis de Góngora y Argote.

Then in his early twenties, Góngora was already writing in the *culturanista* form which provoked violent debate in literary circles for a generation. He appeared to be moving away from the traditional pastoral mechanism toward a new, anti-populist design. It was sonorous, stylized poetry, ambiguous, delighting in acrobatically distorted metaphors and a system of inversions based on Latin syntax. *Culteranismo's* very ambiguity reflects the malaise of his time; it was turned away from the world, interiorized, *desengañado*. Góngora's "biggest" works, the two *Soledades* (*Solitudes*), share not only a common atmosphere, but also a common ideological structure with the conventional pastorals of his time. They were eclogues for the literary elite.

Cervantes would pay tribute to Góngora in *La Galatea* as

> a rare, bright and matchless wit;
> I am rejoiced by his works, and enriched—
> not I alone, but all the wide world. . . .[7]

That he maintained this opinion all his life says much for Cervantes' much-maligned critical ability; in the *Voyage to Parnassus* (Chapter Two) praise is renewed of the poet "I fear my meager praise may wrong." He even tried to imitate the *culturanista* style, though he soon gave it up; the Góngoran angularities were evidently too uncomfortable to sustain. For the Córdoban's other imitators, however, Cervantes had little patience. Their double-jointed rhetoric is satirized in Reponce's greeting to his mistress in the playlet *The Salamanca Cave:*

REPONCE: Oh how welcome are the Automedons and conductors of the cars of our pleasures, the lights of our shadows and the two reciprocal determinations which serve as the pedestals and columns for the amorous fabric of our desires!

LEONARDA: That's the only thing that annoys me about him. Reponce mine, by your life, speak in modern style so that I can understand you, and do not reach for what you cannot grasp.

All pastoral literature was built around the tribulations of courtly, elegant, university-schooled shepherds whose sole occupation—no one is ever seen plowing or planting or milking in a pastoral romance—is to talk about love, usually unrequited love. Nostalgia for bygone times has driven them to the meadows and glens, where they seek to revive the Golden Age which all poets agreed had existed in some vague antique time. This had been standard doctrine even before Virgil's wistful forecast of the coming of "a second Tiphys" bearing in "her hero-freight a second Argo."[8] The pastoral's central device was to contrast the disharmony of the shepherds' spiritual agonies with the harmony of nature and, by drawing the correct logical inferences from the lesson, to establish a Golden Age of reason.

It was no simple wife-and-kiddies romance the Renaissance poets yearned for, however. They had in mind a philosophic love as synthesized in the Neoplatonism of Castiglione in *The Courtier* and, especially, by Leone Ebreo, an exiled Spanish Jew, in his 1535 *Dialogues of Love.* Ebreo's influence on his time as a popularizer of Neoplatonism has been likened to that of Freud on twentieth-century literature. Combining elements from Plato, Plotinus, Proclus and the Pseudo-Dionysius, the system posed a hierarchy of love rising through successive stages of sensual-corporeal, intellectual-philosophic and, finally, spiritual or perfect love through the ennobling passion of idealized, selfless devotion. With the appearance of Montemayor's *Diana,* this abstraction was humanized and the faith expressed became the spiritual-emotional energy fired by profane love itself. Secularization of the religious mysteries brought down on the pastorals the anathema of Catholic moralists, prodding poets from Cervantes to Lope de Vega to try, with only limited success, to identify the last stage in love as a mystical union with God.

Underlying the naturalism of pastorals was the assumption that the countryman was possessed of perfect innocence and, therefore, had an inherent knowledge of perfect love. Cities, they postulated, were evil and corrupt, places of sour bedsheets and poisonous air where love of money and worldly accomplishment displaced divine love. Nature, pure and refreshing, was the setting in which—barring accidents—a perfect unity of souls might be achieved. Luis de León thought Christ lived in the fields; he asserted that "though people may talk better in the city, finesse of feeling belongs to the fields and to solitude."[9]

Not, of course, the nature around them, with its droughts and stony fields and its mindless savageries. Theirs was an artificial nature, a perfect poetic nature in which the perfect natural man acted out the spiritual drama of perfect love. Thus properly idealized, nature became what Don Quixote described as "God's major-domo."

Despite sixteenth-century readers' easy identification with these erudite shepherds, they eventually found constant, unrelieved restatement of the lovable old theme a trifle wearing. From the midcentury on, the prose narration in pastoral novels was given vivifying injections of blood and thunder distilled from the Byzantine novels and the tales of medieval chivalry. The shepherds and shepherdesses even went in for what one critic has described as parlor games[10]—viz. the riddles in Book Six of *La Galatea*—so as "not to weary their ears listening eternally to lamentations and doleful songs of love."

No one took such goings-on literally. In the *Diana,* all the shepherds join Selvagia in a chorus of weeping, the shedding of tears "being an occupation in which they were highly experienced."[11] In a mischievously purple passage in *The Dogs' Colloquy,* Cervantes ridicules the pastoral genre, including his own *Galatea* and Lope's *Arcadia.* He reflects with the dog Berganza

that what I heard about the life of shepherds could not be true, at least about those that my master's lady read about in books when I went to her house, all of which told of shepherds and shepherdesses, saying that they spent their whole lives singing and playing on bagpipes, flutes, rebecks and flageolets and other extraordinary instruments . . . she would go on about how Amphrysus' shepherd sang so marvelously well in praise of the peerless Belisarda, there being not a tree in all the mountains of Arcadia at whose foot he had not sat to sing from the moment the sun emerged in the arms of Aurora until it set in those of Thetis. And even after black night had spread its black and dusky wings over the face of the Earth he did not cease his well-sung and better-wept laments. . . . I was led to see how different were the manners and customs of my shepherds and all their crew from those of the shepherds I had heard about in books. If mine sang, their songs were not harmonious and well composed, but "See where the wolf doth go,

Jenny" and other such things, nor was this done to the sound of flageolets, rebecks or bagpipes, but to the clacking of crooks or of tiles held between their fingers. And their voices were not delicate, tuneful and delightful but hoarse growls which, alone or in chorus, sounded more like shouts or grunts than singing. Most of the day they spent delousing themselves or mending their sandals. . . . I finally understood . . . that all those books are well-written imaginings for the entertainment of the idle, with not a shred of truth in them.

Cervantes was being ingenuous in this. Again and again, over the years, he promised a sequel to *La Galatea*—in both parts of *Don Quixote,* in the dedication of his *Eight Plays and Eight Interludes;* the promise was in the very last line he wrote, a few days before his death, in the dedication of the *Persiles.* This consistency expresses more than the longing of a sick old man for the serene orderliness of that other, younger, world.

It seems clear that he was dissatisfied with the book. He indicates in the prologue to it that he dithered about releasing it for publication: ". . . I could not decide which of two evils was the greater—that of someone who, anxious to display his heaven-sent talent, ventures too soon to offer the fruits of his wit to his country and his friends, or that of the person who, purely through fussiness, laziness and procrastination, forever questioning what he does and understands, holding as certain only what he cannot achieve, never resolves to unveil and release his writings. . . . Fleeing from both these evils, I withheld publication of this book until now, but I did not wish to keep it to myself any longer. . . ."

"This Cervantes has been a great friend of mine for many years," the priest says in the book-burning sequence in *Don Quixote,* "and I know he is better versed in misfortunes than in verses. There is some originality in his book; it proposes something, but comes to nothing. We must wait for the Second Part (of *La Galatea*) he promises; perhaps with improvement it will be granted the mercy now denied it. . . ."[12]

Cervantes may, too, have recognized the debt the rest of his work owed to *La Galatea.* His pastoral was the marble from which all his subsequent monuments were carved. The themes running through it repeatedly reemerge, often with the emphases shifted, as though each new work offered a way to examine his ideas from a vital new perspective: reality-illusion, truth-falsehood in art and life, free will-moral law, idealism-skepticism, "natural" (semi-divine) man vs. Worldly (semi-demoniac) man, all the bulging agenda of Renaissance speculation. And the revolutionary technical brilliance of the later works glows dimly in *La Galatea;* both *Don Quixote* and the *Persiles* are prose distortions of the pastoral form, more authentic (the scene in the *Persiles,* for example, in which shepherds make a bed in a hollow tree trunk for Feliciana, newly delivered of a child, has the true country flavor along with the mythical quality of a divine myth) but still recognizable as *Galatea*'s children.

The book opens with Elicio the shepherd singing a self-righteous complaint about his love for Galatea. "The mountain, meadow, field and stream sound a bitter echo of my weary spirit," he wails. In this he is joined by the humbler, simpler goatherd Erastro, who also loves the protagonist but whose rusticity (class distinctions in the classless pastoral society?) disqualifies him from serious consideration. This makes him the purer love. It also frees him from Elicio's jealousy, a naturally epidemic sentiment in the pastoral world.

Poor Galatea! She has been called passionless, frigid, sexless, marble-hearted. This is too hard on a girl who also has to carry the book's message. She is purity, divinity, chastity, the ideal to whom love is owed for no reason but her perfection. She is freedom incarnate, as impossible to confine within a single relationship as divine grace itself. "I promise you, Elicio," says Erastro,

> that I would give
> everything I have left in life
> to Galatea if only she would return
> the soul and heart she stole from me;
> and, along with my flocks, I would add
> my dog Gavilan and the other, Manchado;
> but, since she must be a goddess, it is my soul
> she will want more than any other thing.

Galatea *is* a goddess, as immortal as her namesake, the Nereid who toyed with and deluded her rustic suitor Polyphemus the Cyclops. She is a majestic, an imposing figure in her first appearance in the book, at dawn at the crest of a hill, her long tresses streaming in the wind; "the very sun seemed to envy them because, wounding them with its rays, it tried to dim their light if it could." She is love itself, the benign figure in whose arms the fleeing hare finds sanctuary from its hunters, the confidante to whom the shepherds come to unburden their souls. Diana she is, Mary even more. Galatea is that unascertainable point at which all ideals converge; her function is not to love but to be loved.

The forlorn debate on the subject between Elicio and Erastro is suddenly interrupted when a shepherd, Carino, bursts out of a nearby woods in flight from another pastor, Lisardo. Carino is stabbed to death by his pursuer with, it transpires, a dagger still stained with the blood of Lisardo's lover, Leonida, the glory of the Guadalquivir, unwittingly murdered by her own brother Crisalvo the Cruel because of Carino's trickery. From this point on the story becomes a tangle of loves, rejections, abductions, resignations, pirate raids, mistaken identities, impersonations, tied together by a shameless string of coincidences. Most of the novel is taken up with the trials of Timbrio and Silerio, the Damon and Pythias of Jerez de la Frontera, whose friendship survives even their rivalry for the love of the beauteous Neapolitan Nisida. A cunning confusion sends the desperate lovers on separate Odysseys which, two tempests, one naval battle, a shipwreck and five books later, are harmonized in a happy ending.

The ranks of the blessed are thin, however; man's condition, the pastorals maintain, is a struggle toward the light. Most of the seventy-two characters in *La Galatea* are unhappy, with the notable exception of the two philosophers-in-residence, Damon and Tirsi, whom reason has liberated from the amorous grind. There is Rosaura, whose flirtation with Artandro almost costs her the love of Grisaldo and who is reduced to threatening suicide before his eyes to win him back—only to be kidnapped by the vengeful Artandro. Darinto loves Blanca, who marries Silerio. The foreigner Artidoro is in love with Teolinda, whose twin Leonarda marries Artidoro although she really loves *his* twin Galercio, who pines for Gelasia. Gelasia loves no one. Orompo the Sad weeps for the dead Listea, Crisio is separated from Claraura, etc.

The action stops periodically for a debate on philosophical issues. One of these pits Lenio against Tirsi in the novel's pivotal discussion of the nature and value of earthly love. Lenio, caustic, superior, self-deluded, derides love as a "yoke to lower the proudest neck," an "invisible thief" which destroys empires and sets brother against brother. To support his argument, he lifts a thirty-five-line passage intact from Ebreo's *Dialogues* arguing that love is a passion and thus harmful to the soul. Tirsi's reply, Platonic at first but growing more frankly Christian as his song progresses, urges Lenio to embark on the process toward perfection. Love, he contends, is the "spirit of fire which gives light to him who is blindest, the sole remedy for hate and fear, never-sleeping Argos however much he is lulled by the counsels of some spurious deity." He pleads that love "is life, is glory, is pleasure, happy tranquillity of the soul." The opponents finally compromise in an appeal for *"un amor templado,"* a moderate, reasoned love. Later Cervantes' heroes would ignore this stricture to their perdition—Carrizales the Jealous Extremaduran, Anselmo the Curious Fool, Don Quixote himself. And Lenio's moderation is soon shattered by his sudden, hopeless love for his female counterpart Gelasia, whose love of nature—"of roses and of jasmin are my chains; I was born free and I believe in liberty"—precludes more limiting attachments.

It would be pointless to try to follow in detail the involutions of a plot in which even Cervantes occasionally lost his way. Nor can a few lines penetrate the thick layers of references, symbols, images, ideas with which the book is textured.

Elaborate allegory lends itself to elaborate subtleties of interpretation. Consider the question of whether *La Galatea* is a converso's novel. To assert that it was could mean that the book was not merely an entertainment, but that Cervantes intended it in some measure as a New Christian's novel of protest, or of exhortation.

The book's frank debt to the *Diana* has been thought suggestive; Montemayor, a Portuguese who wrote in Castilian, was almost certainly of Spanish Jewish ancestry and this heritage has been seen in the intensity of the *Diana*'s melancholy, in an edge of bitterness staining its pastoral tranquillity.

When the same divining rod is passed over *La Galatea* its magic seems to fail; Cervantes' novel is, if anything, less plaintive than the species required. It is a tormented book, not at all the epic of sweetness and youthful enthusiasm it is sometimes taken to be, but its violence is not surprising in view of Cervantes' recent history.

Wonder does arise, nevertheless, when some of the relationships in *La Galatea* are examined closely. Among the most provocative of these, because it involves personages clearly meant by Cervantes as axial to his meaning, is the companionship in love and frustration of Lenio and Galercio, both enamored of the "cruel" Gelasia. Lenio, we notice, is the spokesman of Leone Ebreo—Leon the Hebrew. Lenio's "conversion" to love strongly recalls the image—recurrent in Cervantes' work, insistent— of the conversion of Saul of Tarsus. "See how my former presumption has changed," Lenio urges, "and is converted to amorous intent." So might Saul have spoken of his discovery of Christ. Lenio calls Gelasia *"endurecida,"* hardhearted, or stiff-necked, as the Jews are sometimes called. Why, demands Lenio-Paul in Books IV and VI, does she flee from her follower, why reject him who seeks to serve her? "Hard as that high rock . . . proud as a tiger . . . Oh harder than marble to my lamentations." He decries her excessive pride, as Paul decried the Jews'.

Lenio is joined in this by Galercio, who sings of a Gelasia of "strange hardness"; she is a "mountain . . . rock or steel, hard marble or diamond; a rock's lover am I, I love and adore a mountain. . . ."

What does all this bring to mind? Perhaps Paul's exhortation of the Hebrews: "Today, if ye will hear his voice, harden not your hearts. . . . For ye are not come unto the mount that might be touched . . . and if so much as a beast touch the mountain, it shall be stoned. . . . Ye are come unto Mount Sion and unto the city of the living God. . . . See that you refuse not him that speaketh. . . ."

We are not obliged to see in Gelasia a symbol of the synagogue, or to recognize the golden calf of Aaron in Cervantes' statue imagery; the pleas of Gelasia's lovers need not be interpreted as entreaties that she receive the softening message of Christian love. We can choose to be haunted or not by the converso preoccupation with the Pauline lesson. But we cannot help wondering about it.

Custom dictates that *La Galatea* be swept aside as a weak effort, interesting only because it was Cervantes' first major work. The verse is uneven in quality, with the mediocre far outweighing the good. Why, then, should *La Galatea* be one of the few pastoral novels which can still be read with interest?

Not all the verse is watery. When, for example, Orompo vents his jealousy (Book III), there is angry power in the lines:

> *Salid de lo hondo del pecho cuitado*
> *palabras sangrientas, con muerte mezcladas:*
> *y si los suspiros os tienen atados,*
> *abrid y romped el sinestro costado. . . .*

(From the depths of my anguished breast, break, bloody words, mixed with death! And if thou be constricted by my signs, then open and crack my heart's side. . . .)

Cervantes' prose in *La Galatea* is subjected to the stereotypes of pastoral writing—the exaggerated use of adjectives to modify nouns, for example: meadows are always pleasant, water invariably crystalline, trees, should city-dwellers have forgotten, consistently green. But, for the first time in pastoral history, the prose language is crisp, virile, active, in sharp contrast to the static oratory of its predecessors. Cervantes arrogantly addressed himself in the prologue to those "narrow minds who wish to limit the abundance of the Castilian language to the brevity of its ancient forms"; he would give them "to understand that they have an open field, fertile and spacious, through which they can freely course with fluency and sweetness, gravity and eloquence. . . ." In *La Galatea* he began the process of transforming the language of Spanish imaginative prose from a passive, ponderous tool to an instrument—supple, terse, expressive, dynamic—of unparalleled resonance.

No other European language owes its literary impetus so wholly to one writer's stylistic enterprise as Spanish to that of Cervantes, and the first charge of this impulse is in *La Galatea,* where the language, perhaps less pungent than it would become, nevertheless flows with a smooth, natural grace.

Structurally, even ideologically, the book reveals a Cervantes exploring the possibilities of his medium, breaking out of the standard mold. It begins *in medias res,* a device borrowed from the Byzantine novelists. *La Galatea*'s movement of action-counteraction follows the approved Aristotelian pattern, but not slavishly; the rhythm is frequently interrupted, reversed, suspended.

Broken pastoral rules litter the pages. Cervantes' grumbling about women (they are inconstant, heartless, prudish, finical, covetous, "lovely but fickle—fickle but lovely," sighs Mireno in Book III) disregards the largely hypocritical Renaissance reverence for womanhood; he may have meant them no flattery in making them more human, more capricious, giving them a richer gamut of emotions than their besotted shepherds, but at least he did not consign them to a pedestal where they might be conveniently ignored.

Despite Lauso's railing against city life, the urban backgrounds of some of the shepherds are left for what they are. Cities are presented as habitable and even admirable places: the "ornamental gardens, white houses and gleaming chapels" of Genoa are objects of affection.

Beginning the action with a murder was daring; failing to punish an act of violence was a pastoral heresy which Cervantes blithely refused to repent. Moreover, Cervantes succeeds in knotting his narrative strands without the help of nymphs, satyrs, fauns, magical springs, giants and spells typical of the form—a trap Lope later failed to avoid in his *Arcadia*.

The adventures enlivening the story are closely woven into the book's texture, not simply thrust into convenient holes as they were in the *Diana* (and as, in his weaker moments, Cervantes would do in Part One of *Don Quixote*). Clumsy and groping as it is, this virtuosity gives his treatment of the theme of love a new naturalness, a layered luxuriance of implications.

The personages in *La Galatea* are individuals. They may live in a distant Eden, but they are aware that their secluded garden exists in a real world, dotted with real cities and dominated by private emotions. How revolutionary a departure this was from the pastoral norm is not easy to appreciate at our remove from it. It meant discarding the convention which made each personage no more than an envelope for a philosophical message. This in turn forced Cervantes to develop his plot with both the book's ideological imperatives and with individual characters consistently in mind. The result is a tension of contrasts infinitely more absorbing than the mechanical conflicts in other pastorals. The (moral) punishment for Lenio's disdain of love represents an orderly philosophic-theological progression, but its meaning is given dramatic power by Lenio's personal beliefs, his sarcastic pride, his intellectual arrogance.

Characterization is reflected in a linguistic hierarchy going beyond the requirements of Aristotelian decorum: the calm, polished discourse of Damon and Tirsi contrasts with the aggressiveness of Artandro's lines as much as it does, predictably, with that of rude Erastro. The differing styles distinguish a character's philosophical level as much as they do his mentality: Tirsi has climbed higher on the ladder to spiritual purity than, say, the passionate Mireno despite the lover's protests of unwavering faith. Cervantes achieves this with none of the Aristotelian condescension which forever excluded the lowly from the higher thought and finer emotions of persons of exalted station. Erastro may be a peasant among courtiers, but the muscular directness of his speeches shows him to be farther along the spiritual path than the more literary Elicio.

The vague forms of future characterizations are here. Don Quixote's shadow lurks in Lauso's progression from madness (love) to sanity (reasoned detachment)—but it is also visible in Tirsi's plea in favor of love, in defense of madness. The gradual merging of the personalities of the poetic, aristocratic Elicio and rustic Erastro foretell the growing interdependence of the knight and Sancho Panza. Dulcinea emanates from Galatea. We see the pilgrimage from sin to sanctity of Persiles and Sigismunda, we anticipate the suffering of Carrizales in his dark journey from egotistical blindness to the open-eyed—but fatal—"reality" of reason.

If Lope de Vega's *Arcadia*, despite the skillful fluency of its verse, despite the Salamanca-inculcated ease of its classical allusions, sounds wooden and trite to us, it is because Lope could not match the range and subtlety of individualization found in *La Galatea*. In fact, Cervantes' originality may be partly ascribed to the lack of university training he had otherwise so much cause to regret. It freed him from any scholarly commitment, allowing him, almost obliging him, to take his story away from the abstractionism of other pastorals—where he might have been uncomfortable—toward realism, action, characterization.

This is not a reflection Cervantes would have enjoyed. There are signs that he tried to cover up for his dilettantism: a conscious effort at Latinization, the use of erudite language, archaisms (often given new meanings) and Italianisms. There are traces of Plautus, Horace, Torquato Tasso, Petrarch, Ausías March in *La Galatea;* classical references are scattered through the text like birdshot in a partridge. The story of Lisandro and Leonida was taken from Matteo Bandello's *Novelle;* great chunks are carved verbatim from a 1551 translation of Pietro Bembo's *Gli Asolani* and the excerpts from Mario Equicola's *Book on the Nature of Love* published in Spanish in 1553. Much of the plot for the story of Timbrio and Silerio is taken from the *Decameron* (Eighth Day) and fragments of Ovid's *Metamorphoses*—Cervantes may only have known fragments of it—are used, but out of context and with their sense changed. Contributions were accepted from Garcilaso, Montemayor and Virgil (via Sannazzaro) as well as Figueroa and Laínez.

Cervantes' reservations about *La Galatea* notwithstanding, it was a critical success which established him as a major artist. Espinel wrote a poem in praise of it in his *Diversas rimas* calling Cervantes a "rare wit" and lauding his "Minerva-inspired fancy." Gracián Dantisco approved its "very pure style" and its "felicitous inventiveness"; Vargas Manrique was impressed by the liveliness of its language. Padilla, in his *Spiritual Garden,* referred to Cervantes as being among "the famous poets of Castile."

Even Lope respected it:

> That is *La Galatea;*
> if it is a good book you want,
> you cannot ask for better.
> Its author was Miguel Cervantes,
> who long ago in the *Naval* lost
> a hand. . . .[13]

In *La dama boda* (Act III) he ranked it above Camoëns' *Os Lusiadas* and just below his own volume of *Rhymes,* and he repeated his praise in his *Apollo's Laurel* and in his novel *La Dorotea.*

The book's influence on French literature was stronger than it was in its author's own country. We learn in Francisco Màrquez Torres' approval of Part Two of *Don Quixote* that a party of French noblemen visiting Spain in 1615 knew the pastoral "almost by heart"; César Oudin, who published a 1611 Paris edition of *La Galatea,* complained that he could hardly find a copy for translation. Delight in the book remained constant among poets and critics until the pressure of gathering reality in the nineteenth and twentieth centuries made the hothouse preciousness of the pastoral genre seem intolerable.

If all these words of praise were ducats, Cervantes might have retired on them. But with neither patron nor publisher in sight for the book, his triumph was limited to the Madrid literary world which imploded daily to gossip and argue and listen to its denizens' writings in the bookstores clustered around what is now the Plaza Mayor. Cervantes' soul may have swelled with its praises, but, at thirty-six, he was all too aware that "the heart's delight consists far more in possession than it does in hope."[14] And of possessions—the negotiable kind—he was depressingly short.

22

In the Cruel Patio

Think of Cervantes standing near the entrance to a Madrid corral on an afternoon, probably in the autumn, of 1583 to watch a fragment of his life unfold as he had dramatized it in the first of his plays to be staged. It is just after lunch; the performance would be timed to end well before dark so that playgoers could get home before the cutpurses take over the streets. Although it is still early, the benches in the stalls are nearly full. In the pit behind them, the groundlings—the *mosqueteros*—are unlimbering their pipes, whistles, rattles, bells and clappers should these instruments be needed to express their owners' disapproval of play, actors or anything else which might irritate the sensitive nerve ends of their self-esteem.

The raised *gradas* are still largely empty; these are for unaccompanied gentlemen whose gravity would be disarranged by a too apparent eagerness to be entertained. In the *aposentos* and *desvanes* (the grilled windows in the buildings along either side of the open patio), servants are setting out the dainties and flagons of wine chilled with snow from the Sierra de Guadarrama for the fashionable ladies who will arrive modishly late in a clatter of compliments from their gallants. The rearmost section of the corral, by contrast, is bedlam. This is the *cazuela* (stewpan), reserved for the women of the town, who are anything but reserved. It is also known as the *jaula* (cage) and some of the birds in it, those concerned for their reputations if not for their virtue, have come masked. Raucously cheerful advances are being made to the men below them, under the interested gaze of two sergeants at arms present to deal with the (occasionally fatal) brawls which so frequently compete with the play for public entertainment. Vendors are already doing a brisk business in water, fruit, nuts, quince paste, wafers, dates, nougat, syrupy anise liqueur and a kind of mead, snow-cooled.

Cervantes may be surveying this fauna with detached amusement, but he is probably eying the pit more anxiously. For the moment, the mosqueteros' fire is aimed at the plumage in the cage, but he knows these are the men called the "wild beasts," whose noisy whims can make or break a playwright's reputation, sometimes driving a play from the stage in midperformance. Even the most confident poets feared and hated them. Lope would complain repeatedly of the *vulgo* who idolized him; Ruiz de Alarcón, in the prologue to the collection of his plays published in Madrid in 1628, would invite them to treat his works "as is your wont: not justly, but according to your fancy, for they face you fearlessly and with contempt . . . if they displease you I shall rejoice, for it will be proof that they are good." Calderón courted "the mosqueteros, whose whistles are already on the tips of their tongues."[1]

What was the play? It may have been *Life in Algiers;* its autobiographical story and primitive technique stamp it as an early work. But we can only guess. *Life in Algiers* is one of the two survivors, with *The Siege of Numantia,* of the "twenty or thirty comedies"[2] Cervantes wrote between 1583 and 1587. Among the missing: *La Confusa, La batalla naval, La gran turquesca, La Jerusalén, La amaranta o la del Mayo, La única o la bizarra Arsinda, El bosque amoroso, El trato de Constantinopla y muerte de Selim* and "many others I've forgotten"[3] but which "even if they were not mine would seem worthy of praise."* History has forgotten them too; not even their titles remain to us. Time, be it noted, has been no more spiteful in this toward Cervantes than it was to his contemporaries. As much as two thirds of Lope's output may have been lost, four fifths of the hundreds of plays written by Tirso de Molina.

Logic tells us that much was at stake for Cervantes personally that afternoon in the corral. Success might open doors which were still closed to him, put him on his feet financially, attract a publisher for his novel, perhaps a patron. It could magnify what was as yet the whisper of *La Galatea* into a shout all Spain (why not all Europe?) might hear. But it is no mind-reading trick which lets us suspect that he had a more splendidly immodest cause to be nervous: the desire, simply, to be the greatest playwright in the history of Spain. Years later, when his active career in the theater had ended, he would still pronounce himself able to write the best plays ever seen in Spain; at the close of his life we will find him defend-

---

* *Eight plus Eight,* Prologue. A few of the lost plays may have been reincarnated in later plays which were never staged. *La Gran Turquesca* may have become *La Gran Sultana; La casa de los celos y selvas de Ardenia (The House of Jealousy and the Forests of Ardenia)* may disguise *El bosque amoroso.* Cervantes' personal favorite, the one "of which I am proudest, called *La confusa,* which, if I do say so, can be singled out as good among the best of all the cloak-and-dagger dramas presented up to now" may be hidden in *El Laberinto de amor (Love's Labyrinth).*

ing his skill against what he felt—admittedly with less of the old assurance—was unfair criticism.

But we must understand that something more than personal glory
moved him. Cervantes plainly longed to give the Spanish stage the dignity and grandeur of antiquity, of that golden age of which he would
come to view the Golden Century as a mockery. He clearly believed that
poetry had a social mission, that a priestly role as the giver of moral law
devolved on the poet. He obviously saw himself as a tragedian in the
Sophoclean-Senecan tradition.

We may now recognize that, to realize such an ambition, he was writing in the wrong place at the wrong time. Cervantes was Spanish enough
to conceive of his plays as morally exemplary vehicles; it would never
have occurred to him to attempt the pure drama of the Elizabethan
stage. It is in terms of his ambition, then, not of his achievement,
that we must interpret his later complaints about the low state of Spanish
drama. The substance of these is contained in the curate Pero Pérez's celebrated discussion with the canon of Toledo in *Don Quixote*.[4] Most of
the current plays, the canon says, were "notorious nonsense, monsters
without feet or head," staged only because "the crowd likes them that
way and not otherwise." Authors who write drama properly merely please
"three or four men of sense . . . while all the rest are left unsatisfied and
cannot fathom their subtlety." The canon says he has "tried to persuade
the managers that their judgments are erroneous and that they would
draw bigger crowds and forge sounder reputations by playing comedies
that follow the rules," but they prefer to "earn their bread from the
many" than to win the elite's approval.

What is wrong with the plays? Pero Pérez is eloquent on the subject:
plays which should be mirrors of human life, patterns of manners and images of truth are "mirrors of absurdity, patterns of nonsense and images
of lasciviousness." Children appear in a play's opening scene in swaddling
clothes and in the second as bearded elders. What is more ridiculous, the
priest demands, than "a valiant old man and a youthful coward, an eloquent servant, a statesmanlike page, a king disguised as a porter or a
princess as a scullery wench?" The unities of time and place are frac-
tured too: "I have seen a play in which the first act was set in Europe,
the second in Asia and the third wound up in Africa."†

Sacred drama fares still worse. Plots are muddled, saints confused, miracles sprinkled over the action like pepper on stale fish, all of which is
"prejudicial to truth" and "detrimental to history." How can audiences
come away from such plays "instructed by their seriousness, amazed by

† Cervantes would later bring himself to disregard the rules, but tentatively, with
so uneasy a conscience that he would waste an entire scene in *The Happy Rogue*
apologizing for it.

the plot, enlivened by the speeches, alerted by the ruses, wiser for the moral, angry at vice and in love with virtue"?

Much of this diatribe is specifically aimed at Lope de Vega. The truth of what the curate has said, Cervantes insists, "is visible in the infinite number of plays written by one most fertile genius of these realms with such splendor and grace, such well-wrought verses, such choice language, such lofty thought . . . that his fame fills the world, and yet, in trying to suit the taste of the players, not all his pieces have achieved (though some have) the perfection art requires."[5]

He goes on to borrow an idea from Plato's *Republic* for censorship of all plays before they could be performed—actually no more than the approval and licensing to which books were already subject. His admirers can do no more than shrug and apologize for this display of bad temper and contend that, had the rule been adopted, Cervantes himself would have been the first to chafe under it. The outburst should not distract us, however, from the more laudable impulse behind it. It is common to see in his complaints no more than a pedantic failure's ill feeling toward a successful rival. But Cervantes did not see himself as a failure; the drama, he manifestly believed, had failed him and the principal conspirator was Lope de Vega.

Whatever Lope's personality might have made him, he was a true artist and a fine poet. His reaction to Cervantes' criticism was one of acute outrage precisely because, one suspects, he recognized the truth in the implication that he had trivialized a high calling, that the populist tone and direction he had imposed on Spanish drama had debased it. History has largely supported Cervantes in the argument, dropping Lope in universal value well behind Shakespeare, Jonson, Molière, Calderón, even Tirso. Cervantes was a failed Euripides. Lope was Lope.

Playwrighting when Cervantes adopted it was a shapeless bundle of an art, its features still blurred and its character undefined. Some conventions did exist: plays were invariably in rhymed verse, although they had not yet been definitively corseted in the rhythmic patterns Lope considered appropriate to specific functions (hendecasyllables for dignity and solemnity, romances for action and some kinds of narration, and so on). Despite Cervantes' claim to have been the first who "dared to reduce comedies to three acts from the five they had been before,"[6] plays of three and four acts as well as five had been appearing for half a century.

Stagecraft was rudimentary. The new permanent theaters, or corrales, differed little from the

> cruel patio,
> blazing forge in summer,
> in winter a frozen river . . .[7]

in which Rueda played. Things had improved a bit since the old days when the devil went in and out of a barrel and Judas slid to perdition down a bell rope. There were trap doors in the stages of the later corrales; proscenium arch and front curtain were still in the future, but a back curtain might mask a simple second set. A few steps at the rear of the stage led to an upper gallery which served as anything from a balcony to a city wall.

Some attempt was made at verisimilitude. Painted backdrops were used, pasteboard fountains and trees appeared, but furnishings were usually limited to a table and a few chairs. The two phantom voices singing unaccompanied from behind a blanket in the old days had been brought out front and given the comfort of accompaniment by a vihuela and a viola and an occasional oboe. Scene changes were considered superfluous; people's imaginations were thought to be adequately stimulated by a few spoken lines, or the kind of stage business called for by Cervantes in Act II of *Numantia:* "Noise is made under the platform with a barrel of stones, and a rocket is fired." Clothes were rich, but costumes were almost unknown. Interiors and exteriors, nationalities, locales were largely indistinguishable except by a simple prop—a javelin in an actor's hand, for example, identified him as a hunter, placing the action out of doors. People in Cervantes' day went to hear a play, not to see it. In this they were encouraged by a system dominated as nowhere else by the incentives of penury and haste.

Plays in Cervantes' day were consumer goods, as perishable as fresh meat. Ten days was a long run for a new work, two or three the average. Naturally, then, plays were staged with all the care of an emergency appendectomy on a farm-kitchen table. They were written hastily. The prolific Lope seldom spent more than a month writing a play and some were ground out in a day or two. It is this Herculean productivity on the part of Spanish playwrights which largely explains why they rarely turned out a play strong enough to survive the voyage across the centuries with its grandeur undiminished. Earlier estimates of their output may now be considered excessive; the eighteen hundred plays once thought to have been churned out by Lope, for example, are now believed to have numbered "only" around five hundred. Compare this awesome record with the thirty-seven plays written partly or entirely by Shakespeare and we begin to see why Spanish drama fades so easily from the memory. Example: both Lope and Shakespeare went to Italian sources for the plot of a play, Lope to Luigi da Porto's *The Lovers of Verona* and the Briton to Matteo Bandello's *Novelle,* probably via Arthur Brooke's narrative poem *The Capulets and the Montagues.* The Spaniard, whose international fame was then far greater than Shakespeare's, labored a few days and brought forth his *Castelvines y Monteses,* which no one now troubles to read; Shakespeare spent nearly a year on it and came up with *Romeo and Juliet*.

The reason for this was not Spanish heroics. It was money. Should anyone cavil about his plays and think that he wrote them for fame, Lope admonished (not entirely candidly) in a letter in 1604, "undeceive him and tell him I wrote them for money." But not much money. At the height of his fame, when admirers followed him through the streets and he wrote admiring little notes to himself in the margins of his manuscripts, even Lope received no more than five hundred reales for a new play; he usually had to settle for three hundred. And at that, as Cervantes complained, a writer had to become embroiled with the managers in "look-here's and I-tell-you's"[8] before he could collect his fee.

Like books, plays were sold outright to an *autor* (the player-manager of a strolling company, so-called because, in the early days, he also wrote the plays he staged) to do with as he pleased. Often only a step away from debtors' prison himself, the autor had to defend his acquisition in that theatrical jungle like a jackal its bone. Rival managers regularly stole plays by copying them, more or less accurately, during a performance. Actors, noted Quevedo, "took (plays) to read and stole them and, by adding an idiocy and removing something well said, presented them as their own."[9] Writers themselves were play snatchers; Calderón, for example, cannibalized at least three of Lope's plays and presented them as his own, greatly improving them in the process. Managers had a stake in keeping purchased plays out of print and so becoming public property.

Actors were no better off. There were a few stars among the two thousand or so players who performed during the late sixteenth and early seventeenth centuries: Agustín Solano was paid three thousand reales a year as a young leading man; Juan de Seguía received one hundred ducats plus his room, board, laundry and transportation on horseback instead of in the common cart for one gawdy season. Generally speaking, however, actors would have agreed with the complaint of Agustín de Rojas, one of the better-paid performers of the day as well as a playwright, that "there is no Negro in Spain or slave in Algiers but has a better life than the actor."[10] Most of them were satisfied with three or four reales a day, their keep and linen, and they usually insisted on being paid every afternoon as soon as the play ended.

As though this were not trouble enough, players and dramatists had the opposition of the Church to contend with. As it had everywhere, Spain's theatrical tradition had originated in religious drama. It had developed along two parallel lines, one slightly more dignified than the other, but both exasperating to the pious. One led from the medieval monastery cloister, where the monks performed mystery plays on feast days, to the university patio, where it was bathed in Renaissance humanism, drenched in student irreverence and wrapped in the pastoral hand-me-downs of antiquity before being cast into the streets in the late fifteenth and early sixteenth centuries. The second emerged through the churches on the *rocas,* platforms carried by twelve men on which impersonators of the Holy Family, the saints and evangelists enacted biblical scenes while escorts of prophets and angels ran tootling alongside.

These were the forerunners of the *autos sacramentales,* religious playlets performed on the major holidays, especially Corpus Christi. When church services ended, the actors, including at least a few paid professionals, boarded large carts which were towed to the town's main squares for repeat performances. By the late sixteenth century these "festivals of the cars" had become extravaganzas, enlivened as in secular theaters by profane interludes, singing and dancing. In Plasencia in 1578 a fully rigged ship floated in a tank sixty feet long set up in the central square for a depiction of *The Shipwreck of the Prophet Jonah;* spurts of flame from gunpowder set off under the tank heightened the realism of the vessel's foundering.

The cartload of players, led by one Angulo the Bad, whom Don Quixote meets,[11] were bringing an auto called *The Parliament of Death* to the villages of La Mancha. The episode gives Cervantes a fine opportunity to speculate on the osmosis of reality and illusion and the absurdity of worldly attainment—the actors, he reflects, "look like princes when they have their makeup and costumes on"—while taking a whack at the real-life Angulo, perhaps for having spurned beginner Cervantes' offerings to him. And the encounter ends, as the autos frequently did, in rows and confusion.

The Church had never been happy about such goings-on. It had reluctantly allowed public dramatization of the mysteries only in an effort to come to terms with the popular love of theater. It was not pleased that women took part in them; it grumbled at the sacrilege of paying actors to promote the cause of religion. Autos often got out of hand. Fitzmaurice-Kelly cites a cathedral ceremonial in which a miter-bearing ass wearing vestments paraded to the music of grotesque canticles and hee-hawing from the congregation.[12]

The rise of a secular theater seemed to confirm the Church's darkest fears. Ecclesiastical uneasiness at the employment of women in the autos changed to indignation at their presence in the corrales, where they appeared regularly decades before their English and French sisters were allowed onstage and centuries before the practice was adopted in Germany. From the mid-century on, Spanish theatrical history largely records the tension between popular demand and Church opposition.

It was its popular character that gave the Spanish theater its vigor and its weaknesses. Writing plays was not considered "serious" work. Plays were amusements, tours de force of poetic agility. A poet's respectability in pre-Lopean days was established by pure poetry printed in a book. Nevertheless, young poets, encouraged by the same escapist impulse which was repopularizing the pastorals, were finding the stage a promising new field. Pride, poverty and lack of other opportunity to make a living may have been their immediate motives. To a few of them (Cervantes was one of these), something else beckoned, some dream of distant wonders still unseen, of glory waiting to be won. Besides, books were even less profitable than plays.

It is hard for us to appreciate how small the reading public was in Cervantes' lifetime. Probably fewer than one million people in the peninsula could write well enough to sign their names; fewer still could read, perhaps no more than 1 per cent of the population. The book-buying public was in turn only a fraction of the literate total. Merchants rarely owned books; even the wealthiest seldom possessed more than one or two, usually devotional works. Exceptions can be found: a cobbler in Valladolid named Diego de Agüero left a library of twenty-five volumes when he died in 1571.[13] The greatest of the private Spanish collections, belonging to the Count of Gondomar, contained fifteen thousand volumes, as many titles as Spain produced in the sixteenth century. The average man of learning, however, had fewer than one hundred books in his study.

But anyone could go to the theater. It took no schooling to look and listen. Gradually, drama entrenched itself as Spain's most popular art form, a single medium which did for the time the service television, movies and the stage together do for us now. By the end of the seventeenth century, the volume of Spanish dramatic literature would be reputed larger than that of the rest of Europe combined.

At its peak, from Lope's early cloak-and-dagger epics to the statuesque melodramas of Calderón de la Barca, the Spanish theater exemplified the give-'em-what-they-want theory of entertainment. A Lear, a Hamlet, a Phèdre would have been unimaginable in such plays; most Spanish dramatic characters were types, not individuals, faces in a national crowd. In vain does the non-specialist try to recall a single outstanding personage from among all the thousands in Lope's plays. This does not mean that Spanish playwrights lacked psychological insight. Their work is full of shrewd understanding of human nature. But their observations are as generalized as those in a psychology textbook. They could count on their audiences to grasp subtle interplays of characters and situations— provided the situations were familiar to the playgoer.

As in modern detective stories, it was plot and atmosphere that counted with Spanish audiences, ingenuity rather than depth. People clamored to be excited, stirred, horrified, exalted, but they wanted no doubts about who everyone was and where he stood. It was confirmation they sought, not provocation. *Non nova sed nova:* the playwright was expected to find clever new ways to dramatize the accepted national values—faith, patriotism, reckless courage, personal dignity, daring, all turning on a spit of personal honor. Love, adventure, violence, sprinkled with fresh blood and seasoned with a touch of buffoonery—these were the requirements. Conflicts were to be resolved by poetic justice satisfying the code of popular morality. In other words, the good guy always won, even if he had to ambush his best friend in a dark alley to do it.

Emotion became stylized, thin, balletic, strangely impersonal to modern readers. In a play attributed to Lope called *La estrella de Sevilla (The Star of Seville)*, a soldier, Sancho de Ortiz, is ordered by the king, for ignoble reasons, to murder Busto Tavera, an oppressively upright character who is Sancho's best friend and his prospective brother-in-law. Sancho is troubled, but he decides that his honor requires that he follow the order. Do we then witness a Sancho tormented by remorse, questioning the meaning of it all, anguished about truth, justice, good and evil? No, no. He is almost maddened by the king's failure to live up to his part of the bargain, as honor dictated. At the end of the play, no one is punished because everyone's honor is satisfied, including that of the deceased's sister, who declines to marry Sancho on the reasonable ground that she would be ill-disposed to face her brother's killer daily across the dinner table. The late Busto remains tastelessly dead.

Such plays resembled highly structured ballads, as appealing as ballads can be, and as superficial. Within these boundaries, the best of the Spanish playwrights acquitted themselves as well as might be expected. They were keen observers, poets of extraordinary facility who often wrote verse of high tensile strength despite rigid verse forms which foiled any effort at the naturalism and individualism that marked Shakespeare's late plays.

But all this was later. In 1583, all of what we now think of as the world's great plays were still to be written except, of course, for those of Greek and Roman antiquity, and fewer of these had yet come to light than are known today. Cervantes knew nothing about writing for the theater. Neither did anyone else then. This was part of the excitement of literature in those days. Shakespeare was nineteen years old, Jonson ten, Lope twenty-one. Stage fever raged in Madrid. A ban on theatricals decreed on the death of Queen Ana in October 1580 had finally been lifted on November 30, 1581; the fast had left the Spanish so hungry for plays that some abandoned theaters were briefly reopened to house them. Between 1582 and 1587 some thirty players' companies appeared in the capital. Scores of lesser attractions—gypsy song-and-dance groups, lone recitalists, puppeteers, mini-companies of two to four actors as well as the major troupes of fourteen or more players—toured the villages and provincial towns as Cervantes shows them to us in so many of his works.

A lot of steam for so small a fire. What was lacking was the fuel: the plays, the talented playwrights. Where was a serious playwright to learn his trade? A few plays by Euripides, Sophocles, Plautus, Terence, Seneca were available in translation. But the grand contemporary works were rare. The workhorse of the Spanish stage then was the Sevillian Juan de la Cueva. In the little more than a year in which the theaters functioned between 1579 and the end of 1581, fourteen of his plays were staged in Madrid. Not one is readable today. They are crude, pompous—"commonplace" stories, sniffed one critic, "recited by a number of blind men who gave each other the floor by turns."[14]

The Italian farces of the commedia dell'arte were well known in Madrid. Cervantes may even have seen the Ganassa company, which is said to have forced a smile even from Philip II. Its trace in some of Cervantes' comic interludes is manifest: Pantaleone certainly went Spanish, for example, in the Pancracio of *The Salamanca Cave*.

That Cervantes never mastered the techniques of writing for the stage is conceded by all but his most unconditional admirers. His plays are like elderly tavern waiters: flatfooted, halting, frequently garrulous. Climaxes are misplaced, then sloughed off; his characters often seem to have no more to do with each other than people on a city bus do. There is real feeling in many of his speeches; some scenes crackle with dramatic tension. Cervantes knew how to use silences to convey the turbulence of unspeakable emotion, as in Act II of *The Dungeons of Algiers*, when the doomed boy Francisco pleads with his father to teach the singers

> that song my mother sang
> in our village
> What say you? Will you not, Father?

The old man's confusion is clear as he struggles to dominate his grief.

> How do the words go?

he asks, stalling for time. And Francisco sings a popular ballad:

> I am in love,
> I'll not say with whom. . . .

But, after raising readers' imaginations to a decent pitch of expectant emotion, Cervantes is all too likely to leave them hanging there like drawers on a washline while he putters at something else. His temperament was not suited to the swift, straight lines of playwrighting, a limitation he obliquely confesses in a passage in *Don Quixote* in which he muses on subjects through which "a good understanding could show itself . . . because they gave a broad and spacious field in which one's pen could run unblushingly, describing shipwrecks, storms, skirmishes, battles; portraying a valorous captain with all the details required for such a creature . . . now a lamentable and tragic event, then a happy and unexpected one; there a beauteous lady, honest, wise and chaste, here a Christian knight, brave and courteous, farther along a swaggering barbarian. . . ."[15] This leisurely approach to writing will not do in the theater. And the clumsiness of the plays' narrative passages shows us a prose genius straining at the confinement of verse forms.

Life in Algiers suffers from all the infirmities of Cervantes' stage style, complicated by the appearance of having been hastily written. The plot is a loose account of how a betrothed slave couple deflect the amorous advances of their masters by acting as each other's procurer. It is better not examined too closely.

The play must have been at least moderately well received. Cervantes assures us that none of his plays were consecrated by "offerings of cucumbers or other throwable items" and that they "ran their courses without whistles, jeers or uproar." Are we to see in this no more than the benevolence of a theater-happy age? Not entirely.

Spastic as it is, *Life in Algiers* did present Spanish audiences with a new kind of theatrical experience: a writer's own life used with obvious emotional sincerity as material for the stage. Cervantes was interested in real people, in real contemporary events, and for the first time, these appear in Spanish drama not as types, but as individuals, crudely drawn but surprisingly alive. Despite the structural weight they must carry, such personages as Saavedra, Leonardo, Silvia were more real than any seen before. Moreover, they are mostly ordinary people; the imposing procession of grand names and lordly personages clumping through so many Golden Century plays is as rare in Cervantes' dramas as in his stories.

Cervantine characters do not think according to rigid, traditional codes. It is a private conviction of what is right and proper in life that motivates them, of what a man owes himself. Cervantes' cutthroats and prostitutes, Moors and Jews and Gypsies are as solicitous of their honor and good name (by their own definitions) as his captains and caballeros.

This may seem perfectly natural to us, but it may not have struck Spanish playgoers as altogether desirable. At a time when largely preproletarian audiences were eager to identify themselves with the powerful, the wealthy, the aristocratic—in short, with the fortunate—Cervantes offered them themselves, sometimes idealized, as often not. He was turn-

ing up a side street while the parade went straight ahead, to where Lope
was preparing to lead it.

It is an irony that the only other play of Cervantes' early career to have
come to light, the most impressive, perhaps, of all his full-length works
for the theater, sacrifices individual characterizations to its heroic stance.
This is *The Siege of Numantia,* an epic tragedy in the Greek manner,
stalked by allegorical figures performing the service the chorus rendered
the Greeks. It is lofty, majestic, still moving to read; were it ever staged,
it would certainly be deadly to watch. Its spirit is national; the patriotic
fervor which breathes in *Life in Algiers* is here elevated to the intensity of
a canticle to Spain, glowing with the sincerity of Cervantes' love of country and his conviction of its moral heroism. *Numantia* is the only one of
his works in which Cervantes is unrelievedly solemn, but the simplicity
and directness of the emotion it conveys, along with the loftiness of its
tone, have consistently evoked comparisons with the works of Aeschylus
and Sophocles. Goethe and Shelley marveled at it; Schlegel thought it
"divine." Schopenhauer mysteriously drew from it the lesson that "all
that remains to us is to return to Nature."[16]

Cervantes' play generally follows the historical facts concerning Numantia, a Celtiberian fortress on an isolated plateau near what is now
Soria, in northern Castile. The town formed the center of resistance to
the Roman campaign of conquest, withstanding repeated attacks for
twenty years before succumbing to starvation under a siege by Scipio
Aemilianus and a Roman army of sixty thousand men in 133 B.C. Most of
its four to seven thousand defenders committed suicide—some sallying
out to die fighting, others falling on their swords or immolating themselves in huge bonfires—and the rest were sold into slavery. Cervantes'
play tells of the defenders' final hours, relating the city's demise partly
through the doomed love of two young Numantines, Lira and Marandro.
At its end, all the city's thousands are dead, Scipio, unfairly but skillfully,
is made to appear a savage and Spain is promised that

> . . . a time will come . . .
> when these Romans will be oppressed
> by those they now hold prostrate. . . .

So much is fine about the play. It raises tragic horror to heights no
other Spanish play has ever reached. The sense of destiny, of moral grandeur it conveys makes the best of Lope's work seem petty. In its depiction
of courage and sacrifice, its powerful evocation of the ancient mysteries, it
has no parallel in classical Spanish literature. Some of its scenes are
lighted by effects of Faustian dreadfulness, as that in Act II in which the

wizard Marquino calls forth the spirit of a dead soldier to predict the
city's fate. Marquino is dressed in a billowing black robe; he is barefoot
and his flowing hair is unconfined; flasks of water dangle from his belt,
one black, one clear, one "dyed with saffron," and in his hands he holds a
black lance and a book of spells. The young soldier's shrouded body rises,
its face "a discolored mask, as of a corpse," to protest his recall to "this
painful life" and to announce with angry despair the city's impending
ruin.

Nevertheless, *Numantia* is closer in spirit to epic poetry than it is to theater. There is very little action in the play. Only occasionally is the horror
made real and sickeningly personal, as Shakespeare made it in *Macbeth*.
Because Cervantes failed in his effort to focus his emotion—Lira and
Marandro are too busy at their heroic posturing ever to become convincing characters—*Numantia* remains distant and rhetorical. The allegorical
figures which he later claimed to have introduced into Spanish drama
impede its movement.‡ The idealism of *Don Quixote* is already in
Numantia, but it is slathered over in the play with the gummy stickiness
of Cervantes' still-youthful romanticism.

Numantia did set a pattern for heroic tragedy which had not existed in
Spain until then. Had it not been ignored by the—less ambitious? less
high-minded?—playwrights who succeeded Cervantes, the trend might
have carried Spanish drama to an eminence it never entirely attained.
Certainly there was felt to be a place for it; the play is known to have
remained in the standard repertory for at least a century and its popularity revived after its publication for the first time in 1784, two centuries
after its composition. Indeed, its greatest triumph on the stage came during the Spanish War of Independence from the French early in the nineteenth century, when it was read to Spanish troops besieged in Saragossa.

Just when *Numantia* was written is not known. But its glorification of
Spanish military honor so curiously coincides with a Cervantes family
event that a case can be made for dating the idea from late 1583 and its
execution early in 1584. If so, it was *Numantia*, in all probability, which
established Cervantes early in his career as one of the princes of the pre-
Lopean stage. And the stimulant for it may have been his brother
Rodrigo.

Rodrigo is an easily forgettable character, a bit player in the family
drama. But he did have one scene to himself, a brief moment in which he

---

‡ "I showed, or to put it better, I was the first to represent concepts and the soul's
hidden thoughts, to bring moral figures to the stage . . . ," he declared in the
prologue to his *Eight Plays*. He is not being quite honest in this; he was certainly
aware of how far back the tradition of allegorical figures went in religious drama.
He may even have appeared in such plays in Jesuit school. One can only suppose
the claim is based on a shaky technicality: that he was the first to represent them
on the *commercial* stage.

emerged from the shadows to become a personage of record. Even then, his performance was a pantomime of heroism; nothing is heard from Rodrigo himself; only the chronicles exist to commemorate his bravery— and, perhaps, *Numantia*.

In 1581 Rodrigo had been with Alba in Portugal. When Antonio of Crato, with French backing, organized a government-in-exile in the rebellious Azores in 1582, Rodrigo (along with Lope de Vega) was among the troops sent with the Marquis of Santa Cruz to secure the islands for King Philip. In July 1582, in the bay of São Miguel Island, the Spanish defeated a French fleet put at Antonio's disposal by Catherine de Medici. When Santa Cruz sailed back to Spain, Rodrigo was among the 2,600 men left in garrison at São Miguel.

A year later, the marquis was back to complete his conquest. French money had bought Antonio an army of nine thousand men who had entrenched themselves along the rugged cliffs ringing Terceira Island. At dawn on July 26, 1583, the anniversary of the battle of São Miguel, a Spanish assault force of four thousand men stormed ashore at a small inlet called Las Muelas.

"The barks quickly reached the shore," reported eyewitness Cristóbal Mosquera de Figueroa, Santa Cruz's auditor-general, "and the Spanish jumped to earth in a rush amid the rocks, flanking the forts. Some sought their footing on a reef to escape the undertow, which was strong. Others, impatient of such devices, leaped into the water up to their waists. . . . Because he had run his bark into the beach, Francisco de la Rua, *alférez* to Francisco de Bobadilla, threw himself into the water with his banner, and behind him came Captain Luis de Guevara and Rodrigo de Cervantes, who was later rewarded by the marquis. . . ."[17]

The battle brought promotion to the rank of alférez for Rodrigo in 1584. After that he melts back into the shadows, not to be heard of again until July 2, 1600, when, still an alférez, he was killed by a harquebus ball in Flanders.

It may be, as Astrana Marín suggested, that Rodrigo came home on furlough later in 1583, laden with his share of Portuguese booty. If so, it is easy to imagine the brothers refighting the campaign across a table, reliving the old days in Italy. The talk could hardly have failed to reawaken Miguel's dreams of military glory, perhaps—only perhaps— planting in his mind the seed of a play to vent his feelings. The conviction burning through the lines of verse suggests they were written under the spur of a strong emotion which his experiences of the previous three years were not likely to have aroused. The play seems to have been a success; Cervantes tells us that his introduction of allegorical conceits—was probably in *Numantia*—brought "general and appreciative applause."[18]

He would later represent this period as a time of satisfactions; "it is a vastly pleasurable thing," he recalls in the appendix to the *Voyage to*

Parnassus, "and no less important (than earning money) to see the crowds emerge contented from the play, and the poet who composed it standing at the door receiving everyone's congratulations." Bright autumn mornings were spent at the *mentidero de los representantes,* the daily gathering of the theater crowd in the small, tree-lined square in the Calle de León, near the Plaza de Santa Ana, in the heart of what is still Madrid's theater district. From time to time, perhaps, a manager might now find it expedient to buy the new playwright a bowl of steaming *olla podrida,* the rich, meaty Castilian stew which was sold out of simmering caldrons on street corners along the Calle Mayor.

Yet there was probably more appraisal than admiration in their eyes when they talked about him. His plays were setting no worlds afire; they knew it and, for all his public vanity—"Oh Adam of poets, Oh Cervantes!"[19]—he must have known it too. Although he was to turn out plays at the rate of a new one every six weeks or so over the succeeding eighteen months,[20] he would never achieve the recognition his ambition craved. This is the time, one suspects, when he began to sense his failure as a poet, to feel the frustration which would eventually drive him to the shameful expedient of writing "poetry in prose." Some Cervantists believe this was the period when he wrote the first of his short stories, *The Liberal Lover,* as well as a first draft of "The Captive's Tale." The theory is wobbly, but it is not impossible that Cervantes may have tried his hand at prose. If so, he may have been surprised at how much more comfortable he was in the form. So comfortable that he may have wondered whether it was worth doing at all.

It would not do to exaggerate his position at this point. We are guessing at subtle states of mind, suspicions, intimations. Cervantes had won recognition. His *Galatea,* licensed for publication February 22, 1584, still lacked patron and publisher, but it was widely known among the literati. With his plays, it stands as a symbol of the tremendous burst of creative vitality that swept through him in those few years.

Creative and sexual: two phases of the same dynamic adventure. For this is also the period of Cervantes' only documented affairs of the heart (the cumbersome phrase suggests how hesitantly we must follow the trail he leaves). To assert that Cervantes was in love, then or ever afterward, may do no more than trample faint clues. To most artists, love is an emotional luxury to be paid for, unwillingly, from the carefully hoarded fund of emotional energy creation demands. We know only that two women now enter Cervantes' life, that one of them, the wrong one, gave him his only acknowledged child and that his relations with them led to his flight into self-imposed exile.

23

Idyllomania

In 1594, a visitor described the lower-class women of Madrid as snappish, quick, bold and arrogant. Their manners, he noted, were scandalously free; they would talk to anyone, even a stranger in the street. Crude language did not shock them. On one occasion, he recounted, a party led by the papal nuncio was aghast to see a woman bathing nude in the Manzanares River. She was untroubled. "Gentlemen," she called to them, "you've now see how much meat there is in the stew"; with that she proceeded unhurriedly to dress.[1] Although the situation had not yet reached the freewheeling conditions of a generation later, when slightly over half the city's estimated ten thousand houses were classified as in some degree houses of ill fame,[2] sex in 1583 was already a major industry in the imperial capital.

It may be unfair to lump Ana de Villafranca, or Ana Franca de Rojas, as she was also known, together with this brawling herd. When she became Cervantes' mistress, probably late in 1583 or early in 1584, she was around twenty years old. The little which is known about her suggests that she was an easygoing, kindly girl, already accustomed by life to expect that, with a little patience, she would see even the good things that happened to her eventually grow rank.

Her father, Juan de Villafranca, was an impecunious vendor of sweet wafers, apparently a familiar figure on the streets of Madrid. When she was about fourteen years old she was put into service with a more prosperous cousin whose wife grew so attached to her "servant and kinswoman" that, when she died in 1579, she willed Ana one hundred ducats as a dowry. It was a decent sum for a poor girl; it might have been enough to bring her a correspondingly decent husband. Instead, almost immediately, it brought her an illiterate Asturian trader named Alonso Rodríguez.

The general inclination among Cervantists has been to despise Ro-dríguez. He was certainly barren of the graceful gestures by which the dead command our affection. A greasy-ruffed man with ill-patched hose, probably, one of the scramblers thrown up by the thousands by every large city, dealing marginally in odd lots of grubby merchandise, making out, but barely. He had apparently impressed Juan de Villafranca as a man who was careful with his *quartillos*,[3] a tendency confirmed by his marriage contract with Ana: instead of matching her dowry, he brought to the union an almost insulting ten thousand maravedis, just over twenty-six ducats.

It is unlikely that anyone was offended. This was a business deal. Ana may never have set eyes on the man before it was negotiated. There is reason to believe she entered into it unwillingly, but she could have been under no illusions about it: Alonso's function was to protect her "for-tune" and marriage was the safest way to hold him to the bargain. He seems to have tried to live up to his side of the agreement. When Cervan-tes met her, the couple probably already ran the tavern in the Calle de los Tudescos which, like the Mermaid Tavern in London, seems to have at-tracted a crowd of actors, authors, managers and theatrical hangers-on along with the normal complement of ruffians and local residents.

The mechanics of that meeting are unknown. It may have come about through a random visit to the tavern; Cervantes could have known Villafranca as a wafer vendor in the playhouses. One suspects he was not the first in the line of Ana's lovers, perhaps not the last, either. After all, she owed no emotional loyalty to Rodríguez and he was probably compla-cently matter-of-fact about her adventures.

Given Cervantes' over-all history of sexual diffidence, it was probably Anica who did the heavy work in this seduction. In the eyes of a young-old barmaid he may have appeared as a glamorous figure—in his middle thirties, a celebrity in the world she daily inhabited, with the poised assur-ance of a man who had seen the world, had been to the wars. He was aristocratic-looking, too, with his broad forehead, his long, lean face, the thin beak of a nose jutting aggressively forward over the trim, chestnut-colored beard. Perhaps, too, there was something in his eyes which at-tracted her, a dark reserve which, even when those at the table roared with laughter at his stories, suggested that the man had learned enough about pain to be gentle. Gentleness, one guesses, was a quality she had need of in a lover.

Ana must have had something to offer in return besides an accessible body and credit at the bar, some sweetness which set her apart from the arrogance of her kind. Barmaids were not in the Cervantes line. It would have been more natural for Miguel to have looked for an alliance in his own world of the theater, the sort of connection Lope was then cementing with Elena Ossorio. But women like Elena were tough, vain, demanding, sophisticated; perhaps they frightened a sexually unenterprising Miguel de Cervantes. They may even have shocked the moralist in him which must always have been perceptible just under the façade of soldierly bonhomie he turned to the world. It would have amused them, this innocence, almost prudishness. Did they tease him, laugh at him, mock him? In any case, they would have known, as he surely knew, that he was not one of them, not really one of them.

Ana, then. Was she in love with Cervantes, or he with her? Probably not. She seems to have expected nothing from him. An occasional outing, perhaps. To watch, for example, the entry into the city of the two strange, outlandishly dressed little men sent under Jesuit escort as ambassadors from Japan? To lounge on a bench in the elm-lined Paseo del Prado and poke fun at the elegant madrileños riding smugly up and down on warm spring afternoons? Small things, certainly, for both she and Cervantes would have been conditioned to the diversions of the poor. Perhaps an occasional celebration. What more likely place than the tavern on the Street of the Germans to toast Cervantes' agreement on June 14 to "cede, sell, renounce and assign to Blas de Robles, bookseller resident in this city, a book of prose and verse containing the *six books of Galatea* which he composed in our Castilian language."[4]

Robles, like his new author a native of Alcalá de Henares, seems to have been a cut above most booksellers of the time. Beginning with a family business in Alcalá, he had grown prosperous enough to open a second shop in Madrid. A relative prosperity, to be sure—booksellers worked on so narrow a profit margin that even one bad guess could bring them close to ruin—but at least he seems not to have needed to sell the antiques and curios with which most of his colleagues then supplemented their earnings from publishing.

Technically, what Robles bought was the royal license the author had obtained. Cervantes was paid 1,336 reales (just over 120 ducats), 1,086 down and the rest to be paid at the end of September. This was all the author would ever realize from his book; rights were sold for a flat fee then, with all profits from sales going to the publisher. If there was to be any more reward for those years of work, it would have to come from a patron. While the manuscript was sent off to the print shop of Juan Gracián in Alcalá, Cervantes continued to seek one.

Patronage was as difficult and humiliating as it was essential to find. The gold in the Golden Century was mainly artistic. For every Count of Lemos or Duke of Sessa genuinely interested in letters there were dozens, scores of semiliterate lordlings obsessed with the magnificence of their persons who collected dedications—sparingly—as airlines today collect testimonials. But, complained Suárez de Figueroa, rewards from patrons were scant, grudging, late and uncertain. And Baltasar Gracián complained that "they think that to celebrate them is a debt owed them and so they disdain the praise; they believe it is mere justice when, truly, it is only a favor. . . ."[5]

Cervantes may have thought of dedicating his book to Marcantonio Colonna, but the general was already suffering from the illness that would carry him off that August. Colonna's son Ascanio, however, was living in Alcalá de Henares. Cervantes may have gone to see him there, perhaps by arrangement with Gálvez de Montalvo, who was then in Ascanio's service. Titular bishop of Santa Sofia, the younger Colonna was more conscious of his standing as a Renaissance prince than most of his Spanish counterparts; he was already a friend and protector of such writers as Gálvez and Rey de Artieda. In the autumn of 1584, he accepted a dedication from the soldier who had "marched for several years under the victorious banners of that sun of the militia who but yesterday was snatched by the heavens from before our eyes. . . ."[6]

How much money this produced for Cervantes is not known. Surely not the five hundred gold escudos Philip II had granted Rufo for *La Austriada;* enough, perhaps, to allow Cervantes to settle his debts, but with not much left over, for he is to be found shortly afterward without the hundred ducats he needed to pay his marriage portion.

Patronage, fame of sorts, a mistress—if he and Ana were still together —and even a little money. Was Ana carrying his child then, and did he know it? It would be gentlemanly to say no, he did not. But we cannot be sure.

The chain of events leading to that turbulent autumn began the previous March with the death of Laínez. He and his young wife Juana Gaitán apparently had been on cool terms for some months before he died. She had squabbled with his family. She may already have become too friendly with a twenty-year-old named Diego de Hondaro, the son of a Burgos merchant who is thought to have spent most of his productive life mincing along the edge of ruin.

When her husband died, Juana seems to have reacted with a keen sense of priorities: she fled at once, perhaps as soon as he was buried, to her house in Esquivias. She took with her all his possessions, including two of his manuscripts, a *cancionero*—a collection of lyric poems—and the *Engaños y desengaños de amor* (*The Snares and Disillusionments of Love*). By June 12 she was married to Hondaro. He may or may not have married Juana for her money; it can be noted that the dowry she formally ceded on that day, consisting almost entirely of Laínez's consid-

erable estate, made him the only prosperous member of the Hondaro
family.

That the marriage set tongues clacking from the palace courtyard in
Madrid to the farmyards of Esquivias seems not to have disturbed Juana.
The portrait of her left by history is almost effaced; only a few strokes
remain to suggest a self-centered, impulsive, unconventional woman, a
prefiguration of George Sand minus the trousers and the beaver hat.
Whether it was Cervantes who persuaded her to let him help edit Laínez's manuscripts or she who sent for him in a passing paroxysm of guilt
for her too joyous rejection of her late husband's memory is not known.
All that can be said is that, probably in mid-September, Cervantes rode
out on the main Toledo road to stay with the newlyweds in their house in
Esquivias.

There are few less memorable landscapes than that of the Sagra, the
bowl of the Mancha spreading mainly east of Toledo, but it is an intensely Castilian patch of earth, austere, silent, empty, where God is the
nearest neighbor. The villages prowling among the vine- and grain-
covered undulations are low and loose-jointed, as though, having been
knocked sprawling by the undeflected fury of the Castilian climate, they
now peer wistfully at the blue shadows of the far mountains to the west
and north, barely visible in September through the heat haze. It is not a
region to go to without a compelling reason.

The setting of Esquivias can be seen as a saddle: a slight rise, supporting a hermitage dedicated to St. Barbara, forms the cantle, from which
the village projects to the pommel of the parish church tower. Behind the
village rises a hill that in Cervantes' time was covered with oak trees from
which Sancho Panza's wife may have gathered the acorns she sent to the
Duchess in *Don Quixote*.

Around 2,500 people live in Esquivias today; in 1584 the population
was about 750, including five Morisco families. The villagers are still
solid, insular, restrained, courtly, suspicious of strangers but hospitable to
friends. Despite the surprising number of large, square houses showing ar-
morial bearings above their doors—Cervantes spoke ironically of Esquivias' "illustrious lineages and . . . its very illustrious wines"[7]—it is a poor
place now and it was poor then. Of its 175 families, 37 were gentry; with
few exceptions, the households which were not aggressively poor managed
to do no more than break even. No one grew rich from his holdings in
Esquivias, despite the patronage of Our Lady of the Good Milk.

The Cervantes whose writing shows such indulgent fondness of young
people doubtless enjoyed himself in the village that September. He probably had few illusions about Hondaro; Astrana Marín thought his opinion

might have been summed up in the observation in *The Faithful Sentinel* that

> Women always choose
> the most unworthy man,
> because their bad taste
> surpasses any merit . . .

although Cervantes might as easily have been thinking wryly of himself. But he obviously did not share the general criticism of Juana, with whom he would maintain a cordial friendship for at least twenty more years. He had already learned—from his sisters, from Ana, perhaps from Silena— the answer to the question he asks in *Love's Labyrinth:*

> . . . could it not happen
> without arousing our amazement
> that a woman might seek a man
> just as a man does a woman?

Only a moment's walk from Juana's house was the church where Cervantes heard mass. Facing it across a tree-shaded square was the house of the Salazars, whose daughter, then not quite nineteen, may have been a friend of Juana's.

Three months later, the girl was married to Cervantes.

Doña Catalina de Salazar, or de Palacios y Salazar, or de Salazar y Palacios, or de Vozmediano, or de Salazar Vozmediana (she signed herself in all these ways at various times). Eldest child of Doña Catalina de Palacios and the late Fernando de Salazar Vozmediano (died February 1584). Baptized November 12, 1565. Of hidalgo lineage, with at least one converso branch on the family tree. Physical appearance: no details available, but the women of the Sagra are generally short, dark, fine-featured, with clear complexions. When first seen by Cervantes, she was undoubtedly dressed in mourning black; may never have emerged from it. Educational background: literate (unlike her mother), probably through the efforts of her maternal uncle Juan de Palacios, parish priest of Esquivias; no evidence of extensive learning or literary inclination. Brothers: Francisco, born 1577, later presbyter in Esquivias, and Fernando, born 1581, later Fray Antonio de Salazar in the Toledo monastery of San Juan de los Reyes. Family's financial position: cash-poor; approximately five hundred acres of land in Esquivias, plus houses in Toledo and several nearby villages, including a number in Yeles held from the chapter of Toledo Cathedral for an annual tribute of three hens.

Why did he marry her?

14.   Another view of Algiers. (New York Public Library Picture Collection)

FIGVRA DEL THEATRO ANTIGVO DEL PRINCIPE Año de 1660.

15.   The Corral del Principe in Madrid. Although the engraving is dated 1660, the theater was still as it had been when Cervantes was writing for the stage in 1583–85. (Photo MAS)

16.

Félix Lope de Vega Carpio, probably the greatest playwright Spain has ever produced. His feud with Cervantes entertained the Spanish literary world for over twenty years. (The Hispanic Society of America, New York)

17.　The home of Cervantes' wife, Catalina de Salazar, in Esquivias, near Toledo, where he lived in 1585–86 and again, probably, in 1602–3. The stream that once faced it has been paved over, but the setting is otherwise not much changed from what it was then. (Photo MAS)

18. Antonio Carnicero's late-eighteenth-century illustrations of Sancho's trick in persuading Don Quixote to accept a Tobosan peasant girl as Dulcinea show some of the ethnic types among the people of La Mancha. The girl in the middle is probably of Morisco origin, as Dulcinea herself may have been. (From *Historia gráfica de Cervantes y del Quijote* by Juan Givanel mas y Gaziel)

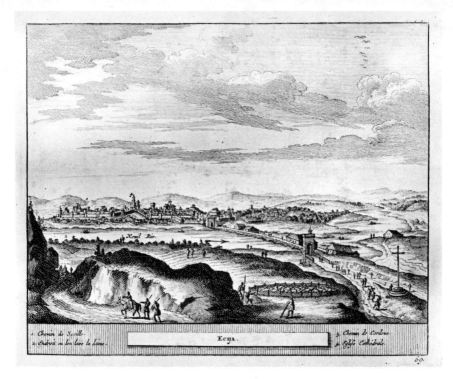

19. Écija as Cervantes knew it. The town probably supplied the models for some of the country people within *Don Quixote*. (The Hispanic Society of America, New York)

20.
Mateo Alemán, whose novel *Guzmán de Alfarache* rivaled the *Quixote* in popularity in the early seventeenth century. He died in obscurity in Mexico. (The Hispanic Society of America, New York)

The simplest answer, the one the Spanish prefer, is that he fell in love with the girl, violently, impetuously. The ideal, a biographer has commented in a fine display of intellectual tidiness, worked mesmerically on Cervantes' optimistic mind, consistently submerging reality.[8] With the lines from his *Galatea* still buzzing in his mind, he is seen as bringing to the affair his supposed disgust with court life, investing it with the lyricism of a pastoral romance. In late summer, the wheat lies like honey over the fields. The wine grapes are harvested in early September in the High Mancha; cart wheels sing on the roads and trains of donkeys, almost invisible under huge baskets of grapes, slip daintily toward towns smelling of must. High, fleecy clouds scud overhead announcing the coming change of seasons. "There is no love without advantage in the big city," he would aver.[9] Did Cervantes see Catalina as Galatea come to life, himself as a conquering Elicio? How musical the notion that, for once, it might have been life which corrected the injustice of art!

Evidence of such passion is perversely elusive. The union would produce no children; indeed, it was hardly given the chance to do so: Cervantes would live with his bride for less than three of the first eighteen years of their marriage, surely an original way to show his devotion. They would be reunited when she was thirty-seven and he fifty-six, in a small apartment in Valladolid shared with Cervantes' daughter, his sisters and his niece. A few years later they would both enter lay orders, taking formal vows of chastity which by then, one imagines, represented no sacrifice to either. Under these circumstances, and given the impossibility, the inconceivableness, of divorce, we may prefer to discount the assurance so aften offered that, after all, the marriage endured for thirty-two years.

For money, then? In *Don Quixote,* a student on the way to the wedding of Quiteria* and Camacho notes that "some curious folk who know everyone's lineage by heart like to say that the lovely Quiteria's is better than Camacho's, but I pay no attention to this; riches have the power to solder many a crack."[10] But Catalina was almost poor. Fernando de Salazar had been no model of husbandry. His estate consisted chiefly of debts, to his brotherhood, his neighbors, relatives, workmen, priests, innkeepers, tradesmen. His three servants were seldom paid, his house and vineyards were in pawn. Such plate and jewels as he owned, and some he did not own, were scattered around the province of Toledo as security for some of these debts. Even the funeral he had ordered for himself had been—so noted Astrana Marín—a little too elaborate for good taste.

Catalina possessed some inherited land her father could not touch. She had the use of the property he left until her brothers came of age. In the meanwhile, the family had its bread and oil, hogs and hens and wine. There were no sugar plum fairies in Esquivias.

* Quiteria was a common name in Doña Catalina's family.

The standard images we are given of Cervantes in the late summer of 1584 are simple and heartening: Cervantes strolling placidly to the tree-shaded Ombidales fountain at what was then the village's edge, murmuring to his farmyard Dulcinea; Cervantes merrily regaling openmouthed Esquivians with tales from his glamorous past over draughts of the Palacios' white Albillo wine in the cool darkness of Diego Ramírez's *mesón* on the main square. All is peace, stability, optimism.

Yet he was on the brink of that plunge into a spiritual wilderness which, despite the flourish of documentation it offers, constitutes the central puzzle of his life. Within six months of his marriage he would vanish from the theaters. Except for very occasional prefatory sonnets in other men's books, he would not publish a line for twenty years. He would shortly abandon his priest-walled Galatea and her hogs and orchards for a solitary big-city existence and a series of wretched employments. Whatever inspired this sudden impulse to marry seems closer in nature to panic than to love.

Cervantes had returned from Algeria blinded by the miracle of his deliverance, ready to conquer the world. Unaccountably, the world was resisting conquest with Numantian determination. How can we avoid thinking of him as being discouraged and disillusioned? How not imagine him as a man losing his bearings, baffled by the challenge of what to do, where to go to find the talisman he had lost in the dark waters between Algiers and Valencia? After all he had suffered, hoped for, dreamed of, he was sunk in a mediocrity he would have been the first to recognize. That immense thrust of courage which had carried him through exile, hardship, disability, which had sustained him in his effort to launch himself on a career—was it now exhausted? We can only probe clumsily in the search to uncover his sense of loss: of faith in himself, in life, perhaps in his very God. Optimism? Like that, perhaps, of Unamuno's atheist priest Don Manuel, who preached the gospel for his flock's sake while agonizing in the private conviction that Christ Himself had died an unbeliever.[11]

Cervantes was just turning thirty-seven, middle age in the sixteenth century. What more natural instinct than to rest, to escape the future in the soothing unreflectiveness of the present? The obvious adulation of a pretty (let us assume she was pretty) girl in a peacefully rustic setting could have induced a temporary onset of idyllomania.

There is also the disturbing question of Ana de Villafranca and of the child thought to have been almost ready then to burst from her womb. It is generally believed that Cervantes said nothing to Catalina of Ana, preferring to ignore mother and child rather than risk blighting the fragile bud of an innocent country girl's adoration. The hero of Lepanto and Algiers, the Cervantes who time and again would assume responsibilities he might have shrugged off, seems in this crucial passage to have been a moral coward. But then, as far as we know, sex was not a problem for him at Lepanto or in Algiers.

We can never establish—could he have done so himself?—how much uneasiness was bred in Cervantes' conscience by the aimless sordidness of his affair with Ana. Nor can we know with what stratified anxiety he may have craved a marriage that would cleanse him of it. To imagine a silent festering of guilt may be to misapply a twentieth-century intellectual fashion to the sexually open society, in fact if not in formula, in which Cervantes lived. He would have known, for example, that his sisters, whatever sexual misdemeanors they may have committed, were merely decently unhappy women. For all that, we remain with an impression, from his history and his work, of a Cervantes who viewed sex as a symbol of worldly evil, unavoidable but unfortunate, a degradation of humanity's creative impulse. As a suitor, such a man would have insisted in corseting his Catalina in all the stays of conventional rectitude.

Suppose he had blurted out the whole business to her. She probably would not have been shocked. Pious morality was—is—a specialty of Sagra villages. But village morality also has a spongelike ability to absorb sin and live with it. The region was a familiar pasture for the farmed-out bastards of toledano and madrileño nobles. Among the recent Esquivias scandals had been one involving Catalina's kinsman Don Luis de Salazar y Rojas, an upstanding knight of the Order of Santiago who had seduced and had a child by another man's maidservant. Catalina would certainly have known of the incident, would have thought it regrettable, but not remarkable. Cervantes was surely aware of this. Yet to proceed on this knowledge and contaminate (for so he would have viewed it) his marriage by public confession of his transgression would have been to concede a cynicism in himself against which all his instincts rebelled.

The possibility must also be considered that Cervantes did not know Ana was with child when he proposed to Catalina. No one knows exactly when Isabel de Cervantes was born. In a statement she made on June 30, 1605, she declared her age as twenty. This could mean that the child had been conceived as late as September of 1584 and that Ana did not realize she was pregnant until shortly before Cervantes' marriage. This was Ana's first child. She may have wanted to keep it, may even have feared that her husband was incapable of giving her one; he had not, after all, succeeded in it so far. Her subsequent actions show that Ana had no wish to spoil her lover's marriage. When she learned of her pregnancy, she may very well have convinced a willing Cervantes that it was kindest to let everyone believe the child was legitimately hers by Rodríguez. Isabel would grow to puberty thinking this was the case; had she not been orphaned in 1599, she might never have known her true parentage, never recognized her father's hostility toward her or learned to hate him because of it.

The business with Juana Gaitán which had brought Cervantes to Esquivias was quickly concluded. On September 22, before the village notary, she gave him power of attorney to seek approval and license for the publication of Laínez's poems. A privilege for the *Cancionero* was eventually issued, but the book was never published; the manuscript is now in the National Library in Madrid. The manuscript of the *Engaños y desengaños de amor* was later lost.

Cervantes presumably shuttled back and forth between Madrid and Esquivias in pursuit of his courtship. It could not all have been roses. Some of the village elders may have mistrusted him as an outsider, resented his big-city ways. Local opinion may have split along class lines: most of the Esquivian hidalgos were active or retired army officers who would have approved of Cervantes' military record, respected the wound he showed. There are indications that the union was unpopular with Catalina's family; Cervantes seems never to have been unreservedly accepted by them. We must assume that Catalina was in love with him, for who but she could so quickly have overcome the family's resistance? Another factor: Cervantes did not formally receive Catalina's dowry until some eighteen months after they were married. This is usually taken to signify that he was too anxious to bed his Catalina to waste time in tedious negotiation. The Palacios clan would not have felt so pressed; for all their cherished hidalguía, they were close-fisted, back-country people, as mean as any peasant. If, as seems arguable, the delay was due to Cervantes' lack of the hundred ducats he needed as his marriage portion, their suspicion of him would have been all the livelier. It would be ungallant to infer from their pliability in the matter that Catalina was otherwise unmarriageable. Then who, if not she, could have persuaded them to waive financial considerations for the time being? Perhaps Catalina was drawn to this older man as a replacement for the father she had so recently lost. If so, it was merely one more bond on which this marriage would default.

They were married by her uncle Juan de Palacios in the Esquivias parish church of Santa María de la Asunción on the morning of December 12, 1584. No members of the Cervantes family attended. There is even some doubt that the bride's mother was present. No wedding feast was held in Esquivias; the twelve months of formal mourning for Catalina's father had not yet expired. That afternoon or the following morning the couple probably left on the traditional wedding trip to Madrid, where they may have stayed with Cervantes' family.

Sometime early in the new year, they settled in with Catalina's family in the big Palacios house in Esquivias. Winter in the Sagra is very cold, very damp; the sky on most days has the mottled, rubbishly look of a dead campfire. It may have been raining when the Adam of poets took possession of his Eden.

24

Esquivias

It was a typical Castilian house,[1] of mud and plaster given the look of slightly stale wedding cake by generations of annual whitewashings. On one side it abutted the home of Catalina's aunt, María de Cardenas. On the other, the corral side, a little stream separated it from the square on which stood the parish church, another family fief. The main entrance to the house—heavy, double-leaf doors high enough to admit a mounted rider—stared across a narrow street at the walled Perales orchard owned by Cervantes' wife.

Life inside the house revolved around the pebble-paved, plant-strewn patio. Shallow flights of steps led down from it to the wine cellar, with its massive wooden press, and the storeroom lined with clay oil jars probably made in Dulcinea's town of El Toboso. Past the well and the stone washing trough, broad stairs flanked by a carved-wood banister led to the upper story, around which ran a wooden balcony resting on the stone columns that reinforce Castilian patios' secretive, cloistral look. Windows and doors swung on finely wrought iron hinges; iron grilles covered windows looking out over fields which, in winter, are silent, empty, monotonous.

Cervantes was now administrator of his wife's property, which to a considerable extent involved deferring payment of the debts against it. There were few guests: inviting people in for meals was not usual then. But he presumably had his books, and there was still a great deal he and his wife had to tell each other. Local gossip and such word of greater affairs as percolated through to the village gave adequate reason for gathering in Ramírez's in the late afternoon or, on mild mornings, under the arcades of the village hall.

It was there, no doubt, that he heard about Catalina's distant ancestor

Alonso Quixada, the monk who, in the first decades of the century, believed that the romances of chivalry were true; Quixada was to be one of Don Quixote's "real" names. Cervantes would also have collected details of the long-standing feud between the Quixadas and his wife's branch of the Salazars. If the hypothesis of his converso origins has any validity, his instruction in this family ritual could have helped explain his relationship with his in-laws. For in the Quixadas' veins, Salazar blood was forced to concide with a New Christian stream, a grievance which Catalina's father Fernando de Salazar handed down intact to her unlovable brother Francisco. The Quixadas were also the richest people in Esquivias, and they may have compounded the sins of their wealth and lineage by lending Fernando money.

It was in August that year that a mass was sung at the Escorial to celebrate the monastery's completion after twenty-three years. Its hundred miles of corridors were already echoing to gibes at this desert mausoleum which had given rise to a proverb describing a sluggish transaction as "lasting as long as the building of the Escorial." Philip had put Spanish backs up by limiting attendance at the mass to demonstrate that this was his house, not the people's, and now anonymous wits were describing it as a place where "plants wither and trees do not grow . . . the cold is insufferable, the heat intolerable, the meat lean, the fish rotten."[2] A childish whim, Quevedo called it; a boring place, said another critic, full of hunters "thinking to refresh themselves in the waters of its favors and pretensions" while, in Madrid, their wives "make new moons grow in their foreheads."[3]

From the capital came word of new edicts to reinforce Esquivian conviction of big-city sinfulness: blasphemy, dueling, brawling and gambling were again forbidden on pain of one hundred lashes; a decree of December 4, 1585, forbade prostitutes to attend church with pillows or to have pages or pimps carrying their trains, from wearing hats of satin or silk or embroidered with gold or silver. They could not sit near women of prominence, nor walk the streets with their faces veiled. There were edicts against short-weighing bread and watering wine; tramps continued to clog the streets despite a command to find work or leave the city. In October 1586 Philip issued a decree putting order in the luxuriance of titles flaunted by his idle aristocrats.

There was grave talk, too, of England. In January 1586 an increasingly indignant Marquis of Santa Cruz had renewed his plea of three years earlier to chastise the impertinent English. Philip had replied that his case was "well thought out,"[4] and his principal secretary, Idiáquez, had added an invitation to the old sea fighter to submit a detailed plan. Santa Cruz did so in March, calling for an impossibly costly force of eight hundred ships and some ninety thousand men to invade England. Annoyed

by Drake's raids, infuriated by lackluster Spanish resistance to English in-
cursions into Spanish trading areas, convinced that no peaceful solution
to his rivalry with Protestant Elizabeth was possible, Philip this time ordered planning to go forward.

In Esquivias, the pull of even such momentous events was probably
weak, serving chiefly to stir the memories of the village's hidalgos with
the swords of their rank hanging uselessly at their sides and their rosaries
dangling from their fingers. As much excitement was probably generated
by village squabbles over the dwindling supply of firewood from the oak
forest on the ridge above the village. And money was scarce; a dry, sear-
ing summer had evolved into a dry, freezing winter, ruining crops and
producing in village records a rash of loan and mortgage agreements.
Nothing, one supposes, intruded on the minuscule rivalries of the village
wives who, as Teresa Panza comments, think that "because they are
hidalgas the wind has no right to touch them."[5] Cervantes, listening to
the chattering of the poor women washing their clothes in the stream outside his windows, may have felt that the dozen leagues from Madrid to
Esquivias covered the distance from the center of the earth to its end.

He seems, in fact, to have lived for a while with only one foot in Arcadia. Trips to Madrid were frequent. On March 5, 1885, he contracted
with player-manager Gaspar de Porres to write two plays, *La confusa*
(*The Confused Lady*) and *El trato de Constantinopla y muerte de Selim*
(*Life in Constantinople and the Death of Selim*). The first was to be
completed within two weeks and the second a week after Easter Sunday.
The fee: a respectable forty ducats for each play.

The plays, the last by Cervantes known to have been accepted for production, may already have been on paper. Cervantes says *La Confusa* was
a hit, "if one rightly credits its renown."[6] He made no comment on *Life
in Constantinople;* so little was heard of it, in fact, that one suspects it
was a failure.

It is a strange, sad situation, that of a writer who, even as he handles
his first novel, fresh off the press, can feel himself receding inexorably toward the antipodes of his literary world. *La Galatea* came out early in
March, 375 octavo folios with the Trajan's Column crest of the Colonnas
on the title page and laudatory sonnets in it by Maldonado, Gálvez and
Vargas. In February, in Padilla's *Spiritual Garden,* Cervantes had been
ranked among "the famous poets of Castile." He may have frequented
the Academia Imitatoria, along with Lope de Vega and a "stupid poet
and mock academician" named Mauleon, who was taken over the coals in
both *Don Quixote* and *The Dogs' Colloquy,* where we are told that his
Art of Poetry is "about what Archbishop Turpin didn't write about King
Arthur," all in "dactyls of nouns at that, without a single verb."

All this was being literary; it was not writing. Worse, *La Galatea* was not popular with the Spanish public. The press run had been small, perhaps no more than five hundred copies; the book was to be reprinted only twice in the author's lifetime, in Lisbon in 1590 and in Paris in 1611.

Cervantes was probably in Madrid when his father died. Rodrigo made his will on June 8, 1585, "being confined to bed." It is a touching document. As his heirs, he named all his children (including Juan) except Luisa, who, as a nun, could not legally inherit, but listed no assets to bequeath to them. He declared he was free of debt. His executors were to be Doña Leonor and Doña Catalina de Palacios, Cervantes' mother-in-law, whom he may never have met. As a gesture of good will it was pathetic—and unrequited. When Doña Catalina came to make her own will, shortly before her death in 1588, she would specifically forbid her daughter to alienate her share of the bequest "in order," Catalina later explained, "that my husband might not profit by it."[7] There was gentle futility, too, in Rodrigo's courtliness toward his wife: "At the time of my marriage . . . to the said Doña Leonor de Cortinas, my wife, the aforesaid conveyed into my power certain dower possessions, I do not remember how much nor what they were. I leave the declaration of them to the said Doña Leonor de Cortinas, my wife, that her statement and declaration be held as valid, for she will say no more than the truth in this . . . and it is my will that this be given and paid (to her) from my possessions, with no impediment whatsoever."[8] One imagines Doña Leonor listening impassively to this fanfare of gallantry. He would leave this chore to her as he had so many others; she would take from his no doubt non-existent estate the dowry which had surely long since been dispersed among bailiffs, creditors, court secretaries, tradesmen. Rodrigo died five days later, on June 13, at the age of seventy-five.

Cervantes is found in Madrid again on August 1, in the heart of the growing season in Esquivias, witnessing an annuity agreement for Inés Ossorio, the actress-wife of author Jerónimo Velázquez and mother of Lope's beautiful Elena. This may mean Cervantes was a visitor in their home on the Calle de Lavapiés and on good terms at the time with the young man he had praised in *La Galatea* as one whose skill belied his youth. Although, given Lope's amateurishness then, the encomium was more than generous, the young man was said to have found it a shade too cool for his liking. But then, he was one day to say that he knew only two extremes, to love and to hate, and nothing in between. In his *Filomena*, finished in 1621, he would draw a picture of a spring on Parnassus where three poets had drunk, Homer, Virgil and one other whose name was not given but who was "sure he was unequaled"; in the margin of a copy now in the Spanish National Library is a note in Góngora's handwriting: "If thou sayest it of three, Lope, thou art a fool without art or judgment."[9]

Young Lope may have had cause to be sensitive in the summer of 1585. He had been writing plays for nearly a decade, had been a student, a soldier and a courtier; he was becoming known not only as a man-about-town and procurer for his employer, the Marquis of Las Navas, but also as a poet.

Extravagant stories have been told to explain a supposed falling-out of Lope and Cervantes. The older man is alleged to have witnessed a face-scratching, hair-pulling match between Elena and her mother over Lope; Ana Franca and Elena were said to be the reigning beauties of the Madrid stage, dragging their lovers into their ferocious rivalry; Cervantes allegedly wrote and circulated a scurrilous letter about Lope's love life. A row did take place between Inés and Elena, but in 1587, when Cervantes was in Andalusia. Ana Franca would have been flattered by her elevation as the toast of Madrid. As for the letter, there is no proof that it ever existed. Writing poison-pen letters was not Cervantes' style, but in the predatory theatrical world of Madrid there were many ready to commit to paper their resentment of Lope's elegance, his brio, his conceit, his luck, his aristocratic friends, above all his success with women.

Falling-out is probably strong language to describe the two men's relationship at that stage. To Lope, Cervantes was already a has-been, a never-was who offered no threat and to whom he could therefore afford to be insolently civil. Cervantes recognized Lope as a "monster of nature";[10] he was perceptive enough to know that, for the time being at least, he himself had no place in the theater. Cervantes seems to have been in no mood to fight the future. Pausing only long enough to sell the cloth he had pawned two years before—the sale brought in an additional twenty-three ducats for his sister—he withdrew once more to Esquivias.

He turns up next in Seville, where, on December 2, he appeared to pledge repayment within six months of a loan of 204,000 maravedis made by a *letrado* named Gómez de Carrion. One of the witnesses was Cervantes' boyhood friend Tomás Gutiérrez, who had given up the stage as a full-time occupation and now owned a luxurious hostel on the Calle de Bayona, opposite the cathedral. Cervantes' financial transaction had the mysterious complexity such arrangements so often had then. In another notarial act dated the same day, Carrion, as agent of one Rodrigo Zamorano, authorized Cervantes to collect 100 ducats owed to Zamorano by Juana Gaitán's young husband Diego de Hondaro. Three days later Cervantes turned all but 17,000 maravedis over to merchant Baltasar Gómez in return for a letter of credit, as most travelers did rather than carry large amounts of cash through bandit-infested country. The letter was cashed in Madrid December 19.

Somewhere in the negotiation figures Laínez's travel-weary *Cancionero*. In August 1585, Hondaro had gone to Seville to try to market the privilege Cervantes had obtained for it, and he did sell it to a merchant named Llorente de Santantón, presumably as a speculative property—it would dance through various traders' hands for years before coming to rest. Hondaro, still legally a minor, may have tried some wheeling-dealing on his own which, with the traditional luck of the Hondaros, left him 100 ducats in the red. What Cervantes planned to do with the 204,000 maravedis (51 ducats) *he* borrowed is anyone's guess. Having collected the amount of Hondaro's debt from Juana, Cervantes returned to Seville in June 1586 to repay both loans.

On August 9, 1586, Cervantes took formal receipt of Catalina's dowry. Many of the peasants in Esquivias could have brought as much: a single bed; a cradle; the usual assortment of bed linens and hangings, all embroidered by Catalina; an embroidery frame; a brass brazier, probably with its crude pine *mesa de camilla* (the round, aproned tables with holes in their bases for braziers) to huddle around against the winter cold; a single brass candlestick with five pounds of wax, presumably cut with the listed three extractors from the four beehives included; two chairs; some benches and stools; a few wine jars; some straw matting for the floors; kitchenware, but no forks or spoons—country people ate, as many still do, with their fingers out of a common bowl. There was an alabaster Virgin and Child in a walnut chest, another of silver, two images of the Christ child "with their little clothes and their little shifts," a small quantity of wheat and 73 reales' worth of flour.[11] "I am content with little," Cervantes would write, "though I wish for much."[12] The lot was valued at 428 ducats, plus the 10 ducats Cervantes contributed. In addition, his mother-in-law undoubtedly contributed some of the family land, perhaps the two small plots his wife later willed to him.

On the same day, Doña Catalina gave gave her son-in-law full power of attorney to administer her property. This may not have been as trusting a gesture as it is sometimes taken to have been; there was simply no one else free to run her errands. There is a record of Cervantes' presence in Toledo soon afterward to collect the rent on a house there from Catalina's cousin Isabel de Cardenas. This was the trip on which he may have met El Greco, who was then painting his "Burial of Count Orgaz" on a commission from Cervantes' friend the New Christian priest Andrés Nuñez de Madrid for the church of Santo Tomás; the painter's mistress, Jerónima de las Cuevas, was related to the curate and it is Nuñez de Madrid who is shown conducting the burial service in the painting. He may have arranged for the painter and the writer to meet, perhaps at Cervantes' request.

Cervantes' interest in knowing the painter is obvious, especially since El Greco was at the center of that group of Toledo artists and intellectuals who met regularly in the country houses around the city. The notion that

Cervantes posed for one of the portraits in the "Burial" is more fanciful. El Greco had virtually completed the work by that time; most of the portraits in it which might fit Cervantes' description have been identified as those of other people. And the haughty, arrogant, intellectually austere painter seems not have been sufficiently impressed with Cervantes' reputation to cultivate his acquaintance, much less paint his portrait.

Nothing is heard of Cervantes from early August 1586 until the following spring, except for an appearance in October as godfather at a local christening. Then, in April 1587, news came that the remains of St. Leocadia, Toledo's patron, were to pass through Esquivias one night in the last week of the month. The relics were near the end of their four-year migration from Flanders and the whole village turned out to receive them. Hundreds of people lined the streets. Bonfires blazed and bells were rung to summon the faithful from neighboring villages.

On April 25 Philip II, his children and his sister, Maria of Hungary, arrived in Toledo to welcome the saint. The high point of the ceremony was the splendid procession which wound the next day from the cathedral to the tiny, reconsecrated mosque of the Christo de la Vega, where the remains lay in state. Among those present was Luis de Vargas Manrique, in whose father's house, facing the tabernacle, the king and his family heard mass. Pedro de Padilla was there too, to receive the privilege for publication of a new book of poetry, and so was Dr. Francisco Díaz, whose forthcoming book on kidney and urinary medicine contained a prefatory sonnet by Cervantes.

Cervantes was there, without Catalina. With a number of Esquivians, he had probably joined the crowds flooding into the city behind the cortege for the great celebration. We may hear an idealized echo of that day in Cervantes' account in the *Persiles* of the pilgrims' arrival in the "Spanish Rome":

> Almost at the same moment there resounded in their ears the sound of countless joyous instruments extending through the valleys surrounding the city, and they saw coming toward them not armed squadrons of infantry, but crowds of damsels, lovely as the very sun, dressed in peasant clothes, hung with pearls and with patens on their breasts . . . all had long locks, as blond as very gold, which, although it fell loose on their shoulders, was bound on top with green garlands of fragrant flowers. . . . Truly, their rustic finery outshone the richest habiliments of the court, because, though it showed their honest humility, by the same token it revealed their extreme cleanliness: all were flowers, all roses, all grace and all together composed a decorous dance. . . . Around each squadron, but apart from it, came many youths dressed in the whitest linen, with embroidered kerchiefs on their heads, their kins-

men or friends, or neighbors from their villages; some played timbrels and pipes, others the psaltery, one the bells, another the cymbals, and all these sounds blended into a single one which gladdened them with its harmony, which is the purpose of music.[13]

Other notes, angrier and more urgent, underlay this merry chirping, however. The talk among the courtiers was still of the execution of Mary Queen of Scots on February 18, an act Philip had at least pretended to take as a personal affront, arranging for solemn funeral services to be held in the Escorial and ordering all speed in the gathering of his invasion fleet. Treasury Counselor Antonio de Guevara had been appointed commissary general for the collection of supplies for the Armada, chiefly Andalusian grain and oil; transfers of troops from Italy had been worked out while, in Cádiz, in Lisbon, ships were being readied too slowly for Santa Cruz's liking. Philip had finally come around to agreement with his admiral's outrage that "while Your Majesty lives in this world, a heretic woman should live and reign who has caused so much harm in that kingdom."[14] Now that the decision was made, the king was growing impatient to have the thing done. He was reasonably confident of its success. The Spain of Lepanto and the Azores was considered stronger than England, richer, more populous. His ambassador in London, Don Bernardino de Mendoza, had persuaded him, quite wrongly, that England was torn by religious dissension, that English Catholics would rise in revolt at the first sight of Spanish flags in the Channel.

A warning that the Enterprise of England was already in deeper water than Philip would have liked was about to be signaled. While fireworks bloomed in the night sky over Toledo in honor of the returned saint, an English squadron of some twenty-six ships led by El Draque was nearing the port of Cádiz. Drake was about to demonstrate his theory of pre-emptive warfare: by striking along the Spanish coast, he believed he could spare Elizabeth's navy the risk and expense of a pitched battle.

April 29, 1587, Philip was settling in for his annual month's sojourn among the roses at his palace at Aranjuez. At four o'clock that afternoon, Drake's ships sailed into the Bay of Cádiz. In the forty-eight hours they remained there, the English gunners destroyed or captured between twenty-four (Spanish estimate) and thirty-seven (Drake's count) vessels, including Santa Cruz's great galleon and a number of roundships loaded with supplies for the Armada at Lisbon. Not a single English ship was lost.

"The greatest pirate in the West," fumed the first of two *Songs to the Invincible Armada* attributed to Cervantes. Philip's public reaction was more restrained—"the loss," he said, "was not very great, but the daring of the attempt was very great indeed"[15]—but he was privately furious at the town's defenselessness. Nor had the loss, estimated at approximately 172,000 ducats, been so slight. Drake noted soberly that he had singed the king of Spain's beard.

At the hour when Drake's ships came in sight of the forts at Cádiz, Cervantes was probably already on his way to the commissary general's headquarters in Seville to apply for work as a fleet commissary.[16] That he had been given a commitment in Toledo is unlikely; probably he had surmised from what he heard there that Guevara would be hiring men. He seems to have acted on the spur of the moment: on April 28 he had appeared before a Toledo notary to give full power of attorney to Catalina, whose absence from the city is recorded. Then, probably on borrowed money, he left—ran might be a better word for it; a feeling of escape, almost of panic, pervades the whole episode. He did not return home with his document; instead, he sent it to Esquivias with witness Gaspar de Guzmán, a Palacios kinsman soon to be appointed young Francisco's tutor.

His flight from Arcadia unsettles Cervantists who might not themselves, in similar circumstances, have fled. He needed money, they guess, and Esquivias was not the place to find it; never mind that others— curate Juan de Palacios, the Quixadas, Francisco de Palacios later on— had no trouble earning livings there. If it was simply a matter of finding work, or operating as a small-business man, one would think that Madrid and Toledo were closer to home; besides, in both places he had friends, some contacts, places to stay. The work to be found in Seville would take him a long social step down from the state of landed proprietor. It was converso's work, demanding, hard, grubby and ill paid. Obviously, none of this troubled him. If a man were looking for a situation which would guarantee his freedom, that of fleet commissary was nearly perfect.

No, Cervantes was on the run. Everything known about his subsequent actions tends to confirm the notion. For example: he arrived in Seville at the end of the first week in May, but his commission did not begin until September; did he spend the interim at home, saving expenses and helping out around the family homestead during its busiest season? There is no indication that he did anything but loiter in Seville during those four torrid months.

Catalina made no attempt to join him. She was needed at home, it is pointed out, to care for her mother, who was old and doubtless ill; there were the boys to look after, and the property. She would not join him the following year, after her mother's death, by which time both brothers were old enough to be entrusted to tutors. It was Uncle Juan who in fact managed the estate and did so with competence and reasonable honesty. There is no evidence that the woman who later professed her "great love and friendship" for Cervantes was with him in any of the trials, disappointments, disgraces, imprisonments he was to undergo in the following fifteen years. But, as Sancho Panza reminds us, "An honest mind and a broken leg are best at home."[17]

Biographers are wary of assuming that the quarrel between Doña Guiomar and her soldier husband in Cervantes' interlude *The Divorce Court Judge* is directly autobiographical. No doubt they are right to question that such a row ever actually took place. We do not know that Catalina was a shrew, or self-righteous, or a snob, as Guiomar is accused of being. There is nevertheless a ring of emotional truth about the speeches in the play, a sound of reproaches rehearsed repeatedly in Cervantes' conscience. The sins he attributes to the soldier were by and large his own. The very fact of the play's impossible setting, in a divorce court, hints at a continuing ruefulness at how irremediable a mistake he had made; in the context of his experience, the lines seem to confess that he was not, had never been, a man for marriage. In this indirect way they may very well be autobiographical. Perhaps, too, they are Cervantes' wry (but not abject) apology to Catalina for being the man he was. Listen:

GUIOMAR: I tell you, my lord, they married me to this . . . man, since your honor insists I call him one, but this is not the man I married.

JUDGE: How's that? I don't understand.

GUIOMAR: I mean that I thought I'd married a right sort of man, a live wire, but in a few days I discovered I'd married a block of wood. . . . Because he doesn't know his right hand from his left, he neither seeks nor contrives to store up so much as a real to help support his house and family. He spends his mornings at mass and hanging around the Guadalajara Gate gossiping, picking up the latest news, telling and listening to lies. Afternoons, and even mornings too, he makes the rounds of the gambling dens to join the kibitzers who, I'm told, are a breed the gamblers detest extremely. At two o'clock he comes home to eat without having received even a real in tips because it's now out of fashion for the winners to give any. Then he's off again, comes back at midnight, eats if he finds anything to eat, and if not, crosses himself, yawns and goes to bed to twist and squirm all night. I ask him what's the matter. He tells me he's composing a sonnet in his head for a friend who's asked him for one, and he puts on airs of being a poet, as though this office made him exempt from worldly cares.

SOLDIER: In everything she has told you, my wife, Doña Guiomar, has not once strayed from the truth. And if I were not as reasonable in what I do as she is in what she says, I would long since have sucked up to the nobodies around and managed to set myself up as other sharp little hustlers have. . . . But since I have no trade and no pension, I don't know what to do with myself, because no gentleman will take me on account of my being married. . . .

GUIOMAR: And there's more, your honor. Seeing that my husband is so worthless and good-for-nothing, I kill myself to help him. But I can't, because I'm a decent woman, after all, and I'll not do anything base.

SOLDIER: For this alone this woman deserves to be loved. But under this nice honorability lies hidden the foulest disposition on earth. She's jealous for no reason, shouts without provocation, she's pretentious about wealth she hasn't got and, because she sees I'm poor she treats me as though I were dirt. And the worst of it is, your honor, that because she's faithful to me, I have to stand without a murmur for the thousands and thousands of rude and nasty things she has to say.

GUIOMAR: Now I won't take that. Why shouldn't you treat me with decency and respect when I'm such a good woman?

SOLDIER: Listen, my lady Doña Guiomar, I want to tell you something before all these gentlemen: why burden me with your virtue when you have to be virtuous anyway because you come of such good family, because you are a Christian and, besides, you owe it to yourself? A fine thing! Women want their husbands to respect them because they are pious and virtuous as though this were all they needed to be perfection itself. But they pay no attention to the breaches in that wall through which a thousand finer virtues leak out. What's it to me if you're so chaste yourself? I care more that you don't insist on it in your servant, or that you're forever sour-faced, grouchy, jealous, suspicious, wasteful, dull, lazy, quarrelsome, grumbling and other such impertinences. . . .

To end the interlude, Cervantes introduces a pair of musicians to sing the decision he and Catalina seem to have reached: that, with patience, "dead honor and pleasure are revived" and that, in the meanwhile, "better the worst agreement than the best divorce."

Biographers like to cite the observation of Don Quixote that a man about to set off on a long journey, "if he is prudent, will seek some staunch and pleasant companion before setting forth on the road; why, then, would a man beginning a lifelong journey to his final resting place not do as much, especially since his companion must be with him in bed, at table and everywhere, as a wife is with her husband?"[18] The quotation is usually lifted from its context, however; when the entire paragraph is reproduced, the comment, deliberately or not, takes on a crustier texture:

> For love and fancy easily blind the mind's eyes, which are so needed in choosing one's condition; the condition of marriage carries a high risk of error, and great caution and heaven's special favor are needed to hit the mark. A man wishing to set out on a long journey, if he is prudent, will seek some staunch and pleasant companion before setting forth on the road; why, then, would a man beginning a lifelong journey to his final resting place not do as much, especially since his companion must be with him in bed, at table and everywhere, as a wife is with her husband? The companionship of one's own wife is not merchandise which, once bought, can be returned or bartered or exchanged; for it is a circumstance from which one can never be separated, one which lasts as long as life lasts; it is a noose which, once tossed around the neck, becomes a Gordian knot which cannot be untied except if death's scythe sever it.

Part IV

FREEDOM'S CAPTIVE

] 25 [

The Sanchos of the Earth

Know you, my lucky friend, to whom
God grant a spacious life, if you
should sometime seek lodging in an inn
in Seville . . . the first . . . is in
the Calle de Bayona, where
princes stay; there they will give you
a charming upstairs chamber
and a spring bed, tapestry-hung,
and, in summer, a room downstairs,
draped in taffeta and damask,
and a silver table service
of saltcellar, ewer and cup:
this, with a pair of candlesticks,
they will unfailingly give you.
But, to save embarrassment, ask
on arriving at the inn how much
you will have to pay for all this. . . .[1]

Tomás Gutiérrez was a grand personage now. He was not yet a gentleman in Sevillian eyes, but he was trying. He rode a forty-ducat horse, and
he sternly banned muleteers from the big establishment on the Calle de
Bayona[2] which he refused to think of as anything so vulgar as an inn. He
had, he affirmed, six thousand ducats in silver and furnishings and, if he
said so himself, went about in great personal style.

Sevillian society patronized his house, drank with him, consulted him
on public affairs and steadfastly closed its doors to him. Gutiérrez was
becoming refined, perhaps a little too noticeably to the señores who had

once paid to hear the former hosier perform on the stage. Did they find
the rings on his fingers a shade too visible, his doublets just faintly on the
rakish side, his voice too vibrant, too frankly emotional in tone for the
comfort of Sevillian *gravitas?* To Gutiérrez's honor, he made no secret of
being an actor fellow; in 1585 he is known to have taken out his own cart
for the Corpus Christi celebration, possibly to act in his own auto, *The
Coming of the Antichrist.* But since he was now paying the freight himself instead of receiving wages for entertaining his fellow citizens, he
clearly felt respectable enough to play host to the likes of the Dukes of
Alba and Osuna, the Marquis of Priego, generals, magistrates, inquisitors,
even a papal nuncio.

Into this select company he took the Prince of Wits—on the cuff. Cervantes would not have rated a cool, damask-hung downstairs room; he
would have had to make do with poor man's pewter in the kitchen instead of ducal silver in the public rooms. But the address was impeccable,
rather like a maid's room at the Ritz, and even a board bed would have
seemed luxurious after ten days on the old Silver Road, the Ruta de la
Plata, which then ran generally west of today's main Toledo-Seville high-
way. Once past the Toledo inn described in *The Illustrious Serving
Wench,* some of the foulest ventas in Spain were to be found on that
road. A fifteen-century treatise had urged that meat carvers in public inns
be not only washed and shaved and wear chamois gloves while at work,
but that they wash their mouths with a paste of mastic, aloe, the lees of
cider, lemon leaves and rosemary flowers. Such niceties were unheard of
in most of the thirty ventas lining the route.

Cervantes' stories are truffled with the names or descriptions of places
on the road: it was at the Venta del Molinillo, near Almodóvar del
Campo, where Rinconete met Cortadillo; the big Venta del Alcalde may
have been the enchanted castle where Don Quixote received his knighthood; he may have watched Grisóstomo's funeral at nearby Fuente de Al-
cornoque. It is here, in the foothills of the Sierra Morena, that Don Quixote, sitting by the goatherds' fire munching roasted acorns, pronounces
Cervantes' moving evocation of the "happy age and happy centuries to
which the ancients gave the name of golden, not because gold, so prized
in our age of iron, was then to be had without toil, but because those who
lived then did not know the meaning of those two words *thine* and
mine. . . ."[3]

Cervantes found Seville busier and bigger than he had known it, at
least on the surface, in fact more corrupt, more indolent, more irre-
sponsible than ever, a prosperous bawd of a city increasingly dependent
on the percentages it took from foreign, chiefly Dutch, merchants. He
would have noticed how the landmarks had changed. Hernán Ruiz's new
lantern, topped by Bartolomé Morel's colossal weather vane, had added a

hundred feet to the Giralda in his absence. Business deals were still being closed and news relayed on the steps of the cathedral and in its Patio of Oranges (for "whether on God's business or the world's," Pedro de Mexía had noted, "it seems a man has to visit this church once a day,"[4]), but the temple's days as a countinghouse were numbered. Episcopal complaints had persuaded Philip to begin building the high-vaulted merchant exchange, La Lonja, alongside the cathedral, transferring his Escorial team to do the job. Most of the windows in the cathedral, Cervantes might have noticed, were new; the old ones had been blown out by a powder-magazine explosion in 1579. At the end of the Calle de las Sierpes, work on the royal prison had long since been completed; Cervantes probably passed it every morning going to or from Fernando Díaz's bookshop on the same street.

Cervantes' first problem was to assure himself a living. This was not as easy as he may have thought it would be. Despite the king's impatience and Santa Cruz's fuming, collections for the Armada were at a standstill throughout the summer of 1587 for lack of the cash with which to pay for requisitioned grain. While Guevara remained at court trying to root the funds he needed out of the undergrowth of jealousies and incompetence strangling the Enterprise of England, his place in Seville was filled by a local magistrate, Diego de Valdivia. It was doubtless Gutiérrez again, Old Friend Gutiérrez, who alone among Cervantes' guardian angels was never thanked by so much as a line in his books,[5] who introduced him to Valdivia, just as it must have been Gutiérrez who helped him to round up the guarantors he needed if he was to receive a commission.[6]

Once the business of applying for work was taken care of, there was nothing for him to do but wait until operations were resumed. Whether, in the meanwhile, he infiltrated the city's artistic contingent is moot. Many of the Sevillian poets he had praised in *La Galatea*—Cueva, Fernando de Cangas, Cristóbal de Villaroël and others—were in Madrid. Others among the city's cultural authorities, Francisco Pacheco, for example, make no mention of Cervantes although their writings comprise a catalogue of Sevillian luminaries. He is known, on the other hand, to have been acquainted with Baltasar del Alcázar, the lyric poet whose most famous work is an ode to a luncheon of blood sausage. Since he had established his reputation as a professional poet with a published book to his credit, Cervantes probably did join the daily reunions in the city's leading bookshops, such establishments as Clemente Hidalgo's place on the Calle de la Plata, where Francisco Arias' *The Imitation of Christ* was later published, and Díaz's outlet, where the books of Juan de Mal-lara and Mexía were first produced.

Early in September, misled by reports of bumper crops in Andalusia, Guevara ordered collections of wheat and fodder to begin "on promise to pay but with no cash down."[7] Sometime around September 18 Cervantes set out on his first commission, to Écija, with a staff of justice in his hand and riding a hired mule

> gray in color and of stumbling gait . . .
> big-boned but slight of strength,
> shortsighted though long in the tail,
> its flanks withered, but its hide
> harder than those a shield is made of . . . ,[8]

one of those beasts the Spanish called *máquinas de sangre*—blood engines. Fortunately, the new commissary later noted,

> . . . any critter can support the burden
> of a poet, which is always light
> because he carries no baggage.[9]

His assignment was to find wheat and fodder, in the town or on the farm, to collect the quota fixed by the crown, sign receipts, mill, store and transport the grain; he had the power to force doors and locks if need be, to sequester goods, intercept merchandise and baggage in transit, order imprisonments, decree fines and see to the acquisition of storehouses and equipment along with such minutia as oil for lamps, baskets, brooms, paper and ink, locks, etc. For this he was to receive twelve reales a day, payable when funds were available.

A latter-day reaction against the romantic emphasis on Cervantes' life-long poverty has created some misunderstanding about how much buying power this represented. Twelve reales would buy six live hens then, we are apprised, or nearly fifteen gallons of rotgut wine; today those hens would cost better than 4,500 reales. This is true, but misleading. Had Cervantes worked steadily, six days a week, fifty-two weeks a year, he would still have been ill paid. A scale worked out for the year 1556 shows that an income of under 20 ducats a month was a poverty wage; from 20 to 40 ducats a month was considered low pay, 40 to 150 "reasonable."[10] But a commissary's pay did not cover the intervals between contracts. In the nineteen months—494 workdays—between September 1587 and April 1589, when his first series of commissions ended, Cervantes was credited with 276 salaried days for which he was theoretically owed 3,312 reales (theoretically because the figure was later whittled down by royal auditors and even the revised total was never fully paid). Projected on a full-time basis, this represents an average salary of 15 ducats a month, well below the poverty line established for 1556 and even more depressed by 1587, for inflation had reduced the value of the ducat by approximately one fourth in twenty years. It is a fact that this was supposed to constitute net income, since his expenses—again in theory—were entirely covered during his working time. Had they been paid in full, they would have put him over the poverty line. Just over it.

Nothing is lost on the curious, however. When, for example, Don Quixote replies to Sancho's desire to be rewarded according to his merits by reminding him that one must first wander the world "on probation, so to speak,"[11] he might have had his creator's experience in mind. The instructive nature of Cervantes' new occupation was affirmed in Écija, where he was introduced to a world of absurdity in which even a Quixote might have lost his bearings.

The notes of a town council meeting on September 22 cite the presence of a royal commissary (Cervantes' name is not mentioned) who proposed to collect all the wheat in the place, "leaving only what is needed for food and planting." The indignation is almost audible through the officialese. These were country men, reluctant at any time to deal with a remote government. Because they sat on the richest wheatland in Andalusia, they were natural targets for royal exactions. With the crown chronically in pawn, it was a royal reflex to try to bleed the Écijanos and their neighbors; the answering reflex was for the townspeople to wheedle and whine and drag their feet. True, the councilmen were jealous of their prerogatives, anxious to protect the country folk they preyed on from outside interference. True, laymen and ecclesiastics habitually hid their produce, trying to create artificial shortages to drive prices up. But even at the best of times there was never plenty, and in 1586–91 the shortage was real and acute. Contrary to what Guevara thought, the hot, dry weather had again burned out much of the crop. No one in Écija had yet seen a maravedi for the 7,500 *fanegas** of grain taken the previous February from the 1586 harvest; appropriations from earlier crops had been only partly paid for. Now this "foreigner" from the north was there with a fistful of blank certificates promising to pay money his masters did not have for grain the town insisted it could not spare to supply an Armada which, if the king's commands meant anything, might very well sail before the grain could be gathered, paid for, processed and transported to Lisbon.

For the absurdity began at the top. His Majesty had ordered his Armada to sail for England January 18, 1588. Santa Cruz's anguished protests that the fleet was unprepared won a delay, to February 15. Philip, who had once written that "in so great an enterprise as that of England, it is fitting to move with feet of lead,"[12] was now issuing flurries of orders

---

* A fanega equals approximately 1.5 bushels.

frantically urging speed. Without waiting to learn if Santa Cruz was ready, he had ordered the Duke of Parma, his commander in the Low Countries, to invade England at once; Santa Cruz was ordered to sail whether Parma was ready or not to make the junction on which everyone agreed the success of the venture depended. Parma, trying to get peace negotiations going with Elizabeth, poured objections into his sovereign's deafened ears: he had no deep-water ports from which to launch his assault, his "invasion fleet" consisted almost wholly of barges and these were bottled up behind Dunkirk by fast-moving Dutch flyboats. In Lisbon, the Captain General of the Ocean Sea, promising to be ready soon, sooner, almost at once, was now convinced there was no way to avoid disaster. He had once thought of an Armada of eight hundred ships and ninety thousand men; by the end of January he would have collected some fourscore vessels, many of them leaky, clumsy and slow. He had wanted fifty galleons; he had thirteen, one of them unseaworthy, all of them undermanned and, considering the opposition they were to face, critically undergunned. Artillery, powder, shot, food, water, supplies arrived erratically when they arrived at all, and such was the chaos in Lisbon that they were loaded aboard whatever vessels were nearest, with the result that some ships were so loaded as to be dangerously low in the water while others rode high and virtually empty.

Recruitment for the Armada had been crippled by prophecies which, gathering force for over a century, converged on 1588 as the year of the Apocalypse, when the Seventh Seal would be broken open and the Last Judgment come. Europe was subject to these cataclysmic visions at roughly semi-millennial intervals and this time, as usual, they were supported by ominous heavenly acrobatics—baleful planetary conjunctions, a strange new star that appeared and disappeared, forecasts of unusual concatenations of eclipses—and the inevitable rumors of unnatural births and monstrous portents. The king of Spain dismissed the prophecies as impious nonsense, but the desertion rate in the fleet rose so alarmingly that press gangs were turned loose around ports in Spain and Portugal to fill the holes. To cap his despair, Santa Cruz was outraged by the appearance of the Count of Fuentes to supervise operations and check Santa Cruz's accounts. The marquis, whose devotion to his king was, or should have been, unquestioned, was made literally apoplectic by the humiliation; he would die of it, suddenly, on February 9, 1588.

Agitation in high places was no business of the Écijanos, however. Their problem was to deal with the new commissary—or, rather, to avoid dealing with him. Cervantes was at once informed that he had come at a bad time: the town's annual festival had started September 20; no question of dealing with other problems until the fiesta ended. Come back in three weeks, or not at all.

Cervantes was obviously feeling uncomfortable. He was no Fugger's man, one of those tough, methodical, zealous Germans used by the German banking house of Fugger to collect taxes awarded as interest on loans to the Spanish crown. His subsequent efforts to avoid the use of force attest to his horror at having to extort grain from people who claimed to need it. Experienced collectors functioned almost as brokers, bargaining with their superiors and putting pressure on the peasantry (whose cries, as the proverb went, did not reach to heaven) ; the crows among this flock of sparrows managed to turn a profit for themselves from the negotiation and the Écijanos had no way of knowing that Cervantes was not one of these. He saw one friendly face among those eight thousand hostile Écijanos: the town's corregidor, Cristóbal Mosquera de Figueroa, then composing his book on the Azores campaign, to which Cervantes would contribute a sonnet in praise of the Marquis of Santa Cruz. Mosquera, who had been among the multitude of poets hailed in *La Galatea*, certainly gave him details about his brother's courage in battle. Unfortunately, this was nearly all he could offer; his term of office expired October 1.

It may nevertheless have been under pressure from Mosquera that the town council forgot its fiesta long enough to hold the September 22 meeting. This concluded with a resolution to draw up a bill of particulars explaining the town's financial crisis and send it in appeal to Valdivia, the deputy commissary general, in Seville. Indulgence was not the order of the day, however. Pressed from above, Valdivia, then in the process of sequestering wheat in nearby Andújar, told Cervantes to get on with it or he, Valdivia, would come and do it for him. A second town meeting was convened September 26 at which it was agreed that the town would deal with Cervantes if he would take no more than a token contribution "because of the great shortage of wheat in this city." The proposition was delivered to Valdivia by two of the councilmen.

Valdivia was by profession a criminal-court judge; the experience had no doubt dried out the soggier reaches of his sentimentality. He knew the Écijanos' history of passive resistance. To come away from the town empty-handed, or virtually so, would mean he had failed in his job, and he was aware that Philip II neither forgot not forgave such failures. His answer was an order to Cervantes to proceed as directed.

Cervantes squirmed. Still trying to avoid using force, he proposed that the Écijanos themselves assign quotas to each landowner and submit the list to Valdivia. Refused. When, early in October, the judge gave the screw another turn, his commissary realized he had no choice: flanked by a scribe and a detachment of sergeants at arms, Cervantes began to seize all the grain he could find, distributing payment certificates as he went. By the end of the month he had collected and stored some two thousand fanegas, none of which could be legally processed for the Armada until it was paid for.

If he thought his troubles were over, he was quickly undeceived. About half the wheat taken was owned by the Church, including some 525 bushels seized from property owned by the dean and chapter of the Seville Cathedral. Never mind that his orders specifically authorized him to take grain "wherever he might understand it to be found . . . from the custody of any person who might possess it, of whatever status and condition, ecclesiastical or secular." Embargo Church property? Retaliation came by special messenger: an order from the vicar-general of Seville excommunicating Miguel de Cervantes and, for good measure, directing that the order be prominently posted, quickly putting everyone on notice that to deal with him was to sin against Holy Church.

Astrana Marín recalls the scene in *Don Quixote* in which the knight and his squire entered El Toboso at midnight in search of Dulcinea's house. " 'See there, Sancho,' Don Quixote exclaimed, 'either my sight fails me or that great shadowy bulk looming there must be Dulcinea's palace.' " When they came up to it, however, he recognized his mistake.

" 'It's the church we've stumbled on, Sancho.'

" 'So I see,' replied Sancho. 'And please God we've not stumbled on our graves. . . .' "[13]

This linking of darkness and death—not excepting the spiritual death of excommunication—with the Church is methodical in Cervantes' writings. It is more squarely touched on in the adventure of the corpse.[14] In it we ride with Don Quixote and Sancho through the terrifying night to encounter a procession of riders dressed in white. Behind them, revealed by the light of their torches, moves a bier escorted by six more riders shrouded in black to their mules' feet. Taking the riders for "evil things from the other world" and convinced that here was a wrong for him to right, the knight charges and disperses the column, wounding two of the horsemen, only to learn that they are monks escorting a corpse to its tomb.[15]

" 'I believe, Sancho,' he said, 'that I have incurred excommunication for laying violent hands on holy things. . . . I did not consciously offend a priest or anything sacred to the Church, which I respect and adore like the Catholic and true Christian I am, but I thought they were phantoms and monsters from another world.' "

Cervantes might also have remembered that Charles V had been excommunicated; the same lightning struck Philip II twice in his lifetime. No permanent disability was noticed in either case. The Church was in the habit of scattering excommunications freely, especially against crown officers impious enough to obey their orders. Cervantes appealed to Seville for help in removing the anathema and went on working as though nothing disturbing had happened.

On November 2 the townspeople addressed another appeal to Valdivia to "suspend the collection, since (Écija) had already contributed 8,000 fanegas this year." All this accomplished was to bring the magistrate to the scene in person, breathing fire. On November 14, he extracted a commitment from the Écijanos for 5,400 fanegas of wheat, including the grain already taken by Cervantes. Then, with his commissary in tow, he rode off to the town of La Rambla, in the province of Córdoba, in search of more grain.

There they heard the same story, but with variations. No one in the town had yet been paid for the exactions of 1579—eight years earlier. One commissary had appropriated a number of hams "in the king's service" and kept them for his own use. Some 1,500 fanegas of grain had already been exacted from the town that year by one Pedro de Salazar Vivanco, a magistrate of the village of Benamejí who functioned as a regular crown commissary; he had also seized a quantity of hams, cheese and beans for which his sole authorization, probably, was that his wages had not been paid either.

Despite their grievances, town officials promised Valdivia that within twenty days they would collect and store another five hundred fanegas of wheat, "dry, cleaned and winnowed," against payment by the crown. Within hours it became evident that the townspeople had no intention of living up to the agreement. Valdivia rode off to Córdoba, leaving Cervantes behind to handle matters in La Rambla. And he did handle them: by November 22 he had not only begun to seize wheat, but he had imprisoned growers who had tried to stand in his way. An appeal went out from the town council to Valdivia to release the prisoners in return for a renewal of the original agreement. Instead of a reply, the terrible magistrate of Benamejí reappeared and proceeded to embargo wheat and fodder on his own. A plague of locusts would have been more merciful.

How Cervantes arranged matters is not known; the record merely indicates that he had not yet collected his full quota when, in December, on orders from the industrious Valdivia, he went on to Castro del Río, a town of approximately six thousand inhabitants some twenty miles to the northwest. There, while sequestering about 1,700 fanegas of wheat, he once more laid violent hands on Church property; a sacristan who resisted the seizure was consigned to jail. Cervantes was excommunicated again, this time by the vicar-general of Córdoba.

From Castro del Río to nearby Espejo, then to Cabra, where he hired his young cousin Rodrigo as an assistant. He took Rodrigo to La Rambla and left him to complete the collection there while, around January 10, his commission expired, he returned to Seville via Écija. He had worked 112 days, for which the crown owed him 1,344 reales in salary. Payment was indefinitely deferred. Spain's expenditure on the Armada in 1588 would average 900,000 ducats a month. Payment of the .00013 per cent of that sum represented by Cervantes' salary might, it seemed, have ruined the nation.

Word from home awaited him. Alonso Rodríguez, the complaisant tavernkeeper of the Calle del Tudesco, had died in October, leaving Ana, who had two daughters now, to run the business alone. Doña Leonor was living in something like comfort, thanks to her daughters. One item of news probably stirred Cervantes' not altogether kindly interest: Lope de Vega had gone on trial in December for libel. Someone had written a poison-pen sonnet defaming Jerónimo Velázquez and his daughter Elena, with whom Lope's amorous converse had run dry. A number of possible authors whose pens were deadly enough to have written the poem—Cervantes was one of them—were suggested to the court, but all the evidence pointed to Lope as the culprit. Around February 21, word reached Seville of Lope's conviction and exile—eight years away from Madrid, two from the Kingdom of Castile—and of his intention to volunteer for the Armada.

But Cervantes had problems of his own. Commissary General Antonio de Guevara had at last arrived on the scene in January to replace Valdivia, and on January 22, citing Cervantes' "practice and experience in such things and because of my satisfaction with him,"[16] he had commissioned the commissary to draw four thousand arrobas† of olive oil . . . from Écija. Unfortunately, Guevara had brought no money with him; there was just cash enough available to pay for transporting the oil to Seville, but none to pay for its purchase, none to buy the wheat which was beginning to rot in the storehouses. Cervantes was probably back in Écija when Seville heard that, as Santa Cruz's successor, King Philip had chosen the city's first citizen, Alonso Pérez de Guzmán el Bueno, seventh Duke of Medina-Sidonia.

Jingoist historians have dealt roughly with Medina-Sidonia. He has been made the scapegoat for the loss of an Armada with which no one else, not even the hallowed Santa Cruz, could have produced a victory. Until very recently, however, references to him revealed an oddly personal hatred of the man of the kind usually reserved for traitors and apostates. "Ugly, short and bandy-legged," one calls him[17] (he was of average height and rather mild-looking); "inept and cowardly," says another;[18] "dominated by avarice to an atrocious degree . . . despicable and mean-

† A variable liquid measure equal to about 4.2 gallons.

spirited," raged Astrana Marín, who found in him "not a single estimable quality."[19] Sneering references to Medina-Sidonia as the "Duke of the Tunas," because of his highly profitable trade in salted tuna fish, were frequent even in his own day.

Recent reappraisals, chiefly from abroad, have recognized him as affable, intelligent, efficient, sensible, honest with himself and courageous. As captain general of Andalusia for ten years, he had shown himself to be a capable administrator; if he is now seen to have been more corrupt than his peers, it is mainly because, as the official responsible for the ports of Seville, Sanlúcar de Barrameda, Málaga, Cádiz, his opportunities for corruption were ampler than most. Thirty-eight years old, one of the first lords of the realm, he was, on paper at least, Spain's richest magnate. He was also that queer fish among Spanish aristocrats, a man indifferent to personal glory. Staying home and making money was what interested him, not playing soldier. His appointment to lead the Armada, then, came as an unpleasant surprise to him.

He tried to wiggle out of the honor, pleading a tendency to seasickness, inexperience in land or sea warfare, a predisposition to colds, and poverty. He protested in his reply to the king that, because his family was 900,000 ducats in debt, "I could not spend a real in the king's service";[20] historians have scoffed at the excuse from a man whose income was probably 150,000 ducats a year, but it was true and it largely explained his undeniable greediness for money. Philip, however, would have none of this; he took the trouble to reply point by point to the duke's objections in an affectionate letter insisting on the appointment and admonishing that "it is for me to judge your ability and endowments, of which I am so satisfied."[21]

That Cervantes viewed the appointment, when he heard of it sometime in March, with the prescient dismay often attributed to him is doubtful. Santa Cruz's death may have saddened him; only Parma was left now of the great soldiers he had known at Lepanto. He would not have enjoyed the intimations of advancing age one feels when death reaches too voraciously for people one has known. But Medina-Sidonia's prestige, especially in Seville, was still enormous then and this could not have failed to impress Cervantes. In the duke's veins, he would note in his first *Song to the Armada,* ran "the blood of Austria"—of the Habsburgs. Besides, the king's commissary had more immediate preoccupations—four thousand arrobas of them.

From January to mid-May, when his second commission expired, he went gingerly in Écija, wringing oil out of the town almost drop by drop. He had learned not to expect to find his own patriotism matched in the much-put-upon peasantry. "For, as I ought to have known from long experience," says Don Quixote, "there is no peasant who keeps his word if he finds it does not suit him."[22] He tried nevertheless to deal honorably with them. There is a hint here of the man's immense understanding, of his open-eyed compassion for these people who were both his victims and his persecutors. It is true that many of the peasants he would later depict are Old Christian simpletons, cunning and avaricious, with names like "Sneeze" and "Cabbage" and more than the then conventional literary allotment of vain stupidity. They were also the blood kin of Sancho Panza and Cervantes loved Sancho, respected his earthiness and his humanity, admired the humorous resilience with which he faced the hourly violence of his life. Like his Quixote, Cervantes forced himself to play out the role he had chosen for himself. But he knew he could throw over that part when he pleased, could go peacefully back to his gentlemanly pursuits and his books. The Écijanos, these Sanchos of the earth, had no such choice and Cervantes mourned for them even as he laughed at them and, more often, with them.

The ambiguity of his position, cutting him off from the structured society which touched but never absorbed him, thrust him increasingly into the company of the no-accounts of his new world, the rootless, shifting population of carters, weighters, watchmen, goatherds, servants, ruffians with whom he shared the heat and the cold, the dust and the verminous beds and the central ordeal of non-belonging. Yet while, to judge from his writing, he understood these people, identified with them as no other writer of his time could, he never learned to love them as he did the poor farmers whose oppressor he knew himself to be. Their attitude toward him was equally ambivalent. The fact that on March 23 nine of the town's wheatgrowers named him as their agent in collecting the money owned them by the crown has been taken as proof of the esteem his rectitude had earned for him in Écija. Perhaps. Later developments would show the Écijanos' malice toward him as well as their grudging respect for his probity. It is just possible that their appointment of him as their collection agent was a way of putting Cervantes in the awkward position of dunning his own employer. There is no record that he ever negotiated any payment for his "principals."

Leaving cousin Rodrigo to act for him in his second excommunication trial, in Córdoba, he returned to Seville in late May. His mother-in-law, he learned, had died May 1. She had left a personal estate of 78,879 maravedis, entailed, as we have seen, to keep it out of Cervantes' hands. Although he would later admit that "no poet can hang on to his money,"[23] Doña Catalina's gesture was largely gratuitous; she had also left debts of 202,810 maravedis, about equal to the total value of the family's property. Cervantes seems to have felt no compulsion to rush home empty-handed to console his wife.

A never-never atmosphere envelops Cervantes' activities at this juncture. Guevara was willing to give him more work, but this time he insisted that Cervantes find additional guarantors. Was this because of the nature of the commission (to arrange for the milling and transportation of grain which could not legally even be removed from storage before being paid for)? Or simply protection for them both against the lawsuits he expected would arise?

So a Cervantes presumably still living on Gutiérrez's money set out to find strangers willing to guarantee his honesty with money they probably did not have either so that he might mill grain to which the crown had no right in order to supply an Armada which, by the time he found his guarantors (June 12), was nearly two weeks out of Lisbon on its way north, with its supplies already rotting in its green-wood casks.

Cervantes' new assignment was different from anything in his previous experience. "First of all he will find out which of the said city's (Écija's) mills . . . are the best and most expeditious . . . he will store the said wheat in the most suitable sites and places . . . where it will not be damaged"; before the wheat was milled he was to test each lot of five hundred fanegas by "dividing each into three piles and choosing at random three fanegas from each," having first weighed them and had the grain cleaned and winnowed, "receiving the oath of those persons who are to do the work that they will do it well and loyally." Elaborate instructions were given for weighing the grain, its chaff, even the dust from it, in the presence of town officials. After milling, the flour was to be entrusted, with the usual precautions, to one Jerónimo Maldonado for conversion into biscuit. Careful records, "noting down each thing in detail," were to be kept of all transactions.[24]

It was Cervantes' job to persuade the Écijanos to consent to this "despite the order that (the grain) not be withdrawn before being paid for" because, although Guevara was "at present" without funds, he was expecting money to arrive at any time; "to wait until it came . . . with the hot weather setting in" would mean loss of the grain. Cervantes, he said in the commission he issued on June 15, "because he is so wholly satisfactory" and "in the light of his practice and experience in things of this sort is the person best suited to do this with the care and speed the business requires."

Very flattering. And to accomplish this impossible function he gave Cervantes an assistant, Miguel de Santa María. Apparently it did not strike him as insulting to give Santa María the same rate of pay, twelve reales a day, as he gave the "practiced, experienced" commissary with whom he was so completely satisfied. Perhaps this explains why Guevara was at pains to instruct Cervantes to maintain good relations—"*buena correspondencia*"—with his assistant. In the event, neither commissary nor assistant was to get a maravedi to squander on himself; their expenses would have to come out of their own pockets.

"Poor me," explains the much-battered Sancho Panza, "if this adventure be with phantoms, as it begins to seem, where will I find the ribs to endure it?"[25]

The town council, meanwhile, was being as obstructionist as ever. His Sevillian guarantees might be adequate for Guevara, he was told, but they cut no ice with the Écijanos. Local guarantees were demanded, from people they knew and could reach. That this was no more than nuisance-making quickly became obvious. Cervantes found his two guarantors easily; on June 20, Fernando López de Torres and Francisco de Orduna affirmed with their persons and property that he would give good account of "all the grain, maravedis and other things turned over to and entrusted to him" and pay the crown's bills promptly and honestly. Inadequate, replied the council. That very afternoon, Cervantes found two more backers, Juan Bocacho and Gonzalo de Aguilar Quixada. He won that round on points.

Money did begin filtering down from Madrid. On June 14 Cervantes approved payment of 34,450 maravedis to Don Gutierre de Laso in Écija for 96.5 fanegas of wheat collected from him in 1587. Among the first to be paid were the churchmen whose wheat Cervantes had distrained. Probably in late June or early July, the chapter of the Seville Cathedral rescinded its excommunication order against him. And on July 1, in Seville, in response to his increasingly insistent claims, 500 of the 1,406 reales owed him in back wages and expenses for his first commission was paid. From that, although it still owed him over 900 reales, the crown deducted 62 reales for postal charges.

In early July, with money in his wallet to cover milling costs, he was back in Écija with Santa María and Salazar. Summer is a trial anywhere in Andalusia, soggy and suffocating. In the Écijan plains—for good reason the town is called the "frying pan of Andalusia"—it is a horror. From late June until mid-September, the white houses, their windows, doors, blinds shut against the belligerent heat, lie like bleached bones in the bleached fields. Dirt roads turn to dust, fetlock deep. As the day burns on into afternoon, human movement gradually ceases, to resume slowly, reluctantly, in early evening. No one sleeps much in summer; it seems almost sinful to waste the few cool hours the Lord allots the land. It takes lean, dry men to withstand high summer in the Écijan plains.

Cervantes got the worst of it. There is nothing quite like the air in a wheat barn in Écija in July and August. Dust rasps at the lungs, sticks to sweating skin like plastic. The grain he inspected had been sitting there, stored in the sheaves, for nearly a year; most of it had rotted—what the weevils had left of it—and the stench, like that of a mountain of moldy bread, was nauseating.

The town council had sent more emissaries to Madrid and Seville to plead that this reeking pile be allowed to go on disintegrating until it was fully paid for. They were certainly not expecting the blow which then fell on them: a stern new order to Cervantes from Guevara to attach more wheat and fodder, "all that can be found," to have all the grain milled at once and shipped with the fodder to Seville.

Cervantes, dressed in his woolen breeches and his woolen hose, can be envisioned riding through the incandescent countryside in search of grain, persuading, quietly arguing over cups of wine cooled in patio wells, forcing doors when he had to. Meanwhile, a torrid storm of orders and counterorders was whipping between Seville and Écija. Direct appeals were made to Philip II to suspend collections; Guevara was urged to find his wheat in the neighboring province of Jaén, where exaggerated reports spoke of a bumper harvest. But the commissary general was disbursing cash now, never quite enough, but something, and his orders to Cervantes were to proceed with utmost rigor. Word of his severity panicked towns throughout the region. Córdoba appealed in advance to the king's confessor against the "damage and extortion" it feared would visit it if Cervantes were sent there.

In Écija, the commissary must have been aware that the tone of resentment around him had risen in pitch. To protect himself against charges of fraud, he began on July 11 to have the stored wheat publicly weighed. Nearly four fifths of it was found to be unusable. Milling began in August, over the town's protests. Cervantes was now surrounded by a dusty, ragged cloud of millers, weighers, carters, laborers, boys eager to earn a few maravedis for doing odd jobs; and again, like a fly on a sugar cookie, a notary appeared, distastefully brushing dust from his correct black clothing.

We have the minutely detailed records Cervantes kept from July 1588 through February 1589: "six reales for oil for the lamps burning in the storehouses. . . . On paper and ink for two months, six reales . . . for more paper and ink, four reales . . . to shelter five hundred fanegas of wheat which were in a patio, uncovered, to make a test with, and it rained and we had to gather it up quickly and I hired people to help in addition to those working on the milling, six reales . . . for a locksmith who went with me to the farms and unlocked some rooms in which there was wheat, six reales. . . ."[26]

Biographers insist on these records not only because they are among the rare documents in Cervantes' handwriting, but because of the honesty apparent in them, in contrast to the usual practice of his corrupt trade.

With what amazed satisfaction do we find that Cervantes' arithmetic is wrong, and that the errors were in the crown's favor! With what vicarious self-righteousness do we read the notation above his signature that all this "and many other things I have not set down" were bought with his own money on the crown's behalf.

No doubt the Écijanos, if pressed, would have confessed their wonderment at this sheep among wolves. They would also have observed that sheep are for shearing, and they were about to give a demonstration of this truth.

The council's appointment of regidor Luis Portocarrero on August 8 as its advocate in appeals to the crown seemed, at first, just one more in its tireless efforts to prove its poverty. Cervantes was in Seville at the time, reporting on his progress and checking payments against his requisition list. On August 17 he signed a receipt for 6,600 reales from Guevara's paymaster, Agustín de Cetina, to cover milling expenses. At least part of the money was to be used to hire local labor, perhaps in the hope of forcing the council to soften its objections to him; he should have known that the kind of people who needed odd jobs were not those the regidores felt they represented. Another document places him in Écija on August 18, indicating that he rode all night to get there. A new commission followed him there four days later, to attach more oil in Écija.

On August 25 Portocarrero returned from Seville. He had not been able to persuade Guevara to stop pillaging the cities, but he had come away with a promise to lift all embargos still in force and to cause no difficulties for the Écijanos (that is, to stop all seizures). Portocarrero was given to right to decide if any townsman was in a position to part with the wheat demanded of him; the promise was accompanied by a letter ordering Cervantes, a king's commissary, to defer to him on all such questions. Écijan officials, all gentlemen, then assigned modest quotas to their fellow citizens, a total of 2,500 fanegas, taking as much as possible from the poorer farmers and a bare minimum from the gentry.

Cervantes thought the quantity ridiculously small and he so informed Seville. Guevara in turn informed Portocarrero that the contribution was indeed rather small, but, to show his good will, he directed Cervantes to accept the offer.

The Écijanos saw this as a breach in the wall and a group of them went to work immediately to widen it. They drafted a new petition to the king, drawing a tragic picture of the misery in which Écija was left by Cervantes' exactions; townsmen were reduced to such penury, they alleged, that they were forced to abandon their homes.

King Philip was moved to react. Guevara was summarily ordered to make amends to those he had victimized and to remain henceforth within the strict letter of his instructions; Cervantes was criticized by name.

Philip is probably not to blame for assuming that Cervantes was just another ruffian in a band of thieves. For the time being, the king was too busy elsewhere to take the disciplinary action he knew was needed in Andalusia. But the name Cervantes, vaguely unsavory, may have stuck in his mind.

On September 2 the Écijanos gave the knife another twist. A new complaint was lodged intimating that Cervantes had lied about the quantity of "fodder and other things" he had taken from the town. It may have been discretion on Guevara's part to issue a new commission to him on September 5, sending him to Marchena, twenty-three miles to the southwest, to search for oil. Since, notwithstanding the writhings of the royal conscience, he brought no money with which to buy the two thousand arrobas of oil at which the Marchena quota had been fixed, Cervantes found himself on the familiar carrousel of guarantors, locksmiths, notaries, all the desperate recourses of a tattered administration of which his, as usual, was the prominently exposed backside.

The road to Marchena then was hardly more than a muletrack through empty fields; here and there a shabby mound marked a venta, hardly more than a goatherd's refuge. A long day's ride, probably two days in that weather. The dense heat of the month-long period "from Virgin to Virgin"—July 16 to August 15[27]—had lightened a bit. But the annual Andalusian miracle, when the first autumn rains overnight cover the sun-blasted fields with a carpet of yellow and purple and blue, as though it had rained wildflowers, was still weeks away. At the end of this track was a town of approximately ten thousand souls, none of them believed known to Cervantes and none eager to welcome him.

A good time and place, it would seem, to dream of that larger world beyond this withered landscape. Did he imagine himself in the "northern mists" of his first song to the Armada, once more glaring into hell's doorway while, around him,

> bodies flew through the air
> propelled by the fiery machines of war,
> (where) the waters changed their color
> and the blood that pulsed from intrepid breasts
> soaked the enemy earth . . . ?

Lepanto again! Again the exhilaration of a fulminating triumph over death. And the first reports concerning the war against England spoke of victory for the Armada. A broadside hawked through the streets of Seville on September 5, the day Cervantes received his commission there, gave an account of the dispatches, more fantasy than fact.

Most of this data had been forwarded by Don Bernardino de Mendoza, the former ambassador to England who had shifted his attentions to Paris; it was through him that Spanish money and Spanish troops bolstered the uprising of the Duke of Guise against France's King Henri III which, it was hoped, would neutralize France while Spain fought the English. Mendoza was one of those men who are all too ready to take their desires for objective fact at the drop of an encouraging rumor. Since neither Parma nor Medina-Sidonia had bothered to keep him informed of developments in the Channel, the ambassador had been forced to piece his summaries together from fragmentary data filtering through from the coast. His first dispatches were jubilant: Drake himself had been killed, captured, wounded! Fifteen of England's great galleons had been sunk in a single engagement!

A second packet of reports was less confident, but by that time Cervantes was in Marchena, where news arrived slowly when it arrived at all. And when he returned to Seville via Écija some two weeks later, he found himself facing a crisis which may have relegated the Enterprise to the back of his mind.

The Écijanos had been inspired to new heights of ingenuity during his absence. The councilmen had consulted the prior of the town's Dominican monastery and had been assured by him that it was sinful to demand wheat of anyone who had none, even though he be a rich man. His opinion, confirmed by Franciscan, Mercenarian and other ecclesiastics to whom the council had appealed, convinced corregidor Juan de Zúñiga y Avellaneda that it would be improper to sign the order putting Portocarrero's agreement with Guevara into effect. The commissary general soon received a letter reminding him of the king's commands; in the light of these, they suggested, the figure of 2,500 fanegas agreed on was really too high. In fact, under the circumstances, they could not in conscience ask anyone to contribute anything at this time, in view of the town's well-known balancing act on the brink of ruin.

"I would never think," Guevara replied, "of asking wheat of those who have none, but of those who have it to sell." He had been moderate in his requests, he asserted. The grain was there. Charging that the growers were selling their stocks clandestinely for spot cash, he warned that if the town did not live up to his agreement with Portocarrero "it will have to be done by my commissary's hands, with much commotion."[28]

At the same time, Cervantes demanded that they prove their allegation of fraud against him or retract it. The council backtracked; on September 30 it declared him entirely innocent. In the interim, he saw for the first time the royal reprimand in which he was accused of abuses of office. Back he went to the council. One may assume that the man who declared that "an ounce of good fame is worth more than a pound of pearls"[29] and that "the man without honor is worse than a dead man"[30] was furious at the smear. Again the council complied, putting it on record that "as is well known, the said Miguel de Cervantes, during the time he spent in this city . . . last year (1587), carried out his job of attaching wheat here with great rectitude, and he has done the same in this present year of eighty-eight. . . ." The council, it insisted, had not solicited the royal criticism of Cervantes (this was officially true) and "although the city has tried diligently" to find out who did, "it has not been able to learn or know it thus far." On October 3 it reaffirmed that Cervantes "had not been seen or heard to do anything improper; instead, he had fulfilled his office of commissary well and diligently."[31]

Having won his skirmish in that sector, Cervantes shifted his fire to Seville, appointing Guevara's chief sergeant at arms, Juan de Manzanares, to collect the salary and expenses owed him. The 438 reales he had received could not have gone far; the life he lived—perpetually on the move, living in inns and rented rooms, carrying no more than would fit in his saddlebags—was expensive even then. In fact, every peasant in Écija would be paid for his produce before Cervantes collected a truncated version of his pay.

It has been suggested that the only way he could have survived was by snipping petty cash for his own and Santa María's expenses from the operational funds allotted him, perhaps with Guevara's tacit connivance. The charge is impossible to disprove. Corollary hints that Cervantes really was guilty of the larger frauds of which the Écijanos accused him, however, will not hold water. Not only did the city repeatedly and publicly clear him of guilt, but he was among the few commissariat officers on whom no suspicion would later fall during an official investigation of Guevara's operation.

In mid-October, with the air around him temporarily cleared, he was again able to join the throngs on the cathedral steps in excited speculation about the Armada's fate. Seville was still far behind events. Mendoza's second packet of news, confessing that his earlier reports may have been overoptimistic, was soon followed by a third in which he had regained all his former confidence. Parma, he reported, had linked up with Medina-Sidonia; by the time Philip received his letter, Spanish troops would certainly be fighting alongside Catholic insurgents on English soil.

But late in August disturbing word had come from other sources; Spanish ships had been seen fleeing before the English fleet, horrible damage—much exaggerated—had been done by the English fire ships to the Spanish in Calais harbor. Now, in October, more baleful rumors were drifting south from Spain's northern coast, although Seville had yet to learn that the Duke of Medina-Sidonia himself, half-starved and burning with fever, had already been carried ashore in a litter in Santander.

The uncertainty is reflected in Cervantes' long *Song Arising from the Various Reports Which Have Come of the Catholic Armada That Went Against England.* "Fierce fame," it pleads,

> by the beating of thy swift wings, break
> the choking mists coming to us from the north,
> on lightest feet, come and utterly destroy
> the confused rumor of evil tidings; let
> your radiance disperse the shadows falling
> on Spanish renown, which is fleeing from you. . . .

There is no need to linger over the poem. Except for the historically valuable recapitulation it makes of the rumors then current, it makes scarcely a mark even on Cervantes' poetic scale; despite its high flights of rhetoric, it is a distressing poem to read. Cervantes was plainly out of practice. This fact, perhaps more than any other document, tells us how far he had strayed from literature. "How easily the poetic imagination discourses," only to be "cast down and shattered by a thousand impossibilities. Upon what weak cement are towering chimeras raised!"[32]

For the present, however, it was back to the fanegas for him. A new commission was issued October 20, 1588, to attach more supplies in Écija. He was to "try to collect all you can without force and without seeking to obtain it from him who has no wheat, because this is not just" —Guevara was looking over his shoulder here—but to see to it that the business "is done with no fuss or complaints, even if the whole quota (1,500 arrobas of oil, 3,000 of grain) is not filled. . . ."[33]

This was easier ordered than done. Cervantes had made enemies as well as friends in Écija; sometime in December or early January 1589, one of them again accused him of taking more than the authorized quantity of grain. We learn of the charge from a formal petition by Cervantes entered in the minutes of a city council meeting on January 23. "It has reached my notice," he protested with some irony, "that a regidor on this city's council, moved by *buen celo* (high zeal, but the phrase also means both suspicion and jealousy), has insistently attempted . . . to find out how much wheat and fodder I took from the householders of this city, imagining that I took more than the 2,500 fanegas of wheat and 500 of fodder I had to attach in fulfillment of the agreement Don Luis Portocarrero . . . made with Antonio de Guevara; and because the said affirmation reflects ill on my reputation and the honesty with which I have conducted and do conduct my office, and to spare the said regidor's labor, I here present the list (of attachments). . . . I request and beseech that the city cry it through the streets and post it in public places so that all may ascertain how much wheat and fodder I have taken . . . which still has not reached 1,000 fanegas taken and paid for. . . ." Anything else he might have collected under the commission, he swore, came from "the tithe barns and ecclesiastics and does not enter into the requisitioning from the householders of this city."

He urged the Écijanos to apportion the remainder so that "the service of our lord the king might be done with less tumult." Failing this, he warned, "I will search for the wheat and fodder wherever I can to comply with (the accord) without regard to the allotments made. . . ."[34]

The city, as it had to, recanted. It sought an accounting, if only for payment purposes. When, after a trip to Seville to present his accounts (on February 6) and assure himself of Guevara's support, he returned to Écija, a public call was issued by the council to "all those householders to whom Miguel de Cervantes, commissary, has issued certificates to bring them and show them . . . because the city is certified to compensate them. . . .[35]

In February Guevara returned to Madrid, presumably to try to explain why the biscuit made from rotten wheat in Écija was so bad that much of it had simply been thrown into the sea. Presumably, too, he was to begin to suspect how much of the thousands of ducats sent to him from Madrid had been diverted into the pockets of men around him.

In all fairness, it should be noted that everyone involved in the operation—the commissaries, the growers, the crown's auditors—was faced with an almost impossible bookkeeping situation, especially given the crude accounting methods of the period when some old-fashioned merchants were still doing their accounts in the Roman numerals standard earlier in the century. The treasury sent Guevara what funds it could; he in turn doled them out to Cervantes and his fellow commissaries to pay not only for supplies purchased, but to compensate carters, millers, warehousemen, bakers, temporary employees, etc. Operations were carried out chiefly on credit; payment was almost invariably partial and usually a year or more overdue. Damage, spoilage, accidents and waste had to be kept track of under the most primitive and approximate conditions. All this was to be done by the commissaries, many of them non-professional field operatives, while they were collecting supplies, hiring men, arranging for processing and transport, filling out and issuing scores of forms to dozens of growers in half a dozen cities and fending off the hostile criticism of people who were no less baffled than they by the procedure. That despite his undoubted repugnance for what he had to do, Cervantes accomplished this juggling act to the satisfaction, if not the applause, of his superiors at court is testimony both to his honesty and his application.

From January through April 1589 Cervantes was mainly occupied in

winding up his commission. This involved constant shuttling between
Écija and Seville, but much of the time was actually spent in the big city.
It was probably in one of these intervals that he wrote his second *Song of
the Loss of the Armada That Went Against England.* The magnitude of
the disaster had been slowly revealing itself, like a monster uncoiling,
as the ruined ships—fewer than half the number that had set out
from Spain—crept back to Spanish and Portuguese ports. It was all
known finally: the Armada, outgunned and unsupported by the helpless
Parma, forced to flee; the killing voyage home through icy Hebridean
storms; the carnage on the coast of Ireland; the fainting men dying of
dysentery, scurvy, typhus, influenza, of hunger, thirst, cold. Most of this
was known in Seville when, in mid-November, a closely curtained horse
litter at last brought the Duke of Medina-Sidonia back to his rambling
palace among the still green oranges in Sanlúcar de Barrameda to brood
on his disgrace.

Cervantes' lament is a better piece of work than its predecessor, oddly
prosy, perhaps, but full of genuine feeling. Its interest nevertheless lies less
in its poetic virtues than in what it tells us about Cervantes' character
and about the national mood.

Certainly he is speaking with the voice of all Spain when he bids the

> Mother of valiant men of war, archive
> of the warriors of Catholicism,
> crucible in which the love of God is purified . . .
> O Spain, our great mother, see
> where your sons return to your bosom, leaving
> the sea clogged with their misfortunes. . . .
> Open your arms and receive in them those men
> who return confounded but undefeated,
> for there is no forestalling what heaven wills.

The time, he insists, is not for resignation, but for determination.

> Lion, they have trod upon your tail; shake
> off now the mangled tufts, wheel about to seek
> your just revenge for the offense, not yours alone,
> for if it were, you might pardon it, but strike
> for God's honor. . . .

That Philip was planning just such a revenge shows how avidly both
king and people were still sucking at the drying breast of the past. One
account related that, when a horrified secretary broke the news from San-

tander to him, the king said, "I give thanks to God, by whose hand I
have been so endowed that I can put to sea another fleet as great as this
we have lost whenever I choose. It does not matter if a stream is choked,
as long as the source flows freely."[36] The quotation is probably an em-
bellishment of the truth—other reports talk of him as being red-eyed with
weeping—but it accurately communicates his policy.

Despite the illness which had visibly aged him that summer and autumn, Philip asserted that he would indeed build another, stronger, fleet,
if he had to melt down every silver candlestick in the Escorial to finance
it. Before 1588 was out, he was ordering construction of new ships, the
casting of new guns. It was the winds of God, not English cannon or English ships, certainly not the irrationality of the Enterprise itself, which
had become—and largely remains—the official explanation for the upset.
God had punished Spain for her sins, whatever they might have been (so
Mendoza insinuated), but God and Spain were all square now; the country had only to confess, repent and start building and surely this time the
deity would cease His exasperating traffic with the Antichrist and come
home where He belonged.

It has been said that Philip, sobered by the orgastic loss of his fleet,
once again became the Prudent King, planning minutely every detail of
his new Armada with fastidious disregard of the realities of leaping
inflation, surging labor costs, shortages of such essential materials as timber and hemp, made more acute by the success of England's economic
offensive against the Spanish. Famine and national bankruptcy were
again plotting their violence against the nation. God's pedagogy had not
only made the winds to blow for the enemy; it had caused the rain to fall
at the wrong times, making food increasingly scarce in Spain. In Seville,
that spring, religious processions were almost constant in supplication for
good weather; it is not clear whether Cervantes was there on April 19 for
the biggest of them, when the image of Our Lady of the Waters was paraded through the city, but he was there to see God's reply: storms which
demolished fruit crops and filled the hospitals with the sick. There were
reports that the weather-vane statue of Faith atop the Giralda was kept
spinning so hard by the wind that it was twisted off its socket and fell to
the ground. There is something almost ironic, against this background of
wreckage and distress, in the joyous proclamation in the Seville Cathedral
on May 4, 1589, of the gift to the city's cardinal archbishop of a thorn
from Christ's crown.

Many people in the country were aware that something in the imperial
obsession would have to give; impotent appeals from the Cortes that
Philip abandon the Low Countries, cut his losses there, attest to the secret
drought in Spanish hearts. But few thought to question the rightness of

another blow at England. Philip II represented the continuing presence of the glorious past; as long as he was alive, the dryness would remain imminent, but hidden. When he died—but that is another era. In the last decade of his reign, not realizing or not choosing to realize how exhausted they both were, king and country would continue, as economist Martín González de Cellorigo commented in 1600, to live "outside the natural order."[37]

Cervantes, at any rate, was certainly living "outside the natural order" that spring. After a total of 276 days of work, he was back in Seville. In May he drops out of sight. But late in June, with his salary still unpaid,[38] he reappears rolling in cash like a foal in clover and obviously preparing to leave Seville for an extended period.

June 25 was a busy day for him. It began with Tomás Gutiérrez in a notary's office, the first of four Cervantes visited that day, to pay Tomás all the money he owed him in loans, lodging "and other things," a total of 2,160 reales. The arrangement was deliberately complicated. A debt in that amount, the document explains, was owed to Cervantes by one Alonso de Lerma, but "for certain reasons" had been assigned to Gutiérrez. "Although he had not collected the money" from Lerma, Tomás had advanced the sum to Cervantes, who was now reimbursing his generosity. No other money changed hands, but the friends declared themselves satisfied, each discharging the other "forever" of all obligations he may have incurred.

Why all the obfuscation? We do not know who Alonso de Lerma was or whether, if he existed at all, he brought anything other than his name to the transaction. Astrana Marín suggested that Cervantes may have wanted to hide the asset from his creditors. What creditors, other than Gutiérrez? Where and how had he acquired 2,160 reales to lend to anyone?

Act II of the mystery takes place in a second notarial office, where Cervantes offered himself as guarantor for the subrental of several houses in the Magdalena district of Seville by an illiterate woman named Jerónima de Alarcón. The sum involved was appreciable—thirty-five ducats. In the agreement, Cervantes identifies himself as a resident of the same district, the first indication we have that he was no longer living in the palatial guesthouse on the Calle de Bayona, in the Santa María quarter. Why not? Subsequent events tell us that he was still Gutiérrez's friend. Are we to wink knowingly back at the leer from the great-lover school of Cervantine scholarship and suppose that the enterprising Jerónima was his mistress?

Note that one of the witnesses to the arrangement was Cervantes' assistant, Miguel de Santa María, whose bit part here grows to that of a leading role as the action unfolds.

Act III: before still another notary, Santa María gave Cervantes a receipt for the sum of 1,600 silver reales "in advance on the salary owed me as his assistant and companion in the milling of which he had charge."[39] Santa María would not actually collect his wages from Guevara until November 10 of that year. Obviously he needed the money at once, and the likeliest explanation for this is that Jerónima de Alarcón was his responsibility, not Cervantes'. The two men, with weighmaster Salazar, had shared a house for at least three months in Écija and in that time they seem to have grown to like each other. A solvent Cervantes may have offered to help Santa María as he himself had been helped by Gutiérrez.

A final document issued June 26 gives Cervantes' power of attorney (via a fourth notary) to Santa María to collect all debts owed him, not only in money but, the authorization specifies with legalistic panache, also in "jewels, clothing, merchandise, slaves, wine, oil and hens and other things. . . ." In this assignment, in which, as in the settlement with Gutiérrez, he sheds his Sevillian identity to become a resident of Esquivias, he also empowers Santa María to present his accounts to Guevara and to stand for him in any lawsuits that might be brought.

With that, Cervantes vanishes from sight for seven months.

All right: where did the money come from? That ex-soldier, whilom author and commissary-at-liberty Cervantes might have turned a fast four thousand-plus reales on a business deal is, given the economics of that era of sinking profits, not to be considered. And we know too much about the family finances in Madrid and Esquivias to imagine a contribution from home.

Astrana Marín thought he might have won it at cards. While not provable, the proposition is admissible. Gambling was (if we exclude aristocratomania and military adventuring) the national vice. Scholars wrote learned treatises on such sports as *el parar* (like modern monte), *quínola*, *pintas* (Góngora's nemesis, according to Quevedo), *veinte-uno* (twenty-one) and others of the sort. The Spanish spent more money betting on chess, checkers, dice and especially cards than they did on food, despite repeated prohibitions of gaming by a government which was simultaneously picking up fifty thousand ducats a year from its monopoly on the manufacture of playing cards.

Among writers, the fever was epidemic. Góngora squandered his fortune at cards, as Quevedo did a good part of his. Rufo bet the last fifty ducats of the five hundred received from Philip II for *La Austriada* on the turn of a card so that, he explained, "the remnant of my soldiery might win or die fighting rather than be wasted by a long siege."[40] Lope de Vega derides the habit affectionately in Act I of his play *El perro del hortelano:* "May it please heaven that he who gambles never lack for money of one man's or another's," he exclaims, going on to explain:

> In olden times, kings learned
> some skill so that, should they lose
> their country and their kingdom
> in war or on the sea, they knew
> something that would earn their living;
> happy were those who in childhood
> learned to gamble! For in lean times
> gambling is a noble art, one
> that, with little effort, provides
> their sustenance. Why, you will see
> a great painter from his bubbling
> brain create a living image,
> only to have some fool declare
> the thing's not worth ten escudos;
> the gambler, by merely saying
> "no more cards," if luck is his, earns
> a hundred for a hundred bet.

That Cervantes was a gambler and had been since his soldiering days would be silly to deny. The knowledge of card games manifest in his stories is encyclopedic. *Primera,* the poker of the time, was probably his game as it was Falstaff's. ("I never prospered," complains Sir John in Act V of *The Merry Wives of Windsor,* "since I foreswore myself at Primero.") In a broken-worded prefatory poem to *Don Quixote*[41] he uses its scoring system (in which the face cards were lowest in value) to ridicule the coat of arms Lope de Vega bestowed on himself. Further along in the book[42] Altisidora teases the knight in primera terms. The meeting of Rinconete and Cortadillo provides a brief lexicon of cardsharper's jargon. References are made to one Vilhan, a Barcelonan to whom Spanish legend attributes the invention of playing cards. The card shop run by the Frenchman calling himself Pierre Papin in the Calle de Las Sierpes in Seville, one of the busiest of its kind in the world and a rendezvous of the Seville underworld, appears in *Don Quixote*[43] as well as in the play *The Happy Rogue.*

Years later, it is believed, Cervantes would frequent gaming houses run by the wife of merchant-banker Lope García de la Torre in Valladolid and, in Madrid, by his friend and publisher Francisco de Robles at the Puerta de Guadalajara. In Seville in 1589 he would have had some three hundred gaming rooms to choose among, most of them in private houses and many run through seedy front men by aristocratic owners. The city had more casinos than it did churches, although the balance was to some extent restored by the devoted attendance of clerics (real and false) at the tables, where their presence inspired confidence in the pigeons they plucked.

Suppose, then, that it was in one of these chambers that Cervantes made his pile. A question still nags at our imaginations. We have seen him commit or dispose of over four thousand reales in one day; enough was left in his pockets, presumably, to see him in decent, perhaps even splashy, style to his destination. Barring a fantastic run of luck, he did not win that kind of money by starting with the few reales he might logically and legally have had. He would have needed a stake. Where did he get it?

Had Cervantes been as familiar with the Sevillian *hampa*, the underworld, then as he was later, we might wonder if that was where his luck had its roots. Probably not yet. Gutiérrez might have lent it to him. The innkeeper's—pardon! hosteler's—theatrical past had doubtless narcotized his middle-class righteousness about money. But he was a businessman again now anxious to persuade Sevillian respectability to forget about his boisterous past. And businessman Gutiérrez may reasonably have doubted the soundness of investing in the luck of a man, friend though he was, who was already some two thousand reales in debt to him.

Unless we let ourselves become bemused by visions of fat wallets found lying in the street or a sudden access of generosity on the part of the notoriously uncharitable Uncle Andrés, we must consider the possibility that Cervantes, with or without Guevara's knowledge, lifted the money from the government funds at his disposal in Écija.

This can never go further than conjecture, stirred partly on what appears to be Cervantes' effort in his accommodation with Gutiérrez to disguise the source of his money. It can be objected that, if the royal auditors found nothing criminal to charge to his record, why should we, with the meager documentary remnants we have, presume to reopen the books. The possibility nevertheless existed. No one will ever know into how many hidden streams the millions of maravedis from Madrid finally seeped. The opportunities for rigging accounts made the operation an embezzler's dream. In this case, the sum involved would have been trifling, probably no more than a few hundred reales, and the motives understandable. Cervantes had been doing a dirty job under odious conditions to earn money which seemed to land perversely in every pocket but his own. He conceivably was not in a mood to haggle over money he could feel was rightfully if not, strictly speaking, lawfully his.

Yet, as we struggle ludicrously to impose logic on life, we remind ourselves that this single aberration in what was demonstrably an otherwise honorable record is just as inexplicable as the puzzle over a pocketful of silver coins. It seems somehow more reasonable to believe that after all, Cervantes came by his windfall in some now unaccountable but reputable way. We are left, at the end, to reflect on Goethe's observation that one acquires everything from solitude except character.

26

"Full of Care, yet Nonchalant"

In the opening scene of Cervantes' interlude *The Faithful Sentinel,* a tattered soldier and a down-at-heels sacristan boast of their attentions to Cristina the upstairs maid. The hapless trooper offers his clincher:

> The other day I sent her a love note written, if you please, on the back of a petition I gave His Majesty outlining my services and my present needs (for the soldier who admits he's poor has nothing to be ashamed of). The petition was approved and passed on to the Chief Almoner. But, scornful of the fact that the document was worth four to six reales,* my incredible generosity and remarkable nonchalance prompted me to write my letter, as I say, on the back.

In a petition submitted, probably by his sister Magdalena, to the Council of the Indies dated May 21, 1590, to which were joined his military service record and the Algiers *Información,*

> Miguel de Cervantes Saavedra says he has served Your Majesty many years in the campaigns on sea and land which have occurred in the past twenty-two years,[1] especially in the Naval Battle, in which he received many wounds, including the loss of a hand from a harquebus ball. And the following year he was at Navarino and later in the action at Tunis and La Goleta. And en route to this Court with letters from my lord Don Juan and from the Duke of Sessa so that Your Majesty might show him favor he was captured in the galley *Sol,* he and his brother, who also served Your Majesty in the same campaigns, and they were taken to Algiers, where they spent such heritage as they had

* That is, the value of the paper it was written on.

in ransoming themselves, along with their parents' whole estate and the dowries of two maiden sisters, who were impoverished through ransoming their brothers. And after their liberation, they served Your Majesty in the Kingdom of Portugal and in the Terceiras (Azores) with the Marquis of Santa Cruz, and are even now serving Your Majesty, one of them as an alférez[2] in Flanders and (the other) Miguel de Cervantes, was the one who brought the letters and information from the Mayor of Mostaganem and went to Oran on Your Majesty's orders; and since then he has served in Seville on business of the Armada, under the orders of Antonio de Guevara, as stated in his records. And in all that time no favor whatsoever has been granted him. He requests and beseeches as humbly as he can that Your Majesty be pleased to favor him with *a post in the Indies*,[3] one of these being the comptrollership of the new Kingdom of Granada, or the governorship of the province of Soconusco in Guatemala, or auditor of the galleys of Cartagena,[4] or corregidor of the city of La Paz; for he will fulfill any of those offices Your Majesty might grant him because he is an able and competent man and deserving of Your Majesty's favor and because his wish is to continue to serve Your Majesty always and to end his life in it as his forebears have (sic), for in it he will receive great favor and reward.

Scribbed above Cervantes' signature is a notation by a council member: "Let him look closer to home for such favor as may be granted him."

"Did you send her anything else?" the sacristan asks the Faithful Sentinel.

"Sighs, tears, sobs, paroxysms, swoons. . . ."

Cervantes had left Seville at the end of June 1589, probably (where else would he have gone?) for Madrid via Esquivias. We lost track of him until February 12, 1590, when he reappears in Carmona, near Seville, with a commission from Guevara's substitute, Miguel de Oviedo, to find four thousand arrobas of oil there. In the interim, he may reasonably be supposed to have discussed his situation with Catalina, consulted with Guevara in the capital, enlisted his sisters' sympathy. If he did any writing, we are unaware of it. The impression is strong in this period of a man adrift, the feeling that breathes in a poem later reproduced in *Don Quixote*,[5] the one beginning "I am a mariner of love," which was set to music by Salvador Luis in 1591 and may have been written at this period:

> I am following a star
> I can see from afar,
> I know not where it's leading me,
> and so I sail bewildered on,
> my soul watching it intently,
> full of care, yet nonchalant. . . .

He has left no record of when he began thinking of his petition. News of the vacant offices in America would have reached Spain with the dispatch boat in the late summer or early fall of 1589. He could have heard about them in Madrid, but, if so, why did he let so many months go by before applying for them? It is more likely that he knew nothing of them until his return to Seville, where such news was common knowledge within hours of the boat's arrival.

"Refuge and haven of the desperate in Spain, swindlers' sanctuary, safe-conduct of murderers, protection and shelter of the gamblers called *sharpers* by the practitioners of the art, ruse of loose women, false lure to many and personal salvation of the few." America! It was in Seville that Carrizales, the Jealous Extremaduran, had hit bottom and took ship for the Indies to recoup his wasted fortune; it was from Seville that Mateo Alemán would realize his Guzmán de Alfarache's curse on the world by sailing to oblivion and an unrecorded death.

That Cervantes would petition for important posts in the Indies, and these posts particularly, is a measure not of his quixotry, as has (predictably) been suggested, but of his desperation. It is hard to believe he invested any serious hope in his application. These were profitable offices and they were bought and sold for thousands of ducats—often repeatedly, if the bids were high enough—to men expected to milk them for thousands more. In a monarchy strapped for cash, paying up to 70 per cent of its budget to service its debts, money was the key to advancement.

And what training had Cervantes for comptrollerships and auditorships, other than his primitive accounting for paper and ink and locksmiths and hired help to shovel rotting wheat out of the rain? What legal training, except his constant bickering with officialdom, qualified him to function as a corregidor, which was a lawyer's job? Hindsight may give a graceless tone to the notation that he look closer to home for favor—that, in effect, he stay where he was and not grow too big for his britches—but this was business and Cervantes may have expected just that kind of response. At best he might have hoped the petition would generate some kind of fallout, perhaps lead to a slightly less antipathetic office than the one he held. But no, not even that.

Carmona, then, and the ritual protests of municipal poverty, all too justified by the previous year's crop failures. So far, Cervantes' only traceable contribution to the war effort had been 2,002 arrobas of Écijano oil put aboard the Atlantic escort squadron. But only nine farmers in Carmona were disposed to help the commissary improve his showing, try as he might to find a method of painless extraction. After two weeks of futile negotiation, he was forced to expand the search to Écija and other towns. If he salvaged anything from the experience, it may have been the finished version of "The Captive's Tale," which some critics think was written around this time. The beauteous Moorish renegade Zoraida, who absconds with Captain Ruy Pérez de Viedma in the story (and repeats the stunt with Don Lope in *The Dungeons of Algiers*) was a living presence in Carmona. The town was then the home in exile of the "Black Prince" Muley Malek, the dethroned poet-Sultan of Morocco who had been made a grandee of Spain by Philip II after his conversion to Christianity. In Cervantes' play "Muley Maluco" appears as Zoraida's betrothed and a generally admirable fellow,

> a famous Moor,
> and in his sect and wicked law
> well versed and most devout;
> he knows the language of the Turks,
> speaks Spanish and German as well,
> and Italian and French, sleeps
> in a bed and eats at table
> seated in the Christian manner;
> above all he's a great soldier,
> generous, wise and cool-headed,
> adorned with a thousand virtues.[6]

The fictional Zoraida may in fact have been a blend of the real one—who was, as Cervantes described her, the daughter of "Agimurato" (Haji Murad) and a legendary beauty, but who never left Algiers—and a feminized version of the newly baptized Prince Philip of Africa who Cervantes might have seen, though probably never addressed, in the streets of Carmona.

By early April 1590, Cervantes was out of work again. He had a little money: 400 reales had been borrowed, at a usurious rate of interest payable in advance, from Diego de Zufre, one of Guevara's custodians of supplies and paymaster of the king's galleys in Andalusia. Zufre agreed to recover the money from Guevara out of the salary owed Cervantes. One hundred eighty more came from the commissary general on May 18 to cover Cervantes' work in Carmona. Cash on hand: between 550 and 600 reales; balance still owed him by his reckoning: 3,312 reales. The 500—or

438—reales paid him in July 1588 was apparently forgotten. On July 14 he assigned a power of attorney to his wife, whom he described as a resident of Madrid (which she was not), and his sister Magdalena to collect any monies owed him.

Cervantes, apparently, was not a practical man with a real. Early in July, he is to be found in company with Agustín de Cetina at an auction in Seville. This is one of the rare moments in which, through the trail dust and the haze of wheat chaff and screen of legal documents, glints the life of Cervantes the private man. He could pass up the plate put on the block; the paintings and sculptures seem not to have tempted him, perhaps because they were too costly. But the late Father Jerónimo de Herrera, whose possessions were being sold for the benefit of the Seville Cathedral chapter, had been a bibliophile, and when his books came up for auction, Cervantes bit. A record exists of his purchase of *"cuatro libritos dorados, de letra francesa,"* four small books in gilt bindings in French—in *French?*—for eighteen reales.[7] On the following day he acquired a *Life of St. Dominic* for a whacking thirty reales, nearly three ducats. How expensive these volumes were can be judged from the fact that, fifteen years later, Part One of *Don Quixote,* a fat, 332-folio book, would sell at retail for only eight and one half reales.

That he was specially devoted to St. Dominic, the founder of the Inquisition about which Cervantes has nothing good to say in print, is doubtful; surely it was that thirty-real binding which dazzled him. Just as surely as those four little books in French seduced him with the gleam of gilt on fine leather. There is not a scrap of evidence that Cervantes could read the language; if he had been able to, he would not have been up to keeping the achievement to himself, but not a single French phrase joins the rabble of Latin and Italian hangers-on in his writing.

And why does a man so poor he will shortly have to borrow the money for a decent suit of clothes spend nearly half the amount of that loan on books which, as far as content was concerned, meant little or nothing to him? Booklovers will understand; he will be understood by those who have ever hungered for a flash of gold in a dreary room, something of beauty with which to disguise an unbeautiful life.

Once more, in August, we catch a glimpse of this unofficial man in the company of Juan Martínez Montañés, the sculptor who may have been a distant relative of his. Martínez was twenty-two then, not yet the majestic figure praised by Valáquez, "the god of wood" who would renew the moribund school of Sevillian religious sculpture for such disciples as Juan de Mena and Alonso Cano.

On August 27 Martínez formally accepted a commission from a Portuguese, Alonso Antunez, to carve a figure of a dying Christ, about eighteen inches high, in cypress wood, for a price to be settled later by arbitration. One of the witnesses to the contract was Cervantes, describing himself for some reason as a native of Córdoba then resident in the Santa María district—that is, he was back on credit in the hostel on the Calle de Bayona. Cervantes may have found the Portuguese among Gutiérrez's silver salvers; it may have been he who, learning that the man was in the market for a not-too-expensive statue to take back to Portugal, had led him to the studio on what is now the Calle de O'Donnell. Whether he received a finder's commission is not recorded.

On the same day, Cervantes turned in his final accounts for wheat collected and milled in Écija in 1587–88, along with a pay claim for 112,608 maravedis. He is short 24,594 maravedis (723 reales) in his reckoning, he reports—no explanation seems to have been needed—so the actual salary owed him is 88,014 maravedis (2,589 reales). (In fact, the claim probably should have come to 82,008 maravedis.) The statement, he swears in the ritual formula, is free of "fraud, deceit or deception of any kind. . . ."

The king's auditors were not so sure. They challenged his figures on a milling operation—the mix-up would later be straightened out—and reduced the salary balance to 55,222 maravedis.

It must be remembered that the presumption of fraud or incompetence on the commissaries' part was automatic in Madrid, partly because they so frequently occurred and, too, because no one alive was capable of making complete sense of the state's finances then. Investigation by Special Commissioner Hernando de Alcázar had already found glaring evidence of grand larceny among some of Guevara's closest subordinates; one by one, they were being ushered into the prison at Puerto de Santa María where Alcázar had his headquarters. Among them was Cervantes' moneylender, Diego de Zufre. Guevara himself had been fired and, although nothing but poor management had been attributed to him so far, he was being held under virtual house arrest until the inquiry was over. To take his place, Philip had named Pedro de Isunza, a Basque who had amassed a private fortune in business in the Netherlands and who had now come home to enjoy it. Isunza was in no hurry to assume his duties, however, obviously preferring to wait until the investigators had cleaned out the nest of thieves in Andalusia. In the meanwhile, commissariat operations were at a standstill; the treasury was harrying commissaries to bring their accounts up to date and fine-combing the figures for error . . . or worse.

Accordingly, on October 7 Cervantes submitted his statement on oil requisitioned in 1588 and began to ponder the inevitability of having to go to Madrid in person to settle the business. The administration expected its functionaries to appear periodically, at their own expense no matter how far they had to travel. Cervantes, it seems, had more to consider than travel costs alone. For while it was all very well to protect that "a monk is not made by his habit, and a soldier made ragged in war is as honorable as a student who wears a tattered gown to show how long he has been studying,"[8] the fact was that he could not show up at court without a new suit of clothes.

His credit rating had declined, however, from the time a year ago when he had stood surety for Jerónima de Alarcón. On November 8 he bought ten ducats' worth of cheap, sturdy cloth on credit; Gutiérrez guaranteed the loan in a bond signed before no fewer than four notaries, enough manpower to certify the national debt.

But when the time came to make the trip, Cervantes apparently found he could not face it. He was broke. He may have suspected that, with his head for figures, he could not have argued convincingly with a trained accountant. Anyway the thing was unpleasant. On December 3 he authorized Guevara's secretary, Juan Seron, to appear for him and obtain approval of his accounts. The decision spared Cervantes the ordeal of having to explain himself again to his family and friends. It meant not seeing Catalina and that was too bad.

Irritation on behalf of Doña Catalina is not habitual among Cervantists, most of them male and all satisfied by their notion of the appropriateness of woman's martyrdom to genius. The very emptiness of the record concerning her points up how bleak her life must have been in the big, bare house in Esquivias, alone except for her two young brothers and her servants—a world circumscribed by chats with aging Uncle Juan and appearances at the village baptisms at which, sadly, she was increasingly a fixture. It was in 1590 that she joined the wealthy new Sisterhood of the Most Holy Sacrament. Chastity was among the virtues recommended to the sisters, a provision she might be pardoned for accepting with some bitterness. Membership would help to structure her busily formless existence, and it would reinforce the social position her husband's conduct was doubtless eroding.

"And how do you know, my lord, that Periandro is not married?" the Princess Sinforosa asks her father. Why, replies the king, "that he is not I judge from seeing him roam through foreign lands, a thing intolerable to close marriage. . . ."[9]

What *was* her husband up to? He was living. Being free. Watching. Seville's theaters were busy and even Cervantes could have scraped up the half-real entrance fee. A number of literary academies were functioning; it is safe to assume that he frequented the one led by Juan de Arguijo, whom he praised in the *Voyage to Parnassus*.[10] Along with most of the poets of his day, however, Cervantes probably passed most of his time exploring the lower world of the pícaros.

The picaresque world had its own geography, marked by such way stations as the fishermen's quarter called the Perchel in Málaga, the Olivera

354 CERVANTES: A BIOGRAPHY

in central Valencia, the Ventillas in Toledo. But Seville, the country's richest and most show-off city, was its capital. An anonymous romance of the *germania*—the word describes both the "brotherhood" of the underworld and its slang—tells of a rogue who

> came fleeing from Seville,
> which is the Cyprus of the brave,
> for I know not what foolishness:
> robberies, thefts and murders.[11]

The names of the thieves' courts of Seville ring through Cervantes' stories like challenges: the Compás, Triana, the Alamillo, the Corral de los Olmos. The education of an accomplished *pícaro* began on the steps of the Seville Cathedral, where Cortadillo filches the sacristan's lace handkerchief. It is a world worth peering into.

The *picaresca* formed the inferno of that vast Cervantine universe of the dispossessed where humanity is seen at its nakedest and thus at its most legible. It was in that turbulent area of reconnaissance between conventional society and its marginalia—its thieves, ex-officio saints, madmen, false prophets, whores, Gypsies, prodigal sons, Moriscos, peasants sly and starveling, disaffected intellectuals, Jews, corrupt officials and pietistic hags—that he built a shelter of personal values to live in. Cervantes and his universe, inseparable as the rock from the mountain, comment on each other and on the "real" world around them.

It was an increasingly tilted world they saw. The symptoms of incipient social sickness visible in the two preceding decades developed from the 1590s onward into a wasting disease. A tax load further weighted by the strain of Philip's wars against England and Holland, and soon to be saddled with war against France as well, pressed ever more cruelly on the poor; such imposts as the *millones*, an excise tax on staple goods, fell chiefly on food (meat, oil, wine) by the end of the century. Decrees such as that giving Mesta members permanent rights of tenancy over any field in which they chose to pasture their livestock destroyed whole farming communities, cut the output of food in a country beset by periodic famines, reduced the national tax base, spurred the inflation which multiplied prices by a then unprecedented 400 per cent in a century. The polarization of Spanish society into a small, wealthy aristocracy and an impoverished mass of workers and peasants deprived industry of the consumer public it needed for growth; with profits dwindling, taxes oppressive and foreign competition so severe that imported goods were often cheaper in Spain than domestically produced items, bankruptcies increased and unemployment soared.

That Philip II and his successors were aware of the public discontent can be gathered, for example, from the growing profusion of sumptuary laws they decreed. These were not, as might be supposed, aimed at instilling a sense of wholesome restraint into prodigal aristocratic souls. They were aimed primarily at the poor. The attempt (unsuccessful) to limit the number of dishes served at meals in wealthy houses to a basic three meat courses was not designed to protect the rich from the sin of gluttony, but to shield them from the violence of the hungry poor who subsisted on a steady diet of bread, oil, garlic and onions. Mostly, the laws —like the decree forbidding artisans to wear aristocratic silk and the measure making it a crime for whores to ride in coaches—were designed to keep the classes visibly distinct. In "this vale of tears, this evil world of ours where hardly anything can be found untainted by villainy, deceit and roguery,"[12] there was no honor for the poor. Ruined peasants streamed to the big-city slums to compete with the urban poor. A few crashed the exclusive ranks of the hampa, the hard criminal core of this underworld; most overflowed into the huge demimonde of the picaresca.

For in this hermetic, authoritarian society, the poor were voting, pointlessly but savagely. Crime now came to represent the aspirations to social justice of a people denied any other means to express them or any organic channel for achieving it. The pícaro was by popular definition a rebel. Some were. Others were merely the refuse discarded by any civilization. "Oh filthy, fat and shining kitchen rogues," Cervantes bellows in *The Illustrious Serving Wench*, "imposters of poverty, pretenders of paralysis, purse-snatchers in the Zocodover or the Plaza de Madrid, prayermongers feigning blindness, errand boys of Seville, ragtag of the hampa and all that innumerable swarm enclosed in the name pícaro!" They shared a guiding philosophy: survive in an unjust world, since, as Alemán's Guzmán de Alfarache assures us, everyone steals, everyone lies and cheats and all are proud of it. In a society of misfits, the pícaro embraced his misshapenness; in a world of the uprooted, he wandered deliberately, stopping occasionally, briefly, working sometimes, scrounging, but always moving on, refusing to subside into the inertia of docile poverty. In a country where labor brought no reward but social disgrace, he lived by his wits, as scornful of work as any lord.

Students were regular recruits to the picaresca. Many sent by relatively poor families to work their way through the schools toward better lives developed a taste for the "free" life and a neo-aristocratic disdain for manual labor. We see them everywhere in Cervantes' stories, from the merry "wizard" in *The Salamanca Cave* to the pseudo-captives in the *Persiles* whose make-believe adventures in Algiers are treated with fatherly disapproval by the author. With them came the rich men's sons looking for thrills and a reprieve from the serious business of conformist adulthood. Diego de Carriazo is one of these and, until love herds him back into respectability as the husband of the Illustrious Serving Wench, he revels in the life. He was "so pleased with this free life," Cervantes tells us, "that despite the discomfort and the poverty it entails, he did not regret the abundance of his father's house, nor did walking tire him, or the cold disturb him, or the heat irritate him; to him, all the seasons of the year were mild and gentle springtimes; he slept as well in a haystack as on a mattress. . . . So well did the pícaro's life suit him that he could have been a professor in the famous Alfarache's university."

Delight in this life of creative unproductivity is expressed again and again in the literature of the period. Guzmán, despite his anathema against a universe which had decreed that he be poor and others not, could nevertheless exclaim: "Oh twice, thrice and fourfold happy thou who rise when you will in the morning, not having to care about serving or being served, free to keep what you have without fear of losing it . . . with nothing to pay, nor anyone to answer to. . . ."[13] To which the whore La Pizpita (the Wagtail) breathes a cheerful amen in Cervantes' *The Widowed Ruffian;* "it's better to have God's help," she observes, "than to be an early riser." The true pícaro saw separation from this good life as an exploratory trip to purgatory. This Lagartija (Little Lizard) in the Mexican monastery where, as Friar Antonio, he still serves the reformed pícaro Lugo. Admonished to fast for the good of his soul, he complains in Act II of *The Happy Rogue* that when he does

> I feel rotten,
> listless, undevout and moody.
> Of another cut and fashion
> was I in Seville when I was
> your sidekick. . . . Would I were now
> a proper pimp in Seville,
> with two mares out to pasture
> and maybe even three, all trained
> in the arts of mischief.

A modern Spanish historian, wondering whether the picaresca could have flourished anywhere else as it did in Spain, concludes that it could not have because, alone in Europe, "we lacked in a bourgeois conscience capable of offering an ideal of life other than the heroic ideal and its picaresque reverse."[14] Picaresque society, then, is not to be viewed as a counterculture. It was an inversion, a reconstitution of the "decent" society in which the pícaro had failed to find his place; its aspirations mimicked those of normal life and its structure was a deadly parody of conventional society. It had its trade associations, its guilds, students, artists, solidery, even its "universities" and its "military orders of knighthood."

The innkeeper who knights Don Quixote boasts that "in his salad days he had given himself to that honorable office (of knight-errantry), wandering through divers parts of the world in search of adventure . . . where he had exercised the fleetness of his feet and the quickness of his hands doing many wrongs, wooing many widows, dishonoring sundry maidens and tricking the odd minor and, in sum, making a name for himself in all the courts, criminal and civil, to be found in Spain."[15]

If the cathedral steps in Seville were a pícaro's grade school, matriculation led to the Corral de los Olmos—the Elmyard—placed conveniently close to the church's east door to allow fugitives to dive quickly into sanctuary behind the chains surrounding the steps. It was also so close to the cathedral's Court of Oranges that the two enclosures were said to form "the two cloisters" of the church. Since the universities were organized around cloistered patios as well, the image is picked up by a pander in Salas Barbadillo's novel *Wise Estacio* who explains that he is "a graduate of the Corral de los Olmos, which is the Salamanca of our germanía." Had he chosen to continue into higher studies, he would have progressed to Cervantes' childhood playground in the Córdoban Plaza del Potro, where, "after having been a student, a page, a soldier," Estebanillo González "lacked only this degree for my doctorate in the calling I professed."[16] The summit of a pícaro's occupational training was achieved if he emerged intact and respected from Zahara de los Atunes, an Atlantic fishing port up the coast from Algeciras. This, reports Cervantes, was "the world's end of the picaresca." And he advises: "Do not call yourselves pícaros if you have not taken two courses in the tuna-fishing academy. There, the dirt is clean, the fat roly-poly, hunger quick, satiety abundant, undisguised by vice; gambling is ceaseless, rows sporadic, death lurks from moment to moment, there is a coarse jest at every step, dancing as though it were a wedding, *seguidillas*[17] as in the prints, refrains in the romances and the poetry unfettered. Here they sing, there they swear great oaths, farther along they brawl or gamble, and anything at all is stolen. There is freedom's altar, lighting this world's work; it is there that many rich fathers or their servants go to seek their sons—and find them, and these are as desolate to be torn from that life as though they were going to their death."[18]

On the lowest level of the scale were the beggars, the official ones "licensed" by their parish priests and thus given legal status, and the freelance mendicants, some 150,000 altogether throughout the country. Above them were the blind who sold prayers to a regular clientele; they were grouped in municipally authorized associations which fulfilled the duties of sick members, cared for them through their illnesses and, if they recovered, saw to it that their customers were returned to them. That prayer-mongering was not an honest man's trade may be judged from the dialogue in Act I of *The Happy Rogue,* when the not yet saintly Lugo calls:

	Hey there! Blind man, thou good man.
BLIND MAN:	Who calls me?
LUGO:	Take thou this real, and for it say seventeen prayers, one after the other for the souls which are in purgatory.
BLIND MAN:	Gladly, sir, and I will do my best to say them devoutly and with clarity.
LUGO:	See thou neither gobble them nor tailor snippets from them.

From there it was just a step to the picaresca proper, a huge floating population of servants like Guzmán de Alfarache, who fed their friends in their masters' kitchens and sold off the less conspicuous of their masters' goods; sneak-thief errand boys (the jumping-off place, as Rinconete and Cortadillo found, for higher achievement in crime); vendors of the stripe of Estebanillo González, who hawked everything from "imported" soap made from scraps of refuse on the banks of the Guadalquivir to "sandalwood" toothpicks of smoked Spanish ash; pimps and whoremasters, the special field of ex-soldiers like Estebanillo and Alonso de Contreras; the unemployed and the underemployed who drifted into the swamp because there, at least, there were no explanations to make, no apologies to offer, no standards to meet. This was the province, too, of the street hustlers, the tavern lizards; Loaysa, the devil incarnate in *The Jealous Extremaduran,* is one of these and we meet him clothed in the flamboyant finery of his kind: fawn-colored taffeta breeches worn wide, sailor-fashion, taffeta doublet decorated with gold embroidery, fawn-colored satin cap and starched lace-and-cutwork ruff. Cervantes does not tell us that the edges of this plumage are dark with grime, but we imagine them to be.

The flimflam artists and professional gamblers, operating in houses often run by invalided soldiers—the kind who, in modern Spain, would be put to selling tickets in the national lottery—constituted the minor gentry of the hampa. Such specimens were lower in rank than the ducal burglars, robbers, highwaymen, the "apostles" who, like St. Peter, were never without their bunch of keys, and the "satyrs" who rustled livestock.

The stupidest and bravest villains formed the true aristocracy of the hampa, the bravos (*valentones*) and the professional killers (*matones*). In them we find the crowning burlesque of the conventional ideal, the warrior ethic of the Reconquest by which the country was, if uneasily now, still possessed. They lived by courage and swordsmanship and they took their trade seriously; they were arrogant, cold-eyed men who wore broad-brimmed hats and buffalo-hide doublets over coats of mail and had swords longer than the law allowed stuck in their wide sashes. Reputations for *valentía*, bravery, were carefully cultivated; these were the people, noted Espinel's Marcos de Obregón, "who did not seem to be Christians, nor Moors, nor Gentiles, but whose religion consists in adoring the goddess Valor."[19] What did it matter that the "Moors" they slew were the husbands of discontented wives, rich old men who refused to die soon enough to settle their heirs' debts, cowards eager to avenge their slighted honor on the point of a thug's sword? What difference did it make that these robber barons went to war to steal purses instead of a weaker neighbor's land? The objective, they reckoned, was the same: aristocratization through aggression. They allied themselves in orders as difficult to crash as the Order of Calatrava. It was among these warrior princes, probably, that the notion of honor among thieves took on its full meaning: honor, not honesty, obedience to the same code of personal honor to which the aristocracy paid such bloody service in Lope's plays. A bravo could be cheated, fooled, bilked, hanged, this was all part of the process of existence, but heaven help the man who reflected slightly on his courage or failed to address him with the proper respect.

The hampa had its heroes, whose memories were revered as fervently as those of the Cid and the Great Captain. In the *Buscón*, Quevedo recounts the martyrdom of one of these in a romance as simple and touching as a flamenco couplet:

> Pero Vázquez de Escamilla,
> that glory of swordsmanship,
> died of the rope sickness
> encircled by policemen.

Both Cervantes and Quevedo knew Alonso Álvarez de Sória, the François Villon of the Sevillian hampa. It may have been he who taught them the ancient trick of writing the broken-footed verse used in the preface to *Don Quixote,* in which the final syllables in a line are omitted for no discernible reason yet discovered. Álvarez's last poem was written shortly before his death of the same rope sickness that had carried off Pero Vázquez:

> Three hours of life they give me,
> those who would escort me to death,
> and since the road is a long one,

they press for an early departure. . . .
Ah, how brief a time it is!
Who owes so much can never pay but little![20]

The insistence in picaresque literature on official corruption helps explain the disillusionment of the age. Honest policemen are as scarce as
lemons in Lapland. The cop in *The Dogs' Colloquy,* who works with a
prostitute to fleece foreign sailors, has "pretensions to being a terror" and
he "maintained his bravery with no danger to his person but at great cost
to his purse." In *The Happy Rogue,* a constable swears he is "blind and
mute" where the hampa is concerned. Some of the choicest expletives in
the picaresque vocabulary were reserved for the Santa Hermandad—the
Holy Brotherhood—the centuries-old rural constabulary which by the
late sixteenth century was known as little better than a corps of
uniformed thieves. By putting the words in a "madman's" mouth, Cervantes is able to fume at them as a "filthy and low-born rabble," an "infamous brood" of "vile and low intelligence . . . pack of thieves . . . not
troopers but highwaymen licensed by the Holy Brotherhood."[21]

Rinconete is "shocked by the law's laxity" in Seville, "where such per-
nicious and perverse people" as Monipodio and his gang "can live almost
openly." A pícaro in *The Illustrious Serving Wench* complains of the
Court of Puñonrostro† who "has a devil in him" because he has "swept
Seville and the whole country for ten leagues around it clear of valiants;
not a thief ventures into his jurisdiction." A more frequently encountered
type was Don Alonso Nuño de Castro, the Mesta magistrate who helped
the governor of the Valladolid prison to rape an inmate, supplemented
his considerable fortune by selling the goods his agents confiscated, took
bribes to let prisoners spend their nights at liberty, forced peasants to tend
his vines under threat of false imprisonment, etc., etc. [22]

While the picaresca was poking its thousand malicious fingers into the
ribs of conventional society, it was absorbing an astonishing amount of
Spanish artists' moral energy. It would be exaggerated to identify the
proliferation of picaresque novels the age produced as protest literature in
the sense we understand today. Their primary objective was literary, not
social. It is nevertheless true that the best of them were written by men
with outraged social consciences; they were expressions—incidentally—of
anger at the malfunctioning of society as viewed through the picaresca.
There was no conscious protest against authority. The feeling was rather
that the country had gone out of harmony with God's machinery. The
new wave of devotional literature coming off Spanish presses in the 1590s
indicates a national mood of confessional anxiety. But what were these

† He really existed; the name literally means "Fist in the Face."

sins? Libertinism, corruption, self-indulgence, lack of dedication, of gravity. The sins of the picaresca.

To Espinel, to Estebanillo González, Contreras, life was a contest in which survival was good and defeat was evil. By and large, for all their talent, these writers do little more than flit over their world, hungry birds wheeling above an empty landscape. Only two, Cervantes and Alemán, fulfilled the grand artistic function of creating a world as momentous and complex as the real world around them.

While Alemán's book will be considered in its place, it is useful to bear in mind how different these two men were in their attitudes toward life and how unique Cervantes' accomplishment was. The terrain over which Guzmán de Alfarache stumbles is a battlefield of stunted trees and crippled bodies. The Creator is indicted for fraud for confecting a worthless humanity and giving it the illusion of divinity. There is nothing to do in Alemán's universe but to suffer, survive—why?—and perish. Triumph consists in the ability to kick life in the teeth before you go, knowing as you do so that life will never feel the blow.

Cervantes' stare was just as unwavering, just as candid, but it remains indulgent, sadly affectionate, the look of an errant world's best friend. Where his contemporaries created symbols, puppets, as gorgeously wooden as religious statuary, his people appear to us as real creatures in all their corrupt nobility, the people of the Fall and the Promise. He too found in the picaresca the defiant presence of evil, to be battled by Quixote and redeemed, as for Carriazo in *The Illustrious Serving Wench,* as for Don Juan de Carcamo in *The Little Gypsy Girl,* by humility and love and the miracle of poetry.

Whether Cervantes was a pícaro in fact as well as in spirit, he showed no profit from his year of idleness. We know that on March 22, 1590, he paid the ten ducats he owed for cloth, but we can assume that he lived mostly on credit, primarily Gutiérrez's. Finally, on March 12, 1591, he persuaded surrogate paymaster Juan de Tamayo to pay him his salary arrears more or less in full: 110,400 maravedis. Like almost all the arithmetic of Cervantes' functionary career, the figure makes little sense. It was 2,208 maravedis short of his total claim (112,608), but it was far above the 88,014 he had claimed in his statement of August 27, 1590, and even that figure is of questionable accuracy.

The money could not have gone far; probably most of it went to pay his debts. When operations started up again under Pedro de Isunza, Cervantes accepted a commission to distrain wheat in the area around Jaén. His reputation for honesty seems not to have suffered from the wave of arrests which was rapidly filling the small, scabrous prison in the town of Puerto de Santa María. In a letter to the king dated January 7, 1592, Isunza described Cervantes as one of the group around him who "were honorable men and highly trustworthy." There was an edge of sincerity on the ritual recommendation this time; because of the scandals surrounding Guevara and his officers, Isunza was making a great display of scrupulousness not only in choosing his men, but in cleaning out the mare's-nest his predecessor had bequeathed him. Despite his efforts, the scandal uncovered by royal inspectors was taken by the towns as an incitement to resist the commissaries openly, thus making collections all but impossible.

Nor had the atmosphere been lightened by a blunder made in the fall of 1591 by Cervantes' new assistant, Nicolás Benito, who had been sent to the village of Teba in search of grain. He found it in a royal granary (one of those used to store grain for distribution in times of famine) and had summoned the official in charge of it, a minor magistrate named Salvador de Toro, to surrender the contents to him. Toro naturally refused, whereupon Benito, with more zeal than discretion, forced the doors and seized a quantity of barley which he immediately sent off for processing.

Toro seems to have been one of those incendiary, officious men who reveled in lawsuits, but he reacted to the seizure at first with no more than normal belligerency, laying a compensation claim against Isunza's office for 645,563 maravedis. Unaccountably, Isunza ignored it; probably he thought Toro was just one more irate peasant bawling for his money. Toro jumped to the conclusion that "his" grain had been milled into a private profit for Isunza; since Cervantes' signature was on the distrainment order Benito had waved in Teba, the magistrate's suspicion blanketed commissary and assistant as well. He was being injudicious, but his "insight" was doubtless stimulated by the disclosure coming out of Puerto de Santa María. Without investigation of any kind, he took his case to Madrid.

How much Cervantes knew of this until he returned to Seville in late May 1592 is open to question. All we can surmise is that he was broke again; he had collected part of his pay in January, but he had lent Benito more than half of it in salary and expenses which he still had not recovered. He managed to dislodge another nugget of cash, six hundred reales, on May 29, but this was the last payment he was to see for four months. He was averaging fourteen ducats a month in income now, a rate at which no muleteer, no water vendor, would have consented to work.

July 14 found Cervantes, probably ill—a document that day was drawn up in Gutiérrez's hostel rather than in the notary's office—still petitioning for funds. He knew now that he and Isunza were in trouble. Toro, infuriated by the commissary general's bad manners, had asked for royal authority to slap a lien on Isunza's personal possessions, hinting to treasury officials of more dirty work in Seville. Permission was granted June 15 and a notice to that effect probably reached Seville at the end of the month.

Cervantes would spend most of the rest of 1592 trying to keep from being ground up in the official machine. On August 5, apparently still confined to his room, he formally affirmed his responsibility for sending Benito to Teba. At about the same time, he was informed that part of his Écija expense claim had been disallowed by the king's auditors, making him 27,046 maravedis short in his accounts. The mistake was the auditors', not Cervantes', but it was months before the fact emerged. The sum was not huge, but it was more than he had. The treasury did not wait for him to find it; on August 18 it collected the money from Cervantes' guarantors in Écija.

If he did not have seventy-five ducats with which to satisfy the treasury's demands, neither, presumably, did he have one hundred ducats with which to guarantee a merchant's transaction. Yet we see him, from his sickbed, doing just that on August 5. This was not just any transaction, however, and the merchant was a very special figure in Cervantes' past. This was Juan Fortuny, the Valencian to whom Doña Leonor had sold the export license to help pay for Cervantes' ransom, the same man who had fed, clothed and housed him during the two months he spent in Valencia on his return from Algiers, the Fortuny who had advanced four thousand escudos of his own money to help ransom Fray Jorge del Olivar. Fortuny, it is true, was a commission man, exacting a fee for his efforts on behalf of the captives he helped. But he earned his money: negotiating with the Algerians was risky; advancing funds to captives— even those of good credit standing—was equally risky. It was with one of these that he now had to deal. One Antonio Centeno, a knight of the Order of St. John, had welched on more than four thousand reales owed the merchant in ransom money and other loans which Fortuny was trying to recover. By law, he had to present a guarantor before he could press his claim. This function Cervantes filled. Of course, Fortuny was good for the money, provided that he escaped all the sudden disasters to which sixteenth-century traders everywhere were subject, and the possibly fatal ones attendant on prolonged dealings in North Africa. The risk does not seem to have troubled Cervantes. He owed a favor and he was paying his debt. In trying to decide how honorable Cervantes was in his handling of the king's funds, surely we must keep in mind his readiness to help his friends—Fortuny in this case, but also his assistants Santa María and Benito—when his sense of responsibility so dictated. How many notarial documents serve, in Cervantes' life, the unaccustomed function of character witnesses for him!

By late August he was probably up and about—to do what? Watch the free bullfights in the Plaza de San Francisco? Stand and gawk with the credulous at the silver-crowned statue of the Virgin which had "miraculously" appeared in a cave in his old parish of San Nicolás? Laugh with the Sevillians at the Cardinal Archbishop Rodrigo de Castro, who was so annoyed with city authorities for refusing to change a festival date to suit his convenience that he threatened to excommunicate the entire city council? (Having held their celebration as scheduled, the municipal officers later went barefoot and laden with chains to ask his absolution. The archbishop, by order of the papal nuncio, is reported to have spoken gently to them, and to have distributed sweets.)

It was sometime around then that Cervantes learned that, man of high trust and practical experience that he was, his pay was to be docked from twelve reales a day to ten. The news was probably broken to him shortly after he left his sickbed. That the move was part of a general governmental belt-tightening which applied to all commissaries may not have consoled him appreciably; the fact remained that, after five years of hand-to-mouth living, he was going backward. He was forty-four years old and he was beginning to outlive too many of his friends. Mateo Vázquez had died in May 1591, still in semi-disgrace. Gálvez de Montalvo had perished, stupidly, the same year, when an overloaded pier collapsed in Palermo. How much longer did he have? And what was he to do to inject some sense, some meaning into the remaining time?

Player-manager Rodrigo Osorio's company was appearing then at the Corral de Doña Elvira, in the Barrio de Santa Cruz; he may even have lodged with his old friend Gutiérrez. Biographers' projections of an acrid discussion (over a flagon of Gutiérrez's best wine) of the state of contemporary drama, with Cervantes insisting he could write a better play than any of Lope's, are gratuitous, but not impossible. On September 5, 1592, Cervantes signed his formal pledge to write six of "the best plays ever presented in Spain"—the public was to be the judge—for fifty ducats each from Osorio.

Both were gambling men and this, seemingly, was a bet neither could lose. And yet . . . The price was good, too good, well above Cervantes' top price, the forty ducats Porres had paid him in 1585 for each of his last two plays to be staged. There is not much doubt of what was in Cervantes' mind, although we can question how seriously he took his promise. But what was Osorio thinking of? It is true that managers were always hungry for new works. But did he really expect ever to see anything from Cervantes? Or was he, perhaps at Gutiérrez's nudging, simply trying to buck up a lag whose career as an artist everyone, even Tomás, probably considered finished? There is no evidence that Cervantes had written a line in at least three years. The occasional literary scraps by him which appeared then had been gathering dust for years. One of these, a poem called *Jealousy*—"which I esteem," he would comment in the *Voyage to Parnassus*, "among others that I hold to be ill favored"—turned up in a 1591 edition of an anthology edited in Valencia; to judge from its pastoral references and its forced, artificial tone, it was a refugee from the *Galatea* period. Under the circumstances, the laudatory *octavo real* devoted to Cervantes in Espinel's *Diversas rimas*, published that year, may have sounded (to all ears but his?) like a tribute to a dead man.

None of the plays, as far as is known, were ever delivered to Osorio. And Cervantes very quickly found more urgent problems to distract him. Getting out of jail, for one thing.

A warrant issued by Corregidor Francisco Moscoso of Écija caught up with Cervantes on September 19 in Castro del Río, the same town in which he had once been excommunicated for putting a sacristan in jail.[23] The charge: illegal seizure of three hundred fanegas of wheat, for which he was ordered to make restitution (some 3,000 reales) and pay court costs (about 175 more) within two weeks. Moscoso had made no investigation of the charge; Cervantes had been "tried" in absentia in a kangaroo court; the corregidor's authority to arrest much less judge a king's officer was doubtful. In view of the offense—not theft, but simply unauthorized attachment—the sentence was unusually harsh. Moscoso and Salvador de Toro would have understood each other. Both were riding the shock waves emanating from Puerto de Santa María that had already claimed a casualty in Madrid: the news that at least five of his principal officers had been condemned to hang had been too much for Guevara; on September 23, still under house arrest and with investigators closing in around him, he died.

Cervantes was not held for long, probably no more than a week or so. An appeal to Isunza procured his release on bail. Was it malice or defiance on both men's parts that put Cervantes back on the circuit in October, distraining oil—in Écija?

Isunza himself was in serious trouble. A petition to Madrid that the treasury straighten his accounts with Toro out of operational funds had been rejected. The commissary general would have to answer to Toro's allegations of fraud. When he learned that the magistrate was on his way to Madrid to press a lien on Isunza's personal property, he collected Cervantes as a witness and, in mid-November, carted him off in pursuit.

"Fortune," moans Don Quixote, "not satisfied with the harm she has done me, has cut all the roads over which any small contentment might reach the miserable soul still left in my body. . . . I was born to be an example of misfortune, to be the target and mark at which the arrows of ill chance are aimed and where they stick."[24]

Fortune was taking angle shots at Cervantes now. During the week of November 20, royal auditors in Seville appropriated supplementary records concerning his commissions. On November 24 they decided that his accounts were short not the 27,046 maravedis they had supposed in August, but 128,281 maravedis. No coherent accounting procedure could have made so many errors in so little time. They were, of course, inherent in the system: accounts were gone over again and again, by different men, often in different places; documents were shifted, were lost; the piles of paper grew as understanding dwindled. Conscientiousness was not lacking in the royal accountants; humility was.

For good measure, they disallowed 1,734 maravedis in expenses claimed by Cervantes, with no explanation. This was auditing by instinct. Worse still, they declared his salary was payable "for 260 days at 12 reales each, which represents a reduction from the 295 (claimed)."[25] Two hundred ninety-five? But Cervantes had only claimed wages for 276 days. The same penalty was ordered for Miguel de Santa María. In neither case was explanation offered. *Fecit!*

On the same day, in Madrid, Isunza presented his case to Philip II. Benito was not to be blamed, he insisted, since Toro had not deigned to prove his own authority, although he was given two weeks in which to do so. If any grain was taken from Teba, it was the magistrate's own fault. The commissary general offered proof that the grain had indeed gone into bread for His Majesty's galleys. Isunza was indignant at the offense to his honor contained in Toro's allegations; he insisted that he be formally exonerated and that Toro be reprimanded and sentenced to pay the costs of contention.

Toro was a stubborn man, as proud as his antagonist. He refused to back down although he must have known by then that he was on shaky ground. He repeated his insinuation that Isunza was a crook and called for detailed evidence of what had happened to the money appropriated for the grain in question. Toro, in fact, was having a high old time; the accounting he wanted might have taken years to complete, years during which he could indulge his combativeness where it might show a man to good advantage—at the king's court, far from the oblivion of Teba.

Enter Cervantes, sounding oddly as though he were in Hassan Pasha's throne room in Algiers instead of a Madrid hearing room. On December 1 he submittted a routine statement confirming his authorization for Benito to seek grain in Teba. Two days later he submitted a petition in his clear, elegant handwriting:

Sir: I, Miguel de Cervantes Saavedra, declare that it has come to my attention that Your Majesty's prosecutor and Salvador de Toro demand of Pedro de Isunza, Commissary General of the Galleys of

Spain, that he pay from his private estate the value of the wheat and fodder taken in Your Majesty's service from the said Salvador de Toro, and that a decree to that effect has been issued; and it is suggested that the said wheat was sold for private profit and was not converted in Your Majesty's service. And I, as commissary for the said commissary general, had it attached by my assistants and turned over to the warehousemen and bakers in the cities of Málaga and Antequera, for which I have the receipts, and the fodder was sold to pay the shipping and transport, and I took charge of that, and it is for me to justify everything, as it is for everything entrusted to me. And it is not just that such things be said of the said commissary general or of me as those being laid to us, nor that the said commissary general be unjustly disturbed. And so that this truth might be affirmed, I offer to account for it in this court or in any place it might please Your Majesty, and to post substantial bonds for it, in addition to those I have provided the said commissary general in this matter, with which to pay any judgment and sentence, and may it please Your Majesty, that in my posting the said bonds and making an accounting as offered, the said commissary general and his possessions be spared any disturbance, since he owes nothing, and in this I ask that justice be done.

Moreover: I beg of Your Majesty that the magistrate's action be suspended until the truth of this business be known. For it is not just that he be believed on a mere statement of accusation, with no other evidence whatsoever, and especially against so faithful a servant of Your Majesty as the said Commissary General Pedro de Isunza.

Miguel de Cervantes Saavedra[26]

On the following day the decree against Isunza was suspended. Toro, obviously a man who did not like to lose an argument, pursued his suit until Isunza's death in 1593 and beyond, petitioning for a lien on his estate, but nothing more came of it. Documentalist Pérez Pastor was undoubtedly right in assuming that the treasury had simply transferred the account from one ledger to another and closed the case.

Isunza returned the favor some days later, so effectively testifying for Cervantes before the War Council against Corregidor Moscoso's judgment that the charge was dismissed.

Cervantes did not linger in Madrid. Did he visit his daughter? If so, he may have been relieved to find Ana reasonably prosperous, the owner of a fine two-story house, her tavern filled with its regular crowd of artists, actors (cadging drinks then, for the theater was in a slump), soldiers and gentry who thought it chic to go slumming among the bohemians.

There is no evidence that he even stopped in Esquivias on his way south. Let us assume that he did. It was not, probably, an encouraging visit. He would have learned at first hand that when Catalina's cousin María de Salazar married cousin Gaspar Tello de Guzmán, priest Juan de Palacios provided the bride with a dowry far richer than Catalina's had been. He would have heard of the kidnapping of another cousin, another Catalina, by a frustrated suitor in November and of her escape from the villain's clutches. (Out of this, perhaps, grew the goatherd's story in *Don Quixote* of the braggart soldier Vicente de la Roca's elopement with the innocent Leandra, found three days later in a mountain cave clad only in her shift.[27]) He would have seen the houses standing empty in the village, heard the tales of hard times that were rapidly emptying the Sagra of its young people.

Nothing he saw or heard seems to have enticed him into spending the holidays with his family in Madrid or in Esquivias. What had he to contribute to Christmas gaiety? With Isunza ill, perhaps of a heart attack brought on by strain and worry, Cervantes went on alone to Seville around the middle of December. He may have reached there by December 22, when Guevara's lieutenant, Francisco Benito de Mena, was hanged in Puerto de Santa María, one of half a dozen who met the same end within the week. The state had owed thousands of ducats to each of them.

Cheer was in generally short supply at the new year. "This year entered with a great excess of rains," Zúñiga noted, "which continued unabated, and, the Guadalquivir adopting its customary arrogance, its flood was one of its most notable. . . ."[28] On January 10 and again on January 17, Cervantes sloshed through the watery mud to answer questions put by his faithful auditors concerning work he had done on the orders of Benito de Mena. They were true to form, having made a hash of what should have been a relatively uncomplicated affair; Cervantes' commissions had been ascribed to other men and theirs to him; dates, even years, were confused. Miguel de Oviedo, filling in for Isunza, had to step in to clear up the mess and Cervantes was again absolved of wrongdoing.

Although he was still out of work and had received no money since collecting six hundred reales in back pay on September 28, he was no longer living with Gutiérrez. That they were still friends of sorts is suggested by Cervantes' testimony for Tomás in a suit against the Hermandad del Santísimo Sacramento del Sagrario for refusing the hosteler's application for membership.

For Gutiérrez, admission to the brotherhood would have put an official seal on the respectability he seems to have pined for. But, it appeared, in spite of his fine horse and his gentleman's clothes and princely lodgers, he had not yet made the grade. He was still a man who had been an actor and who now, damask hangings notwithstanding, was an innkeeper. This, at least, was the official excuse when, on March 21, 1593, thirteen of the brothers met to consider the application; all thirteen beans cast were black. The matter came up again on April 14, Ash Wednesday; this time there were twenty-four members voting, and twenty-four black beans cast. Not unreasonably protesting that the membership already included "many laboring men, cobblers, tavernkeepers and others in such trades," Gutiérrez appealed the decision in an ecclesiastical court. He was intent on proving that he was "an honorable man, of equal quality and of lineage as good as any brother's."[29] The key to the dispute is almost certainly here: hosier-player-tradesman Gutiérrez—the very name was suspect— was thought, probably rightly, to be a New Christian.

The suspicion lights Cervantes' testimony. He described himself as a native of Córdoba—the better, presumably, to support his claim of life-long friendship with the plaintiff. As the "son and grandson of familiars of the Holy Office," he lied, he could reliably attest to the spotlessness of Gutiérrez's lineage. He spoke from experience of the establishment in the Calle de Bayona which, he maintained, was not a common inn but "a hostel like the ones in Madrid, honorable and distinguished. . . ." Most of the testimony consists of an oration on "the origin of theatrical plays": he knew, he told the court, that "in ancient times actors were not held as infamous, as were the mummers and mimes, a type of minstrel who appeared in the plays with comical and pleasing gestures and business to make the people laugh. Not so those who portrayed grave and honorable things. And the said Tomás Gutiérrez, although he has acted in public, has always portrayed roles of gravity and wisdom, maintaining all honest decorum. . . ." Besides, Cervantes declared, a little anticlimactically, he had left off that life years ago and was now entirely devoted to the governance of his house.

So the proceedings skittered around what must have been the central issue; no one appears to have been willing to question publicly the purity of the innkeeper's blood, probably because the charge would have been almost impossible to prove. Exasperated, the court excommunicated the entire Hermandad. In February 1594 Gutiérrez was admitted as a member in good standing. And in June the brothers assigned two carts to him for the performance of autos at Corpus; he was, after all, a professional actor.

Cervantes was back on the circuit when this happened. Oviedo, who had taken charge of commissary operations after Isunza's death in June 1593, had immediately commissioned Cervantes to collect what wheat he could in the area around Seville, no easy feat considering that a poor harvest had pushed the free-market price nearly 25 per cent above what the government was paying. Thus he was probably on the road when word reached Seville of Doña Leonor's death on October 19, at the age of seventy-three.

Death had come suddenly, for she left no will. There could not have been much to bequeath, although she seems to have lived her last years in comfort; the big house she shared with Magdalena in an outlying district of Madrid was rented for a respectable 50 ducats a year. Her daughters provided a lavish funeral, paying an almost showy 1,122 maravedis, nearly three times the price of an ordinary burial of people in their position. Andrea, clearly; no one else in the family was in a position to contribute significantly to their mother's support. This may have been the period of Andrea's mysterious marriage to "Santi Ambrosio, a Florentine," of which passing mention is made in a deposition taken from her in 1605 and again in her death registration. No trace of his existence has ever been found, a strange silence around a man who, like most of the Italians in Madrid, would have been a merchant with a froth of legal documents in his wake. This has led some Cervantists to believe he was merely a fiction invented by Andrea to enhance her own and Constanza's respectability. The conclusion is understandable, but it leaves us with no explanation of Andrea's evident prosperity; that she could have maintained two separate households in something like style on her earnings as a seamstress strains the imagination. Almost as farfetched is the notion that, at the age of fifty, she was still a temptress able to keep lovers on a string. Santi Ambrosio, obscure as he was, seems the most logical probability.

We have no way of knowing how Cervantes reacted to his mother's death. Perhaps we can do no more than view the question in a wider context, of Cervantes' consistent shying away from women who had a claim on his emotions—mother, mistress, wife, daughter. None would have had so direct a claim as Doña Leonor. It may be, too, that none pressed the claim so clamorously as she; silent heroism was not a family trait. Whatever Cervantes may have felt—grief, relief, guilt or all of them together— he seems to have considered himself the "son of his hands," a world unto himself in which, as in any universe, neighboring planets were at best remote. With his mother's death, and that of his Uncle Andrés a few days earlier in Cabra, an epoch had ended for him. He may not have noticed it passing; the death of the past can be meaningless to a man with hardly any present and, as he was soon to learn, a sickly future.

In April 1594, in response to the Guevara scandals and to outcries for a change in the commissary system, Oviedo's operation was closed out and all commissions revoked. In June, Cervantes' accounts were approved. His career as a commissary was over. He had very little money, the vaguest of prospects, and an army of characters in search of a story.

Perhaps, after all, he had come away from his job richer than any of his colleagues. At least two of these characters can be traced to their origins.

In the *Persiles*,[30] we meet a garrulous old woman, a pilgrim making the rounds of Spain's shrines. Pug-nosed and pop-eyed, she was dressed "in a torn pilgrim's cloak which kissed her heels, over which straggled a mozetta half of leather, but so torn and rotten that it was impossible to tell if it was Córdoban or sheepskin; her belt was an esparto cord so thick and strong it seemed more like a galley's anchor cable than a pilgrim's cord; her toque was coarse but clean and white; her head was covered by an old hat without band or trimming and her feet by torn *alpargatas*." An enormous rosary hung from her neck and in her hand was a pilgrim's staff; in short, "all of her was torn and all was penitent." She is on her way to the festival at the sanctuary of Nuestra Señora de la Cabeza, in the Sierra Morena near Andújar, which she describes in exhausting detail. That Cervantes had actually seen his pilgrim is obvious. That he saw her at or near the sanctuary on festival day, the last Sunday in April 1592, is likely, since he is known to have been within half a day's ride of the place at the time.

The other personage was equally garrulous, but otherwise a very different bag of bones. As Berganza the dog describes her, she was over seventy years old, "more than seven feet tall and all bones, covered with blackened, hairy, tough hide; her belly, which was of sheepskin, hung down to cover her private parts and even reached halfway down her thighs; her nipples looked like two cow's udders, dry and wrinkled; her lips were blackened, her teeth worn down, her nose hooked and twisted, her eyes bulging, her hair disheveled, her cheeks sunken, neck shriveled and breasts withered. . . ."

This is La Cañizares, a witch masquerading as a hospitaler, although she denies the charge with a certain elegance of invective: "Scoundrel, charlatan, cheat and son of a whore, there's no witch here. If you were thinking of La Camacha, she has paid for her sins, and is God knows where; and if you were thinking of me, you coarse lout, I have never been a witch in my life"; her reputation, she protests, was given her by "false witnesses and an arbitrary law and a hasty and ill-informed judge. . . ." The scene of the action is Montilla, a wine town near Córdoba, where Cervantes had gone in search of wheat in December 1591.

La Cañizares of folk legend was long gone by then; so were her companions La Montiela, whose children had been turned into dogs, and the archsorceress La Camacha. Local lore identified them as Elvira García, who ran a tavern on the Calle de Mesones, and her sister and daughter. Cervantes, the collector of popular ballads, legends, myths, superstitions, was clearly delighted with this one. Elvira, it was said, had turned one

Alonso de Aguilar into a horse about the year 1555. This is not unflattering to Alonso, since the case was probably one of common procurement,
with Elvira—La Camacha—functioning as the local Celestina. It is a
matter of record that Elvira, her daughter and the noble stallion were imprisoned and whipped by the Inquisition for their joys. But the songs of
the blind beggars in the streets had confirmed the case as one of witchcraft, and so it is offered by Cervantes in *The Dogs' Colloquy* to serve,
obliquely, the cause of social justice—in anticipation of that time when a
bestialized humanity sees

> the mighty speedily brought down
> and the humble exalted
> by that hand which has the power to perform it.

By the end of June, he was on his way to Madrid, having left ahead of
the cyclone that hit Seville on June 22, scattering the stock of a poor vendor in Triana all over the city. Some people are just unlucky.

27

Variations on a Theme

Cervantes had thought of Agustín de Cetina as a friend. They had attended that book auction together, had drunk together. How helpful Cetina had been to him as Guevara's paymaster is questionable, but Cervantes did not have so many contacts in high places that he could afford to harbor such doubts. So it was to Don Agustín, who had survived the Seville massacre to become a member of the royal council of auditors, that he applied for help in finding work on his arrival in Madrid at the end of June 1594.

He may have hoped for something in Madrid, or at least a sedentary post in Seville. The maggoty thistle which friend Cetina tossed him might have appalled even a veteran of the Écija wars: collecting 2,557,029 maravedis in wildly snarled tax arrears in the old Kingdom of Granada. The job was Cervantes' for the asking—no one but a desperate man would ask for it—provided he could find someone to guarantee his honesty.

Probably again through Cetina, he found a guarantor, Francisco Suárez Gasco. Suárez's standing in court circles had declined notably since 1591, when he was suspected (though never convicted) of having tried to poison his wife. But *Don* Francisco, as he would later style himself, had been tolerated because he was reputed to be a wealthy man of respectable family. Now he was close to bankruptcy, and such secrets were hard to keep in the Madrid administrative village. Even though Cetina formally vouched for Suárez's solvency, Cervantes was asked to find additional guarantors.

That was on August 5; two weeks later, still unable to find backers, the candidate tax farmer was obliged to represent that he was himself a married man of established creditability. On August 20 he was granted the commission on condition that he and his wife jointly pledge their personal fortune to supplement Suárez's surety.

To have to enlist his wife's aid has been presented as bitter medicine for Cervantes' pride to swallow. He is seen as having to wheedle, persuade, even beg Doña Catalina's help. The timing alone suggests the process was not so demanding. She appeared with him on the following day, August 21, before notary Jerónimo Félix, jointly pledging their "persons and goods, present and future" against any shortages in his accounts. Catalina obviously expected no enrichment from the venture: a commission of fifty days plus travel time at a postrider's pace of eight leagues a day was to be compensated by sixteen reales four maravedis a day, the sum to be paid by the towns out of the taxes due. Neither, probably, did she anticipate having to pay anything out. Perhaps her husband encouraged her to hope (did Cetina encourage *him?*) that the commission could lead to some more settled arrangement which would enable them to live together in Madrid. We have no way of knowing if she tried to dissuade him from accepting work which, by its very nature, could only damage their social standing. This was Jew's work, contemptible. Well, her husband was going his own way. Since there was no help for it . . .

Perhaps we should see him as he saw the ex-soldier in *The Divorce Court Judge,* "with a staff of justice in my hand and, under me, a stunted, shriveled, ornery hired mule" with a small saddlebag strapped behind him, "a collar and shirt in one and, in the other . . . half a cheese, (his) bread and wineskin, without anything else to convert (his) street clothes to a traveling outfit than a pair of leggings and a single spur. And with (his) commission and the vermin biting at (his) chest," he went "slipping and humping over the Toledo bridge despite the cunning of that reluctant mule."

By September 7 he was in Guadix, his first stop on an itinerary which was to include Granada, Loja, Alhama de Granada, Baza, Motril, Almuñécar, Salobreña, Vélez-Málaga, Ronda and a plague of villages between them. This was still Morisco country, the mountain valleys and rocky coast dotted with white, flat-roofed towns, often, as at Guadix, surrounded by warm, dry troglodyte homes scraped with knives and hoes out of the soft limestone hills.

The ease with which Cervantes dispatched his business in Guadix may have stirred a flare of confidence in him. If so, it died quickly, suffocated by the bazaar-stall stratagems he had to contend with in the towns he visited. By the time he reached Ronda he was already behind on his quota, and there he was assured by no less a personage than the district tax official that Madrid's arithmetic was faulty—a charge Cervantes could well believe—and he was given 24,975 maravedis less than his directive had specified. In Vélez-Málaga he had no choice but to accept the local tax officer's oaths that, with profits falling, crops failing and costs rising, the full 277,040 maravedis he had come for was simply not to be had; he settled for 136,000. The confusion, retracing of steps, arguing, checking of figures entailed repeated reports to the king and two twenty-day extensions of his commission. It was not until early December that he was free to ride through the icy air of snow-choked passes to the coast; on December 15 he exchanged the last of the money he had collected for a letter of credit for 4,000 reales in Málaga—the sierras were dangerous for a man with money—and departed for Seville.

We must insist on these wretched figures; because of them, Cervantes will end his career as a functionary in prison; he will be bedeviled by them for years afterward and made to suffer centuries of accusation of muddleheadedness, dishonesty, irresponsibility—none of them true. Along with the vivid images of Morisco and Gypsy life carried into his stories from his Granada travels, he should have returned to Madrid with a decent profit for his ninety-day commission of just under 50,000 maravedis (about 1,450 reales). Instead, because of a flourish of incompetence by the royal auditors, he was a loser in time, money and reputation. A review of his accounts will measure both the depth of his indignation and the breadth of the wrong done him.[1]

The assigned tax debt of 2,557,029 maravedis was reduced to 2,525,958 maravedis by the auditors, who allowed the shortages in Ronda and Baza, a total of 31,071 maravedis, as uncollectable. Cervantes turned in 2,384,918 maravedis; a delayed payment of 92,307 maravedis raised the total receipts to 2,477,225 maravedis. This is the figure credited to Cervantes. So far, this is how the account should stand:

Total revised debt	2,525,958
Total credited to Cervantes	2,477,225
Deficit	48,733

But Cervantes was charged with a deficit of 79,804 maravedis, not 48,733! Having written off the Baza-Ronda shortfall, the auditors made the schoolboy error of failing to carry the revised debt over to the calculation of Cervantes' account and subtracting the credit from the original debt: 2,557,029. In any case, their second error made nonsense of the first.

Although they had allowed the Baza-Ronda shortfall, the auditors failed to deduct the Vélez-Málaga deficit, 141,040, from the total debt assignment. The provisional figures should have read:

Total revised debt   2,384,918 (the original 2,557,029 minus
the uncollectable Baza-Ronda/
Vélez-Málaga shortfall of 172,-
111)
Total collected   2,384,918
Total deficit   0

Finally, with receipt of the delayed payment, the account properly reckoned:

Total revised receipts   2,477,225
Totaled revised debt   2,384,918
Credit owed Cervantes   92,307

The auditors, having misread his accounts and mislaid a few entries of their own, later alleged that Cervantes had not reported his failure to collect the full Vélez-Málaga assignment. The charge was not only untrue, it was incoherent. Cervantes did indeed report collection of 136,000 maravedis there. Had he not done so, the deficit attributable to him would have been 141,040, the amount of the shortfall there; if, in addition, we repeat the auditors' failure to subtract the Baza-Ronda deficit from his account, he appears deficitary by an even wilder 172,111 maravedis. Instead, he was charged for 79,804, a figure which no amount of account juggling can produce.

With this fiscal wizardry still in the future, however, Cervantes may have felt reasonably satisfied with his situation when, in January 1595, he gave 6,000 reales in tax receipts and 1,400 reales of his own to merchant-banker Simon Friere de Lima in Seville in exchange for a letter of credit to be redeemed in Madrid. He then went on to the court to turn in his accounts and, presumably, to try to unhook another assignment.

There he waited, probably fretting about his money, about his future. And about his niece Constanza. Because Constanza, like her mother and her aunt Magdalena and her great-aunt María, had learned the language of amorous converse and the dialogue was invoking ghosts from the past which an already nervous Cervantes might have preferred not to contemplate.

The young man in question was Pedro de Lanuza y de Perellos; he might have been lost in the gilded oblivion of history along with the Ovandos and Pachecos and Don Martín "the Gypsy" had his family not wandered into Philip II's quarrel with the fallen archsecretary Antonio Pérez.

Pérez and the Princess of Eboli had been arrested in 1579. The princess was confined in her own palace of Pastrana, where she would die, half-mad, in a bare tower room a dozen years later. Pérez was eventually tried and imprisoned for the murder of Don Juan's secretary, Juan de Escovedo. In 1590 he escaped and fled to Saragossa, where Philip, as king of Aragon, was bound by other laws than those to which he was subject as king of Castile. When, balked in his request for Pérez's extradition, the king tried to accomplish through the Inquisition what his secular law had failed to achieve, he touched off a popular uprising in Aragon. A Castilian army easily restored order, but Pérez escaped to France, where he was to spend the rest of his life plotting revenge against Spain. Philip found another scapegoat, the former archsecretary's principal ally in Saragossa, Don Juan de Lanuza, Viscount of Rueda y Perellos, Aragon's justiciar or chief justice. Don Juan was more or less legally decapitated and then given a state funeral.

When the excitement subsided, the crown moved against Lanuza's family. The justiciar's twenty-four-year-old brother and his mother were accused of conspiracy in the uprising; their possessions were confiscated and they were ordered to stand trial in Madrid. The brother's name was Pedro de Lanuza y de Perellos, and when Constanza de Ovando, then nearly thirty years old, fell in love with him he was flat broke and in disgrace.

The affair followed the Cervantes family pattern: Pedro was innocent of the charges and when, in the spring of 1595, it became evident that his family was to be rehabilitated, he decided he could dispense with Constanza's consoling presence. On July 5 he formally promised to pay her 1,400 ducats . . . when he could.

That Cervantes, who was fond of his pretty blond niece, did much more than fuss over this unpleasantness is improbable. Andrea would not have welcomed his meddling; she was, she would hardly have needed to remind him, more experienced in such matters. He could stick to his poetry and let her take care of her own daughter's difficulties.

Cervantes was indeed writing poetry. One of his efforts was submitted as an entry in a poetry contest organized by the Dominicans in Saragossa to celebrate the canonization of San Jacinto. The awards offered were typical of these exercises: three silver spoons as first prize, with a length of purple taffeta for the runner-up and a gilt book of hours as the third prize. It was not the prizes that enticed poets to these contests, but vanity. A century later, such events would become as common as radio quiz shows were in the 1950s, and as ridiculous. In Cervantes' time, however, the mass of recognition-starved mediocrities they attracted was often joined by good poets—Lope, Tirso de Molina, Calderón, Guillén de Castro—who viewed them as championship matches in which the veterans reaffirmed their supremacy. It is true that no distinguished verse ever came out of a poetry contest, and Cervantes' offering to the Dominicans was in depressing conformity to the rule. What commands our notice of it is the evidence it offers that writing was again tugging at his imagination; the same stirrings which prompted his offer of three hundred ducats' weight of plays to Ossorio seem to have persuaded him to try for three silver spoons. What point was there, after all, in pursuing a sinecure that would enable him to write if, in the pursuit, the writing itself were abandoned?

The poem was a plodding conceit playing on one of the meanings of *jacinto* as a precious stone and it was judged the best of the lot. On May 7 the jury's decision was announced in doggerel so crude it must have made Cervantes wince, but it told him what he doubtless wanted to hear:

> Miguel Cervantes arrived,
> so masterly that he confirmed
> in the second competition
> the opinion the world holds of him. . . .[2]

He had brought this on himself, but he can perhaps be forgiven his showing. There were other problems pressing on him, notably Freire's failure to appear with the 7,400 reales he was holding for Cervantes. A letter to the merchant, probably in March, had finally drawn a written apology; orders had been given, Cervantes was informed, for the money to be paid in his name by Freire's Madrid correspondent, a Portuguese named Gabriel Rodrigues. This, however, Rodrigues declined to do. In April, fending off the treasury's impatient demands for a final accounting of his Granada mission, Cervantes had written again to Seville. He was still without an answer.

In Esquivias, meanwhile, a weeks-long watch ended May 5 with the death of Juan de Palacios. Cervantes may not have been on the best of terms with the priest, but her uncle had been Catalina's mainstay and probably her confidant. His death left Cervantes, like it or not, the head of the family. Uncle Juan had not liked that idea, at any rate. His bequest to Catalina was no more than a token: two parcels of nearly worthless land, some French hangings, a bed with two wool-stuffed mattresses, a pair of blankets and "one of the two small winecasks." Richer bequests, in wine, books, clothes, vineyards and cash, went to her brothers and to others in the family. A trust established out of Francisco de Palacios' heritage, designed to pay off some of the family debts, was accompanied in the will by an express order that no one in the family "or any other person on their behalf" shall sue to recover this money. A slap at Cervantes? Perhaps, though not certainly. The priest might already have seen in his nephew Francisco, then studying for the priesthood in Toledo, signs of that greedy acquisitiveness which would ultimately make him the wealthiest as well as the worst-tempered member of the tribe.

Cervantes is known to have been in Toledo on May 19, probably in connection with the will. But his tenure as functioning head of the family was short. Probably around the end of the month, word did arrive from Seville: Freire, he was informed, had gone bankrupt and absconded with 60,000 ducats, including the approximately 670 ducats Cervantes had deposited with him.

The news sent Cervantes hurrying to Seville, where he found that Freire's creditors had already closed in around the ruins. He tried to assert the priority of his claim on the grounds that he was acting for the crown (he seems to have kept very quiet about the part of the money that was his), and was challenged to prove it. Stopping only long enough to formalize a statement in which witnesses testified that he had indeed deposited the money with Freire, he rushed to Madrid to petition for endorsement of his priority.

Not until August 7 did the king order a Sevillian magistrate, Dr. Bernardo de Olmedilla, to attempt collection of the money in response to Cervantes' plea. But the terms of the order must have startled the petitioner: Olmedilla was instructed to collect the money if no prior claim to it existed, and to deposit the entire sum, including Cervantes' wages, to the treasury's account; if he found that prior title to the money did exist, he was authorized to sequester the 7,400 reales and claim restitution from Cervantes and his guarantor, Suárez. All this was to be done at Cervantes' expense.

Back to Seville steamed Cervantes through the awesome August heat. As feared, Freire's creditors moved to block the payment. Cervantes' actions over the next few weeks are confusing. On September 20, he sent his sister Magdalena an order for 149,600 maravedis for remission to the treasury against future collection of the debt. This was followed on October 23 by a second order for 37,500 maravedis, to be remitted through Fernando de Lodeña, whose friendship with the Cervantes family had somehow survived his long-dead and still unpaid-for affair with Magdalena. The total, some 5,500 reales, represents nearly all he actually owed the government.

Why was he so anxious to discharge the debt quickly? Had he been threatened with prosecution? (The sum, including Cervantes' wages, was recovered, but not until fourteen months later, on January 21, 1597; it was all turned over to the treasury.) And where had Cervantes found the cash? Any reserve he might have had and more was exhausted by the expense to which he was being put. Probably it was the accumulated proceeds of a month's feverish scrounging: loans, maybe liquidation of some of Catalina's belongings, even help from Francisco de Palacios at a suitable rate of interest.

His career in public service was over, no doubt to the general indifference. It was poor man's work no poor man could afford to do. Cervantes still had not been paid in full for the work he did for Oviedo in 1593–94 and he never would be. The salary he had earned in Granada had vanished into the "chest with three keys" in which the king's treasure symbolically lay, never to reappear. And, with it all, he was treated as though he were a thief while men of substance, such men as Simon Freire de Lima, were trusted and honored, at least until they ran off with other people's money.

"For three things is it proper for a prudent man to weep," Cervantes comments in one of his mock-solemn moods: "first, for having sinned; second, to obtain forgiveness for his sin; third, out of jealousy; no other tears are seemly in a serious face."[3]

] 28 [

To Fall and Rise Again

King Philip seemed demented. Like Mad Orlando, he was striking out everywhere. At home, famine was spreading; Spain's trade was in ruins, its hold on the Americas was weakening under pressure from its northern rivals, its economy was close to bankruptcy. Because of the crown's failure to prosecute the war vigorously in the Low Countries, the economy—and the loyalty—of its Catholic provinces was rotting. The country desperately needed peace. Instead, in the spring of 1596, it was simultaneously at war with France, England, Holland.

Blind imperialism, religious fanaticism, economic beleaguerment, personal egocentrism—the motivational lines in Philip's thinking blur and seethe. It was almost as though the sickness in his gout-riddled kidneys (and, according to Antonio Pérez's biographer Dr. Gregorio Marañon, syphilis as well) had loosened his hold on reality, walling him into a private world of pain and brooding fantasy in which, increasingly, salvation lay in the one bold move, the magisterial stroke which would set everything to rights.

Everywhere but in the northeastern corner of France, Spanish troops were being pushed steadily backward. But when, in April, his soldiers captured Calais, the last shreds of Philip's prudence went flying to the winds. Now he was readying his new fleet for an invasion of Ireland; with that island in hand and a Channel port at his command, he reckoned wildly, he could make good the attack on England which had failed eight years before.[1] Was it an omen that his most dreaded opponents were being removed from play? Sir John Hawkins had died of yellow fever during an expedition against the Isthmus of Darien in 1595; Drake expired in February 1596 in Portobelo.

In his bleary peering across the Continent, the king somehow missed a movement occurring in Plymouth. An English naval squadron sailed from there on June 13 under the joint command of Thomas Howard, Earl of Effingham, and Elizabeth's favorite, the young Earl of Essex. On June 25 the ships were sighted off the coast of Portugal and the alarm was raised. There was hardly anyone to hear it.

When the English ships (estimates of their number vary from sixty to one hundred sixty, but there may have been no more than twenty ships of the line involved) sailed into the Bay of Cádiz on June 30, they found eight Spanish galleons, eighteen galleys and scores—perhaps more than one hundred—vessels of the New Spain fleet. Within twenty-four hours, having sunk some forty cargo vessels and thirteen fighting ships, the English were masters of the harbor. Artillery fire from the forts fell short of the marauders; many of the land guns were assigned ammunition that did not fit them; a number simply blew up.

The next day, July 1, the English commanders began landing some of their sixteen thousand English and Dutch troops. The sack of the city got under way at once. It was done in very orderly fashion; there were no rapes, no murders, nothing but four-square pillaging.

Legend has it that the Duke of Medina-Sidonia was fishing for tuna when word reached him of the English landing. As Defender of Andalusia and High Admiral of Spain, he was responsible for the defense of Cádiz. He has, of course, been excoriated for not rushing troops to the city. But what troops? About a thousand men were available. He may have believed that this was no mere raid, but the long-feared invasion of Spain by the English. If this were so, he did exactly as he should have done: he sent riders to all the towns in the region and to Madrid appealing for reinforcements; when Lord Howard feinted toward Seville, Medina-Sidonia led 750 men to the city's relief—and found that Seville's defensive equipment consisted of around four hundred harquebuses and a beplumed, swaggering, comic-opera troop of hastily recruited militiamen drilling under the leadership of one Marco Antonio Becerra.

For an incredible sixteen days the English occupied Cádiz, sacking and burning, while Medina-Sidonia and his handful of men danced around the environs, not daring to attack, waiting for the levies to arrive from the towns to which appeals had been sent. When the attackers at last withdrew, they left only 290 of Cádiz's 1,203 houses standing; millions of ducats in treasure along with 156 prisoners sailed with them. It was not until July 25, ten days after the English departure, that Medina-Sidonia dared to enter the ruined city.

All this seems a very great machine with which to trap a fleeting glimpse of Cervantes, but he surfaces so seldom between the autumn of 1595 and the winter of 1603-4 that all such contraptions are legitimate. He is thought to have spent the interval from 1596 to 1600 chiefly in

Seville; from time to time confirmation glimmers—a loan for a suit of clothes in December 1598, collection of a debt in February 1599—before he disappears again. In such a desert, the wanderer uses the landmarks he finds, and accepts the risk of being fooled by them. One of these high dunes on the horizon is his sonnet *To the entrance of the Duke of Medina into Cádiz in July 1596, with the support of troops trained in Seville by Captain Becerra after evacuation of that city by English troops who had sacked it for twenty-four (sic) days under the command of the Earl of Essex.*

Cervantes had certainly watched Becerra's bravos cavort (the name Becerra means "calf"), had probably watched the duke march them off, more to the relief of the Sevillians than of Cádiz (Zúñiga would later comment that "on feast days they could be seen in the Campo de la Tablada practicing the use of arms, to the alarm of many, because the militia began to act like soldiers, giving the forces of justice much to do"[2]). The sonnet bespeaks old soldier Cervantes' scorn:

> In July we saw another Holy Week,
> confirmed by certain brotherhoods
> which soldiers call companies,
> of which the populace, not the English, were terrified.
> Such a panoply of plumes was there
> that in less than fourteen or fifteen days
> its pygmies and Goliaths took flight
> and all its edifice toppled to the ground.
> The calf bellowed and dressed them into line;
> the earth rumbled, the heavens darkened,
> threatening wholesale ruination;
> and when, at last, the earl, untroubled,
> left the place, into Cádiz, with all prudence,
> triumphant marched the geat Duke of Medina.

Cervantes would later find kind words for the English in the story he based on the raid, *The Spanish Englishwoman*. In it, a seven-year-old girl is taken secretly to London by one of the English captains, a crypto-Catholic who raises the girl as his daughter. Elizabeth of England is a principal figure in the tale and she is presented, in knife-edged contrast to the then reigning Philip III of Spain, as a monarch kindly, compassionate and honorable, tolerant, wise and open to the outside world. She enjoys speaking Spanish and receives complacently the disclosure that the heroine, Isabel, is Catholic; "I esteem her the more for that," the queen replies, "because she so faithfully obeyed the law her parents had taught her." Isabel is the Spanish form of the name Elizabeth; in making the

girl an idealized image of Spain and identifying her with the English
queen at a time when the Inquisition was hanging Protestant sailors who
landed in Spanish ports and naked imperialism had replaced Spain's
crusading morality, Cervantes was clearly criticizing the narrow militancy
of his own rulers.

In Madrid, meanwhile, Cervantes' niece Constanza was conducting another kind of siege. Rehabilitation of Lanuza's family had begun in February 1596 with the bestowal on Pedro by Philip II of an estate worth
nearly half a million maravedis a year. The family's debts were heavy and
none of the money was diverted to his former mistress' claim against him.
In the autumn she sued and, in December of that year, won a promise of
payment: two hundred ducats a year for seven years, or the whole balance in a lump sum should his income suddenly be increased. One of the
documents remaining—Andrea's hand is visible here—gave Constanza a
lien on Lanuza's estate if he died before the debt was paid. It was as
foolproof an agreement as could be obtained in such circumstances, but
no record has ever been found that Constanza ever collected a maravedi.

Heaven knows what Cervantes lived on in those days when, resisting
return to the captivity of Madrid or Esquivias, he floated anonymous and
unrecorded through Seville. He may have taken odd jobs, may have acted
as a jobber, a broker (biographers quote—hopefully—Andrea's remark in
1605 that her brother was "a man who writes and deals in business and
who, for his great ability, can count on good friends"). Not with any consistency, probably, since his name has not yet cropped up in any commercial documents of the period.

It has even been suggested that he picked up a few coins writing ballads for the blind beggars to sing in the streets ("hunger," he would later
comment, "turns the wits to things which are not on any map"[3]). We
may still hear some of these in the delightful songs in his *Exemplary Stories*, some of them so charming that one wonders if Cervantes was not,
after all, a fine lyric poet gone astray into rhetorical mediocrity:

Hermosita, hermosita,
la de las manos de plata,
mas te quiere tu marido
que el rey de las Alpujarras.
Eres paloma sin hiel;
pero a veces eres brava
como leona de Orán
o como tigre de Ocaña. . . .

(Little beauty, little beauty, she of the silver hands, your husband loves
you better than the king of the Alpujarras. You are a gentle dove, yet at
times you are as fierce as a lioness of Orán or as a tiger of Ocaña. . . .[4])

Did he find some refuge in the democracy of letters in 1596–98? To some Cervantists, asking this is like wondering if Nebuchadnezzar ate vegetables: he did because he must have, even if there is no direct evidence. They point, with perhaps more eagerness than justice, at the stylistic simplicity of some of his stories—*The Liberal Lover*, "The Tale of Foolish Curiosity," *The Two Maidens*, *The Lady Cornelia*. These, they surmise, must have been early efforts because they lack the psychological subtlety of Cervantes' later work, again a questionable verdict. Some of these stories may in fact have been drafted long before 1596; internal evidence places others at a later date.

Tenuous stylistic reasons can be found to suggest that he committed little to paper in a finished state in those years. There is, for one thing, the uniformity of tone of the works published from 1605 onward: resolved, controlled, quizzical. Then too, the themes of his late plays, of the *Exemplary Stories* and of the vast, symphonic *Quixote*, which in so many ways gathers them up and elaborates them, show a compactness of vision and feeling usually indicating compression in time. The man who wrote those stories had come to some kind of terms with himself.

There is no evidence that he had yet reached that state. More than his Pedro de Urdemales, more than his Quixote, Cervantes was his own creation.

> *Yo soy hijo de la piedra,*
> *padre no conocí . . . ,*

says Pedro, "I am a son of the stone, I never knew a father." So Cervantes appears through the haze of the centuries still imprisoned then, like a sculpture in the block of whatever personal illusions had taken him to Andalusia—freedom, or direct experience of life or perhaps simply the pragmatic hope of finding an economic cushion on which his poetic ambitions might recline. Who knows now if the form was already beginning to emerge from the mass, whether lines, verses, situations, concepts were already being stocked for use, or if a preliminary version of *Don Quixote* had already been outlined? Before he could stand free and in the round, before he could exchange the delusion of freedom that confined him for a voluntary servitude to art, one more sharp tap of the mallet was required on the stone. It came in the late summer of 1597.

In August, auditors wrestling with Cervantes' Granada accounts summoned him, along with Doña Catalina and his co-guarantor, Suárez Gasco, to appear before them in Madrid. Although the money left with Freire, including the part of it owed to Cervantes, had been fully recovered, it was decided that he was still short in his accounts. This not because his arithmetic was any faultier than the auditors', nor because any fraud was suspected, but simply because it was decided that he should have collected all the money owed in Vélez-Málaga. Having arbitrarily deducted his pay from the shortfall, they charged him—somehow—with a debt of 79,304 maravedis.

Two courses were theoretically open to Cervantes: he could return to Vélez-Málaga and try to pry loose enough money there to cover the debt, or he could go to Madrid and try to convince the auditors that there was absolutely no more blood to be squeezed from that stone. Either journey would have to be made at his own expense. Probably he did not have the cash to swing it and, to judge from her sale of a plot of land in Esquivias earlier that year for a paltry twenty ducats, neither did Doña Catalina. Perhaps, too, his long experience with auditorial bumbling had persuaded him that no real urgency lay behind the summons.

In Madrid, however, Suárez Gasco panicked; he had collected his commission as guarantor, but he probably had neither the intention nor the cash to make good on his pledge. Instead he secured a royal order for Cervantes to post a satisfactory bond and to appear in Madrid within twenty days; if no bond was posted, Cervantes was to be returned under guard to the court and there lodged in the royal prison.

The order was received in Seville by Gaspar de Vallejo, one of the nine summary-court magistrates. It is difficult to determine whether Vallejo was a venal judge or merely a stupid one. Probably both. The most powerful man in Seville then was the city's chief magistrate, that Count of Puñonrostro who in *The Illustrious Serving Wench* was said by the city's thieves to be "poking his fingers in our souls." He was particularly hard on the monopolists who, protected by certain magistrates, took advantage of crop failures to corner the market on staple foods and further gouge already rising prices. If Vallejo was, as is suspected, involved in this traffic, his severity toward Cervantes may have been no more than an idiot display of zeal to deflect suspicion away from himself.

Cervantes' writings are larded with complaints about the corruption of Spanish magistrates, and Cervantists usually apply them to Vallejo. In *The Illustrious Serving Wench,* the innkeeper assures Tomás that "he knew people in Toledo of such importance that they had great influence with the forces of justice, especially a lady nun who was related to the corregidor and who had him wrapped around her little finger, and that a washerwoman for that nun's convent had a daughter who was a great friend of a sister of a monk who was very close to the said nun's confessor . . . and if she asks her daughter . . . to talk to the monk's sister who will talk to her brother who will talk to the confessor who will talk to the nun, and if the nun pleases to write a note . . . there will be no lack of unguent to grease all the ministers of justice; for those who are not greased squeal louder than cartwheels."

An old Gypsy woman in *The Little Gypsy Girl* accepts a gift of gold with the excuse that, should one of the tribe fall into the hands of justice, "will any influence as effectively reach the ear of the judge and the scribe as these escudos if they reach their pockets?" She herself, she points out, had on three occasions "almost been seated on the ass, ready to be whipped, and I was freed the first time by a silver pitcher, the second by a string of pearls and the other by 320 reales. . . ."

A collection of such observations could fill a small book—or a large one if we add supporting testimony from other artists of the time. Perhaps the most succinct comment was to be found in a fresco Cervantes might have seen in the courthouse in Monsaraz, on the Portuguese border south of Badajoz, showing honest justice and a crooked magistrate carrying a bent baton.

Although the wording of the royal order was confusing, the least that can be said is that Vallejo placed the most ungenerous possible interpretation on it. Assuming, erroneously or knowingly, that Cervantes had turned in no money at all to the treasury, he fixed the bond at the full amount of the Granada assignment, 2,557,029 maravedis instead of the 79,304 maravedis of the alleged deficit. This despite the fact that, with a little time, Cervantes could have produced the documents he needed to prove Vallejo's error. Cervantes might have been able to find a bondsman who would guarantee the lower sum; no one would risk two and a half million on him.

At this point, Vallejo made his second mistake, this one so flagrant that it must be presumed deliberate. Although the king's order clearly directed that Cervantes be returned to Madrid, the magistrate ordered him confined in the royal prison in Seville, within convenient bribing distance. In late September or October, Cervantes entered the prison he had so often passed on the Calle de las Sierpes,[5] that place "where all discomfort had its seat and every sad sound made its home" and where, if some—by no means all—Cervantists are to be believed, *Don Quixote* was born. Thanks to a number of detailed descriptions of prison life by Cervantes' contemporaries, we can follow him there.[6]

Had the devil wished to instruct men in what hell was like, the demonstration model might very well have been the Cárcel Real de Sevilla. Purgatory was a narrow passage between the Audiencia (local) and royal prisons, a stinking alley usually abustle with prisoners and their visitors, wives, whores, lawyers, guards, beggars, hawkers.

Cervantes, one of eight or ten prisoners admitted every hour, was led into the larger building, the royal prison, where as many as eighteen hundred persons might be held at a time. At the first of three gates opening into the place, he was registered. This was the so-called Puerta de Oro, the Golden Gate, where the wealthiest prisoners were allowed to buy their way into the more comfortable antechambers of the prison proper and the private and semi-private quarters of the upper floor. Everything was for sale in this prison, including freedom (for a ducat or two a day inmates could come and go at will; daytime "passes," good until the gates were locked at 10 P.M., could be had for a real); all the prison officers, down to the lowliest porter, bought their jobs and they considered the purchase price an investment.

From there, Cervantes, presumably out of the Golden Gate class, mounted a long flight of steps to a second gate, the Copper or Iron Gate. As he climbed, the guard's voice floated up behind him:

"Hooolaa!"

"Hooolaa!" came the answering shout from above.

"Prisoner coming."

"What's he in for?"

Language was part of the process of diminution. If a debtor arrived, for example, the guard would yell, "There goes Mr. Hundred Ducats!" Not infrequently, the prisoner would pause on the steps to shout back, *"Mentis vos! Voto a Dios!"* (You lie! I swear to God!) or *"Eso niego!"* (I deny that!).

A second flight of steps led to another gate where the major offenders entered. It was called the Silver Gate because it was there that the institution's traffic was centered. Silver coins were needed if a prisoner wished to avoid having chains placed on his wrists and ankles; it was to the guards there that inmates paid their silver reales to be released for the day or to gain entrance for their women at night.

Cervantes presumably did not reach those heights. Technically he would have been held in what was known as *prisión primera,* a kind of preventive detention imposed until he could post the bond set. Let us assume, then, that it was through the Copper Gate—the tariffs here, copper and alloy coins, were more modest, in keeping with the paltriness of the services offered—that, in a sort of daze of shock and squalor, he acceded to the inner prison.

Cervantes had been a soldier, he had lived for months at a time in a war galley, had lain in chains in Algiers dungeons. But in all these situations he had been considered a decent man in honorable confinement; the spectacle that confronted him on the other side of that iron door could only have horrified him.

It was a tumult. Since it was the custom in the Seville prison to allow the prisoners free run of the premises until lockup time at night, there were thousands of men milling around, prisoners, visitors, officials, lawyers. Men were shouting at each other in the stentorian bellow that passed for a normal conversational tone. Men were laughing, arguing; there may have been a brawl going—there usually was—and the shouting of the guards intervening, the grunting of the combatants, the cries of warning if hidden knives or clubs were brought into action would have angled sharply above the exclamations of the gamblers in the prison casinos (the prison governor took his cut of the winnings), the bawling of songs obscene and plaintive in the prison's four taverns (wine supplied, at outrageous cost, from the governor's vineyards, although the prisoners who rented the concessions were expected to supply holy water free for baptisms). In time these would all be familiar to the new man, along with the drone of mass from the upstairs chapel in the mornings, the hum at lights-out, when the men would leave off their scuffling and cursing to kneel in prayer before the chapels in each chamber. He would grow accustomed to the complaints as the *animeros* passed among the men at noon; these were the trustees appointed to cut up the three-pound loaves of bread alloted to every three prisoners, and who always cut four pieces keeping the middle part, the *anima* or soul, for themselves.

The newcomer would get used to the frequent rounds of men up for the gallows, saying goodbye, shaking hands and, if possible, stealing a copper or two in the shadow of death as a last act of defiance; when the guards and officials came for their victim, the men would pelt their tormentors with a hail of excrement before forming up, each with his candle, to march in procession around the patio chanting a litany for the dead. A new man would become inured to the almost daily auctions among the prisoners (with a cut to the governor) of the day's haul of loot stolen from new prisoners, visitors, from anyone who had anything to steal and who had not protected himself by bribing the self-appointed protectors in each block.

That very night, Cervantes would have learned that the racket was muted but not quenched after lights-out. This was fun-and-games time: the *culebra,* a kind of blindman's buff played with blows, and the *mariposa,* a splinted stick set alight between a sleeper's fingers, and the mock trials in which the condemned (no one was ever acquitted) were paraded around the bunks on two men's shoulders (representing the penitential ass on which prisoners were whipped) and then "fined" drinks for the "court." There were the gruntings and thrashings of the copulators in the dormitory bunks, the screams of whores being beaten by their men because the day's take was suspiciously light.

Within a day or two, Cervantes would have recognized the internal order in this apparent chaos. The inner prison was a three-story edifice built around an open central patio some thirty paces square in which stood a fountain of clear spring water. There were few individual cells and these were reserved for the nobility and the rich; humbler prisoners were lodged in common dormitories each containing from a dozen to over one hundred inmates. It was probably to the mezzanine, where the petty offenders were held, that Cervantes was assigned. From the balcony running around the floor he could look down on the flower of the prison's population below—the thieves, the murderers, the bare-chested valientes in their slashed doublets and heavy rosaries, those men at whom Guzmán de Alfarache sneered because they thought "a clean, starched ruff and an upturned moustache were all they needed for salvation."[7]

He would have learned that prison rations were minimal, but that they could be supplemented by purchases of fresh produce from the governor's lands, sold in the two prison shops at no more than triple the going market prices.

The notion that in this atmosphere, given what must have been his state of depression, his uncertainty about the future, his resentment at the injustice done him, his sheer physical exhaustion, he began to write *Don Quixote* is highly indigestible. When all the pages of argument are winnowed, the grain of justification remains the phrase in the book's prologue: ". . . what could my sterile and ill-cultivated wit engender but the story of a dried-up, withered, fantastical child, full of myriad fancies never imagined by anyone else, very much like someone engendered in a prison . . . ?"

The dangers of taking any single remark by Cervantes too literally are recognized by most modern critics. Pierre Guenoun also objects that the conditions of Cervantes' imprisonment argue against his being able to do more than toy with ideas and possibly outline a few scraps of incident. Américo Castro believed the prison referred to was moral and psychological, that Don Quixote was the Jew storming at the bars of social ostracism. However unsatisfying this may be as a theory, it at least takes us a step toward a metaphorical reading of the line. We may reach surer ground if we consider how immense a transformation those months in prison wrought in Cervantes.

The process would certainly have developed in phases. It may have begun by reaming from his mind any lingering fantasy about a free life among the pícaros. The pícaros! Here they were! He had only to inspect them in their natural habitat to recognize that, for all the sympathy they may have wrung from him, he really had no place among them. Only in one area would he have felt himself one of them: in the resentment any man feels when he is thrust behind bars, especially, as in his own case, when he has committed no crime. For them, as well as for himself, would have risen the complaint we read in the *Voyage to Parnassus* (Chapter Three), where, with mock self-deprecation, Cervantes is left standing in Apollo's presence after all the minor poets and parapoets

> in infinite number, found seats
> before I did; and so I remained standing,

indignant, angry and diminished.
I said to myself: can it be that angry fortune,
which offends many and fears no one,
is going out of its way to persecute me?

His impulse to protest might have given Cervantes a motive to write a story about a man who righted wrongs and rendered justice. Oh, not one who actually righted wrongs—Cervantes was too wryly realistic to think this was possible—but who *tried* to do so, who was mad enough to want to do so. Under the circumstances, it is difficult to see how more than an embryo of an idea, hardly more than a yen, could have developed. And what, after all, was there in his surroundings to suggest specifically the idea of a man whose wits are turned by reading the romances of chivalry?

The phase that followed would have been decisive for him and it gives the measure of his heroism. Any prisoner must make a mighty moral effort to push back the walls enclosing him, to encompass the injustice and violence of imprisonment. Either he will emerge from the struggle embittered, a hardened criminal, or he will be purified and enlarged. In prison, Cervantes was forced to face his grief, his past, like a dying soul reviewing its life, to examine his own sins and analyze his relationships with God and humanity. This is a perilous ordeal; only a hero can emerge from it sound and triumphant. Cervantes, we know, was a fighter. He would have made that moral effort, climbed that upward path.

An uncannily evocative echo of what we may imagine went through his mind comes to us from another prison, in the words of another writer who faced a similar crisis:

I also recall an ardent desire to be resuscitated, to be reborn into a new life, that gave me the strength to resist, to wait and to hope. . . . I still remember that, surrounded by hundreds of comrades, I was frightfully alone, and that I came to love that solitude. Isolated amid the crowd of prisoners, I reviewed my former life, I analyzed its slightest details, I pondered it and I judged myself pitilessly; sometimes I thanked the destiny which had granted me that solitude, without which I could never have judged myself nor plunged back into my past life. Some hope sprouted in my heart then! I thought, I decided, I swore to myself never again to commit the mistakes I had made and to avoid the falls that had broken me. I drew up my future program, promising myself to abide by it. I believed blindly that I would accomplish, that I could accomplish anything I wished. I waited, I looked joyously forward to my freedom. . . . I wanted to try my strength again in a new struggle. . . . I write this because I think everyone will understand me, because everyone will feel as I did, who has the misfor-

tune to be sentenced and imprisoned in the prime of life, in full possession of his strength. . . .

The book is *The House of the Dead*,[8] the writer, of course, Fyodor
Dostoyevsky, who once declared Quixote to be the most perfect Christian
hero in all literature.

If we accept these as, in substance, Cervantes' thoughts—and how
could they not have been?—we arrive at two answers in one: his review
of his past, his resolve for the future would at last have thrust him irrevo-
cably toward the self-fulfillment in art he must always have awaited. In
this sense, *Don Quixote,* the first of his works to appear in this new stage
of his life, was indeed "engendered in a prison"—and so were all the
other plays, stories, poems, novels that pressed so tumultuously against
each other in the elation of those climactic decades to come. Those
months in prison marked his own rebirth as well.

Doubtless the transformation was halting; the next phase may have
been marked by the angry defiance toward life we hear in the opening
lines of his poem called *Disdain:*

> So accustomed is my heart
> to your disdain, ungrateful one,
> that it has come to feed on it
> like the asp on its own venom.
> I thought to lose myself in your love;
> in your flame I thought to be consumed;
> but I no longer fear your embers,
> nor of your iciness am I afraid.
> Torments to me are bonanzas
> and dread shipwrecks, safe harbors. . . .

Soon, however, his courage and his conscience together would generate
an irresistible current of moral energy, poised, serene, confident. How do
we know? We have the books to prove it.

For the moment, Cervantes had other problems. One of his first acts
was to write an appeal to the king citing Vallejo's error in setting his
bond so high and noting that as a prisoner away from home, the sum
fixed made it impossible for him to comply with the order to report to
Madrid. He asked the king to order the bond reduced to correspond with
the sum at issue. On December 1 the king obliged, ordering Vallejo to reduce the bond to his own "satisfaction." The magistrate was to see to it
that Cervantes arrived in Madrid within thirty days. Should the prisoner
fail to appear, the order stipulated, the sum would be collected from his
bondsmen and Cervantes be released since "he was not being held for any
reason other than the aforesaid."

What came of this order is uncertain. We do not know how long Cervantes remained in prison because the institution's entry and release records were destroyed in a riot in 1652. Astrana Marín believed that Vallejo, still hoping to screw a bribe out of Cervantes, refused to reduce the bond to manageable proportions and that the prisoner remained behind bars for seven months, until late April 1598. This allowed the biographer ample scope for developing his argument that *Don Quixote* was conceived as a novelette consisting of what are now the book's first nine chapters. He even had cousin Juan de Cervantes bringing books, especially books on chivalry, to Miguel in his prison of thieves.

In fact, all that is verifiable is that Cervates was free April 28, 1598, because on that day he presented his Teba accounts in Seville. He seems simply to have picked up his old life in Seville, all thought of his returning to Madrid dismissed from his mind. Strangely, no further official mention of the case is to be found in treasury records until 1599. The death of Philip II on September 13, 1598, and the ensuing raffle of public office by Philip III's favorite, the Duke of Lerma, may have temporarily paralyzed government operations.

Cervantes drops out of sight. He was almost certainly at work, at least spasmodically, on *Don Quixote* and on some of the novelas later published as the *Exemplary Stories*. If he thought of writing plays, a total ban decreed May 2, 1598, on all theatrical performances in Madrid except puppet shows, would have vetoed the plan.

One would have thought that the death of Ana de Villafranca on May 12 might have flushed him out of the underbrush. His daughter Isabel, then fourteen, was sent to live with her grandmother and, although money seems to have been left to her under the terms of Ana's will, the girl drew no immediate benefit from it. But no. Cervantes may have feared imprisonment if he set foot in the capital. He was undoubtedly short of cash. The girl was in good hands for the time being. He stayed put.

If we believe Andrea's declaration that he was a businessman with good friends, we can suppose he scraped by on marginal dealings. The documentary file is meager: a record that he acted as a middleman in a deal involving two quintals (two hundredweight) of biscuit, with Seville public prosecutor Jerónimo de Vanegas as guarantor. That his affairs were not prospering is evident from an agreement on September 15, when he was given three months of credit by Jerónimo Luis de Molina for enough coarse brown cloth to make two suits of clothes; this was probably a bit of veiled usury to make guarantor Francisco de Avila Sotomayor, a local attorney, pay double the value if Cervantes defaulted on the loan.

By this time the number of his "good friends" may have been reduced by one: Tomás Gutiérrez. The last document in which the two men ap-

pear together is the record of Gutiérrez's lawsuit in 1593. Never again
would Tomás post surety for his old friend; no further reference is seen to
Cervantes' residence in the hostel on the Calle de Bayona. Perhaps
Tomás finally grew weary of playing guardian angel; Cervantes may
have been hopelessly in debt to him; a quarrel might have arisen over
Cervantes' imprisonment, possibly in connection with the bond set by
Vallejo. The evidence is all negative and far from conclusive. If the
friendship did decay, however, the long-term reason must be found in
Clodio's observation in the *Persiles* that "friendships can endure between
poor men because equality of fortune is the chain that links their hearts;
but there can be no durable friendship between the rich and the poor because of the disparity existing between wealth and poverty."[9]

Yet, for all his difficulties, he seems to have been in crisp spirits, perhaps because he was writing and enjoying it, letting the stories build up
from character in a way no one in literature had ever done before. Judge
from the confident tone of one of the poems he wrote then, to the tomb
built in honor of Philip II in Seville.

News of the king's death after a reign of nearly forty-three years
reached Seville on September 18. It had not been unexpected; the king
had been an invalid for more than two years and he had stoutly endured
his death agony through fifty-three days of stench and horror. But his
reign had exceeded many of his subjects' lifetimes and the sense of loss, of
confusion and uncertainty that followed his death prompted exaggerated
signs of grief. Seville rose to the occasion like the huckster city it was. An
honorary tomb was to be built for Philip II. No expense was to be spared.
Archbishop Rodrigo de Castro's instructions to architect Juan de Oviedo
were to design "one of the most outstanding tumulary apparatuses human
eyes have ever chanced to see."[10]

For the fifty-two days the work required the whole city was draped in
black. By law, everyone wore mourning; even horses and mules were
shrouded in fine black cloth provided by the authorities when necessary.
Trade in all but basic commodities was halted. Gradually, the edifice
took shape: a three-story spectacular filling the space between the two
choirs of the church, crowned by a vault supporting an obelisk topped by
a great ball on which sat a phoenix in the flames, its head scraping the
roof of the nave. Lanes of arches flanked it on either side running the
width of the huge cathedral. The entire machine was of wood and plaster
painted to look like mauve-colored stone. It was crowded with paintings,
statues, inscriptions, altars, pyramids, globes, columns (nearly five hundred of them). In the center of the second level, under a crown of gold
and jewels on a crimson pillow, was the tomb itself, destined never to
hold any remains but those of the Sevillians' affection for a king whom,
in his lifetime, they had consistently swindled and duped.

The "apparatus" became the talk of Spain. In Act II of Lope's play *The Grateful Lover,* Leonardo tells Juan about it in 175 lines of meticulously recorded detail beginning:

> In honor of King Philip,
> stout column of the church,
> Seville, in its great grief,
> built this worthy memorial . . .
> a tomb which would abash
> the Pyramids of Egypt
> if it came to a contest. . . .

On November 24 this funerary bonbon was formally dedicated. On the twenty-fifth, each order paraded around the church bearing aloft its heavy silver and gold crosses. Then they filed into the sanctuary to hear the memorial mass, trailed by the city's secular priests, the doctors of the city's university, the sixty members of the Inquisition court, the royal magistrates and officers and municipal authorities with their men at arms.

Then the trouble started. Don Pedro López de Alday, the president of the royal court, seated himself on a low bench draped in black cloth. Ignoring the service in progress, the Inquisition objected on grounds of protocol: this, it insisted, was too much honor for him. When Don Pedro refused to budge, the Inquisitors excommunicated him on the spot. Efforts to make peace failing, the mass was completed behind closed doors in the sacristy to confine the scandal. All that could be wrung from the angry Inquisitors was temporary absolution while the quarrel was referred to the Royal Council for decision.

There the situation rested until after Christmas, while Seville in its thousands jammed the cathedral day after day to gape at the tomb. From time to time, poets would declaim respectful verses to the glory of the structure and its subject.

"On Tuesday, 29 December of the said year," wrote eyewitness Francisco de Ariño, "the order came from His Majesty that the services be held, and it seems that the Inquisition was sentenced to pay for the candles burned on the first day, and the city those used in the masses, and that the magistrates not be seated on a dais; and on that day, while I was in the holy church, a swaggering poet entered and recited an octave on the grandeur of the tomb."[11]

The "swaggering poet" was Cervantes and the "octave" was a sonnet which might very well have miffed the right-thinking Ariño:

> I swear to God that all this grandeur frightens me,
> and I'd give a crown to describe it.

For who would not be struck with wonder
at this remarkable machine, this richness?

By the living Christ, each piece
is worth a million, and it is a sore thing
that it might not endure a century. Oh great Seville,
triumphant Rome in wit and in nobility!
I bet that, to enjoy this seat,
the dead man's soul has abandoned
his eternal life in heaven's splendor!
A bravo heard this, and said, "It's true
wotcherhonor says, Sir Soldier,
and if anyone says different, why—he lies!"
And then he leered,
clapped his hat on, fondled his sword,
peered around him, left, and that was the end of it.

Within weeks the sonnet was being circulated in copies and broadsides everywhere in Spain. Lope de Vega, who would later scoff at Cervantes as the worst of poets, said it would be more famous than any of his own poems. Cervantes himself called it the "chief honor of my writings."[12] Its very popularity makes us wonder at how subtly we have gauged popular feeling when we insist on how beloved Philip was by his subjects. It is true that Seville is the immediate butt of the gibe and that Spaniards were always eager to make fun of that peacock of a city. The poem evokes an image of a Cervantes not long out of prison, broke, with no visible future, exasperated with the tough, moneyed, ostentatious Sevillians, at their skin-deep emotions and overweening pride.

But beyond Seville lay another target, Philip II himself, as ruinously extravagant as any vainglorious caballero in Seville. Cervantes was manifestly among those who felt that Philip's imperial vanity and narrow piety had left his country weakened, impoverished, as isolated as a disaffected cloister. Américo Castro traced a line of what he saw as slighting references to the king beginning in La Galatea;[13] if some of his proofs seem unconvincing, it is hard to fault his connection of the sonnet with another funerary poem by Cervantes included "because they are his" in a celebrational volume on the ceremonies by the licenciado Francisco Jerónimo Collador:[14]

Doubtless they will have to call you
a new and peaceful Mars,
since in repose you won
most of what you wanted.

And that is much the least of it. . . .
That the treasure chests,
in which were stored the gold
they say you gathered, are empty
shows us that you were hiding
your treasure in heaven. . . .

Later, his estimates of Philip's profligacy reinforced by his observation of Philip III's prodigality, Cervantes would urge what we would now recognize as an elective constitutional monarchy. The wise Mauricio tells the pilgrims in the *Persiles* that in his homeland the throne "is not inherited nor handed in succession from father to son; the inhabitants elect (their king) at their pleasure, striving always to find the most virtuous and best man"; by "common consent," he then rules absolutely for life "so long as he does not worsen. . . ."[15]

It was on the day following Cervantes' recitation, December 30, that the memorial services for Philip at last took place. The magistrate's bench was draped with the same black cloth that had started the quarrel, but Don Pedro remained standing throughout the service. The compromise satisfied everyone, for which we should rejoice, because a terrifyingly high number of the mourners would themselves be dead before the autumn.

Isolated cases of bubonic plague had been recorded in Seville as early as 1596. By late 1598, the incidence of the disease, the usual result of famine caused by a series of bad crop years, was becoming disturbing despite municipal efforts to ignore it for fear of driving trade away. "God spare you," says Guzmán de Alfarache, "the sickness that comes down from Castile and the hunger that goes up from Andalusia."[16] For three years, the sickness had been drifting down through Castile from Britain, Flanders and Normandy, saving its most venomous bite for Spain. A good crop in 1598 could not have held it off, but ample food might have softened its killing blow. Instead, drought that year sent grain prices to their highest level of the century, and the following year was to be no better. "This was a year of great calamities in this city," Zúñiga would record for 1599, "because in addition to the plague, which clung to it, there was a great drought."

The plague of 1599–1601 has been called the first of the three great offensives of death in the seventeenth century and it was probably the worst of them. Together they caused at least 1,250,000 deaths—half of them in the three years at the turn of the century: 600,000 dead, according to a probably accurate contemporary source,[17] 8 per cent of the country's population. An equivalent mortality today would wipe out nearly 4.5 million people in Britain or France, nearly 18 million in the United

States, 80 million in China. It has been thought of as the coup de grâce to a decadent Spain and while there were surely other claimants to the deed, it is true that nearly a century was needed to make up the population loss.

Between 1600 and 1620, foreigners, mainly French, came to fill the gaps the disease had left among Spain's corps of merchants, artisans, financiers, manufacturers, taking control of the Spanish economy for quick profits sent abroad rather than reinvested at home. Spain's army became largely a mercenary force. The obliteration of whole peasant families, even entire communities, accelerated the process of land absorption by the relatively lightly touched aristocracy. For plague made clear the class differences in Spain, and intensified the hatreds. It was the rich who left contaminated cities to hide on their country estates, leaving the poor locked into the cities to die. Many city authorities fled, leaving a few public-spirited men to organize what countermeasures they could. Priests not infrequently refused to attend the dying. Archbishop de Castro hid in Écija for four months until the first great wave of death began to ebb with the passing of the hottest part of the summer. He declined even to receive emissaries from his stricken diocese.

By the spring of 1599 the epidemic could no longer be kept secret. The doctors, those who had not fled to the country, were now too frequently seen rushing through the streets of Seville, disseminating their obscene pharmacopoeia: sudorifics and tonics, borage distilled in sorrel water with lemon syrup and dittany leaves, sulphuric acid in an infusion of viper grass and other such natural remedies. The magicians left off hiding letters in eggs and making roast pigs grunt and turned their hands to nostrums for the disease which so frightened Sancho that he refused even to name it, sensibly preferring to run away and hide from it.

The doctors were calmly confident and, surprisingly, not as ineffective as might be thought. Their recommendation that people wear leather clothing and eliminate sex had the beneficial side-effects of helping people keep their plague-bearing fleas to themselves. Despite the leeches the doctors placed on abscesses and the filthy blades with which they lanced buboes, the recovery rate in the hospitals was decent, largely because there, at least, the sick were fed regularly. Most of those who died received no treatment at all. Many of these had refused care, refused to admit they were ill—the rich because they thought it dishonorable to suffer from a disease of the hungry poor, the poor out of shame or fear of isolation or dread of the hospitals.

In Seville, five thousand perished in May and June of 1599 and the total for the year there exceeded eight thousand. When the first wave of plague waned in September, an epidemic of tertian fever took its place to carry off many of those already weakened by their fight against the black death. Then, with the return of torrid weather in 1600, bubonic returned, driving Vicente Espinel's Marcos de Obregon out to the fields where pirates captured him. Only the nobility, shut into their high towers behind the walls of their country fortresses, the traditional laws of hospitality suspended until the threat finally receded late in 1602, were relatively safe. They, and the rapidly rising number of bandits besieging the roads on the prowl for refugees from the cities.

In this atmosphere of hunger, death, corruption and cruelty, the first part of Alemán's *Guzmán de Alfarache,* which appeared in March 1599, was an immediate success, going through twenty Spanish editions alone by 1604.

Guzmán might qualify as the most bitter book ever written. A story of a rogue boy growing up in a rogue world, it remains the archtypical picaresque novel. The lean, staccato brilliance of its language, its inventiveness and erudition, the depth of its emotional sincerity and Alemán's talent for storytelling make it the greatest of the Golden Century's prose epics, after *Don Quixote.* More: it is considered a landmark in the history of prose fiction, the first large-scale work to present a picture of real life and manners set against the times in which it was written.

There are points at which Alemán's life mirrors that of Cervantes. They were born only a few days apart; Alemán's father was the official surgeon at the Seville prison, but no less a bonesetter for that than Rodrigo de Cervantes. Alemán was probably of converso origin. And he was twice a prisoner in the Seville prison, in 1580 and again—for debt despite his book's popularity—in 1602. Both writers were victims of what was then current practice, the appearance of spurious sequels to their novels.

The differences between these two giants of literary history are equally striking: Alemán attended the University of Seville before going on to study philosophy and medicine at Salamanca and Alcalá. He toiled for seventeen years as a royal auditor. In 1608 he wangled a post in Mexico, where he wrote mainly devotional works before disappearing sometime after 1613. His book is so different from Cervantes', however, that the two men seem to have existed in different centuries, almost on different planets. *Guzmán* is a Gothic work, a dead end of a book about a world that has come to a dead end; *Don Quixote* is a doorway to the future. *Guzmán* is a long complaint, a tract in fictional form; *Don Quixote* is an epic poem in prose. One is a simulacrum of life, the other, although it was conceived as literature, is life itself.

For the effect of Alemán's novel is oddly two-dimensional, like a Byzantine icon. There is no doubting the accuracy of his delineation of picaresque society, but—is this all there is to reality? *Guzmán* is a book to satisfy those who believe that feces are real and a rose, somehow, is not.

Its hero—anti-hero—lives in a curiously stagnant world of wanton cruelty and total corruption, a hopeless place in which man is condemned by God's creative incompetence to a life of lawless struggle against injustice. In this trickster's world, morality is wholly pragmatic: "Although I was evil, I wanted to be good, if not to enjoy that benefaction, at least so as not to see myself subjected to any grave harm."[18] Nothing humanity can do will change this iron order of savagery in which change itself obeys no law but that of inconstancy. In the most profound sense, nothing happens in the book; its wealth of incident is really only a series of examples testifying to man's inherent depravity: "Everything was, is and will be the same. The first father was perfidious, the first mother mendacious; the first son a thief and a fratricide. What is there now which did not exist before, or which might be hoped for in future?"[19] The boy Guzmán we meet at the start of the book and the full-grown rascal sentenced to the king's galleys for theft are the same person, unaltered and essentially undynamic. He is one of those who learns nothing and forgets nothing, chiefly because his universe, totally without elasticity, neither affects him nor is affected by him. Guzmán is there to tell us, in windy sermons which have long since lost the popular following they had then, that man's sole hope is to secure his personal moral and spiritual salvation. Yet this too, he warns, is futile.

In a passage in Part One,[20] Alemán imagines a congress of the gods at which Jupiter expresses his anger at men and his impulse to destroy them. After all, he comments in a line denying the very basis of Christ's mission, "there need not be any." Castro has noted the anecdote's parallel in Genesis, in which Jehovah, furious at men's wickedness, threatens to "destroy man whom I have created from the face of the earth; both man, and beast, and the creeping thing, and the fowls of the air; for it repenteth me that I have made them."[21] Apollo dissuades Jupiter, however, reasoning that "you must either give them free will or not; if you do give it to them, they will necessarily be what they were before; if you take it away, they will not be men and you will have created in vain all this machinery of sky, earth, stars, moon, sun, composition of the elements and other things you made so perfectly. . . ." He advises Jupiter simply to deprive men of the god Contentment he had left with them.

God thus becomes a disgruntled father who will receive the repentant sinner with open arms—but who will not lift a finger to help him, who will stand by in regretful inactivity if the sinner stumbles and falls in the attempt, as he inevitably must. Worse: He deliberately places obstacles in men's path. Alemán explains ironically that "since his divine Majesty sends us trials as they serve and for reasons He knows, all designed for our greatest good if we wish to profit from them, we should give thanks for them all, for they are signs that we have not been forgotten." In this,

God is cheating: the trials he visits on men are "gilded pills which, tricking the sight with false appearance of succulence, leave the body disordered and wasted. They are green pastures full of venomous vipers, stones which seem of great value and under which are nests of scorpions, eternal death tricked by brief life."[22]

This was a conclusion to which Cervantes could not have subscribed. No doubt he admired Alemán's work; lines from it were imbedded in Gines de Pasamonte's speech in Don Quixote's adventure with the galley slaves, and Cervantes, we recall, referred directly to Guzmán in *The Illustrious Serving Wench*. Certainly he shared Alemán's view of man's bestiality—to a point. Guzmán's cynicism regarding the first family seems to receive a vote of assent in *The Dogs' Colloquy* when Berganza (for these talking dogs are Cervantes' symbols of man as enlightened beast) asserts:

. . . we inherit the tendency to do and speak evil from our first parents and suck it with our mother's milk. You can see this clearly in the fact that the child has barely got his arm out of his swaddling clothes before he raises his hand as if he wanted to take his revenge on the person he thinks has offended him; and with almost the first words he utters he calls his nurse or his mother a whore.

But the two men were too profoundly different in personality to agree philosophically. Alemán had wit where Cervantes had humor. There is a basic softness in Alemán, an almost romantic self-pity which collides with the tougher, more resilient core of Cervantes' nature. Maybe this reflects no more than a difference in fundamental vitality—that force which so identifies with life as to be beyond the dismal pressures of reason. "Melancholy was always kin to death," observes Cristina in Act I of Cervantes' *The Dalliance,* and so is Guzmán's cynical pessimism.

It has been alleged that Cervantes never tried to explore the metaphysical problems of illusion-reality. Even if we note that novelists are seldom philosophers, that their function is to crystallize problems, not to establish systems, the fact remains that Cervantes probed more deeply than all but a handful of major novelists into the organs of metaphysical thought. And the area of his search is to be found in the contrast between Guzmán de Alfarache's "reality"—the reality of a man to whom the world owes not only a living, but a meaning as well, a purpose—and the "illusion" of, say, a Quixote that if he can fashion reality into a meaning of his own, it may later be confirmed by divine endorsement.

It takes no special perception, Cervantes seems to insist, to see the world's injustice or recognize that man is a wretched creature, more beast than god. The trick is to go beyond this, to find in this cesspool a method that will justify man's persistent intimations of his sublimity. Cervantes, in other words, begins where Alemán leaves off.

Their difference centers in the two men's appreciation of free will. Where Alemán saw it as God's error, Cervantes thought of it as man's salvation. Cervantes was the first in a long line of writers (Ibsen, Pirandello, Unamuno, Camus and many more) who believed one must create one's own being, that one must assume God's function in order to fulfill God's purpose—or to supply a purpose if, in fact, God had none. Cervantes did not, like Alemán, lament that God has not done man's work for him; he clearly believed that, having supplied the tools and the raw materials, God left it up to man to use them, to model himself in what he innately knew to be the Lord's likeness. Only thus, Cervantes believed, could he create an equilibrium between the talking, weeping, laughing beast he is and the divinity from which he emerged and to which, if he is a good and skillful workman, he will return.

The difference between Alemán and Cervantes was, finally, one of spaciousness of mind: the ability to fuse abstract intellectual problems with experience to project a new and heightened reality.

Cervantes was determined to join the ranks of the epic poets. He subscribed, at least in theory, to the classical definition of an epic as a recital of heroic deeds and perfect love expressed in masterful language through characters who are larger than life in order to instruct and delight the reader. He accepted the classicists' rules for epic writing: decorum (appropriateness of sentiment and tone to a personage's station in life), imitation (a vague term roughly meaning creative imitation of human nature as presented in an admirable model), verisimilitude of plot line, *admiratio* (wonder and amazement), variety and vigor of characterization.

He was also keenly aware that the rules were under attack. The romances of chivalry which, especially since the invention of the printing press, had become Europe's favorite form of fiction, were going out of style then, but their popularity had impressed the serious poets. So had Lope's anti-Aristotelian revolution in the theater. The old guard's absolute obedience to Aristotle's *Poetics* and Horace's *Ars Poetica,* their total devotion to the artificial perfection of the divine Virgil were beginning to get in the way of literary experimentation. Besides, something was obviously wrong with standards that held even Homer to be vulgar because of his closeness to nature.

Cervantes had been following the debate. He knew Gian Batista Guarini's argument, put forth in 1586, that the *Poetics* was a beginning, not an end, that the new concept of tragicomedy purged spectators' minds of melancholy more effectively than archaic tragedy did. More important, Cervantes had certainly read Tasso's 1587 *Discourse on the Art of Poetry,* in which Europe's leading literary theorist urged the need for historical truth—realism—in the epic; arguing that the classical epic could be revitalized only by incorporating in it the features that made the romances of chivalry so pleasing, he defined the writer's task as the expression of human nature through universal truth (things as they might be) based on history (things as they are) in a varied and pleasing way.

In Spain, Fernando de Herrera had a foot in each camp, but Cervantes is known to have been influenced by his defense of Spanish literature and his championship of the Spanish language as an epic instrument. More influential still, probably, was Dr. Alonso López-Pinciano's first Spanish-language commentary on the *Poetics,* the *Philosophía antigua poética,* which appeared in 1596. While basically advocating the old criteria—the book's avowed purpose was to combat Lope's dramatic innovations—Pinciano did adopt some of the new criticism's recommendations. He endorsed comedy as an instrument for morally instructive ends. And his book asserted that prose could be as suitable to the epic as poetry. "What rustics, what plebeians, what city dwellers speak in meter?" Pinciano demanded.[23] "For the epic may be written as well in prose as in verse," agrees Cervantes in *Don Quixote.*[24]

Cervantes lined up with the avant-garde. He had no intention of slavishly following even Pinciano's enlightened conservatism. The doctor's dictum in Dialogue Nine that comedy is imitation of the worst in men as tragedy is of the best is made visible nonsense in *Don Quixote.* The laws of decorum limiting eloquence and wisdom to characters of noble presence are repealed by Sancho's eloquence and his wisdom as a governor. Small details shatter the rule that the noble must never be held up to ridicule—the knight's embarrassment, for example, at having to mend the run in his black hose with green thread, thus literally knitting up a raveled dream of glory with the thread of reality.

The problem Cervantes set himself to solve was colossal: to reconcile "historical" and poetic truth. This was the vital distinction Alemán missed. The storytelling tradition into which *Guzmán* fits would do to depict the reality of mutilated hopes, of crooked officials, foolish rulers and the glutinous despair of the picaresca. It was too static to deal simultaneously with the poetic truth of harmony and beauty, of ideal goodness and the spotless refuge of perfect love. Yet, Cervantes recognized, as Alemán could not, that historical and poetic truth are interlocked in a constant tension of assault and riposte, of impingement and redressment.

To express this, Cervantes would have to create a dynamic new technique of change and interchange. To satisfy the masters of the new criticism to whom his book would really be addressed, his method would have to contain all the epical ingredients of unity and grandeur and moral power and still appeal to a public primarily interested in a good story.

His own experience had taught him to know that public in the inns between Madrid and Seville. "On feast days in harvest time," says an innkeeper in *Don Quixote*, "many of the reapers gather here, and there is always one who can read, and he will pick up one of these books and there will be more than thirty of us clustered around him and we listen to him read with such pleasure that it relieves us of a thousand worries." To please both these illiterate villagers and the neo-Aristotelians: it was an exciting challenge. *Don Quixote* would be a logbook of the author's experiments, failures, regressions, breakthroughs, the laboratory in which the modern novel was developed. Beside it, *Guzmán* seems, for all its intense feeling and masterful language, a lifeless exercise. Its personages are smaller than life, not larger; both heroism and love are suckers' games in this catalogue of corruption.

The impression of lifelessness is reinforced when we understand that the literary argument then raging was no hothouse debate among aesthetes. Behind it loomed the great scientific-secular upheaval which, in the late sixteenth and early seventeenth centuries, brought two worlds into conflict. The old hierarchical world of Aristotle and Galen and the fixed Ptolemaic heavens was losing its hold on men's minds. This had been the world of miracles and revealed truth, a world of poetic reality. Opposing it was the new "historical" reality of Kepler's third law and Harvey's pumping heart, of a cuckoo-clock Cartesian universe—itself, had men but known it, as illusory as the old. Cervantes struggled to create a form which would contain the old literary universe and the new, as Kepler worked to reconcile the new astronomy with the astrology of the ancients. No such gigantic striving informs *Guzmán de Alfarache*.

What was Cervantes up to while plague, famine, corruption and literary gloom swirled around him? It depends on which biographer you read. The documentary gaps are wide enough to drive armies of theories through:

FEBRUARY 10, 1599: Styling himself "a servant of His Majesty" although he is not known to have been officially employed then, he takes notarized receipt of ninety ducats from Don Juan de Cervantes in repayment of a loan. No one is certain of who the Don Juan de Cervantes was.

FEBRUARY 20: Treasury officials again call on Cervantes to account for the Ronda leg of his 1594 mission, claiming reimbursement of 27,000 maravedis he had already paid. The summons was sent to Seville, but there is no record of his having responded to it either there or in Madrid.

AUGUST 9: Isabel appears for the first time as Isabel de Saavedra in a document appointing Bartolomé de Torres as her guardian. She is still, however, referred to as the daughter of "Alonso Rodríguez and Ana Franca, his wife."

AUGUST 11: Torres places Isabel in service to Magdalena de Sotomayor, "daughter of licenciado Cervantes de Saavedra," for two years, committing her to render "good and faithful service" to Cervantes' sister in return for her food, drink, a bed, a clean nightgown and twenty ducats in cash. Cervantes may have been in Madrid to engineer this pseudo-adoption, but he nowhere appears in the process and it is equally possible that it was carried through without his presence. Magdalena was then living alone, but apparently, like Andrea and Constanza, earning her living as a seamstress, a skill she contracted to teach Isabel.

MAY 2, 1600: Cervantes appears in Seville as a witness supporting a petition for residency by Agustín de Cetina. This places him in the city at least from March 18, when the petition was presented, to May 2.

JULY 2: Rodrigo de Cervantes, still an alférez, is killed in Flanders at the battle of Nieuport, a foolish and unnecessary engagement in which tired, outnumbered Spanish forces were routed by a strongly entrenched Dutch contingent. At his death, his arrears in pay came to over 238,000 maravedis, which would occasion lawsuits by three generations of heirs. Litigation trails off in 1651 with 36,000 maravedis still due.

AUGUST 19: The will of Cervantes' brother-in-law Fernando de Palacios is heard in Toledo, as was customary when a novitiate entered holy orders. As Fray Antonio de Salazar, the boy, then nineteen, was going into the Franciscan monastery of San Juan de los Reyes. Among the will's provisions: "I order that no accounting be required of Doña Catalina de Salazar and Miguel de Cervantes, her husband, for their administration of my maternal and paternal inheritance in regard to the income thereof, because I give them dispensation for it (*se lo perdono*)." His estate is to be shared equally by Catalina and his brother Francisco;[25] as executors, he names Francisco and Cervantes. The presumption, again with no formal proof, is that Cervantes attended the ceremony to accept his executorial responsibility, possibly remaining in Toledo at least until September 17, when Fernando entered the monastery.

JANUARY 15, 1602: Catalina de Palacios Vozmediana, under a power of attorney from her absent husband, sells a plot of land to Gabriel Quixada de Salazar for 10,200 maravedis. Since Francisco has now come into his inheritance, the sale may have been imposed by creditors' claims against the family estate.

JANUARY 27: Cervantes stands as godfather in Esquivias to the daughter of Bartolomé de Uxena and Ana de la Peña. For once, the godmother is not the assiduous Catalina, but Juana Gaitán. Apparently as wistful as ever for the children she would never have, Catalina would return to the font—alone—for other neighbors in September and again, for the last time in Esquivias, in January 1603.

SEPTEMBER 14: The question of Cervantes' 1594 accounts is revived in an interoffice query in which it is still maintained that he owes the government 79,804 maravedis. No new summons is known to have been issued to him.

JANUARY 14, 1603: Royal auditors return to Cervantes' 1594 accounts, getting their figures wrong again. Ten days later, a commission of accountants complains that he still has not appeared to answer for them, but he cannot be summoned because his whereabouts are unknown.

FEBRUARY 8: In Madrid, Andrea de Cervantes formally declares receipt of 788 reales for sewing done for the Marquis and Marchioness of Villafranca, an immensely rich couple who would later ruin themselves trying to keep up with the Lermas. An itemized bill included as a supplementary document is signed by Cervantes as a witness.

A dozen documents in four years, and in only four of them does he appear in person. Rodríguez Marín, noting his absence from the property sale in January 1602 and unaware of his presence in Esquivias less than two weeks later, thought Cervantes might have been in jail at the time. The idea has since acquired a life of its own, as though some Cervantists had a vested emotional interest in the man's continuing disgrace.

Many of those who reject the idea have no doubt been too quick to conclude that it was junked by Astrana Marín's discovery of the 1602 baptismal registration; the blocks of time still unaccounted for allow for any theory, including a second and, as some have proposed, even a third jail term in 1601–2. Cervantes had not, after all, legally acquitted himself of the charge that had put him in prison in the first place. Yet those who so meticulously insist that no proof has yet turned up to keep him out of jail seem too willing to forget that no evidence exists to clap him into it.

Those who will have Cervantes trundled in and out of prison like a hound in heat being dragged back to its kennel must agree that the burden of proof lies on them. They have their work cut out for them. Cervantes, we now know, was not in prison in January 1602. Probably he had not been in prison when he was appointed executor of Fernando's estate; even on the unlikely presumption that he was not in Toledo then, it is too improbable that Fernando would have made the appointment had his executor been sitting in a cell. Nor, in all probability, was Cervantes in prison on August 22, 1602, when he "dated" the composition of Chapter 25 of *Don Quixote*, Part I, in the knight's love letter to Dulcinea. And it is a good bet that he was still a free man in the autumn of 1602, when a new romance of chivalry was published in Valencia. The book, Juan de

Silva y Toledo's *Don Policisne de Boecia,* was the last of its kind to be published in Spain (subsequent publications were all reprints). Parts of it are imitated in Chapters 28 and 30 of *Don Quixote,* Part I, and knowing Cervantes' vacuum-cleaner work habits, we can reasonably assume he saw it soon after its publication that September. It was as characteristic of Cervantes to incorporate contemporary events into his stories as it was for him to use whatever date he happened to be writing on when the need for one arose.

Astrana Marín's proposition is equally unproven, but it is more plausible. He saw Cervantes run out of Seville by the plague early in 1599. Relying, perhaps too creatively, on Cervantes' tendency to turn autobiography into incident, he had Cervantes so eager to flee that he left a trunkful of books and manuscripts in the Venta del Alcalde, on the main north-south road, where "The Tale of Foolish Curiosity" might conveniently be discovered by Don Quixote's priest in Part I, Chapter 32.

Cervantes would spend the ensuing two years, according to this scenario, shuttling between Seville, Toledo and Madrid with salutary intervals in Esquivias. Presuming on no more evidence than an acquaintanceship between Cervantes and Fernando de Toledo, lord of Higares, it has him employed by the nobleman—as, heaven help them both, an accountant—in Toledo. Sometime early in 1602, Cervantes is seen as leaving Andalusia for the last time.

As a working hypothesis, it will do. However the facts are arranged, the all-important event is unchanged: Cervantes, then fifty-four years old, had finally made his break. He had escaped from freedom. He could work now.

Part V

THE JOURNEYMAN

29

Harlequin's Slapstick

When King Philip III died in 1621, irreverent madrileños said he had been killed by the heat of a brazier because the proper official was not on hand to remove it. The story was apocryphal, but it summarizes the atmosphere of rigidly ceremonious indolence in which that inglorious man lived.

Philip had always been a disappointment to his father. Flabby-faced and sickly, he had been considered too fragile for serious training in government. In some ways he took after the old king: he was a solitary figure, gluttonous and dyspeptic; he drank no wine, only water—boiled cinnamon water according to Venetian ambassador Simon Contarini, water from a spring in Alcalá de Henares which was carried to him everywhere he went, if we believe Bartolomé Joly. He was something of a linguist, disliking war but versed in the use of arms, a womanizer on a moderate scale, a composer of undistinguished music, so devout he would be called Philip the Pious. All of this recalls his father's character. The differences between them were few, but fundamental. Young Philip had an inferior mind and he detested work. Probably his poor health drained his energy, made him unable to concentrate. So, having inherited his father's absolutist philosophy and his imperial pretensions, he was incapable of doing anything on his own to preserve them. Philip II had been all too aware of his son's deficiencies. On his deathbed, he had complained to Don Cristóbal de Moura that "God, who has given me so many kingdoms, has not granted me a son fit to govern them."

Twenty years old when he mounted the throne, Philip III was very pleased to be king but not in the least willing to put in the office hours the job required. For months at a time he would hold himself aloof from his subjects; all those with business to transact were dismissed with the excuse that "their majesties have come here to amuse themselves and not to deal with business."[1] It is said that while the pleasure-hungry sovereign danced, gambled at cards and cultivated the crude practical jokes of the time, monitors posted in the palace corridors kept anyone from disturbing him with affairs of state.

The right way to rule, as far as he could see, had been at hand for years: revival of the old system of government by *privados* or *validos*— royal favorites—which had virtually ruined medieval Spain until it was painfully uprooted by Isabel the Catholic.

Philip had just the man: Don Francisco Gómez de Sandoval y Rojas, Marquis of Denia, soon to be Duke of Lerma. Hardly anyone else liked him. Just over fifty, swarthy, with a lustrous, melancholy gaze, he could indeed be tactful, charming, mild-mannered, affable. He could also, said Contarini, be envious, jealous, inconstant, given to impetuous temper tantrums and avid for flattery. He was hated, it was said, for never listening to anyone or letting them speak, which he knew but was too vain to do anything to remedy. Of impeccable Valencian lineage, he was descended from both St. Francis Borja and King Ferdinand; he was also as impoverished as a marquis could be. His assessment of his new responsibilities was forthright: see to it that Philip was amused, keep things going somehow and make the house of Sandoval very, very rich. He was to succeed in these deceptively simple objectives for nearly nineteen years.

Every possible event—a baptism, the sanctification of St. Raymond, a birthday—became the occasion for celebrations of unprecedented sumptuousness at a time when the country was nearly prostrated by poverty and overtaxation. Philip's marriage to his cousin Marguerite of Austria in 1599 cost nearly a fifth of the annual national income. New taxes were devised, of course, but they did not begin to bridge the deficit in a royal budget in which expenses regularly exceeded receipts by some 60 per cent a year. With all the state's ordinary revenues for 1599–1600 pledged in advance to the moneylenders, Lerma persuaded Philip to do what his father had stubbornly refused to allow: debase the currency. By the end of 1603, the price of a candle was nearly three times the weight of the candle itself.

Gifts, gratuities, titles quickly made the new Duke of Lerma rich. He arranged for a vacancy in the See of Toledo by dismissing Archbishop García de Loaysa, who died of the shock; Don Pedro Portocarrero was relieved of the Inquisitor-generalship, and both posts were awarded to Lerma's uncle, the unassuming Bernardo Cardinal de Sandoval, Cervantes' future patron. The Toledo prelacy alone was said to be worth over 300,000 ducats a year. The court was turned into a souk in which almost every office in the land was sold (and frequently resold) to the highest bidder. At its peak, the Lerma fortune would be estimated at an incredible 44 million ducats, enough money to float even Philip's swollen state budget for eight years.

Perhaps nothing proves Lerma's absolute sway over the king more astoundingly than the decision to move the national capital from Madrid to Valladolid.

Rumors of the planned move had been giving Madrid the jitters for nearly a year. On the night of January 10, 1601, it was officially announced. The very next day the long convoys of bullock carts carrying the royal possessions began clogging the two main roads toward the new royal palace in Valladolid, built of shoddy plaster painted to resemble brick and dotted with fine blue-and-gold balconies. Official excuses, equally shoddy, were also in luxuriant supply. Although Charles V had chosen Madrid partly for its salubrious air, it was now decided (with some justification) that the air of Valladolid was kinder to the king's delicate health. Prices, it was argued, were lower in the old northern capital, and so they were until the court arrived. Lerma's decision was bought by Valladolid for hard cash, 400,000 ducats, as Madrid would buy it back five years later for nearly ten times that price. In 1601, however, the duke was anxious to remove his sovereign from the influence of the royal grandmother, the powerful Dowager Empress Maria of Austria, who had retired to the Reformed Carmelite convent in Madrid and who hated Francisco Gómez de Sandoval.

Andrea de Cervantes and her daughter depended for their living on proximity to the court, where the rich and fashionable were concentrated. By the time they moved to Valladolid, probably with Magdalena, in 1603, Madrid had become a ghost town where the poor were paid to inhabit abandoned mansions to keep them safe. Sometime in the summer of 1604 Cervantes followed them there, perhaps not so much to join them as to be near the bulging manuscript of *The Ingenious Gentleman Don Quixote of La Mancha,* which may already have made the trip north with bookseller Francisco de Robles.

For the book—what we now know as Part I—was finished. It seems from this remove almost to have sprung full-grown from Cervantes' thigh, so little do we know about the circumstances of its creation. Occasional dates and incidents in it, none earlier than 1597,[2] mark the work's progress. Cervantes is thought to have spent most of 1602–3 completing it in Esquivias, in the big house facing the church. Since he is known to have been a slow, deliberate worker, we may reasonably suppose that he arrived there with a rough draft, perhaps hardly more than a bundle of anecdotes, which he then settled down to thread together, but this can only be conjecture. The important fact was that, after some seven years of work and nearly twenty years of all but total literary silence, he had a book to sell.

Robles, the son of the Blas de Robles who had brought out *La Galatea*, had undoubtedly been hearing about Cervantes' book for years; parts of it had certainly been read aloud to gatherings of writers, perhaps in the shop the publisher maintained in Madrid when he moved his head-quarters to Valladolid. Signs of hasty last-minute revisions suggest that Robles was now pressing Cervantes to seek a privilege for publication as quickly as he could.

What was the author paid for his years of work? We can only guess, because the contract for it has been lost. Since *The Ingenious Gentleman* was a longer book than *La Galatea*, he presumably collected more than the 1,336 reales he got in 1584. But Robles was known to drive a sharp bargain. In 1603, despite the inflation which was soaring again after a few years of relative price stability, he bought Agustín de Rojas' *Viaje entretenida* for a miserly 1,100 reales plus thirty copies of the printed book. We can hope that Cervantes received at least the 1,600 reales he would collect for his *Exemplary Stories* in 1613. Even at that he was being cheated. Compare the figure—slightly under 150 ducats—with the fee El Greco received for his painting "The Burial of Count Orgaz" in 1586. The canvas had taken less than a year to complete and the painter, having asked 1,600 *ducats* for it, had to settle for 1,200 ducats despite an appeal to the pope.

Cervantes' feelings about booksellers were, understandably, not tender. In *The Glass Scholar*, Rodaja chides a dealer for "all the 'i's' they dot and the 't's' they cross when they buy the privilege of a book." An author explains to Don Quixote that he is printing his book at his own expense and expects to make a pile of money on it. When the knight suggests that he'll be no match for the wily publishers, he draws an irritated retort: " 'What would you have me do, then?' said the author. 'Does your grace expect me to give it to a bookseller, who might give me three maravedis for it and think he's doing me a favor at that?' "[3]

The "three maravedis" Cervantes did get, however, enabled him to move bag, baggage and Doña Catalina to Valladolid; in the autumn of 1604 he was living in a still-unfinished building in a low-class district of the new capital, on what is now the Calle del Rastro. The move is not surprising; after so many years in the frothy atmosphere of Seville, the air of decay, genteel in Toledo, morose in Madrid, would have been untenable. On July 21 he had been present for the formal division of his mother-in-law's estate and had watched most of it filter through Francisco's hands into the pockets of the family's creditors. After his enforced isolation in Esquivias, Cervantes would have been eager for excitement, to wander streets crowded with people, to gamble, to talk shop with the writers thronging to the court. Practically everyone who wasn't actually working there passed through regularly—Quevedo (complaining acridly about the displacement of the court), Góngora, Vélez de Guevara, Espinel, Salas Barbadillo, Bartolomé Leonardo de Argensola, Suárez de Figueroa, who would be among Cervantes' most scurrilous critics, and Francisco López de Ubeda, who would be the first among them to praise *Don Quixote* publicly.

The building Cervantes inhabited was one of five new houses jerry-built by a small-bore speculator hoping to cash in on the influx of riffraff into the city. It was an instant slum. A noxious stream, its banks buried under piles of rubbish, ran some twenty yards from the door, spanned by a rickety wooden footbridge leading to the municipal slaughterhouse. On the building's ground floor was a tavern, much frequented by the butchers. Adjoining the row of three-story buildings was the Hospital de la Resurrección, a hospital for the poor.

What is more surprising is to find Cervantes presiding in patriarchal authority over an entire colony of family and friends from Esquivias, Madrid and Toledo. In the apartment over the tavern lived Cervantes, Doña Catalina, Andrea, Constanza, Magdalena and Isabel. Perhaps a servant as well; he is known to have hired a serving-girl named María de Ceballos early in 1605. Opposite them on the same floor lived Cervantes' cousin Luisa de Montoya with her two sons and a daughter. Above, over the Cervantes household, were friend Mariana Ramírez, her mother and two young daughters. And across the landing dwelt Juana Gaitán with her husband Diego de Hondaro, her sister Luisa de Ayala and a niece, Catalina de Aguilera. After Hondaro's death in March 1605, his widow stayed on in the apartment, taking in, as boarders, María de Argomeda, her servant Isabel de Islallana, and Jerónima de Sotomayor, the wife of a yeoman of Lerma's guard. Finally, in a mansard room lived a local gossip and part-time procuress named Isabel de Ayala. A total of twenty-two people living in thirteen rooms, some tiny, some no more than alcoves. An instant slum, with servants.

Yet this clustering reinforces the impression of liberation emanating from the facts of Cervantes' life. With solid work behind and before him, he now appears to have thought himself strong enough, sufficiently poised, to allow him to shelter among his own without fear of suffocation.

Probably, too, a more sinister motive helped force him to it. Almost certainly he had been feeling increasingly run-down. His muscles were not obeying him as they once had. Cervantes had always been a lean man, but he was probably becoming emaciated despite an increasingly voracious appetite which, like all the poor of Spain, he would have tried to appease with ever larger portions of bread and gruel. His eyesight was not what it had been, either; the few teeth he had left were rotting and this, he may have thought, probably accounted for the permanently parched mouth which "not all the water of the Ocean sea" seemed to moisten. Worst of all was the frequent feeling of fatigue, of drowsiness. This was interfering with his work. He would increasingly have had to hoard the energy left to him. He no longer had the time or the strength to shift for himself; the irksome problems of daily existence would have to be moved to other shoulders. The natural degeneration of age, he may have thought; at fifty-seven a man was old. His weakness, his increasing dependence on others, may have contributed to the testiness and depression he undoubtedly felt. No more than the doctors could he have understood that, as far as we can judge, he was already suffering from the diabetes that would kill him, or that with every mouthful of gruel he wolfed down he was literally gumming his way to the grave.

His irritability may have contributed to the row blowing up with Lope de Vega. In the vicious picture of him given in the prologue to the "false Quixote"—the sequel published in 1614 by a defender of Lope signing himself Alonso Fernández de Avellaneda—there is probably some truth: ". . . And besides, Miguel de Cervantes is now as old as the castle of San Cervantes (sic) and so discontented with his life that everything and everyone irritate him, and this is why he has so few friends that when he wants to adorn his books with laudatory sonnets he has to ascribe their paternity, as he says, to Prester John of the Indies or the Emperor of Trapisonda. . . ." The sermon pelts him with St. Paul's admonition that "charity suffereth long and is kind; charity envieth not; charity vaunteth not itself, is not puffed up. . . ."[4] And, referring to the "errors" of Part I, chiefly, one presumes, the "errors" in estimation of Lope, Avellaneda excuses them for having been written in prison,[5] from whence they "could not have helped emerging groggy . . . plaintive, backbiting, impatient and choleric, as those in prison are."[6]

By comparison with the guerrilla warfare among the intellectuals Cervantes knew, modern cocktail-party sniping is as a chirping of nightingales. And Lope was a natural target. His unending bustle, his appeal to women, his now legendary popular success were incitement enough to the envious, but his social pretentiousness and, most of all, his tumescent ego made him fair game for the scalp-hunters.

Rey de Artieda let fly at the self-styled Apollo and his court in a letter to the Marquis of Cuéllar:

> Beneath the Lord of Delos's burning heat
> spring little poets from the putrid pool,
> with such agility, 'tis quite a treat;
> And marvelous it is, beyond all rule
> to see a comedy writ by some wight
> whom yesterday Minerva put to school.

> Since his invention is but wind outright,
> in eight short days, or in less space of time
> the mode and matter are in keeping quite. . . .[7]

Góngora referred patronizingly to Lope as "Lopico" and "Lopillo" (little Lope); when the playwright, a future familiar of the Inquisition, indulged himself in what seems to have been one of his favorite forms of insult, hinting at impurities in a rival's lineage, Góngora retaliated by clawing at the coat of arms Lope devised to give himself a spurious aristocratic ancestry:

> By your life, Lopillo, do erase
> the nineteen towers from your shield
> for, windy as you are, I doubt
> you've wind enough for so many towers. . . .
> Build no more towers on sand
> unless you mean, now that you are wed
> a second time, to make towers out of bacon strips. . . .[8]

For some reason, however, no barbs seemed to work as deeply under Lope's hide as those planted by Cervantes. The two men had never been close friends; until lately their relationship had been correct, amicable enough to allow them to trade tepid public compliments. In Lope's pastoral novel *La Arcadia*, which appeared in 1598, Cervantes is included in a listing of Spain's foremost poets; as recently as 1602, a laudatory sonnet by the older man prefaced Lope's *La hermosura de Angélica*. Indeed, it was to be a strangely on-again off-again quarrel; praise of the *Arcadia* is to be found in *The Dogs' Colloquy;* Cervantes is mentioned, coolly, in Lope's 1630 *La Dorotea,* in the *Laurel de Apolo* and in the 1635 play *El premio del bien hablar.* In Act I of another play written the same year, *Amar sin saber a quién,* a maid refers to Don Quixote—for which "may God pardon Cervantes"—as "a knight of the wilder, erring kind the chronicle magnified so." Cervantes would pay tribute to Lope's genius and industry in *Don Quixote,* Part II, and would flatter him by appropriating some of his songs for *The Jealous Extremaduran.*

Each was too skillful not to recognize the other's abilities. Nevertheless, to Lope's mind, Cervantes was a *lego,* a lightweight, as a prose novelist little more than an entertainer, whereas he, Lope, was a *científico,* a serious artist, a university man and a poet of the grand school. We know the distinction nettled Cervantes; inevitably, criticism from this ragamuffin *lego,* and on theoretical grounds at that, drove the *científico* wild (though not speechless) with anger.

Don Quixote really started the row. It was probably early in 1604 that those among Lope's friends who had heard about the priest's discussion of Lopean theater with the canon of Toledo in Chapter 48 of Part I gleefully passed the word along. This was lèse-majesté.

Revenge came quickly. In a play called *Esclavos de Argel,* probably written that year, Lope borrowed the character of Saavedra from *Life in Algiers* and transformed him into a cowardly, unheroic grifter who is accused of having shadowy dealings with his masters. The shot obviously hit home. A second Cervantes salvo, the one which seems to have caused the greatest number of casualties among the Lopeans, was discharged in mid-1604: the prologue to Part I of *Don Quixote.*

Here Cervantes presents a mock picture of himself as stumped by the need to write an erudite preface he is too ignorant to document: "I would have wished to give you (this book) naked and pure, unadorned with a prologue or the usual endless catalogue of sonnets, epigrams and eulogies it is the custom to place at the beginnings of books. For I can tell you that, though (the book) cost me some labor to compose, I deemed nothing in it more laborious than making this preface you are now reading. Many times I took up my pen to write it and many times I put it down, not knowing what I would say. . . ." Besides, he confesses with purse-lipped solemnity, "I am too cowardly and lazy to go looking for authors to say what I can say without them." There he is, then, "with the paper before me, the pen in my ear, my elbow on the desk and my cheek on my hand" when a friend enters and offers a solution: make up the verses and give them any paternity he chooses.

Oh, Lopico! Oh, Fernández de Avellaneda! It was common knowledge that Lope composed self-laudatory verses and tacked real names to them, even when the "authors" were known never to have written a line of poetry in their lives—such masters as his current mistress, actress Micaela de Luxan, whose "sonnets" appear in Lope's prose-and-verse adventure novel *El peregrino en su patria* and in his *La hermosura de Angélica.* Another of his habits was skewered on Cervantes' lament that *Don Quixote* lacked prefatory poems by "dukes, marquises, counts, bishops, ladies or famous poets." Not that Lope had trouble finding others to write poems for him; he simply felt safer reinforcing these with some of his own: no one else was as good a poet or as unfettered a friend.

The poems Cervantes produces on his "friend's" advice add insult to injury: foolish efforts, deliberately fatuous, most of them broken-footed frivolities which deride Lope's verse by their very form. Not content with this barrage, Cervantes goes on to snipe at the científico's lavish displays of erudition, making fun of it through driveling marginal notes, Latin allusions known to any schoolboy and a few unknown to the supposed authors themselves, all elaborately useless. The *Peregrino en su patria,* which received a mixed reception when it came out in Seville in March 1604, was graveled with such trivia, 150 of them by actual count; in the very first paragraph of Book Three, Lope managed to cite Boetius, Seneca, Terence, Plato, Aristotle, Tully and Demosthenes. And this was a model of restraint when compared to the 267 classical references in the 1599 *Isidro,* a life of St. Isidore.

Lope, already out of temper, seems to have taken his vexation out on Cervantes, who replied through the mouth of the "poet" Urganda the Unknown that it is a foolish thing

> to take stone in hand
> to throw at one's neighbor
> when one lives under a glass roof. . . .

Lope is counseled to abstain from "giving birth to pamphlets to entertain maidens." A potshot is also taken at the nineteen towers pictured on the title page of the *Peregrino en su patria.* In fact, there is scarcely a line in the prologue, the last part of the book to be written, that is not aimed at Lope; sure of his ground, Cervantes uses it to whack at Lope's works in general, and especially at the *Peregrino,* like Harlequin wielding his slapstick.

The full impact of this onslaught would not be felt by its target until he could read it for himself early in 1650. It would do his famous temper no good. In an often cited letter to an unidentified friend in Valladolid, Lope remarked, speaking of poets, "many are coming out for the coming year, but there are none so bad as Cervantes, nor any so stupid as to praise *Don Quixote."* He goes on to assert his dislike of satire, "a thing more odious to me than my little books are to Almendarez[9] and my plays to Cervantes."

Cervantes in turn unlimbered a broken-footed sonnet.[10] Too many references are packed into it for convenient citation here. It manages in sixteen lines to attack nine of Lope's books—all he had written to date—and to include a gibe at the uncredited borrowings from other poets in his *Rhymes.* A Lopean sonnet is dismissed as foolishness.

At this, scholars believe, the little restraint left to Lope cracked. A torrent of vituperation was spilled into an obscene sonnet—presumably (but not certainly) by the phoenix—sent to Cervantes through the mail.[11] It is disgraceful:

> I, who know nothing of la-, or li-, or le-[*]
> nor know if you, Cervantes, are co- or cu-[†]

[*] That is, of the childish device of broken-footed verse.
[†] Various meanings have been offered for the broken words; Astrana Marín proposes *coco,* or bogeyman, and *cucú,* or cuckold. Equally possible, in view of the poem's tone, are *coño* (vagina) and *culo* (anus).

I say only that Lope is Apollo, and you
a horse for his chariot; and a pig on the hoof.

    To prevent you from writing, the order was given
in heaven that you lose a hand in Corfu.‡
You spoke, ox, but all you said was *moo.*
I will give you a bruising Quixotada!**
Honor Lope, you aging juvenile,†† or—watch out!—
for he is the sun, and if annoyed he'll rain on you.
    And as for your nothing of a *Don Quixote,*
it goes from asshole to asshole through the world
hawking spices and bastard-saffron‡‡
and it will come to rest on a dung heap.

This was not the sort of thing a Cervantes replied to—at any rate not in kind. When the riposte did come, years later in the appendix to the *Voyage to Parnassus,* it was devastating in its sweetness:

When I was in Valladolid, a letter for me was sent to my house with a real in postage due on it. A niece of mine accepted it and paid the postage, which she should never have done, but she offered as her excuse that she had often heard me say there are three things worth spending money on: giving alms, paying a good doctor and paying the postage on letters, whether they are from friends or enemies; for those from friends bring news, and from our enemies we can get some indication of what they are thinking. They gave me (the letter) and it contained a poor, feeble sonnet, with no flair or cleverness at all, speaking ill of *Don Quixote;* and what I regretted was the real, and from then on I resolved never to accept a letter with postage due on it. . . .

In January 1605, however, Cervantes had a triumph to savor: a fat, eighty-three-octave (664 pages) volume fresh off Juan de la Cuesta's press[12] and now on sale in Robles' shops in Madrid and Valladolid. Robles had been doubtful about the book. Privilege had been asked for Castile only. A rapid first edition had been run off—probably no more than 750 copies—on the cheap paper made by the Jesuits of El Paular in Segovia instead of on fine rag paper. But there it was, with Robles' motto *Post tenebras spere lucem* in its oval border, with a lion and an arm and

‡ Lope is taking liberties with historical fact, but nothing else was handy to rhyme with "moo."
** A reference to the pummelings administered to the knight throughout the book.
†† The Spanish word, *potrilla,* can also mean a scrotal hernia.
‡‡ Like the "pig" reference in line four, this is meant to suggest that Cervantes was a "Jew."

fist holding a hawk. Of course, it was studded with mistakes, the most egregious of them the omission of the words "Don Quixote" from the title. Everybody had been in a hurry to get the thing done with; even the approval by corrector Francisco Murcia de la Llana had errors in it. Since authors never saw proofs of their work, Cervantes had no control over the printing process. Besides, this was a cheap edition, priced at 290.5 maravedis, or about three quarters of a ducat, paper-bound; a parchment binding would cost half again as much. Robles may have doubted he could sell the five hundred copies needed to break even.

If Cervantes had thought to profit from his dedication of the book to the Duke of Béjar, he was disappointed. Don Alonso Diego López de Zúñiga y Sotomayor, Duke of Béjar, Marquis of Gibraleón, Count of Benalcazar and Benares, Viscount of La Puebla and Lord of the Boroughs of Capilla, Curiel and Burguillos, was a mean-spirited young man of twenty-seven, thick-witted and inordinately fond of flattery. Cervantes may not in fact have hoped for much; he hadn't bothered to write the sort of fulsome tribute the duke might have appreciated. Instead, he copied it almost intact from one written by the admired Fernando de Herrera. In the event, Béjar apparently concluded either that it was not flattering enough or that Cervantes was too insignificant a creature to waste much money on.

They were all wrong—Robles, Béjar, probably even Cervantes himself. To everyone's surprise, the book was an immense success. Almost overnight, its author became one of Spain's most famous men.

30

Don Quixote

Nearly four centuries ago, for reasons still being debated, a lean, dry country squire nearing fifty but still tough and vigorous "thought it would be fitting and incumbent, both to augment his honor and to serve his country, to become a knight-errant and ride armored through the world in search of adventures, following in every way the practices of the knights-errant he had read about and righting all manner of wrongs." The reason for this venture, we are told, is that "from little sleep and much reading, his brain dried up and he lost his wits," but scarcely anything in his history can be taken for granted.

Our gentleman ("his name was said to be Quixada or Quesada—there is some difference of opinion on this among authors who have written about the case—though the most likely conjectures point to his being called Quexana") takes down a rusty old suit of armor from the wall and applies himself to polishing it as best he can. A visor for the helmet is patched together of pasteboard and strips of iron. It is a symbolic action to match his new resolution: this moldering armor is the virtue of long ago, now rusted and fallen into disuse; its steely purity must be refurbished and brought back into service if humanity is to re-create its golden age. For, as the iron strips in the visor suggest, this is an "age of iron," a "detestable age."

This done, he turns his attention to his horse. The poor beast has "more cracks in its hooves than a real has quarters," but to its master it is "the equal of Alexander's Bucephalus and the Cid's Babieca." With a nice sense of the realities of the situation, he renames it Rocinante,* "a name which seemed to him grand and resounding." Another week of cogitation produces an equally sonorous name for himself: Don Quixote de la Mancha.

* From *rocín,* a nag or hack.

One problem remains: he must find a lady to love. A knight-errant without a lady, he reflects, is "like a tree without leaves or fruit and a body without a soul." He recalls that in a nearby village there lives "a very handsome peasant girl with whom he had once been smitten, although it is generally supposed that she never knew or suspected it. Her name was Aldonza Lorenzo . . . and, searching for a name that would not be too far from her own and would carry the suggestion of a princess and great lady, he resolved to call her Dulcinea del Toboso, because she was a native of El Toboso. . . ."

One morning before dawn he rides out. He goes surreptitiously, aware of how strange a figure he would cut in his neighbors' eyes. Before he returns for the last time he will be an old friend over whom we are never sure whether to laugh or cry, but there will be no doubt in our minds that he is a great man, the noblest man we are ever likely to meet.

Don Quixote is a magic book, as close to being a living object as any work of art has ever been. It has a life of its own which is like our lives, if we think about it, a game of mirrors, an impression of receding depths, of truths just beyond our grasp, of planes of reality shifting and blurring. In all the garrulous annals of human expression, only a handful of characters—Quixote, Hamlet, Faust, Don Juan, perhaps Oedipus—have so perfectly summarized areas of the human condition as to embed themselves as symbols in humanity's unconscious. Of these, arguably none have lived so intensely on every level of experience as Cervantes' knight.

Time and place dissolve in *Don Quixote*† so that even today we feel we are sitting in the semidarkness of a Manchegan venta watching this gaunt, oddly accoutered apparition stride into the ring of light cast by the fire on the hearth, his dust-streaked face barely visible behind the clumsy visor. He is in a state of great agitation, for "scarcely had he reached open country when he was assailed by a thought so terrible that he almost abandoned his enterprise": he had never been knighted and so had no right to bear arms against another knight. It suits his humor to assume this inn is a castle, and he is here to beg the castellan to give him the accolade.

We are already at the heart of the book's axial irony. "Mad" Quixote, we will come to suspect, is not mad at all, at least not in the way everyone takes him to be. The evidence will accumulate that he is a brilliant actor consciously playing a part. His purpose in doing this is serious: to impose his ideals—of God, truth, love, fidelity, service, justice, all man's highest aspirations—on a materialistic world by the sheer force of his will and the energy of his creative imagination.

† Although ten years separated the publication of Parts I and II of *Don Quixote,* the halves are too closely joined to be considered separately. Chronology— "historical" truth—will have to cede here to poetry.

Quixote is a cultivated man, an intellectual who has dabbled in everything, thought about everything; he is a natural teacher whose knowledge is as spacious as his mind, as passionately savored as his language. He has prepared carefully for his role, has studied his predecessor's performances and memorized every detail he will need to improvise as he goes along, to create a life in action. He is the poet militant, messenger of the divine mysteries, but he knows the world will tolerate him only if it believes he is mad.

He will not succeed in this. Those, like the innkeeper, who do not know him will humor him for their own amusement; others, the ones who love him (but love themselves more), will go to great lengths to restrain him. They mean well, the priest Pero Pérez, Master Nicolás the barber, the bachelor Sampson Carrasco, the beautiful Dorotea. Freedom itself is a form of madness, is it not? To ride the world alone, to go one's own way is the devil's path; safety, thus sanity, lay in remaining together, in hewing to the norm. "You will be safer in the fold . . . even if you are not so happy," a goatherd scolds his errant billy. "If you who should guide them go unguided and astray, what will become of them?"[1]

In the process of helping Quixote, however, they will bring their own sanity into question. Is it sane, after all, for a priest to dress up in women's clothes to lure Quixote home? Is Carrasco entirely sane when he swathes himself in armor stuck with bits of mrirror to joust with Quixote? And how well balanced is his lust for revenge for the knight's fluke victory? When Sancho Panza literally makes an ass of himself in a braying contest, is he really all there? Surely the sanity of the Duke and Duchess in their vicious encouragement of the knight's obsession is open to doubt, a point their ferocious chaplain emphatically makes.

And yet—Cervantes' joke is at the triple-take stage—perhaps poor Alonso Quexana or Quesada is mad after all. Even if the person of Quixote is a deliberate work of art, who but a madman would set about rousing an inert world to heroism by prodding it with the point of his lance? The knight's madness does not lie simply in conceiving truth in terms of predetermined ideas, that is, in interpreting observed phenomena. We all do that. It is how we impose order on irrelevant events; it is how we *maintain* sanity. Nor does it derive from the discordance of his vision with objective fact, a failure of reason. The logic of the world outside the book is as illusory as the knight's imagined world: windmills were not giants, admittedly, but neither was the earth the center of the universe, as many of his contemporaries still believed. This was reason relegated to its proper place, as the servant of poetry. Quixote clearly hopes to teach the world that his madness is a higher form of sanity.

Perhaps his true madness was rooted in sin, the Aristotelian sin of ignorance, or what a Marxist would think of as objective error. In trying to do good, Quixote does harm, to himself chiefly, but to others too. He faces the activist's dilemma, accepting responsibility for promoting justice, but learning that the very act of redressment distorts right and wrong; his human perceptions will ensure that action turns out badly. Quixote refuses to face what Cervantes saw as the basic contradiction of human effort: man may not be God. To presume to try is madness. Yet he is impelled to usurp God's function by the God within him. Only God can administer justice justly. Art is vanity, imagination idle, vison a delusion; God is the only perfect artist, the great creator. But to resign himself to this leaves man no choice but death; the vision must still be sought in life, for it is the act of striving that confirms his divinity. Without such a vision and, more important, without its active prosecution, existence is sterile, man a stone.

It is the knight's gradual perception of this paradox that holds the story together. And it is his obstinacy almost until the very end in refusing to accept the paradox that so appeals to us.

Let us follow him as, newly knighted and pleased with his own ingenuity, Quixote rides out of the inn literally looking for trouble. The world quickly provides a cause for him to champion. He finds a wealthy farmer (very like the ones Cervantes knew in Écija) whipping a boy, Andrés, who is tied to a tree. Quixote forces the man to release his victim and wrests a promise from him to pay the boy the wages he claims are owed him. Social justice having been done to his satisfaction, the knight rides on until he meets a party of merchants on the road, six of them, riding under parasols, with their servants and muleteers. He challenges them to concede Dulcinea's superiority over all other maidens. The merchants, being merchants, haggle over the terms of the proposal. They will take nothing on faith; they insist on seeing a picture of Dulcinea. This so enrages Quixote that he lowers his lance and charges. But when, we are invited to reflect, have honor and the beauty of an ideal stood victorious against the hard practicality of common sense? The knight is left senseless in the road.

When he regains consciousness he sees a figure bending over him. It is a neighbor from his own village. Quixote must be taken aback, but he recovers himself quickly. He identifies the man as the legendary Christian hero Rodrigo de Narváez and himself as the noble Moor Abindarráez. The good neighbor reminds him that "your worship is not . . . Abindarraez, but that worthy gentleman Master Quixada." Quixote ad-libs his part. "I know who I am," he roars, "and I know too that I can if I please be not only the personages I have mentioned but all the Twelve Peers of France and the Nine Worthies as well. . . ." With that, he allows himself to be slung ignominiously over the neighbor's ass and carted home for treatment.

There the parish priest, Pero Pérez, and Master Nicolás the barber (representing the secular arm of the law) conduct an auto-da-fé over Alonso Quexana's offending library, consigning to a bonfire in the patio those volumes the inquisitors consider to have sinned by their foolishness and lured the knight to madness like an *iluminado* seduced by heresy. Some of the books are acquitted, others do penance and are reconciled. *Tirant lo Blanch*, a fifteenth-century Catalan novel which, for its attempt at realism and its heavily ironic tone, can be considered a distant ancestor of *Don Quixote*, is spared as "a rare treasure of delight and a mine of entertainment." One book, the *Galatea* of Miguel de Cervantes, is placed on probation because, says the priest, "Cervantes has been a great friend of mine for many years and I know that he is more versed in misfortunes than in verse." Most of the rest are relaxed to the flames.

Some Cervantists think that it was here, at the end of Chapter 6, that Cervantes originally planned to end what they believe had been designed as a short story. Introducing the character of Sancho Panza, they contend, was an inspired afterthought which made the novel's structural development possible; for the knight's personality, ideas, yearnings are honed and refined against the resistance of his fat-bellied, long-shanked squire. Others agree that the book began as no more than a novela, but they place the junction at the break of Chapters 8 and 9, during Quixote's stupendous battle with the Basque. And in fact something strange does happen to the story here. As though he were holding a movie camera on the scene, Cervantes stops the action with the combatants' swords upraised. Suddenly we are told that his account came from an old manuscript and that Cervantes—now no longer the author but merely a research scholar—has run out of material:

> It is true . . . that the second author of this work could not bring himself to believe that so unusual a chronicle would have been consigned to oblivion . . . (and) he did not despair of coming upon the end of this pleasing story and, with heaven's favor, he did find it, as shall be related in the second part.

The chance discovery of a manuscript in a shop on an old Jewish street in Toledo introduces us to Cide Hamete Benengeli, the endearing "Arab historian" whose honesty defies his origins. At a stroke, the narrative suddenly recedes several planes from reality, becoming as fragmented as a Cubist painting; the tone, the very pace of the writing become more spacious, more varied, as though Cervantes were in awe of the vast perspective stretching dimly ahead of him.

He probably had only the vaguest idea of where he was going when he began to write his story. Almost certainly he had a long work in mind; a short prose epic would have been a contradiction in terms. Why should he have brought Sancho into the action if he planned to end his story one chapter later? How explain that the elaborate game of shifting perspectives, of hide-and-seek with reality, is played from the opening lines?

Cervantes seems simply to have moved from one happy discovery to the next, playing with their possibilities as he went along. Plotting was relatively simple, since each of Quixote's adventures parodies an incident in a romance of chivalry. New tricks were found: irony is integrated into the story as a motor of action; events occur in Quixote's absence which will affect him later, thus, by implication, stretching the action to infinity without breaking the story's organic unity. For the first time, a long work is written from multiple points of view, sometimes the protagonist's, sometimes that of other characters, even the reader's, occasionally the author's. Cervantes himself flits in and out of the novel like a comic detective with a trousseau of false beards and cardboard noses. He will be seen as author, translator, personage (the Saavedra of "The Captive's Tale"), as author of *La Galatea,* as a mysterious traveler who has left a trunkful of stories in manuscript (including a draft of *Rinconete and Cortadillo*) in an inn on the Madrid-Seville road. He is everywhere at once and nowhere, as God is. Fantasy and reality, separate but inseparable, are interwoven not only for the literary polyphony this creates, but to promote a philosophic purpose. At one point, the nonsense personage of the Princess Micomicona is assumed by the "historical" Dorotea, who is a character in Benengeli's "history" of Don Quixote invented by Cervantes. The knight's unremitting struggle against his "enchanters"—the resistance opposed by experience to his imaginative will—turns reality itself into illusion; experience becomes a conspiracy to thwart the "real" fantasies he conjures.

When Quixote regains his strength, he sets about recruiting a squire, a

> neighbor of his and an honorable fellow—if a poor man may be called honorable—but without much salt in the old noodle. In the end, he talked so much, persuaded so hard and promised him so much that the poor rube agreed to go with him and serve as his squire. . . . Among the other things Don Quixote told him was that . . . an adventure could take place that in the batting of an eye might win him some isle of which he would leave (his squire) governor. . . .

Another set of resonances begins to sound here. The relationship of Sancho to Quixote is strangely like that of Peter to Jesus. The dumpy little squire with his straggly beard and straggling strings of proverbs will appear to us entirely a man, but he is also a distorted mirror held up to his master, a Quixote, so to speak, in a state of nature, and man and master will come to form a single whole in our minds, as the human and divine identities coincide in the figure of Christ.

Quixote will forever be trying to instruct the little peasant in the secrets of his faith. He is often formal and didactic: "The cleverest role in a play is the fool's," he will explain in a flash of candor, "for a man who wants to be taken for a fool must never be one."[2] He never really comes to understand his squire. We hear him declare over the sleeping Sancho,

> "Oh you, fortunate above all who dwell on the face of the earth, for without envy or being envied you sleep with a quiet mind. . . . Ambition does not trouble you, nor the vain pomps of the world worry you, for the limits of your desires extend no further than the care of your ass. The care of your own person you have laid on my shoulders, a compensatory burden which nature and custom have ever imposed on masters. The servant sleeps and the master watches. . . ."[3]

Nor does Quixote's intellectual pride ever wholly accept the peasant as equal: "I was born, Sancho, to live dying, and you to die eating. . . ."[4] But an affection will grow in him for his squire, rather, Cervantes suggests, like God's affection for mankind:

> "I would have your lordships understand that Sancho Panza is one of the drollest squires that ever served knight-errant. Sometimes his simplicities are so shrewd that it gives me no small pleasure to consider whether it is simplicity or shrewdness that prevails. Some rogueries in him convict him of knavery; and his indiscretions confirm him a fool. He doubts everything and believes everything. When I think he is going to tumble into folly he comes out with clever sayings which exalt him to the sky. In fact I would not exchange him for any other squire. . . ."[5]

Sancho, lured by visions of wealth and power into following his neighbor, is nevertheless skeptical. When a Quixote bruised by his encounter with the windmills explains that it was the enchanters who overthrew him, the squire answers with a noncommittal "God send it as He will" and helps his master to remount. Greed drives the little man on after his first drubbing, and a peasant's belief in the bravery and learning of the gentility. But he never completely loses his sense of the realities. When Quixote presses him to sit beside him at the goatherds' fire, to "eat from my plate and drink from the cup whereof I drink, for it can be said of knight-errantry as of love: that it puts all things on the same level," the squire refuses. "Let the honors your worship means to confer on me . . .

be exchanged for something of more use and profit to me."⁶ Later, as both lie bruised after their run-in with the Yanguesan herders, the knight's admonition that nothing is won without pain elicits the squire's acid reminder that "I'm more in need of poultices than of sermons." We can imagine Sancho's silent protest when Quixote observes that a peasant's shoulders "were made for such a storm (of blows), but as mine were nurtured between cambrics and fine linen, clearly they are more sensitive to the pain of this misadventure."⁷

Sancho's hopes rise and fall with events. When the servant Maritornes asks his master's name at the inn, the squire informs her with new self-importance that he is Don Quixote, a knight-errant, "one of the best and bravest the world has seen for a very long time."

> "What's a knight-errant?" asked the maid.
>
> "Are you so green that you don't know that?" replied Sancho. "Then I'll tell you, my girl, that a knight-errant . . . is beaten up one day and made emperor the next. Today he's the most unfortunate and poverty-stricken creature in the world; tomorrow he'll have two or three kingdoms to give his squire."⁸

A fresh beating soon dampens his optimism.

> "Sancho, my friend, are you asleep? Are you asleep, friend Sancho?"
>
> "Sleep, confound it," replied Sancho in gloom and despair. "How can I sleep when all the devils in hell must have been at me tonight?"
>
> "You are right about that, for certain," replied Don Quixote. "For if I know anything, this castle is enchanted. You should know . . . but what I am going to tell you now you must swear to keep secret until the day I die."
>
> "I swear," replied Sancho.
>
> "You must swear, because I hate to take away anyone's reputation," continued Don Quixote.
>
> "I do swear, I tell you," repeated Sancho, "that I will keep silent to the very last days of your honor's life. And please God I may be free to speak tomorrow."⁹

Revelation is advanced when Quixote stands prudently at a distance while his squire is tossed in a blanket.

> "But I do know that since we have been knights-errant—or your worship has, for I cannot count myself of that honorable number—we have never won a battle except that one over the Basque, and even

from that one your worship came off with the loss of half an ear and half a helmet. But since then it has been nothing but beatings and still more beatings, punches and still more punches. . . ."

"That is an affliction which I bear and you must bear, Sancho," replied Don Quixote. "But from now on I will try to have at hand a sword of such craftsmanship that no kind of enchantment can be worked against its bearers. . . ."

"With my luck," said Sancho, "when this happens and your worship finds such a sword, it will be of use and profit only to knights. . . ."[10]

Some of the scenes are pure slapstick and they have never been surpassed, not even in the great days of the Hollywood one-reelers. One such is the scene in an inn in which Maritornes, fumbling through the dark toward her tryst with a carrier, is waylaid by Don Quixote:

She was gliding modestly and silently, groping with out-stretched hands for her lover, when she stumbled into the arms of Don Quixote, who seized her tightly by one wrist and, drawing her to him, she not daring to say a word, forced her to sit on his bed.

Then he felt her shift and, although it was of sackcloth, it seemed to him of the finest, most delicate satin. The glass beads she wore on her wrist had for him the sheen of rare Orient pearls. Her hair, which was as coarse as a horse's mane, seemed to him strands of the most glistening gold of Arabia, whose splendor eclipsed the very sun. And her mouth, which, no doubt, reeked of the stale salad of the night before, seemed to him to breathe out a sweet and aromatic odor. In short, he bestowed on her the several features of that famous princess who came, in the books he had read, to visit the sore-wounded knight whom she loved so well. . . .

Maritornes was bathed in a sweat of anguish at finding herself grasped by Don Quixote and, without understanding or paying the least attention to his protestations, tried silently to break away. As for the good carrier, whose lusts kept him awake, he had heard his wench from the moment she came in, and had been listening to the knight's every word. Suspecting that the Asturian maid had broken her promise to him in favor of another, he edged nearer and nearer to Don Quixote's bed . . . when he saw the maid struggling to break loose and Don Quixote trying to hold her, the jest seemed to him to have gone too far. Whereupon he raised his arm and dealt the amorous knight so terrible a blow on his lean jaws that his mouth was filled with blood; and, not content with this, he trod on his ribs and trampled him briskly up and down.

The bed was rather weak and supported on no firm foundations. So, unable to bear the additional weight of the carrier, it gave way with a loud crash. . . .[11]

Such broad comic interludes are simply part of a dazzling balancing act Cervantes maintains between the sublime and the grotesque, the real and fantastic, all dancing across a line of the ebullient knight's conversations with everyone he encounters. Comic scenes end in drama, elevated rhetoric dissolves in strings of proverbs, drama turns to ridicule and unpoetic figures crash heavily into lyrical passages. Everything is true and nothing is true. There are scenes of great tenderness and a sort of twilight sadness. We hear Quixote's rhapsodic elegy on the golden age delivered, as no one else in literature ever could, to a troupe of goatherds around a fire. The atmosphere is quiet, mystical, mythical. Only the goatherds' polite incomprehension reminds us that his golden age never really existed outside of man's longing.

Suddenly the story is carried to a pinnacle of intensity, like the swelling of a Wagnerian theme. Everyone attends the burial of Grisóstomo, the Arcadian shepherd who has died of unrequited love. We are far here from the gilded mists of *La Galatea;* the goatherds accompanying Quixote and Sancho are real country people and the gentlemen they meet on the road wear riding clothes and are bent on thoroughly urban business. There is a flash of comic wonder, and then the mood changes. Marcela, the dead Grisóstomo's beloved, delivers a powerful oration in defense of Platonic love. I am beauty, she warns the mourners, "I am that distant fire, that faraway sword."[12] Marcela is one of the many manifestations of Dulcinea; her defense of the inviolability of beauty defines Quixote's relationship with truth, explaining man's corrupt perception of perfection and commenting on Cervantes' idea of the poet's priestly function. It is Quixote the poet who protects Marcela from the crowd's anger.

Cervantes' supreme skill as a storyteller can even use the vast panorama of his Spain to his purpose. Quixote sees a dozen men walking on the road, "strung by their necks like beads on an iron chain and all in handcuffs." They are escorted by two mounted men with muskets and two more on foot armed with swords and javelins. Sancho identifies them:

"There's a chain of galley slaves, people on their way to forced labor in the king's galleys."

"What do you mean, 'forced'?" Don Quixote asked. "Is it possible that the king uses force on anyone?"

"That's not what I mean," Sancho replied, "but that they are people who have been condemned for their crimes to serve the king in his galleys, and go they must."

"In short," replied Don Quixote, "however you put it, although these men are being led, they are going by force and not of their own free will."[13]

The exchange reverberates in a way no translation can relay, for the Spanish traditionally refer to an individual's volition as a man's *real gana,* his "royal wish." The knight, whose proud will it is to create his very existence, is naturally outraged. In a scene ripe with the stench of the Seville prison—but with a compassion wholly removed from Mateo Alemán's bitter toughness—he questions each man as to the reason for his misfortune. One says he was sentenced for "falling in love," then quickly explains to the astonished Quixote that the object of his affection was a basketful of white linen. Another was there "for being a canary, that is, as a musician and singer"; his singing was done on the rack, where he confessed to cattle-rustling.

The obvious leader of the group is a striking figure. He is about thirty years old, of very good appearance except for being a little cross-eyed. When Quixote inquires why he is more heavily chained than the others, he is told that the man—Gines de Pasamonte is his name—has committed more crimes than all the others together. And, unlike the others, he is tough, cocky, defiant. Thinking the knight means only to give them alms and go on his way, Gines loses patience with all the questioning. "Mr. Gentleman," he snaps, "if you have anything to give, then give it to us now and may God go with you, for all this prying into other men's lives is annoying."

This is not only Cervantes' reflection on a writer's dilemma. It is the Tridentine admonition: do your good works and do not try to penetrate the mystery of God's grace; man's justice is not God's. This will not satisfy Quixote; he sees only that these men are there through ill fortune and a human judge's twisted understanding. Politely he requests that the guards release the prisoners, for "these poor devils have committed no wrong against you. . . . Each of us will have to answer for his sins in the other world . . . it is not right that honorable men be other men's executioners for something that does not concern them . . . it seems to be a hard thing to make slaves of those whom God and nature made free."[14] The guards refuse, Quixote attacks, the prisoners scatter. The knight is stoned for his pains and left for dead.

Quixote accepts his martyrdom; as he said, there can be no achievement without pain. But the persistency of failure has begun to soften him. His attitude toward Sancho is gentler. He consents to the unflattering name given him by his squire of Knight of the Mournful Countenance and even resolves to use it as an attribute on his shield. When Sancho, like some cartoon Scheherazade, undertakes to keep his master amused throughout the night and so defer the attack on the fulling mill until daybreak, Quixote puts up with his bumbling and his intestinal indiscretions with anti-Aristotelian mildness. He admits to being terrified by the "sound of regular blows and a sort of clanking of iron and chains . . . the darkness, the roaring of water and the rustling of leaves."

With morning, and the realization that the danger is no danger at all, Sancho cannot help laughing. When Don Quixote looked at his squire

> and clearly saw from his swollen cheeks and his twitching lips that he was on the point of exploding, despite his own gloom he could not help laughing. And as soon as Sancho saw that his master had begun, he let loose. . . . At this Don Quixote wished him to the devil, especially when he heard him say, as though mockingly, "Friend Sancho, you must know that by the will of heaven I was born into this iron age to revive the age of gold." . . . Seeing that Sancho was making fun of him, Don Quixote lost his temper . . . he raised his lance and dealt him two blows. . . .[15]

Peace is made, but the knight's awareness of the damage to his prestige is accompanied by Sancho's recognition that his master is, after all, just a man who can be afraid. References to blanket tossings and fulling mills will henceforth recur in his conversation. Quixote is aggrieved: "You are a bad Christian, Sancho; you never forget an injury once done you . . . noble and generous hearts set no store by such trifles."[16] Yet it is probably Sancho's recognition of his master's fallibility that allows him to love the man he had heretofore dared only fear and respect.

Irony commands that the knight will go on from this sorry showing to his greatest triumph—an involuntary one. His conscience prompts him to do solitary penance in the mountains for what he imagines must be Dulcinea's wavering faith in him. Again he is the conscious artist at work, reviewing the various accounts he has read of knightly penitence and adopting the revered Amadis of Gaul as his model, with convenient modifications. While in the mountains he encounters the love-crazed Cardenio (who is probably no crazier than Quixote) and the sorrowing Dorotea. There is a grand gathering of strands in the parlor of an inn—lovers, neighbors, the Captive and his Moorish bride and an assortment of servants, policemen and victims of previous knightly ministrations. It is Quixote, through the grandeur of his wisdom, his generosity and high sense of honor, who provides the catalyst by which all conflicts are resolved. As thanks, all, including Sancho, conspire to trick him into returning to his village to be "cured." The lesson of his encounter with the galley slaves is confirmed: his good works can only redound to his discomfiture. This is brought home in a meeting with Andrés, the boy Qui-

xote found being whipped in his very first adventure. Proudly the knight
turns to his companions and recites the story of his first great act of justice. Andrés listens impatiently to the recital.

> "All that your worship has said is quite true," he replied, "but the
> end of the business was very much the opposite of what you suppose."
> "How the opposite?" demanded Don Quixote. "Did not the peasant
> pay you, then?"
> "Not only didn't he pay me," replied the boy, "but as soon as your
> worship was out of the wood and we were alone, he tied me up again
> to the same oak and beat me again so hard that I was left flayed like
> St. Bartholomew. At every stroke he gave me, he mocked and gibed at
> your worship. . . . In fact, he gave me such a welting that I've been in
> a hospital ever since. . . ."

Quixote vows revenge, but the boy waves this aside.

> "I don't believe in these vows. I'd rather have something now to get
> me on to Seville than all the vengeance in the world. Give me some-
> thing to eat and to take with me, if you have anything here. Then God
> bless your worship and all knights-errant and may they be as good er-
> rants for themselves as they have been for me."[17]

In the Don's final adventure in Part I, the clash of his knightly sword
is like the clanging of a bell. A group of penitents is spied dressed in
white and carrying a holy image swathed in mourning clothes. They are
in procession to pray for rain, but Quixote decides they are ruffians kidnapping a lady of quality. He rides to meet them, ignoring Sancho's
warning cry: "Where are you going, Don Quixote? What demons have
you in your heart that incite you to assault our Catholic faith?" The incident ends in the inevitable mayhem, leaving the knight dazed and docile.
The very stars are arrayed against him, he concludes, and, at least for a
while, he must submit. He is stuffed into a wooden cage like the lion he
will later face and dominate. Sancho is uneasy, for he has fallen under
the knight's spell. "Take care," he warns the priest, "that God doesn't
call you to account for imprisoning him this way." To no avail; Quixote
is trundled home in his cage under the benevolent guard of his inquisitors.

The years of trial and error, of searching, that separated Parts I and II
produced a masterpiece. Part II is an astonishing display of control over
a seemingly limitless range of devices; "the author," says the prologue,

"asks that his work not be despised and that praise be given it not for what is written but for what was left out."

Perspectives become hallucinatory. Cervantes had begun work on his *Persiles* before *Don Quixote* was finished, and his last book is here prefigured in Part II's accent on marvelous happenings, its strongly redemptionist tone, its heightened mannerism. Truth and deception are consubstantial, fusing in a surrealistic world of strange visions, cruel laughter and moral courage. Tautened by the discipline of novela writing, the language was unlike anything seen in Spanish before: lean, elegant, juxtaposing high rhetoric and gambler's slang, saturating every character with his own identity. Who would be more waspish than the chaplain who lashes out at "Don Quixote or Don Dunce or whatever his name is," bidding him "go back to your home and see to your children if you have any . . . and stop wandering the world like a gaping ninny"? Righteous smugness breathes in every word uttered by the Gentleman in the Green Coat, a good old Tridentine boy concerned with his dogs and his table and his handful of devotional books and nervous about his son's being an intellectual. Generations of stupidity have gone into the Duke's praise—to Sancho—of big-game hunting as an exercise for war, "and the best thing about it is that it is not for everybody, as other kinds of hunting are, except for falconry, which is also reserved to kings and great lords."[18] Not even Shakespeare produced a passage of more passionate beauty than Cervantes gives Quixote when, pressed to describe Dulcinea, this "continent and Platonic lover" declares:

> "If I could pluck out my heart and place it before Your Highness's eyes, here, in a dish upon this table, I would spare my tongue the toil of expressing what is hardly conceivable, for in it Your Excellency would see her fully portrayed. But why should I try now to delineate and describe the beauty of the peerless Dulcinea, feature by feature and in all exactitude? That is a burden fitter for other shoulders than mine. . . ."[19]

Cervantes' mastery of his technique is now so absolute that he can afford to open Part II with a bravura bit of sleight of hand. Quixote and Sancho, back on the road, are informed of the success of Part I and a discussion ensues criticizing its failings and reviewing the range of public opinion on the knight's personality. Readers thus become characters in the novel, considering events happening outside its scope. The protagonists speculate on whether there will be a second part to their story and make recommendations to the author (which author?) as to how it should be told—a comment on a written record of events which have not yet happened by protagonists only partly informed of their own pasts. The sequence has been compared with Velázquez's painting of "Las Meninas," in which the artist, the princess he is painting and his royal onlookers are so placed as to put the viewer himself simultaneously inside and outside the room.

We soon find Quixote and Sancho setting out to find Dulcinea and speak to her. The knight is on shifting ground. He is not as sure of himself as he once was and he is trying to recoup his position with a bold stroke: an appeal for Sancho's help. The moment is fatal to Quixote. Events will increasingly escape his control; increasingly he will open himself to criticism and with every attempt to justify himself he will become less convincingly mad, more desperately rational. He has already hinted to Sancho that Dulcinea is a creature of his imagination: "for what I want of Dulcinea del Toboso, she is as good as the highest princess on earth."[20] Later, in his conversations with the Duke and Duchess, Quixote will have to go a step further: "God knows if a Dulcinea exists on earth or not, or if she is fantastic or not. Nor are these matters that can be fully verified. I neither begot nor bore my lady, but contemplate her in her ideal form. . . ."[21]

For the moment, though, he sees no other way out. He tells Sancho that he will wait on the outskirts of the town while the squire goes in search of his lady's palace. When the little man protests that he can't be expected to find in the dark a palace he has seen only once—knowing, as they both do, that it doesn't exist at all—while Quixote "must have seen it thousands of times," the Don expostulates:

"Sancho, you will drive me to despair. Come here, *heretic*.[22] Have I not told you a thousand times that I have never in all the days of my life seen the peerless Dulcinea, nor ever crossed the threshold of her palace, and that I am enamored of her only by hearsay and her great fame for beauty and wisdom?"[23]

Not even Quixote the poet, the "diviner,"[24] the squire is being warned, may probe too deeply into the occult mysteries, yet Quixote the actor is being carried toward this reef by the onrushing logic of his role. The little peasant sees the danger; a few pages further on he will wish God to "deliver me from mortal sin, for that is what He would be doing if He delivers me from this perilous calling of squire. . . ."[25]

Sancho is sent to find Dulcinea and bring a message of encouragement from her to his master. Faced with an impossible task, he resorts to trickery. Sighting three peasant girls, one uglier than the next, riding their asses along the road toward where Quixote is waiting, he represents them as the princess and her retinue. If his master is really mad, he can be fooled into believing it is true. If not, he will have to go along with the ruse. The knight sees only a squalid country girl on an ass instead of a beautiful princess on a palfrey? Enchanters have blinded his eyes, he is told, for Sancho can see her "as she is." She reeks not of costly perfumes, but of raw garlic? The enchanters again. Quixote is hoist on his own petard.

Sancho feels himself more his master's equal now. When their encounter with the Cart of Death, the actors' company headed by Andrés del Angulo costumed as Death, launches Quixote on a pompous speech about death being the great equalizer, Sancho quickly deflates him. "A fine comparison," he comments, "though not so new I haven't heard it often before. . . ." The knight, in spite of himself, is amused: "Sancho, you grow wiser and less simple every day."[26]

The truth is that the two have learned to love each other. "There's nothing of the rogue in him," Sancho will declare of his master.

"His soul is as clean as a pitcher. He can do no harm to anyone, only good to everybody. There's no malice in him. A child might make him believe it's night at noonday. And for that simplicity I love him as dearly as my heartstrings and I can't bring myself to leave him, for all his foolishness."[27]

A point is nevertheless being made in the Cart of Death speech which eludes Sancho. The encounter is one phase in a chain of reflections on death that continues with the pair's introduction to the Gentleman in the Green Coat. To Sancho, Don Diego is "the first saint I have ever seen riding with short stirrups."[28] But Quixote is exasperated by the way this model of prudence and obedience disparages his son's poetry; the knight will dismiss him with a curt "Pray go away, my dear sir, and see to your quiet pointer and your bold ferret and leave every man to do his duty."[29] He encourages the son to write and is hesitantly shown the young man's latest effort. To die, it says, is better than to live, but we are afraid to die because "our after griefs may be too great."

An answer is already at hand in the Cart of Death: death is a sham. The response is developed in the incident of the country wedding. A poor peasant, Basilio, feigns suicide to win from the rich Camacho the bride Camacho's money had enticed from him. When Quiteria satisfies her "dying" suitor's last wish by marrying him, Basilio leaps up hale and triumphant and carries her off. Death here is patiently a fake. Moreover, it seems that great love brings rich rewards after the ritual of death is accomplished. An intimation, this, of Quixote's disillusionment, and a preview of his end.

The adventure of Montesinos' cave is the pivot on which the story turns. The knight insists on exploring the famous chasm of which so many marvels are told. He is lowered down into it on a rope. Crows and jackdaws fly out as he hacks his way through the brush blocking the entrance. Then he disappears from sight. Half an hour later he is hauled up, asleep. But when Sancho wakes him, he exclaims: "God forgive you, friends, for you have taken from me the sweetest, pleasantest existence that ever mortal has seen or experienced. Now indeed do I begin to understand that the pleasures of this life pass like a shadow or a dream and wither like wildflowers."[30]

He proceeds to tell a bizarre story: that he had been in the cave not half an hour but three days. Of course he had not been dreaming! He had dozed off, it's true, but he awoke and "I rubbed my eyes . . . felt my head and chest" to satisfy himself that he was awake again. He was, he said, in a lovely meadow before a sumptuous crystal palace. Received by the bearded sage Montesinos, he is shown the talking corpse of the fabulous knight Durandarte, whose salted heart ("so that it would remain, if not fresh, at least dry") is in the keeping of his lady Belerma. The lady appears: flat-nosed, beetle-browed, her teeth "few and uneven, but white as peeled almonds," the "reality" of the Dulcinean ideal. She is, moreover, a flesh-and-blood figure who is saddened, Quixote is told, not because she long ago stopped menstruating, but because of the oppressive weight of that shriveled heart she carries. For death has been annulled in the cave of Montesinos; everyone there has been placed under a spell by Merlin which they hope—without much conviction—the great Don Quixote de la Mancha can break. "And even if it should not be," Durandarte groans, "I say, patience and shuffle the cards."[31]

The Don's amazement reaches its climax when he spies Dulcinea gamboling with her maidens in the meadow. He knew her, he explains, because he recognized in them the peasant girls Sancho had presented to him. One of her ladies in waiting approaches him and, her eyes brimming with tears, tells him she has come on behalf of Dulcinea to ask if he will lend her half a dozen reales on a petticoat. Want, Montesinos explains to the befuddled Quixote, is to be found everywhere, even among the enchanted nobility. The poor knight has only four reales, which he willingly bestows.

The story has been called Quixote's hoax, a deliberate lie. Was it a dream, a hallucination of a mind under great strain? Or was Quixote forced to embroider on the scenario Sancho had begun for him? The squire, certainly, is skeptical: "God—I was about to say the devil—take me if I believe a word of your worship's story."[32] His master swears he is telling it as he saw it, but even Cide Hamete Benengeli breaks in to doubt the truth of his recital; since everyone knows, however, that Quixote is incapable of lying, they all leave it to the reader to judge.

The adventure teems with associations. We think of the descents into the underworld of Orpheus, and of Jesus; there is a suggestion of abandonment of the half life of the senses to plunge into the mysteries of creation. At one point during Quixote's stay in the cave Sancho had wished him back "free, sound and unharmed to the light of this life, which you have left to bury yourself in that darkness you are seeking." He refers to the cave as "that hell" and, although Quixote the poet, enthralled by his vision, demurs, even he admits to journeying through an "obscure nether region on no certain or definite road."

This is the point at which the great cycle of the knight's progress from the insanity of life turns toward the reality of death and its promise of an afterlife. Quixote himself doubts that he saw what he says he saw, but it was so real, so real. He had even noticed the green university ribbons Montesinos wore across his chest—Cervantes' mocking gesture toward Aristotelian verisimilitude.

It is no mere flourish that Quixote's adventure with Master Peter's puppet show begins with an interview with the puppeteer's divining monkey. He asks the beast if what he saw in the cave was true or false, and is told by a curiously indulgent Gines de Passamonte—for he is Master Peter—that it was "partly false and partly credible." Quixote is so taken in by the show that he leaps to the heroine's defense and hacks the puppets to pieces. A brilliant improvisation by the knight—or revenge for his stoning by the galley slaves?

The trials of Quixote and Sancho at the ducal court are savage. Here they enter a world of dreams, of the subconscious. Nasty practical jokes build through an infernal torchlit charade to the pair's "diabolical aerial voyage" aboard a wooden horse, scenes of Faustian delirium. On the "voyage," a Sancho already placed in a state of severe emotional confusion by the tricks played on him takes his own excursion into quixotry. Although he has never left the ground, he describes all the sights he has seen in the heavens. His master is amazed, but he quickly seizes the occasion: "Sancho," he whispers, "if you want to be believed about what you saw in the sky, I want you to believe me about what I saw in Montesinos' cave."[33]

Only later, at the end of the book, do we realize that the most touching speech in the sequence is Sancho's unconscious anticipation of Quixote's deathbed resumption to grace. It also sums up the book's central theme, and as though this were not already a sufficient weight for a speech to carry, another burden seems to tug at it, that of Cervantes' longing for immortality in this world and the next. For, Sancho pointedly asks the duke,

"what greatness is there in commanding on a mustard seed, or what dignity or empire in governing half a dozen men the size of hazelnuts, for it seemed to me that is all there were on the whole earth? If Your

Lordship were gracious enough to give me a tiny patch of the sky, even one no more than half a league across, I would take it more gladly than the biggest island in the world."[34]

His Grace regretfully replies that such a grant is beyond his power to make. Perhaps the implied slight adds to the duke's relish in fulfilling the little squire's dream of a governorship. This is the most pathetic of the court's brutal jokes. The "isle" is a town in the duke's domain. Its very name is an announcement of what the new governor can expect: Barataria, from *barata*, meaning barter or trade, but also cheap, sham, fraudulent. In his two-day administration, Sancho shows himself to be a surprisingly able executive, a defender of the oppressed. Much good it does him. Through the machinations of the duke's servants, he is taught that the democracy of the soul so vaunted by the Spanish may be a spiritual truth, but it is certainly a practical illusion. Starved, mocked, bruised, he now recalls his peasant's life as one of carefree simplicity; he renounces his office, to his subject's involuntary sorrow. We cannot help but recall that Sancho's creator was also unwilling to master the geometry of a bureaucratic career. On his way home, the squire falls into a pit—a mirror image of the Montesinos cave—and is hauled out by Quixote.

Swiftly now the story reaches its climax. Knight and squire journey to Barcelona. There the Don is defeated in a joust with the bachelor Carrasco, who is this time disguised as the Knight of the Moon and eager for revenge for his earlier defeat at the Don's hands. Quixote is unhorsed. With the victor's lancepoint at his throat, the fallen knight refuses to deny his faith:

> In a faint, sickly voice, without raising his visor, as though he were speaking from the grave, the battered, stunned Don Quixote said: "Dulcinea del Toboso is the most beautiful woman in the world, and I the most hapless knight on earth, and it is unjust that my weakness defraud her truth. Drive your lance home, knight, and rid me of my life, since you have already taken away my honor."[35]

Instead, Carrasco orders him to return to his home and abandon the exercise of arms for a full year. The cure is definitive. Quixote, his vulnerability proved, is too weary of life to cling to it. He has made a fool of himself, he thinks: "I quit this life with an uneasy conscience at having given (the author) an excuse for writing (so many gross absurdities)." Not even Sancho's tearful plea that they play at being shepherds, as Quixote had once wildly proposed, can revive his appetite for living. A greater hope now lies before him. He ruefully acknowledges the disproportion between man's small allotment of divinity and the totality of

God's power: "And if when I was mad I was party to giving him (Sancho) the governorship of an isle, now that I am sane I would give him a kingdom if I were able. . . ." How heavy the phrase is with implication! The lesson of humility has been learned and it has taught Quixote that God will bestow what it was not in the knight's power to give: the kingdom of heaven.

Quixote's death, with its promise of loving redemption, is one of the most moving scenes in all literature. Appropriately, it ends on a note of irony. Soon after his master's death, Sancho is cheered by a bequest to him in Quixote's will. Legacies, notes Cervantes, "help to erase or dull in the heir's memory the sorrow with which death should afflict him."[36]

Cervantes' hope that the novel would consecrate his position among the epic poets of his day was only partly satisfied. A respectable number of Spain's literary leaders recognized the *Quixote*'s daring. The redoubtable Quevedo, who saluted the book's appearance with a romance in which the knight dies mad, conceded its technical virtuosity; years later he would reproach a young writer for presuming to compose novels "with scant fear of and reverence for those printed by the most ingenious Miguel de Cervantes."[37] Recognition from other sources was sometimes oblique. Lope denigrated the book, but he set himself—unsuccessfully—to outdo it. Espinel heaped scorn on it and imitated it in his *Life of Squire Marcos de Obergon;* Estebanillo González, in his *Autobiography,* would acknowledge the debt with better grace. In his *Los Cigarrales de Toledo,* Tirso de Molina would call Cervantes "our Spanish Boccaccio" and mean it as a compliment. Cervantes would gratefully accept flattery from his peers in whatever form it took. He would not, however, be pleased by praise from sources he considered unworthy of the serious business of poetry; a tribute to the *Quixote* in a giddy book called *La Pícara Justina,* published in 1605, failed to save its author, Francisco López de Ubeda, from consignment in Cervantes' *Voyage to Parnassus* to the ranks of Spain's bad poets.

Even Quevedo shared the literary establishment's view of *Don Quixote* as an entertainment, having little to do with either poetry or philosophy. Cervantes himself may not have fully understood the revolutionary impact of a book which was the upstart novel's challenge to verse as the dominant form of epical expression in Western literature. He even contributed to the illusion of the book's simplicity with his (no doubt ironic) observation that "no comment is needed to understand my story because it is so clear that there is nothing in it to create difficulties; children browse in it, young men read it, mature men understand it and the old praise it."[38] Its popularity was so widespread that Descartes could later issue a pompous warning in his *Discourse on Method* against "falling into the extravagance of the paladins in our romances and conceiving aims which exceed their strengths." Yet no one then would have predicted that Cervantes' "entertainment" would go through approximately 2,300 editions to date in sixty-eight dialects and languages, including Korean, Welsh, Kashmiri and Esperanto, making it, after the Bible, the world's most widely translated book.

For two hundred years, Cervantes' admirers, especially abroad, took him at his word and wrote burlesques copying the *Quixote*'s surface devices while ignoring its complex aesthetic and philosophical understructure. Not until the nineteenth century was the *Quixote* rehabilitated as a superb tragedy of the human spirit, but in their fondness for melodrama the Romantics came almost to regret that it is a funny book. Victor Hugo admonished Cervantes' readers to "observe carefully and you will note that there is a tear in his smile."[39] Heine thought it the greatest of the epic poems. Madame Bovary (who has been called a Quixote in skirts) was directly inspired by it. Melville wrote a poem comparing himself to Cervantes' knight. Pickwick and Sam Weller are Quixote and Sancho gone to England.

The *Quixote* revival produced a series of often wistful exegetic studies. The book has been dissected for possible anagrams; concealed codes have been detected lurking in it like so many bewitched frogs waiting to be turned back into princes. The density which invites such probing explains why the book is still being studied. It is read primarily for another reason: Cervantes realized the greatest of poetic accomplishments, that of creating another poet who takes over the work of creation, who is no longer his author's image, but an independent being seemingly capable of building his own life from within himself. Somewhere in the kaleidoscope of illusion and reality Cervantes disappears, Cide Hamete Benengeli disappears, leaving Quixote on his own. The knight's conversion of the lusty Aldonza Lorenzo into the fabulous Dulcinea seems to us to be his idea, not Cervantes', based on his own recollection of a handsome girl with whom he had once been mutely infatuated.

"For me alone was Don Quixote born," concludes Cide Hamete ben Cervantes in the book's final paragraph, "and I for him; his was the power of action, mine of the word, and we two are one. . . ."

El oji ygualacuebant...

Relacion delos gastos menudos q̃ se ã en la molienda q̃ tiene
gasto el g̃º g̃ostos en la Ciudad de Eçija Por comyson del g̃º Ant.º de guebara los
años de 88 y 89.

Comencela molienda el mes de agosto y gaste en aquel
mes y en el d setrembre seys Reales de agente

Para los Candiles q̃ ardian en los almazenes ————— 2 o 4   m

De papel q̃ tinta en dos meses · y Reales ————— 2 o 4

De quatro palas seys Reales ————— 2 o 4

De sondas y escobas seys Reales ————— 2 o 4

De Alquile de vnas steras para vn almazen
seys Reales ————— 2 o 4

De mas steras Para el segundo almazen
Porq̃ estuuese bien acondiçionada la Sarina
seys Reales ————— 2 o 4

De azeyte para otros dos meses seys Reales ————— 2 o 4

De mas tinta y papel quatro Reales ————— 1 3 6

De encerrar quinientas f̃ de trigo q̃
estauan en vn patio descubiert para
hazer vn ensaye y lleuo y fue menester
de cogello con priesa y fue Jente q̃ a
yudase de mas de la q̃ seruia en la ha
çienda seys Reales ————— 2 o 4
                                        ‾‾‾‾‾‾‾
                                        ·1768

---

21. Part of Cervantes' accounts, in his own handwriting, of his activities as a fleet commissary in Andalusia in 1588–89. (Archivo de Simancas)

Ara Cerrajero q̃ fue con migo a los cortijos
del Campo y çerrar algunas aposentos
donde sacar trigo seys reales _____ 204

De Alquile de quatro candados para los
almaçenes de la harina y çer trigo ocho rr _____ 272

otro dia q̃ fuy al campo di a un cerrajero seys _____ 204

de mudar dos mill fz de trigo a otro almaçen
por q̃ le corria de goteras y cogi mas gente
de la ordinaria seys reales _____ 204

mas en otros dos meses seys reales de goteras _____ 204
de maço pague y trinta quatro tz _____ 136

a otro Cerrajero q̃ se coma con migo en la
Ciudad muchos al mazenes y aposentos
buscando trigo seys tz _____ 204

otro dia le di quatro tz _____ 136

de alquile de tres Salvas q̃ se hizieron
para la çanolienda seys tz _____ 204

mas a otro Cerrajero quatro tz _____ 136

Mas de alquile de una Romana q̃ sirvio
en toda la molienda ocho tz _____ 272

otra vez mide el trigo por la misma occasion
del gorgojo y cogi seys reales _____ 204
                                          _____
                                           2380

de mas y gaste seys reales _____ } 204

de tinta y papel quatro reales _____ 136

de mas escobas tres reales _____ } 102

de vn alla de de loba dos reales _____ 68

de otros dos palos dos re _____ 68

de mas gente quatro reales _____ 102

de papel y tinta tres re _____ 680

todo lo qual jure a dios gastte + q lo
gaste en bene ficio de la molienda y
otras cosas muchas mas que no a sente que
se lo firmo de mi nonbre fecho a seys
de setienbre de 1580   Miguel de cerbantes
                                        saavedra

680
2.380
1.760
4.328

22.
Luis de Góngora y Argote. (The Hispanic Society of America, New York)

23.
Francisco de Quevedo y Villegas. (The Hispanic Society of America, New York)

Philippus der drith König
auß Spanien.
1602.

24.
King Philip III of Spain. His expulsion of the Moriscos from Spain in 1609 completed the work of social vandalism begun with Queen Isabela's ejection of her country's Jews in 1492. (The Hispanic Society of America, New York)

La Doña Musniera.

L'hoste

D. Tolosa

Don Quixote
Pour pniquon luy donne
lonuult quituuc cargy ay regarde

Huitntable d'hoste
et fe seruy parson hoste

25. This scene in the inn in *Don Quixote* where the hero is knighted is taken from the oldest known *Quixote* album, *Aventures du fameux Chevalier Dom Quixot de la Mancha et de Sancho Pansa, son escuyer.* The album, in the Bibliothèque Nationale in Paris, probably dates from the late seventeenth century. (From *Historia gráfica de Cervantes y del Quijote* by Juan Givanel mas y Gaziel)

26.

The Romantic age idealized both Quixote and Roque Guinart, the outlaw chieftain he meets on the road to Barcelona, as social revolutionaries. Witness this nineteenth-century notion of the knight looking visionary in bandit's costume. (From *Historia gráfica de Cervantes y del Quijote* by Juan Givanel mas y Gaziel)

27.

With Maritornes: a German Romantic vision of the seduction scene in the inn in *Don Quixote*. (From *Historia gráfica de Cervantes y del Quijote* by Juan Givanel mas y Gaziel)

28.   Quixote and Sancho arrive in Barcelona. The drawing is by Gustave Doré. (From *Historia gráfica de Cervantes y del Quijote* by Juan Givanel mas y Gaziel)

29. The last return: Rocinante and Dapple, looking more determined than
dejected, bear the defeated knight and his squire homeward through a
desolate landscape. (From *Historia gráfica de Cervantes y del Quijote* by
Juan Givanel mas y Gaziel)

31

A Closing of Circles

His Excellency of Lerma was pleased. If all went right—and why should it not?—he would soon acquire effective control of all royal patronage. Plans to remodel his entire town of Lerma in the style of Juan de Herrera's Escorial were going ahead satisfactorily; not only would this reflect admirably on him as a forward-looking patron of the arts, but the new houses he was building around the square fronting the palace there were going at suitably outrageous prices to the elect chosen for his private court. And now, in the spring of 1605, not one but two events occurred in Valladolid to justify the kind of damn-the-expense celebrations with which King Philip was kept bemused.

On April 8, Good Friday, a son had been born to Queen Marguerite. In happy ignorance of the cynicism of history, people were gravely confirming each other's conviction that, as a Good Friday child, the future Philip IV was endowed with the powers of a soothsayer and diviner.

As though this prospect were not cause enough for festivity, the court was also awaiting the arrival of Lord Howard of Effingham, created Earl of Nottingham for his exploit against Cádiz in 1596, with a retinue of some five hundred persons to ratify the peace with England concluded in London the previous year.

Cervantes was to be directly concerned with the joint celebration. Doubtless to cash in one his new popularity, Robles commissioned him to write an account of the ceremonies for a news sheet. For his ramshackle author had suddenly become a celebrity. So famous had Cervantes' creation become that before the end of the year Don Quixote and his squire would figure in carnivals as far away as Peru. In Valladolid, tall, skinny men were now liable to be called Don Quixote, just as fat, dumpy ones were greeted as Sancho, and every trace-galled nag in the city was automatically a Rocinante. If the men of letters who gathered in the late morning at the mentidero del Corrillo did not take Cervantes as seriously as he might have wished, he was at least received as a person of standing. Fame was, after all, a salve to heal many a small cut.

Perhaps the surest sign of the book's success was the speed at which pirate editions were appearing. When it became clear that it was selling rapidly, Cervantes had quickly obtained and sold to Robles an extension of his privilege to Aragon and Portugal, but not in time to head off two pirate versions in Lisbon, two more being readied in Valencia and another in Barcelona. Robles had ordered a second printing from Cuesta almost at once; this would bring the number of editions in 1605 alone to seven.

Cervantes' description of that lively springtime of 1605 has been lost, but a poem later embedded in *The Little Gypsy Girl* may have been written for it. Done in ballad form, it contains a few pleasant touches:

> There goes furious Mars
> in the odd persons
> of more than one young gallant
> startled by his own shadow. . . .

On the whole, though, it demonstrates that his talent as a poet laureate had evolved only slightly since his first effort nearly thirty-seven years before. The royal mother is compared with the Virgin Mary and . . . well, never mind.

Not everyone was happy about the coincidence of the soothsayer's birth with Howard's visit. A sonnet attributed to Góngora protests:

> The queen gave birth; the Lutheran came
> with six hundred heretics and heresies;
> we spend a million (ducats) in two weeks
> on jewels for them, on hospitality and wine.
> We staged a pageant, pure folly,
> and a sleight-of-hand fiesta
> for the angelic legate and his spies
> who swore by Calvin to make peace. . . .
> We remain poor; Luther was enriched;
> and to record these feats, order was given
> to Don Quixote, to Sancho and his ass.[1]

Even the court admitted to some official trepidation. On the eve of Howard's arrival, the decree was cried through the streets of Valladolid that no woman was to go out at night except on her husband's arm, presumably on the theory that rape by a heretic had farther-reaching consequences than a properly Catholic assault. Fortunately for Spanish souls, the English were surprisingly well behaved, possibly because Howard had threatened that troublemakers would be delivered over to punishment by the Spanish Inquisition.

There were the usual hijinks of public rejoicing, such antics as emptying baskets of ashes on the heads of passers-by, loosing snakes and rats in the crowd and hurling eggshells filled with odorous essences. Spirits had been raised to great heights by suspension of the sumptuary laws for the celebration, allowing the artisans' wives to break out the gold baubles and velvet skirts with which their grandmothers had so dazzled Rodrigo de Cervantes fifty-four years before.

The true beneficiaries of the decree were the nobles. A banquet given for the English on May 31 by the constable of Castile put things in proper perspective. The doors to the huge banqueting hall were left open so that all could gawk who would. Amid hangings of silk and gold, three hundred guests sat down to—four hundred? a thousand? twelve hundred?—courses piled up to twelve deep on platters of gold and silver; fish had been rushed in relays from the coasts. The constable's plate was prominently exhibited on the walls and more treasure was displayed in adjoining rooms. A number of pieces were afterward found to be missing.

In these few hectic weeks, it seemed that all the world had been pressed into service to spur the joy in Valladolid. On June 4 the streets rang with music to announce the election of a new pope, Paul V. Three days later, not to be outdone by his own creature, Lerma gave a banquet. On a purely statistical basis, he won going away: 2,200 dishes, not counting the dried fruits, preserves and pastries "in a thousand shapes of castles and ships, all gilt and silvered."[2] Beer was thoughtfully provided for the English, which, as far as the Spanish were privately concerned, put the heretics in their proper social place. In three rooms, cupboards stretching to the ceilings were stuffed with gold and silver plate, gold-chased rock crystal, fountains, Venetian and Catalonian glass, Portuguese ceramics. Afterward, in a canopied garden where, in wanton luxury, the windows in the surrounding arches were all glazed, the guests were shown a play, Lope's *El caballero de Illescas.*

June 9, Corpus Christi, was chosen as the day of formal ratification of the peace treaty. The bullfight which is traditionally a part of Spanish Corpus celebrations took place on the following day, on the sanded floor of the city's Plaza Mayor. The great entered the square in their coaches that day. Sunlight flashed on thousands of jeweled gold collars, chains, bracelets, buttons, decorations, sword hilts. It is to be hoped that Cervan-

tes was present (not seated, certainly, not at the specially reduced price of
two hundred reales a ticket). For, as his admirer Tomé Pinheiro de
Veiga described it, he was one of the stars of the show:

> And that an *entremés* not be lacking in that universal celebration, a
> Don Quixote appeared in the foreground, alone and with no one at his
> side, with a big hat on his head and a baize cape and sleeves, shag hose
> and good boots with "sparrow's-beak" spurs, beating the flanks of a
> miserable gray hack with ribs galled by a coach harness and a coach-
> man's seat; and before him came Sancho Panza, his squire. He (Don
> Quixote) wore spectacles to increase his gravity and presence, and an
> upturned beard. . . .[3]

The bulls were brave that day and the aristocratic *toreros* on their
beribboned horses were elegant, according to a contemporary chronicler:
"nothing unfortunate happened except to the common people."[4] One incident did occur to mar the courtly tone: a Navarrese gentleman named
Gaspar de Ezpeleta fell off his horse while trying to lance a bull. According to Góngora, who seemed unable to comment on a public event except
in verse,

> . . . the fool fell off
> to show all who he was.
> It might be said the gentleman,
> given his seedy look and air,
> had seldom entered a bullring,
> and his steward less often still. . . .[5]

The incident is mentioned only because Don Gaspar is shortly to reappear in this narrative, in a much sorrier state.

When the English left on June 18, Cervantes was presumably ready to
settle back into an everyday routine of work, church, visits to the mentidero del Corrillo, the small-business activities on which, with the proceeds from the women's sewing, the family is thought to have lived. Now
that the fierce winter wind, the *cierzo,* was holding its snowy breath, dusk
might find him on a stone bench on the new Prado de la Magdalena,
watching the fashionable promenade in their coaches and eavesdropping
on the irreverent comments of the young lovers who favored the place.
This new craze for coaches probably amused Cervantes, especially when
he saw one of these great vessels, mirrored, tasseled and gilt, parked ostentatiously before its owner's house, covered with oilskin and with its
traces poking through a window and anchored indoor. When Sancho's

wife, euphoric at learning she is a governor's lady, asks leave to travel to her husband's court, she assures him that "I will try and do you honor there by going about in a coach."[6] So essential a prestige item had the vehicles become that people too poor to keep one but too proud to admit it would walk along the street leaning on a squire's arm and wearing the scapular of some obscure religious order to indicate that they were afoot through piety, not poverty.

In the evenings, when he was not sitting convivially at *quínolas* and *el parar* at the gambling rooms run by old friend Juan García de la Torre, he might be found at home entertaining a business associate—Fernando de Toledo occasionally, or the Genoese trader Agostino Raggio, or the Portuguese Simon Méndez, a treasury official.

Shortly before 11 P.M. on June 27, this routine was interrupted.

The Calle del Rastro, well out of the city center, was dark and normally deserted at that hour. Cervantes had already gone to bed. In the apartment above, twenty-three-year-old Luis de Garibay thought he heard a clash of swords; this was soon followed by cries for help from the street. Because such alarms would normally have gone unheeded, especially in so violence-prone a quarter as the Rastro, the voice may have called by name to the young man's mother, Luisa de Montoya. Luis and his younger brother Esteban rushed down the stairs. At the building's entrance they found Don Gaspar de Ezpeleta, the "fool" of Góngora's poem, bleeding and near collapse. From his right hand dangled a naked rapier; a buckler was clutched in his left.[7]

In response to an appeal from Luis, Cervantes went down and helped take Ezpeleta to the Montoya apartment, where the wounded man was stretched on a mattress on the floor in the main room. Magdalena appeared, wearing the homespun habit of the lay sister she had now become; she would not leave Ezpeleta's bedside for the next thirty-one hours. While she and Luisa did what they could to make him comfortable, Luis and Esteban went for help.

Soon afterward, surgeon Sebastián Macías arrived. With him was a priest who heard Ezpeleta's confession. Macías found two deep sword wounds, in Ezpeleta's left thigh and the lower abdomen; presumably, the surgeon pushed things into place, cauterized the wounds against bleeding and applied the usual white-of-egg balm under compresses.

By this time the law had arrived: Cristóbal de Villarroël, one of four ordinary Valladolid magistrates, with constables Francisco Vicente and Diego García. On hand as well was Ezpeleta's patron, the Marquis of Falces, as well as the victim's page, Francisco Camporredondo, age nineteen. Villarroël proceeded, as the police say, to take a preliminary statement from the groaning figure on the floor. It was extremely unhelpful: Ezpeleta said he had supped with Falces, leaving the marquis around

10 P.M. At the corner of the Hospital de la Resurrección, he said, he had been accosted by a man dressed in black who asked him where he was going (there is no indication that the magistrate asked the same question, or that Ezpeleta volunteered the information). "Why do you want to know?" Ezpeleta said he replied, drawing his sword. The other man also drew, they fought, Don Gaspar was wounded. His assailant fled. No, Ezpeleta had no idea who the man was.

From the first, magistrate Villarroël's conduct of the case is exasperating. He seems to have gone out of his way to avoid asking the normal questions: what was Ezpeleta doing in the Rastro district, walking away from the direction of his lodgings in what is now the Calle de la Manteria? Had his assailant's voice sounded familiar? Did Ezpeleta have any enemies, had he quarreled with anyone recently? Records of the case preserved in the archives of the Spanish Royal Academy of History recount that the page, Camporredondo, told the investigator that Ezpeleta had a mistress, Inés Hernández, the wife of a royal scribe named Melchor Galvan, and that the man in black was undoubtedly Galvan or a kinsman. The marriage was known to be in trouble; the couple's debts were high and Inés' reputation for chastity correspondingly low. They lived near the Rastro, in the direction in which Ezpeleta seemed to have been heading.

Villarroël made no attempt to call the woman for questioning; he did not even note her name and address. Witnesses also testified that a note found folded in the victim's hose was taken by the magistrate before anyone else could see it and was never produced again. Constable García took possession of the money Ezpeleta had with him, along with two small gold rings, one set with six brilliants, the other with three small emeralds. The man's clothes—waistcoat, satin shirt, taffeta sleeves, hose and braid-trimmed doublet—were left, for some reason, with Cervantes.

Everyone in the building was questioned. Oddly, there is no record of interrogation of Doña Catalina; no one in the Cervantes family mentioned her, although all the other witnesses said she lived there. Equally curiously, when asked to name the inhabitants of Cervantes' apartment, the servant María de Ceballos listed Catalina, Magdalena, Constanza, Isabel and Cervantes, but not Andrea, whose residence there was confirmed by other witnesses and whose testimony appears in the dossier.

Witnesses told Villarroël they had seen the fight, that they saw one man fall crying, "Ah, thief, you have killed me," and saw the other combatant run away. Isabel de Islallana, servant to María de Argomeda, who, with her sister Luisa, boarded with Juana Gaitán, said she saw the assailant's face and would recognize him if she saw him again. Although this presumably eliminated, at least tentatively, any of the building's residents, all of whom were known to the girl, Villarroël ignored the statement. He had apparently made up his mind to seek his swordsman among the building's tenants or their familiars. His interest was aroused by the maid's statement that she had seen Ezpeleta with her mistresses a month earlier and had spotted him loitering in the street before the fight the assertion was at least questionable, but it tells us what attitude the magistrate had adopted.

Villarroël's handling of the case has convinced many historians that he was deliberately covering up, one supposes for Galvan, that pressure was brought to bear on him to direct his inquiry along lines that were socially innocuous. This may be putting too crude a light on the business. Perhaps the truth lies in what might be called the average of his character and Ezpeleta's.

Quite a bit is known about Don Gaspar, little of it inspiring. Born of a noble Pamplona family, he had accompanied the Armada as an adventurer, had attached himself to the army sent to Saragossa by Philip II and later, as a commissioned officer, had fought briefly but bravely in Flanders. At one point in his past he had been named a member of a delegation to the Low Countries, but had ditched the party to carouse in Paris with a group of politically doubtful friends he met en route; a providential visit by the constable of Castile rescued him from what might very well have been a long career in a French prison or a short one on a French scaffold. Although he had long since run through his family fortune, his family's rank had secured him a knighthood in the Order of Santiago and an allowance from the crown of fifty ducats a month. This might have suited, say, a Cervantes nicely, but it represented misery to a man of Don Gaspar's habits. When the crown, noting that "because of his manner of governance and conduct he deserves little," refused to augment the allowance under conditions suitable to him, he attached himself to the Marquis of Falces, captain of the guard of the king's archers. Ignoring the wife and son he had left in Navarre, he spent as much time as he could at Falces' table, eating too little, drinking too much and acting as a sort of court fool to the marquis and his friends.

Of Villarroël there is much less to be said. He was new at his job, which probably means that he had recently bought it. He was also one of those self-important, opinionated men whom every bureaucracy produces and in whom Mediterranean bureaucracies sometimes seem to specialize. That he was incompetent is less clear. He was an officer of the law—but of whose law?

Murder in that Spain of sudden violence and fragile honor, of dwindling moral certainties and almost constant famine, was as common as the pox. We remember that in his autobiography, Alonso de Contreras tells of stabbing a schoolmate to death when he was twelve years old with the knife he used for trimming goose quills—for which he was exiled from Madrid for one year. In royal Valladolid, crime was so common that terrified citizens habitually went armed whether or not they were officially licensed to do so.

Villarroël would have known that a goodly number of the local pícaros were renegade priests and noblemen and that no good could come of pressing such fellows too closely; they were seldom punished and they were addicted to revenging themselves on troublemakers. He would of course have known Ezpeleta's reputation as a bravo and an idler; everyone in Valladolid knew it. But Ezpeleta was a person of rank, a Knight of Santiago, a frequenter of influential tables. It is to be noted that Falces remained, quite improperly, at the magistrate's elbow throughout the interrogations conducted that night, a presence of which a Villarroël would have been acutely conscious.

These people in the Rastro, however: they were something else again. They were poor. They kept sordid company. There was doubtless a public service to be performed in inquiring into what he later termed the "freedom" in which these women lived "without visible means of support. . . ." To find Don Gaspar's assailant among them would be a feather in his cap. The magistrate persisted in his line of investigation.

He returned to the charge twice the next day, insisting that Ezpeleta tell him who his attacker had been. Twice the wounded man told him that he did not know, that he could only say the man had fought fairly, that he wished to be left in peace. Villarroël again turned to the building's tenants. And he began to receive answers that gratified him. Esteban de Garibay, probably trying to deflect attention from his mother's too obvious connection with the victim, said that both Mariana Ramírez and Juana Gaitán had caused gossip by receiving gentlemen. Some of Juana's guests had been noblemen, the Duke of Pastrana, the Duke of Maqueda, the Count of Concentaina. Both Pastrana and Maqueda had been in trouble with the law before. No attempt was made to question either man. Juana's explanation that she had hoped to persuade one of these gentlemen to accept the dedication of Laínez's still unpublished volume of poetry was received without comment by the investigator. As for Mariana Ramírez, she and her lover Diego de Miranda had already been punished for concubinage.

Esteban also mentioned Raggio and Méndez as visitors to the Cervantes apartment. This information was made more appetizing to Villarroël by the testimony of the pietistic widow in the attic, Isabel de Ayala. We can almost see her—bony, black-clad arms emphatically gesticulating, toothless jaws working steadily, crisply, like a garlic press in a cheap restaurant. The visits of men to the Cervantes family by day and by night were scandalous, she said—why, it was common knowledge that Isabel de Saavedra was Méndez's mistress. Señora de Ayala had repeatedly rebuked Méndez, the magistrate was told, but he of course had denied that his calls had been anything but friendly.

Ezpeleta died at 6 A.M. June 29. On June 30, Villarroël ordered the arrests of Cervantes, his daughter, Andrea, Constanza, Juana Gaitán, María Ramírez, Diego de Miranda, María and Luisa de Argomeda and the niece who lived with them. An order also went out to arrest Méndez, until it was found that he was already in prison, for debt. The magistrate had excused Magdalena de Cervantes despite what seemed a suspicious circumstance: before he died, obviously in payment for her faithful nursing, Ezpeleta had bequeathed her a silk gown. What, Villarroël demanded, was a woman her age, a woman of religion, to do with a silk gown—unless it was to be passed to a younger woman on the victim's instructions, perhaps to Isabel? The witlessness of the question suggests he felt his case was slipping away from him.

Meanwhile, however, the owner of the rooming house in which Ezpeleta had lodged, a bedridden woman named Juana Ruiz, summoned the police to her bedside to hear her evidence. The deceased had indeed lodged with her, although, she added, in the three months he had been there "he had not slept there fifteen nights." More to the point, she told them a complicated story of a mysterious veiled woman who went to Don Gaspar's room in his absence, swearing vengeance on him for having taken two rings from her. The description of the rings matched those the police had taken from Ezpeleta's hands.

When the veiled woman was found in his rooms after his death, there was no help for it: she had to be interviewed. The magistrate talked to her alone; his clerk was told to delete her name and address from the record. The woman had said she was merely visiting poor, invalid Juana Ruiz and had wandered into Ezpeleta's rooms by mistake. Villarroël did not press the point. It is not known if Inés Hernández—certainly she was the woman in the veil—ever recovered her rings.

For Cervantes, arrest was a closing of concentric circles. The prison in which he was lodged had held his father and his grandfather; he had continued this progress of the generations from cell to cell through Algiers, Castro del Río, Seville and now back to the ancestral starting point. Ten years later, in the *Persiles,* he would remember the incident with an outrage barely softened by time. In Book III (Chapter 4), the party of pilgrims led by Periandro and Auristela stops to rest by a stream near Cáceres, in Extremadura. Suddenly, from the surrounding bushes, staggers a young man transpierced by a sword from back to breast. With a cry of despair, he falls dead before their eyes. Periandro, the first to reach his side, withdraws the blade and searches the body for identification, but finds nothing. At that moment, a patrol of the Santa Hermandad erupts into the clearing. One calls:

"Hold, thieves, murderers, highwaymen! Rob him of nothing more, for your time has come to be taken to where you will pay for your sins."

"Don't be stupid," retorted Antonio. "There are no thieves here; all of us are enemies to such folk."

"A pretty show you make of it," said the officer. "The man dead, his effects in your possession and his blood on your hands, all are witness to your misdeeds. You are thieves, you are highwaymen, you are murderers, and you will soon pay for your crimes, nor will you be saved by those capes of Christian virtue with which you cover your evil deeds, dressing yourselves as pilgrims."

Impulsive Antonio puts an arrow through the officer's arm. The others call for help and more than twenty patrolmen converge on the spot, taking the pilgrims prisoner. They are brought to Cáceres, where the corregidor, hearing the police evidence, seeing Periandro bloodied, proposes to put them to the torture. Ricla tries to bribe a court official to defend them, which makes things worse, "for the satraps of the pen, sniffing golden fleece beneath the pilgrim homespun, resolved to shear them to the bone, as is their habit and custom." They are saved only by one of those miraculous strokes of luck so frequent in the book; the real murderer is identified, but never arrested.

Much the same denouement was unfolding in Valladolid. If Villarroël had hoped that interrogation in a grim official atmosphere might be more productive than it was in the familiar surroundings of the Rastro, he was quickly undeceived. The women falsified their ages, but their stories were unshakable. Yes, Ezpeleta had been known to a few of them—Luisa de Montoya, Juana Gaitán, the Argomeda sisters—but none could be suspected of his murder. No, Isabel de Saavedra was not involved with Méndez; Isabel de Ayala, they agreed, was a liar and a malicious busybody. Juana's aristocratic visitors were indeed being consulted about the proposed dedication of the Laínez book; Pastrana had been a friend of the poet's in Madrid.

Only two surprises—to us—were revealed in the testimony. One is Andrea's declaration that she was "a widow, wife that was of Santi Ambrosio, Florentine." The second, that Isabel de Saavedra, alone among the women in her family, was illiterate. The "servant" had been taught to sew, but not to read. Although her status as Cervantes' daughter was openly conceded—she is described in the case records as his natural daughter—no one seemed to feel that this entitled her to any special consideration.

Within twenty-four hours, all those arrested were sent home under house arrest. On July 5 they petitioned for unconditional discharge; at the same time, Cervantes requested the authorities to relieve him of Ezpeleta's clothes, "which are rotting with the blood on them." By July 18 the case had been dropped, but in gratuitously humiliating fashion: Miranda was ordered to leave the city and to have no further communication with his Mariana; Méndez, on no grounds but Villarroël's spite, was forbidden to enter the building on the Rastro. The prohibition effectively tarnished Cervantes' reputation by publicly insinuating that he was the complaisant father of an erring daughter. Melchor Galvan, the husband of Inés Hernández, was never questioned. Magistrate Villarroël was no doubt congratulated by his superiors for his prudence and discretion; murders were commonplace in Valladolid, but scandal touching the court, however remotely, was to be assiduously avoided.

Almost everyone left the house on the Rastro shortly afterward. Cervantes is thought to have been away from Valladolid in November 1605 because he did not join Andrea and Magdalena in petitioning for a formal accounting of the pay arrears due their brother Rodrigo. Citation of specific details about the city of Salamanca in *The Glass Scholar,* which Cervantes is believed to have written in 1606–7, has prompted speculation that he was there at the time, presumably on business.

In January 1606, the ruin of Valladolid begun by Philip II's departure from the city nearly half a century before was completed by his son's decision to move the court back to Madrid. Reasons of health were again given: the plague still lurked in Valladolid. More to the point was the tonic Madrid prescribed for the crown's fiscal anemia: 250,000 ducats a year to Philip for ten years, plus one sixth of all house rents for the same period; to sweeten the pot and help subsidize the grant, municipal authorities approved the doubling and tripling of all rents in the city. In addition, Madrid volunteered to pay the cost of moving the royal household, no mean offer, it has been pointed out, considering that four hundred teams of oxen were required merely to haul the royal wardrobe across the rain-mired, snow-clogged thirty-three leagues to Madrid.

Cervantes' sisters probably left Valladolid at once, following their livelihood. He and Catalina may have spent some months in Toledo and Esquivias before rejoining them. It may be that he needed a spell of peace and quiet to finish the work he had on hand. This period, once thought to have been so sterile for him, was in fact highly productive; from it probably date some of the best of his novelas, works examining in virile new forms the problems set forth in *Don Quixote.*

32

"A Rich Heritage of Carols"

Half a man's soul resides
in his sons, but his daughters
take half and more besides,
and a father must look sharp to guard their honor. . . .
Disobedient daughters,
that anticipate the pleasure
reserved to the unfolding years,
may God destroy you, the heavens curse you![1]

These lines were probably written in 1607–8 and they burn with the
heat of personal experience. Perhaps this was because Cervantes had
recently learned that Isabel was pregnant, but not by the man who is
thought to have been her husband at the time. Coming on top of the
business in Valladolid, this was really intolerable.

It may have been the unpleasantness there that prompted the family to
seek a husband for her almost as soon as they returned to Madrid; the rumors involving Méndez had been a warning that unless she were safely
disposed of, the girl was headed for trouble. Ample precedent on both
sides of the family taught them what to expect. They had not bargained,
however, on the intensity of Isabel's hatred for them—a feeling which
would presumably have extended to any man they chose as her husband
—or for her drive toward the security she had missed so far.

The husband they gave her was named Diego Sanz or Diego Sainz del
Aguila. He is almost as shadowy a figure as Andrea's Santi Ambrosio. We
know about him only through references to him in the contract for her
second marriage and in a will she made in 1639. If there was a dowry in
the hand Isabel gave him it would have been minimal; we know Cervan-

tes was broke again because an inventory of Francisco Robles' assets dated November 23, 1607, lists an outstanding loan to the author of 450 reales.

Whether Isabel was already married when she met Juan de Urbina is impossible to affirm. It would not have mattered to her. If, as we suppose, Sanz was as unprosperous as her own family, Urbina represented a chance for a taste of luxury, a surreptitious fondling of the courtly life she had no hope of acceding to legitimately.

Urbina was secretary to Spain's client House of Savoy. He was probably in his early forties when he met Isabel, married, the father of at least one daughter and already a grandfather. A shrewd head for business had enabled him to profit from his position to acquire lands, bonds, what would now be called company directorships, houses and an accumulation of cash and finery.

If he felt any affection for Isabel, it was short-lived. She appears to us as conniving, greedy, not very bright, almost totally without charm. No gracious action by her is recorded, although a number are known that linger disagreeably in the memory. In 1639, for example, she would stand up in an Inquisition court to accuse another woman, a mentally deficient creature named María Baptista, of illuminism. The defendant, Isabel declared, had told her that one day in church a golden thread had emerged from the rib of Christ crucified and bound her to him; on another occasion, the accused had said the king (then Philip IV) must do penance for his sins and that things would go badly because of his maladministration. The Inquisitors, recognizing that poor, witless María Baptista was merely parroting the rumors then current in Madrid, gave her absolution.

Isabel became pregnant in March 1607. A daughter was born in December who was christened Isabel Sanz del Aguila y Cervantes. Whether Sanz knew the child was Urbina's is moot. Innocent or complaisant, he did contribute one final, soundless act of good taste: he died quickly, possibly in June 1608. On June 24 the widow and her infant daughter moved into a house owned by Urbina at what is now 33 Pasaje del Comercio. The secretary's subsequent actions would show that he no longer felt bound to the mother, but he was concerned for his daughter's well-being.

Cervantists easily adopt the rhetoric of closet snobbery: what could be expected of the daughter of Ana Franca, a tavern wench, a loose woman? This may be unfair to Ana, about whom, after all, very little is known, but it serves to shift responsibility for Isabel away from where it belongs: with Cervantes himself.

He probably did not care whether she turned out to be a model daughter. He may hardly even have thought about her, and when he did, one suspects, it was with disgust at her existence and, it is to be hoped, a feeling of guilt at the way in which she had been raised. The fiction of her "service" to Magdalena had been maintained until, with the gathering of the clan under one small roof in Valladolid, it could no longer hold. The guilty secret this implied was the atmosphere she grew up in, and revelation of the truth, when it finally came, could only have confirmed her disgrace in her own mind. It would not have escaped her that while her cousin Constanza's illegitimacy had been immediately accepted—because she was an Ovando and not a Villafranca?—her own had been resented and disguised.

Constanza was cherished by everyone, especially Cervantes, whose favorite she was. Not so Isabel. That Doña Catalina would never take to the girl might be expected. But there is no evidence that anyone else loved her either. To anyone reading Cervantes' stories (the appendix to the *Voyage to Parnassus,* say, or the prologue to the *Persiles*) his fondness for young people is apparent. It seems not to have extended to Isabel. She may have been made to feel a stranger, an unloved burden. There may be a harsh recall of Cervantes' antipathy toward her in *The Dogs' Colloquy,* which is set in Valladolid: Montiela, who "abandoned many vices and did many good works" although "in the end she died a witch," had two children by a man named Rodríguez who were turned into dogs by a jealous rival.

Illiterate, undowered, made subtly but constantly to feel her father's distaste for her, Isabel came to womanhood detesting them all. It is indicative that, despite the financial ease of her later years, she refused to mark the anonymous graves in which her father and her "foster mother" Magdalena lay.

By 1607–8 Cervantes' self-respect was almost wholly derived from the work for which, increasingly, he would have hoarded his waning emotional and physical energy. His reluctance to involve himself in the problems of those nearest him would have been deeper than ever. Scandal was a distraction and distractions were unwelcome. Now, damn it, something would have to be done about that girl.

On August 28, 1608, rather like a bundle of old clothes being stuffed into a box for shipment to some far-away charity, Isabel was auctioned to a smalltime trader named Luis de Molina.

The marriage contract signed that day is an exercise in black humor. No one trusted anybody. A dowry of two thousand ducats was provided for Isabel, technically by her father, but obviously by his guarantor, Juan de Urbina; Molina, however, insisted on holding mortgages against the sum on Urbina's property until the dowry was paid. He promised to marry Isabel within a month, on pain of a thousand-ducat fine which would in no case release him from his agreement. If Isabel balked, she was to pay *him* one thousand ducats and be stuck with him anyway.

Molina and Isabel were granted free lifetime occupancy of the house she lived in, which was represented as belonging to her father, but neither was to hold the deed. The property would belong to the child Isabel until her marriage; if she predeceased Cervantes, her mother retained the use of it, but on her death ownership would revert to Cervantes to do with as he pleased. This, of course, was no more than a device to give him some means of control over his daughter; a separate, secret agreement would be signed in which Cervantes conceded that the property was Urbina's. Half the dowry was to be paid within a month, the rest within three years, but Molina was taking no chances: formal betrothal might take place at the appointed time, but he would not consummate the marriage until half the dowry was in his hands, thus leaving a way open to annulment.

Isabel, who seems to have been taught to sign her name for the occasion (a feat which had been beyond her in 1605), is referred to variously in the document as Isabel de Saavedra, Isabel de Cervantes, Isabel de Cervantes y Saavedra, Isabel Sanz and Isabel de Sanz. She is described as the "legitimate" daughter of Cervantes and Ana Franca, a designation in which Doña Catalina conspired as a witness. No doubt Catalina would have preferred to have no part in the proceedings. Nevertheless, she had every interest in seeing to it that her stepdaughter be gotten rid of as quickly as possible and with a minimum of scandal. It was not mere prudishness which made her dislike Isabel. An event occurring about the same time suggests that she might have been willing to overlook mere immorality.

Sometime that autumn, Constanza de Ovando went into court again, this time to sue one Francisco Leal for the usual unspecified offense, and was granted a writ of execution for eleven hundred reales (which Leal perforce would pay December 18). This, as we know, was not Constanza's first venture into love's boggy corners, although it would be her last of record. Yet she remained in Doña Catalina's affections and was a beneficiary in her aunt's will—a document in which Isabel is not so much as mentioned. Even more oddly, Catalina would establish such good relations with Molina that he became the executor of the very will in which his wife was snubbed.

Molina has not been loved by historians. They point out that he was venal, shifty, self-indulgent, spendthrift. The Madrid agent for a Genoese banking family named Strata, he had been ransomed from Algerian captivity in 1598 for a bargain-basement 1,250 reales. When he sold himself into bondage to Isabel he was thirty-eight years old, in debt and likely to remain so.

Isabel, needless to say, despised him. She would promptly give public notice of the fact in an attempt to recover what she believed was being

withheld from her by the executor of Ana Franca's estate. The chore
would normally have been assigned to her husband; instead, she asked
Magdalena to take charge of the suit. Her undoubted coolness toward her
pious aunt made the move a double slap at Molina.

That antagonism would grow with the years. In 1631, only seven
months before Molina's death but twenty-one years before her own, she
was to make a will which seethed with her dislike of him:

> . . . When my marriage to the said Luis de Molina, my husband,
> took place, I conveyed into his power in dowered goods 36,743 reales,
> of which 2,000 ducats was in silver coin and the rest in furnishings,
> and today the said dowry has been diminished by half or more, and be-
> cause of this I found myself obliged to exclude (him) from a share in
> my household goods; but since Our Lord God was pleased to give him
> to me as a companion, I wish . . . that he may receive 200 ducats from
> my estate. . . .

The sum was an insult. Isabel was reasonably well off by then (thanks,
admittedly, to her own shrewdness); the will assigns four times that
amount to the monks of San Basilio for prayers for her salvation. Another
clause complains that some of her jewels had been pawned, an indis-
cretion to which Molina confessed in his own testament. Her slave
Gracia, whom she refused to liberate, was barred from her husband's
service because "if she remains in the power of the said Luis de Molina
some evil will certainly come of it." Not only did she fail to make her
husband an executor, but she made a point of saying, "And if perchance
the said Luis de Molina . . . should oppose the provisions of this testament . . . any bequest or favor provided under its terms is to be considered null and void. . . ."[2]

Molina probably never knew Isabel had made the will. But in his own
testament, dated December 25, 1631, he appoints Isabel his executrix
with a humble admission: "I declare for the relief of my conscience that
my estate, such as it is, belongs to the said Isabel de Saavedra, my wife,
and that I have consumed and wasted much of her dowry, for which
reason I name her my sole heir,"[3] a disposition going well beyond the
legal requirements.

There is a redeeming side to Molina's character which is often
overlooked. He did establish himself as a reputable crown scribe; he
seems to have tried hard to administer his wife's money fruitfully. If he
failed, it was partly because he had a strangely trusting nature that made
him the natural prey of more wolfish competitors. Not long after the
marriage, he would establish a solid friendship with Cervantes. His
dealings with Urbina were turbulent, but that was as much Urbina's

fault as it was Molina's. He would remain a friend to Constanza after Doña Catalina's death in 1626 despite the testamentary snub to Isabel. But Isabel held out. She clearly thought of Molina as a jailer to whom she had been delivered up by Urbina with her own family's complicity. She was never to forgive any of them for it.

The act of incarceration was their formal betrothal in the church of San Luis on September 8. The ceremony constituted a legal marriage, but when it was over Isabel and Luis returned to their separate beds. When, on December 8, Molina collected part of the dowry, he warily declared his *intention* to consummate the marriage. At the same time he acknowledged receipt of 14,753 reales brought by Isabel in jewels, clothing and furnishings, a gift from Urbina in addition to the 2,000 ducats. The list of effects is ducal: diamond and ruby rings, gold bracelets, silver plate, mirrors, linens, a complete trousseau for the bride. Only one item in the dowry inventory might have come from Isabel's father: "six books of collected stories, valued at 100 reales"[4] for an Isabel who could not read them.

Not until March 1, 1609, after the agreed half of the dowry had been paid, was a formal nuptial mass said and the marriage consummated. Cervantes and Doña Catalina were present in the church. Relations with Isabel were suspended almost immediately afterward.

That Cervantes managed to remain relatively serene through the turmoil can be attributed to the standard tranquilizers, work and, increasingly, religion. And both point, through the work he had in progress, to a growing philosophical resolution that absorbed and comforted him.

His fame was spreading far beyond Spain's frontiers. In 1607 a new edition of *Don Quixote,* Part I, issued in Brussels, the best and most error-free to date, would move Robles to put out a third Madrid edition in July 1608. Thomas Shelton's first "true" translation, based on the Brussels version and in many ways the most flavorful ever done, was completed "in the space of forty daies" in 1607 although it would not be published until 1612. In the same year, the knight and Sancho were represented, along with the priest, the barber and the Princess Micomicona, in a festival in Peru in which Quixote wore a helmet stuck with cock feathers and "a pair of hose from the year one." Nicolas Baudovin's French translation of "The Tale of Foolish Curiosity" appeared in 1608. The following year saw Jean Richer's French version of excerpts from *Don Quixote,* notably the incidents of Grisóstomo's funeral and Don Quixote's discourse on the relative merits of arms and letters. Its publication inspired César Oudin to undertake the first French translation of *La Galatea.* Cervantes was at least as famous abroad as Lope de Vega.

Whatever satisfaction this may have given him, it brought no money into the household. Cervantes had entered his sixties; there was no question now of humping along broken roads on lumpy hired mules even if he had wanted to, and the spasmodic business dealings which had helped sustain him in the past were increasingly victims of his age and failing health. There are indications that he was evicted from the small house the family occupied on the Calle del Duque de Alba, perhaps for nonpayment of rent; in 1609 he appears with his wife and sisters in a house at what is now 21 Calle de la Magdalena, one of six in which he is known to have lived in the last seven years of his life. At the same time, his old troubles with the treasury rose from their bureaucratic grave: on November 6, 1608, an order was issued to Cervantes and his Granada-mission guarantor, Francisco Suárez Gasco, to pay the wretched deficit charged to him within ten days, along with a sixty-ducat fine. Cervantes was notified of the order November 24; this time he acknowledged it, sending a reply in which he presumably justified his accounts. The document vanished around the beginning of the twentieth century; judical records of the case were lost even earlier, for Martín Fernández de Navarrete, who had seen them, was unable to relocate them in 1819. In any event, nothing further was made of the case.

There is no record that Cervantes had yet found a patron, but some help may already have been going to him from the Count of Lemos. Robles is thought to have given Cervantes an advance on his fee for the *Exemplary Stories,* which were nearing completion. It may also have been Robles who pressed him to begin work on the sequel to *Don Quixote,* on which he is known to have been working in 1607, and this may have produced a second advance.

With the little money his sisters may still have been able to earn, this trickle of silver was enough to keep the coarse, blackish bread of the poor on the family table, but it offered no security. This partly explains why, when the theaters reopened in 1607 after another period in limbo, Cervantes was tempted to try his hand at playwrighting again. Probably the memory of his 1592 defection still rankled. More to the point, the theater still allowed a writer to earn as much in three months of work as he could make in years of toil on a novel.

A commission was wangled from a doubtless reluctant Gaspar de Porres, probably for old times' sake. Between the late summer of 1607 and the spring of 1608 Cervantes churned out at least three plays for him. They were "captivity" dramas: *The Dungeons of Algiers* (a salad of *Life in Algiers* and "The Captive's Tale" dressed with dashes of *The Liberal Lover*), *The Spanish Gallant* and *The Great Sultana.* Cervantes, preoccupied with other work in progress, was clearly short of new theatrical ideas, but he was in a hurry to deliver something to Porres.

All three were rejected. Porres really is not to be blamed for the decision. Although there were good moments in all three plays, they were nonetheless old-fashioned, often confused, the plotting trumped up; there was little in them of Lope's smooth-flowing, neatly assembled carpentry in which action occurred, if not always naturally, at least with seeming inevitability. The three plays' themes, shopworn, did not correspond with the inflated escapism of the public mood, nor with the emotional nostalgia Lope so confidently fed to audiences more wistful than ever for the formulary grandeur of an earlier time.

With his customary blindness to his own theatrical failings (or, again, was it stubborn defiance? Was the world, after all, to bow to Quixote's will, or would it annihilate him with its own?), Cervantes deeply resented the rejection. Direct revenge took the form of Sancho's·ungentlemanly dig at the player-manager who "can be arrested for two murders and come out free without paying costs."[5] Porres, his son and three actors were in fact accused of murdering a priest named Pedro de Villavicioso, but the manager did not get off quite as easily as Sancho alleged; buying his family's way out of the jam cost him 950 ducats.

Repeatedly, in later works, Cervantes would harp on his disappointment. In the appendix to the *Voyage to Parnassus* he would declare that his plays went unstaged "because the managers did not seek me out, nor will I go to them." Elsewhere in the work he grumbles that they "have their black-bread-and-butter poets and . . . they do not look for whiter loaves." His comment in the prologue to his *Eight Plays and Eight Interludes* comes closer to candor: "I found no birds in old nests; by that I mean I found no manager to solicit my work."

This may have been the period in which Cervantes wrote the enchanted *Pedro de Urdemales.* Yet for all its superb poetry, its subtlety and emotional intensity, *Pedro de Urdemales* is a closet drama, almost unplayable. Moreover, the personages who interest us in it are Gypsies, vagabonds, peasants, people with whom Spanish playgoers were in daily contact—precisely the people they did not wish to see on a stage.

Cervantes' thinking at this period might be likened to the traditional designation of the king's treasury: "the chest with three keys." *Pedro de Urdemales* opens one of the locks. Two closely related works dating from about the same period provide the other keys: *The Dogs' Colloquy* and *The Little Gypsy Girl.* Together they seem to comprise Cervantes' justification of his years of impotence, his gradual return to creativity.

Pedro de Urdemales was a Spanish folk figure, a symbol even in the late Middle Ages of the pícaro, with what that implied of a free spirit, more than a little demonic. He is a will-o'-the-wisp, changing yet immutable, wily, almost preternaturally wise, unconfined; he is forever aspiring, inching interminably along the crumbling trail bordering the pit of defeat.

As the hero of Cervantes' play he is first seen in peasant's clothes but functioning as a Mr. Fixit, arranging love matches, advising Cervantes' comic village officials. "You are wiser than a priest and a doctor," the mayor tells him, assuring him that if Pedro will counsel him "you will no longer be my hired man, but my brother." Such promises are dolefully familiar to Pedro, but hope is his natural condition and he will try.

Pedro is in love with Belica, a beautiful Gypsy girl who turns out not be a Gypsy after all but a person of "noble and rich folk engendered." So he listens willingly when Maldonado, the lord of the Gypsies, presses him to join the tribe. The argument, spoken in the habitual Spanish Gypsy lisp, is strangely set apart in the play, as though to accentuate its importance:

> Look you, Pedro, our life
> is unfettered, free, curious,
> broad, vagabond, wide-ranging,
> in which nothing that we seek
> or ask for is ever lacking . . .
> for (the Gypsy) is a diviner of hidden fruit,
> full of industry and spirit,
> agile, ready, unconfined and sound.

Pedro is tempted. What has he to lose? For, he explains, he was raised in some forgotten place where, "with the hunger and the blows which are always abundant there, I learned to say my prayers, and I learned to be hungry." A cabin boy to the Indies, errand boy in Seville, apprentice to a thief, a brandy-seller, a blind beggar's helper, a muleteer—he has made the round of the pícaro careers. Then one day, he recounts, he met a fortuneteller who read in his hand that

> . . . you are destined
> to be king, monk, and pope, and clown,
> and through a Gypsy it will come
> to pass—this I know—that kings
> will listen to you, and take
> pleasure in the hearing.

Maldonado's promise to give him Belica as a wife sits hard with the girl. Haughty, subtly conscious that her life, too, is a masquerade, she warns:

> Do not try, Pedro,
> to frustrate my will,

> for I spy a far-off hope;
> its brilliant light envelops me
> and bears me toward my desire.

When **Maldonado** complains of her presumption, Pedro silences him:

> Let her be; she very rightly does. . . .
> I too, dunce that I am,
> dream of being prince and pope,
> emperor and monarch,
> and my fantasy even has me
> master of all the world.

Pedro achieves his heart's desire when he sees a company of players re-hearsing a performance. His Protean destiny will be realized as an actor. "I have become a chimera," he announces.

> Now I can be patriarch,
> pope and student,
> emperor and monarch,
> for the actor's trade
> is the vessel to all these. . . .

A sound plucks at the memory, of Don Quixote's voice bellowing that "I know who I am." Pedro is more modest than the knight; he will ac-cept the means as the end. His observation to Belica might equally have been addressed to Quixote:

> Your presumption and mine
> have arrived at their term:
> mine, only in fiction,
> yours, as it had to be. . . .

The Dogs' Colloquy, with its companion piece *The Deceitful Mar-riage,* probably dates from 1605–6. We can more or less trace the seeds from which it sprouted. Cervantes undoubtedly knew Baltasar del Al-cázar's short satirical poem *Dialogue Between Two Pups,* written before 1586, in which a canine pícaro named Zarpillo mocks his masters. The poem can reasonably be supposed to have occurred to him when, from his window in Valladolid, he watched the two animals known as "the dogs of Mahudes" begging for alms near the Hospital de la Resurrección. Mahudes was a poor man whose life had been saved *in extremis* in the hospital, and so grateful was he for his salvation that he devoted the next half century to soliciting charity for the institution. It was he who led the hospital watchdogs out at night to accompany the friars of La Capacha on their begging rounds. "You will also have seen or heard," Cervantes tells us, "the stories told about them: that if by chance people throw alms out of the windows and it falls on the ground, they rush up immediately with a lantern to look for it, and stop in front of the windows where they know people usually give them alms. . . ."

The Deceitful Marriage is in itself little more than a picaresque short story, close in spirit to Cervantes' interludes. It concerns a vain, fatheaded soldier named Campuzano who is so sickened by a courtesan's trick on him that he takes to a bed in the Hospital de la Resurrección. There, in telling his story to his friend Ensign Peralta, he sets the scene for the main body of the narrative, *The Dogs' Colloquy*.

As in other areas where the truthfulness of the story is subject to extreme critical doubt, Cervantes here is at his most ambiguous, wrapping his story in mystery, strewing contradictory clues, using questionable references, making a point of his own "doubt." In recounting the conversation he claims to have overheard between the two watchdogs, Campuzano warns Peralta that "you must be prepared to believe it without crossing yourself or raising objections."

We are quickly won over by the dogs. The story we hear is Berganza's, and it takes so long to tell that poor Scipio never gets in his licks. The dogs themselves are amazed to find themselves talking. "Brother Scipio," says Berganza, "I hear you speak and I know that I am speaking to you, and I cannot believe it, for it seems to me that our speaking goes beyond the bounds of nature." Scipio agrees and goes on to observe that "this miracle is greater in that not only are we speaking but we are speaking coherently, as if we were capable of reason, when in fact we are so devoid of it that the differences between the brute beast and man is that man is a rational animal and the brute irrational."

Unsure of how long this divine gift will last, they resolve to spend all night talking. Berganza recounts his adventures under a succession of masters. Like Pedro, he has run the pícaro gamut, beginning with a murderous butcher at the Seville slaughterhouse and going on through a band of thieving shepherds, a Sevillian merchant and his schoolboy sons, a crooked police officer and his prostitute protégée, a ragamuffin army drummer, a tribe of Gypsies, a Morisco and a poet-playwright before he is taken in by Mahudes. The migration allows Cervantes to fire full broadsides at the Church's rapaciousness, its formalism and what he saw as its hypocrisy; the law in all its craven corruption takes its lumps; we pass through the temptation of Satan in Berganza's brush with the witch Cañizares, and, in the playwright eating crusts of bread and dreaming of extravagant scenes, a blunt-tipped missile is loosed at that favorite target,

Lope de Vega. Again we hear of Maldonado, the lord of the Gypsies who, as Cervantes identifies him (with, it appears, some vague historical justification), was in fact a non-Gypsy, "the page of a gentleman of this name" who "fell in love with a Gypsy girl who would not return his love unless he became a Gypsy and took her to be his wife."

Which leads naturally to *The Little Gypsy Girl*, the story Cervantist Ángel Valbuena Prat called "Carmen in a state of innocence."[6] More conventional in form than the *Colloquy* or *Pedro de Urdemales*, it tells of Preciosa, the fifteen-year-old Gypsy girl (or is she a Gypsy? lavish hints warn us that she may not be) whose wit, beauty and talent enslave all who see her. She is Belica as Pedro would have dreamed of her. Preciosa sings, dances, tells fortunes, she is prophet, poet, virtue itself. Unlike the other Gypsies, she will not steal, will not lie, will tolerate no licentiousness: "None of the Gypsy women, old or young, dared sing an improper song or say a coarse word in her presence."

A rich and handsome young nobleman, Don Juan de Carcamo, falls in love with her and begs her to marry him. But, Gypsy or not, Preciosa is a free spirit. Like Pedro, like Belica, like Quixote, "I have a certain fancy inside me which carries me on to great things." She warns Don Juan that "my liberty must never be restricted."

She insists that this new Maldonado join the Gypsy band for a two-year "novitiate." Passion cools with satisfaction, she warns, and in the meanwhile "you may recover the sight which now must be lost to you . . . and you might then see that you must flee from what you now so zealously pursue. And when once you've recovered your lost liberty, any fault can be pardoned if you truly repent."

Taking the name Andrés Caballero, Carcamo agrees to run away with the Gypsies. To reconcile him to his plunge down the social ladder, the Gypsies' headman extols the free life in a speech much like the one Pedro de Urdemales heard: "We are lords of the fields and crops, of the forests, the woods, the springs and the rivers," he says, ". . . our courage is not daunted by bonds, nor damaged by pulleys[7] or stifled by gags. . . . We make no distinction between yes and no when it suits us. . . . We are not bothered by the fear of losing our honor, nor are we disturbed by the ambition to increase it. . . . or do we lose sleep trying to write petitions . . . or ask for favors. . . ."

Once more we are reminded of Cervantes' extraordinary sympathy with the oppressed and the outcast. We remember the Morisca Ana Felix, the Jew of Algiers. A line from *The Jealous Extremaduran* sticks in our minds, surely one of the most terrible epigrams about black anguish ever written: when the slave girl Guiomar is ordered to stand watch while the rest of the household sings and dances, she says with bitter resignation, *"Yo, negra, quedo; blancas van: Dios perdone a todas"*—I, black,

remain; whites go: may God forgive us all. Guiomar might nod in understanding at Preciosa, "who," Cervantes notes ironically, "beautiful as she
was, was a Gypsy after all." She perceives Andrés shame and calls him on
it.

> "If all men's souls are equal,
>   then can a plowman's
>   be rival in its worth
>   to any that's imperial"

she sings, but this is an equation Andrés must learn through love.

The story's climax is precipitated when an innkeeper's daughter, Juana
Carducha, falls in love with Andrés. She begs him to marry her, but he,
of course, is unavailable. Still, he hurries away "for he could clearly read
in the Carducha girl's eyes that she would willingly give herself to him
without bonds of wedlock and he had no wish to find himself alone in
hand-to-hand combat on that palisade. . . ." Furious, the girl frames
him for theft; an altercation leads to a killing for which Andrés is about
to be hanged when it is discovered that Preciosa is really the magistrate's
kidnapped daughter and Andrés is, after all, a Knight of Santiago.
"When the mayor, the dead man's uncle, learned (the news), he saw that
his paths to vengeance were blocked, for the rigor of the law could not be
brought to bear on the chief magistrate's son-in-law."

A number of common factors weld these stories together: the recurrent
emphasis on marginality, criminality and escape from the confines of conventional society; insistence on the semidivinity of poetry; the omnipresence of the Gypsies. A whiff of sulphur hovers over all of them. And
all three tales conclude with some form of redemption, necessarily ambiguous; there was to be no total redemption on earth.

Sin is the identifying mark of conventional society. It may take the
form of murder: Berganza begins in the stockyards, where "they put a
knife in a man's stomach as readily as if they were killing a bull." Or it
may concern other commandments: the king in *Pedro de Urdemales*
conspires to commit adultery. Even where no actual crime is delineated,
the guilt of turning one's back on convention is clear: Andrés is so afraid
his defection to the Gypsies will be found out that he insists on secrecy,
even to the point of killing and burying his hired mule for fear it may be
recognized. Pedro is an outcast figure from the start, a bastard, a drifter,
a pícaro.

Sex appears as the symbol of worldliness, the natural product of sin. It
is Juana Carducha's come-hither eyes that nearly cost Andrés his life;
Berganza is starved, beaten and finally routed by the lasciviousness of the
slaves in the merchant's household, only to fall into equally deep disgrace

through a prostitute's trickery. The king's lust in *Pedro de Urdemales* turns incestuous, which leaves him balked but unrepentant.

In such circumstances, reason is not an unalloyed value. Cervantes' homonid dogs wonder at it: ". . . it seems that some have believed we have a natural instinct, so lively and acute in many things that it almost seems to demonstrate that we possess some sort of understanding which is capable of reasoning." They do not understand it, but there it is and "there is no point in our beginning to dispute about how or why we are talking." The idea of reasonable unreason which animates Quixote is here recognized by the dogs; accept it, then, without falling into the in-tellectual-spiritual convention which makes reason sovereign among the irrational. This tension between the illusion of reason and the reality of unreason is emphasized even by the personalities of the two dogs: Ber-ganza is a pícaro, but he is poetic, intuitive, impulsive, mordantly intel-lectual; Scipio is the voice of reason, right-minded, sensible, seemly, as stuffed with the prudence of folk wisdom as Sancho Panza.

In this dark forest, man must find his own way, Cervantes suggests. The Church is of little help in dispelling the confusion. Criticism of the established Church and the nobility is constant in *The Dogs' Colloquy.* "Not a beast is killed" by the slaughterhouse thieves, Berganza declares, "without their carrying off their *tithes and first fruits*";[8] thieving *shepherds* constantly cry wolf—that is, decry heresy—when "the very ones who were supposed to guard the flock were tearing it to pieces"; the episode of the bacon-toting Breton sailor victimized by the whore and her constable pimp "studded with Moorish brass" spoofs the mutual bum-scratching by the Inquisition and the secular law which are both contaminated by her-esy. Berganza, an idol of truth and honesty in the Cervantine pantheon, is happy with the merchants' sons in the Jesuit school until he is expelled for "reasons of state"—the masters' fear that he might distract their pupils—and chained up in the merchant's home; the implication is una-voidable that the day of free thought in the schools is over, that truth must now lie in chains.

The theme is treated more delicately in the other two works. Direct references are rare, as in the implicit mockery of biblical sacrifice—of sterile ritualism—in Pedro's attempt to swindle a peasant of his chickens. For the most part, the Church simply does not exist in these works; it is, so to speak, aggressively absent. It is in them negatively, however, in Cervantes' sympathy with the Gypsies. "Gypsy" in Cervantes' day was synonymous with "atheist"; folklore identified the Gypsies as an elfin peo-ple, kin to the devil, and Cervantes emphasizes this with his seemingly gratuitous account of the old Gypsy woman's impish trick on the greedy Triguillos in *The Little Gypsy Girl.* No exorcistic zeal is brought to bear on the figure of Pedro, whose destiny is mapped for him by a soothsayer's prophecy and who listens sympathetically to the Gypsies' call to freedom. Preciosa is virginal, Marian, but she bypasses the Church to become virtue itself, beauty itself, poetry incarnate. She has, we are told, a "rich heritage of carols, songs, seguidillas and sarabands." When she thumps her tambourine, the sounds are "pearls scattered from her hands" and her songs are "flowers darted from her lips." Poets beg her to sing their ballads. She has the faerie imagination, the sweet volatility of the poetic spirit.

"One must use poetry like a most precious jewel whose owner does not wear it every day or show it off to everybody all the time, but when it is appropriate and right to display it," Clemente tells her. "Poetry is a maiden of great beauty, chaste, pure, discreet, shrewd, modest and extremely circumspect. She is a friend of solitude: the fountains give her pleasure, the meadows consolation, the trees comfort, the flowers delight; and, in short, she brings pleasure and profit to all who come into contact with her."

Clemente's description fits Preciosa, and spills over to the Gypsies, Cervantes' pre-Rousseauan symbols of natural man. For Cervantes, as, later, for Pushkin and Byron, their very thievery made them rebels against the circumscriptions of conventional society. They were a people corrupt but free, unhampered by guilt, possessed of a mysterious, elemental consonance with a creative, even holy, vitality. They are the unrefined but essential stuff of poetry, the "diviners of hidden fruit," and in Preciosa that potential has become real, pivotal.

What, then, are we being told? Perhaps that truth does not lie in conventional wisdom; rather it is a mysterious, miraculous thing, as profoundly hidden as a sacred vessel in a deep cave. That man must strip off the confining corruption of society, divest himself of his worldly trappings as Andrés Caballero rids himself of his clothes and scatters his purseful of gold crowns. Man must begin again, must return to the guiltless, unfettered, natural state he enjoyed in Eden, before he burdened himself with his heritage of sin. From this he will emerge spiritually enriched, purified, in the path toward that union with God which is the ultimate good. We see here the same Platonic progression toward chaste love, absolute truth, so relatively crudely expressed in *La Galatea* but now deepened and alight with personal meaning; the same concept of a higher spirituality, of higher truth perilously poised between Quixote's reason and "mad" unreason.

The process is specially important for the poet, the artist. Poetry is the most divine of human callings, man's closest approach to prophecy and so to God. The poet must put off worldliness, eschew the joys of the flesh, resign himself to poverty; he must break free of social bonds, penetrate to the lowest, most demonic level of the human soul, become a pilgrim through the unmapped darkness of human duality. And, if he is lucky and truly holy, truly dedicated, and strong enough to withstand the hardships of the journey, he will ultimately return to the light with a knowledge of love, possessed of the divine grace of poetry, a prophet ready to call humanity to redemption.

For redemption is the ultimate objective. Berganza's pilgrimage is explicit: he moves through all the phases of worldly corruption, from the original sin of murder through the Church, business, the schools, the law, the army; he descends into a nether world with the Gypsies, flees in horror from the malevolent witch Cañizares and a heathen, miserly Morisco before resurfacing to gnaw the poet's leavings. In the end, he takes service in the Hospital—of the Resurrection. Andrés Caballero plunges directly into this natural world, lured by the light of virtue, beauty, musicality and purity—in short, of poetry—which causes him to "lose his sight." In the end, the holiness of his love for Preciosa leads to the joy of self-discovery; in celebration, "vengeance was interred and mercy resurrected."

In one sense, the theme's most poignant climax is reached in *Pedro de Urdemales*. Pedro is approaching the blessed state at the play's end. But his status as a personage known outside the work necessarily gives him a more ambiguous destiny. He is hence the most human of them all, the one who is still struggling to find his footing, who has almost, perhaps, found it. Of all the Cervantine heroes, Pedro is the one closest to Cervantes himself. In *Pedro de Urdemales,* we read Cervantes' spiritual autobiography. As such, it becomes not so much a play as an epic poem. Appropriately, its poetry, elegiac, dignified, lyrical and joyous, forms the finest verse ensemble to be found in Cervantes' writing.

Sometime after 1608, a pendant piece was added to the chain which points to an evolution in the developing mysticism of Cervantes' attitudes. This was the play *The Happy Rogue,* again the story of a pícaro, Cristóbal de Lugo, who becomes a Dominican monk in Mexico, suffers the martyrdom of Job—the comparison is specific—and dies a saint. Lugo actually existed. Cervantes took the outline of his story from a history of the preaching order in Santiago de México published by Fray Agustín Davila Padilla in 1596. From this was fashioned a miracle play, really an elaborately "realistic" auto-da-fé.

The play's pivotal scene, in Act II, is the monk's successful attempt to save the soul of the dying Doña Ana de Trevino. The woman is so obsessed with her guilt, so appalled by her sins that she rejects God; her concept of worldly justice persuades her that He could not possibly forgive so great a sinner, nor should He:

> I am bounded by God's justice;
> He is so just He cannot pardon me;
> justice punishes the evil;

hope does not live in the sinner's unjust heart,
nor is it right that it should live there.

To save her soul, Cristóbal makes a contract with heaven: he will assume all Doña Ana's sins and give her all his pious works, his prayers, his self-mortification. God accepts the bargain: as Doña Ana dies in an odor of sanctity, the monk's body is suddenly covered with the sores of leprosy. The final act, very short, traces his thirteen years of devotion in affliction. At his death, the crowd jostles for holy trophies, dipping cloths in the blood of his sores, filching scraps of his robe.

The play is crude and theatrically flawed: awkwardly paced, hardly more than a series of climactic scenes connected by a webbing of static dialogue. Its story is unpalatable to modern appetites.[9] Yet for all its faults, it is a work of great splendor. The very intensity of Cristóbal's conversion underlines its importance to Cervantes. There is a thrilling exaltation in these powerful lines which infects even the skeptical modern reader; the verse is supple yet solid, as gracefully muscular as a great ballerina's leaps. There is no doubt of the depth of belief of the man who wrote it, nor of his absolute need of faith. The world had been no friend to him, but, by his lights, he had doubtless been no better: he had been proud, he had sinned in the flesh, had been ungenerous at times; people had suffered because of him. All apart from what *The Happy Rogue* might be saying to an unrepentant Spain covered with the sores of its own decline, or to humanity in general, we must see in it Cervantes preaching to himself. The exercise was only partly successful.

The Happy Rogue shortens the thematic line of the earlier stories. The flight from conventionalism is here; Lugo's self-alienation is as clear as that of Pedro de Urdemales. But all the intermediate stations in this way of the cross have been eliminated. Simplified, purified, the process now leads directly to faith. The demons in *The Happy Rogue* are no longer symbolic, they are certified demons—Lucifer and his crew. It is as though a decision had been made to leave the world behind, to recognize that even art is vanity, a needless delay in the journey to redemption. *The Happy Rogue* is a broad hint of why the recovery of his "sanity" would be fatal to Don Quixote. It is a preview of the mystery of Periandro, whose story in the *Persiles* is climaxed in a scene of blood and sacrament in Rome, before the church of St. Paul. Poetry, the last relay point on the earthly progress to salvation, seems to have been eliminated.

Redemption was a personal as well as an aesthetic problem. It may be that his dwindling flesh and the weakness to which he was probably increasingly subject reminded him that the religion which had been as natural to him as breathing was now becoming as important as breathing. Death had to be prepared for; some gesture had to be made toward a gradual withdrawal from the world. The women in his family had already taken steps in this direction: Catalina and Andrea, near the end of a preparative year of novitiate, were about to take the habit of the strict Tertiary Order of St. Francis. (They entered June 8, 1609. Unless a clerical error was made, Andrea invented a new husband for the occasion; she described herself as the "widow of General Álvaro Mendaño." No such person is known to have existed.) Magdalena would join the order the following February.

Cervantes apparently was not prepared for such rigor. But on April 17, 1609, he did join a newly organized chapter of a Trinitarian lay brotherhood, the Congregation of Unworthy Slaves of the Most Holy Sacrament. He may have found something hugely satisfying about the duties it imposed: severe simplicity of life and dress, abstinence from sex and stimulants, daily attendance at mass and nightly examinations of conscience, regular religious exercises. He wore the order's scapulary, visited hospitals, followed brothers' coffins when the time came. All this cleansed the mind, redirected one's sense of purpose.

Although Cervantes was one of the first to join, he was soon followed by Lope, Espinel, Quevedo, Salas Barbadillo, Vélez de Guevara and others in the world of letters. The songs and sonnets (some decent, others obscene) and autos they wrote for religious festivals—Cervantes' verses for the 1609 Corpus Christi celebration won a prize from the court—made the brotherhood intellectually fashionable. Cervantes and Lope both worked hard for it, in characteristically different ways. The only meetings of the group Cervantes failed to attend were those at which officers were elected; these were the meetings Lope never missed and he was invariably elected to office.

The brotherhood was a sanctuary in a dreary world. No glamour of royal frippery could disguise the hardship among Spain's poor. Fiddling with the currency had sent prices jumping again. There had been so many crop failures in those years that it sometimes seemed as though the Spanish earth itself were rejecting its inhabitants. To this, in the late spring of 1609, was added the dismal spectacle of thousands of Moriscos moving toward Spanish ports in obedience to a decree expelling them, all of them, from the country.

The move was generally acclaimed. Quevedo protested that their departure "increased not only the number of our enemies, but, among our enemies, the knowledge of many skills,"[10] but he believed the Moriscos had brought it on themselves. Even Cervantes, still clinging to the sense of wrong done him in Algiers and, perhaps unconsciously, to the frustration of his youthful military ambition, joined the public snarling. His description of the Moriscos in *The Dogs' Colloquy* as child-breeding vultures is unworthy of him. Later, touched by the exiles' suffering, he seems to have felt ashamed of himself. His sympathetic portrayals of Moriscos in *Don Quixote* and the *Persiles* can be read as an indirect apology.

Their suffering was indeed epical. They were herded off for shipment to North Africa, to France, to any place that would take them. They were allowed thirty days[11] in which to sell their possessions in exchange for portable merchandise, for they were allowed to take with them only what they could carry on their persons. No gold, no silver, only enough money to cover expenses.[12] Along the exit routes, retaliatory robbery and murder were frequent on both sides; there were the usual church burnings. Many died of hunger and exposure, although others were wealthy enough to begin life comfortably elsewhere. Those sent to North Africa found they were as detested there as they had been in Spain. "Wherever we are," Ricote mourns to Sancho, "we weep for Spain, for after all, we were born here and this is our natural homeland."[13]

By mid-1611, when the movement trailed off, between 250,000 and 300,000 Moriscos had been deported. Towns like Dulcinea's El Toboso, where a third of the population had been Morisco, were ruined and everyone was thoroughly sickened by two years of killing, robbery and violence.

News of such large events flooded into Madrid in surprising volume. It poured steadily out of the palace courtyard to join the flow on the steps of the San Felipe monastery at the Puerta del Sol, the city's main forum of current events. There Cervantes repaired every morning after mass at the monastery of Nuestra Señora de la Merced, across the Calle de Atocha, to listen to travelers recite occasionally truthful eyewitness details of the latest atrocities. Five minutes' walk away was the Puerta de Guadalajara, the city's rumor bazaar, where Cervantes waded through the gossip to Robles's bookshop-casino to read the flyers and chat with his friends. Later there were the academies to attend.

Madrid was a culture in which academies popped briefly to the surface, quickly burst and were succeeded by new growths. They were founded, usually, by aristocrats or high royal officials, often less for love of letters than for the flattery attendant on being a salon-keeper. In them, poetry was not only a sacred calling to be celebrated, but also a bludgeon with which to beat a rival to his knees. The acrimonious quarrels attracted aristocratic spectators hoping for an hour's amusement watching the quaint writer people savage each other. When an academy ceased to be fashionable, it generally ceased to function. Of the first meeting of a new one in 1612, Lope wrote that "there was no gentry; they probably do not know about it yet; it will last until they do."[14]

That Cervantes frequented them is certain. At one of them, we learn from a letter by Lope to the Duke of Sessa, "I read some verses using a pair of Zerbantes' (sic) spectacles that were so ill made they give the eyes the appearance of scrambled eggs, badly cooked."[15] Another met in the local Jesuit school. One evening in particular was memorable.

The program included a series of lectures on letters followed by a talk about medicine and a lecture on testamentary law ("I would have been astonished," Quevedo commented, "if there had not been a testament to follow the physician"[16]). Among the speakers was the Count of Lemos, who dabbled in poetry himself and who liked to surround himself with artists and men of learning. This may have been Cervantes' first meeting with his future patron.

Probably the most uproarious of the literary academies was that founded by Lope's friend Félix Arias Giron. Cervantes was surely present in 1609 to hear Lope give his first readings from his *New Art of Modern Playwrighting*. We can almost see the volleys of challenging glances the two men exchanged when the Phoenix read his half-serious apology for violating the classical rules of the art

> not because I did not know the precepts,
> but because, after all, I found the plays
> in Spain then were not as their first mentors
> thought the world would hear them,
> but as a host of barbarians handled them. . . .[17]

Despite the sting in that word "barbarians," Cervantes may have felt self-justification surge within him. This was Lope's reply to the attack on him by the canon of Toledo in *Don Quixote*. The wound had been deep. And the riposte was hardly more than a parry. Yet if Cervantes was being honest with himself, he would have recognized that Lope had won the argument after all. For the plays Cervantes was writing in that period show that he had, reluctantly, joined Lope's revolution.

33

The Exemplary Stories

Andrea de Cervantes died October 9, 1609, "of a fever," so suddenly that she left no will. The burial registration in the church of San Sebastián, where she was given a barely decent two-ducat funeral, describes her as "the widow of Sante Ambrosi (sic), Florentine, age sixty-five." Six months later, Cervantes' only grandchild, Isabel Sanz, also died. The two events set the tone for the year that followed.

The little girl's death touched off a lawsuit that completed the break in relations between Cervantes and his daughter. This was Urbina's doing. He seems to have learned to dislike his former mistress, but his affection for money was undimmed. With little Isabel's passing, he saw no reason to deliver the unpaid balance of the dowry he had promised only to ensure the child's future. He also moved to reassert his ownership of the house Isabel and Molina inhabited, ceding only their lifetime use of it. To this end, he cooked up an arrangement in which Cervantes was declared the building's legal owner; Cervantes in turn relinquished his fictitious rights to Urbina on condition that the non-existent income from it be devoted to an equally imaginary charity.

It was a nasty business and there is no explaining why Cervantes lent himself to it, unless his animosity toward his daughter blinded him to what he had to know was the honorable thing to do. He should certainly have known that Isabel would put up a fight. As her daughter's legal heir, she sued to break the new arrangement. This was the opening battle in a contest which was to drag on until Urbina's death nineteen years later.

The atmosphere of gloomy uncertainty hanging over that spring of 1610 alarmed Doña Catalina. With Andrea gone and Isabel estranged, she probably felt closer to her harried husband. His defenselessness was all too clear. What would become of him if she were suddenly to die? On June 16, 1610, she appeared before notary Baltasar de Ugena, a fellow Esquivian, to make a will. Most of her goods were bequeathed, as had been arranged, to her brother Francisco; Miguel, her executor, was to receive outright only two small plots of land outside the town, her deathbed and the linens and furnishings of her house "for the great love and good companionship we both have had."[1] But he was to have full use of the bulk of her estate during his lifetime; after his death, the income from it was to go to Constanza for two years before reverting to Francisco. It was a protective arrangement: although her estate was entailed to pay her parents' debts, it deferred the moment of reckoning for as long as Cervantes lived. Given the little value of her possessions, Catalina's will was scarcely more than a gesture and a detail suggests that she made it with some mental reservation: it specifies that she was to be buried not with her husband, but in her father's tomb in the choir of the Esquivias church "alongside the step of the high altar. . . ."* Still, such gestures were rare enough in Cervantes' life to be noticeable. He was more accustomed to the treatment he had received earlier that spring from two admired acquaintances, Lupercio Leonardo de Argensola and his brother Bartolomé.

Lupercio was a scholar of some standing, an excellent Latin translator with something of a reputation as a satirical poet. His career had been moderately distinguished: historiographer of Aragon, secretary to the Empress Maria of Austria, gentleman of Archduke Albert's household in the Netherlands, secretary to the Duke of Villahermosa. He was also a writer of abominable tragedies which Cervantes, with his reverence for high-minded orthodoxy, once declared "filled all who heard them with admiration, delight and interest." This judgment is contained in the sixteen fulsome lines devoted in *La Galatea* to the then unknown Lupercio and to Bartolomé, also a historian and craftsman of pungently witty verse. Early in 1610, when the Count of Lemos was appointed viceroy of Naples, they had a chance to return Cervantes' compliment in practical fashion.

Don Pedro Fernández de Castro y Andrade, seventh Count of Lemos, Marquis of Saria, nephew by marriage of the Duke of Lerma, passes in most ways for a model Renaissance prince. Portraits show us a broad-browed, fine-featured, romantic-looking man; judging from his record as an overachiever among the ladies at court, the pictures are not flattering. He was only twenty-six years old when he was named to the vice-royalty, a post his father had also held, to the family's considerable profit. By then he had acquired a reputation for intellectual eminence and a scrapbook of suspect praise as a man bountiful, tactful and kind. He was in the

---

* She would change her mind after Cervantes' death and request that she be buried with him in the church of Madrid's Trinitarian monastery.

flower of youth, Góngora gurgled dutifully, but ripe in judiciousness. Lemos wrote poetry which poets were at pains to praise when he was within earshot; he was also a Latinist and wrote a manual on law. Lope, his secretary in 1598–99, hailed him as "wise" and devoted sonnets to him in at least two of his books. It is the word "bountiful" which should be retained here, and perhaps "kind" as well: the count not only liked to surround himself with a court of artists, but he was aware of the price such a luxury commanded; his largesse was widespread and generally ungrudging. True, Lope later charged that he was stingy, but the Phoenix was a notoriously greedy bird. Be that as it may, when Lemos received his Naples appointment it was only natural that he should think of stuffing his retinue with as many men of letters as it would hold. The task of choosing them was left to a kindred soul, his new secretary Lupercio Leonardo de Argensola.

Applications poured in. Among them were appeals from Cervantes, Góngora, Cristóbal de Mesa and other leading talents of the day. We need not indulge in romantic fancies of a Cervantes longing to see his Promontorio, to talk to Silena once more; after what he had been through with Isabel, he would probably have been more than happy to ignore them both if in fact they existed. While it is reasonable to think that he would have enjoyed seeing Naples again, the Cervantes who could give his sister nothing better than a two-ducat funeral had causes more compelling than nostalgia for trying to pull any string that came to hand.

Enlistments proceeded apace: Antonio Mira de Amescua, another middle-rank but ponderous playwright on whom Cervantes lavished admiration; the interlude writer Gabriel de Barrionuevo and others of the type. But when the boatload of courtiers left for Naples in June, Cervantes was not aboard, nor was Góngora or Mesa or any other first-rank poet.

The mediocrity of the men chosen has suggested that the brothers Argensola feared strong rivals who might outfence them in the cutthroat competition for the viceroy's favors. In a "Letter to the Count of Lemos, en route as viceroy of Naples," Mesa chided that "you favor some Spaniards who in Italy, as experience will show you, do not reach the foothills of Parnassus."[2] Fair enough, no doubt, but to this motive must be added specific opposition to at least some of those excluded. The Argensolas, second-raters with second-rate judgment, disapproved of Góngora's culturanismo as obscure and artificial. Their dislike for Cervantes seems to have been more personal. Barrionuevo later wrote an interlude in which an unpleasant character named Cervantes is depicted as living off women. Some of this antagonism stemmed from the Argensolas' friendship with Lope (curiously, Lope's friends were often more vicious to his rivals than he was). They may also have thought, with some justification, that Cervantes' shortening temper with those who failed to subscribe to his own evaluation of his poetic talent might be abrasive in the hothouse atmosphere of a Neapolitan court. Moreover, he was a sick man. Altogether a depressing person, they apparently concluded.

Góngora, who had not long before suffered a similar rebuff from the Duke of Feria, publicly shrugged off his disappointment:

> My lord the count went to Naples;
> my lord the duke went to France:
> princes, good journey; this day
> I shall give grief to a dish of snails. . . .[3]

Cervantes took it harder. Some vague promises apparently had been made; he had been put off, then forgotten. In Chapter 3 of the *Voyage to Parnassus* he tells the story in tones of resentment. He imagines himself aboard ship with the god Mercury en route to the battle of the good and bad poets on Parnassus. Mercury sends him ashore with a summons to the Argensolas to join the divine contingent, but Cervantes urges that someone else be sent. Something tells him, he explains, that the brothers'

> "goodwill toward me, like their sight, is short. . . .
> For had some little part of all the promises
> they made me at our parting been fulfilled,
> God knows I'd not have needed to sail with you.
> I hoped for much of the much they promised;
> perhaps a host of new preoccupations
> made them forget what they had told me. . . ."

More sorrow was to follow for Cervantes. Magdalena had been ill for months. On October 11, 1610, she made a will requesting a simple burial "accompanied by as little pomp as my heirs consider fitting."[4] The assets listed are chiefly imaginary: the quarter-century-old debt of three hundred ducats still outstanding from Fernando de Lodeña for breach of promise; her share in the claim on Rodrigo's uncollected pay. Magdalena declared that "I do not have possessions enough to leave for my burial . . . and I name no heirs to my estate aside from the aforementioned because I have no possessions at all, nor is there left to me anything worth anything. . . ." Of Isabel there is no mention.

At the same notarial session, perhaps at his sister's urging, possibly in fulfillment of a promise to Andrea, Cervantes renounced his share of Rodrigo's pay to Constanza. The document twice refers to him as "alférez Miguel de Çerbantes." A notarial error? Or had Cervantes, still hurting from the popping of his Neapolitan dream, simply conferred on himself one of the many distinctions life had refused him?

Magdalena died January 28, 1611, in the house at No. 3 Calle de León. She was buried in her Franciscan habit, with her face unveiled, as was the order's custom. The cost of her pauper's funeral, twelve reales, was paid by the monks.

Sometime early in 1612 the family—Cervantes, his wife and Constanza —left the house in the Calle de León for another at what is now No. 18 Calle de las Huertas "facing the houses where the Prince of Morocco used to live."[5] The new house was virtually around the corner from the old, in the theater district; the neighborhood was known as the "quarter of the muses." Lope lived nearby, in what is now the Calle de Cervantes, surrounded by a scattering of his past and future mistresses. Juana Gaitán was a neighbor, and so were, or would be, Quevedo, Vélez de Guevara, Ruiz de Alarcón. But the new house was much smaller, darker, dingier. "My humble cottage," Cervantes calls it in the *Voyage to Parnassus*. At the end of the poem, Cervantes leaves the sacred mountain "indignant and dejected"; he

> returned to my decrepit and lugubrious lodging
> and threw myself, fatigued and battered, upon the bed;
> how wearying it is to fight a long campaign!

The "decrepit and lugubrious" room was probably in the Calle de las Huertas. Its sole advantage: it may have been given him rent-free by a friend, Juan de Acevedo, a kinsman of the Alonso de Acevedo greeted— in Italian—in the *Voyage to Parnassus*.

The awkward fact was that Cervantes had published nothing in seven years. Ideas were banging around in his mind like flies in a sunbeam. *Don Quixote, Part II* was less than half done; a start had been made on the *Persiles*, but it was scarcely past the planning stage. Stories, poems, full-length plays, interludes were piling up in his trunk. But nothing was ready for the printer.

Like a flagellant at the approach of Easter, he thought again of the theater. Perhaps he should have known better and perhaps he did. In the appendix to the *Voyage to Parnassus* he remarked that he had completed six plays and six interludes to accompany them. Three of the plays were disabled old veterans of the theatrical wars, dragged out of the files and hurriedly patched up for inspection. *The Dungeons of Algiers, The Spanish Gallant* and *The Great Sultana* all were captivity plays, perhaps revived with an eye toward riding the national feeling against the Moriscos.

Whether anyone even looked at them is impossible to say. Probably not.

Cervantes merely grumbles that no one wanted them. Lope was at the height of his fame in 1611. His name was so legendary that the phrase *"es de Lope"*—it's by Lope—came into the language to describe anything excellent, from comedies to cabbages. Cervantes mocks the phrase in the interlude *The Faithful Sentinel:* when the soldier praises a pair of slippers destined for his beloved, the cobbler replies: "I know little of poems, but these sounded so good to me that they seem to be by Lope, like all things which are or appear to be good."

As far as is known, this was the last time Cervantes would attempt to hawk his plays directly to the managers. Any lingering hopes he may have nurtured of selling them, however, were snuffed out with the closing of the theaters in October 1611 on the death of Queen Marguerite; at that point, he tells us in the prologue to the published plays, he "stuffed them in a chest and consecrated them to perpetual silence."

It was probably in the autumn of 1611 that Cervantes set about putting a final polish on his *Exemplary Stories.* This was a more complicated process for Cervantes than it was for some other writers. He was not a facile writer; "work quickly done," he remarks in *Don Quixote,* "never ends up as perfect as it should be."[6] He worked slowly, carefully polishing and reworking his stories, often revising them radically from one version to the next. Scholars point to the myriad differences between the published versions of at least two of the *Exemplary Stories* and the earlier versions found in the Porras de Camara manuscript. We will have to delve into this manuscript quickly to fish for a Cervantes puzzle.

Licentiate Francisco Porras de Camara was a prebendary of Seville Cathedral, a humanist, traveler, graceful writer and all-round merry fellow. A pleasant man to be with, whose hobby was collecting jokes and stories. Sometime in the first decade of the seventeenth century, he and his secretary copied out an assortment of stories, jokes, anecdotes and other such diversions to beguile the siestas of his archbishop, Francisco Cardinal Niño de Guevara. Each of the entries was attributed as best as the prebendary could. Among them were the tales of *Rinconete and Cortadillo* and *The Jealous Extremaduran,* although neither is attributed. Indeed, Cervantes is not mentioned by name anywhere in the manuscript.

Scholarly banditry gave the collection an adventurous career. Rediscovered in 1788, it was stolen early in the nineteenth century and later sold. A few years later it briefly resurfaced, was lost, found again and finally vanished for good in 1823. By then, however, it had been thoroughly copied and studied.

Because it was compiled before the *Exemplary Stories* were published, it sheds valuable light on the changes Cervantes brought to the two stories. It is in the Porras de Camara version, for example, that we find *The*

Jealous Extremaduran with its original ending, the accomplished seduction of Leonora. Not all the differences may safely be taken as changes. The licentiate clearly did not know Cervantes and could not have taken his copies from the original manuscripts. His were copies of copies, possibly several times removed from their first parent, and this inevitably meant errors in transcription, not to mention the possibility of "improvements" brought to them by arrogant copyists. This fugg surrounding Porras de Camara's sources is no great problem as far as the two authenticated stories are concerned. A third novela found in the manuscript, equally unattributed, has raised a running row between those who firmly believe Cervantes wrote it but declined to publish it and others who just as firmly deny he had anything to do with it.

It is called *La tía fingida* (*The Make-Believe Aunt*). The aunt in question is a madam who sets up shop in Salamanca with her current breadwinner, a pouting beauty named Esperanza, and a retinue of dueñas and servants. The story turns on a lecture by the madam on the techniques of the trade. Complaints by Esperanza, who has already been endowed with three false hymens and who is becoming impatient with her role as an unfinished quilt while auntie pockets all the receipts, lead to a hairpulling match and then to jail, but the girl is rescued and marries an admirer.

It is a scabrous little story, shorter than most of the published *Exemplary Stories*. Cervantists who believe it is the Great Man's work—they perceive similarities in it to *The Jealous Extremaduran*—affirm that when the time came to assemble his stories for Robles Cervantes discarded it because of its lack of exemplarity. Besides, they demand, who else could have written it?

Analyses of style can give highly equivocal results, but they are not to be ignored for that. Scraps of what seem to be Cervantes' style, his phrasing and language do seem traceable in the story. Yet the language is not typically Cervantes'. It lacks his dignity, his suavity. Cervantes, for example, did use slang, but the slang in *The Make-Believe Aunt* is somehow coarser, more vulgar; it is not used, as Cervantes used it, for deliberate effect, but seems rather the writer's natural diction, as it does, for example, in the works of Vélez de Guevara. The sentences generally do not "breathe" as Cervantes' sentences do. More disturbing still is the lack of the Cervantine tone. Cervantes wrote with a smile, a lyrical gentleness and an eye for the telling detail. *The Make-Believe Aunt* leers when it is not guffawing like some high school boy telling a bathroom joke, and its descriptions are flat and meaningless. Take the description the anonymous author gives us of Esperanza (bearing in mind that it follows an equally detailed picture of her "aunt"):

. . . she looked to be about nineteen, with a composed and serious face, more aquiline than round; black eyes, almond-shaped and heavy-lidded in repose; eyebrows long and well shaped; lashes long and cheeks pink; her hair, blond and artificially frizzed, as could be told from the sidelocks; skirt of fine wool, corsage of twill or silk shag; shoes of black velvet studded and edged with burnished silver; gloves perfumed, and not with talcum powder but with amber. Her manner was grave, her glance honest and her step light and birdlike.

Compare this catalogue of semi-trivia with Cervantes' description of Pancracio de Roncesvalles in the appendix to the *Voyage to Parnassus:*

. . . he looked to be twenty-four, more or less, and he was wholly clean, wholly neat and altogether effervescent; but he wore a ruff so broad and so starched that I thought it needed the shoulders of an Atlas to carry it. Sons of this ruff were two flattened cuffs which, beginning at his wrists, climbed and clambered along the bones of his arm as though mounting an assault on his beard. I have never seen ivy so greedy to rise from the foot of a wall to its battlements as those cuffs were to go and trade blows with his elbows. In short, so exorbitant were that ruff and those cuffs that his face was hidden in his collar and his arms entombed in the cuffs.

Were both these descriptions written by the same hand?

Other objections exist, no more conclusive than the stylistic differences, but of more gravity. They center around the fact that *The Make-Believe Aunt* is not merely obscene; it is pointlessly obscene.

So much effort has been lavished on explaining what Cervantes meant by calling his stories "exemplary" that very little energy seems to have remained to tell us why he should have written one that was so flagrantly unexemplary.

It is true that sexual immorality is as common in the published *Exemplary Stories* as beautiful women are. Few of the sinners in them are punished; the immoral usually legitimize their sins and live happily ever after. This has caused some anguish to those who define the genre as necessarily "exemplifying" conventional morality. A critic has noted, however, that a short story in Cervantes' day was defined as a device to "prompt imitation or act as a warning."[7] Cervantes' basic attitude, he believes, is that taken toward the adulterous Luisa in the *Persiles:* "Let her be as free and flighty as a kestrel; the touchstone is not her flightiness but what happens to her. . . ." Cervantes inveighs in the stories against cruelty, pain, suffering, stupidity, insularity, pride, hypocrisy. The acts

482   CERVANTES: A BIOGRAPHY

of immorality he depicts are forgiven if they are instrumental in bringing about a higher moral good which nullifies the original transgression.

No such progression is perceptible in *The Make-Believe Aunt*. The story is scarcely more than a long off-color joke in which no morality is organically present, although a feeble excuse for one is tacked on to its very end for reasons of propriety. Then why would an aging but formally virginal Cervantes—the same Cervantes who regretted the explicit carnality of *La Celestina*—sit down and write a story that makes Rojas' bawd seem prissy by comparison, with no discernible purpose except to wallow in ribaldry? It is much easier to believe that *The Make-Believe Aunt* was written by a younger man with considerable narrative skill but not much else on his mind. It could, for example, have been early story by Salas Barbadillo, who consciously imitated Cervantes' style and who specialized in short, pungent tales of manners with a pronounced picaresque flavor.

By the spring of 1612 the package of twelve stories was turned over to Robles. Official approval was given on July 9, 1612, by a Trinitarian monk named Juan Bautista Capataz, who found the stories "truly diverting" because of their "novelty" and the "exemplary virtues they teach" and because they brought "honor to our Castilian tongue." Cervantes shortly returned the favor with praise in the *Voyage to Parnassus:* Friar Juan, he said, was "barefoot and poor, but well clad in the adornments of fame." It was all very friendly, practically a family affair which spared the monk from having to delve too deeply into how some of the stories might be interpreted.

Cervantes probably received no cash from Robles. Most or all of the sixteen hundred reales† the bookseller had advanced him for the collection was long since spent. While they waited for the royal privilege (it was not issued until November 12) and Cervantes worried the problem of a dedication, Robles pressed him to complete *Don Quixote, Part II;* the merchant was confident it would be a money-maker and he had already shown his willingness to pay for it. In Cervantes' position it would have been the practical thing to do.

But he was in no mood be to practical. There had been too many rebuffs of late, too many slights. He was famous as a clown? Then he would give them all a clown's retort. When he came across a satirical poem called *Viaggio in Parnaso* published in 1582 by a Tuscan poet, Cesare Caporali, he thought he might have the model he needed. *Don Quixote* was laid aside, the *Persiles* ignored. Instead, he began blocking out the broad lines of the *Voyage to Parnassus,* which nobody wanted, in which no bookseller would invest a cuarto. Whatever his private suspicions that his critics might just be right, that

† This was a respectable price for the time, Compare the 1,170 reales Espinel received for his *Life of Squire Marcos de Obregón*.

I who, sleepless, toil constantly
to counterfeit the poet's grace
which heaven refused to give me[8]

he nevertheless had a claim to stake to eminence in Spanish letters.

Cervantes' defensiveness may seem mere oversensitivity on the record. He was, after all, celebrated everywhere in Europe. In Spain, *Don Quixote* had touched a national nerve; it was as though he had been one of theirs forever and he became a reliable figure in festivals, masques, celebrations of all kinds. Cervantes, moreover, was now a personal hero as well as a literary one in the public mind: Haedo's *Topographia,* with its detailed account of his conduct in Algiers, was published in 1612 and was widely read in Spain.

Abroad he was probably the best-known of contemporary Spanish writers. A Spanish edition of *La Galatea* was printed in Paris in 1611, a full four years before any new version of the book came out in Spain. Óudin's translation of *Don Quixote, Part I,* was to appear in 1614, bringing the Frenchman three hundred silver livres, more than Cervantes received for writing the book. Similar attention was being paid to him in Germany and Italy. A second Brussels edition of *Don Quixote, Part I,* came out in 1611. In England Cervantes was virtually a household name. This was a period in which much Spanish literature was being translated into English; *La Celestina, Lazarillo de Tormes, Guzmán de Alfarache,* the *Dianas* and many others competed for stall space with the Shelton *Quixote,* which came out in 1612. But Cervantes' works were and would remain a favorite mine for English writers. A first allusion to "tilting at windmills" is found early on in George Wilkins' *The Miseries of Inforst Marriage.* Ben Jonson, whose library contained a Spanish edition of the *Quixote,* never tired of it. In the *Epicoene, or the Silent Woman* (Act IV, Scene 1), Truewit advises Clerimont that if he would know women well "you must leave to live in your chamber, then, a month together upon *Amadis de Gaul* or *Don Quixote,* as you are wont." The two knights are paired again in *The Alchemist* (Act IV, Scene 4), where Kastril orders Surly out of the house:

KASTRIL: Sir, if you get not out o' doors, you lie;
and you are a pimp.

SURLY: Why, this is madness, sir, not valour in you;
I must laugh at this.

KASTRIL: It is my humour; you are a pimp and a trig,
an Amadis de Gaul or a Don Quixote.

DRUGGER: Or a knight o' the curious coxcomb, do you see?

In 1611 John Fletcher had taken his play *The Coxcomb* from "The Tale of Foolish Curiosity" as had Nathaniel Field his *Amends for Ladies*. The industrious Fletcher also joined Francis Beaumont that year in writing a coarse farce, *The Knight of the Burning Pestle*. A dedication to the play notes that "Perhaps it will be thought to bee of the race of *Don Quixote:* we may both confidently sweare, it is his elder above a yeare; and therefore may (by vertue of his birth-right) challenge the wall of him." This was faking it; the dating refers to the publication of Shelton's translation, but Fletcher read Spanish easily and knew the book before he began working with Beaumont in 1607–8. It was Fletcher again who in 1612 or 1613 collaborated with Shakespeare on a play, since lost but known to have existed as late as 1653, which was apparently based on the story of Cardenio in *Don Quixote*.

Cervantes certainly knew little or nothing of all this. Nor did his countrymen. Not a single Spanish poet could read English; the volcanic vitality of Elizabethan literature was unknown in Spain. What was happening in France was hardly better known. In his official approval of *Don Quixote, Part II,* Francisco Márquez-Torres would feel called on to "certify" the author's popularity with a group of French aristocrats who, while on a visit to Cardinal de Sandoval, inquired as to what good books were then current in Spain.

> We thereupon fell to discussing those that I was at the time engaged in censoring, and no sooner had they heard the name of Miguel de Cervantes than they at once began speaking most enthusiastically of the high esteem in which his works were held not only in France but in neighboring kingdoms. They mentioned in particular the *Galatea,* the first part of which one of them could almost repeat from memory, and the *Stories.* So fervent, indeed, was their praise that I offered to take them to see the author of those works, an invitation which they eagerly accepted. They went on to question me in great detail regarding his age, his profession, his rank and worldly state, and I was obliged to inform them that he was an old soldier and an impoverished gentleman, whereupon one of them replied to me most gravely, "How comes it Spain does not see to it that such a man is maintained in luxury out of the public treasury?" One of the others then made this astute observation. "If," he said, "it is necessity that obliges him to write, then God grant that he never be possessed of abundance, in order that, while poor himself, he may continue to enrich all the world."[9]

Even if Cervantes had been aware in 1612 of how highly thought of he was abroad, he was enough of a Spaniard to have felt that the praise that counted was praise at home, from the poets of Spain.

Like Shakespeare, Cervantes is a depressing figure for later writers to contemplate. This is partly because of his genius, of course. But partly, too, because so little had been done in literature before he came on the scene; the high likelihood is that no one ever again will have the chance to do so many new things that are important in writing as he did. Cervantes was not the first story writer, any more than Columbus was the first navigator or Copernicus the father of all astronomers. But we would not recognize our world as we do had his *Exemplary Stories*, first published in August 1613, not existed.

The stories, at any rate the seven best of them, confirmed how far ahead of his time he was. Again he is to be found going his own way, following the sources of a main stream of writing no one else in Spain then was able to find. Even today, a reader can still recapture the excited sense of formal adventure the stories exude. There is about them that experimental air, that tentative, step-by-step but confident probing of new regions of art that we perceive in a Leonardo painting or a Schoenberg opera. It was not simply that Cervantes' dialogue was solid, that his language was richer, his style purer, his ideas more complex than other prose writers'. What was important was that he brought a new dimension to prose fiction, the breakthrough structure which has carried it with relatively little fundamental change into the twentieth century. Like most such discoveries, it was deceptively simple: he placed his characters in society and gave them psychologies of their own with which to deal with their situations. The stories are open to the sights and sounds of everyday life, habits, clothes, attitudes, the random comings and goings of people and events in a lived-in world. His characters exist and act in the context of that world; their problems are created by it, its accidents change their lives and they in turn stir the general air.

This interaction between fictional characters and a real world seems so natural to us now that we do not easily see how it could not always have been so. But short stories before Cervantes occupied an almost airless middle distance; their personages lived closed in on themselves, concerned wholly with the dreamy universe in which their action evolved, vaguely conscious of the world as a hum of faraway bustle drifting through a farmhouse window. Boccaccio's people, trading their "in" gossip and their encapsulated anecdotes in their country hideaway, have nothing directly to do with life in plague-stricken Florence. Bandello's Romeo and Juliet dance their tragic ballet as though they were in the middle of an open, moonlit meadow, not in the thriving city of Verona. The Moor Abendarraez crisscrosses the Kingdom of Granada without ever encountering a peasant or a traveler. These were like the saints in Gothic paintings, dehumanized, oversized, saved from caricature only by the gravity of the general values they represented.

In Cervantes' stories the world crowds in. Try as they may, his personages cannot prevent society from forcing its way into their lives. In the guise of Loaysa it thrusts its heedless snout into Leonora's cloistered existence. Andrés Caballero thinks he is sealed into the Gypsy hive, but the world is a constant, threatening presence which crashes into it with Clemente, with Juana Carducha. It is the random, spontaneous lust of Rodolfo that shatters Leocadia's world in *The Call of Blood*. In *The Glass Scholar*, society is the tormentor, the street crowd that hectors Rodaja in his madness and persecutes him when he returns to sanity. *The Illustrious Serving Wench* is set in a roadside inn near Toledo and it is the shifting pageantry of normal inn life that provides the story's incidents. The moiling, shouting, struggling presence of society is the breath of these stories.

Yet, against all logic of the time, Cervantes did not disperse his narratives when he opened them to the unruly outside; despite their individual experiences, their personal problems, their almost journalistic reality, his characters' humanity enhances their universality instead of diminishing it. This was art working directly on personal experience, boldly exploring the unmarkable frontier between the "lie," or fiction, and "truth," or "history"—life itself. When Cervantes boasts in his prologue to the *Exemplary Stories* that "I was the first to write novelas in the Castilian tongue," he is exaggerating only in a semantic sense: he was redefining the "novela" to mean not a tale or an anecdote (Juan de Timoneda, for example, called his stories *patrañuelos*—tall stories), but longer, more complex pieces, closer in spirit to what we now call novelettes. He was very much the first to condense the broad vitality which he and Alemán and Quevedo were giving to the novel into the shorter, denser container of the story.

Scene after scene in these stories glitters with the lightning play of psychological insight: Loaysa's use of music to dominate the childishly amoral slave Luis, La Cariharta's row with her pimp Repolido, riotous as a modern musical comedy. Indeed, they are rightly thought of as scenes; an enemy of Cervantes shrewdly called the *Exemplary Stories* plays in prose and they do have a theatrical fascination which Cervantes was never able to convey intact to the stage; the silences, the descriptions, the subtleties so impressive in the stories become dead spots, loquaciousness, obscurities in his plays.

Not all of the *Exemplary Stories* are on this level, though there is not a dull story among them. Some (*The Lady Cornelia, The Liberal Lover, The Two Maidens*) are reworkings of early efforts which, despite revision, never achieved the level of sophistication the others reached. *The Call of Blood* may have been written around 1600, but its remodeling was more successful.

In at least one story, Cervantes' experimentation got out of hand. For all its potential power, *The Glass Scholar* is a failure because it lacks a framework of compelling action. It involves a Salamanca scholar driven mad by a courtesan's poisoned quince; he fancies he is made of glass. The idea was not original with Cervantes; there is a reference to such a case in Boccaccio's stories and in the writings of Frenchman Simon Goulart; there seems even to have been an actual case concerning an alchemist at the University of Valladolid, although there is no proof that Cervantes ever heard of any of these cases.

Since he is too fragile to work, Rodaja is reduced to roaming the streets hurling epigrams, to the delight of the crowds that flock behind him. Superficially, then, he is related to the court buffoons and the harlequins and *graciosos* of the theater whose supposed simplicity gives them license to tell home truths to the world.

But only superficially. We must not forget that Cervantes' seamless stories are not only experiments in prose alchemy, but they are designed to explore moral and philosophic problems. The prologue hints that the stories are to be taken both individually and as a group and that there is in them an esoteric meaning or system of meanings for elite readers to dig out:

> I have given them the name *Exemplary,* and if you look closely, there is not one from which some fruitful example may not be drawn . . . if in any way I thought the reading of these stories were indeed to induce an evil desire or thought in whosoever reads them, I would rather cut off the hand that wrote them than expose them in public. At my age, one does not play tricks with the other life. . . .

The notes they strike reinforce—exemplify—the ideas in his other works: it is man's condition to live in society, but society is worldliness, corruption. This is how men are, and it is not their fault. They live locked into a world which is evil by definition. This theme of confinement, in its various aspects, runs through the great stories as, perhaps, it ran through Cervantes' mind on the roads and streets of Andalusia. Leocadia shuts herself up in her parents' house for fear "that her disgrace could be read in her brow." Leonora is cloistered by Carrizales, who himself is locked into his pinched and stunted values. Rinconete and Cortadillo confine themselves in Monipodio's warped brotherhood. Rodaja is twice confined, first in his madness, then in his sanity. In all these cases, society is satanic in both its individual and collective incarnations, as Rodolfo the rapist, Loaysa the pícaro, the crowds around Rodaja. Life is hazard, mutely evil yet often joyous. The world has no patience with reason. Rodaja cured of his madness pleads with the crowd to stop following him around. "Ask me now at home what you used to ask me in the squares and you will see that the man who gave you good improvised answers, so to speak, will give you better ones for having thought them out." It is no use. Reason is prudent; it is not amusing. He is forced to flee to Flanders, where he dies a soldier.

Notwithstanding the omnipresence in them of the world's unthinking evil, the *Exemplary Stories* are not pessimistic. As we have seen, Cervantes prescribed a course of treatment of the disease: self-examination, cultivation of man's reason and his will, active pursuit of the ideal of love. None of this will change the world, but it will put man in readiness to receive the divine grace which will surely, sometime, be offered him. What was true for individuals, moreover, might also be true for societies, as Cervantes may have suggested in *The Jealous Extremaduran*. In its story of a jealous authority (the aged husband Felipe de Carrizales) attempting to isolate a subject people (the child bride Leonora and her attendants) from the contamination of worldly evil (the pícaro Loaysa), we are surely meant to understand the uselessness—indeed, the offensiveness—of efforts to seal Spain off from foreign, i.e. heretical, thought. However carefully the doors are locked, Cervantes tells us, the outside will enter. Even the husband's name, *Philip,* is significant when we find that in his picaresque past he squandered his birthright in Spain, Flanders and Italy. Philip dies not of the truth, but of his false perception of the truth; it does not occur to him that Leonora, tempted by an alien seducer, might refuse to succumb to him.

The stories were a commercial success, going through four editions within ten months, including a pirate edition printed in Pamplona and a forgery done in Lisbon. On August 9, 1613, a privilege for Aragon was granted, with an enthusiastic approval of their "invention and language" and their capacity to "instruct and amaze." That the praise came from a man less than half his age and still little known outside of the Madrid intelligentsia would not have bothered Cervantes in this case. Its author was Salas Barbadillo, to whom, said Cervantes in the *Voyage to Parnassus,* "I bow and for whom my appreciation is limitless." Salas Barbadillo was then thirty-two years old and just settling down to full-time writing after an unruly youth which had brought him three prison terms (once for fighting a duel and twice for satirizing sensitive officials). Cervantes was his literary idol, one he imitated even to the depth of his poverty. The prose and verse novel *El caballero puntual (The Punctilious Knight)* he was to publish in 1614 in imitation of *Don Quixote* brought him a wretched one hundred reales, probably because he was desperate for money and in no position to bargain. This was to be followed in 1615 with a collection of seven stories, the *Correction of Vices,* clearly patterned on the *Exemplary Stories.*

Salas Barbadillo was an exception among Spanish writers, however. Despite the openings the stories offered for fictional exploitation, hardly anyone in his own country followed Cervantes' lead. The Spanish were too committed to their scholasticism, too obsessed with the showy emotionalism and rapid virtuosity of Lopean theater to go adventuring into Cervantine realism.

As usual, it was the English who most freely read and plundered Cervantes' stories. Thomas Middleton wrote a play called *The Spanish Gypsy*, which transplanted episodes from *The Call of Blood* into the plot of *The Little Gypsy Girl*. The indefatigable Fletcher also converted *The Lady Cornelia* into the play *The Chance*, reworked *The Deceitful Marriage* into *Rule a Wife and Have a Wife*, transferred *The Two Maidens* to the stage as *Love's Pilgrimage* and returned to *The Call of Blood* for *The Queen of Corinth*.

Among the prefatory sonnets to the *Exemplary Stories* was one by young Fernando de Lodeña, a friend, one of the two men who would write epitaphs at Cervantes' death. A merely touching detail, had Fernando not been the son of the older Lodeña, Magdalena's former lover. The past also returns, more fruitfully, to haunt the dedication to the Count of Lemos. It is dated July 14, 1613; by that time, the count's jealous secretary Lupercio Leonardo de Argensola was dead, the viceregal subsidies may have been flowing steadily to Cervantes.

The volume went to press, however, without the portrait of himself Cervantes says he had hoped to see on the frontispiece. He blames the omission on a friend who "could very easily" have done the engraving, for "the famous Juan de Jáuregui would have given him my portrait," so satisfying the curiosity of "those few who would have liked to know what kind of face and figure he has who dares lay so many inventions" before the world. Failing this, he supplies a word portrait of himself with "chestnut hair, a smooth and lofty brow, merry eyes and a curved but well-proportioned nose, a silvery beard that not twenty years ago was gold; the moustache is sweeping, the mouth small, teeth neither short nor long, for he has but six and those in sorry condition and worse seated, for none of them meet; the figure is average, neither tall nor short; his color is high, rather pale than swarthy, he is somewhat stooped in the shoulders and not very light on his feet. . . ."

Taking Cervantes literally when he is in this mood is not usually a safe course. When he goes on to remark that "since this friend I complain of could think of nothing else to say about me, I could set up a couple of dozen testimonials to myself and say them anonymously, so spreading my fame and vaunting my wit," we are on familiar ground. In Lope de Vega's *Jerusalem Conquered* appears a portrait of the author by Francisco Pacheco accompanied by a eulogy beginning: "This is the effigy of

Lope de Vega Carpio, to whom a rightful place is granted among the eminent and famous men of our time. . . ." If Lope did not write the testimonial himself, as he probably did, Cervantes at any rate assumed he had and he was letting his rival know it. To conclude from this that Cervantes had actually asked Jáuregui to paint his portrait, or that the picture had actually been done, is riskier.

Sevillian Juan Martínez de Jáuregui y Aguilar had returned from Rome shortly before 1610 with a double reputation as painter and poet. Cervantes probably met him in the Madrid academies and, at a time when the Lemos incident had brought Italy back into his mind, was probably attracted by the young man's Italianate culture. Jáuregui's translation of Tasso's *Aminta* is lauded in *Don Quixote, Part II,* as one of the two best of its kind Cervantes had ever seen, and his poetry receives its share of unmeasured praise in the *Voyage to Parnassus.*

Did Jáuregui do a portrait or even a sketch of Cervantes from which the "friend" failed to take an engraving? The uneasy conditional tense of the prologue—"Juan de Jáuregui *would have given* him my portrait"—is ambiguous. It can as justifiably be read to mean the painter would have done one had he been asked to do so. The confusion has extended to the two extant portraits said to be of Cervantes and attributed to Jáuregui. The one most often seen, showing a ruffed Cervantes looking rather like a stale boiled egg with an absurd spun-sugar beard lying on a bed of lettuce, has created the livelier fuss. Academic caution requires that it be described as "almost certainly" a forgery, perhaps out of deference to the Spanish Royal Academy, which for many years defended its authenticity and still has it on public display in Madrid. No one who maintains that it is a modern fake, cooked in an oven, probably in Oviedo, to give it an "authentic" antique surface in the first decade of the twentieth century, would be exposing himself to much censure.[10] It was allegedly painted in the year 1600—when Jáuregui was seventeen years old—but depicts a "Cervantes" who looks closer to seventy. As a painting it is an offense to Jáuregui's memory.

A second portrait attributed to the Sevillian and now in the collection of the Marquis of Casa Torres has had a more peaceful history and was endorsed as "probably authentic" by Astrana Marín and other scholars. Aside from the Habsurg look it gives its subject, however, it suffers from a serious drawback: although Jáuregui could not have done a portrait of Cervantes before 1610 and probably not until 1611, the painting shows a man who looks some fifteen years younger than Cervantes would then have been. If the Royal Academy treatment is a crude caricature of the description contained in the *Exemplary Stories* prologue, the Casa Torres version unaccountably shows an idealized "Cervantes" with the golden beard of "not twenty years ago" and a nose Romanized by the painter's cosmetic vision. Portraitists painting from life do not generally depict their subjects as they might once have been. In the absence of conclusive evidence to the contrary, it is more prudent to assume that neither is genuine; either Jáuregui failed to do the portrait, or he did one and it has been lost.

In the prologue to the *Exemplary Stories,* Cervantes refers to the *Voyage to Parnassus* as completed—the appendix, an afterthought, would be written in the summer of 1614—and promises the rest of *Don Quixote,* the *Persiles* and a book called *Semanas del jardín*—literally *Weeks of the Garden*—of which nothing has ever been seen, if indeed any of it was ever composed. This should have meant he was now free to respond to Robles' pleas for *Don Quixote.* Probably he did—when other business permitted. On July 2, 1613, Cervantes was in Alcalá de Henares, where he became a novice in the Venerable Tertiary Order of St. Francis, following the example of his wife and sisters. Back in Madrid, he presumably wasted some time in seeking a publisher for the *Voyage to Parnassus* before convincing himself that no one would have it.

If it seems incredible that only a scattering of dates remains to show that Cervantes, then at the peak of his fame, was alive at all in 1614, the reason must lie in part with the quality of that fame. Mementos were not kept because few people felt they were worth treasuring. After his death his papers, notes, unfinished manuscripts—there must have been these—came into the keeping of Doña Catalina, who could do nothing with them. And the hands that took them from her were unsympathetic: perhaps Isabel de Molina's, more probably those of Francisco de Palacios. Into the fire with them, or sell them as scrap for a few maravedis. Cervantes, after all, was not Lope de Vega.

The dates are soon listed:

JULY 20: The dating of Sancho's letter to his wife tells us that Cervantes had then gotten only as far as Chapter 36 of *Don Quixote, Part II,* halfway through the book.

JULY 22: The "letter from Apollo" is written concluding the appendix to the *Voyage to Parnassus.*

SEPTEMBER 25: A jury of which Lope was a member declined to award a prize (a silver jug for the winner, the usual fabrics for the runners-up) to Cervantes for his song to St. Teresa of Ávila.

OCTOBER 18: A privilege is granted for the *Voyage to Parnassus.*

The poem went on sale in November at forty-four maravedis, preceded by the kind of pompously academic Latin epigram (this one was by Don Agustín de Casanate Rojas) Cervantes had derided in *Don Quixote.* The dedication was to one Rodrigo de Tápia y Alarcón. Tápia was the compleat aristocrat: strong, arrogant, a fine rider and fearless bullfighter. At the age of nine he was made a Knight of Santiago; he had been a page to Queen Marguerite. Was there anything odd about dedicating a long poem to him? Well, yes, there was: Rodrigo was only fifteen years old in 1614 and had probably never read a poem in his life. In fact, the dedication was designed to flatter the boy's father, Pedro de Tápia, a magistrate for the Royal Council and the head of a family reputed to be among the most successfully corrupt of the realm. The Count of Villamediana, the (probably homosexual) Don Juan whose satirical doggerel made him one of the most feared and hated men of his time, treats the elder Tápia, his daughter Ana and her husband as "thieves" who "stink of fear." Quevedo supported the charge in his *Grandes anales de quince días* with the observation that much of the Tápia fortune was "usurped." As for young Rodrigo, wrote Villamediana, he was

> Rodrigo, and not the one of Vivar,‡
> but Rodrigo the sponger,
> a very sluggish bill-payer
> but lively enough at collecting. . . .[11]

A strange crew, surely, to be honored by a Cervantes who prided himself on his uprightness. But he had devoted a year to writing the *Voyage to Parnassus*, a year he could ill afford, and months more convincing himself that no bookseller was prepared to pay him so much as a compliment for it. To finance its publication on his own was out of the question. Yet it had to be printed. The *Voyage to Parnassus* was not simply a poem, it was Cervantes' manifesto, an advertisement for himself and a statement of defiance. So when Don Pedro de Tápia, no doubt feeling himself in the need of a little positive publicity, agreed to defray the cost of producing this irreproachably high-minded item, Cervantes' order of moral priorities adjusted to the situation.

The *Voyage to Parnassus* is a narrative of its author's imaginary journey to the sacred mountain where Apollo, as the god of poetry, lords it over the Muses. Cervantes confesses his doubts about his poetic merit, describing himself with mock modesty as

> swanlike in the color of my hair,
> in voice a black and raucous crow.

If only he could drink from the sacred spring Aganippe[12] on Apollo's mount (the sexuality of the image is certainly accidental), he fancies he

‡ The reference is to Rodrigo Díaz de Vivar, El Cid Campeador.

would then be an "illustrious poet—or at least a splendid one." Having read of the voyage by the "trifling Italian corporal" (Caporali) to Parnassus on a broken-down hired mule, he determines to do the same. He is poor, however, and will have to go "on the flanks of destiny" for lack of any other conveyance; like Sancho's, his pack holds only a loaf of bread and eight bits of cheese (for the eight chapters of the poem). Will his resolution survive so long a journey afoot? A sudden whiff of fame steels his determination; he half expects to be disappointed:

> but because I always start out
> mistakenly believing in my desire, I set
> my feet on the road and bent my head to the wind.

Reaching Cartagena on his way, which prompts him to relive the battle of Lepanto, the traveler encounters Mercury in a galley made entirely of poetry, from the poop of stout sonnets to the parrel of slender redondillas. Cervantes is called aboard to learn that the god is rounding up the good poets to repel a threatened invasion of Parnassus by "more than twenty thousand puny, foolish poets." Mercury shows him his list of recruits and asks Cervantes to select the best. This gives rise to the first of a series of verses praising poets of the day. Most of them have been forgotten, but a few names are familiar: Villamediana, Cabrera de Córdoba, Jáuregui, etc. The tribute to Quevedo, teasing him gently about his lameness, is obviously addressed to a friend:

> "For Don Francisco de Quevedo to come would be
>   difficult," I thereupon said, but he (Mercury) told me:
> "Leave without him I cannot;
>   he is Apollo's son, son of the Muse
>   Calliope; we cannot part without him
>   and on this I shall be adamant.
>   He is the scourge of dreary poets;
>   his strokes of wit will rout from Parnassus
>   the dull wits with us and those expected."
> "Oh, my lord," I said, "his step is halting;
>   a century's not time enough for him to arrive."
> "That matters not to me," said Mercury.
> "A knightly poet will ride a cloud
>   part gray and part resplendent. . . ."

This peroration is cut short by a sudden squall of poets; from this the galley is rescued by the sirens, who apologize for being late: they'd been listening to one Sancho Panza discourse. A cloudburst on the horizon rains down toads and frogs and strange human shapes; these are the poets on Mercury's list, "many poorly clad." From another cloud falls

> . . . the great Lope de Vega,
> distinguished poet, whose verse and prose
> no one surpasses, nor even equals.

The praise is correct, but formulary, cool.

There is a further series of adventures: the defenders narrowly escape boarding by the bad poets' galley; they are caught in a storm in the Strait of Messina in which Cervantes' old Italian acquaintance, the garrulous bard of Sardinia, Antonio de Lofraso, is nearly thrown overboard to propitiate the waves. At last they reach Parnassus, where Apollo, dressed like a burgher in doublet and hose, greets them at the shore and summons them to assembly on the mount. At Aganippe the poets drink; some of them wash their hands and feet "and other things somewhat more indecent" in it.

Arrived at the high place, the poets are seated in order of merit. Only Cervantes is left standing. He asserts his right to a place, listing his claims to eminence—almost everything he'd written: his lost *Filena*, the *Galatea*, his romance on Jealousy and his sonnet on King Philip's tomb, the *Persiles* "which is almost ready for the printer" and especially his plays. He pleads his lifelong love of poetry, the seemliness and honesty of his verse, even his personal rectitude. Typically, he seems proudest of the wrong achievements: his verse, his plays, the *Persiles*. *Don Quixote* is dismissed—perhaps more fearfully than candidly—as an entertainment, although his judgment on his stories is sound:

> I opened in my stories a way
> through which the Castilian tongue
> can show a folly with propriety. . . .

Despite his misfortunes, he says, he is not bitter,

> although seeing myself standing as I am
> and in such a place, I wonder if I should not be.

The reply is harsh:

> You alone have forged your fortune,
> and I have sometimes seen you lucky,
> but luck is brief for the improvident.

Aware of how much an outsider he is, Cervantes offers himself an ironic solution: if there is no place for him, he has only to fold his cloak and sit on it. But he protests:

> "Clearly, my lord, you have not noticed,"
> I replied, "that I do not have a cloak."
> He said: "Even so, I am pleased to see you.
> Virtue is the cloak with which poverty
> covers and conceals her shame;
> in it she is safe and free from envy."
> I bowed my head before this sterling counsel;
> standing I remained; for there is no good seat
> that's not by favor fashioned, or else by wealth.

Some among the poets protest the injustice, but they are interrupted by the appearance of the Parnassian nymphs escorting the blinding beauty of poetry. Cervantes fails to recognize her arrayed in so much splendor; "I've always seen her swathed in poor rags," he explains.

The action builds up theatrically from there. A boatload of poets winnowed by Cervantes from Mercury's list heaves into sight and, charging him with bad faith and worse taste, threatens him with revenge. He, appalled, replies it was the god who chose; he complains that

> Some hate me because I put them on the list.
> Others, because I left them out of it,
> are determined to cause me sorrow. . . .
> I have never been content or satisfied
> with hypocritical modesty. I have bid openly
> for praise for those things I did well.

In one of his most poignant passages, he begs that Apollo

> . . . so that the dark fear besetting me not end
> my life with the end of this contentious day,
> cover me with your mantle and with your shadow
> or mark me with a sign that all might understand
> that I am your creature, and am of your house,
> and then there will be no one to offend me.

Apollo obligingly appeals to Neptune, who sinks the vessel in a scene recalling the lines on Lepanto.

After all this tumult, Apollo puts his troops to sleep to rest them for the coming battle. Cervantes dreams of a figure, ambiguous at first, beautiful from afar but less so close up, her words "rich in suavity but poor in science." The figures grows bigger and bigger—there is a diabetic's reference to "the disease known as dropsy"—until its arms span the space from sunrise to sunset. This, he is told, is the daughter of fame and ambition, who "aspires to be first in greatness," who believes luck is constant and who, in her boldness, can do a thousand impossible things: she is vaingloriousness. Her natural sustenance is air and this is why she grows so rapidly. Anyone who tries to imitate her will see his own glory scattered to the winds. Cervantes found his consolation where he could.

The battle of the poets is a burlesque, and a funny one, in which poems and books serve as missiles. The good poets win, but Cervantes is not one of those Apollo crowns with laurel. So, after a dose of the new medicinal drug tobacco—described here as the sacred droppings of Pegasus—to restore the faint, Cervantes goes back to sleep.

When he wakes he is in Naples with Promontorio "who called me father and I called him son"; the young man, bastard son or symbol of Cervantes' youth, wonders what great cause brought him there "old and half-dead as you are." We never get a proper answer, for the chapter wanders off into flattery of Lemos and a fresh squadron of poets. Then, suddenly, as one is in dreams, Cervantes is back in his "dismal room," throwing himself exhausted on his bed.

It is competent, occasionally brilliant verse, full of funny sequences— Apollo in doublet and hose slapping his favorites on the back *is* a funny image—and vibrating with Cervantine irony. One biographer, noting its witty mixture of humanized gods and deific mortals, indulgently compares it to Velázquez's "Vulcan's Forge," in which the god's divinity hardly distinguishes him from the smiths around him, and "Los Borrachos," showing a Bacchus as human as he is immortal.[13] Thus Mercury in the *Voyage*—a bit of a gossip, a little pompous. Cervantes, however, does what the more detached painter refused to do: he opens his heart, reveals himself in lights and shadows more reminiscent of a Rembrandt.

A multitude of classical puns and wry personal digs do not obscure the verses' clarity and directness. Yet the form, the idiom, even the concepts of these thousand-plus tercets are of another day; they reek of Garcilaso's Italianisms and, despite their humor, of Herrera's pedantry. That Cervantes could publish the *Voyage to Parnassus* the same year in which Góngora's complex, abstruse *Soledad primero* appeared suggests how arrested his technical notions were. The irony is almost conscious: Góngora is praised no fewer than three times in the poem; one of the references has been seen as tribute to the Córdoban's *Fable of Polyphemus and Galatea,* which would make it one of the first public endorsements of this difficult work. Góngora's poem, he says, will

> . . . leave your scar
> and with the sharp edge, on the poet's face
> who will not take you as his guiding star.

One feels almost as though Cervantes were telling us that he knew good poetry when he saw it, that his critical sense alone deserved recognition, but that it was not in his nature to write that way.

The brief prose appendix is pure Cervantes, glowing with rakish charm. It tells of his meeting while on his way home with young, extravagant Pancracio de Roncesvalles. The dialogue which follows chiefly concerns why poets are poor. Finally Pancracio reaches into his bosom and extracts a letter with seventeen maravedis due in postage on it. Cervantes is scandalized by the cost, and recounts the incident of Lope's scurrilous sonnet. Pancracio, though a poet, is rich and, though rich, is perceptive enough to see through the subterfuge; he volunteers to pay the seventeen maravedis.

The letter is from Apollo with all good wishes from the god and his friends and an admonition that Cervantes "take care of your health." Enclosed with it is a burlesque code of divine ordinances for Spanish poets—containing such provisions as:

ITEM: if a poet arrives at the home of a friend or acquaintance and the family is at table and invites him to join them, even though he swears he has already eaten, under no condition is he to be believed; rather should he be forced to eat, for not much force will be needed under the circumstances. . . .

A few of the bad poets cited in the poem did try to take their revenge; one of them, Esteban Manuel de Villegas, who at twenty-four considered himself the greatest of them all, wrote to Bartolomé Leonardo de Argensola,

> You will go to conquer the Helicon
> more easily than Cervantes the bad poet;
> there it will not serve him to be *quixotista*. . . .[14]

Some of the good poets were grateful for his praise, but for the most part, the *Voyage to Parnassus* was ignored, at least publicly. By that time, a fresh offense had reddened the Cervantine cheek: the "false Quixote."

] 34 [

Avellaneda's Folly

In October 1614 a volume went on sale in Madrid entitled *Second Volume of the Ingenious Don Quixote of La Mancha, which contains his third sally, and is the fifth part of his adventures.*

It went on to say: *Composed by the Licentiate Alonso Fernández de Avellaneda, citizen of the Town of Tordesillas.*

Fanciful scenes have been written to depict Cervantes' horror at this new villainy: Cervantes entering a bookshop, being silently handed the volume, feverishly donning his glasses to leaf through it with trembling hands; Cervantes seated at his table writing his own Second Part when a friend enters, white-faced, and wordlessly places the volume before him. . . . Such words as "wickedness," "brigand," "treacherous" leap nimbly to Cervantists' tongues. Before we are too carried away by our modern sense of property, however, it might be prudent to understand in what the outrage—for it was an outrage—actually lay.

The notion of artistic individualism, of an artist's creation as somehow belonging to him, was just beginning to take root in Cervantes' time. For centuries before that, art was largely thought of as common property, not, to be sure, to be stolen outright, but to be modified, adapted, imitated at will. A work of art was a theme on which anyone was licensed to supply variations. The apocryphal *Quixote* was not plagiarized as the term was understood then. "Avellaneda," if that was his name, nevertheless felt obliged to defend himself in his prologue: "Let no one be shocked that the Second Part comes from a different author, for it is nothing new for different people to continue a tale. How many have told of the loves of Angelica* and her adventures? The *Arcadias* have been the work of various writers; *Diana* is not all by the same hand." He (perhaps carefully) avoided mentioning the spurious Second Part of *Guzmán de Alfarache*

---

* The heroine of Ariosto's *Orlando furioso*.

published by one Juan José Marti under the name of Mateo Lujan de Sayavedra in 1604; the impertinence so infuriated Alemán that in his own Second Part he introduced a character named Sayavedra, a rogue and liar who robs Guzmán, becomes his servant and finally goes mad and drowns. Nor, apparently, had "Avellaneda" yet seen the *Voyage to Parnassus,* else he might have cited Cervantes' pilferage from Caporali's poem.

Yet Cervantes was right to be irate, all aside from any feeling he might have had of violation or his fears of what effect this apery might have on the public's view of his own Second Part. For not only had Avellaneda gone out of his way to be personally insulting to his victim; his very book was an offense against Cervantes' artistry. And its cloddishness was a wounding confirmation of how little people understood what Cervantes was driving at.

A small Avellaneda cult has grown up over the years. It is typified by the comment of one Agustín de Montiano y Loyendo, a founder of the Spanish Academy of History, that at least the book is not "cold and graceless," as Cervantes' is. Don Agustín apparently shares the mentality of those who feel so dwarfed by Shakespeare's shadow that they would rather attribute his work to anyone else than concede his genius. Avellaneda's book bears no trace of the original's poetic truth, its aesthetic searchings, not a whisper of its philosophic or moral strivings. No real sense of beauty relieves its grossness, no ideal illuminates it. Avellaneda's personages are shallow caricatures of their betters. Quixote here is a windbag, a vulgar lunatic with none of his forebear's saving dignity, no hint of his humanity; he is a comic-strip character, as Sancho is a caricature of a sly and stupid rustic, a glutton, drunkard, clown—worse, an unamusing clown.

It is significant that, in Chapter 2 of the book, Avellaneda's Quixote is reproached by Dulcinea and abandons her as faithless and demanding. With her went the point to the characterization, but such delicacies were beyond the author's sensibilities. She had to be eliminated because she had no function in this book; she simply got in the way of the gags; her presence would have made the ribaldry in which Avellaneda reveled meaningless and disturbing, pornographic. The book has the soul of a long practical joke in the bawdy, fat-footed, flushed-cheeked student manner of the time. Its author, we suspect, may not have been physically out of the university for very long; mentally, in any case, he was still in it.

Who was this wattle-and-daub comic, this raucous pickpocket of an author? No one knows; if Cervantes knew, he kept the secret. If the name was not invented, he was an incredibly discreet man, for the most diligent search has uncovered no trace of such a person. The full arsenal of scholarly machinery, including cryptography and mathematics, has produced guesses ranging from Lope de Vega via half the minor literary figures of Cervantine Spain . . . to Cervantes himself.

That he was an Aragonese is evident from his book's language. Avellaneda's familiarity with theology, his insistent references to monastic routine, his fluent if decadent Church Latin and certain incidents in the book suggest he may have been a monk, and his reverence for the Inquisition focuses attention on the Dominicans. Finally, he was a devoted admirer of "the excellent poet Lope de Vega Carpio, familiar of the Holy Office."[1] A glance back at the defense of his piracy in the prologue indicates why he cited *Angelica* and the *Arcadias:* Lope had appropriated both of them. The implication is plain: if Lope did it, it must be all right. Avellaneda—we have no other name for him—appears as a vain man who prided himself on being "in" with the great, a busybody with a taste for conspiracy and, for some reason, angry.

His prologue, he protests, is less "boastful and aggressive" than Cervantes' to *Don Quixote,* "more humble" than the foreword to the *Exemplary Stories.* He mocks his victim for being one-handed, and pretends to be "speaking in a way for everyone" when he describes him as being "as old in years as he is young in spirit, with more tongue than hands." Cervantes, he charges, "offended" him by the means he chose to his end— presumably a reference to the attacks on Lope, since he goes on to regret the "offense" more keenly on behalf of "one who is so justly celebrated in the most foreign of foreign countries and to whom ours owes so much for having most creditably and fruitfully maintained the theaters of Spain for so many years with stupendous and innumerable plays, with the rigorous artistry the world seeks and with the authority and purity to be expected from a minister of the Holy Office."

The sulking continues: he has decided, he says, to make a comic interlude of Sancho's simplicity, but without "offending anyone." He then goes on the offensive himself:

And then, Miguel de Cervantes is now as old as the castle of San Cervantes and his age has made him so discontented that everything and everyone infuriate him, and that is why he is so lacking in friends that when he wished to adorn his books with resounding sonnets he had to ascribe their paternity, as he admits, to Prester John of the Indies or the Emperor of Trapisonda, because there is probably no titled person in Spain who would not be offended at having his name in the mouth of . . . the author about whom there is so much gossip and please God he may be left alone now that he has rallied to the shelter of the Church.[2] Let him be content with his *Galatea* and his plays in prose, for these are what most of his stories are, and may he cease to weary us.

The crowning slur occurs in Chapter 4, where Avellaneda alleges that Cervantes has been cuckolded by Doña Catalina—thus the allusions to the feathers planted in the castle of San Cervantes.

A lover creeping under middle-aged Catalina's Franciscan homespun? Nonsense! The tone is so like that repugnant sonnet mailed to Cervantes in Valladolid, the allegations so similar—Cervantes' cuckoldry, his lineage—that one wonders if Lope should not be blamed for it after all. Avellaneda seems to have known Cervantes at some time—it is not easy to work up so much animosity against a total stranger. Could it have been in Valladolid? To dismiss out of hand the notion that Catalina might have been unfaithful to Cervantes there (but would this have escaped the gossip in the attic?) or, more conveniently, in the long loveless years alone in Esquivias, is impossible in view of how little is known of her life. But the odds are so long against it that we can only assume Avellaneda and the anonymous sonneteer of Valladolid were indulging a particular form of Latin viciousness.

Cervantes' reaction was characteristically restrained. He was at work on Chapter 59 of his own Second Part, the first in which "the other" book is mentioned.

> "Why would Your Grace have us read such nonsense, Señor Don Juan," came the reply: "anyone who has read the First Part of the history of *Don Quixote de la Mancha* cannot possibly take any pleasure in this second one."
>
> "For all of that," said Don Juan, "it would be well to read it, since no book is so bad that there is not some good in it. What displeases me most about it is that it depicts Don Quixote as being no longer in love with Dulcinea del Toboso."
>
> Hearing this, the knight, filled with anger and resentment, raised his voice and roared, "If anyone says that Don Quixote has forgotten or ever can forget the peerless Dulcinea del Toboso I will make him understand by force of arms that he is far from speaking the truth. . . ."

Quixote takes the book, leafs through it and hands it back to its owner, saying:

> "In this bit I've seen of it I have found three things in this author worthy of reproach. The first, in a few words I read in the prologue; the second, that the language is Aragonese, because he sometimes writes without articles; and the third, which most confirms his ignorance, is that he errs and deviates from the truth in the fundamental things in the story, for here he says that the wife of my squire Sancho Panza is named Mari Gutiérrez and that is not her name; it is Teresa

Panza,[3] and it is to be feared that who errs in so essential a fact may be wrong in the rest."

From that point on, the theme becomes obsessive. In Chapter 61 Avellaneda's book is "false," "apocryphal," not the "true, legal and faithful" version. In 62 Cervantes refers to "so-and-so, citizen of Tordesillas" to whose book "St. Martin's Day will come as it does to every swine."[4] In 70, one devil says to another, "What book is this?" When told it is the false *Quixote* the devil cries, "Take it away and put it in the depths of hell so that my eyes may no longer see it." "Is it so bad?" asks the other devil. "So bad that I could not do it worse if I tried." Cervantes even borrows a character from Avellaneda, Don Alvaro Tarfe, to insist on the authenticity of Cervantes' version.

Even in his replies, Cervantes showed himself to be the finer craftsman of the two. The point has been made that, like Part I, the other *Quixote* is a fact outside the true Second Part and comes to intervene in it in the same way. This, the critic noted, "sets up an uneasiness in the heroes," who have not only to deal with enchanters, false knights, bogus duennas, lackey champions, etc., but "with travesties of themselves" as well. Don Quixote's reply to this is to call on other characters to witness that he and Sancho are the true knight and squire—that is, that he is believable as a character whereas the other is not, that he had a poetic existence as much denied the other as it was denied the extravagant heroes of chivalry. And all of this is integrated in the novel in masterly fashion.[5]

Cervantes' own prologue is wholly given over to a direct reply. He solemnly resents being called

> . . . old and one-handed, as if it were in my power to make time stand still for me, or as if I had lost my hand in some tavern brawl instead of upon the greatest occasion the past or present has ever known. . . . If my wounds are not resplendent in the eyes of the chance beholder, they are at least respected by those who know where they were received. . . . So strongly do I feel about this that even if it were possible to work a miracle in my case, I still would rather have taken part in that prodigious battle than be today free of my wounds without having been there.

While ostentatiously praising Lope, he upbraids Avellaneda as a sneak and, indirectly, as a thief and a fool. One of his gibes is in the form of an anecdote:

> There was in Seville a certain madman whose madness assumed one of the drollest forms ever seen in this world. Taking a hollow reed

sharpened at one end, he would catch a dog in the street or somewhere else; and, holding one of the animal's legs with his foot and raising the other with his hand, he would fix his reed as best he could in a certain part, after which he would blow the dog up round as a ball. When he had it in this condition he would slap it on the belly a couple of times and let it go, remarking to the bystanders, of whom there were always plenty, "Do Your Worships think, then, that it is such an easy thing to inflate a dog?" So you might ask, "Does Your Grace think it is such an easy thing to write a book?"

In February 1615, when Part II of Cervantes' *Don Quixote* was completed, its author had for all practical purposes divorced himself from the world to live in the hurrying, tumultuous universe of his work and his illness. Only absolute concentration and stubborn defiance of his emaciated body can account for his prodigious output: half of Part II had been written in six months, as much as he had done in the seven years before that; he must have been well into the *Persiles;* at least two plays and two interludes were rewritten or revised. Time had nevertheless been found to turn out at least two prefatory sonnets for friends. One was to Juan Yagüe de Salas for his interminable verse recital—20,400 verses!—of *The Lovers of Teruel,* another to the *Minerva sacra,* a slim volume of sophisticated poems by a nineteen-year-old nun, Doña Alfonsa González de Salazar. Enough work to exhaust a healthy man in his prime. Cervantes was caught in the gears of that paradox which has broken so many men and women with so much still to do and so little time in which to do it, so little strength: the harder the racer tries to run, the faster the body's clock runs out. Visits from his doctor may now have been more frequent; there was not much the man could do but gaze disapprovingly at his bottles of cottony urine and recommend rest—impossible!—and decent wine, well watered. As well feed him medicinal sugar and be done with it. But, then as now, medicine was a blend of faith and art; only the proportions have changed. Governor Sancho's fury at the doctor trying to starve him suggests that Cervantes may have dismissed one for putting him on a diet —or, at any rate, that he thought of doing so. References to "wicked doctors" and "quacks" stud the Barataria sequence.

Part II of *Don Quixote* was moving stormily toward publication. Approval by Cervantes' friend Márquez-Torres on February 15 was followed on March 17 by the obligatory second approbation, this one from José de Valdivieso, who paid his debt for praise in the *Voyage to Parnassus* with a handsome description of the work as "fully worthy of (Cervantes') great inventiveness, honor and luster of our nation, wonder and envy of those abroad." A privilege, for twenty years covering the whole Spanish Empire, was granted March 30.

We do not know how much Robles paid Cervantes for Part II. Perhaps no more than the sixteen hundred reales he had given for the *Exemplary Stories*. Most or all of that had already been advanced to the author, but Cervantes may have hoped for enough more to give him a breather from his financial worries. Because Part II was the last of Cervantes' works Robles would publish, Astrana Marín guessed at a falling-out between them over the price. An issue might also have been the bookseller's refusal to take the plays whose "perpetual silence" Cervantes was now itching to break.

If the issue was money, his hand was soon strengthened by a stroke of luck for which his experience had not prepared him: a flow of unsolicited funds from a new patron, Cardinal de Sandoval y Rojas. It may have been the French nobles' visit described my Márquez-Torres in his approval of Part II that opened the prelatic purse. Certainly the primate's spontaneity was unusual enough to provoke surprise; nine years after his death, Salas Barbadillo would refer to him as a "haven in all needs and true father of the poor" who gave Espinel a daily allowance for his old age and "exercised the same piety with Miguel de Cervantes because it seemed to him that helping virtuously occupied men was a charity worthy of the Primate of the Spains."[6]

Contarini described Sandoval as a man "who affects justice and reason," truthful but "flighty," fond of flattery, by which the ambassador meant his ineptitude as a negotiator. Venetian diplomats made a profession of seeking the flaw in the stone. Once safely cured by his nephew Lerma's dynastic benefactions of the personal insecurity literally inherent in his status as the second son of a second son in a primogenitive caste, Sandoval relaxed naturally into the role he liked best, that of fatherly churchman. Perhaps because he had never had to develop his predatory side, he was among the few Sandovals to remain openhanded and courtly: one of the touches which most astonished his clients was his habit—unheard of in a prince of the Church—of sending personal letters with his gifts.

At about the same time, Cervantes found a publisher for his plays: Juan de Villarroël, a small operator who escaped obscurity mainly by the extent of his debts. In his prologue to the volume of *Eight Plays and Eight Interludes, New and Never Performed*, the author explains offhandedly that when "in good time a bookseller told me he might buy them from me" despite being warned against them, "I grew weary" of arguing with managers and sold them to the publisher; "he paid me a reasonable price; I took the money meekly, happy not to have to put up with the actors' haggling. I wish the plays were the best in the world, or at least reasonably good." The proud contract of 1592 to write six of "the best plays ever seen in Spain" was a long, sobering time behind him. He knew that Villarroël, even by using the cheapest paper and the most ill-cut type, expected to take a loss on the book, calculating that it was worth the little he undoubtedly paid Cervantes to acquire an author with two commercial successes to his credit and a novel, the *Persiles,* in the works. The bookseller may have hoped that anything Cervantes wrote now would sell on his name alone. He would have had some reason for optimism: a French translation of the *Exemplary Stories* came out in 1615 and pirate editions of the Spanish version were beginning to appear; in January Guillén de Castro had adapted *The Call of Blood* for the Madrid stage, the latest of a series of theatrical versions of Cervantes' stories. A ballet based on *Don Quixote,* the first of scores of musical compositions the book would engender, had been a success in Paris in 1614. Cervantes was a highly desirable property.

So, while Cuesta was rushing the printing of Part II of *Don Quixote,* the plays were hurriedly being set in cheap type in the nearby shop of the widow of Alonso Martín de Balboa. It was the plays that won the race to the bookstalls. There, for the most part, they remained.

A powerful protective impulse seizes Cervantists when they contemplate their hero's interludes. These one-act marvels are so much more *successful* than the full-length plays (in a purely literary sense; it was years before any of them were staged). The explanation is partly formal. The Cervantes whose mind's eyes crossed under the strain of his poetic responsibility could relax in the freedom of prose and blank-verse interludes. These short, sharp glances at life did not require the tightly orchestrated plotting that forever escaped him in the longer plays. Dramatic conflict did not have to be built up in them; it is instantaneous by the mere juxaposition of characters. Moreover, by a tradition so firm that it had become law, interludes dealt with the commonalty—scheming whores, ex-soldiers, starveling students, grimy sacristans—with whom he felt comfortable, whereas plays had to do with personages of suitably Aristotelian gravity and stature, in whose presence he was always ill at ease, never having understood how rank could overshadow even the smallest virtue.

At first reading, the interludes[7] seem hardly more than elaborate epigrams jabbing at standard human vices—hypocrisy, vanity, credulousness, social conformism, prejudice. But their apparent simplicity is deceptive. In them Cervantes was teaching the Lopean stage the same lesson *Don Quixote* was giving Spain's novelists about the unity of the creative mystery in life and art. The characters in the interludes are Quixotes in miniature, Sanchos drawn to scale, all playing the same game of hide-and-seek with truth. The space each personage inhabits is his own, but where do the edges lie? Each is, but not quite, a representative of a social reality. Each is—almost—absurd, for Cervantes was one of the very few artists the world has known who made absurdity a positive value, the saving humanity of a social statistic. Thus the Faithful Sentinel is a typically scarecrow figure, the ex-soldier spending boasts for lack of cash, but he is also a man struggling to maintain his self-esteem as the loser he knows all along he will be. The hardheaded whore Cristina in *The Make-Believe Basque* is tricked by her own greediness, but she defies both theatrical and social custom by turning out to be a good egg after all. No one in these interludes is punished for his follies, no one loses face; "a joke's not funny if it makes a person look contemptible," says Solorzano in *The Make-Believe Basque.*

An effect of receding mirrors blurring the nature of reality gives these tiny comedies of manners a feeling of enormous scope. First there is, of course, the pretended reality of the situation in tension with the accepted, even emphasized, convention that these are actors playing roles. When tricks are played on the personages, as they are in most of the interludes, the audience participates in a double illusion: its "knowledge" of what is "really" happening and of the victims' "deception."

The subjects themselves are part of the illusionism. Many are simply comic reworkings of serious stories: *The Jealous Old Man* is clearly a companion to *The Jealous Extremaduran; The Widowed Ruffian* is a baby brother of *Rinconete and Cortadillo; Choosing a Councilman in Daganzo* brings us the same rusty-breeched rustics met with in *Pedro de Urdemales;* Chanfalla in *The Wonder Show* is kin to the Master Peter of *Don Quixote,* here free to triumph over reality without the knight's interference. Again we see how fascinated Cervantes was by the game of reshuffling forms, ideas, situations into new orders to reveal new glintings of ambiguous truths.

Some of the playlets are almost surrealistic. In *The Jealous Old Man,* Lorenza complains to her neighbor Hortigosa that her aged, jealous husband keeps her incommunicado; she wishes he were dead despite his gifts, his jewels and money. Hortigosa proposes a scheme for introducing a lover into Lorenza's room under the very nose of her husband, Cañizares. Lorenza and her equally exasperated niece Cristina discuss the problem:

"And honor, niece?"
"And delight, aunt?"
"And if we are found out?"
"And if we are never found out?"

A trick involving a leather hanging allows a lover to slip into Lorenza's bedroom. So thoroughly gulled is Cañizares that he will believe what he thinks he sees—the figures in the hanging—even while his wife tells him what is actually happening. Lorenza then accuses him of representing lies as realities, while she clearly plans to continue converting reality into a lie.

The Wonder Show is even more hallucinatory, as befits an examination of the power of poetry to evoke what is not "really" there. Chanfalla the showman brings to town a "charity" spectacle devised by a mythical Tontonelo el Sabio, the Learned Fool, who is famous for having a beard that falls to his waist. ("For the most part," observes Mayor Benito Repollo, "people with long beards know everything.") He warns the local notables invited to a free trial performance that unless they are legitimately born and pure of blood his tableaux will be invisible to them. He has really nothing to show but a bare stage, but the townspeoples' anxiety to fulfill his conditions makes them imagine they are actually seeing what the narrator tells them is happening. Only the governor, who preens himself on being "a bit of a poet," admits to himself that he sees nothing, but he pretends to "for my wretched little honor."

A detachment of the king's cavalry arrives demanding billets. The mayor assumes they are part of the show, envoys from the Learned Fool (the dig at King Philip III is obvious), and shoos them away. When the quartermaster, seeing nothing, asks what all the dancing is about, he is accused of being *ex illis;* "he's one of them (a Jew)," shouts the notary; "he's one of them, one of them," shouts the governor, not to be outdone. In the ensuing free-for-all, Chanfalla drops the curtain, burbling of "our victory in this battle. . . ." Victory? Over whom? Over the blindly fatuous, to be sure, over hypocrisy and conceit. But these are merely the infantry of illusion. This was a battle won for poetic truth.

In *The Salamanca Cave* even the sleight of hand is illusory: the denouement turns on a pretense of black magic to trick a fatuous husband. *The Widowed Ruffian* is an inversion of reality in which a pimp and his gang spout Latin phrases, make casual allusions to Greek mythology and generally—almost persuasively—conduct themselves like solid, respectable burghers. Is this socially real? And how real is social reality?

Cervantes is an awesome figure to contemplate at this point in his life. Never had this magnificent fighter waged such a campaign. One feels that he was beating back death by main force, overwhelming disease with a tide of ideas, plots, incidents, plans, confusing time itself in his web of subtleties. Mysterious reserves of vital energy swept up through him and were dissipated like the wanton scattering of erupting lava, as though he thought he were going to live forever, or not survive another month. In October 1615 he wrote the prologue to Part II informing his readers to "expect the *Persiles,* which I am now completing, and the Second Part of *La Galatea.*" His dedication of the book to Lemos, dated October 30, seems serenely confident:

When, some days ago, I sent Your Excellency my plays, printed instead of being performed, I said if I remember rightly that Don Quixote was about to put on his spurs to go and kiss Your Excellency's hands; and I can now say that he has put them on and is on his way, and if he arrives I believe I will have done Your Excellency some service, for I am being pressed from every side to send him and thus get rid of the loathing and nausea caused by another Don Quixote who, disguised under the name of Part II, has been wandering about the world.

Cervantes comforts himself that "I have the great Count of Lemos in Naples who, without so many collegiate titles and rectorships, supports, protects and favors me beyond anything I could desire." He promises his patron *The Labors of Persiles and Sigismunda,* "a book which I will complete within four months, *Deo volente,* and which will either be the worst or the best written in our language, at any rate among those designed for entertainment. Indeed, I repent having said 'the worst,' for according to my friends' opinion it will certainly be extremely good."

In the late summer or early fall of 1615, Cervantes, Doña Catalina and their servant María de Ugena—Constanza had by now set up on her own —moved to another house at the corner of the Calle de León and the Calle de Francos, the present Calle de Cervantes, only a few steps away from where Lope de Vega would die. It was a newly rebuilt house owned by royal scribe Gabriel Martínez, a pious, kindly man who lived on the second floor with his wife, four children and servant. The quarters occupied by the Cervantes family were on the ground floor, crowded to one side of a central staircase to make room for Martínez's office. It was not a luxurious place—vestibule, large main room with a sleeping alcove and a kitchen backing on a patio and an abandoned stable. But it was an improvement on the "humble cottage." The three windows of the main room looked directly out on the actors' mentidero. The family was installed there by mid-November, when Part II of *Don Quixote* went on sale in Madrid at 292 maravedis.

] 35 [

Magnificat

April 2, 1616. Through the bolted shutters of the three windows the sound of theatrical voices drifts on shafts of sunlight from the Calle de León and splashes against the drone of prayers inside the darkened room. Cervantes stands shakily in the center of a group of figures in brown Franciscan robes. In his right hand he holds a white candle; the cord and habit of the Tertiary Order of St. Francis are in his left hand, "which he could not move," specifies the order's chronicler, "because of his wound at Lepanto."

"When they came to dress him in the habit," the account details, "he got as far as the cassock, of serge, yoked and hooded, with a cord that hung to his knees, for the breeches would not cover him. . . ."[1]

His profession in the order might almost be considered a post-climax to the now completed *Persiles*, as though Periandro-Cervantes had stepped out of the half life of literature to affirm his transience through the physical world and his readiness for the permanency of the next. In his ear might be the distant, prophetic voice of Aurelio observing in Algiers that

> Whether my life is much or little
> is unimportant; only he who dies holy
> can say his life was long,
> and he who dies evil, a measureless death. . . .[2]

The Congregation of Slaves was too secular now to suit his needs. Not that Cervantes had abandoned it; he was past questioning his old, soul-deep ties to the Trinitarians. There may have been mornings missed now, but whenever he could do so, it was to the convent of the Discalced Trinitarian nuns, a stone's throw from his doorstep, that he walked, leaning increasingly heavily on Catalina's arm, to hear mass. The Congregation, however, had abandoned him. So fashionable had the presence of so many leading artists made it that the membership was soon swollen by an influx of aristocrats—Lerma himself was a brother—with a resultant worldliness in its religious observances. In 1615 the monks had let it be known that such luxury of appointments, such glitter of ornament in the processions, so gorgeous a display of gold lace and jeweled sword hilts were unbecoming a redemptionist order consecrated to poverty and humility. There was to be no more poetry in their festivals, they decreed; lavish processions were forbidden. Since the poets were unwilling to stop versifying, and since ostentation was the nobles' chief way of asserting *their* priority, the governing junta rebelled. The brotherhood was placed under the patronage of the Brothers Minor of the Holy Spirit, whose monastery stood on the present site of the Cortes.

Such business was unfitting a man with his "foot in the stirrup." Cervantes had few illusions about his chances of survival. On March 26, in a hand still surprisingly firm, he wrote his farewell letter to Sandoval:

Most Illustrious Lord,

I received your Most Illustrious Lordship's letter a few days ago and with it new favors. If there were a remedy for the illness I complain of, the repeated marks of favor and support your Illustrious Person has dispensed to me were sufficient to obtain it. But it has lately so increased its hold that I think it will be the end of me, though it be without my consent. May our Lord God preserve you, executor of such Holy works, that you may enjoy the fruits thereof there in His Holy glory, as is the wish of your humble servant, who kisses your very Magnificent hands. At Madrid, the twenty-sixth of March of the year one thousand six hundred sixteen.

Most Illustrious Lord

Miguel de Cervantes Saavedra

Not that he had lost contact with the life literally outside his door. Although his work and his rapidly declining health largely confined him to his home that winter and spring, he was able to take part in the actors' mentidero from his window. Friends came to see him and hear part of his *Persiles*. Tertiary brothers, led by his landlord's son Francisco Martínez, the chaplain of the Trinitarian nuns, came to pray with him and to pump up his faith in the eternal life.

The Labors of Persiles and Sigismunda had been finished in early March. To anyone knowing Cervantes' history, the *Persiles* is a terrifying book to read. It is a condensed record of man's struggle to achieve, to live, to accede to divinity. Death hangs over it, black wings twitching impatiently. "Death is deaf," Quixote had said, "and when it calls at the doors of our lives, it is always in a rush, and it will not be stayed by prayers nor by force. . . ."[3] Yet what a joyous turbulence there is in this book, what a tidal overflowing of ideas, characters, events, aspirations! Too many: it is an exhausting book to read, a feast more for gluttons than for gourmets. But we feel in it, we know the excruciating tension of Cervantes' will to complete it. This, he thought, not the *Quixote,* was to be his monument. And his contemporaries agreed with him.

He had lived up to the promises he had made to himself in the prison in Seville, had reshaped his life. His depleted body was not, after all, equal to the contest with that black angel; the Moon Knight, death's messenger, was to triumph again. Yet, like Don Quixote, Cervantes would concede his opponent's strength, but not his right. Death had no right over him!

Miguel de Unamuno once declared that he found the notion of an insubstantial immortality unsatisfying, that when he died he wanted to present himself in Paradise in recognizable form, wearing his hat and gloves. Miguel de Cervantes was even more demanding. He wanted to leave a chip of himself behind him, alive and imperishable. The *Quixote,* he felt, would not serve the purpose. It had been an experiment, flawed by the very premise of its originality: its attachment to real experience. It had not been written in full conformity with the canons of advanced criticism and it was these, in the long run, that would win Cervantes acceptance by the epic poets he had courted since his boyhood in Madrid.

He certainly saw *The Labors of Persiles and Sigismunda* as a rectification of the *Quixote.* In creating a "true harmony" between poetic truth and the "lie" of verisimilitude,[4] it would affirm that, although "historical" reality made up the pattern of a novel, poetic reality made its substance. He had long ago laid down the rules it was to follow, in the discourse by the canon of Toledo:

> The perfect chivalric romance would offer a broad field in which the author could roam, a variety of unusual events and characters exemplifying changes in fortune patterned in a pendular tragic-happy, comic-marvelous rhythm; the hero was to be exemplary, the subject matter lofty and touching on all the arts and sciences, the style ingenious, varied, pleasing, unified, the whole designed to instruct and delight.

Cervantes' model, as recommended by Pinciano, was a work of irreproachable intellectual respectability, the prose novel by the Byzantine writer Heliodorus called *An Ethiopian History of the Loves of Theagenes and Chariklea,* often referred to simply as the *Aethiopica.*

The book was immensely admired by serious poets everywhere in

Europe. Tasso based part of his *Jerusalem Liberated* on it. To intellectuals of the late sixteenth and early seventeenth centuries, it embodied
the grandeur of true epic writing. To anyone conditioned to today's more
concentrated structures, the book is a cyclonic bore, but in Cervantes'
time it was considered a suspenseful, exciting, splendidly textured example of how to write a great Aristotelian poem. Here was a book that
seemed, if not to resolve, at least to point the way to that ideal synthesis
which the poets of the late Renaissance had been debating for over a generation. Then too, although in their ignorance of history they could not
have confirmed it, they may instinctively have felt a vague parallelism between the world of Heliodorus and their own.

Heliodorus was a Greek born in Syria who may or may not have lived
in the third century A.D., may or may not have been bishop of Tricea, in
Thessaly. Like Cervantes, he lived in a time of profound change, when
the old chains of causality, the old established forms were cracking.
Heliodorus may have been as sensitive to the signs of Rome's decay as
Cervantes was to Spain's, as Tasso was to the erosion of the High Renaissance. Increasingly, both eras seemed to see man being abandoned to the
whims of fortune, seemed to lose the pattern of events. Things happened
without reference to character or morality; the interrelationships between
the inner and outer worlds of human existence which only a few years before had seemed so vital were disrupted. There is even an oblique comparison to be argued between the revolutionary impact of third-century
Christianity on Roman civilization and the struggle of the Reform to rev-
olutionize Tridentine Europe. At such times, artists felt a responsibility to
demonstrate a moral order, to prove that, despite appearances, there were
divinities shaping man's ends.

Heliodorus' technique for achieving his mission was surprisingly like
the one the Jesuits would later use to win souls for Rome: to shock minds
awake and thus open them to the acceptance of a moral truth. His vehicle was what Pinciano endorsed as the perfect Aristotelian formula for a
tragic plot: complication so snarled that it seems impossible to untangle
until, when it is at its tightest, the process of unraveling begins, moving
toward a final paroxysm of catastrophe leading to relaxation and recognition—that is, the "true" nature of the personages and events portrayed.
The devices used were deliberately obscurantist: delayed exposition, a beginning *in medias res,* fragmentation of the story through the interweav-
ing of more or less relevant episodes and subplots, each relatively simple
but made complex by their sheer number and, often, their provisional
irrelevance to the main story line.

The *Aethiopica* is full of rhetorical embellishments, psychological solil-
oquies, tirades against the whims of chance, descriptions of works of art,
cities, natural phenomena and others not so natural; there are learned

digressions into religion and science, all designed to add color to the story while retarding and confusing the plot. Above all, Heliodorus used—abused—*admiratio,* astonishment, wonder, surprise, awe through representation of the marvelous and the exceptional. He made only passing acknowledgment of realism or naturalism. Everything important is larger than life, a Colossus of Rhodes guaranteed on every page.

This was the paragon Cervantes chose to improve on. He made no secret of his model; on the contrary, he advertised it, a little nervously, as a warning of his intentions. The *Persiles,* he had announced in his prologue to the *Exemplary Stories,* was to be "a book which dares to compete with Heliodorus, although its daring may bring it out holding its head in its hands."

Critical acclaim of the *Persiles* was virtually unanimous. The book would go through nine printings within a year, would be available in all the major Western European languages within less than a decade. Cervantes was never to savor fully this vindication of his self-esteem; the book was published posthumously. But, like all such works, it was well known among the literary elite before its publication. Cervantes' last months of life were months of triumph.

Probably Part II of the *Quixote* had been a sort of dress rehearsal for the *Persiles.* Although, in writing it, Cervantes was largely a prisoner of Part I, the later book's influence is evident, as we have seen, in the multiplication in Part II of the marvelous, the bizarre, in the lift of its rhetorical tone and in its final accent on salvation and redemption. Just when Cervantes read the *Aethiopica* is not known—the book had existed in Spanish since 1554, but the edition he probably used was the superior translation published in 1587—but we may not be far off in connecting it with Quixote's misadventure in the cave of Montesinos. In any case, his debt to it in the *Persiles* can be followed almost chapter by chapter, despite the influence of other sources, notably a second Byzantine novel, *The Loves of Clitophon and Leucippe* by Achilles Tatius Alexandrinus. The character of Antonio, the "barbaric" Spaniard in the *Persiles,* is based on that of the "barbaric" Greek Knemon in the *Aethiopica;* the swamp fire in Heliodorus' book became the blaze on the barbarians' island in Cervantes'; the games at the court of the Spaniard's King Polycarpus parallel those in Book IV of the *Theagenes.* On and on the echoes rumble.

The book's central plot line is simple enough. Persiles and Sigismunda are royal lovers who have sinned in thought but not in deed. Fleeing from their mysterious Northern lands as brother and sister under the assumed names of Periandro and Auristela, they embark on a pilgrimage to Rome. Rather like diners without appetite at a Gargantuan smorgasbord, they filter through tribulations, trials, reparations, narrow escapes, injuries, perfidies, bewitchments, poisonings, shipwrecks, attempted and successful seductions, murders, suicides until they reach the Holy City with the band of pilgrims they have gathered along the way. There, after some last-minute backing and filling, all lovers are united, all enmities expunged in preparation for what one is confident will be lives of unflinching rectitude.

Critic Alban Forcione has called the book "a quest romance in which the heroes must abandon an imperfect society, journey through strange worlds full of menacing forces and suffer numerous trials and struggles before reaching their destination," where "their sufferings are rewarded with superior wisdom and they can return to elevate their society to the state of perfection which they themselves embody."[5] It can also be described as Cervantes' grail story, *Tristan and Isolde* with a happy ending, the perfect romance of chivalry and Cervantes' *Divine Comedy* with the action confined to this world. Joaquín Casalduero has seen in it, among other things, an elaborate allegory on the Fall and the Redemption. There is general agreement that it represents a cycle of bondage and liberation—Cervantes' old theme—on which the main plot and most of the subepisodes are hung. At times the allusion to bondage is direct: Taurisa says she was "thrown into the light of the world," that she had "thought I would freely enjoy the sunlight in this life, but my thoughts deceived me, for I see myself about to be sold into slavery."[6] The students pretending to be former Algerian captives escape genuine captivity in a Spanish jail only through Periandro's intercession. Bartolomé the baggage boy is seduced by the dissolute Luisa into the free life of the pícaro, and is saved by Periandro from hanging in Rome. Transgression, repentance, redemption, salvation—the movement is fugal, fragmented but unified.

Again, as in the *Exemplary Stories,* in the *Quixote,* Cervantes here is to be found working at the outer limits of the known literary world, innovating, exploring, finding ingenious solutions to the enigma of how to reconcile variety and unity. He is daring not merely in the number and disposition of his digressions, but in their length and, often, their studied irrelevance to the main line of action. His plotting is hair-raising: around the central strand is woven a thick cable of plot and incident, all of it on a gigantic scale, from the barbarian's outsize arrow on the opening pages to the correspondingly grand magnanimity of Maximiliano at the close and, throughout, the protagonists' awesomely monumental virtue. All of this is kept under perfect control, united by a web of inner relationships; Bartolomé's escapade with Luisa, for example, is meant to point up the heroes' immunity to temptation.

Cervantes knew he was pushing his technique to its limits, at times coming close to shattering the work's coherence. But the Cervantes who could never bear to waste a good line or a good idea again took his cue from Pinciano, who had confirmed in Aristotle's name the importance of pleasure—variety—in poetry. "Tell your story," Periandro tells the Pole, "with all the details you please to use, for often the inclusion of them will heighten the story's gravity."[7]

Intermingled with the narrative are mini-treatises in support of Tridentine Catholicism, on geography, astronomy and other such recondite matters. Cervantes had prepared himself carefully to document factually the absurdities of his story. Although it was then popular in the Latin world to think vaguely of the North as a mysterious, primal region of perpetual mists, of ice and monsters and witchcraft—"the latitudes," Riley observes, "of the poetically possible"[8]—the geography in the *Persiles* conforms closely to existing maps and geographies. Cervantes may have had the Venetian Niccolò Zeno's 1380 map of the Northern seas before him, may even have heard of Willem Barents' grueling expeditions into the Arctic Circle, details of which were published in Amsterdam in 1598. Traces are visible of the work of Olaus Magnus, Pedro de Mexía, the Inca Garcilaso and others. Much of Cervantes' pseudo-science came from Antonio de Torquemada's 1570 *Jardín de flores curiosas* (as, for example, the episode of the witch assuming a wolf's form in Book I, Chapter 3).

For all its sophistication, Cervantes' science occasionally reveals that the poetic truth he endorsed in fiction extended to the physical world as well. In Book III, Bartolomé finds it hard to accept that the sun, "though it looks no larger than a shield," is many times larger than the earth and that despite its size, "people say it is so light that in twenty-four hours it travels more than three hundred thousand leagues. The truth is that I don't really believe any of it, but so many learned men say it that, although it strains my understanding, I do believe it." To this calculatedly skeptical presentation of the no longer new Copernican-Galilean cosmology Periandro objects an authoritative orthodoxy: "I want you to understand that it is an infallible truth that the Earth is the center of the heavens. . . ."[9] Cervantes the Franciscan Tertiary clearly had decided, like Dostoyevsky's Stavrogin, that "reason and science have always performed, and still perform, only an auxiliary function in the life of peoples, and it will be like that till the end of time."[10] To Cervantes, it is the dream that is important, the poetic marrow of existence. Periandro dreams a marvelous vision of beauty and light, of luscious fruits and emerald fields through which wind processions of lovely women. The vision vanishes when he awakes. "Were you asleep, then, my lord Periandro?" Constanza asks. "Yes," he replies, to the obvious annoyance of the rationalist Mauricio, "because all my treasures are in dreams."

Some of Cervantes' best narrative writing is lavished on the *Persiles*, although much of it is curiously stagy in the Cervantine manner. When Periandro suddenly breaks off a soliloquy,[11] fearful that he has been over-

heard, he does what can only be imagined as a double take. Set speeches
are more important than dialogue. Scenes are painstakingly set, but to the
casual reader they function as scenes, tied to the main plot by literary
rather than active connections. This seeming haphazardness, faithful to
the Byzantine concept of accidental events, enormously heightens the feeling that the *Persiles* is a dream floating on a misty sea of reality. The impression is reinforced by the beauty of such sequences as that in which
Ricla the barbarian and Antonio the Spaniard discover each other—her
initial fright and astonishment, her joyousness when she touches him, her
gift of bread and water. "She makes him a fortress against the hostility
around him," Casalduero has noted, for Ricla is a "serpentless Eve," innocent and good.[12]

Flashes of the old Cervantine mordancy are occasionally seen. In the
boat-race allegory,[13] Interest outstrips Love, is in turn overtaken by Diligence, but it is Luck that wins the race. There is self-mockery in his por-
trayal of himself as a pilgrim collecting aphorisms from other pilgrims
near Rome in a volume like some kind of religious guest book. Why such
a book? "I, gentlemen, am a curious man," he explains.

> Mars dominates half my soul and Mercury the other half; I gave a few
> years to the art of war and others, the most mature, to that of letters;
> in those of war I earned a reasonably good reputation and in those of
> letters I have won some little esteem; I have published a number of
> books which the ignorant have not condemned as bad nor the wise
> failed to consider good. Since necessity, as they say, is the mother of in-
> vention, my wit, which has something of the fantastic and inventive in
> it, has devised something a bit new and strange, and that is that I want
> to bring out a book at someone else's cost, the work on which, as I say,
> will be someone else's and the profit mine.[14]

Thematically, the *Persiles* is a summing up of the philosophic ideas,
Platonic, Augustinian, Pauline and the rest, expressed in his earlier works
—so much so that the novel has, perhaps too broadly, been described as a
summary of Cervantes' life. Certainly it is a summary of his work. The
note of confinement, physical in the captivity stories, more subtly spiritual
and social in the *Exemplary Stories*, imaginative in the *Quixote*, here becomes a great organ chord of release and redemption. Man, bound to
God by chains of guilt, threatened at every turn with an unrepentant
death, constantly confined and as constantly liberated by a loving Creator, is brought by his own perseverance into the bony bosom of a purified,
ascetic Church. In Auristela, Dulcinea comes hazily into our field of vision although she never comes as alive as Quixote's invisible lady. Ricla is
the final reincarnation of Zoraida, Zahara and all the other crypto-Chris-

tian barbarian women of the earlier tales. The almost reluctant mysticism infiltrating Cervantes' later works, so fundamental to the *Persiles,* is encapsulated in the hermit Soldino's praise of his rocky retreat as a place where "I am my own master; here I bear my soul in the palm of my hand, and here I direct my thoughts and my desires directly to heaven. . . ."[15]

In modern eyes, the book fails—splendidly, but it fails. While it is no doubt useful to remind ourselves, as modern critics do, of the lofty daring of Cervantes' intentions in the *Persiles,* it must also be borne in mind that the intentions of the author of an unsuccessful work of art provide mitigation, not justification, of his failure. Noting, too, that criticism is "now wary of modern preconceptions of what constitutes literary quality"[16] is judicious, and a touch indulgent, more historically than artistically relevant; a work of art must pass the final test of time, as the *Quixote* does, whatever its immediate reception. The choir of the cathedral of Beauvais, in France, might have been the finest ever built had it not collapsed forty-seven years after its construction.

The *Persiles* has always haunted Cervantes' admirers. Despite its undeniable virtues, the book is a bore, so much so that efforts have even been made to prove it was really an early work hauled out of a chest, dusted and aired by a Cervantes sliding into senility. The argument can be dismissed, but the problem remains: how could the man who wrote *Don Quixote* and the *Exemplary Stories* have then produced this literary barrage balloon? It has all the baroque theatricality of Tintoretto's paintings, yet we continue to look at Tintorettos and we do not read the *Persiles.* It has the cool, colored grace, the mystical serenity we find in El Greco's canvases, but . . .

For all its marvels and shocks, clashes and alarums, the *Persiles* is a strangely placid book compared to *Don Quixote;* to read them in sequence is like visiting a cemetery after the war is over. The inner conflict that made the *Quixote* exciting is gone, replaced in the *Persiles* by an elaborate clockwork mechanism. In breaking the dynamic pattern of the *Quixote,* in rooting its center of gravity in a poetical ideal instead of the historically possible, Cervantes regresses, so to speak, to a picaresque universe in which all things are preordained. With no real inner conflict to animate it, the *Persiles* is emotionally feeble, a piece of science fiction in which events, phenomena are more striking than the characters. All its whirlwind movement does not, paradoxically, save the *Persiles* from being a static, sluggish book. The personages are wooden, rolled out on schedule to strike the hours. Auristela-Sigismunda drifts erotically through the book exciting desire in the men she meets while remaining as chaste as a holy image. It is hard to think of Periandro-Persiles without recalling comedienne Anna Russell's description of Siegfried as "very big, very strong, very stupid." If there is any modern interest in him at all, it derives from the faint aura of homosexuality he exudes (at one point he is called "this Ganymede"), a suggestion Cervantes certainly had not meant to make. At that, the hero merely runs true to the sexual neutrality of most epic heroes. Cervantes, one believes, did not love the population of the *Persiles*.

This passionless mannerism makes the *Persiles* unsympathetic. What makes it nearly unreadable is precisely that variety of which Cervantes was so proud. The novel is as overstuffed as a Victorian parlor in which no single item is distinguishable. There are too many events, too many thoughts, too many allusions, symbols, references. More than any other of Cervantes' works, it is to blame for the reputation he has been given for indecisiveness, an unwillingness to make final decisions. Although Cervantes' life, especially the last twenty years of it, hardly supports the charge, a reader of the *Persiles* cannot help being impatient with the man's compulsion to get it all in, to satisfy every critic, reconcile every rule.

All "big" writers dream of writing the definitive novel. Most of them are too wise to attempt it; they know that, like a fighting bull, a story with too much weight on its bones tires fast. In the *Persiles*, Cervantes deliberately abandoned his own rule of claiming credit "not for what I have written but for what I left out." Ignored is the warning by Master Peter the puppeteer to his young narrator in *Don Quixote* not to "go in for flourishes. . . . Go on with your plainsong and don't wander off into counterpoint, for that's the way the strings are broken."[17]

Can we, however, really blame Cervantes for the prolixity he himself had so often condemned? This old man who had undertaken a project that would have frightened most of his juniors was not so much writing a book as fighting a battle, his last battle, for the recognition and acclaim he felt he deserved—for what he undoubtedly thought of as simple justice. He was fighting, what's more, not on his own turf, but on the uncongenial terrain dictated by Heliodorus and his advance man Pinciano. It was like charging with a hood over his head. The wonder is that Cervantes came as close to succeeding as he did. For, after all, he did win the fight as far as his contemporaries were concerned.

Defensively perhaps, Cervantists like to compare the *Persiles* with Shakespeare's late plays. In *The Tempest, A Winter's Tale, Cymbeline*, the Briton is seen as moving in the same Northern mists which enshroud the Spaniard. Shakespeare had also read and been influenced by the Byzantine novelists. In the plays, as in the *Persiles*, noted Astrana Marín, "the characters wander with no fixed destination, inclined to lose themselves, to dissolve. . . . Nothing is more spiritual, finer and more delicate, more mysterious. The quiet, concentrated happiness, the suave, refined

anguish. . . . Memories of their authors' lives are mingled with phantas-
magorical visions. . . . The styles shed all superfluous adornment. Images
are scarcer and glow fire-red. . . . All is drenched in a stern asceticism
. . . the words more just and precise, the thought deeper and loftier . . .
(as in) the last quartets of Beethoven."[18]

The similarities are unquestionably there. So are the differences, chief
among them the fact that Shakespeare, working in a more condensed medium, avoided—had to avoid—the tangle of minutiae which ensnared
Cervantes. Another contrast moves us more, however: Shakespeare, successful, admired, financially comfortable, soaked his last plays in misan-
thropy; they are funerary monuments of gloom and despair. Cervantes,
living on charity, still struggling to assure his rightful ranking, made the
Persiles into a Magnificat, a great cantata to the joyous complexity of life,
a marvelous anticipation of redemption.

Nothing in his life more clearly illuminates the epical splendor of Cervantes' spirit than the end of it. The *Persiles*, for all its faults, is the record of that climax.

For a brief time, Cervantes' family and friends may have thought he
could defer the irreversible moment, if only for a little while. Shortly
after he wrote to Sandoval his condition seemed to improve. The doctor
attending him recommended that he be moved to Esquivias for a change
of air. The spring was hot and dry after a dry winter, and people walked
with their faces muffled against the fetid dust of the Madrid streets. Good
wine, the physician urged, and good food might cure what he had
vaguely diagnosed as "dropsy," a condition about which he knew nothing
whatever and so felt unqualified to treat.

How seriously Cervantes took this is moot. Assuming the Franciscan
habit may have seemed more reassuring to him than his physician's
forced optimism. But on April 4 or 5, the Monday or Tuesday of Easter
week, he dutifully rode the six leagues to Esquivias. Probably nothing he
did would have saved him, but of all the possibilities, this trip was the
most damaging. The fatigue of the journey, heaps of spice-laden country
sausage, above all the refreshing tankards of cool, white Esquivian wine,
destroyed him. Within a week he was back in Madrid, more dead than
alive.

Presumably he made a will, drawn up by landlord Martínez, but it has
since been lost with all the rest of the notary's papers. On April 18 his
condition caused such alarm that he was given extreme unction by priest
Francisco López, who had performed the same service for his sisters. Yet,
amazingly, on the following day, a Tuesday, he wrote the gallant dedication of the *Persiles* to Lemos:

I would have preferred that those old couplets, famous in their day,
which began

"With my foot already in the stirrup"
were not so apt in this my letter, for I can begin with almost the same
lines, saying

> With my foot already in the stirrup
> and with the anguish of death upon me,
> great lord, I write thee this. . . .

Yesterday they gave me extreme unction, and today I am writing
this; time is short, anguish grows, hope dwindles, yet I live on the
desire I have to live and I would not wish to bring it to a close until I
kiss Your Excellency's feet; for perhaps the pleasure of seeing Your Excellency well in Spain would be so great that it might restore me to life.
But if it is decreed that I must lose it, let heaven's will be done; at least
I would have Your Excellency know my desire and that you had in me
a servant so faithful that he wished to show his devotion even beyond
death. Nevertheless, as though in prophecy, I am happy at Your Excellency's arrival, I rejoice at seeing admiring fingers pointed at you,[19]
and I am doubly glad that my hopes, spread by the fame of Your Excellency's kindness, have been realized.

Some relics and presumptions of *Weeks in the Garden* and of *The
Famous Bernardo* remain in my mind. If by luck, by my very good luck
—indeed, this would be more miracle than luck—heaven should grant
me life, you shall see them, and with them the end of *La Galatea,* of
which I know Your Excellency is fond. And with this, and my continuing good wishes, may God preserve Your Excellency as He may ordain.
At Madrid, the nineteenth of April, one thousand six hundred sixteen.

Your Excellency's servant,

Miguel de Cervantes.

That day, or on Wednesday at the latest, he drafted the prologue, the
last in his lifelong series of intimate confidences to his "dearest reader." It
tells of his return with two friends from Esquivias. As they neared
Madrid, Cervantes recounts, a student gray with road dust and struggling
vainly to keep his Walloon collar straight came racing after them. On
learning that one of the riders was Cervantes, he leaped to the ground,
scattering his saddle pad and portmanteau in his eagerness, and seized the
writer's crippled hand, exclaiming:

"It is, it is! This is the healthy cripple, the most famous of them all,
the delight of the Muses!"

The acknowledgment is edged with resentment that he was no more
than the jester of the gods. "This," Cervantes comments, "is an error into
which many ignorant admirers have fallen." Nevertheless, they embraced
courteously—"the gesture achieved the total perdition of that collar"—

and rode slowly on together. The talk turns to Cervantes' illness and, with a student's innocent arrogance, the young man "at once dashed all my hopes," saying:

"Dropsy is your illness, and not all the water in the ocean sea will cure it however greedily it's drunk. Your Worship, Señor Cervantes, must cut down on your wine-bibbing, don't forget to eat and with this you'll recover without any other medicine whatsoever."

"Many have told me this," I replied, "but it is as impossible for me not to drink my fill as though I had been born for no other purpose. My life is ending, and by the tempo of my pulse beats, I estimate they will end their race this Sunday at the latest, and mine with them. Your Worship has met me too late, for I've no time left in which to show my appreciation of the good will Your Worship has manifested toward me."

At the foot of the Toledo bridge they separated. Cervantes and his young admirer embrace once more, the student spurs his donkey and is gone, "leaving me as ill-humored as he was gallant on his donkey who had given my pen so fine an occasion to write a gracious passage."

But times change. The day will come, perhaps, when, knotting up this broken thread, it will say what I cannot say here and what I know should have been said. Farewell sprightliness, farewell wit, farewell merry friends, for I am dying and hope soon to see you happy in the other life.

Sometime that night he lapsed into a diabetic coma. On Saturday, April 23 by the new calendar,[20] he died, probably without ever regaining consciousness. On the same date, but ten days earlier because of the difference in their calendars, William Shakespeare, in his time his only peer, had died in England.

No account remains to us of Cervantes' funeral. As a Franciscan Tertiary, he would have been carried in his coarse brown habit, face uncovered to the sky, on the brothers' shoulders to his grave in the Trinitarian convent. It can be supposed that most of the Tertiary brothers and the Slaves of the Most Holy Sacrament fulfilled their duty and attended the ceremony. No stone or cross was set to mark the burial place.[21] Not one of the famous poets among his congregational brothers contributed an epitaph for publication with the *Persiles*, as custom invited them to do. The two poems included were written by obscure friends, Fernando de Lodeña and a poet-priest, Luis Francisco Calderón.

Bookseller Juan de Villarroël bought the privilege for the *Persiles* from

Doña Catalina de Cervantes for an unknown sum in September 1616. The book, printed by Cuesta, went on sale in January 1617 and was so well received that its hitherto obscure publisher became, virtually over-night, a leader in his trade. When Doña Catalina died in 1626, Villarroël still owed her four hundred reales on the sale price.

Notes

There are no few facts for Cervantes experts in this book. Strenuous efforts were made to ensure its accuracy. As many of the fruits of recent research and critical comment are included as can conveniently be stuffed into a single volume. But the book was not written with the scholars in mind. It is aimed at general readers, both those who know Cervantes' works and those others who, it is hoped, will be enticed by it into reading them. The facts in it were all taken from printed sources; while random discoveries of original material are occasionally being made, no significant concentration of Cervantine documentation, as far as the author knows, has yet come to light which has not already been printed in one or another form. When, at some future date, the still unsifted matter in official Spanish archives is classified, important new data about Cervantes' life will certainly be uncovered. Until then, Luis Astrana Marín's seven-volume *Vida ejemplar y heroica de Miguel de Cervantes Saavedra* will probably remain the most exhaustive summary of what is known on the subject. While that monumental compilation is inaccessible to the general reader, and the judgments it advances are often unsatisfying to those interested in an unsentimental, if affectionate, portrait of its hero, it is nevertheless the quarry from which all subsequent biographies must be mined. A glance at the notes that follow will confirm this book's indebtedness to it.

For convenience, abbreviations are used to designate works frequently referred to. Aside from Astrana Marín's *Life* (AM in the notes), these are all works by Cervantes:

DQ: *Don Quixote*
ES: *Exemplary Stories*
PS: *The Labors of Persiles and Sigismunda*
VP: *Voyage to Parnassus*
8 plus 8:   *Eight Plays and Eight Interludes*

The Spanish texts of all quotations from Cervantes' works translated for this book were taken from the 1967 Madrid edition of the *Complete Works* edited by Ángel Valbuena Prat (CW). All translations not specifically attributed are the author's.

PRELUDE

1. AM I, pp. 251–52.
2. The building now standing on the site is a recent reconstitution; all that remains of the original building are the pillars in the patio and the well shaft.
3. Birth dates were generally recorded only for royalty and the high nobility.
4. "Información de Argel," prepared by Cervantes in Algiers in 1580 and published for the first time by Pedro Torres Lanzas in the *Rivista de archivos, bibliotecas y museos XII* (3a época), Madrid, 1905.
5. Consuegra, Seville, Córdoba, Lucena, Madridejos, Herencia, Madrid, Toledo, Esquivias and Alcázar de San Juan.
6. Riguero Montero, José Maria: *Estudio acerca de la verdadera cuna y oriundez de Miguel de Cervantes Saavedra,* La Coruña, 1910, cit. Fitzmaurice-Kelly, James: *Miguel de Cervantes Saavedra: a Memoir,* Oxford, 1913, pp. 8–10.

1. SO VAST A DREAM

1. Ortiz de Zúñiga, Diego: *Anales eclesiásticos y seculares,* Madrid, 1677, p. 505.
2. Bataillon, Marcel: *Érasme et l'Espagne,* Paris, 1937, p. 591.
3. Riley, Edward C.: *Cervantes's Theory of the Novel,* Oxford, 1962, pp. 16–17.
4. *Obras,* 1690, cit. Peers, E. Allison: *Studies of the Spanish Mystics,* New York, 1951, II, p. 247.
5. Castile, Aragon, Valencia and Catalonia.
6. Lynch, John: *Spain Under the Habsburgs,* Oxford, 1964, I, p. 35.
7. Montoto, Santiago: *Sevilla en el imperio, siglo XVI,* Seville, 1938, introduction, p. ix.
8. As a philosopher, Vives was ranked by his contemporaries with Erasmus. Nearly a century before Francis Bacon, he suggested the need to base knowledge on direct observation of nature; he also advocated redistribution of the world's wealth so that all might share in it.
9. Luis Escudero y Perosso, cit. Montoto: *Sevilla,* p. 247.
10. Defourneaux, Marcelin: *La vie quotidienne en Espagne au siècle d'or,* Paris, 1964, p. 108.
11. Nykl, A. R.: *Hispano-Arabic Poetry and Its Relations with the Old Provençal Troubadours,* Baltimore, 1946, p. 240.
12. Sánchez-Alborñoz y Menduiña, Claudio: *Los Españoles ante la historia,* Buenos Aires, 1958, pp. 85–86.
13. Hayes, Francis C.: *Lope de Vega,* New York, 1967, p. 89.
14. Lope de Vega: *La estrella de Sevilla.*
15. DQ Part I, Chap. 28.
16. Giovio, Paolo: *Lettere,* Naples, 1535, fols. 97–98, cit. Croce, Benedetto: *La Spagna nella vita italiana durante la Rinascenza,* Rome, 1921, pp. 211–12.
17. Saavedra Fajardo, Diego de: *Empresas políticas,* 1640, cit. Defourneaux: *Vie Quotidienne,* p. 46.

18. Bemelberg, Baron Conrad von: *Travels in Spain,* 1599, cit. Pfandl, Ludwig: *Cultura y costumbres del pueblo español en los siglos XVI y XVII,* Barcelona, 1929, pp. 326–27.
19. In theory, it was illegal for commoners to wear swords. The rule was widely ignored.
20. Joly, Bartolomé: "Voyage en Espagne (1603–4)," *Revue hispanique XX,* New York-Paris, 1909, p. 616.
21. Cambon, J.: *The Diplomatist,* London, 1931, cit. Petrie, Charles: *Don John of Austria,* London, 1967, p. 124.
22. *Lazarillo de Tormes,* New York, 1966, p. 91.
23. DQ Part I, Chap. 45.
24. Menéndez Pidal, Ramón: *Los Españoles en la historia,* Madrid, 1947, p. 33.
25. Ibid., p. 40.
26. Lynch: *Spain,* I, pp. 66–67.
27. Ibid.
28. Bataillon: *Érasme,* p. 529.
29. Espinosa de los Monteros, Pablo de: *Historia y antigüedades de la gran ciudad de Sevilla,* Seville, 1627–30, fol. 89.
30. Castro, Americo: *Los Españoles: como llegaron a serlo,* Madrid, 1965, p. 229.
31. Lloyd, Alan: *The Spanish Centuries,* New York, 1968, p. 18.
32. Bernaldez, Andrés: *Memorias del reinado de los Reyes Católicos,* ed. Juan de Mata Carriazo, Madrid, 1962, pp. 94–103. (This is a late fifteenth-century chronicle.)
33. Castro: *Los Españoles,* pp. 21–22 (note).
34. Kamen, J.: *The Spanish Inquisition,* New York, 1965, pp. 106–7.
35. Fernández del Valle, Agustín Basave: *Filosofía del Quijote,* Mexico City, 1968, p. 14.
36. DQ Part II, Chap. 42.

2. HOLES IN THE FAMILY COAT

1. While no record exists of Rodrigo's baptism, it is likely that the family had always lived in that parish.
2. See Fernández de Navarrete, Martín: *Vida de Miguel de Cervantes Saavedra,* Madrid, 1819, for fanciful genealogical research.
3. *The Dogs' Colloquy;* the Latin has been corrected.
4. From testimony given by Fernando de Antequera, of Alcalá de Henares, cit. AM I, pp. 279–82.
5. DQ Part II, Chap. 21.
6. DQ PART I, Chap. 4.
7. DQ PART I, Chap. 18.
8. *The Dogs' Colloquy.*
9. DQ PART I, Chap. 21.
10. DQ PART II, Chap. 8.
11. DQ Part II, Chap. 45.
12. It becomes still more urgent when references to Don Quixote hint that the knight himself came of New Christian stock. They begin with the hero's very name, Don Quixote de la *Mancha*. Among the meanings of "mancha" is that of spot or stain; the word is frequently encountered in attestations of blood purity. Cide Hamete Benengeli, the mysterious Arab "author" of *Don*

Quixote whose references run so much more glibly to St. Paul than they do to the Koran, is carefully identified as a "Manchego"—which means both "stained" and "from la Mancha." The "manuscript" is discovered in the Alcana, the high street of Toledo's Jewish quarter. Its Morisco translator is convulsed by the description of Dulcinea as the best ham-salter in El Toboso, a town with a high percentage of Morisco inhabitants, suggesting that Quixote's ideal was of questionable pedigree. The knight is trampled by a herd of swine as "punishment" for being a knight-errant, a context that makes the very word "errant" suggestive.

In his *Cervantes par lui-même* (see Bibliography), Pierre Guenoun noted that silences can be as telling as words. When Sancho argues for forgiveness because he is an enemy of the Jews, Quixote, usually so prompt to take him up on his foolishness, remains strangely silent. Among the persons singled out repeatedly as living models for the knight was one Alonso Quixada, a great-uncle of the woman Cervantes married; he was known in his home village of Esquivias as being of Jewish origin. Alonso Quixada is one of Quixote's "real" names and the connection is reinforced by the knight's claim to descent from Gutierre Quixada, an ancestor of the historical Alonso.

13. DQ Part II, Chap. 32.
14. DQ PART I, Chap. 36.
15. DQ PART II, Chap. 58.
16. PS Book III, Chap. 11.
17. DQ Part II, Chap. 54.
18. DQ Part II, Chap. 52.
19. From a manuscript in the National Library in Madrid, cit. Ortega y Rubio, Juan: *Cervantes en Valladolid*, Madrid, 1905, pp. 21–22.
20. DQ Part II, Chap. 55.
21. DQ Part I, Chap. 22.
22. DQ Part II, Chap. 6.

3. THE UNMAKING OF A GENTLEMAN

1. The range of Spanish coinage in Cervantes' lifetime was broad and varied widely in type and value. The *maravedi*, its most common if not its smallest unit, declined in value from 340 to the ducat to 400, then to 440. The *real* also depreciated in value, from 10 to the ducat to 11.76. In 1534 the ducat became a money of account, being replaced in the coinage by the *escudo*. It is impossible to calculate in any general way the worth of these moneys in terms of twentieth-century currency (estimates have varied from 100 to 400 times their sixteenth-century valuations), even though the prices of specific items can occasionally be compared.

2. Rodríguez Marín, Francisco: *Nuevos documentos cervantinos hasta ahora inéditos,* Madrid, 1914, p. 142 (declaration by Diego de Alcalá).

3. This is an assumption; he may have bought annuities and government bonds as well, but he never, at any rate, used the money to buy a lucrative public office.

4. Cabezas, Juan Antonio: *Cervantes, del mito al hombre,* Madrid, 1967, p. 35.

5. When Gaspar de Guzmán, the future Count-Duke of Olivares and favorite of King Philip IV, went to Salamanca as a student, he brought with him a

governor, preceptor, eight pages, three valets, four lackeys, a chef, physician, barber and dozens of lesser servants and grooms.

6. A work of the first half of the sixteenth century, traditionally attributed to Cristóbal de Villalón, but now believed to have been written by Andrés Laguna.

7. One of the witnesses to the child's baptism on June 23 was a medical student named Francisco Díaz. In 1588, Cervantes would write a sonnet in honor of a treatise on diseases of the kidney and bladder written by a then famous Dr. Francisco Díaz, probably the same person. Lope de Vega also contributed a poem to the work.

8. Joly: "Voyage," p. 536; he was talking about the prostitutes in Zaragoza, but their sisters in Valladolid must have been even more regal.

9. Bennassar, Bartolomé: *Valladolid et ses campagnes au 16e siècle,* Paris, 1967, pp. 212–13.

10. Cock, Enrique: *Jornada de Tarascona hecho por Felipe II en 1592,* in García Mercadel, J.: *Viajes de estranjeros por España y Portugal,* Madrid, 1959, I, p. 249. (A collection, translated into Spanish, of sixteenth- and seventeenth-century travel diaries.)

11. Archivo de Protocolos de Córdoba (12-22-558), in AM I, pp. 286–87 (footnote).

4. THE FATHERS

1. Cabezas: *Cervantes,* p. 66.
2. P. Silverio de Santa Teresa: *Vida de Santa Teresa,* I, p. 25, cit. Auclair, Marcelle: *Theresa of Avila,* New York, 1959, p. 183.
3. Valbuena Prat, Ángel: *La vida española en la edad de oro,* Barcelona, 1943, p. 91.
4. DQ Part I, Chap. 9.
5. AM I, p. 360.
6. DQ Part II, Chap. 11.
7. Archives of the City of Córdoba, 20, 7, cit. AM I, p. 365.
8. Ortiz de Zúñiga: *Anales,* p. 518.
9. Ibid.

5. GREAT BABYLONIA

1. AM II, p. 53.
2. AM I, pp. 466–67.
3. PS Book III, Chap. 4.
4. Guenoun: *Cervantes,* p. 91.
5. PS Book III, Chap. 8.
6. *La entretenida.*
7. A unit of measure, equal to about twenty-five pounds.
8. DQ, prefatory verses.
9. The passage, an almost verbatim citation of Leone Ebreo's Neoplatonist *Dialoghi d'amore,* is in Book IV of *La Galatea.*
10. Lürssen, Dr. Ernst: *Psychoanalytic Observations About Cervantes' Don Quixote,* lecture given to the Sigmund Freud Society of Vienna, January 26, 1975.

11. Cit. Pfandl: *Cultura,* p. 128.
12. *El arenal de Sevilla.*
13. Morgado, Alonso: *Historia de Sevilla,* Seville, 1587, I, p. 142.
14. Toward the end of the century, Spain was drawing 5 million ducats a year and more from the Latin Americans mines. A shipment in the spring of 1595 filled a total of 1,018 carts—1,730,000 tons of gold, silver and precious stones.
15. *Anales,* pp. 523–24.
16. Ibid.
17. DQ Part I, Chap. 6.
18. PS Book II, Chap. 9–10. It was chiefly the conversos who, for obvious reasons, objected to the Inquisition's practice of hanging offenders' penitential robes in the naves of their parish churches for generations; *sanbenitos* from Cervantes' period were still to be found, their inscriptions faded but still legible, in some Catalonian churches in the late nineteenth century.
19. DQ Book II, Chap. 59.
20. Standard comic figures of the time, as the Scot once was to the English or a Brooklynite to Americans.
21. 8 plus 8, Prologue.
22. Rueda's first wife, an actress-dancer named Mariana, had been the solace and elixir of the melancholy Gaspar de la Cerda, third Duke of Medinaceli, for six years. She danced for His Grace, sang for him and, presumably, provided such other consolatory services as circumstances allowed. Dressed as a page and with her hair cut short, she accompanied him on his travels, trusting in his promise to endow her and to find a good marriage for her. The duke died before he could bring himself to carry out his promise. Mariana married Rueda soon afterward and he sued the duke's successor for the promised dowry, winning a judgment of sixty thousand maravedis.
23. PS Book I, Chap. 5.
24. Welsch, Hieronymus: *Descriptions of a Voyage,* Stuttgart, 1664, p. 234.
25. Ramssla, J. W. Neumair von: *Voyage in Italy and Spain,* Leipzig, 1622, cit. Pfandl: *Cultura,* p. 205 (note).
26. DQ Part I, Chap. 16.
27. Armiñán Odriosola, Luis de: *Las Hermanas de Cervantes,* Barcelona, 1957, p. 126.
28. Ibid., p. 126.
29. Ibid., p. 115.
30. Ibid., p. 144.
31. 8 plus 8, Prologue.

6. TURNING POINT

1. Grierson, Edward: *The Fatal Inheritance,* New York, 1969, p. 75.
2. Menéndez Pidal: *Los Españoles,* p. 183.
3. Ibid., p. 184.
4. Ovando died sometime before 1596. Astrana Marín recorded the existence of a Nicolás de Ovando who took the habit of a Benedictine monk in Salamanca in May 1569 and wondered if this might have been Andrea's lover. Probably not; it is doubtful that a thoroughly secular Nicolás, half-trained in the law and young enough to hope for a worldly career, would have thrown up his hopes so quickly. Such sudden vocations were not un-

known then, however, and the shock of finding himself poor could have driven him to it.

5. AM II, p. 175.

6. Ibid.

7. His ordeal was protracted. He was imprisoned in the castle in Segovia, then, on apparently trumped-up charges of plotting to escape, was transferred to the royal prison at Simancas; probably his presence in Segovia cast a pall on Philip's marriage there to his fourth wife, Anna of Austria, in the spring of 1570. In the months that followed, rumors were put out that he was seriously ill; a great show of doctors' visits was made, much display of medicine. On Saturday, October 14, 1570, an astonished Montigny, who had been expecting an order for his release, heard instead an order for his execution. He was forced to write a statement that he was dying of illness, but he was not allowed to make a will or order payment of his debts, so ensuring that his estate would revert to the crown. Between midnight and 2 A.M. on October 16 he was strangled. The body was dressed in Franciscan robes to hide the marks of the garrote. Until the end, he had maintained his faith in his king's wisdom and good will.

8. AM II, p. 170.

9. AM II, p. 171.

10. The Frenchman Pierre Cosin, who with his Spanish business partner Alonso Gómez had set up the capital's first print shop in 1566.

11. VP Chap. IV.

12. AM II, pp. 171–72.

13. AM II, p. 179.

14. AM II, pp. 178–81. A *copla castellana* is a ten-line stanza in the classic octosyllabic Spanish romance line, rhyming *abbab;* a *redondilla castellana* is a tandem of five-line stanzas in the same meter but rhyming *ababa.*

15. AM II, pp. 185–86.

16. PS Book I, Chap. 5.

17. Cervantists cite his mention of southern France in a number of writings as witness that he knew the area and so must have gone overland to Italy. Much romancing is devoted to following him as he sneaked across the Pyrenees, through France and down into Piedmont disguised as a pilgrim to Rome. There are any number of reasons to doubt this. For one thing, his writing does make it clear that he did visit Barcelona, but no other occasion in his life seems to allow for such a visit. Again, all his references to France are flattened by an un-Cervantine muzziness, as though he knew no more of the place than what he gleaned from hearsay or casual reading. The notion of a young, impatient Cervantes begging his way slowly across France and dodging constables in Milan—if, indeed, he was on the run at all—when a galley from Barcelona would have deposited him quickly and safely in Genoa is simply incredible.

18. PS Book I, Chap 5.

19. DQ Part II, Chap. 61.

7. THE CARDINAL'S CHAMBERLAIN

1. Part of the street is still called the Via dei Banchi Vecchi. One of the exchange agents in the street was the correspondent, and perhaps kinsman, of Pirro Boqui, the Cervanteses' friend and/or lodger in Madrid.

2. Pérez Pastor, Cristóbal: *Documentos cervantinos hasta ahora inéditos,* Madrid, 1897–1902, II, pp. 11–16.
3. The fact that Cervantes had to send for certification instead of bringing it with him argues against the theory that he had left Spain in response to a job offer.
4. Sandorno, Amalia Billi de: "El Cardenal Gaspar de Cervantes y Gaete, ignorado protector de Miguel de Cervantes Saavedra," *Anales cervantinos,* Madrid, 1952, II, pp. 335–58.
5. Letter to the court from Don Juan de Zúñiga, the Spanish ambassador in Rome, cited in a number of biographies: see Fitzmaurice-Kelly: *Memoir,* p. 17.
6. Nola, Roberto de: *Libro de cozina,* Madrid, 1968, pp. 38–39. For worm's-eye views of servants' life in noble households, see also Alemán, Mateo: *Guzmán de Alfarache,* Madrid, 1968, Part I, Book III, Chaps. 7–10, and Castro, Miguel de: *Vida del soldado español Miguel de Castro (1593–1611),* Buenos Aires, 1949, pp. 211–21.
7. Nola: *Cozina,* p. 84.
8. Alemán: *Guzmán,* Part I, Book III, Chap. 7.
9. *The Glass Scholar.*
10. PS Book IV, Chap. 5.
11. Bataillon: *Érasme,* p. 83.
12. Croce: *Spagna nella vita italiana,* p. 210.
13. Rodríguez Marín, F.: *"La Filida" de Gálvez de Montalvo, Speech to Royal Academy of History,* Madrid, 1927, pp. 69–71.
14. PS Book III, Chap. 19.
15. DQ Part II, Chap. 42.
16. VP Appendix.
17. DQ Part II, Chap. 16.
18. DQ Part II, Chap. 8.
19. DQ Part II, Chap. 4.
20. DQ Part II, Chap. 58.
21. DQ Part II, Chap. 18.
22. *The Dogs' Colloquy.*

8. THE KING'S CRUMBS

1. Ranke, Leopold von: *History of the Popes During the Sixteenth and Seventeenth Centuries,* trans. Mrs. S. Austin, London, 1840, pp. 361ff.
2. *Correspondance du Cardinal Granvelle (1565–83),* Brussels, 1877, IV, p. 51.
3. Cit. Fernández Duro, C.: *Cervantes marinero,* Madrid, 1869, pp. 20–21.
4. Gallo, Antonio: *Destierro de ignorancias en todo género de soldados de infantería,* Madrid, 1639, cit. AM II, pp. 264–65.
5. *Floreto de anécdotas y noticias diversas,* ed. F. J. Sánchez Canton, cit. Sánchez-Alborñoz y Menduiña, Claudio: *España: Un enigma histórico,* Buenos Aires, 1956, II, p. 84.
6. PS Book II, Chap. 13.
7. Torres Lanzas: "Información de Argel," p. 349.
8. In his play *El castigo del penseque,* Tirso de Molina devoted a bit of doggerel to Cervantes' reportorial bent:
   Has aught occurred of this species?

When Madrid hears what's afoot,
Cervantes will surely put
the happening in his stories.

9. DQ Part I, Chap. 38.
10. Ibid.
11. Serrano, Luciano: *Correspondencia diplomática entre España y la Santa Sede*, Madrid, 1914, IV, p. 347, cit. Dennis, A.: *Don Juan of Austria*, Madrid, 1966, pp. 149–50.

9. AN ARMY OF PARROTS

1. AM II, p. 256.
2. Isaba, Marcos de: *Cuerpo enfermo de la milicia española*, Madrid, 1594, p. 30.
3. Croce: *Spagna nella vita italiana*, p. 279.
4. Isaba: *Cuerpo enfermo*, p. 114.
5. Ibid., p. 140.
6. *The Dogs' Colloquy.*
7. The princely title so shrewdly bestowed on him here was not formally granted to Don Juan by the Spanish Council of State until 1575, three years before his death.
8. Martínez-Hidalgo, José-María: *Lepanto*, Barcelona, 1971, p. 14 (footnote).
9. The flag, along with Don Juan's 485-foot-long oriflamme, are still hung once a year, on October 7, the date of the battle of Lepanto, in the nave of Toledo Cathedral.
10. Cabrera de Córdoba, Luis: *Relación de las cosas sucedidas en la corte de España desde 1599 hasta 1614,* Madrid, 1857, p. 96.
11. Stirling-Maxwell, Sir William: *Don John of Austria,* London, 1886, pp. 374–75.
12. AM II, p. 292.
13. Armiñán Odriosola: *Las Hermanas,* pp. 91–92.
14. Personnel statistics for the League force are necessarily approximate because of the standard practice of cooking payroll figures. Estimates of the number of soldiers have varied from twenty thousand to thirty thousand.

10. THE SEA EAGLES

1. Bauer y Landauer, Ignacio: *La marina española en el siglo XVI,* Madrid, 1921, p. 85.
2. Warships, as such, were scarce in the sixteenth century. Standing navies were small; at the peak of his shipbuilding program, Philip's fleet amounted to only about one hundred vessels of all types. In wartime, commercial galleys were rented from private individuals who provided supplies and crew but not armament. Warships carried more troops, their artillery was heavier and they carried no mechandise except gold, silver, precious stones—and contraband. But in peacetime even these were often used as merchantmen.
3. Until well into the century, most of the other men-of-war were variations on the light galley. The great galleass was simply a larger galley, usually 170–75 feet long by 25 feet wide, a floating fortress with a reinforced hull.

mounting from thirty to seventy-six guns and manned by three hundred oarsmen and as many as five hundred soldiers. It functioned chiefly as an artillery platform, moving ahead of the line of galleys and firing broadsides in an attempt to disorganize the enemy formation. A similar mission was given to the galleon, a slow, clumsy, high-hulled, twin-deck giant, forerunner of the great sailing ships with which the Dutch and the English were already beginning to wrest command of the seas from the Mediterranean powers. The galleon was the only Mediterranean fighting ship of the day which operated entirely under sail; it generally had to be towed into firing position—as did the galleass. Galiots, fustas, brigantines and frigates were smaller versions of the galley, little more than glorified long boats propelled by up to twenty-four oarsmen and used chiefly for patrol and liaison work.

4. Guevara, Antonio de: *Libro que trata de los inventos, del arte de navegar y trabajos de la galera*, Zaragoza, 1545, p. 51.
5. *The Glass Scholar.*
6. Letter to Miranda de Ron, cit. Castro y Bravo, F. de: *Las naos españolas en la carrera de las Indias*, Madrid, 1927, pp. 135–38.
7. Castro y Bravo: *Naos Españolas*, p. 193.
8. DQ Part II, Chap. 63.
9. DQ Part I, Chap. 39.
10. Petrie: *Don John*, p. 165.
11. Ibid., p. 167.
12. Ibid., p. 168.
13. Melo, Francisco Manuel de: *Política militar en avisos de generales*, Madrid, 1638, cit. Penna, Mario: *Il 'lugar del esquife': apunti cervantini*, Perugia, 1965, p. 254.
14. DQ Part I, Chap. 38.
15. Many sources; see Rodgers, W. Ledyard: *Naval Warfare Under Oars from the Fourth to the Sixteenth Centuries*, Annapolis, 1939, p. 199.

11. LEPANTO

1. *Documentos inéditos para la historia de España*, XXI, p. 348, cit. AM II, p. 324.
2. AM II, pp. 324–25 (footnote).
3. Many writers have assumed that the pinnace in which Cervantes fought was afloat alongside the galley. Recent research has shown that the boat remained on deck throughout the engagement. While small boats were often lowered in small-scale sea fights to provide flanking action, in fleet action, as Alonso de Chaves noted in his c. 1530 *Espejo de navegantes* (cit. Bauer y Landauer: *Marina española*, p. 471), to lower them would have exposed them to the danger of being crushed between the closely packed galleys.
4. Torres y Aguilera, Gerónimo: *Chrónica de varios sucesos de guerra que ha pasado en Italia y partes de Levante*, Zaragoza, 1579, p. 75.
5. Marmol Carvajál, Luis de: *Primera (y segunda) parte de la descripción general de Africa*, Granada, 1573, I, pp. 291–92.
6. The terms port and starboard, while occasionally used in the Mediterranean galley fleets, were usually reserved then for the sailing vessels of the Atlantic armadas.
7. Given in a number of accounts; see Martínez-Hidalgo, José María: "La batalla de Lepanto," *Historia y vida 41*, Madrid, August 1971, pp. 58–85.

8. Various sources; see Petrie: *Don John*, p. 175.

9. *Lettere del clarissimo Girolamo Diedo*, Venice, 1588, fol. 10 verso.

10. Garnier, François: *Journal de la bataille de Lépante*, Paris, 1956, p. 180.

11. Ibid., p. 182.

12. Diedo: *Lettere*, fols. 19–20.

13. Herrera, Fernando de:; *Relación de la guerra de Cipre y suceso de la batalla naval de Lepanto*, Seville, 1572, Chap. 27.

14. Diedo: *Lettere*, fol. 23.

15. Translation by J. Y. Gibson, London, 1863. Cervantes loses heavily in the transaction; the translation of line six is mine.

16. Diedo: *Lettere*, fols. 18–19.

17. Valbuena Prat, Ángel: *La vida española en la edad de oro*, Barcelona, 1943, pp. 136–37.

18. Diedo: *Lettere*, fol. 19.

19. *The Gallant Spanishwoman*.

20. Bauer y Landauer: *Marina española*, pp. 104–5.

21. Chrónica, p. 74.

22. Rosell, Cayetano: *Historia del combate naval de Lepanto*, Madrid, 1853, p. 112.

23. Various sources; See Rosell: *Historia*, p. 115; Rodgers: *Naval Warfare*, pp. 210–11.

24. Gravière, J. B. E.: *La guerre de Chypre et la bataille de Lépante*, Paris, 1888, II, pp. 186–87.

25. Scetti, Aurelio: *Diary 1567–75*, cit. Garnier: *Journal de Lépante*, p. 200.

26. Caracciolo, Ferrante: *Commentarii della guerra fatta coi Turchi da D. Giovanni d'Austria dopo che venne in Italia*, Florence, 1581, p. 39.

27. *The Turkish History*, London, 1687, cit. Petrie: *Don John*, p. 181.

28. Euldj Ali was a Calabrian shepherd named Giovanni Dionigio Galeni when he was taken prisoner at the age of fourteen, nearly half a century before Lepanto. For fourteen more years he rowed as a slave in North African galleys, mocked as El Fartas—The Scurvy One—by his fellow slaves for the infection (probably ringworm) which left him bald and covered with scabs. Only his thirst for vengeance on a galley boss who struck him convinced him to convert to Islam. His rise to prominence was meteoric. A skillful seaman—his contemporaries said he could maneuver his galley like a rider on a show horse—he quickly won wealth and notoriety as a pirate. In 1560 he defeated the Spanish at Gelves, in what is now Libya. It was he who, in 1570, filched Tunis from Spain. His success in saving his own skin at Lepanto won him promotion to the Turkish captaincy of the sea. Responsible for rebuilding the Ottoman fleet, Euldj Ali also busied himself with more grandiose projects. He urged the piercing of a canal across the Isthmus of Suez to facilitate the Sultan's Red Sea and Indian campaigns; work was in fact begun on it, but the project was never carried through. He made a deliberate policy of encouraging piracy, giving it a scope which was to harass Europe for centuries. On his death in 1587, he was buried in the splendid mosque he had built on the shores of the Bosporus.

29. *Epistle to Mateo Vázquez*.

30. DQ Part I, Chap. 39.

31. *Vray discours de la bataille des armées chrétienne et turquesque etc.* (anonymous), Paris, 1571, p. 28.

32. Various sources; see Rodgers: *Naval Warfare*, p. 210.

33. Swinburne: "Hymn to Proserpine."
34. The true beneficiaries of the battle of Lepanto were the slaves: in addition to those released from the Turkish galleys, nearly five thousand on Christian oars won their freedom in combat, although, for many of them, the respite was brief if heady. Hundreds probably emulated El Marquesillo, who had fought with such daring that his officers not only liberated him but allotted him two hundred ducats from the spoils; true to his caste, he gambled away the whole sum the next day and, by nightfall, was back in his old place at the oar.
35. PS Book IV, Chap. 1.
36. Fitzmaurice-Kelly: *Memoir*, pp. 22–23.
37. Ibid.

12. "FOR THE GREATER GLORY OF THE RIGHT"

1. *Vray discours etc.*, p. 20.
2. Various sources; see Menéndez Pidal, Ramón (ed.): *Historia de España*, Madrid, 1966, XIX, p. 129; Stirling-Maxwell: *Don John*, pp. 445–46.
3. Caracciolo: *Commentarii*, p. 54.
4. Stirling-Maxwell: *Don John*, p. 447.
5. Ibid., p. 456.
6. Ibid.
7. Don Juan was to complain bitterly to Philip against charges that he had enriched himself at Lepanto, quite accurately pointing out that the campaign had in fact left him out of pocket.
8. *Commentari della guerra di Cipro*, written c. 1600 though not published until 1845 in Monte Cassino, cit. Rodgers: *Naval Warfare*, pp. 210–11.
9. González, Estebanillo: *Vida*, Madrid, 1968, p. 55.
10. Ibid., pp. 55–58.
11. Navarro y Ledesma: *El ingenioso hidalgo Miguel de Cervantes Saavedra*, Madrid, 1958, p. 72.
12. *Epistel to Mateo Vázquez*.
13. *Memoir*, p. 31.
14. *Life in Algiers*, Act II.
15. The protagonist of Cervantes' "The Captive's Tale" was at Navarino at the time, "rowing in the (Turkish) admiral's flagship" (DQ Part I, Chap. 39). Through him, Cervantes would insist that the Turks were ready to give up without a fight. The opinion is not to be taken seriously.

13. THE SAND CASTLES

1. *The Dogs' Colloquy*.
2. Byron: *The Corsair*.
3. Contarini, Giovanni Pietro: *Historia delle cose successe dal principio della guerra mossa da Selim Ottomano a' Venetiano etc.*, Venice, 1572, fol. 221.
4. *The Liberal Lover*.
5. DQ Part I, Chap. 39.
6. Dennis: *Don Juan*, pp. 218–19.
7. Various sources; see Navarro y Ledesma: *El ingenioso hidalgo*, p. 78.
8. AM II, p. 384.

9. DQ Part II, Chap. 23.
10. Trans. J. Y. Gibson in *Journey to Parnassus,* London, 1883.

14. AN ISLAND IDYLL

1. Virgil: *Aeneid,* Book X, 791–824, trans. J. Rhoades, London, 1962.
2. VP Chap. IV.
3. DQ Part II, Prologue.
4. Dennis: *Don Juan,* p. 230.
5. Ibid., p. 232.
6. Archivo general de Simancas, cit. Braudel, Fernand: *La Méditerranée et le monde méditerranéen au temps de Philippe II,* Paris, 1966, I, p. 234.
7. "Relación de sucesos," *Colección de documentos inéditos para la historia de España,* Madrid, 1847, II, 389.
8. Despite their names, these are Italian wines; Cervantes gives them in the Hispanicized Italian the soldiers spoke.
9. Ciudad Real, in the Mancha.
10. *La Galatea,* Book V.
11. PS Book III, Chap. 8.
12. PS Book III, Chap. 18.
13. Archivo general de Simancas, cit. AM II, p. 414.
14. DQ Part I, Chap. 27.

15. "SUCH POINTS OF DESPITE"

1. Woolf, Virginia: *Orlando,* London, 1949, p. 168.
2. *The Glass Scholar.* Spanish literature of the period abounds in allusions to the fat land of Italy, the place hungry Spaniards went when they died, and they are often couched in the barracks Italian Cervantes used. It may be, as some criticis have assumed, that Cervantes deliberately used this patois to burlesque Spanish soldiers' struggles with the language. But there is at least a strong suspicion that his own Italian, like his Latin, was collected like porcelain, a piece at a time and often a little chipped and mended. "La macatela" or *maccatella* is a kind of meatball; "manigoldo" a pastry, *manicotto;* "li polastri," *le pollastre,* fowl.
3. DQ Part II, Chap. 63.
4. *Cancionera,* Zaragoza, 1562, cit. AM I, p. 376.
5. Various sources; see Navarro y Ledesma: *El ingenioso hidalgo,* p. 89.
6. AM II, p. 449.
7. *La Galatea,* Book IV.
8. PS Book II, Chap. 22.
9. AM II, p. 441.
10. AM VI, p. 507 (footnote).

16. CAPTURE

1. *Epistle to Mateo Vázquez,* trans. J. Y. Gibson in *Journey to Parnassus.*
2. *La Galatea,* Book V.
3. *The House of Jealousy,* Act III.

4. DQ Part I, Chap. 63.
5. Villalón: *Viaje,* pp. 36–37.
6. *Epistle,* trans. J. Y. Gibson in *Journey.*
7. *The Dungeons of Algiers,* Act II.
8. Haedo, Fray Diego de: *Topographía e historia general de Argel,* Valladolid, 1612, fol. 17.
9. Ibid., fol. 17.
10. Ibid., fol. 22.
11. Fisher, Sir Godfrey: *Barbary Legend: War, Trade and Piracy in North Africa (1415–1830),* Oxford, 1957, pp. 102ff.
12. Haedo: *Topographía,* fol. 100.
13. Dan, R. P. Pierre: *Histoire de Barbarie et de ses corsaires,* Paris, 1636, I, p. 400.
14. Haedo: *Topographía,* fol. 120.
15. Ibid., fol. 120.
16. Ibid., fol. 118.
17. Ibid.
18. Ibid.
19. Act I.
20. Haedo: *Topographía,* fol. 23.
21. Bernaldez: *Memorias,* p. 267.
22. *Life in Algiers,* Act II.
23. Sosa, cited in Haedo: *Topographía,* fol. 128. One of Cervantes' closest friends in Algiers, Sosa was captured in the Maltese galley *San Pablo* in April 1577. The incident is referred to in *Life in Algiers,* Act II, as are some of those captured in her. Sosa contributed heavily to the Cervantes legend in Algiers.
24. Dan: *Barbarie,* I, pp. 398–400.
25. DQ Part I, Chap. 22.
26. Madariaga, Salvador: *Don Quixote: An Introductory Essay in Psychology,* London, 1961, p. 17.
27. Unless otherwise specified, all the quotations in Chapters 16 through 19 are from the *Información de Argel* as reprinted (with minor corrections) by Pedro Torres Lanzas in the *Revista de archivos, bibliotecas y museos 12,* Madrid, 1905, pp. 346–97.

17. "BE THOU A SHEPHERD"

1. ES, Prologue.
2. This was one of the two principal religious orders (with the Trinitarian Brotherhood) devoted to the ransoming of Christians from Moslem captivity. Each order periodically did the rounds of the Moslem capitals from Constantinople to Fez, negotiating for the release of as many slaves as their funds would cover. To supplement such moneys as the captives' families could contribute, the orders besought alms; they were also helped by a royal liberation fund set aside from tax revenues, as well as by private bequests.
3. AM II, p. 519.
4. Pérez Pastor: *Documentos cervantinos,* II, p. 32.
5. AM II, p. 523.
6. Act II.

7. *Memoir,* pp. 50–51.
8. Morell, John Reynell: *Algeria: The Topography and History, Political, Social and Natural, of French Africa,* London, 1854, p. 326.
9. DQ Part I, Chap. 21.
10. Italics mine.
11. The standard Algerian refreshment of water, grapes and lemon syrup.
12. Act II.
13. DQ Part I, Chap. 16.
14. DQ Part II, Chap. 50.
15. DQ Part II, Chap. 27.
16. *La Galatea,* "Calliope's Song," Book VI.
17. Memorandum prepared in Algiers by Sosa and signed by several captives, including Cervantes, cited in AM II, p. 531.
18. DQ Part II, Chap. 40.
19. Nephew of the Duke of Alba.
20. Dan: *Barbarie,* I, pp. 43–44.
21. Haedo: *Topographía,* fol. 86.
22. DQ Part I, Chap. 40.
23. Act IV.
24. Ibid.
25. Buchanan, Milton J.: *The Works of Cervantes,* Ottawa, 1938, p. 27.
26. Menéndez Pidal: *Historia de España* XIX, p. 192.
27. Diego Castellano in *Información de Argel,* p. 365.
28. Haedo: *Topographía,* fol. 184.
29. Act IV.
30. Ibid.

18. THE AUTHOR OF IT ALL

1. From her will, cited by a number of sources; see Arbó, Sebastían Juan: *Cervantes,* Barcelona, 1956, pp. 396–97.
2. Información of 1578 in *Información de Argel,* p. 352.
3. Petition of May 21, 1590, in *Información de Argel,* p. 345.
4. AM III, p. 16.
5. Grierson, Edward: *King of Two Worlds,* London, 1974, p. 210.
6. Menéndez Pidal: *Historia de España* XIX, p. 204.
7. AM III, p. 19.
8. PS Book II, Chap. 5.
9. DQ Part I, Chap. 18.
10. PS Book II, Chap. 19.
11. Navarro y Ledesma: *El ingenioso hidalgo,* pp. 116–17.
12. The idea, for example, that the servant of a prominent person was unidentifiable as such is fantasy.
13. Albistur, Jorge: *El teatro de Cervantes,* Montevideo, 1968, p. 21.
14. DQ Part I, Chap. 40.
15. DQ Part I, Chap. 28.
16. *The Two Maidens.*
17. An Algerian coin worth slightly over six Spanish reales.
18. Pedrosa was captured in the rout of Sebastian's army in Morocco. He was not ransomed until 1583.

19. Act II.
20. Act I.
21. Domingo de la Asunción, Fray: *Cervantes y la Orden Trinitaria,* Madrid, 1917, p. 146.
22. The license was to bounce from extension to extension until it was finally sold on December 13, 1584.
23. AM III, p. 63.
24. AM III, p. 64.
25. DQ Part I, Chap. 40.
26. It is not known what part Torres, who is mentioned in passing only once, in Aragonés' testimony, had in the conspiracy. Hassan hoped to be able to appropriate the property of both traders and hold them for rich ransom as well.
27. Italics mine.
28. Italics mine.
29. AM III, p. 61.
30. PS Book I, Chap. 2.
31. Haedo: *Topographia,* fol. 185.

19. FREEDOM

1. His career in Algiers reached an appropriate climax in 1591 when his clumsiness in asking a visiting ship's captain for weapons as stage props touched off another slave-revolt scare in which a number of Christians were killed and Blanco himself put to torture. He was ransomed in 1592 for one thousand escudos.
2. National Historical Archives, *Libro de la Redempçion,* 118-B, fol. 156, cit. AM III, p. 85.
3. Haedo, Fray Diego de: *Topografía e historia general de Argel,* Madrid, 1927–29, II, pp. 208–14.
4. Palafox was still with Hassan when the dey returned to Algiers in 1582; he was ransomed by Juan Gil in 1583 for seven hundred gold escudos. He was then twenty-three years old and had been a captive for eight years.
5. Hassan became the Sultan's general of the sea on Euldj Ali's death in 1587. He was finally poisoned by a rival who succeeded to the admiralty.
6. His word of honor was the only security asked, a unique case in Trinitarian annals. No record has ever been found of repayment. But we have Cervantes' assurance (in Act II of the *Dungeons*) that "the promise of a hidalgo or a caballero is as good as cash."
7. The testimony Blanco collected was never, as far as is known, presented to any official body in Spain.
8. PS Book II, Chap. 5.
9. Cervantes had acted as witness to the act of liberation for one of the five, a man named Juan Gutiérrez, who, in his sixties and with cataracts in both eyes, was ransomed for fifty doblas.
10. DQ Part I, Chap. 40.
11. Of all the friends he had made, all the men he had tried to help, only Sosa, Gabriel López Maldonado and perhaps Andrés Muñoz are known to have maintained their friendships with him after liberation.

20. DIPLOMATIC INTERLUDE

1. *The Liberal Lover.*
2. Francisco de Aguilar, in affidavit dated December 18, 1580; Archivo de Protocolos de Madrid, No. 499, fol. 1399.
3. A Romanic language akin to Catalan, Mallorcan and Provençal.
4. PS Book III, Chaps. 11–12.
5. Rodgers: *Naval Warfare,* p. 215.
6. Euldj Ali's sally had, in fact, been aimed only at punishing disaffection among the janissaries in Algiers; his fleet returned to the Morea a month later.
7. Eraso was the natural son of Francisco de Eraso, principal secretary to Charles V and later secretary of the Council of the Indies, a post to which his son succeeded.
8. Punctuation mine.
9. Francisco de Sopando Balmaseda. Astrana Marín, noting that, on his death in 1596, not a single book was found among Balmaseda's effects, suggests that this was hardly the man to sympathize with Cervantes. In defiance of literary logic, however, the secretary does seem to have received Cervantes kindly.
10. Archivo general de Simancas, *Guerra antiqua,* Legajo 123, fol. 1.
11. "Calliope's Song," Book VI.

21. THE HYPERBOREANS

1. *La Galatea,* Book III.
2. *Lectures on the Dramatic Literature of the Age of Elizabeth,* London, 1821, p. 265.
3. Schlegel, F. von: *Werke,* Vienna, 1822, cit. AM III, p. 251.
4. *Memoir,* p. 105.
5. Trend, J. B.: *Cervantes in Arcadia,* London, 1954, p. 502.
6. The grand chorales of Tomás Luis de Victoria were an exception, but he spent most of his life in Rome and his influence was yet to make itself felt in Spain.
7. "Calliope's Song," Book VI.
8. Virgil: *Eclogue IV,* trans. J. Rhoades, London, 1962.
9. *De los nombres de Cristo,* cit. Bataillon, Marcel: "Cervantès penseur," *Revue de littérature comparée,* Paris, 1928, p. 814.
10. Riley: *Cervantes's Theory of the Novel,* p. 34.
11. Montemayor, Jorge de: *Los siete libros de la Diana,* ed. F. López Estrada, Madrid, 1970, p. 59.
12. DQ Part I, Chap. 7.
13. *La viuda valenciana,* Act I.
14. *Pedro de Urdemales,* Act I.

22. IN THE CRUEL PATIO

1. *Entremeses de Quiñones de Benavente,* cit. Rennert, H. A.: *The Spanish Stage in the Time of Lope de Vega,* New York, 1909, p. 118.

2. 8 plus 8, Prologue. "Comedy" was the general term for any full-length play, comic or tragic.
3. VP, Appendix.
4. DQ Part I, Chap. 48.
5. Lope generally agreed with Cervantes' dicta; he said as much in his *Arte nuevo de hacer comedias en este tiempo* (1609), but he also pleaded the need to satisfy the *vulgo*.
6. 8 plus 8, Prologue.
7. Rufo, Juan: *Las seiscientas apotegmas,* Toledo, 1596, fol. 266.
8. 8 plus 8, Prologue.
9. *La vida del buscón,* Book II, Chap. 9.
10. Rennert: *Spanish Stage,* p. 159.
11. DQ Part II, Chap. 11.
12. *Memoir,* p. 164.
13. Bennassar: *Valladolid,* p. 511.
14. Francisco A. de Icaza: *Sucesos reales que parecen imaginados de Gutierre de Cetina, Juan de la Cueva y Mateo Alemán,* Madrid, 1919, cit. AM III, pp. 318–19.
15. DQ Part I, Chap. 47.
16. Cited by a number of commentators; see Valbuena Prat's introduction to *Numantia,* CW pp. 145–46.
17. Mosquera de Figueroa, Cristóbal: *Comentario en breve compendio de disciplina militar en que se escribe la jornada de las islas de los Açores,* Madrid, 1596, II, fol. 85.
18. 8 plus 8, Prologue.
19. VP Chap. I.
20. He may also have written *autos sacramentales.* In testimony given July 4, 1593, on behalf of Tomás Gutiérrez in Seville, Cervantes described himself as "a studious person who has written autos and many plays." The claim may also have been based on autos written in Algiers.

23. IDYLLOMANIA

1. Borg, in García Mercadel: *Viajes de estranjeros,* II, p. 273.
2. Pfandl: *Cultura,* pp. 214–15.
3. A silver coin worth one quarter of a maravedi.
4. AM II, p. 374.
5. *El criticón,* Madrid, 1664, p. 363.
6. *La Galatea,* Dedication.
7. PS, Prologue.
8. Entwhistle, W. J.: *Cervantes,* Oxford, 1940, p. 50.
9. *The House of Jealousy.*
10. DQ Part II, Chap. 19.
11. *San Manuel Bueno,* Madrid, 1931.

24. ESQUIVIAS

1. Cervantes never lived in the house usually shown to visitors as his. Nor did his wife own property on the street now called Calle de Doña Catalina.
2. AM III, p. 552.

3. Anonymous: "Sátira contra el sitio del Escorial," in García Mercadel: *Viajes de estranjeros,* II, pp. 218–20.
4. AM IV, p. 145.
5. DQ Part II, Chap. 50.
6. VP Chap. IV.
7. Pérez Pastor: *Documentos cervantinos,* I, p. 173.
8. Ibid., I, p. 23.
9. Biblioteca Nacional R-3.074, fol. 98, cit. AM V, p. 512.
10. 8 plus 8, Prologue.
11. Archivo de Protocolos de Toledo, cit. AM III, pp. 469–73.
12. VP Chap. IV.
13. PS Book III, Chap. 8.
14. Letter to Philip from the Azores dated August 9, 1583, cit. AM IV, p. 137.
15. Mattingly, Garrett: *The Defeat of the Spanish Armada,* London, 1970, p. 106.
16. A document discovered in Córdoba indicating that Cervantes was already working as a commissary on April 13, 1587, is probably erroneous. Unsupported by any other record in this most amply documented period of Cervantes' life, it almost certainly reflects a lapse of memory by the deponent.
17. DQ Part II, Chap. 49.
18. DQ Part II, Chap. 19.

25. THE SANCHOS OF THE EARTH

1. Anonymous: *Trato de las posadas de Sevilla,* etc., Seville, 1596, cit. Rodríguez-Marín, Francisco: *Introducción crítica a Rinconete y Cortadillo,* Madrid, 1920, p. 135.
2. At what are now Nos. 13 to 15 of Calle de Federico Sánchez Bedoya.
3. DQ Part I, Chap. 11.
4. *Coloquios,* Seville, 1570, cit. Amador de los Ríos, José: *Sevilla pintoresca,* Seville, 1844, p. 254.
5. Valdivia, on the other hand, is duly remembered in *The Glass Scholar,* where he appears as a soldier and boon companion to Tomás Rodaja.
6. Fleet commissaries were not employees but contractual agents who handled government funds to cover operational costs. They were personally responsible for any disparity between the quantities of supplies collected and those delivered; thus the insistence on co-signers to protect public funds.
7. Cabezas: *Cervantes,* p. 260.
8. VP Chap. I.
9. Ibid.
10. Braudel: *Méditerranée,* I, p. 417.
11. DQ Part I, Chap. 21.
12. Mattingly: *Armada,* p. 180.
13. DQ Part II, Chap. 9.
14. DQ Part I, Chap. 19.
15. Some scholars believe this episode was based on the secret translation of the remains of John of the Cross. The saint died December 14, 1591. The following year, the body was secretly exhumed, hidden in a trunk and spirited out of Úbeda at night by John's disciple Ana de Mercado y Peñalosa, her brother Luis de Mercado, an official of the Council of Castile, and Fray

Nicolas de Jesús María, vicar-general of the Reformed Carmelite Order. According to one account of the journey, Fray Jerónimo de San José's *Historia del venerable Padre Fray Juan de la Cruz* (Madrid, 1641), a notable incident occurred on the night the body left Úbeda. The officer escorting the body, it reported, had decided to eschew the main Madrid road in favor of a secondary route through Jaén and Martos: "Before they reached that town, a man suddenly appeared on a high ridge not far from the road and began to cry loudly, 'Where are you taking the saint's body? Leave it where it was!' " Everyone's "hair stood on end." Then, crossing a field, they were stopped by a lone man who insisted they account for their burden. He was told that, by order of the Council of Castile, no one was to be allowed to inspect it. When the fellow insisted, the escorting officer turned to ask for a bit of silver to offer as a bribe; when he turned back, the man had vanished. He was strongly suspected to have been the devil.

In *Don Quixote,* the body is said to have come from Baeza, which is only five miles from Úbeda, and to be on its way to Segovia, as was that of John of the Cross. Like the saint, the dead man in the novel had been the victim of a "pestilent fever." Cervantes notes that "they all thought this (Don Quixote) was no man, but a devil from hell."

16. Cabezas: *Cervantes,* p. 266.
17. Ibid., p. 268.
18. Navarro y Ledesma, Francisco: *Cervantes, the Man and the Genius,* trans. D. and G. Bliss, New York, 1973.
19. AM IV, pp. 206–7.
20. Mattingly: *Armada,* p. 183.
21. National Maritime Museum, Greenwich, England: *Armada Papers 4,694,* cit. AM III, p. 209.
22. DQ Part I, Chap. 31.
23. *The Little Gypsy Girl.*
24. Pérez Pastor: *Documentos cervantinos,* II, doc. XXXV.
25. DQ Part I, Chap. 19.
26. AM IV, p. 232 (footnote).
27. From the feast of Our Lady of Carmen to Ascension Day.
28. Archivo Municipal de Écija, Actas Capitulares, Cabildo de 26 Septiembre de 1588. The document was discovered by Francisco Rodríguez-Marín and is cited in AM IV, p. 255.
29. PS Book II, Chap. 15.
30. DQ Part I, Chap. 33.
31. Archivo Municipal de Écija, cit. AM IV, p. 257.
32. PS Book III, Chap. 2.
33. AM IV, p. 263.
34. Rodríguez-Marín, Francisco: *Nuevos documentos cervantinos hasta ahora inéditos,* Madrid, 1914, doc. CV, cit. AM IV, pp. 361–62.
35. Ibid., doc. CVI, cit. AM IV, p. 363.
36. Father Famiano Strada, cit. Mattingly: *Armada,* p. 325.
37. Lynch: *Spain,* I, p. 346.
38. Fitzmaurice-Kelly (*Memoir,* p. 75) erroneously identifies the one hundred ducats Cervantes received in Écija on March 14 as a second payment of back wages. In fact the money was earmarked to pay shipping costs.
39. Archivo de Protocolos de Sevilla, oficio 24, libro segundo de 1589, fol. 318, cit. Rodríguez-Marín: *Nuevos documentos,* doc. CXI.

40. *Apotegmas,* fol. 99.
41. The one by Urganda the Unknown, fourth stanza.
42. DQ Part II, Chap. 57.
43. DQ Part I, Chap. 48.

26. "FULL OF CARE, YET NONCHALANT"

1. The phrasing is ambiguous, evidently intended to needle the record, as is the deliberate confusion of Miguel's record with Rodrigo's.
2. Years later, Cervantes would appropriate his brother's rank to himself.
3. Underlined in the original.
4. In Mexico.
5. DQ Part I, Chap. 43.
6. *The Dungeons of Algiers,* Act III.
7. A typeface called French was in use then, but Astrana Marín is surely right in believing that an auctioneer, even if he had recognized the print, is more likely to have made his notation on the language. The fact, too, that the titles are not given suggests they were in a language which was meaningless to the auction master.
8. *The Faithful Sentinel.*
9. PS Book II, Chap. 5.
10. By the time the encomium was published, Arguijo had returned to his monastery en route to a pauper's grave, having exhausted his fortune maintaining the academy and subsidizing its members.
11. Valbuena Prat: *Vida española,* p. 127.
12. DQ Part II, Chap. II.
13. Defourneaux: *Vie quotidienne,* p. 262.
14. Sánchez-Albornoz: *España,* I, p. 573.
15. DQ Part I, Chap. 3.
16. Defourneaux: *Vie quotidienne,* p. 261.
17. The traditional Sevillian dance, often confused with flamenco dancing.
18. *The Illustrious Serving Wench.*
19. Valbuena Prat: *Vida española,* p. 127.
20. Cervantes: *Novelas ejemplares,* ed. F. Rodríguez-Marín, Madrid, 1969, I, p. 226 (footnote).
21. DQ Part I, Chap. 45.
22. Bennassar: *Valladolid,* pp. 548–49.
23. The anathema evidently had been lifted when the government paid its bills to the chapter of Córdoba's cathedral, but no record survives to tell us when this happened.
24. DQ Part II, Chap. 10.
25. Archivo de Simancas, cit. AM V, p. 37.
26. Ibid., pp. 39–41.
27. DQ Part I, Chap. 51.
28. Zúñiga, Lorenzo Baptista de: *Anales eclesiásticos i seglares de la ciudad de Sevilla,* Seville, 1747, p. 579.
29. This and all other details on the case cited here are taken chiefly from AM V, pp. 68–69.
30. PS Book III, Chap. 6.

27. VARIATIONS ON A THEME

1. The following figures are based on Astrana Marín's reckoning, which seems to me irreproachable.
2. Martel, Jerónimo: *Relación,* Zaragoza, 1595, cit. AM V, p. 157.
3. PS Book II, Chap. 5.

28. TO FALL AND RISE AGAIN

1. Despite a state bankruptcy in 1596 and the expense of his Continental wars, Philip sent a second Armada, against Ireland, that year. It was dispersed by gales that sank a third of the fleet. In 1597 a force almost as large as the Armada of 1588 met a similar fate. By that time, the results of Philip's policies were taking shape: the Low Countries lost, a pro-Protestant king on the throne of France, England strong and undefeated, Castile reduced to beggary.
2. Zúñiga: *Anales,* p. 582.
3. *The Little Gypsy Girl.*
4. Ibid.
5. The prison was torn down in 1837; the site is now occupied by a bank.
6. The description which follows combines material from several sources, chiefly Chaves, Cristóbal de: *Relación de lo que se pasa en la cárcel de Sevilla (1585–97),* in Gallardo, Bartolomé José: *Ensayo de una biblioteca española de libros raros y curiosos,* Madrid, 1863–89, vol. I; Morgado: *Historia de Sevilla,* I, p. 191 et passim; León, Padre Pedro de: *Segundo parte del compendio de las cosas tocantes al ministerio de las cárceles,* in AM V, pp. 232–38.
7. Alemán: *Guzmán,* Part II, Book III, Chap. 8.
8. Translated from a French edition (Paris, 1962), p. 295.
9. PS Book II, Chap. 5.
10. Zúñiga: *Anales,* p. 594.
11. Ariño, Franciscode: *Sucesos de Sevilla de 1592 a 1604,* Seville, 1873, p. 105.
12. VP Chap. IV.
13. Castro, Américo: *Cervantes y los casticismos españoles,* Madrid, 1966, pp. 97–99.
14. Collador, Francisco Jerónimo: *Descripción del túmulo y relación de las exequias que hizo la ciudad de Sevilla en la muerte del Rey Don Felipe Segundo (1598),* Seville, 1869.
15. PS Book I, Chap. 22.
16. Alemán: *Guzmán* (Clásicos Castellanos edition), II, p. 24.
17. Dr. Francisco Ruíz y Porcerio, cit. Bennassar, Bartolomé: *Recherche sur les grandes épidémies dans le nord de l'Espagne à la fin du 16e siècle,* Paris, 1969, p. 10.
18. Alemán: *Guzmán,* Part II, Book III, Chap. 4.
19. Ibid., Part I, Book III, Chap. 1.
20. Ibid., Part I, Book I, Chap. 7.
21. Gen. 6:7.
22. Alemán: *Guzmán,* Part I, Book I, Chap. 3.

23. Dialogue III.
24. DQ Part I, Chap. 47.
25. Francisco's acquisitive spirit was by then highly developed. He had recently (1597) won a lawsuit against his cousin Pedro de Palacios over the living willed him in Esquivias by Juan de Palacios.

29. HARLEQUIN'S SLAPSTICK

1. Trevor Davies, R.: *The Golden Century of Spain (1501–1621)*, London, 1967, p. 229.
2. The incident possibly based on the abduction of the body of St. John of the Cross in 1591 (see Note 15, Chapter 25) was obviously drawn from notes or from memory.
3. DQ Part II, Chap. 62.
4. I Cor. 13:4.
5. He is taking Cervantes at his word here; the passages taking Lope to task were written long after Cervantes' departure from Seville.
6. Avellaneda, Alonso F. de: *El Quijote*, Madrid, 1958, p. 13.
7. Cervantes: *Journey to Parnassus*, trans. J. Y. Gibson, London, 1883, p. 362.
8. In most collections of Góngora's poems the verse is merely attributed to him (*Obras completas*, Madrid, 1943, p. 459), but no other plausible author for it has been suggested.
9. Probably a reference to Julian de Armandariz, a minor poet and friend of Cervantes'.
10. The poem has never been documentarily proven to be by Cervantes and has sometimes been credited, if that is the word, to Góngora, but for stylistic and textual reasons I accept it as being by Cervantes.
11. Cited by many sources; see Ortega y Rubio, Juan: *Cervantes en Valladolid*, Madrid, 1905, pp. 21–22.
12. At what is now 87 Calle de Atocha in Madrid.

30. DON QUIXOTE

1. DQ Part I, Chap. 50.
2. DQ Part II, Chap. 3.
3. DQ Part II, Chap. 20.
4. DQ Part II, Chap. 59.
5. DQ Part II, Chap. 32.
6. DQ Part I, Chap. 11.
7. DQ Part I, Chap. 15.
8. DQ Part I, Chap. 16.
9. DQ Part I, Chap. 17.
10. DQ Part I, Chap. 18.
11. DQ Part I, Chap. 16.
12. DQ Part I, Chap. 14.
13. DQ Part I, Chap. 22.
14. Ibid.
15. DQ Part I, Chap. 20.
16. DQ Part I, Chap. 21.

17. DQ Part I, Chap. 31.
18. DQ Part II, Chap. 34.
19. DQ Part II, Chap. 32.
20. DQ Part I, Chap. 25.
21. DQ Part II, Chap. 32.
22. Italics mine.
23. DQ Part II, Chap. 9.
24. DQ Part II, Chap. 1.
25. DQ Part II, Chap. 13.
26. DQ Part II, Chap. 12.
27. DQ Part II, Chap. 13.
28. DQ Part II, Chap. 16.
29. DQ Part II, Chap. 17.
30. DQ Part II, Chap. 22.
31. DQ Part II, Chap. 23.
32. Ibid.
33. DQ Part II, Chap. 41.
34. DQ Part II, Chap. 42.
35. DQ Part II, Chap. 64.
36. DQ Part II, Chap. 74.
37. Castro: *Casticismos*, p. 8.
38. DQ Part II, Chap. 3.
39. Hugo, Victor: *William Shakespeare*, Paris, 1864, cit. AM V, p. 273.

31. A CLOSING OF CIRCLES

1. Góngora: *Obras completas*, p. 463.
2. Cabrera de Córdoba: *Relación*, cit. AM VI, p. 45.
3. *La fastigiana, o fastes geniales*, trans. Narciso Alonso Cortés, Valladolid, 1916, p. 70.
4. Herrera, Antonio de: *Relaciones*, cit. AM VI, p. 50.
5. *Obras completas*, pp. 357–58. The last two lines contain an untranslatable pun on the word "*plaza*," meaning here both bullring and market; the implication was that Don Gaspar was a true-to-life Paredes, hungry but proud.
6. DQ Part II, Chap. 52.
7. The following account of this incident is culled from too many sources to list independently. The most complete single version is, of course, to be found in AM VI, Chap. 72.

32. "A RICH HERITAGE OF CAROLS"

1. *The Dalliance*, Act III.
2. Pérez Pastor: *Documentos cervantinos*, II, doc. 98.
3. Ibid., I, doc. 56.
4. Ibid., II, pp. 434–35 (note).
5. DQ Part II, Chap. 11.
6. CW, p. 774.
7. The reference is to modes of judicial torture.
8. The italics throughout this passage are mine.

9. Its flavor lingers on, however, in Zorilla's nineteenth-century version of the Don Juan legend.
10. *El Chitón de las tarabillas,* cit. AM VI, pp. 342–43.
11. In a few areas this was reduced to three days.
12. Considerable quantities of gold were in fact smuggled out, chiefly to France.
13. DQ Part II, Chap. 54.
14. AM VII, p. 19.
15. Ibid.
16. AM VI, p. 280.
17. Astrana Marín, Luis: *Lope de Vega,* Madrid, 1963, p. 237.

33. THE EXEMPLARY STORIES

1. See AM VI, pp. 395–400 for the complete text of the will.
2. *Rimas de Christóval (sic) de Mesa,* Madrid, 1611, fol. 153.
3. *Obras completas,* p. 420.
4. The complete text is available in AM VI, pp. 409–17.
5. VP, Appendix.
6. DQ Part II, Chap. 4.
7. F. Suárez de Figueroa: *El pasajero,* cit. Riley: *Cervantes's Theory,* pp. 103–7.
8. VP Chap. I.
9. Samuel Putnam translation, New York, 1949, II, p. 502.
10. A fuller discussion of the painting can be found in AM I, pp. LXXXVIII–CXXIII and VI, pp. 63–64; see also Cabezas: *Cervantes,* p. 409 (note).
11. AM VII, p. 103 (note).
12. In Greek mythology, the spring is on Mount Helicon, not on Parnassus, but Cervantes followed the corrupt Renaissance mythology used by, among others, Cueva and Lope de Vega.
13. Cabezas: *Cervantes,* p. 422.
14. AM VII, pp. 147–48.

34. AVELLANEDA'S FOLLY

1. Avellaneda: *El Quijote,* p. 86.
2. An ambiguous phrase, doubtless referring to Cervantes' ingress into the Tertiary Order, but suggesting also that he was a "Jew" who had found the faith.
3. In Cervantes' book, Sancho's wife is called Mari Gutiérrez in the same chapter (Part I, Chap. 7) in which he calls her Juana Gutiérrez; in Part I, Chap. 52, she becomes Juana Panza before adopting the name Teresa. More of Cervantes' deliberate playing with names in order to break the thread of reality.
4. It is the custom to slaughter pigs on St. Martin's Day.
5. Riley: *Cervantes's Theory,* pp. 212–20.
6. Dedication of *La estafeta del dios Momo,* Madrid, 1627.
7. A number of interludes and one auto not published by Cervantes have at various times been attributed to him. One called *The Seville Prison* can

definitely be eliminated. The auto entitled *The Sovereign Virgin of Guadalupe and Her Miracles and Grandeurs of Spain* is another foundling laid on his doorstep and he remains stuck with it until its true parent is found. *Los habladores—The Chatterers*—is a more difficult case; stylistically it is worthy of Cervantes and many scholars confidently accredit it to him. Nevertheless. its lack of thematic continuity with the published interludes suggests that it was not his after all; funny as the piece is, there is nothing below its surface. Much the same reproach can be directed at *The Hospital for the Envious*. The chances are better than even that Cervantes had nothing to do with any of them.

35. MAGNIFICAT

1. *Libro de profesores,* fol. 130 verso; in AM VII, p. 448.
2. *Life in Algiers,* Act I.
3. DQ Part II, Chap. 7.
4. PS Book III, Chap. 10.
5. Forcione, Alban K.: *Cervantes' Christian Romance,* Princeton, 1972, p. 30.
6. PS Book I, Chap. 2.
7. PS Book III, Chap. 7.
8. Riley: *Cervantes's Theory,* p. 91.
9. PS Book III, Chap. 11.
10. *The Possessed,* trans. Andrew R. MacAndrew, New American Library Edition, New York, 1962, p. 237.
11. PS Book II, Chap. 6.
12. Casalduero, Joaquín: *Sentido y forma de "Los Trabajos de Persiles y Sigismunda,"* Buenos Aires, 1947, p. 42.
13. PS Book II, Chap. 11.
14. PS Book IV, Chap. 1.
15. PS Book III, Chap. 19.
16. Forcione: *Christian Romance,* p. 11.
17. DQ Part II, Chap. 26.
18. AM VII, pp. 416–17.
19. After the fall of his father-in-law Lerma in 1618, the fingers pointing at Lemos, as at all the Sandovals, were pointed in vengeance. The count died in disgrace in October 1622.
20. Astrana Marín argues that Cervantes died on Friday, April 22, and that the traditional date of the twenty-third taken from the parish record of the church of San Sebastián is erroneous. This, he argues, was the date of burial, which was when the deceased died as far as the Church was concerned, but that a full day intervenes between death and interment. But the biographer was not consistent; he accepted parish records as the true death dates for other figures of the time—Andrea de Cervantes, for example. Until conclusive proof is unearthed, therefore, the only existing evidence is the statement in the parish register that "on the twenty-third of April 1616 Miguel de Cervantes Saavedra died."
21. When Lope de Vega died in 1635, he was given a princely funeral. The obsequies lasted for three days. Three bishops officiated, dressed in their pontifical vestments.

Bibliography

Agapita y Revilla, Juan: "La familia, lose vecinos y los amigos de Cervantes en Valladolid en 1605," *Boletín de la Sociedad Castellana de Excursiones 12*, Valladolid, 1914, pp. 289–96, 313–20.

Aguilar, P. de: *Memorias del cautivo en la goleta de Túnez, el alférez P. de Aguilar*, Madrid, 1875.

Aguirre, J. L.: *Cervantes y Don Quixote: notas sobre una época y un libro*, Valencia, 1959.

Alba Abad, José: *Historia sintética de Madrid*, Madrid, 1949 (2 vols.).

Albistur, Jorge: *El teatro de Cervantes*, Montevideo, 1968.

Alcalá Galiano, Pelayo: *Servicios militares y cautiverio de Cervantes*, Madrid, 1905.

Alonso Cortés, Narciso: *Casos cervantinos que tocan a Valladolid*, Madrid 1916.

———: *Cervantes en Valladolid*, Valladolid, 1918.

———: "Los Cervantes de Alcalá," *España y America 74*, Madrid, 1922.

———: *Noticias de una corte literaria*, Valladolid, 1960.

Álvarez Guerra, Juan: *Sol de Cervantes Saavedra, su verdadera patria, Alcázar de San Juan*, Madrid, 1878.

Amador de los Ríos, José: *Historia de la villa y corte de Madrid*, Madrid, 1860–64 (4 vols.).

———: *Sevilla pintoresca*, Sevilla, 1844.

Arambilet, Santiago: "Cervantes y la marina," *Diario de la marina 37*, Madrid, May 6, 1905, no. 11285.

Arbó, Sebastián Juan: *Cervantes*, Barcelona, 1956.

Arcaeus, Franciscus: *A Most Excellent and Compendious Method of Curing Wounds*, trans. J. Read, London, 1588.

Archivo General de Indias: *Colección de documentos inéditos*, Madrid, 1875, vol. 25, pp. 386–534:

"Información hecha en Madrid à solicitud de Rodrigo de Cervantes para probar ser su hijo noble y estar captivo en Argel."

"Certificación del Duque de Sessa relativo a los méritos y servicios de Miguel de Cervantes."

"Información hecha en Argel a solicitud de Miguel de Cervantes exponiendo sus méritos y servicios hechos en Italia en la battala naval de Lepanto, y en otras partes, con motivo de solicitar uno de los oficios vacantes en Indias."

Arco y Garay, R. del: *La sociedad española en las obras de Cervantes,* Madrid, 1951.

Ariño, Francisco de: *Sucesos de Sevilla de 1592 a 1604,* Sevilla, 1873.

Armas y Cárdenas, José de ("Justo de Lara"): *Cervantes y el duque de Sessa. Nuevas observaciones sobre el Quijote de Avellaneda y su autor,* La Habana, 1909.

———: *El Quijote y su época,* Madrid, 1915.

Armiñán Odriosola, Luis de: *Las Hermanas de Cervantes,* Barcelona, 1957.

———: *Hoja de servicios del soldado Miguel de Cervantes Saavedra,* Madrid, 1941.

Arsenio y Toledo, J. M.: *El Conde de Lemos, estudio biográfico,* Madrid, 1880.

———: "¿Estudió Cervantes en Salamanca?", *Ilustración Española y Americana 43,* part 1, Madrid, 1883, no. 18, p. 290.

Astrana Marín, Luis: *Lope de Vega,* Barcelona, 1963.

———: *Vida ejemplar y heroica de Miguel de Cervantes Saavedra, con mil documentos hasta ahora inéditos y numerosas ilustraciones y grabados de época,* Madrid, 1948–57 (7 vols.).

Atkinson, W. C.: "Cervantes, El Pinciano and the *Novelas ejemplares,*" *Hispanic Review 16,* Philadelphia, 1948, pp. 189–208.

———: "The Enigma of the *Persiles,*" *Bulletin of Hispanic Studies,* Liverpool, October 1947.

Aubier, Dominique: *Don Quichotte, prophète d'Israel,* Paris, 1966.

Avellaneda, Alonso F. de: *El Quijote,* Madrid, 1957.

Azorín (Martínez Ruiz, J.): *Con Cervantes,* Madrid, 1957.

———: *Un hidalgo; "les racines de l'Espagne,"* trans. G. Pillement, Paris, 1929.

———: *An Hour of Spain Between 1560 and 1590,* trans. A. Raleigh, London, 1930.

Bardon, Maurice: *Don Quichotte en France aux 17e et 18e siècles,* Paris, 1930.

Baret, Eugène: *De l'Amadis de Gaule et de son influence sur les moeurs et la littérature au 16e et 17e siècles,* Paris, 1873.

Barto, Philip Stephen: "The Subterranean Grail Paradise of Cervantes," *Publications of the Modern Language Association of America 38,* New York, 1923.

Bataillon, Marcel: "Cervantès penseur," *Revue de littérature comparée,* Paris, 1928.

———: *Érasme et l'Espagne: recherches sur l'histoire spirituelle de 16e siècle,* Paris, 1937.

Battitessa, Angel J.: "Cervantes y la contrareforma," *Síntesis 4,* Buenos Aires, 1928.

Bauer y Landauer, Ignacio: *La marina española en el siglo XVI,* Madrid, 1921.

Bell, Aubrey F. G.: *Cervantes,* New York, 1961.

———: "Cervantes and the Renaissance," *Hispanic Review 2,* Philadelphia, 1934, pp. 89–101.

———: *Luis de León. A Study of the Spanish Renaissance,* Oxford, 1925.

Bennassar, Bartolomé: "Facteurs sévillans au 16e siècle d'après leurs lettres marchandes," *Annales S.E.C. XII,* Paris, 1957, pp. 60–71.

———: *Recherche sur les grandes epidémies dans le nord de l'Espagne à la fin du 16e siècle,* Paris, 1969.

———: *Valladolid au siècle d'or,* Paris, 1967.

Bertrand, J.-J. A.: *Cervantès et le Romantisme allemand,* Paris, 1914.

Blasquez y Delgado Aguilera, Antonio: *La Mancha en tiempo de Cervantes,* Madrid, 1905.

Boas, Marie: *The Scientific Renaissance (1450–1530)* London, 1970.

Boedo, Fernando: *El Contraquixote,* Madrid, 1916.

Bonello y San Martín, Adolfo: *Cervantes y su obra . . .¿Qué pensaron de Cervantes sus contemporáneos?,* Madrid, 1916.

Bourland, C. B.: *The Short Story in Spain in the Seventeenth Century,* Northampton, 1927.

Bransby, Carlos: "The Personal and Literary Relations Between Cervantes and Lope de Vega," *Transactions and Proceedings of the American Philological Association 67,* Boston, 1912.

Braudel, Fernand: *Capitalism and Material Life (1400–1800),* trans. M. Kochan, London, 1974, vol. 1.

———: "Les Espagnols et l'Afrique du Nord de 1492 à 1577," *Revue africaine,* Alger, 1928.

———: *La Méditerranée et le monde méditerranéen au temps de Phillippe II,* Paris, 1966 (2 vols.).

Brenan, Gerald: *The Literature of the Spanish People,* New York, 1958.

———: *St. John of the Cross,* Cambridge, 1973.

Buchanan, Milton J.: *The Works of Cervantes,* Ottawa, 1938.

Burguete, Ricardo: *Corsarios y piratas: la leyenda del Mediterráneo,* Barcelona, 1903.

Cabezas, Juan Antonio: *Cervantes, del mito al hombre,* Madrid, 1967.

Cabrera de Córdoba, Luis: *Felipe Segundo, rey de España,* Madrid, 1619.

———: *Relación de las cosas sucedidas en la corte de España desde 1599 hasta 1614,* Madrid, 1857.

Cansinos-Assens, R.: *Cervantes y los israelitas españolas, los Quijotes,* Madrid, 1916.

———: *Los Judíos en la literatura epañola,* Buenos Aires, 1937.

Caracciolo, Ferrante: *Commentarii della guerra fatta coi Turchi da D. Giovanni d'Austria dopo che venne in Italia,* Florence, 1581.

Casalduero, Joaquín: *Sentido y forma del teatro de Cervantes,* Madrid, 1966.

———: *Sentido y forma de "Los Trabajos de Persiles y Sigismunda,"* Buenos Aires, 1947.

Castresana, Luis de: *Medicina pintoresca y patética,* Barcelona, 1958.

Castro, Américo: *Aspectos del vivir hispánico,* Madrid, 1970.

———: *Cervantès,* Paris, 1931.

———: *Cervantes y los casticismos españoles,* Madrid-Barcelona, 1966.

———: "Cervantes y la Inquisición," *Modern Philology* 27, Chicago, 1929–30, pp. 427–33.

———: *Le drame de l'honneur dans la vie et dans la littérature espagnoles du 16e siècle,* trans. Y. Billod, Paris, 1965.

———: *De la edad conflictiva,* Madrid, 1963.

———: "Erasmo en tiempo de Cervantes," *Revista de filologia española XVIII,* Madrid, 1931, pp. 329–90.

———: *Español, palabra extranjera: razones y motivos,* Madrid, 1970.

———: *Los Españoles: como llegaron a serlo,* Madrid, 1965.

———: *Hacía Cervantes,* Madrid, 1967.

———: *El pensamiento de Cervantes,* Madrid, 1925.

———: *Realidad histórica de España,* Madrid, 1962.

Castro y Bravo, F. de: *Las naos españolas en la carrera de las Indias. Armadas y flotas en la segunda mitad del siglo XVI,* Madrid, 1927.

Cazenave, Jean: "Cervantès à Oran (1581)," *Bulletin de la Société de Géographie d'Alger et de l'Afrique du Nord 41,* Algiers, 1923.

————: "L'esclavage de Cervantès à Alger (1585–80)," *Bulletin de la Société de Géographie d'Alger et de l'Afrique du Nord 29,* Algiers, 1924, pp 103–35.

Cejados y Franca, Julio: *La lengua de Cervantes,* Madrid, 1905–6 (2 vols.).

"El centenario del Quijote. Hommenaje de la *Revista penitenciaria.* Retrato de Cervantes; la cárcel de Sevilla en 1597 donde se engendró el Quijote; la criminalidad en la época de Cervantes," *Revista penitenciaria 2,* Madrid, 1905, no. 5a.

Cervantes Saavedra, Miguel de: *The Adventures of Don Quixote,* trans. J. M. Cohen, Harmondsworth (Penguin), 1968.

————: *The Ingenious Gentleman Don Quixote de la Mancha,* trans. S. Putnam, New York, 1949 (2 vols.).

————: *Exemplary Stories,* trans. C. A. Jones, Harmondsworth (Penguin), 1972.

————: *La Galatea,* intro. J. B. Avalle-Arce, Madrid, 1961 (2 vols.).

————: *Interludes,* trans. E. Honig, New York, 1964.

————: *Journey to Parnassus,* trans. J. Y. Gibson, London, 1883.

————: *Novelas ejemplares,* ed. F. Rodríguez Marin, Madrid, 1969 (2 vols.).

————: *Obras completas,* ed. A. Valbuena Prat, Madrid, 1967.

Cervantes. A Collection of Critical Essays, ed. L. Nelson, Jr., Englewood Cliffs, N.J., 1969.

Chapman, Charles E.: *A History of Spain,* New York, 1918.

Chaunu, Pierre: *L'Espagne de Charles Quint,* Paris, 1973 (2 vols.).

Chaves, Cristóbal de: "Relación de lo que se pasa en la cárcel de Sevilla (1585–97)," in Gallardo, Bartolomé José: *Ensayo de una biblioteca española de libros raros y curiosos,* Madrid, 1863–89, vol. I.

Chavalier, Maxime: *Sur le publique des romans de chevalerie en Espagne,* Bordeaux, 1968.

Ciruelo, Pedro: *Reprobación de las supersticiones y hechicerías,* Salamanca, 1556.

Cock, Enríque: *Jornada de Tarascona hecho por Felipe II en 1592,* Madrid, 1897.

————: *El Madrid de Felipe II visto por humanista holondés (H) enríque Cock,* trans. V. E. Hernández Vista, Madrid, 1960.

————: *Relación del viaje hecho por Felipe II en 1585,* Madrid, 1876.

Collador, Francisco Gerónimo: *Descripción del túmulo y relación de las exequias que hizo la ciudad de Sevilla en la muerte del Rey Don Felipe Segundo (1598),* Sevilla, 1869.

The Continental Renaissance (1500–1600), ed. A. J. Krailsheimer, Harmondsworth (Penguin), 1971.

Correspondence des Deys d'Alger avec la Cour de France (1579–1833), ed. E. Plantet, Paris, 1889.

Cortines Murube, Felipe: *Cervantes en Argel y sus libertadores trinitarios,* Madrid, 1950.

Cotarelo y Mori, Emilio: *Efemérides cervantinas, o sea: Résumen cronológico de la vida de Miguel de Cervantes Saavedra,* Madrid, 1905.

Cotarelo y Valledor, Armando: *El teatro de Cervantes,* Madrid, 1915.

Crawford, J. P. W.: *Spanish Drama Before Lope de Vega,* Philadelphia, 1937.

Crillon, Louis des Balbes de Bertonde: *Autre véritable discours de la victoire des Chrestiens contre les Turcs, en la bataille navale près Lepantho . . . ,* Paris, 1571.

Crisis in Europe (1560–1660), ed. T. Aston, London, 1970.

Croce, Benedetto: *La Spagna nelle vita italiana durante la Rincascenza*, Rome, 1921.

——: "Scene della vita dei soldati spagnoli in Napoli," *Studi di storia napoletana in onore di M. Schipa*, Naples, 1926.

Crow, John A.: *Spain: the Root and the Flower*, New York, 1963.

Dan, R. P. Pierre: *Histoire de Barbarie et de ses corsaires*, Paris, 1636.

Defourneaux, Marcelin: *La vie quotidienne en Espagne au siècle d'or*, Paris, 1964.

Deleito Pinuela, José: *La mujer, la casa y la moda*, Madrid, 1954.

——: *Solo Madrid es corte*, Madrid, 1968.

——: *Tambien se divierte el pueblo*, Madrid, 1966.

Del Río, Angel: "Quijotismo y Cervantismo: el devenir de un símbolo," *Revista de estudios hispánicos I*, New York, July 3, 1928.

Dennis, Amarie: *Don Juan of Austria*, Madrid, 1966.

Descola, Jean: *Histoire d'Espagne*, Paris, 1959.

Díaz de Benjumea, Nicolas: *Vida de Cervantes, Introduction to Edition of "Don Quijote,"* Barcelona, 1880, vol. I.

Diedo, Girolamo: *Lettere del clarissimo Girolamo Diedo a l' illustrissimo signor Marc Antonio Barbaro*, Venice, 1588.

Domingo de la Asunción, Fray: *Cervantes y la Orden Trinitaria*, Madrid, 1917.

Dominguez Ortíz, A.: *The Golden Age of Spain (1516–1659)*, trans. J. Casey, London, 1971.

Eastman, Jayne Kearny: *Autobiographical Elements in the Works of Miguel de Cervantes Saavedra*, University of Minnesota, 1937.

Eguilez, Martín de: *Discurso y regla militar*, Madrid, 1596.

Elliott, J. H.: *Europe Divided (1559–98)*, London, 1968.

——: *Imperial Spain (1469–1716)*, London, 1963.

Entwistle, William J.: *Cervantes*, Oxford, 1940.

——: "Review of Casalduero's 'Sentido y forma . . . ,' " *Modern Language Review XLIII*, London, 1948, pp. 426–29.

Espejo, C.: "La carrestía de la vida en elsiglo XVI y medios de abarratarla," *Revista de archivos, bibliotecas y museos*, Madrid, 1921.

Espinosa de los Monteros, Pablo de: *Historia y antiqüedades de la gran ciudad de Sevilla*, Seville, 1627–30 (2 vols.)

Fernández Álvarez, Manuel: *El Madrid de 1586*, Madrid, 1962.

Fernández Duro, C.: *Armada española desde la union de los reinos de Castilla y de Aragon*, Madrid, 1897, vol. III.

——: *Cervantes marinero*, Madrid, 1869.

Fernández de Navarrete, M.: *Vida de Miguel de Cervantes Saavedra*, Madrid, 1819.

Fernández del Valle, Agustín Basave: *Filosofía del Quijote*, Mexico City, 1968.

Ferrandis Torres, Manuel: *El mundo que Lope de Vega pudo conocer*, Madrid, 1961.

Fisher, Sir Godfrey: *Barbary Legend: War, Trade and Piracy in North Africa (1415–1830)*, Oxford, 1957.

Fitzmaurice-Kelly, James: *Cervantes in England*, London, 1905.

————: *Miguel de Cervantes Saavedra: a Memoir*, Oxford, 1913.

————: *The Life of Miguel de Cervantes*, London, 1892.

————: *A New History of Spanish Literature*, Oxford, 1926.

Forcione, Alban K.: *Cervantes, Aristotle and the Persiles*, Princeton, 1970.

————: *Cervantes' Christian Romance*, Princeton, 1972.

Ford, J. D. M.: "Plot, Tales and Episode in Don Quijote," *Mélanges offerts à M. A. Jeanroy*, Paris, 1928.

Ford, Richard: *Gatherings from Spain*, London, 1970.

Fourastié, Jean: *Prix de vente et prix de revient*, 13e série, Paris, 1964, pp. 3–58.

Frois, P. Luis: *La première ambassade du Japon en Europe (1582–92)*, Paris, 1942.

Fuller, Gen. J. F. C.: *Decisive Battles of the Western World*, New York, 1961.

Gallo, Antonio: *Destierro de ignorancias en todo género de soldados de infantería*, Madrid, 1639.

García, Ismael: *Cervantes: su saber literario*, Panamá, 1966.

García y Balboa, Pedro José: *Noticia de la verdadera patria (Alcalá de Henares) de Miguel de Cervantes*, Barcelona, 1898.

García Mercadel, J.: *Estudiantes, sopistas y pícaros*, Madrid, 1934.

————: *Viajes de estranjeros por España y Portugal*, Madrid, 1959 (3 vols.).

García Puertas, Manuel: *Cervantes y la crisis del Renacimiento español*, Montevideo, 1962.

Garnier, Francois: *Journal de la bataille de Lépante*, Paris, 1956.

Gilmore, Myron P.: *The World of Humanism (1453–1517)*, New York, 1962.

Girard, A.: "La répartition de la population en Espagne dans les temps modernes, 16e au 18e siècles," *Revue d'histoire economique et sociale*, Paris, vols. III and IV, pp. 347–62.

Gómez, E.: *El Quixote y los libros de caballerías*, Barcelona, 1926.

Gómez de Losada, Fray Gabriel: *Escuela de trabaios*, Madrid, 1670.

————: *Noticias de Argel y su gobierno*, Madrid, 1670.

Gómez-Moreno, Manuel: *La gran época de la escultura española*, Barcelona, 1964.

González de Armezúa, A.: "Una carta desconocida e inédita de Cervantes," *Boletín de la Real Academia Española, 34*, cuad, 142, Madrid, Mayo/Agosto 1954, pp. 217–23.

————: *Cervantes creador de la novela corta*, Madrid, 1956–58.

————: "La vida privada en las obras de Cervantes," *Revista de archivos, bibliotecas y museos 56*, Madrid, 1950, no. 3.

González Aurioles, Norberto: *Cervantes en Córdoba. Estudio crítico-biográfico*, Madrid, 1914.

————: *Cervantes y Sevilla. Estudio histórico-crítico*, Sevilla, 1916.

González Palencia, Angel: "El testamento de Juan López de Hoyos, maestro de Cervantes," *Revista de archivos, bibliotecas y museos 41*, Madrid, 1920, pp. 593–603.

Gosse, P.: *Histoire de la piraterie*, trans. P. Tieillac, Paris, 1933.

Grammont, H. D. de: *Histoire d'Alger sous la domination turque*, Paris, 1887.

Granado, Diego: *Liebro del arte de cozina*, Madrid, 1599.

Grand-Carteret, John: *L'histoire, la vie, les moeurs et la curiosité*, Paris, 1927, vol. 1.

Gravière, Vice-Adm. J. B. E.: *Les Chevaliers de Malte et la marine de Philippe II*, Paris, 1887 (2 vols.).
———: *Les corsairs barbaresques et la marine de Soleiman le Grand*, Paris, 1887.
———: *La guerre de Chypre et la bataille de Lépante*, Paris, 1888 (2 vols).
Grierson, Edward: *The Fatal Inheritance*, New York, 1969.
———: *King of Two Worlds*, London, 1974.
Guenoun, Pierre: *Cervantès par lui-même*, Paris, 1971.
Guevara, Antonio de: *Libro que trata de los inventos, del arte de navegar y trabajos de la galera*, Zaragoza, 1545.

Haedo, Fray Diego de: *Topographía e historia general de Argel*, Valladolid, 1612.
Hale, J. R.: *Renaissance Europe (1480–1520)*, London, 1971.
Hamilton, Earl J.: "American Treasure and the Price Revolution," *Harvard Economic Studies XLIII*, Cambridge, 1934.
Hartzenbusch, Juan Eugenio: "Cervantes y Lope en 1605," *Revista española*, Madrid, 1862.
Hauser, Henri: *La prépondérance espagnole (1559–1660)*, Paris, 1948.
Hayes, Francis C.: *Lope de Vega*, New York, 1967.
Hazard, Paul: *Don Quichotte de Cervantes*, Paris, 1949.
Heer, Friedrich: *The Intellectual History of Europe*, Garden City, 1968, vol. II.
Heliodorus: *An Ethiopian History of the Loves of Theagenes and Chariclea*, London, 1587.
Hermida Balado, Manuel: *Vida del VII Conde de Lemos*, Midrid, 1948.
Herrera, Fernando de: *Relación de la guerra de Cipre y suceso de la batalla naval de Lepanto*, Seville, 1572.
Huarte, Don Juan: *Exam de ingenios para las sciencias*, Antwerp, 1603.
Huizinga, J.: *Erasmus and the Age of Reformation*, New York, 1957.

Isaba, Marcos de: *Cuerpo enfermo de la milicia española, con discursos y avisos para que pueda ser curado, utiles y de provecho*, Madrid, 1594.

Jackson, G. A.: *Algiers, Being a Complete Picture of the Barbary States*, London, 1817.
Jeannin, Pierre: *Les marchands au 16e siècle*, Paris, 1969.
Joly, B.: "Voyage en Espagne (1603–4)," *Revue hispanique XX*, New York, 1909, pp. 460–618.

Kamen, Henry: *The Spanish Inquisition*, New York, 1965.
Kristeller, Paul Oskar: *Renaissance Concepts of Man*, New York, 1972.
———: *Renaissance Thought*, New York, 1961.
Krutch, Joseph Wood: *Five Masters, A Study in Imitations of the Novel*, New York, 1930.

Laínez, Pedro: *Obras*, ed. J. de Entrambasagues, J. de José Prades, L. López Jiménez, Madrid, 1951 (2 vols.).
Lane-Pool, S.: *The Barbary Corsairs*, London, 1890.
Lazarillo de Tormes, New York, 1966.
Lea, Charles Henry: *A History of the Inquisition of Spain*, London, 1906–7 (4 vols.).
León, Fray Luis de: *La perfecta casada*, Madrid, 1968.

León Pinelo, Antonio de: *Anales de Madrid (1598–1621)*, Madrid, 1931.

Lesure, Michel: *Lépante*, Paris, 1972.

Lewis, Dominic B. W.: *The Shadow of Cervantes*, London, 1962.

Liñán y Verdugo, Antonio: *Guia y avisos de forasteros . . . que vienen a la corte*, Madrid, 1620.

Llanos y Torriglia, Félix de: *Apuros de la hacienda y enfermedad de la moneda española en tiempos de Cervantes*, Madrid, 1905.

Lloyd, Alan: *The Spanish Centuries*, New York, 1968.

Longhurst, John E.: *Erasmus and the Spanish Inquisition*, Albuquerque, 1950.

López, Joaquín M.: "Pintura de las immediaciones y pueblo de Esquivias donde escribió Cervantes una parte del Quixote," *Platea*, Sevilla, 1852.

López Estrada, F.: *La "Galatea" de Cervantes*, Tenerife, 1948.

López Madera, Gregorio: *Prática y teoría de cirujía*, Madrid, 1605.

López Méndez, Harold: *La medicina en el "Quijote,"* Madrid, 1969.

López Navío, José: "Tres estudios sobre Lope de Vega y Cervantes," *Anales cervantinos*, Madrid, 1959–60.

López-Pinciano, Alonso: *Philosophia antigua poética*, Midrid, 1596.

Lucas-Dubreton, J.: *Madrid*, Paris, 1962.

Lynch, John: *Spain Under the Hapsburgs*, Oxford, 1964 (2 vols.).

Machado, Manuel: "Felipe V, continuador del Quijote," *Revista de la Biblioteca, Archivo y Museo del Ayuntamiento de Madrid 5*, Madrid, 1928, pp. 365–80.

MacLaurin, Charles: *Don John of Austria, Cervantes and Don Quixote*, New York, 1923.

Madariaga, Salvador de: *Don Quixote: An Introductory Essay in Psychology*, London, 1961.

Maeztu, Ramíro de: *Don Quijote, Don Juan y la Celestina: ensayos en simpatía*, Madrid, 1924.

Major, Ralph H.: *A History of Medicine*, Oxford, 1954, vol. I.

Maldonado, Luis: *Don Quixote en lost estudios de Salamanca*, Salamanca, 1915.

Mal-lara, Juan de: *Descripción de la Galera Real del Serenisimo Sr. D. Juan de Austria*, Sevilla, 1876.

———: *Recibimiento que hizo la muy noble y muy leal ciudad de Sevilla a la C. R. M. del Rey D. Philipe (II)*, Sevilla, 1570.

Marañon, Gregorio: *Antonio Pérez*, London, 1954.

Maravall, A.: *Humanismo de las armas en Don Quijote*, Madrid, 1948.

Marmol Carvajál, Luis de: *Primera (y segunda) parte de la descripción general de Africa*, Granada, 1573.

Martínez-Hidalgo, José María: "La batalla de Lepanto," *Historia y vida 41*, Madrid, August 1971, pp. 58–85.

———: *Lepanto*, Barcelona, 1971.

Mattingly, Garrett: *The Defeat of the Spanish Armada*, London, 1970.

Mayans y Siscar, Gregorio: *Vida de Cervantes*, Madrid, 1750.

Medina, Pedro de: *Libro de grandezas y cosas memorables de España*, ed. D. Pérez de Messa, Alcalá de Henares, 1595.

Mele, Eugenio: *Per la fortuna del Cervantes in Italia nel seicento*, Catania, 1909.

Melon y Ruiz de Cordejuela: *Geografía histórica española*, Madrid, 1928.

Menendez y Pelayo, Marcelino: "Cultura literaria de Miguel de Cervantes," *Revista de archivos, bibliotecas y museos XII (tercera época)*, Madrid, 1905, pp. 309–39.

———: *San Isidro, Cervantes y otros estudios*, Buenos Aires, 1959.

Menéndez Pidal, Gonzalo: *Los caminos en la historia de España*, Madrid, 1951.

———: *Imagen del mundo hacía 1570*, Madrid, 1944.

Menéndez Pidal, Ramon: *Un aspecto en la elaboración del Quijote*, Madrid, 1920.

———: *De Cervantes y Lope de Vega*, Buenos Aires, 1964.

———: *Los Españoles en la historia*, Madrid, 1947.

———(ed): *Historia de España XIX*, "España en tiempo de Felipe II" by P. Luis Fernández de Retana, Madrid, 1966 (2 vols.).

Mérimée, Prosper: "Notice sur la vie et oeuvres de Cervantès," preface to Biart trans. of *Don Quixote*, Paris, 1826, vol. I, pp. 5–80.

Merriman, R. B.: *The Spanish Empire: Philip the Prudent*, New York, 1934, vol. IV.

Mesonero Romanos, R. de: *El antiguo Madrid*, Madrid, 1861.

Miquelarena, Jacinto: *Mesones y comidas en tiempo de Cervantes*, Buenos Aires, 1947.

Montoto, Santiago: *Sevilla en el imperio, siglo XVI*, Seville, 1938.

Montserrat, Santiago: *La conciencia burguesa en el Quijote*, Córdoba (Argentina), 1965.

Morel Fatio, Alfred: *Cervantès et les Cardinaux Acquaviva et Colonna*, Bordeaux, 1906.

———: "Le Don Quichotte come peinture et critique de la société espagnol du 16e et 17e siècles," *Études sur l'Espagne V*, Paris, 1895 (10th series, 2nd ed.).

Morell, John Reynell: Algeria: *The Topography and History, Political, Social and Natural, of French Africa*, London, 1854.

Morgado, Alonso: *Historia de Sevilla*, Sevilla, 1587 (2 vols.).

Mousnier, Roland: *Les 16e et 17e siècles*, Paris, 1967.

Navarro y Ledesma, Francisco: *Cervantes, the Man and the Genius*, trans. D. and G. Bliss, New York, 1973.

Nola, Roberto de: *Libro de cozina*, Madrid, 1968.

Nykl, A. R.: *Hispano-Arabic Poetry and Its Relations with the Old Provençal Troubadours*, Baltimore, 1946.

Olmos García, Francisco: *Cervantes en su época*, Madrid, 1968.

Oman, Sir Charles: *History of the Art of War in the Sixteenth Century*, London, 1937.

Oregaa y Gasset, José: *Meditaciones del Quijote. Ideas sobre la novela*, Madrid, 1964.

Ortega y Rubio, Juan: *Cervantes en Valladolid*, Madrid, 1905.

Ortiz de Zúñiga, Diego: *Anales eclesiásticos y seculares de la muy noble y muy leal ciudad de Sevilla*, Madrid, 1677.

Palacín Iglesias, Gregorio B.: *El Quijote en la literatura universal*, Madrid, 1965.

Pardo Manuel de Villena, Alfonso: *Un Mecenas español del siglo XVII. El conde de Lemos. Noticias de su vida y de sus relaciones con Cervantes, Lope de Vega, lost Argensola y demás literatos de su época*, Madrid, 1912.

Peers, E. Allison: *Studies of the Spanish Mystics,* New York, 1951 (2 vols.).

Penna, Mario: "Il 'Lugar del esquife': Apunti Cervantini," *Annali della facoltá di lettere e filosofia della Universitá degli studi di Perugia,* Perugia, 1965.

Pérez, Joseph: *L'Espagne du 16e siècle,* Paris, 1973.

Pérez Pastor, Cristóbal: *Documentos cervantinos hasta ahora inéditos,* Madrid, 1897–1902 (2 vols.).

Petrie, Charles: *Don John of Austria,* London, 1967.

Pfandl, Ludwig: *Cultura y costumbres del pueblo español de los siglos XVI y XVII,* Barcelona, 1929.

Picatoste y Rodríguez, Felipe: *Don Juan, Don Quijote y Hamlet. Cervantes. Don Juan Tenorio. Estudios literarios,* Madrid, 1883.

Playfair, Sir R. L.: *Scourge of Christendom,* London, 1884.

Poliakov, Leon: *De Mahomet aux Marranos,* Paris, 1961.

Predmore, R. L.: *Cervantes,* New York, 1973.

Querol Gavalda, Miguel: *La música en las obras de Cervantes,* Barcelona, 1948.

Quevedo, Francisco de: "España defendida," *Boletín de la Real Academia de Historia 69,* Madrid, 1915, p. 174.

Ramírez de Villa-Urrutia, W.: *Ocios diplomaticos: la jornada del condestable de Castilla a Inglaterra para las paces de 1604; la embajad de Lord Nottingham a Espagna en 1605,* Madrid, 1927.

Ranke, Leopold von: *The Ottoman and Spanish Empires in the Sixteenth and Seventeenth Centuries,* trans. W. K. Kelly, London, 1843.

Renaissance and Reformation (1300–1648), ed. G. R. Elton, New York, 1970.

Renard, Leon: *L'art naval,* Paris, 1866.

Rennert, H. A.: *The Spanish Stage in the Time of Lope de Vega,* New York, 1909.

Reynier, Gustave: *La vie universitaire dans l'ancienne Espagne,* Paris, 1902.

Riley, Edward C.: *Cervantes's Theory of the Novel,* Oxford, 1962.

Río, Angel del: "Equivoco," *Hispanic Review 27,* Philadelphia, 1959, pp. 200–21.

Rodgers, W. Ledyard: *Naval Warfare Under Oars from the Fourth to the Sixteenth Centuries,* Annapolis, 1939.

Rodríguez-Marín, Francisco: *El andalucismo y el córdobesismo de Miguel de Cervantes,* Madrid, 1915.

————: *El apócrifo secreto de Cervantes,* Madrid, 1916.

————: *El capítulo de los Galeotes,* Madrid, 1912.

————: *La cárcel en que se engendró el Quijote,* Madrid, 1916.

————: *Cervantes en Andalucía,* Sevilla, 1905.

————: *Cervantes estudió en Seveilla (1564–65),* Sevilla, 1905.

————: *Cervantes y la ciudad de Córdoba,* Madrid, 1914.

————: *El ingenioso hidalgo Don Quijote de la Mancha, Nueva edición crítica,* Madrid, 1927–28 (7 vols.).

————: *Introducción crítica a Rinconete y Cortadillo,* Madrid, 1920.

————: *El Loaysa de El Celoso Extremeño,* Sevilla, 1901.

————: *El modela más probable del Quijote,* Madrid, 1918.

————: *Nuevos documentos cervantinos hasta ahora inéditos,* Madrid, 1914.

————: *El retrato de Miguel de Cervantes,* Madrid, 1917.

Rosales, Luis: *Cervantes y la libertad,* Madrid, 1960.

Rosell, Cayetano: *Historia del combate naval de Lepanto, y juicio de la importancia y consecuencias de aquel suceso,* Madrid, 1853.

Rosenkranz, Hans: *El Greco and Cervantes,* trans. M. Aurousseau, New York, 1932.

Sainz de Robles, Federico Carlos: *Breve historia de Madrid,* Madrid, 1970.

Salazar, Adolfo: *La música en Cervantes,* Madrid, 1961.

Salomon, Noël: *La campagne en Nouvelle Castille à la fin du 16e siècle d'après les "Relaciones Topgráficas,"* Paris, 1964.

Sánchez-Alborñoz y Menduiña, Claudio: *España: Un enigma histórico,* Buenos Aires, 1956 (2 vols.).

――――: *Los Españoles ante la historia. Raices medievales del Quijote,* Buenos Aires, 1958.

Sánchez-Arjona, J.: *Noticias referentes a los anales del teatro de Sevilla,* Sevilla, 1898.

Sánchez Canton, Francisco Javier (ed.): *Floreto de anecdotas y noticias diversas (en tiempo de Felipe II),* Madrid, 1948.

Sangrador y Vitores, Matías: *Memoria historica sobre la expulsion de los Moriscos,* Valladolid, 1858.

Santos, Francisco: *Día y noche de Madrid,* Madrid, 1674.

Schevill, Rudolph: *Cervantes,* New York, 1919.

――――: "Cervantes and Lope de Vega: A contrast of two master spirits of the Golden Age in Spain," *Spanish Review 3,* New York, 1936, pp. 1–14.

――――: "Cervantes and Spain's Golden Age of Letters," *University of California Semi-Centennial Publications 1,* Berkeley, 1918, pp. 237–56.

――――: "The Education and Culture of Cervantes," *Hispanic Review 1,* Philadelphia, 1933, pp. 24–36.

――――: "Studies in Cervantes. The Question of Heliodorus," *Modern Philology,* Chicago, 1907, p. 685.

Servía, Miguel de: "Relación de sucesos," *Colección de documentos inéditos para la historia de España,* Madrid, 1847, vol. II.

Sicroff, Albert A.: *Les statuts de la pureté de sang en Espagne au 16e et 17e siècles,* Paris, 1955.

Singleton, Mack: "The 'Persiles' Mystery," *Cervantes Across the Centuries,* ed. A. Flores and M. Bernadete, New York, 1969, pp. 237–48.

Slocombe, G.: *Don John of Austria, the Victor of Lepanto,* London, 1935.

Stirling-Maxwell, William: *Don John of Austria,* London, 1883 (2 vols.).

Sylvia, Esther B.: "Don Quixote's Library," *Bulletin of the Boston Public Library,* Boston, April 1900, pp. 135–52.

Tenenti, Alberto: *Piracy and the Decline of Venice (1580–1615),* trans. J. and B. Pullen, London, 1967.

Teresa of Avila, St.: *The Life of St. Teresa of Avila by Herself,* trans. J. M. Cohen, Harmondsworth (Penguin), 1958.

――――: *Le livre des foundations,* trans. M. Auclair, Paris, 1951.

Thomas, Henry: *Spanish and Portuguese Romances of Chivalry,* Cambridge, 1920.

――――: *Spanish Sixteenth-Century Printing,* Benn, 1929.

Ticknor, George: *History of Spanish Literature,* Boston, 1888 (3 vols.).

Toffanin, G.: *La fine dell' Umanesimo,* Turin, 1920.

Torre, Lucas de: "Un cautivo compañero de Cervantes," *Boletín de la Real Academia Española 3,* Madrid, 1916, pp. 350–58.

Torres y Aguilera, Gerónimo: *Chrónica de varios sucesos de guerra que ha pasado en Italia y partes de Levante* . . . *desde 1570 hasta 1574*, Zaragoza, 1579.

Torres Lanzas, Pedro: "Información de Miguel de Cervantes de lo que a servido a S. M. y de lo que ha hecho estando captivo en Argel . . . ," *Revista de archivos, bibliotecas y museos 12*, Madrid, 1905, pp. 345–97.

Turgenev, Ivan: "Hamlet y Don Quijote," *Revista contemporánea 23*, Madrid, 1879, pp. 453–71.

Trend, J. B.: *Cervantes in Arcadia*, London, 1954.

Trevor Davies, R.: *The Golden Century of Spain (1501–1621)*, London, 1967.

———: *Spain in Decline (1621–1700)*, London, 1965.

Trotter, George D.: *Cervantes and the Art of Fiction*, London, 1965.

Turquet de Mayerne, Theodore de: *Sommaire description de la France, Allemagne, Italie et Espagne avec la guide des chemins et postes*, Rouen, 1529.

Unamuno, Miguel de: *Ensayos (La vida de Don Quijote y Sancho Panza)*, Madrid, 1942, pp. 1–292.

Valbuena Prat, Ángel:; *La vida española en la edad de ora*, Barcelona, 1943.

Valdées, Francisco de: *Espejo y disciplina militar*, Brussels, 1586.

Vaughan, Dorothy M.: *Europe and the Turk. A Pattern of Alliances (1350–1700)*, Liverpool, 1954.

Vilanova y Andreu, Antonio: *Erasmo y Cervantes*, Barcelona, 1949.

———: "El peregrino andante en el 'Persiles' de Cervantes," *Boletín de la Real Academia de Buenas Letras 22*, Barcelona, 1949, pp. 97–159.

Vilar, Pierre: *Histoire de l'Espagne*, Paris, 1965.

Villanueva, Juan Bautista de: *Información sobre actividades de la Liga a Lepanto*, Valencia, 1583.

Vindel, Francisco: *Cervantes, Robles y Juan de la Cuesta*, Madrid, 1934.

Vives, Juan Luis: *Instrucción de la mujer cristiana*, Buenos Aires, 1948.

Watson, R. and Thompson, W.: *History of Philip III*, London, 1786.

Welsch, Hieronymus: *Descriptions of a Journey*, Stuttgart, 1664.

Zúñiga, Lorenzo Baptista de: *Anales eclesiasticos i seglares de la ciudad de Sevilla*, Seville, 1747.

INDEX